Computer Science and Statistics: Proceedings of the 14th Symposium on the Interface

Computer Science and Statistics: Proceedings of the 14th Symposium on the Interface

Edited by
Karl W. Heiner
Richard S. Sacher
John W. Wilkinson

With 179 Figures

Springer-Verlag
New York Heidelberg Berlin

Karl W. Heiner
John W. Wilkinson
Symposium Chairmen

Department of Statistical, Management, and Information Sciences
Rensselaer Polytechnic Institute
Troy, NY 12181
U.S.A.

Richard S. Sacher
Symposium Chairman, Computer Science and Computing Activities

Alan M. Voorhees Computing Center
Rensselaer Polytechnic Institute
Troy, NY 12181
U.S.A.

The Computer Science and Statistics 14th Symposium on the Interface was held July 5–7, 1982, at Rensselaer Polytechnic Institute, Troy, New York.

Library of Congress Cataloging in Publication Data
Computer Science and Statistics: Symposium on the Interface (14th : 1982 : Rensselaer Polytechnic Institute)
Computer Science and Statistics.
Symposium held July 5–7, 1982.
1. Mathematical statistics—Data processing—Congresses. I. Heiner, Karl W. II. Wilkinson, John W. III. Sacher, Richard S.
QA276.4.C58 1982 519.5 83-537

Printed and bound by Halliday Lithograph, West Hanover, MA.
Printed in the United States of America.

9 8 7 6 5 4 3 2 1

ISBN 0-387-90835-8 Springer-Verlag New York Heidelberg Berlin
ISBN 3-540-90835-8 Springer-Verlag Berlin Heidelberg New York

Contents

Preface

The 14th Symposium on the Interface continued the well-established tradition of previous symposia in providing a forum for the interchange of ideas of common concern to statisticians and computer scientists. We chose to convene between Rensselaer Polytechnic Institute's academic sessions, on July 5-7, 1982, so that that the excellent facilities at RPI could be totally dedicated to the Symposium.

A convivial mixer held on July 5 in the Great Hall of the Communications Center greeted early conference arrivals and late registrants. After a few welcoming remarks on the morning of July 6, the conference was excitedly launched by John Tukey's keynote address "Another Look at the Future." Thirten workshop sessions run in parallel in four groups filled the remainder of the two days. The conferees' attentions were also captured by the nineteen poster sessions and several software demonstrations carefully interleaved between the workshops. A time period at the end of each day was also reserved for self-initiated "Birds of a Feather" sessions.

Several workshop sessions took advantage of the link between RPI's Voorhees Computing Center, other computing centers, and the RPI Communications Center by incorporating live computer demonstrations in their presentations. Immediately following the Symposium, representatives of the Royal Statistical Society presented an excellent two-day tutorial workshop on GLIM3.

For those whose schedules were not yet full, we arranged a continuous cycle of tours of Rensselaer's main computing facility--the Alan M. Voorhees Computing Center, and the Center for Interactive Computer Graphics. Each Symposium participant was given a computer account enabling him or her to use the central computing facility.

A visit to the opening night performance of the New York City Ballet, in residence at the Saratoga Performing Arts Center for three weeks each summer, provided the highlight of the social part of the conference. This, coupled with excellent weather, 300 participants from various parts of the USA, Canada and the United Kingdom, the fine facilities at Rensselaer for living and learning, all contributed to a very successful conference.

In closing, we would like to acknowledge the support and assistance of those people involved in the planning and execution of the Symposium:

The faculty and staff of the School of Management (Robert J. Allio, Richard LeMay); Department of Statistical, Management and Information Sciences (Donald P. Schneider, Albert Paulson, Pasquale Sullo); Office of Computer Services (James L. Moss, Harriet Borton, John Bradley, Wilson Dillaway, William Dodge, Peter Frosch, Robert Gallagher, Michael Kupferschmid, Nancy Kutner, Joan LaFleur, Don Moore, Barbara Moses, Dean Nairn, Sharon Roy, Julie Swant); Office of Conferences and University Events (Pat Henry, Robert Metzger); Dining Services (Leo Titus); Communications Services (Linda Lagerroos, Randy Rumpf); Instructional Media (William Ryan); Center for Interactive Computer Graphics (John Kolb); RPI Physics Laboratories (Harold Butner, Thomas Shannon); and the secretarial staff of the Department of Statistical, Management, and Information Sciences (Rose Carignan, Jan Smith).

Furthermore, we would like thank the graduate students who served as administrative assistants, programmers, and on the audio-visual staff: Snorri Agnarsson, Chai-Yi Chou, Kelly Collins, Thomas Delehanty, Karen Fandel, J.P. Fasano, Bill Kelly, Mark Miller, Andre Seiterle, Gary Wade, Jose Zayas-Castro, and for her role as an administrative assistant and GLIM3 teaching assistant, Arilee Bagley.

Finally, we are grateful to the financial supporters of the INTERFACE XIV: the General Electric Company, International Business Machines Corporation, Rensselaer Polytechnic Institute, and the Shell Oil Company

Karl W. Heiner and John W. Wilkinson
Symposium Chairmen

Richard S. Sacher
Chairman, Computer Science Sessions and Computing Activities

Keynote Address

"Another Look at the Future"

John W. Tukey, Princeton University and Bell Laboratories

ANOTHER LOOK AT THE FUTURE

John W. Tukey

Princeton University and Bell Laboratories

Princeton, New Jersey 08544 and Murray Hill, New Jersey 07974

ABSTRACT

It is just ten years since I gave an invited talk at the Interface.

My emphasis then was ***the importance of graphics*** -- which might, it then seemed to me, be for all -- or might be only for a few special centers -- centers that would combine people and graphics systems to teach us about new processes, processes for all to run in batch.

My emphasis is still on ***the importance of graphics, not alone but as one of a number of leaders.*** Today it is clear that everyone will soon have graphics, that the personal computer five to seven years into the future will have good graphics capabilities.

I shall make brief comments in each of 11 areas, about one third of which can involve significant uses of graphics:

A1) Choice among alternation, color, etc.

A2) Better data-modification display systems.

B1) Cognostics.

B2) Better flexibility in re-expression.

B3) Deeper automation in re-expression.

B4) Two-dimensional (?) re-expression.

C1) Software-driven ***verbal*** guidance of ***exploration.***

C2) Expository software, verbal and pictorial, telling what results MAY mean.

C3) Automated cartography of exploration.

D1) Displays and guidance for ***alternative*** analyses of ***factorial*** data.

D2) ***Regression*** tools of flexibility and scope.

1. Introduction.

It is just ten years since I gave an invited talk at the Interface.

My emphasis then was ***the importance of graphics*** -- which might, it then seemed to me, be for all -- or might be only for a few special centers, centers that would combine people and graphics systems to teach us about new processes, processes to run in batch.

My emphasis is still on ***the importance of graphics, not alone but as one of a number of leaders.*** Today it is clear that everyone will soon have graphics, that the personal computer five to seven years into the future will have good graphics capabilities:

- multiple-plane frame buffers
- color monitors
- really adequate memories
- adequate computing power for any reasonable dynamic displays.

*** the real problems ***

Thus our problems must be:

- How do we get ready to use these capabilities?
- What impact will their use have on data analysis/statistics on the one hand?
- And on computing on the other?

2. Projection pursuit.

Ten years ago, as noted above, one possibility for graphics seemed that a few places would use them to generate new techniques. The instance I had in mind was ***projection pursuit,*** whose descendants are already fairly widespread, including:

- Friedman and Stuetzle's (1981) projection pursuit regression
- Peter Huber's seminar at Harvard on projection pursuit as a topic.

Projection pursuit, in its original form, looks for a k-dimensional projection -- $k=1$ and 2 have been implemented -- which optimizes a criterion of "clottedness". The criterion used is equivalent to

$$\frac{\textit{measure of spread}}{\textit{measure of global spread}}$$

to be min

Prepared in part in connection with research at Princeton University, supported by DOE and ARO(D), for ***Interface 14***, 6 July 1982.

The simplest approximation, for $k=1$, would be:

$$[\Sigma\Sigma r(|x_i - x_j|)] \times [var\{x's\}]$$

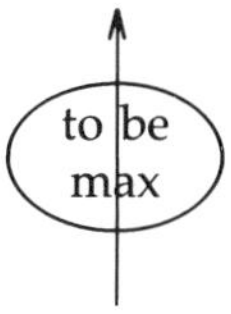

where $r(\ )$ looks roughly like this:

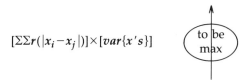

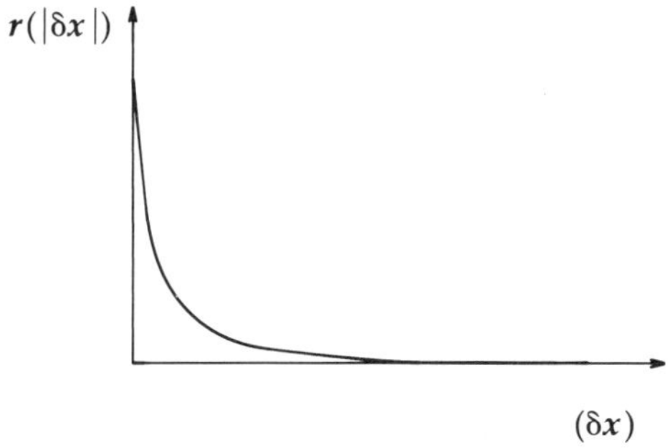

(We actually used a trimmed variance, and a variety of $r(d)$'s including $(1-d/R)$.)

We need two factors -- or a numerator ***and*** a denominator -- in such a criterion, to keep expansions and contractions from having major effects upon the criterion.

*** how did it arise ***

The original projection pursuit came into being because:

- we looked at an effective dynamic display (PRIM-9)!
- the limited imagination that went into the PRIM-9 display system took us as far as rotation, and
- the available "good coordinates" for 3-body-final-state particle-physics data gave us patterns that rotation could do very nice things with.

*** what can its genesis teach us? ***

The lessons we should learn from this include:

- imagine more ways to modify data, and
- seek out unusual kinds of data which may be effectively handled by such additional modifications, and
- start using modifications, old or new, on all sorts of data, looking hard to see what opportunities supposedly familiar data has been offering us without our recognition of these opportunities.

These may not be mentally easy, but they are not physically hard.

3. What will be discussed when?

I will come back again to data-modification graphics at my close, but I want next to put it in its place as ONE of ***many major items*** to which we should attend.

*** the classical interface ***

In the narrowest sense of "what computations should be done to give a desired result", the classical interface joined numerical analysis and formalized statistics.

The last ten years have seen much progress, and the next five will see more.

This is a vital area, where we will depend heavily on both past and future progress, today, tomorrow, and throughout the foreseeable future.

Many people recognize its problems; some are highly skilled in solving them. I can -- and will -- leave all responsibility for progress here, both in depth of insight and in breadth of understanding, to those who are -- or will become -- capable of contribution.

*** the theory-computation interface ***

A similarly important interface arises when a statistical theorist wants a numerically more or less difficult answer. A thousand single integrals (quadratures) are quite bearable. A thousand double integrals (cubatures) still remain a deep pain. A thousand multiple ($\geq$ 3-dimensional) integrals are probably not yet to be borne.

There are many other ways in which computing -- both in terms of numerical analysis and in terms of calculations -- needs to come to the aid of theory, here the theory of data analysis (including the theory of statistics). At this interface, we are not as well organized -- much of reasonable use could probably be said -- but I must put this topic, too, aside with a brief mention.

My task today is rather to bring out a good collection of less-recognized -- and often less-structured -- problems.

*** a four-area breakdown ***

So let me list, and lightly structure, a handful of areas where we are going to need real progress, soon. Four broad areas are diverse in character, each deserving further breakdown.

A) Better picturing.

B) Local guidance as to what's next (often ***not*** seen by the analyst or client).

C) Larger-scale guidance (to the analyst or client).

D) Support for broad data-analytic techniques.

Let us, now, take up the breakdown of these areas from D to A (opposite to many conversions of data)!

4. Support for broad data-analytical techniques.

Under (D), two items seem to me to deserve particular mention:

D1) displays and guidance that are well-related to a number of ***alternative*** schemes for analyzing ***factorial*** data, and

D2) ***regression*** tools of the flexibility and scope we can now recognize as needed.

While some will want to add other broad technologies to this list -- with instances of which I might go along -- it seems to me that the extensive and diverse uses of factorial data analysis and regression earn them the leading places on any such list.

In both cases we are likely to want BOTH pictorial AND verbal guidance, and we will need to have our computer systems go considerably deeper and more broadly than any presently available book or collection of books.

This means (i) large systems, (ii) systems planned both for growth and for easy specialized attachment, (iii) cooperation between a variety of insightful data analysts on the one hand and a variety of computer experts on the other -- each group with diverse skills. Success will not be easy, but starting now poses no major barriers. There are people with enough insights of the needed kinds, though they may be hard to find and assemble. And we can expect the 4th or 5th generations of such systems to be far, far better than anything we have today.

5. Larger-scale guidance to the analyst or client.

Under (C), three items are especially worth our attention:

C1) Software-based ***verbal*** guidance of data exploration on an interactive basis. (This is what "expert software" seems to mean to statisticians today.)

C2) Expository software, verbal as well as pictorial, to ***explain*** to analysts and clients what their results ***MAY*** mean. (Here little, if any, start has been made.)

C3) Automated ***cartography*** of exploration, as a routine tool. (Barely even thought about!)

* interactive verbal guidance *

Today, we are seeing the construction of the first systems intended to counsel their users about which alternative steps seem most reasonable in analyzing that user's data. This counsel is based on a combination of two sources: (a) what the computer can calculate from the data and (b) what answers users give to the computing system's questions. The combination of the information from these two sources -- possibly also both what computations have been tried and which questions have been asked -- is guided by some more or less complex body of rules gathered from the insights of highly competent statistical consultants. (It is in this last that such systems are truly "expert systems".)

* expository software *

Tomorrow we should see the rise of systems that offer bouquets of alternative possible "reasons" for lists of detailed statistical results. This activity fails utterly if it is interpreted as a "since -- hence" process. Quite the contrary, its logical structure is, instead, "seeing this, let's point out a reasonably diverse collection of possible 'reasons' which would more or less account for what we've seen".

Such answers as "possibly the long-run average difference is >0" OR "an event of probability less than p% (two-sided) has happened" are only the very simplest example of incompatible, but result-explaining, alternative answers.

We need systems that suggest 6 or perhaps even 20 alternative possibilities, not just two.

* cartography, forsooth! *

We must explain (C3) carefully.

A competent data analysis of an even moderately complex set of data is a thing of trials and retreats, of dead ends and branches. Today we recognize that we don't know how to satisfactorily describe, in words, a given instance of this process. It seems plausible that we could do better if we described it by a combination of sketches, words, numbers, and pictures, perhaps amounting to several screensful of information (in a tree-like structure?).

Once we can do this, even in only a partially automated way, we will have gained a number of advantages, including:

- we can review our ***own*** work, looking for missed opportunities -- opportunities perhaps to try new branches, perhaps to make new syntheses,
- we can understand much better what others have done in their analysis, judging the completeness of their attacks, and the adequacy of their synthesis.

We are not going to have a very powerful version of (C3) as soon as 1983, but it is high time someone began to put together some early attempts.

6. An unjustified reaction.

There is one all-too-automatic reaction by many statisticians and data analysts, the reaction that automating -- even in part -- such insight-related things as the two D's and the three C's is a threat to their professional position.

The flavor of "the computer will take away our business" is all to likely to drift about.

Fortunately, it is easy to see that this is a serious misconception. For there are TWO reasons, either of which would be enough alone:

- there have never been ***enough statisticians*** to go around -- yet the ***amount of data deserving*** analyses grows ***exponentially.*** No matter how much the computer helps, statisticians/data analysts will still be in short supply.
- the wisdom of Edgar Anderson -- who long ago pressed on me the truth that the best (and often the only) way to get new ideas was to work hard telling the public about the ideas we already have -- applies, I am sure, to data analysts collectively; just as I know, from experience, it applies to individuals.

The process of building more insight into computer systems will bring new ideas and new tasks to the whole profession. Rather than running out of work -- we are likely to run into MORE WORK.

We will, however, have to admit how often and how far we go beyond the

CERTAINTY of MATHEMATICS.

7. Local guidance as to what's next (often not seen by the analyst or client).

Under (B) we will set out 3 items for sure and 1 for maybe:

B1) Cognostics

B2) Better flexibility in re-expression

B3) Deeper automation of re-expression

B4) Two-dimensional (?) re-expression

All of these need a few words of explanation.

*** cognostics ***

A "cognostic" is a diagnostic to be interpreted by a computer rather than by a human. If we tell our system "here is some 100-variable data -- of the 4950 scatter plots of one variable against another, show me the 50 most interesting ones" only a computing system well-fitted with cognostics to reveal the interestingness of scatter diagrams can respond to our request.

Extensions in many directions are much easier to point out than to implement. (Again we are trying to build some of the elementary forms of insight into our computing system.)

*** flexibility in re-expression ***

Re-expression is one of the major tools of data analysis. Its name sounds a little like "regression", which Cochran characterized, 30 years ago, as "the worst taught branch of statistics". The plausible analog of that statement is "re-expression is the worst ***un***taught branch of data analysis!"

One reason for this used to be computational -- but need no longer be so. I can remember when a colleague was so, so proud of his hand-calculator operator, who could invert a 12×12 matrix in one day! Those were the days when everything had to be kept linear, so re-expression had to involve replacing variables by sums of terms, all too often polynomials.

We have got beyond this today -- after all, even our pocket calculators provide logs and exponentials. Indeed, many of us are "into" the "ladder of powers" and regard x^p and $\ln x$ as natural candidate re-expressions.

This is a step forward, but we need to go quite a lot further. How much further is not quite clear, but good bouquets of possible re-expressions involving 1 or 2 more constants than $a+bx$ are badly needed.

I have been pushing (for some time)

"trexes"	$a+be^{cx}$	(2+1 const's)
"trems"	$a+bx^c$	(2+1 const's)

as well as their iterations and extensions, like

"trexexes"	$a+be^{ce^{dx}}$	(2+2 const's)
"trexems"	$a+be^{cx^d}$	(2+2 const's)
and		
"tremtrems"	$a+b(1+cx)^d$	(2+2 const's)

and I still like these choices. (Here "tr" is from **tri**vially, "re" is from **re**-expressed, "x" or "ex" is from exponentials, and "m" is from **m**onomials.)

On another hand, if pictures like those Jerry Friedman has been showing me recently prove to occur in even a small fraction of other real data sets, we must also plan to provide:

$$\text{"monogons"} \quad \begin{cases} a + b_-(x-x_0), & \text{for } x < x_0 \\ a + b_+(x-x_0), & \text{for } x \geq x_0 \end{cases}$$

which also involves "2+2 constants".

If $b_+b_->0$, then the dependence of x on y is of the same general form as that of y on x. To reflect this rather palindromic behavior, we might replace, in this special case, "monogons" by "monogonoms" or "nogons", or "ogos". Whether or not we need to provide further possibilities for non-monotonic re-expressions is not yet clear.

* deeper automation *

(B3) is simpler; it merely requires automatic techniques to try a variety of re-expressions and to select a list of those that are bearably good, with an indication of the quality of their performance.

* a vital GENERAL principle *

We always want to have the machine provide diversity for human resolution, though we want this to happen at higher and higher levels as we build each block of human experience -- a year's or a decade's or a century's worth -- into the machine, so it may resolve the lower diversity and create new diversity at a higher level.

* two-dimensional re-expression *

(B4) is an important aim, but it is not clear we are yet ready to tackle it. We understand a fair amount about one-dimensional re-expression; we can state the problem for two dimensions; but can we yet approach it effectively? We do not know.

One possible approach seems worth mentioning. Let R_1, R_2,... be generalizations of diagonal matrices of a chosen order, k, whose diagonal "elements" are more or less arbitrary, strictly monotone ***functions,*** each of which induces a (nonlinear) reversible re-expression of its coordinate. And let L_1, L_2,... be ordinary non-singular matrices of the same order, k, each of which induces a reversible change of coordinates. Then the concatenation

$$L_n R_{n-1} L_{n-1} R_{n-2} \cdots R_2 L_2 R_1 L_1$$

has a clear meaning, and defines a reversible transformation of one k-space into another. Is this a good way to seek for an answer to (B4)? Who knows?

8. Better picturing.

Under (A), I am going to confine myself to two items:

A1) Effective choices for internally distinguished displays

A2) Data modification, pictorially guided.

These seem to me today's "hottest" items.

* how should we distinguish? *

We have color displays by virtue of multiplane frame buffers. We can have alternating displays just as easily, with or without color cues. All we have to do is to replace one color-look-up table by an automatically cycling series of display-look-up tables, whose outputs may be either black-and-white or color. We do not even have to change what's stored on the bit-map planes.

It is high time we compare, say:

- pure color
- pure alternation
- alternation with color cues.

I hereby stick my neck out to say that what color will most effectively do for us is to ***cue*** -- to TAG what is presented in some ***other*** mode -- rather than provide ***information*** by ***itself.***

* one alternagraphic example *

I shall now turn the microphone over to Richard Becker, who will describe a videotape he produced showing a variety of alternagraphic displays, in each of which something happens to a changing degree.

The first of these is perhaps the least usual. It shows (vertically)

reported value + (puG)(reported s.d.)

for each of 11 determinations of the speed of light (arranged in chronological order), made in the decades before World War II. Exhibits 1, 2, and 3 show some steps in this display.

Here "puG", the possible unit Gaussian deviate, is common to all displayed points, and oscillates back and forth between

-1.36 and +1.36

The bar on the left covers the range of the points displayed at the instant.

The bar on the right would be a confidence limit on the median of the population, if the points displayed at the instant were a sample from a population.

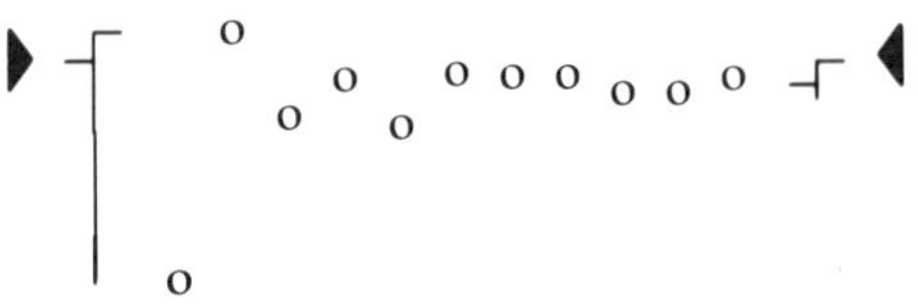

Exhibit 1

1st, 15th, 29th, ... frame: o's at estimates ***MINUS 1.36*** times their standard errors.

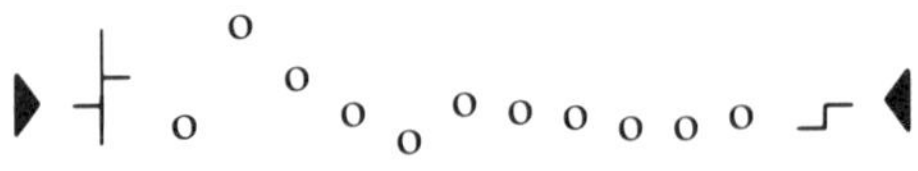

Exhibit 2

2nd, 14th, 16th, 28th, 30th, ... frame: o's at estimates ***MINUS 0.76*** times their standard errors

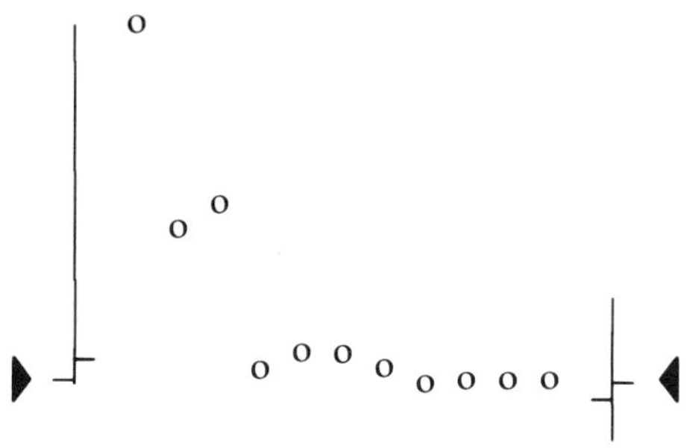

Exhibit 3

7th, 21st, 35th, ... frame: o's at estimates ***PLUS 1.36*** times their standard errors

*** pictorial guiding: PRIM and PTIM ***

Now for (A2), where PRIM-9 and its contemplated extensions have given us considerably more background than in any of the other items. PRIM-9, which I wish to *re*describe today as "**P**icturing, **R**otation, **I**solation, and re**M**embering in up to **9** dimensions" was a data-modification system which modified (a) by introducing new coordinates linearly into, in principle, all of the space concerned, and (b) by subdividing the data and providing boolean operations on the subdivisions. These manipulations share, with those involved in the extension of PRIM to PTIM (which will include axial **T**wists as well as rotation), two important properties:

- the whole space, not just the data (as would be the case for multidimensional scaling, etc.) is modified -- is given new coordinates
- the Jacobian for each step is both constant over all space and non-zero -- so that the same is true of the overall modification -- as a consequence the overall modification is reversible. (We could also include radial twists, without losing these properties.)

Before we are ready to go further, we must first learn to play PTIM effectively. I have had a half hour manipulating a very toy prototype, but even that was enough to lead us into new ideas about what sorts of displays we are going to need to play PTIM well.

Initially, these displays are likely to be split-screened between a direct view and a diagnostic plot, both probably color-cued for greater insight.

Our emphasis on ***twist*** comes, as rotation did earlier, from the nature of a specific kind of particle physics data. For PTIM, the stimulating agent is 4-body final-state data, where the data-points are expected to cluster around 2-dimensional manifolds in 7-space -- manifolds that are likely ***not*** to be flat in the initially chosen coordinates, and which, then, might well be untwisted to make them flat.

*** should we ask for reversibility? ***

Other types of modification will clearly be needed as we proceed, including (see Tukey and Tukey 1981):

- techniques for sharpening and/or blunting point clouds,
- techniques for agglomerating nearby groups of "little points" into "bigger points".

Some of these, including sharpening by excision, and agglomeration, will not be reversible -- and may not make sense applied to the space around the data points.

We will have to learn how important failures to be reversible are -- and how best to reduce their impacts, but we ought not take them as critical or fatal. Both "all-space applicability" and "reversibility" can be dispensed with -- when we must, or merely when, it will help us.

Reversibility is sometimes thought to be important as a way to trace one's steps. This is not so, because our computer systems -- like Gilbert Gosseyn of Null-A fame -- can remember past "locations" and return us to a selected one of them in a flash.

*** snap return to a few past states ***

To have ***snap return*** to perhaps half a dozen past states -- states of both data modification and control setup -- and "semisnap" return to many more -- is both easy and useful -- and requires **no** reversibility!

In fact, the management of how we snap back, and to which previous states, is probably the most important part of the planning of an effective data-modification display system. Ease of going back to the most useful states is highly valuable.

Reversibility may indeed be important as a general analog of monotonicity, as a way to help emphasize or enforce simplicity, as a way to enforce some attention to the space around the data points. We will learn as experience grows, about such questions. But retracing one's steps, step by step, is almost never going to be worthwhile.

In all of this, we should be guided as much as possible by those ***real*** data sets that suggest new modifications to us. Geometric mental pictures underlying rotation and twisting have been very useful -- we should continue to gain as much help from them as we can. But if the "gobblygonk function of three arguments" helps us simplify and understand some class of data, WE SHOULD LEARN TO USE IT EFFECTIVELY, also.

9. Close.

We have talked about 11 areas that seemed to me to deserve special attention, so let's have the eleven back again, namely:

D1. Displays and guidance for ***alternative*** analyses of ***factorial*** data

D2. ***Regression*** tools of flexibility and scope.

C1. Software-driven ***verbal*** guidance of ***exploration.***

C2. Expository software, verbal and pictorial, telling what results MAY mean.

C3. Automated cartography of exploration.

B1. Cognostics.

B2. Better flexibility in re-expression.

B3. Deeper automation in re-expression.

B4. Two-dimensional (?) re-expression.

A1. Choice among alternation, color, etc.

A2. Better data-modification display systems.

REFERENCES

Friedman, J. H. and Stuetzle, W. (1981), Projection Pursuit Regression, ***Journal of the American Statistical Association,*** **Vol. 76,** pp. 817-823.

Tukey, J. W. and Tukey, P. A. (1981). "Methods for direct and indirect graphic display for data sets in 3 and more dimensions". (3 lectures, Conference on ***Looking at Multivariate Data,*** Sheffield, England, 24-26 March 1980. Printed in ***Interpreting Multivariate Data*** ed. V. Barnett, as follows: Chapter 10: "Preparation; prechosen sequences of views," pp. 189-213; Chapter 11: "Data-driven view selection; agglomeration and sharpening", pp. 215-243; Chapter 12: "Summarization; smoothing; supplemented views," pp. 245-275. London: Wiley.

APPENDIX

This appendix is for those who saw the presentation. The transparencies used were .003" thick sheets of cellulose acetate, Projectofilm EP 300, sold by Plastic Suppliers, Blackwood, New Jersey 08012. [Thin sheets will not warp, and thus do not require frames.] Pens used were Staedtler LUMOCOLOR 317 medium permanent. (#317 is being restyled, but remains first class.) [Schramm STABILO permanent has equally good inks, but the caps fall off more frequently, leading to drying up.] Erasures and emendations were done with Pelikan PT20 erasers. [Staedtler LUMOPLAST and ordinary Artgum erasers are next choices.] The use of a ruled sheet (conveniently the top sheet of a ruled pad) under each transparency as it is prepared is essential.

Graphics Software and Techniques

Chair: Peter D. Welch, IBM Watson Research Center

Interactive Statistical Graphics in APL: Designing a Versatile User—Efficient Environment for Data Analysis
Neil W. Polhemus, Princeton University

The Application of Dual Screen Graphics and APL to Interactive Data Analysis
P. Heidelberger, P.D. Welch, and L.S.Y. Wu, IBM Watson Research Center

Graphical Analysis of Regenerative Simulations (Abstract)
P. Heidelberger, IBM Watson Research Center
P.A.W. Lewis, Naval Postgraduate School

INTERACTIVE STATISTICAL GRAPHICS IN APL:

DESIGNING A VERSATILE USER-EFFICIENT ENVIRONMENT FOR DATA ANALYSIS

Neil W. Polhemus
School of Engineering and Applied Science
Princeton University
Princeton, NJ 08544

ABSTRACT

One of the major advantages of interactive data analysis over batch programming is the ability to allow the data to govern the course of the analysis process. This requires a user/machine interface which is flexible enough to adapt itself to the user's demands, while at the same time remaining as nondisruptive as possible. In the application of statistical graphics, it is especially important that graphics be available upon demand with little or no intermediate handling of data and in a manner which does not interrupt the flow of other statistical procedures. In exploratory analysis, it is also vital that the analyst be able to create original displays or to modify standard displays for unusual situations. This paper describes some of the most important aspects of statistical graphics software design as they relate to the overall interactive data analysis environment, user efficiency, and the fostering of creative statistical analysis. These aspects are illustrated using elements of the STATGRAPHICS statistical graphics system.

KEYWORDS: Interactive data analysis, statistical graphics, software design, APL, full-screen programming, nondisruptive graphics.

INTRODUCTION

During the last several years, the statistical community has witnessed dramatic changes in the nature of statistical computing. One of the most visible changes is a shift in emphasis from batch processing to interactive data analysis. Advances in hardware, coupled with a decrease in the ratio of computer costs to analyst costs, have created a demand for statistical analysis systems designed to meet the special requirements of interactive computing.

Interactive data analysis environments impose a different set of requirements on software structure than do batch programming systems. The input/output medium, rather than a punched card or computer sheet, is a rectangular screen of typical dimension 24 rows by 80 columns. Effective user/machine interaction requires careful coordination of screen displays. On-line help facilities, menu drivers, and flexible data structures become important considerations for interactive data processing, as addressed by several authors including Filliben (1979) and Muller (1980).

One of the most important features of any interactive statistical analysis system is the need for flexible, nondisruptive graphics. The user who wishes to analyze data in an interactive fashion requires a more rapid information flow than does the analyst who can ponder at leisure over a printed output. To remain in control, interactive data analysts need to have a wide range of tools at their disposal to query the status of data sets, to determine the results of selected procedures, to interrupt and examine what is happening to their data and decide whether or not to continue, and to try out new ideas which might arise while sitting at the terminal. All of these needs require a graphics system which is available upon demand and in a fashion which does not disrupt other procedures.

This article examines some of the important aspects of statistical software design, with emphasis on those issues which are particularly critical for interactive data analysis systems. STATGRAPHICS, an interactive statistical graphics system written in APL, provides a case study which illustrates the type of system which can be developed to take advantage of modern interactive computer systems.

DESIGN PARAMETERS

In designing any software system, certain parameters determined early in the development process shape the structure of the system. STATGRAPHICS was developed in response to the following broad objective:

> DESIGN OBJECTIVE
>
> To create an interactive data analysis system in which graphical and statistical techniques are fully integrated under flexible user control.

In order to take full advantage of the capabilities of interactive systems, it was decided that no attempt would be made to provide a batch mode of operation. Further, the integration of graphical and statistical methods into common procedures, controllable by users through program function (PF) keys and other flexible mechanisms, insures that graphics will play more than merely a summary role in the analysis process.

Six separate design parameters were established:

(1) Graphics should be available on demand and be nondisruptive.

This requires a careful segmentation of system functions as described later.

(2) User efficiency should be maximized.

While some regard must naturally be paid to computational costs, system design leaned heavily toward the goal of minimizing the amount of user time required to accomplish a given task.

(3) Input/output should be oriented around screen pages rather than a sequence of commands.

With the entire 24x80 screen available for exchange of information on many terminals, program control need not center around a sequence of commands, but rather around a sequence of screen panels.

(4) Data handling by the user should be minimized.

In an interactive session, maintaining control over data is one of the most difficult tasks and must be carefully structured.

(5) Side-by-side comparisons should be exploited wherever possible.

The resolution of many graphics terminals allows for multiple plots on a single screen, which is helpful when making comparative judgments.

(6) User creativity should be encouraged.

The act of "graphics" implies not only display but also creation, and provisions are needed to encourage user creativity.

SYSTEM STRUCTURE

To accomplish the objectives set forth above, a statistical graphics system was developed which had the following major features:

1. multiple modes of function execution
2. extensive use of fullscreen control panels and program function (PF) keys
3. access to graphics primitives
4. frequent "splitscreen" plotting
5. user access to the full power of the host language (APL) at all times
6. a structure which allows for easy addition of user-written functions.

The selection of APL as a host language is highly significant, since it gives the analyst a powerful base upon which the rest of the system can be built. APL differs from most other programming languages in that it is interpretive rather than compiled, allowing interactive access to the source code. The special features of APL which has made it popular for data analysis include:

(1) The ability to dynamically define and modify data arrays.

(2) The ability to transform data arrays, including matrices, via concise equation-like expressions.

(3) The interactive creation and testing of new procedures.

(4) The capability for interrupting procedures, examining the status of functions and arrays, executing secondary analyses, and then resuming execution of the initial procedure.

Some excellent examples of the use of APL in statistics have been given by Smillie (1974), McNeil (1976), and Anscombe (1981).

The importance of building a software system upon an already existing interactive computational system cannot be overemphasized. The user then finds that he or she is not constrained by artificial boundaries, but is free to expand the system in whatever direction is most desirable. Further, the time and effort spent in learning to manage data, modify system functions, or write new code is applicable well beyond the package itself and becomes an advance in overall computer literacy. Self-contained systems too often become restrictive and can stifle creativity.

MULTIPLE MODES OF FUNCTION EXECUTION

To achieve the type of flexibility needed to meet the demands of interactive data analysis, each of the statistical and graphics procedures included in STATGRAPHICS has been developed as a separate APL function which can be executed in any of several manners:

(1) directly from the APL environment after loading the system workspace.

(2) from other APL functions, either already contained in the system workspace or created by the user.

(3) under the control of fullscreen menus, to assist less sophisticated users.

(4) by pressing program function (PF) keys defined by procedure control functions.

This multi-modal feature is made possible by dividing the system functions into several distinct segments. When the system workspace is first loaded, an initialization segment is executed which sets various system flags determined by the type of terminal configuration being used and shares variables with the auxiliary processors needed to drive the input and output devices. The user is then left to operate freely in APL and can execute individually any of the user-documented functions, write new functions, or copy data and functions from other APL workspaces.

Alternatively, menu control can be invoked by executing the function RUN. Menu control serves several basic functions:

(1) It insures that one of many available full-screen panels always fills the display screen, which gives the user a focal point from which to operate.

(2) It lists the available functions in the workspace and can provide information on how to execute them.

(3) It controls the spooling of nongraphics output to an offline printer for later review.

```
                 S  T  A  T  G  R  A  P  H  I  C  S
        AN INTERACTIVE STATISTICAL GRAPHICS SYSTEM IN APL
------------------------------------------------------------------
CONTENTS

  ANALYSIS OF VARIANCE          (A)     NONPARAMETRIC STATISTICS    (N)
  BASIC PLOTTING FUNCTIONS      (B)     NUMERICAL ANALYSIS          (O)
  CLUSTER ANALYSIS              (C)     SAMPLING                    (P)
  DESCRIPTIVE METHODS           (D)     QUALITY CONTROL             (Q)
  ESTIMATION AND TESTING        (E)     REGRESSION ANALYSIS         (R)
  DISTRIBUTION FUNCTIONS        (F)     SMOOTHING                   (S)
  SIMULATION AND RANDOM NUM.    (G)     TIME SERIES ANALYSIS        (T)
  FORECASTING                   (H)     UTILITY FUNCTIONS           (U)
  DATA INPUT/OUTPUT             (I)     STOCHASTIC MODELING         (V)
  EXPLORATORY DATA ANALYSIS     (J)     SYSTEM MAINTENANCE FCNS.    (W)
  BASIC DRAW FUNCTIONS          (K)     EXPERIMENTAL DESIGN         (X)
  CATEGORIZED DATA ANALYSIS     (L)     SPECIAL MATH FUNCTIONS      (Y)
  MULTIVARIATE STATISTICS       (M)     MATHEMATICAL PROGRAMMING    (Z)

INPUT VALID LETTER AND HIT RETURN.
```

Figure 1

Main Menu of STATGRAPHICS Chapters

```
                    ------------------------------
                    CHAPTER D:  DESCRIPTIVE METHODS
                    ------------------------------
CONTENTS

  SUMMARY STATISTICS              (STATS)  FREQUENCY HISTOGRAM    (HISTOGRAM)
  3-DIMENSIONAL HISTOGRAM        (HIST3D)  BOX AND WHISKER PLOT     (BOXPLOT)
  VERTICAL BAR CHARTS          (BARCHART)  PIE CHARTS               (PIECHART)
  SAMPLE MEDIAN                  (MEDIAN)  SAMPLE PERCENTILES     (PERCENTILE)
  SAMPLE AVERAGE                (AVERAGE)  SAMPLE VARIANCE          (VARIANCE)
  SAMPLE STANDARD DEV.              (STD)  SAMPLE RANGE                (RANGE)
  SAMPLE MAXIMUM                (MAXIMUM)  SAMPLE MINIMUM            (MINIMUM)
  GEOMETRIC MEAN                (GEOMEAN)  INTERQUARTILE RANGE      (INTQRANGE)
  FREQUENCY CLASSIFICATION        (FREQ1)  SAMPLE HINGES               (HINGES)


ENTER EXECUTABLE STATEMENT; OR           STATS X
TYPE FUNCTION NAME AND HIT PF KEY.
                                         X = INPUT ARRAY CONTAINING DATA SAMPLE

STATS MYX
```

Figure 2

Chapter D Menu Illustrating Execution of Function STATS and Display of Its Syntax

The first menu panel displayed, shown in Fig. 1, lists the titles of the 26 chapters contained in the system. These chapters group system functions according to their primary application. Requesting a particular chapter causes its menu to be displayed. The chapter menu panels, an example of which is shown in Fig. 2, consist of four fields:

(1) a <u>display field</u> listing the functions contained in that chapter (output).

(2) an <u>instruction field</u> which tells the user what to do next (output).

(3) a <u>message field</u> which can display the syntax of a function or an error message (output).

(4) a <u>command field</u> in which the user enters system commands (input).

The command field, which consists of the bottom two lines of the screen, will accept <u>any</u> executable APL expression including system functions, user-written functions, data vectors and arrays, and APL operators. The statement in that field is executed by APL, and when computation is complete the menu panel is redisplayed. In this manner, the menu control segment is almost completely isolated from the rest of the computational functions. Basic plotting functions such as HISTOGRAM can be executed under menu control, or called by other system functions such as FITDIST which produces the output shown in Fig. 3.

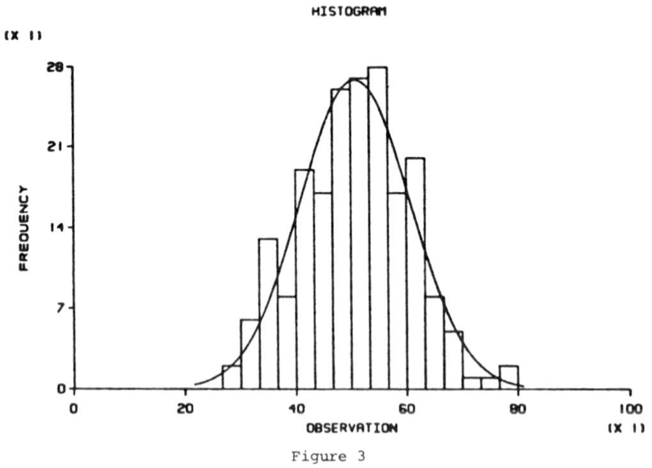

Figure 3

Graphical Output Generated by FITDIST from Internal Execution of HISTOGRAM

FULLSCREEN PROGRAMMING

Many statistical analysis systems which were initially designed for batch processing require the user to enter a sequence of commands. However, to the data analyst sitting at a CRT, the natural unit of input is not a line but an entire screen page. With the introduction of terminals such as the IBM 3270 series which allow multiple input fields to be defined anywhere on the screen, many possibilities arise for developing efficient user/machine interaction control strategies. By moving the cursor from field to field, the user can specify all options at once by simple editing of the screen. On screens with dual intensity, input fields can be made brighter than output fields. On color terminals, they can be a special color.

The menu control panels described earlier represent one use of fullscreen programming, with three output fields and a single input field. A second interesting example is demonstrated in Fig. 4, which shows a fullscreen panel used to control the production of piecharts. The panel consists of 6 input fields:

(a) a field below "TITLE" in which labels for each piece of the pie can be entered.

(b) two fields below "COLOR" and "FILL" to specify color and filltype codes.

(c) a field beneath "OFFSET" to specify radial offset distances for each piece.

(d) fields to the right of "PIE SIZE" and "POSITION" to specify the pie diameter and the location of its center.

Fig. 5 shows the piechart produced by the panel in Fig. 4.

A second example of fullscreen programming is shown in Fig. 6. Upon executing the function FACTORIAL, a screen panel is presented showing a full 4-factor factorial design. By editing the input fields to the right of "BLOCKS", "FACTORS" and "RUNS" and pressing ENTER, fractional or blocked factorial designs can be created.

```
                              PIE-CHART SPECIFICATION
CLASS  TITLE                                     FRACTION      COLOR  FILL OFFSET
  1    ECONOMICS                                   0.10          1      1   0.0
  2    STATISTICS                                  0.40          2      1   0.0
  3    MATHEMATICS                                 0.30          3      3   0.2
  4    HISTORY                                     0.20          4      4   0.0




PIE SIZE:  0.4      POSITION: 0.3 0.3
EDIT SCREEN AND HIT ENTER TO PLOT OR PF KEY TO QUIT:
```

Figure 4

Fullscreen Control Panel for Specification of PIECHART Options

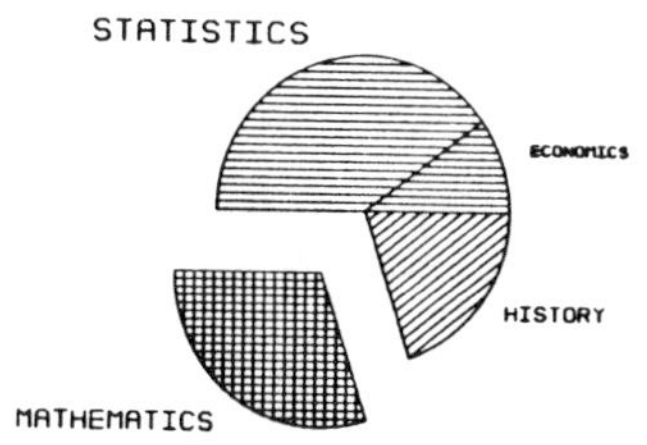

Figure 5

Piechart Created by the Panel in Figure 4

```
                              FACTORIAL DESIGNS
BLOCKS: 1             FACTORS: 5              RUNS: 16             PAGE: 1

RUN    BLOCK   RESPONSE    A B C D E F G H
(12)     1        0        - - - - +
( 2)     1        0        + - - - -
(14)     1        0        - + - - -
( 7)     1        0        + + - - +
( 4)     1        0        - - + - -
(15)     1        0        + - + - +
(16)     1        0        - + + - +
( 8)     1        0        + + + - -
(10)     1        0        - - - + -
(13)     1        0        + - - + +
( 5)     1        0        - + - + +
(11)     1        0        + + - + -
( 3)     1        0        - - + + +
( 1)     1        0        + - + + -
( 9)     1        0        - + + + -
( 6)     1        0        + + + + +
HIT DESIRED PF KEY TO CONTINUE.
```

Figure 6

Fullscreen Panel Displays after Editing of FACTORIAL Input Fields

NONDISRUPTIVE GRAPHICS

One way to insure that graphics can be produced in a nondisruptive manner is to structure common displays as defined program functions within more general procedure control functions. Many terminals now have "soft" PF keys which can be defined by the program in a dynamic fashion, so that the user can choose from a number of different displays by pressing the appropriate keys. Even on older terminals without such special keys, the creation of graphic displays from within another procedure without disrupting that procedure can be accomplished in many different ways.

A good example of nondisruptive graphics is provided by the function MODEL, designed for the analysis of general linear models. This function is controlled by the fullscreen panel displayed in Fig. 7. Five input fields are present on the panel:

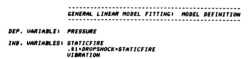

```
                 -----------------------------------------------
                 GENERAL LINEAR MODEL FITTING:  MODEL DEFINITION
                 -----------------------------------------------
DEP. VARIABLE:   PRESSURE

IND. VARIABLES:  STATICFIRE
                 .01*DROPSHOCK*STATICFIRE
                 VIBRATION




STEPWISE:   NO
CONSTANT:   YES
WEIGHTS:

HIT DESIRED PF KEY TO CONTINUE.
```

Figure 7

Procedure Control Panel for General Linear Models Function MODEL

(1) a field alongside "DEP. VARIABLE:" in which the name of an APL vector or any APL expression resulting in a vector can be specified. The values of this vector or expression form the dependent variable. Transformations can be expressed within the field by expressions such as

PRESSURE*.5

individual columns of a matrix can be specified as in

M[;2]

or the field may include the output of user-written functions which return explicit results.

(2) a large rectangular field for specification of independent variables, each delimited by a blank if on the same line. Note the specification of a scaled interaction through an APL expression in the field.

(3) a field alongside "STEPWISE" for selection of stepwise fitting if desired.

(4) a field alongside "CONSTANT" for inclusion or exclusion of an intercept.

(5) a field alongside "WEIGHTS" for specification of an APL vector or expression to be used for weighted regression.

OPERATIONS OF DEFINED PF KEYS

LIST DEFINED PF KEY OPERATIONS	DEFINE THE MODEL	FIT THE MODEL
DISPLAY THE FULL MODEL ANOVA	DISPLAY THE INDIVIDUAL VARIABLE ANOVAS	PERFORM A RESIDUAL ANALYSIS
RESIDUAL NORMAL PROBABILITY PLOT	USE THE MODEL FOR PREDICTIONS	DISPLAY MULTIPLE CONFIDENCE REGIONS
DISPLAY RESIDUAL SUM OF SQUARES SURFACE	DISPLAY PARTIAL REGRESSION PLOTS	EXIT

HIT ENTER TO RETURN.

Figure 8

Defined Program Functions from MODEL, Displayed by PF1

MODEL FITTING RESULTS

MODEL: 1 STEPWISE: NO

VARIABLE	COEFFICIENT	STND.ERROR	T-VALUE	PROB(>|T|)
CONSTANT	10.7131	.5068	21.1402	.0000
STATICFIRE	¯.1123	.0046	¯24.2458	.0000
.01×DROPSHOCK×STATICFIRE	.0314	.0043	7.2954	.0000
VIBRATION	.0233	.0047	5.0041	.0001

HIT ENTER TO CONTINUE.

Figure 9

Summary Table Produced by PF3 from MODEL

The procedure control panel in Fig. 7 is the focal point for execution of MODEL and is repeatedly redisplayed after each user request. Requests are entered by pressing various PF keys which perform the operations indicated by Fig. 8. The PF keys can be executed in any order, with the exception that PF3 (model estimation) must preceed keys of higher number. Examples of the output generated include:

(a) Fig. 9, a summary table created by PF3.

(b) Fig. 10, the ANOVA table from PF4 with information on lack of fit when available.

(c) Figs. 11 and 12, showing the graphical and nongraphical output of PF6. On dualscreen terminal configurations such as the IBM 3277GA, both figures will be displayed simultaneously. With single screen configurations, graphics and nongraphics output are displayed consecutively.

(d) Fig. 13 shows a normal probability plot of model residuals from PF7.

(e) Fig. 14 shows the fitted model with confidence limits for individual expected values of the dependent variable from PF8. This is an example of a splitscreen plot, in which several figures are displayed on a single screen.

(f) Fig. 15 shows joint confidence regions for model parameters generated by PF9.

(g) Fig. 16 shows a 3-D plot of the residual sum of squares surface produced by PF10.

ANALYSIS OF VARIANCE FOR THE FULL REGRESSION

SOURCE	SUM OF SQUARES	DF	MEAN SQUARE	F-RATIO	PROB(>F)
MODEL	2641.5905	3	880.5302	251.5474	.0000
ERROR	70.0091	20	3.5005		
LACK-OF-FIT:	30.2207	8	3.7776	1.1393	.4046
PURE ERROR :	39.7883	12	3.3157		
TOTAL (CORR.)	2711.5996	23			

R-SQUARED = 0.97418
R-SQUARED (ADJ. FOR D.F.) = 0.97031
STND. ERROR OF EST. = 1.8709

HIT ENTER TO CONTINUE.

Figure 10

ANOVA Table Generated by PF4 from MODEL

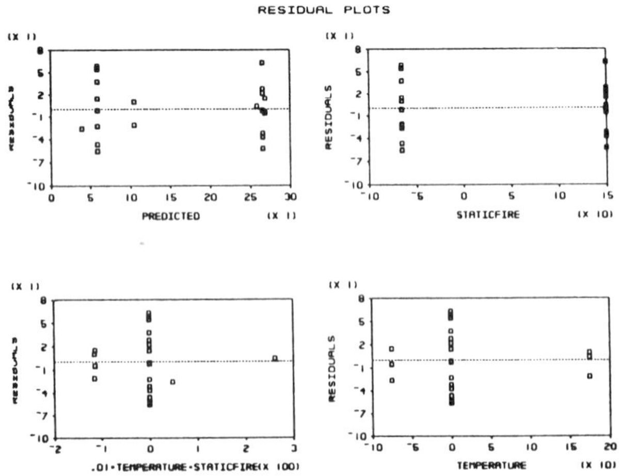

Figure 11

Splitscreen Residual Plot Generated by the PF6 Key From Within MODEL

```
RESIDUAL ANALYSIS

NUMBER OF RESIDUALS= 24
RESIDUAL AVERAGE = 1.0029E¯14
COEFFICIENT OF SKEWNESS = 1.0986   STANDARDIZED VALUE = 2.1972
COEFFICIENT OF KURTOSIS = 4.9109   STANDARDIZED VALUE = 1.9109
DURBIN-WATSON STATISTIC = 1.3500

FLAGGED OBSERVATIONS (INDEX, STANDARDIZED RESIDUAL, LEVERAGE,
                               MAHALANOBIS DISTANCE, DFFITS STATISTIC):
 19         ¯1.0009    0.37206  12.079    ¯0.03010
 21         ¯0.7444    0.51600  22.501    ¯0.76990

HIT ENTER TO CONTINUE.
```

Figure 12

Text Output Generated by the PF6 Key from Within MODEL

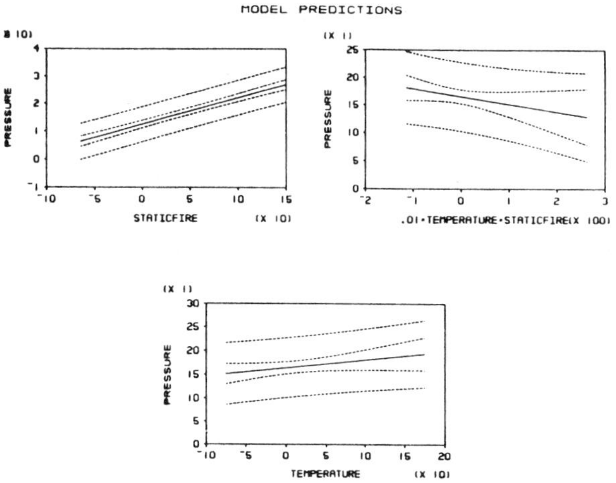

Figure 14

Fitted Model with Confidence Limits Generated by PF8 from MODEL

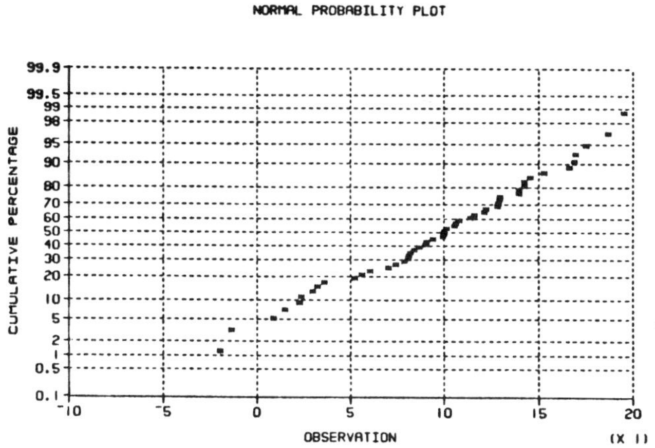

Figure 13

Normal Probability Plot of Residuals from PF7 in MODEL

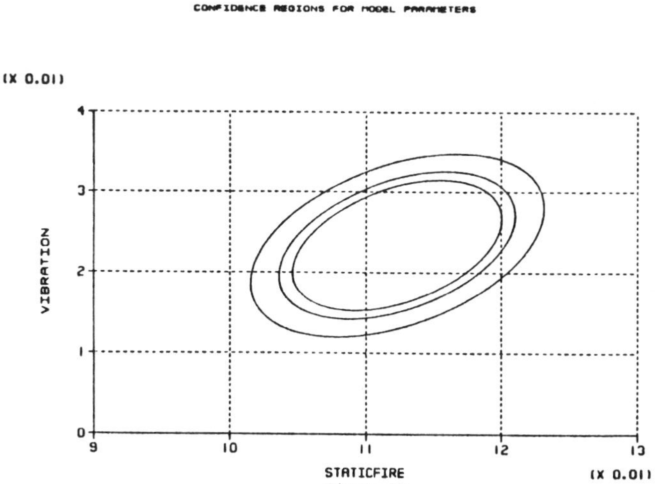

Figure 15

Joint Confidence Regions Generated by PF9 from MODEL

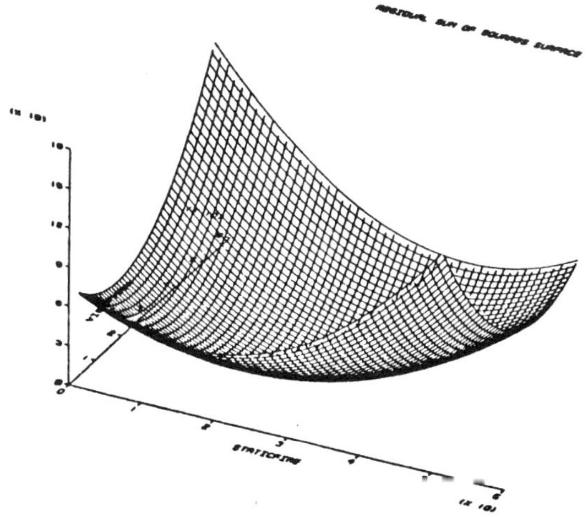

Figure 16

Residual Sum of Squares Surface from PF10 in MODEL

Other examples of fullscreen programming and nondisruptive graphics are illustrated in:

(a) Fig. 17, which shows the stepwise regression panel generated by MODEL if a stepwise fit is selected. Input fields on the panel allow for selection of forward or backward fitting, automatic or manual control, F values, and the maximum allowable iterations. Under manual control, the screen panel is updated at each step. After the algorithm selects a final model, variables can be forced in or out as desired, with the panel updated to show the result.

(b) Fig. 18 shows the fullscreen procedure control panel from ANOVA. Input fields allow the specification of vectors for the dependent variable and factor levels. When additional factors are added to the panel, the table will be automatically updated to show the new numerical results. Fig. 19 shows an example of the graphics output produced by PF keys from within ANOVA.

(c) The procedure control panel from TWOSAMPLE is shown in Fig. 20. Input fields allow for specification of confidence coefficients, null hypothesis values, one or two-sided alternatives, alpha level, and nature of the assumption regarding equal variances.

```
                         STEPWISE REGRESSION
SELECTION:    FORWARD                              CONTROL:     AUTOMATIC
F-TO-ENTER =  4.0             MAX STEPS = 50       F-TO-REMOVE = 4.0
                                 STEP 4
R-SQUARED = 0.97911                          C(P) = 3.0735
R-SQUARED (ADJ.) = 0.97472                   MSE = 2.9007 WITH 19 D.F.
  VARIABLES CURRENTLY IN MODEL              VARIABLES CURRENTLY NOT IN MODEL
VARIABLE               COEFF.  F-REMOVE     VARIABLE          PARTIAL CORR.  F-ENTER
  2. VIBRATION         .01027   13.7367     1. TEMP                 .0072     .1300
  3. DROP              .01065    4.4072     5. TEMP*VIBRATION      ¯.1620     .4051
  4. FIRE             ¯.11152  674.0007     6. TEMP*DROP           ¯.0560     .0565
 10. DROP*FIRE        ¯.00033   66.2952     7. TEMP*FIRE           ¯.2237     .9403
                                            8. VIBRATION*DROP      ¯.2717    1.4353
                                            9. VIBRATION*FIRE       .0007     .0000

                                            FINAL MODEL SELECTED


SPECIFY FINISH, ENTER K, OR REMOVE K: ENTER 0
```

Figure 17

Stepwise Regression Panel from Function MODEL

```
                  ANALYSIS OF VARIANCE - BALANCED DESIGNS
---------------------------------------------------------------------------
                   RESPONSE VARIABLE:  YIELD
---------------------------------------------------------------------------
SOURCE OF VARIATION       SUM OF SQUARES  D.F.  MEAN SQUARE  F-RATIO  PROB(>F)
---------------------------------------------------------------------------
TOTAL (CORR.)                  560.00000    19
---------------------------------------------------------------------------
TREATMENT                       70.00000     3     23.33333    1.239   .33066
BLEND                          264.00000     4     66.00000    3.504   .04075
ERROR                          226.00000    12     18.83333



ENTER DESIRED FACTORS, THEN
HIT ENTER TO FIT OR PF KEY.
```

Figure 18

Fullscreen Panel from Function ANOVA for Specification of Factor Variables

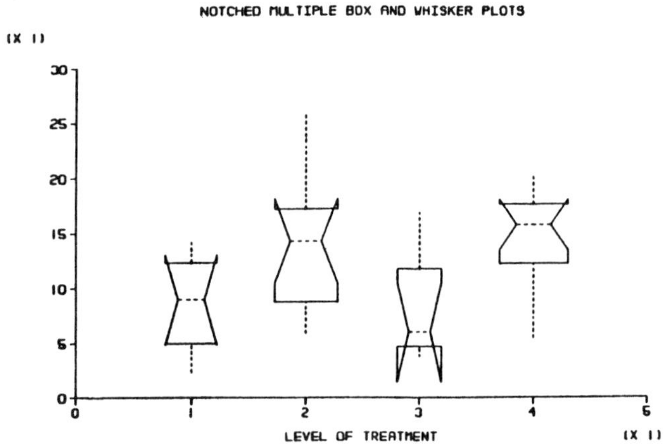

Figure 19

Notched Box and Whisker Plots Generated by PF5 from ANOVA

```
                           TWOSAMPLE ANALYSIS

                                        SAMPLE 1       SAMPLE 2       POOLED
SAMPLE STATISTICS: NUMBER OF OBS.       10             10             20
                   AVERAGE              84.24          85.54          84.89
                   VARIANCE             8.4204         13.325         10.873
                   STD. DEVIATION       2.9018         3.6503         3.2974
                   MEDIAN               84.5           85.4           84.6

CONF. INTERVAL FOR DIFF. IN MEANS:      95 PERCENT
 (EQUAL VARS.)    SAMPLE 1 - SAMPLE 2   ¯4.3901 1.7901      18 D.F.
 (UNEQUAL VARS.)  SAMPLE 1 - SAMPLE 2   ¯4.4094 1.8094    17.1 D.F.

CONF. INTERVAL FOR RATIO OF VARIANCES:  95 PERCENT
                  SAMPLE 1 ÷ SAMPLE 2   0.15696 2.5442       9     9 D.F.

TEST: DIFF. OF MEANS H0: DIFF = 0.0     COMPUTED T STATISTIC = ¯0.88158
                  VS  HA:      ≠        PROB(|T|>0.88158) = 0.38963
                  AT ALPHA =   0.05          SO DO NOT REJECT H0
    EQUAL VARIANCES ASSUMED:  YES

HIT DESIRED PF KEY (PF1 FOR LIST, PF12 TO END):
```

Figure 20

Fullscreen Procedure Control Panel for Function TWOSAMPLE

USER CREATIVITY

One of the most important distinctions between a graphics system and a system capable only of graphic display is the user's ability to define and manipulate basic graphics elements in new and creative ways. Without the ability to be creative, the data analyst loses many of the advantages offered by interactive computer processing. The peculiarities of any particular data set frequently suggest modifications of standard displays or entirely new techniques, which the user should be able to add to the system in a quick, straightforward manner.

User creativity can be encouraged in several ways:

(1) by providing basic plot functions with simple syntax designed to operate on a wide variety of data structures.

(2) by providing a simple mechanism to override default labels and scaling.

(3) by storing results in global variables for use outside the primary statistical procedures.

(4) by providing access to graphics primitives to allow the creation and manipulation of basic objects.

(5) by providing functions which allow the user to exercise primary control over the graphic display surface.

In STATGRAPHICS, a basic plot facility is provided through the syntax:

```
(a)  PLOT Y VS X
(b)  PLOT Z VS X AND Y
(c)  PLOT Y1 AND Y2 VS X
(d)  PLOT (Z1 VS X1 AND Y1) WITH Z2 VS X2 AND Y2
```

where X,Y,Z,X1,X2,Y1,Y2,Z1 and Z2 are APL vectors or expressions resulting in vectors of equal length. (a) and (c) produce 2-dimensional displays as in Fig. 21, while (b) and (d) produce 3-D displays as in Fig. 22. The AND and WITH functions allow for multiple plots on a single set of axes.

To override default labels and scaling, modular functions called TITLE, SCALEAXIS, LINETYPE and POINTTYPE can be executed separately or imbedded in user-written functions. Alternatively, PLOTOPTIONS displays a fullscreen panel (Fig. 23) on which all labels, scaling, point and line types can be specified by screen editing.

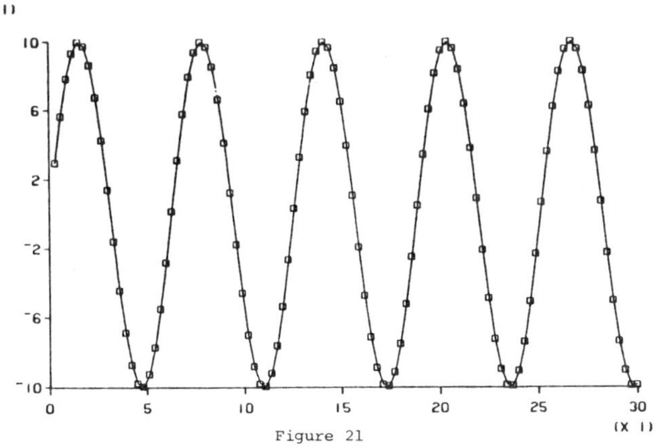

Figure 21

Basic 2-D Plot Created by PLOT Y VS X

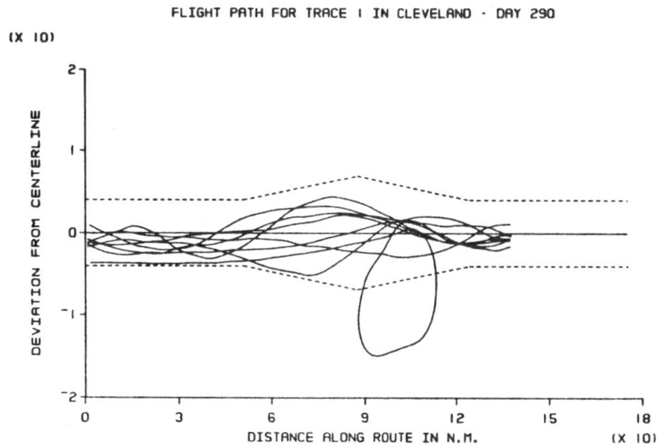

Figure 24

User-Created Display of Flight Traces Along a Jet Route in Cleveland

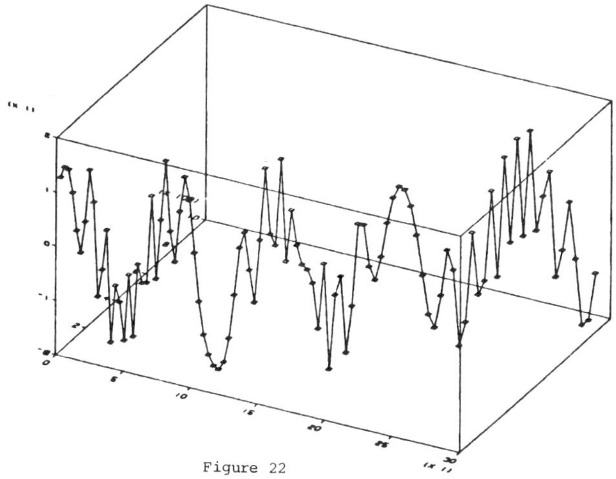

Figure 22

Basic 3-D Plot Created by PLOT Z VS X AND Y

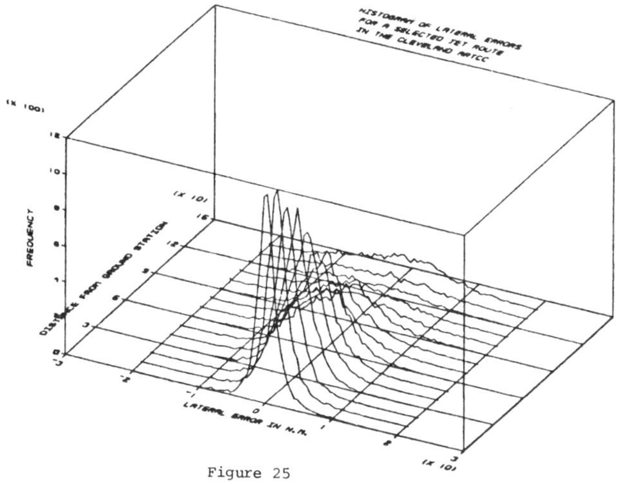

Figure 25

3-D Distribution of Navigational Error Distributions by Distance from Ground Station

```
                         USER SPECIFICATION OF PLOT OPTIONS

TOP TITLE     :   THIS IS THE TOP TITLE
 (ENTER UP TO     IN TWO LINES.
   3 LINES)
X-AXIS TITLE:     X-AXIS TITLE
  (2 LINES)
Y-AXIS TITLE:     Y-AXIS TITLE
  (2 LINES)
Z-AXIS TITLE:
  (2 LINES)

X-AXIS MARKS:     0 4 8 12 16 20 24 28 32
Y-AXIS MARKS:     -2 0 2
Z-AXIS MARKS:

LOG X-AXIS   :    NO
LOG Y-AXIS   :    NO
LOG Z-AXIS   :    NO

POINT TYPES  :    12
LINE TYPES   :    DL

HIT ENTER TO CONTINUE.
```

Figure 23

Fullscreen Panel for Selection of Axis Titles and Scaling from PLOTOPTIONS

By combining these basic functions in the desired order, usually within other user-written functions, unique displays can be created. Figs. 24 and 25 show an interesting example. The first is a plot of nine radar flight traces along a jet route in the Cleveland air route traffic control center (including one holding pattern), while the second figure displays the observed distribution of lateral errors from route centerline (of a larger sample) by distance from the navigational ground station located at the beginning of the route.

SPLITSCREEN PLOTTING

Many of the newer graphics terminals have a resolution high enough to permit multiple plots to be displayed simultaneously. In many statistical applications, side-by-side comparisons can be very informative. The user needs the capability to segment the screen and access various segments for display of desired images.

STATGRAPHICS creates splitscreen plots in several situations. Figs. 11 and 14, illustrated earlier, are examples. Other interesting applications include the display of multivariate control charts (Fig. 26), the display of individual components in a seasonal decomposition (Fig. 27), and the display of sample autocorrelation functions for various orders of differencing (Fig. 28).

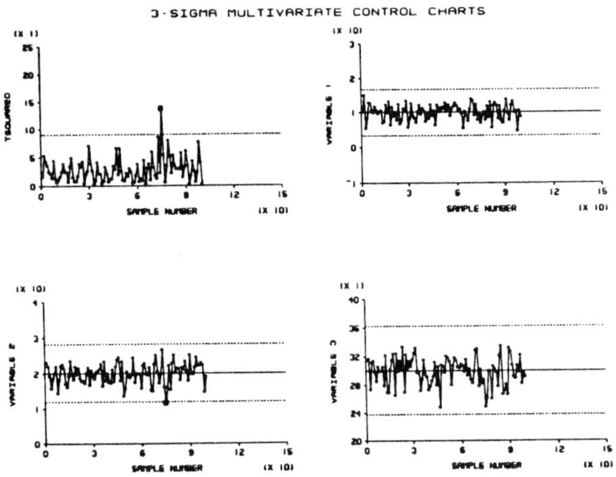

Figure 26

Splitscreen Plot Generated by CONTROLM

HARDWARE CONSIDERATIONS

With the many recent developments in interactive graphics terminals, selecting the best configuration is sometimes a difficult task. Some obvious concerns are:

(a) What type of resolution is required?

(b) Is graphics input as well as output needed?

(c) Would two separate devices, one for text and one for graphics, be desirable?

(d) Should color be available?

(e) What type of hard copies are needed?

(f) Is there a need to dynamically rotate 3-dimensional objects?

For a user who typically creates graphics to serve a summary role, making extensive use of piecharts, barcharts and the like, resolution is less important than color and good hardcopy features. On the other hand, when a major use of graphics is analytical, low levels of resolution can prove to be bothersome. If many original displays are likely to be created, or dynamic manipulation is desired, then a dual-screen configuration is desirable.

The IBM3277 graphics attachment, which consists of a 3270 display terminal for text I/O and a Tektronix storage tube for graphics I/O, has proven to be a powerful configuration for analytical purposes. The two screens allow for simultaneous display of numerical and graphics output, and the high resolution of the Tektronix tube allows for splitscreen plotting and detailed displays. While STATGRAPHICS has been designed to run under many configurations, including IBM3270 and 3279 terminals, Tektronix 4013 and 4015 terminals, and Datamedias, none of those configurations gives the interactive data analyst the same type of power as the 3277GA.

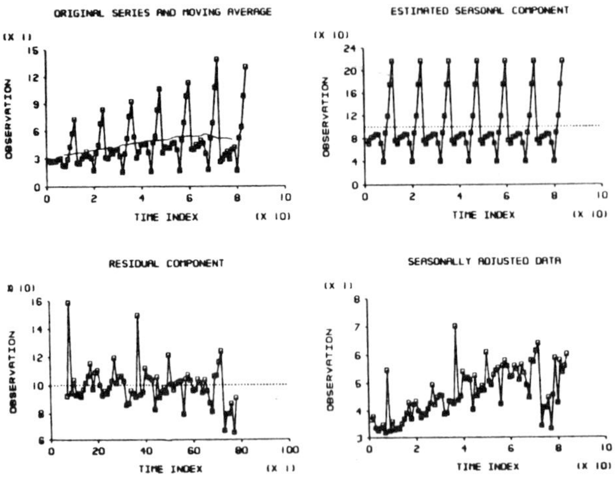

Figure 27

Splitscreen Plot Generated by SEASON

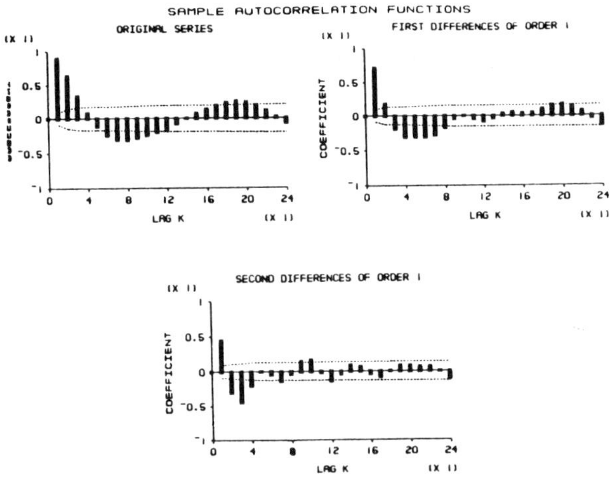

Figure 28

Splitscreen Plot Generated by ARIMA

CONCLUSION

The type of data analysis environment needed to meet the special requirements of interactive computing differs greatly from that of batch-oriented systems. Much more concern must be given to the user-machine interface, particularly with regard to the system control structure and the exchange of information. Fullscreen control panels, program function keys, menu panels, interactive access to source code, functional modularity, on-line documentation, and access to the host language are all important means of achieving efficient interactive data analysis. The statistical software systems developed over the next five years will undoubtedly help determine the most effective use of these various techniques.

REFERENCES

Anscombe, F.J. (1981) Computing in Statistical Science Through APL, Springer-Verlag, NY.

McNeil, D.R. (1977), Interactive Data Analysis, Wiley, NY.

Smillie, K.W. (1974), APL/360 With Statistical Applications, Addison-Wesley, MA.

Muller, M.E. (1980), "Aspects of Statistical Computing: What Packages for the 1980's Ought To Do," The American Statistician, Vol. 34, pp. 159-168.

Filliben, J.J. (1979), "Factors Affecting the Use of Statistical Graphics Software," Computer Science and Statistics: 12th Symposium on the Interface, pp. 147-154.

THE APPLICATION OF DUAL SCREEN GRAPHICS AND APL TO INTERACTIVE DATA ANALYSIS

P. Heidelberger
P. D. Welch
L. S. Y. Wu

IBM Watson Research Center
Yorktown Heights, N.Y.

ABSTRACT:
This paper describes an APL workspace, GRAFSTAT, designed for interactive scientific and engineering plotting and interactive data analysis. The workspace runs with a full-screen editing interface on the IBM 3277GA dual screen terminal. A number of special graphics functions for the description of one, two and three-dimensional data sets are described as well as a general plot routine which, with the support of APL and user developed APL statistical functions, becomes a highly flexible data analysis tool. The workspace also provides for the interactive design of customized graphics which can then be generated from the user's own APL functions. Designed to be user friendly, it has complete on-line help facilities.
Key words: data analysis, graphics, APL, dual screen.

1. Introduction

This paper will describe GRAFSTAT, an APL workspace (developed for use within IBM) for interactive data analysis, scienfific-engineering plotting and graphics output development. GRAFSTAT runs on the IBM 3277GA terminal (see [1]), a dual screen terminal consisting of a 3277 alphanumeric CRT terminal for user interaction and a Tektronix 618 for high resolution graphics display.

GRAFSTAT is a set of generic graphical-statistical functions. There is a one-one correspondence between these functions and a set of 3277 control screens. The user edits default entries in these control screens to provide specific parameters for the functions. The system is PF key driven in that the user moves from control screen to control screen, obtains on line help, makes hard copies, etc. by pressing the PF keys on the 3277.

The workspace was designed to be user friendly with on line help for each entry, a full screen editing interface and carefully designed default controls. Although it has substantial flexibility and power, very little knowledge is required to get started. The workspace is synergistic with APL in that APL expressions, including APL functions, can be used internally as entries to the control screens and in that graphics output designed interactively in GRAFSTAT can be generated externally as part of user written APL functions. Both of these features will be illustrated below.

GRAFSTAT has thirteen different functions. They are:

general plot
general write
scatter plot (with least squares fitting)
cumulative distribution function
concentration function
histogram
empirical density
scatter plot analysis
scatter plot analysis with zeros grouped
category subpopulation analysis
multipopulation confidence interval generation
regression (least squares) analysis
multiple population analysis

In Section 2 we will describe the first of these functions, general plot, and use it to illustrate both the interactive nature of the workspace and the flexibility and power provided through the use of APL expressions as entries in the control screens. Section 2 also contains a description of the general write function. Sections 3 through 7 describe briefly the remaining eleven functions. Finally, Section 8 describes the customized graphics generation capability and Section 9 contains a summary of the paper.

2. The General Plot and General Write Functions

The general plot function provides a full screen interface to an extremely flexible two dimensional plotting facility. More than one set of X coordinate values can be plotted, each against multiple sets of Y coordinate values. Controls are provided for symbol types, line types, axis labeling, plot labeling, axis scaling, axis location, presence or absence of grid lines, position of the plot on the screen, etc. The full screen interface with the default entries is shown in Figure A1 of Appendix A. These entries are edited to generate the controls desired for a particular plot. Help is available by locating the cursor at the entry position in question and pushing PF1. The help responses corresponding to the entries of Figure A1 are given in Appendix A. By studying the full screen interface and the help entries the reader can obtain a appreciation of the capability of the function.

The system is synergistic with APL. For example, the X variable and Y variable entries in the general plot function can be any APL expression which generates an APL entity of the proper type and shape. Hence, if the requirement is for an APL numeric vector of length 10, the following inputs are acceptable.

a) `1 2 3 4 5 6 7 8 9 10`
b) `⍳10`
c) `10↑ DATA` (where `⍴DATA=N≥10`)
d) `.4 FUNCTION X` (where this function with these arguments gives a vector of length 10).

Appendix B contains several examples of user responses to the general plot function frame and the corresponding 618 outputs. The illustrations involve the analysis of a simulated monthly sales sequence. YEAR is an APL vector which gives the time and SALES is an APL vector describing the simulated sales history. In Figure B1, YEAR and SALES have been entered as the X variable and Y variable respectively. The corresponding 618 response is given in Figure B10. Notice that very little user effort is required to get started. Figures B2 through B9 give the 3277 control screens for 8 more plots which represent the types of plots which might be made in the analysis of such a sequence. To equalize the variance, the log of the sequence (using the APL log operator) is analyzed. It is plotted through the control screen of Figure B2. The corresponding 618 output is in the upper left quadrant of Figure B11. In actual practice the four quadrants of Figures B11 and B12 would appear one at a time. We have put them up together to conserve space. Figure B3 illustrates the application of a 23 point cosine arch moving average smoother, (23 0) FILTER, from Anscombe's library of APL functions [2]. This is a low pass filter which removes all seasonal variation. (It has a null at all frequencies which are multiples of one cycle per year.) The 618 output is in the upper right quadrant of Figure B11. Figure B4 illustrates the application of another such smoother, a straight 12 point moving average which is also one of Anscombe's functions. The 618 output is in the lower left quadrant of Figure B11. Notice from the comparison of the plots that the cosine arch yields a much stronger low pass filter. Finally the control screen, Figure B5, generates both the original time series and the cosine arch smoothed series in the lower right of Figure B11. Figures B6, B7 and B9 show how you would use the general plot function to produce the detrended sequence, the periodogram of the detrended sequence and a quantile-quantile plot of the marginal distribution of the detrended values against a unit normal distribution. PERIODOGRAM is an APL function which generates the periodogram, PVALS N generates the sequence 1/2N, 3/2N,..., (2N-1)/2N, INIF is an Anscombe function giving the inverse normal distribution function, and AORDER X orders the vector X is ascending order. The corresponding plots are in Figure B12 in the quadrants indicated. These control screens and plots should give some feeling for the interactive functioning of the workspace and the interaction of it with APL. The histogram of Figure B8 will be discussed below.

From the general plot function (in fact from all the functions) via PF4 one can get to the general write function. This function enables you to write on the screen in a highly flexible manner. Controls are provided for font, size of characters, angle of text, box around text or not, justification of multiline entries, etc. The text can be either written at a specified location on the screen or the location can be controlled by the joystick.

One final feature possessed by the general plot and the general write functions (as well as the other functions) is the ability to store and retrieve the control responses and use the stored responses as variables for noninteractive versions of the function. Through a screen reached via PF10, any set of control responses can be stored by giving it a name. It will be stored as an APL character vector with that name. The vector can also be retrieved from this same screen by using the name previously given. There is an APL function RUN which when given, as an argument, the name of the character vector containing a set of stored responses will produce the corresponding 618 graphics in noninteractive mode. There is also a function creation capability which will generate an APL function containing a sequence of these RUN statements. Hence the user can interactively design a graphics program consisting of a sequence of RUN statements which he can use as to produce customized graphics in his own APL functions.

Thus, although the graphics routines built into GRAFSTAT perform very general graphics and statistical graphics functions, specialized graphics routines for particular application areas can be easily written using GRAFSTAT and then incorporated in user generated APL functions which both process data and produce graphics output. An example of this will be given in Section 8.

3. A Set of Four Functions for Describing One Dimensional Data Sets: Histogram, Empirical Density, Empirical Cumulative Distribution and Concentration

The histogram function generates equal bin size histograms. Controls exist for the bin size, bin boundary locations and line type as well as all the axis, scale, heading, label and position parameters described in connection with the general plot function. A selection input enables the user to reduce the data set by any specified APL binary vector of the same length. Thus suppose the data set were the APL variable X. Then if the selection entry were X≤25 the function would generate the histogram of all those elements of X which were less than or equal to 25. Finally, a set of weights can be specified and a "weighted" histogram produced. The "weighted" histogram accumulates the weights of the points in each bin. If all the weights are identically equal to one then the weighted histogram is identical to the regular (unweighted) histogram. If the data set were the APL vector X and the weight vector were identically equal to 1÷ρX then the weighted histogram would be a probability density estimate. If the user had a frequency table of values versus frequency of occurrence and inputed the values as the data set and the frequencies as the weights, the function would generate the regular histogram. A sample histogram 3277 control screen is shown in Figure B8 and the corresponding 618 output in the lower left quadrant of Figure B12.

The empirical density function generates a smooth representation of the distribution of a data set. If the data set is a sample from a probability distribution with a density, it estimates that density. Let the data set be the APL vector X. Then over each of the points of X it centers a raised cosine arch of area 1÷ρX and takes the summation of these cosine arches as the empirical density. Controls are available for the width of the cosine arch. This width is analogous to the bin width for the histogram function. Again, as with the histogram, a selection entry and a weighted option are available. The weighted empirical density gives a smooth representation of a distribution of weights. If the user had a weight vector W corresponding to the data set vector X then over each point X(I) a raised cosine arch of area W(I)÷(+/W) is centered and the sum these cosine arches is the weighted empirical density. Again all the general plot controls such as axis location and labeling, scaling, position, etc. are available.

The cumulative distribution function plots the standard empirical cdf. Again a selection option and a weighted option are available along with all the general plot controls discussed earlier. In the weighted case it plots the cumulative distribution function of the weight distribution.

Finally, the concentration of a data set X is the proportion of +/X contained in a set of largest values of X as a function of the proportion of elements in that set of largest values. For example, at the abscissa .1 the curve tells you what proportion of +/*X* is contained in the largest 10% of the *X*. Again a selection entry is available and a weighted option exists. Control of all the standard plot parameters is available.

The user can generate tables appropriate to all these functions. These tables are initially put on the 3277 but they can be transferred to the 618 and formatted jointly with the graphics.

4. A Set of Four Functions for Describing Two Dimensional Distributions: Scatter Plot, Scatter Plot Analysis, Scatter Plot Analysis with Zeros Grouped, and Category Subpopulation Analysis

There is a group of four functions for describing two dimensional data sets. There is a scatter plot function for the display of scatter plots and the least squares fitting of either a set of standard functions or user provided functions. Both ordinary and robust techniques can be applied. Again tables of statistics of the data set are available. As with the earlier functions these tables are initially displayed on the 3277 but they can be transferred to the 618 and formatted with the graphics output.

A scatter plot analysis function gives a graph which abstracts major features of a scatter plot. It takes as input a bivariate data set (represented in this discussion by the APL vectors *X* and *Y*) and a partitioning (set of intervals or bins) of the *X* axis given by a bin determination entry. It partitions the data into subpopulations according to the bin (interval) membership of the *X* variable and plots, for each subpopulation selected statistics (mean and quantiles) of the *Y* variable versus the bin mean of the *X* variable. Flexible partition or bin determination options are available. Also available is a box plot option which generates box plots of the *Y* subpopulations above the bin means of the *X* variable. In Figure 1 we have displayed a scatter plot and two scatter plot analysis outputs for the simulated sales data discussed earlier. In the first scatter plot analysis output the .05, .25, .5, .75 and .95 quantiles and the mean is displayed for the division of the *X* variable into 9 bins each containing roughly the same number of points. In the second scatter plot analysis output the box plot option is illustrated for the same set of bins. Notice how these outputs display the major features of the original scatter plot; namely the increase in the location and spread of the *Y*'s with increasing *X*. In this case these features are evident from the scatter plot itself; however, many times the eye cannot integrate the scattered points and successfully extract these features.

Also available from scatter plot analysis is a profile feature. This feature generates one dimensional data set analyses; one for each of the *Y* variable subpopulations. For example, suppose the user wished to have histograms for the *Y*'s corresponding to each of the nine bins in the example illustrated in Figure 1. Further supposed he wished them all to be plotted to the same scale. Then by proper entries in the histogram profile screen he could generate the output illustrated in Figure 2. Notice how the location and spread of the histogram changes, as expected, as the *X* variable increases. In this profile function the user has flexible control over the bin size and scaling. They can either be made common to each plot or not. Profile functions for empirical density, cumulative distribution, and concentration are available. Additional profile capability is available from scatter plot analysis but it will be discussed in connection with the analysis of three dimensional data sets in the next section.

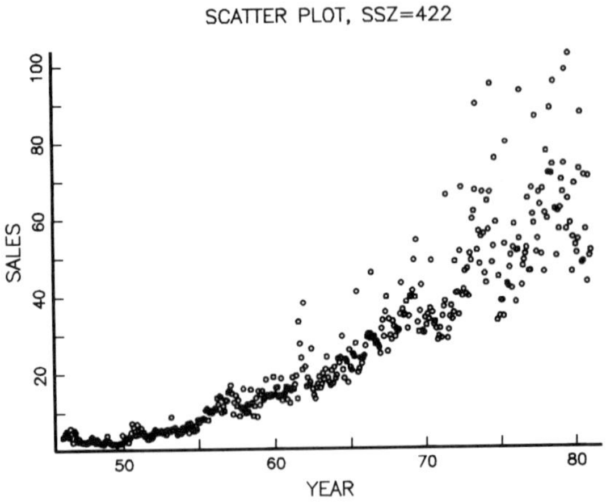

Figure 1a: Sample Scatter Plot

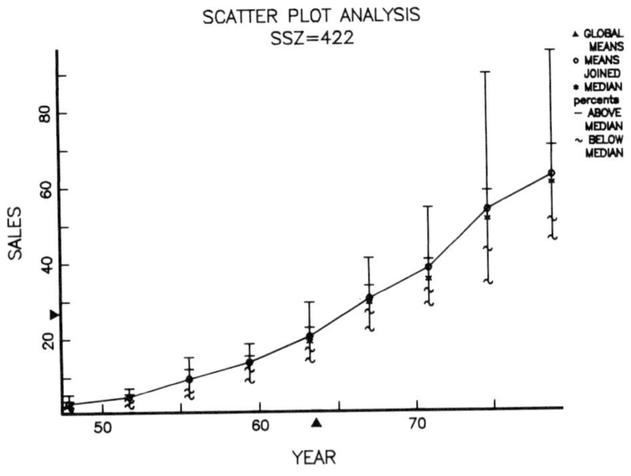

Figure 1b: Sample Scatter Plot Analysis

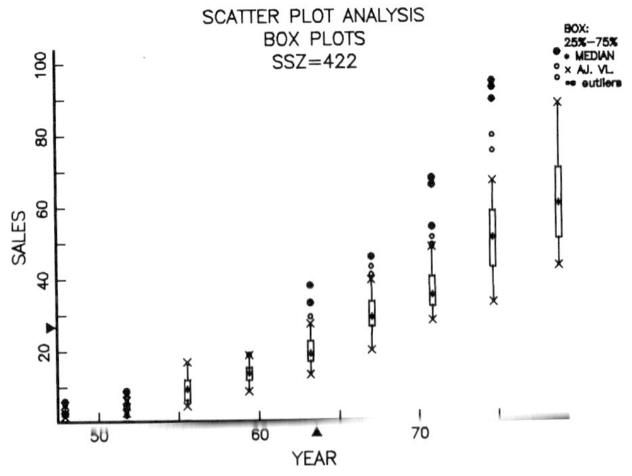

Figure 1c: Sample Scatter Plot Analysis with Box Plots

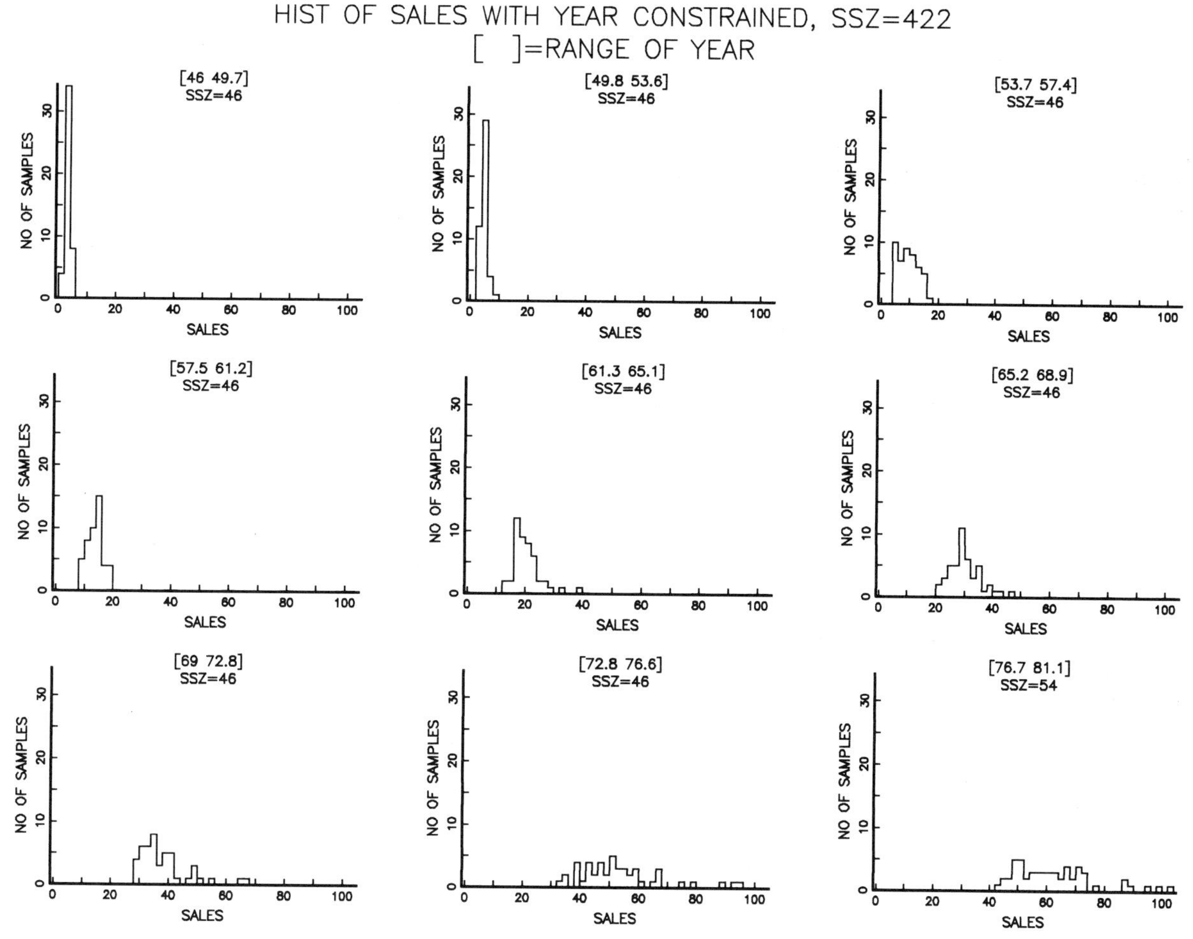

Figure 2: Sample Histogram Profile

There is also a function entitled scatter plot analysis with zeros grouped. It parallels scatter plot analysis exactly except that all the Y values corresponding to $X=0$ are grouped together in a single bin. Control of the bin locations is otherwise identical.

Finally, there is a function category subpopulation analysis. This function analyses the statistics of a data set Y when broken up into categories by a category vector C of the same length. The categories of the Y's are defined by the corresponding values of the elements of C. The statistics (mean and quantiles) are plotted against the corresponding category value exactly as the statistics of subpopulations of the Y's are plotted against the corresponding X value bin means in the case of scatter plot analysis. For example suppose the user had a data set Y of peoples heights and a vector C where the corresponding element was 0 if the person were male and 1 if the person were female. Then through category analysis the two populations could be compared with line graphs similar to the 9 line graphs of Figure 1b. Again box plot output is available as are selection options, weight options, and tabular output. The profile function also operates in a fashion parallel to scatter plot analysis giving one-dimensional analyses of each of the "categories" of Y.

5. The Use of the Profile Capability to Describe Three Dimensional Data Sets

Suppose a user has a three dimensional data set represented by the APL vectors X, Y and Z. He can analyze a family of two dimensional slices of this distribution using the profile capability of the scatter plot analysis function. He first runs the scatter plot analysis function for X and Y and defines subpopulations of the Y's based on the magnitude of the X's. Then he exercises the profile option for each of the subpopulation of the Y's and generates scatter plots or analyzed scatter plots of the Y subpopulations versus the corresponding Z subpopulations. Thus the partitioning on the basis of the X variable generates a set of bivariate Y, Z subpopulations which can be analyzed jointly by means of either scatter plot, scatter plot analysis or scatter plot analysis with zeros grouped. Flexible control of scaling is available and all the resulting plots can be drawn to a common scale or not. This is identical to the "casement window" views proposed by Tukey and Tukey [3].

Profile capability for any of the four two-dimensional functions is available from either scatter plot analysis, scatter plot analysis with zeros grouped or category subpopulation analysis.

6. Two Functions for the Description of Multiple One Dimensional Data Sets: Multiple Population Analysis and Multipopulation Confidence Interval Generation

The multiple population analysis function displays the statistics of multiple populations against a given set of parameter values, one for each population, in a fashion exactly parallel to the way the category subpopulation analysis function displays the statistics of subpopulations against the values of a category vector. Again the box plot option, selection option and weighting options are available as well as tabular output and a profile capability which includes all the one-dimensional functions.

The multipopulation confidence interval generation function generates and plots confidence intervals for either the mean or a quantile of multiple populations. The confidence intervals are plotted against specified parameter values. The elements of the populations can be either independent or serially correlated. A curve fitting capability is available.

7. The Regression Function

There is a linear regression function. The default option is classical unweighted least squares. Other options are weighted least squares and robust regression through the biweight technique as described by Mosteller and Tukey [4]. For a single model it will generate coefficient estimates, coefficient confidence intervals, and a simple analysis of variance table. It can not analyze a sequence of nested models. After the regression is run, the coefficients, the estimated regression vector, and the residuals are available for analysis via a subset of the functions (plot, scatter plot, scatter plot analysis, histogram, etc.) from the remainder of the package.

8. Using GRAFSTAT to Customize a Graphics Output Function

We will now illustrate how the RUN function and the GRAFSTAT function building capability described in Section 2 can be used to generate customized graphics programs. As we mentioned in Section 2 a set of function control entries (the responses to a 3277 control screen) can be given a name and stored as an APL character vector with that name. The function RUN will, when given this name as argument, produce the same 618 graphics output. Hence the user can use GRAFSTAT interactively to generate graphics output functions which can be included in his own APL function. Furthermore there is a function building capability which creates sequences of RUN functions automatically.

To illustrate this we have written a function which when given a time series as argument:

a) plots the series,
b) plots the periodogram of the series,
c) plots the logged periodogram of the series,
and d) plots the sample autocorrelation function out to a number of lags equal to .2 of the length of the original series.

To plot the time series of a generic vector *X* the control responses shown in Figure C1 of Appendix C are created. This set of responses is called TT1 and RUN TT1 is added to a GRAFSTAT function called TSERIES. In Figures C2 through C4 we give the control responses for the other three plots. These are called TT2, TT3 and TT4 respectively. The resulting function TSERIES is:

```
[0] TSERIES
[1] RUN TT1
[2] RUN TT2
[3] RUN TT3
[4] RUN TT4
```

Now all the control responses assume the existence of a sequence *X* hence if we edit the function TSERIES and give it the argument *X* creating

```
[0] TSERIES X
[1] RUN TT1
[2] RUN TT2
[3] RUN TT3
[4] RUN TT4
```

we can get these four output graphs for any sequence by just inputting TSERIES followed by the name of the sequence. For example, `TSERIES (10ρ1÷10) MAV RNORMAL 409` generates the output given in Figure C5. `RNORMAL` is another of Anscombe's [2] functions. `RNORMAL N` generates a vector *N* i.i.d. unit random normal deviates. The expression `(10ρ1÷10) MAV RNORMAL 409` generates 400 unit random normal deviates which are the output of a simple flat moving average filter of length 10.

Thus you can see how, interactively, a user can design a function which gives customized graphical analysis. This function could be further enhanced and edited to provide more graphics output, obtain user input information, conduct and display the results of statistical tests, etc..

9. Summary and Future Plans

GRAFSTAT is an experimental APL workspace for interactive scientific and engineering graphics and interactive data analysis. It also has capability for the interactive creation of customized user graphics programs. It is for IBM internal use. Further development of the workspace is continuing with planned additions which include a new fit function, additional axis control, automatic legend generation, 3-d surface generation, a more sophisticated regression and model building capability, a time series capability including univariate Box-Jenkins forecasting, and a collection of compatible statistical functions.

References

[1] IBM 3277 Display Station, Graphics Attachment RPQ 7H0284, Custom Feature Description, IBM Corporation

[2] Anscombe, F. J., Computing in Statistical Science Through APL, Springer-Verlag, New York, 1981

[3] Tukey, J. W. and Tukey, P. A., "Graphical Display of Data Sets in 3 or More Dimensions", Chapters 9-11, Interperting Multivariate Data, ed. by V. Barnett, Wiley, London, 1981

[4] Mosteller, F. and Tukey, J. W., Data Analysis and Regression, Addison-Wesley Publishing Co., Reading, Mass., 1977.

APPENDIX A: Additional Material on the General Plot Function

```
                         GENERAL  PLOT  FUNCTION

X VARIABLE                     : X
Y VARIABLE                     : Y
SYMBOLS A/O LINES VECTOR       : 0
TYPE OF LINES VECTOR           : 1
SYMBOL VECTOR                  : ∘+×○∇∆⎕⊛⍋⍒
PLOT HEADER (IN QUOTES)        : ∆
SCREEN HEADER (IN QUOTES)      : ''
X AXIS LABEL (IN QUOTES)       : ∆
Y AXIS LABEL (IN QUOTES)       : ∆
POSITION                       : 1
SCALE X-AXIS     : LIN             SCALE Y-AXIS     : LIN
PLOT ONLY (YES/NO)             : N
AXES LOCATION A/O GRID         : 0 1 0 0
```

Figure A1: Full Screen Interface for the General Plot Function

Help Responses for the General Plot Function

X VARIABLE(S): SET OF X COORDINATES ENTERED AS AN APL VECTOR. IF MORE THAN ONE SET, ENTRIES SHOULD BE SEPARATED BY ;'S.
DEFAULT: ANY DEFINED APL VECTOR NAMED X.

Y VARIABLE(S): SET OF Y COORDINATES (ENTERED AS AN APL VECTOR) FOR THE CORRESPONDING X COORDINATE ENTRY. MORE THAN ONE Y COORDINATE SET MAY BE ENTERED AS A MATRIX (EACH COLUMN IS CONSIDERED A SET OF Y COORDINATES). THE LENGTH OF THE Y'S, IF VECTORS, OR THE NUMBER OF ROWS, IF MATRICES, MUST BE EQUAL TO THE LENGTH OF THE CORRESPONDING X ENTRY. IF MORE THAN ONE Y ENTRY (CORRESPONDING TO MORE THAN ONE X ENTRY), THEY MUST BE SEPARATED BY ;'S.
THE NUMBER OF Y ENTRIES MUST BE GREATER THAN OR EQUAL TO THE NUMBER OF X ENTRIES. IF THE NUMBER OF Y ENTRIES IS GREATER THAN THE NUMBER OF X ENTRIES, THE LATTER Y ENTRIES CORRESPOND TO THE LAST X ENTRY.
DEFAULT: ANY DEFINED APL VECTOR OR MATRIX NAMED Y

LINES AND/OR SYMBOLS : 3 OPTIONS

```
        0 = SYMBOLS ONLY (NO LINES)        2 = LINES AND SYMBOLS
        1 = LINES ONLY (NO SYMBOLS)
```

THIS CAN ALSO BE A VECTOR TO CORRESPOND TO THE CASE OF MULTIPLE Y COORDINATE SETS. THE FIRST ELEMENT WILL APPLY TO THE FIRST Y COORDINATE SET, THE SECOND ELEMENT TO THE SECOND Y COORDINATE SET, ETC.
(IF A Y ENTRY IS A MATRIX EACH COLUMN IS A COORDINATE SET.)
IF THIS VECTOR IS TOO SHORT, THE LAST ELEMENT WILL BE USED REPETITIVELY. IF THIS VECTOR IS TOO LONG, THE LAST ELEMENTS WILL BE IGNORED.
DEFAULT: 0

TYPE OF LINES: OPTIONS 1 THRU 30--SEE RGRAFGA MANUAL--FIRST 5 ARE

```
        1 = PLAIN            3 = SHORT DASH          5 = DOT-DASH
        2 = DOTTED           4 = LONG DASH
                 THE LAST 15 ARE BOLDER.
```

THIS CAN ALSO BE A VECTOR TO CORRESPOND TO THE CASE OF MULTIPLE Y COORDINATE SETS. THE FIRST ELEMENT WILL APPLY TO THE FIRST Y COORDINATE SET WITH A LINE AND/OR SYMBOL OPTION SPECIFYING LINES (OPTIONS 0 OR 1),THE SECOND ELEMENT WILL APPLY TO THE SECOND SUCH Y COORDINATE SET, ETC. (IF A Y ENTRY IS A MATRIX EACH COLUMN IS A COORDINATE SET.)
IF THIS VECTOR IS TOO SHORT, THE LAST ELEMENT WILL BE USED REPETITIVELY. IF THIS VECTOR IS TOO LONG, THE LAST ELEMENTS WILL BE IGNORED.
DEFAULT: 1

TYPE(S) OF SYMBOLS : A SET OF SYMBOLS. THIS MAY BE EDITED TO BE ANY SET OF APL SYMBOLS. (A SYMBOL MAY BE REPEATED.) THE FIRST SYMBOL WILL APPLY TO THE FIRST Y COORDINATE SET WITH A LINE AND/OR SYMBOL OPTION SPECIFYING SYMBOLS (OPTIONS 0 OR 2). THE SECOND SYMBOL WILL APPLY TO SECOND SUCH Y COORDINATE SET, ETC.
(IF A Y ENTRY IS A MATRIX EACH COLUMN IS A COORDINATE SET.)
IF THIS VECTOR IS TOO SHORT, THE LAST ELEMENT WILL BE USED REPETITIVELY. IF THIS VECTOR IS TOO LONG, THE LAST ELEMENTS WILL BE IGNORED.
DEFAULT: ∘*+×∇∆○⊛⍋⍒

PLOT HEADER: A HEADING WHICH WILL APPEAR DIRECTLY ABOVE THE PLOT.
ALL TEXT MUST BE ENTERED IN QUOTES. NONE IS ''. ALL THE TEXT CONTROL FEATURES OF RGRAFGA MAY BE USED. SEE THE RGRAFGA MANUAL OR THE HELP COMMENTS FOR TEXT IN THE GENERAL WRITE FUNCTION (PF4). IN PARTICULAR, MORE THAN ONE LINE CAN BE WRITTEN BY USING THE SEPARATOR ¨. ':' MAY NOT BE USED IN THE TEXT.
THE NAME OF AN APL CHARACTER VECTOR MAY BE ENTERED (NOT IN QUOTES).
THIS IS EQUIVALENT TO ENTERING THE VECTOR ITSELF IN QUOTES.
IN RUNNING PROFILE FROM SCATTER PLOT, CATEGORY OR MULTIPLE POPULATION ANALYSIS, MULTIPLE PLOTS ARE CREATED. THIS ENTRY CONTROLS THE HEADINGS ON ALL THE PLOTS.
∆ INDICATES A DEFAULT ENTRY CONSIDERED TOO COMPLEX TO DISPLAY.
TO EDIT THIS EXPRESSION OR INSPECT IT, PUSH PF2.
DEFAULT: THE DEFAULT DEPENDS ON THE FUNCTION.
FOR THE PLOT FUNCTION IT IS ''.

SCREEN HEADER: A HEADING WHICH WILL APPEAR AT THE TOP OF THE SCREEN.
ALL TEXT MUST BE ENTERED IN QUOTES. NONE IS ''. ALL THE TEXT CONTROL FEATURES OF RGRAFGA MAY BE USED. SEE THE RGRAFGA MANUAL OR THE HELP COMMENTS FOR TEXT IN THE GENERAL WRITE FUNCTION (PF4). IN PARTICULAR, MORE THAN ONE LINE CAN BE WRITTEN BY USING THE SEPARATOR ¨. ':' MAY NOT BE USED IN THE TEXT.
THE NAME OF AN APL CHARACTER VECTOR MAY BE ENTERED (NOT IN QUOTES).
THIS IS EQUIVALENT TO ENTERING THE VECTOR ITSELF IN QUOTES.

CAUTION: WILL OVERWRITE PLOT HEADER WHEN POSITION OPTION 1 IS USED.
∆ INDICATES A DEFAULT ENTRY CONSIDERED TOO COMPLEX TO DISPLAY.
TO EDIT THIS EXPRESSION OR INSPECT IT, PUSH PF2.
DEFAULT: ''

X AXIS LABEL: THE LABEL FOR THE X AXIS. A SINGLE LINE OF TEXT MAY BE ENTERED IN QUOTES. NONE IS ''. ':' MAY NOT BE USED.
THE NAME OF AN APL CHARACTER VECTOR MAY BE ENTERED (NOT IN QUOTES).
THIS IS EQUIVALENT TO ENTERING THE VECTOR ITSELF IN QUOTES.
∆ INDICATES A DEFAULT ENTRY CONSIDERED TOO COMPLEX TO DISPLAY.
TO EDIT THIS EXPRESSION OR INSPECT IT, PUSH PF2.
DEFAULT: THE DEFAULT DEPENDS ON THE FUNCTION.
FOR THE PLOT AND SCATTER PLOT FUNCTIONS IT IS THE X VARIABLE(S) ENTRY (AS TEXT).

Y AXIS LABEL: THE LABEL FOR THE Y AXIS. A SINGLE LINE OF TEXT MAY BE ENTERED IN QUOTES. NONE IS ''. ':' MAY NOT BE USED.
THE NAME OF AN APL CHARACTER VECTOR MAY BE ENTERED (NOT IN QUOTES).
THIS IS EQUIVALENT TO ENTERING THE VECTOR ITSELF IN QUOTES.
∆ INDICATES A DEFAULT ENTRY CONSIDERED TOO COMPLEX TO BE DISPLAYED.
TO EDIT THIS EXPRESSION OR INSPECT IT, PUSH PF2.
DEFAULT: THE DEFAULT DEPENDS ON THE FUNCTION.
FOR THE PLOT AND SCATTER PLOT FUNCTIONS IT IS THE Y VARIABLE(S) ENTRY (AS TEXT).

POSITION: POSITION OF PLOT ON THE SCREEN. 3 OPTIONS:

```
FIXED POSITIONS----ONE PLOT PER SCREEN
        1: ONE PLOT ON FULL SCREEN
       10: ONE PLOT WITH DIMENSIONS PROPORTIONAL TO 8 1/2 BY 11
FIXED POSITIONS----MORE THAN ONE PLOT PER SCREEN
    21-22: 2 PLOTS PER SCREEN      41-44: 4 PLOTS PER SCREEN
    31-33: 3 PLOTS PER SCREEN      91-99: 9 PLOTS PER SCREEN
    THE SECOND DIGIT INDICATES THE POSITION OF THE  PLOT ON
    THE SCREEN FROM UPPER LEFT TO LOWER RIGHT RESPECTIVELY.
ARBITRARY POSITION SPECIFIED BY THE USER
    XL YL XU YU: A 4 ELEMENT VECTOR
```

```
        (XL,YL): LOWER LEFT POINT OF PLOT AS PROPORTIONS OF
                 TOTAL SCREEN DIMENSIONS (0≤XL,YL≤1)
        (XU,YU): UPPER RIGHT POINT OF PLOT AS PROPORTIONS OF
                 TOTAL SCREEN DIMENSIONS (0≤XL<XU≤1,0≤YL<YU≤1)
DEFAULT: 1

X AXIS SCALE: SETS THE SCALE OF THE X AXIS
          LIN: LINEAR SCALE
               SETS LIMITS TO FIT DATA WITHIN PLOT
          LOG: LOGARITHMIC SCALE
               SETS LIMITS TO FIT DATA WITHIN PLOT
   LIN(LOG) X1 X2: A LINEAR(LOGARITHMIC) SCALE WITH LIMITS SET AT
               X1 AND X2 (X1<X2). X1 MAY EITHER BE A SPECIFIC
               NUMBER OR THE CHARACTER SEQUENCE XMIN. IN THE
               LATTER CASE THE LOWER LIMIT IS SET TO FIT THE
               SMALLEST X VALUE WITHIN THE PLOT. SIMILARLY, X2
               MAY EITHER BE A SPECIFIC NUMBER OR THE CHARACTER
               SEQUENCE XMAX. IN THE LATTER CASE THE UPPER LIMIT
               IS SET TO FIT THE LARGEST X VALUE WITHIN THE PLOT.
            P: THE X AXIS SCALE OF THE PREVIOUS PLOT
  P LIN(LOG): THE X AXIS SCALE OF THE PREVIOUS PLOT BUT MADE
               LINEAR(LOGARITHMIC) IF IT WASN'T ALREADY.
DEFAULT: THE DEFAULT DEPENDS ON THE FUNCTION.

Y AXIS SCALE: SETS THE SCALE OF THE Y AXIS
          LIN: LINEAR SCALE
               SETS LIMITS TO FIT DATA WITHIN PLOT
          LOG: LOGARITHMIC SCALE
               SETS LIMITS TO FIT DATA WITHIN PLOT
   LIN(LOG) Y1 Y2: A LINEAR(LOGARITHMIC) SCALE WITH LIMITS SET AT
               Y1 AND Y2 (Y1<Y2). Y1 MAY EITHER BE A SPECIFIC
               NUMBER OR THE CHARACTER SEQUENCE YMIN. IN THE
               LATTER CASE THE LOWER LIMIT IS SET TO FIT THE
               SMALLEST Y VALUE WITHIN THE PLOT. SIMILARLY, Y2
               MAY EITHER BE A SPECIFIC NUMBER OR THE CHARACTER
               SEQUENCE YMAX. IN THE LATTER CASE THE UPPER LIMIT
               IS SET TO FIT THE LARGEST Y VALUE WITHIN THE PLOT.
            P: THE Y AXIS SCALE OF THE PREVIOUS PLOT
  P LIN(LOG): THE Y AXIS SCALE OF THE PREVIOUS PLOT BUT MADE
               LINEAR(LOGARITHMIC) IF IT WASN'T ALREADY.
DEFAULT: THE DEAULT DEPENDS ON THE FUNCTION.

PLOT ONLY:    2 OPTIONS
   YES(Y): ONLY THE LINES AND SYMBOLS ARE DRAWN. NO AXES, LABELS, ETC.
    NO(N): EVERYTHING SPECIFIED IS DRAWN
DEFAULT: N

AXES LOCATION A/O GRID: LOCATION OF THE AXES AND PRESENCE OR
ABSENCE OF GRID LINES. A 4 ELEMENT VECTOR. FROM LEFT TO RIGHT:
          X AXIS LOCATION: 0 (BOTTOM)
                           2 (TOP)
                           20 (AT Y=0)
                           10 (TOP AND BOTTOM)
          Y AXIS LOCATION: 1 (LEFT)
                           3 (RIGHT)
                           21 (AT X=0)
                           11 (RIGHT AND LEFT)
   VERTICAL LINES OF GRID: 0=NO GRID, 1=DASHED GRID, 2=SOLID GRID
 HORIZONTAL LINES OF GRID: 0=NO GRID, 1=DASHED GRID, 2=SOLID GRID
DEFAULT: 0 1 0 0
```

APPENDIX B: Examples of General Plot Screens and Corresponding 618 Responses

```
X VARIABLE                      : YEAR
Y VARIABLE                      : SALES
SYMBOLS A/O LINES VECTOR        : 0
TYPE OF LINES VECTOR            : 1
SYMBOL VECTOR                   : ∘+×○∇∆⎕⍟⍋⍒
PLOT HEADER (IN QUOTES)         : ''
SCREEN HEADER (IN QUOTES)       : ''
X AXIS LABEL (IN QUOTES)        : ∆
Y AXIS LABEL (IN QUOTES)        : ∆
POSITION                        : 1
SCALE X-AXIS    : LIN              SCALE Y-AXIS     : LIN
PLOT ONLY (YES/NO)              : N
AXES LOCATION A/O GRID          : 0 1 0 0
```

Figure B1: Simple Control Screen

```
X VARIABLE                      : YEAR
Y VARIABLE                      : ⍟SALES
SYMBOLS A/O LINES VECTOR        : 1
TYPE OF LINES VECTOR            : 1
SYMBOL VECTOR                   : ∘+×○∇∆⎕⍟⍋⍒
PLOT HEADER (IN QUOTES)         : ''
SCREEN HEADER (IN QUOTES)       : ''
X AXIS LABEL (IN QUOTES)        : 'YEAR'
Y AXIS LABEL (IN QUOTES)        : 'REVENUE'
POSITION                        : 41
SCALE X-AXIS    : LIN              SCALE Y-AXIS     : LIN
PLOT ONLY (YES/NO)              : N
AXES LOCATION A/O GRID          : 0 1 0 0
```

Figure B2: Control Screen for Logged Sales Plot

```
X VARIABLE                      : 11↓¯11↓YEAR
Y VARIABLE                      : (23 0) FILTER ⍟SALES
SYMBOLS A/O LINES VECTOR        : 1
TYPE OF LINES VECTOR            : 1
SYMBOL VECTOR                   : ∘+×○∇∆⎕⍟⍋⍒
PLOT HEADER (IN QUOTES)         : ''
SCREEN HEADER (IN QUOTES)       : ''
X AXIS LABEL (IN QUOTES)        : 'YEAR'
Y AXIS LABEL (IN QUOTES)        : ∆
POSITION                        : 42
SCALE X-AXIS    : LIN              SCALE Y-AXIS     : LIN
PLOT ONLY (YES/NO)              : N
AXES LOCATION A/O GRID          : 0 1 0 0
```

Figure B3: Control Screen for Cosine Arch Smoothing

```
X VARIABLE                      : .04+5↓¯6↓YEAR
Y VARIABLE                      : (12⍴1÷12) MAV ⍟SALES
SYMBOLS A/O LINES VECTOR        : 1
TYPE OF LINES VECTOR            : 1
SYMBOL VECTOR                   : ∘+×○∇∆⎕⍟⍋⍒
PLOT HEADER (IN QUOTES)         : ''
SCREEN HEADER (IN QUOTES)       : ''
X AXIS LABEL (IN QUOTES)        : 'YEAR'
Y AXIS LABEL (IN QUOTES)        : ∆
POSITION                        : 43
SCALE X-AXIS    : LIN              SCALE Y-AXIS     : LIN
PLOT ONLY (YES/NO)              : N
AXES LOCATION A/O GRID          : 0 1 0 0
```

Figure B4: Control Screen for Moving Average Smoothing

```
X VARIABLE                       : YEAR;11↓¯11↓YEAR
Y VARIABLE                       : ●SALES;(23 0) FILTER ●SALES
SYMBOLS A/O LINES VECTOR         : 1
TYPE OF LINES VECTOR             : 2 16
SYMBOL VECTOR                    : ∘+×○∇∆□●⍋⍒
PLOT HEADER (IN QUOTES)          : ''
SCREEN HEADER (IN QUOTES)        : ''
X AXIS LABEL (IN QUOTES)         : 'YEAR'
Y AXIS LABEL (IN QUOTES)         : 'SALES AND SMOOTHED SALES'

POSITION                         : 44
SCALE X-AXIS     : LIN             SCALE Y-AXIS     : LIN
PLOT ONLY (YES/NO)               : N
AXES LOCATION A/O GRID           : 0 1 0 0
```

Figure B5: Control Screen for Moving Average Smoothing and Original Series

```
X VARIABLE                       : 11↓¯11↓YEAR
Y VARIABLE                       : DTSALES←(1 23) FILTER ●SALES
SYMBOLS A/O LINES VECTOR         : 1
TYPE OF LINES VECTOR             : 1
SYMBOL VECTOR                    : ∘+×○∇∆□●⍋⍒
PLOT HEADER (IN QUOTES)          : 'DETRENDED ●SALES'
SCREEN HEADER (IN QUOTES)        : ''
X AXIS LABEL (IN QUOTES)         : 'YEAR'
Y AXIS LABEL (IN QUOTES)         : ∆
POSITION                         : 41
SCALE X-AXIS     : LIN             SCALE Y-AXIS     : LIN
PLOT ONLY (YES/NO)               : N
AXES LOCATION A/O GRID           : 0 1 0 0
```

Figure B6: Control Screen for Detrended Series

```
X VARIABLE                       : (¯1+⍳400)÷400
Y VARIABLE                       : PERIODOGRAM DTSALES
SYMBOLS A/O LINES VECTOR         : 1
TYPE OF LINES VECTOR             : 1
SYMBOL VECTOR                    : ∘+×○∇∆□●⍋⍒
PLOT HEADER (IN QUOTES)          : ''
SCREEN HEADER (IN QUOTES)        : ''
X AXIS LABEL (IN QUOTES)         : 'CYCLES PER MONTH'
Y AXIS LABEL (IN QUOTES)         : ∆
POSITION                         : 42
SCALE X-AXIS     : LIN  0 .5      SCALE Y-AXIS     : LIN  0 YMAX
PLOT ONLY (YES/NO)               : N
AXES LOCATION A/O GRID           : 0 1 0 0
```

Figure B7: Control Screen for Periodogram of Detrended Series

```
X VARIABLE                       : DTSALES
UNWEIGHTED (0) OR WEIGHTS        : 0
SELECTION                        : ∆
BIN DETERMINATION                : 0 20
PLOT HEADER (IN QUOTES)          : ∆
SCREEN HEADER (IN QUOTES)        : ''
X AXIS LABEL (IN QUOTES)         : ∆
Y AXIS LABEL (IN QUOTES)         : ∆
POSITION                         : 43
SCALE X-AXIS     : LIN             SCALE Y-AXIS     : LIN 0 YMAX
PLOT ONLY (YES/NO)               : N
AXES LOCATION A/O GRID           : 0 1 0 0
```

Figure B8: Control Screen for Histogram of Detrended Marginal Distribution

```
X VARIABLE                       : INIF PVALS 400
Y VARIABLE                       : AORDER DTSALES
SYMBOLS A/O LINES VECTOR         : 0
TYPE OF LINES VECTOR             : 1
SYMBOL VECTOR                    : ∘+×○∇∆□●⍋⍒
PLOT HEADER (IN QUOTES)          : ∆
SCREEN HEADER (IN QUOTES)        : ''
X AXIS LABEL (IN QUOTES)         : ∆
Y AXIS LABEL (IN QUOTES)         : ∆
POSITION                         : 44
SCALE X-AXIS     : LIN             SCALE Y-AXIS     : LIN
PLOT ONLY (YES/NO)               : N
AXES LOCATION A/O GRID           : 0 1 0 0
```

Figure B9: Control Screen for Quantile-Quantile Plot

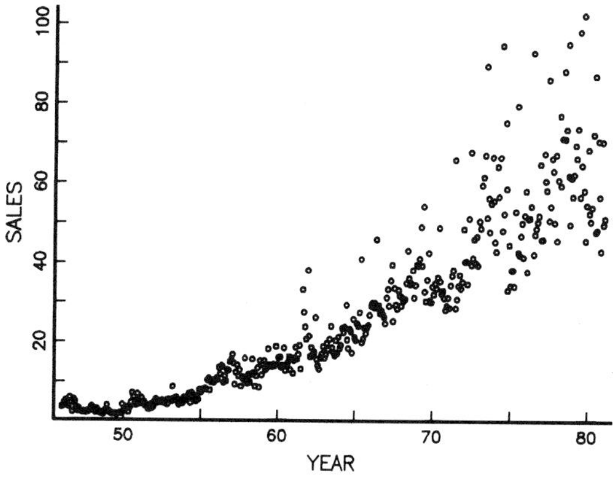

Figure B10: 618 Output Corresponding to Figure B1

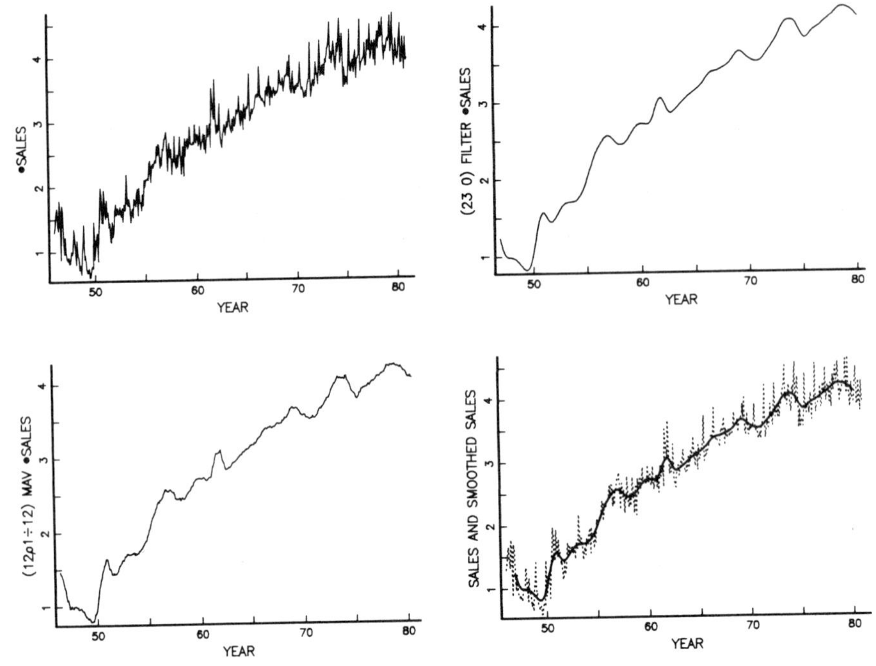

Figure B11: 618 Output Corresponding to Figures B2-B5

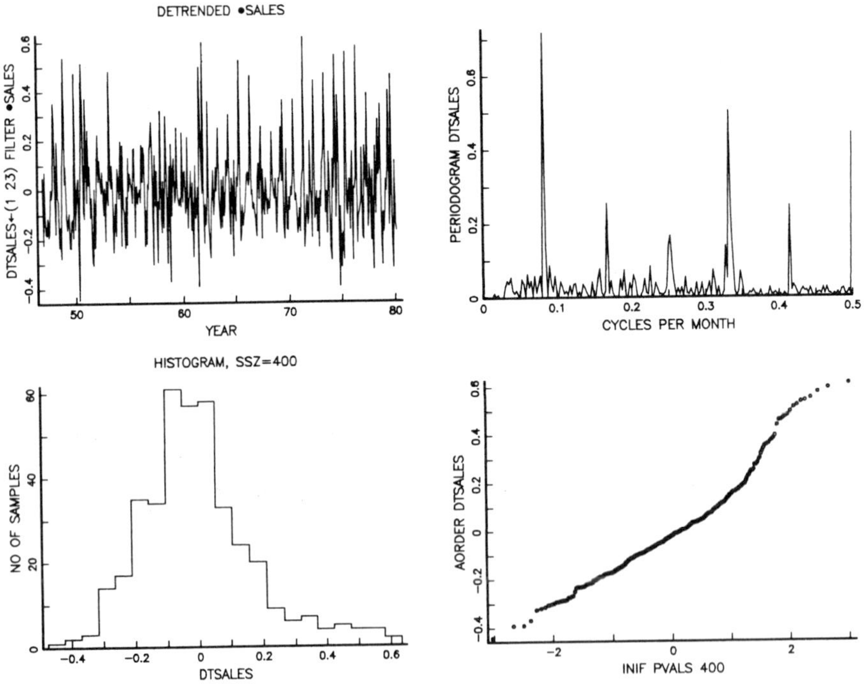

Figure B12: 618 Output Corresponding to Figures B6-B9

```
X VARIABLE                      : ιρX
Y VARIABLE                      : X
SYMBOLS A/O LINES VECTOR        : 1
TYPE OF LINES VECTOR            : 1
SYMBOL VECTOR                   : ∘+×○∇Δ⎕⍟⍋⍒
PLOT HEADER (IN QUOTES)         : ''
SCREEN HEADER (IN QUOTES)       : ''
X AXIS LABEL (IN QUOTES)        : 'NUMBER OF INCREMENTS'
Y AXIS LABEL (IN QUOTES)        : 'TIME SERIES'
POSITION                        : 41
SCALE X-AXIS     : LIN          SCALE Y-AXIS     : LIN
PLOT ONLY (YES/NO)              : N
AXES LOCATION A/O GRID          : 0 1 0 0
```

Figure C1: Control Screen TT1 for Plotting Time Series

```
X VARIABLE                      : (ι((ρX)-1))÷ρX
Y VARIABLE                      : 1↓PERIODOGRAM X
SYMBOLS A/O LINES VECTOR        : 1
TYPE OF LINES VECTOR            : 1
SYMBOL VECTOR                   : ∘+×○∇Δ⎕⍟⍋⍒
PLOT HEADER (IN QUOTES)         : ''
SCREEN HEADER (IN QUOTES)       : ''
X AXIS LABEL (IN QUOTES)        : 'FREQUENCY'
Y AXIS LABEL (IN QUOTES)        : 'PERIODOGRAM'
POSITION                        : 42
SCALE X-AXIS     : LIN  0 .5     SCALE Y-AXIS  : LIN   0 YMAX
PLOT ONLY (YES/NO)              : N
AXES LOCATION A/O GRID          : 0 1 0 0
```

Figure C2: Control Screen TT2 for Plotting Periodogram

```
X VARIABLE                      : (ι((ρX)-1))÷ρX
Y VARIABLE                      : 1↓⍟PERIODOGRAM X
SYMBOLS A/O LINES VECTOR        : 1
TYPE OF LINES VECTOR            : 1
SYMBOL VECTOR                   : ∘+×○∇Δ⎕⍟⍋⍒
PLOT HEADER (IN QUOTES)         : ''
SCREEN HEADER (IN QUOTES)       : ''
X AXIS LABEL (IN QUOTES)        : 'FREQUENCY'
Y AXIS LABEL (IN QUOTES)        : 'LOG PERIODOGRAM'
POSITION                        : 43
SCALE X-AXIS     : LIN  0 .5        SCALE Y-AXIS     : LIN
PLOT ONLY (YES/NO)              : N
AXES LOCATION A/O GRID          : 0 1 0 0
```

Figure C3: Control Screen TT3 for Plotting Logged Periodogram

```
X VARIABLE                      : ¯1+ι⌊1+.2×ρX
Y VARIABLE                      : ((+/⌊.2×ρX) AUTOCOV X)
                                  ÷1↑1 AUTOCOV X
SYMBOLS A/O LINES VECTOR        : 1
TYPE OF LINES VECTOR            : 1
SYMBOL VECTOR                   : ∘+×○∇Δ⎕⍟⍋⍒
PLOT HEADER (IN QUOTES)         : ''
SCREEN HEADER (IN QUOTES)       : ''
X AXIS LABEL (IN QUOTES)        : 'LAG'
Y AXIS LABEL (IN QUOTES)        : 'AUTOCORRELATION'
POSITION                        : 44
SCALE X-AXIS     : LIN  0 XMAX      SCALE Y-AXIS : LIN  ¯1 1
PLOT ONLY (YES/NO)              : N
AXES LOCATION A/O GRID          : 20 1 0 0
```

Figure C4: Control Screen TT4 for Plotting Autocorrelation Function

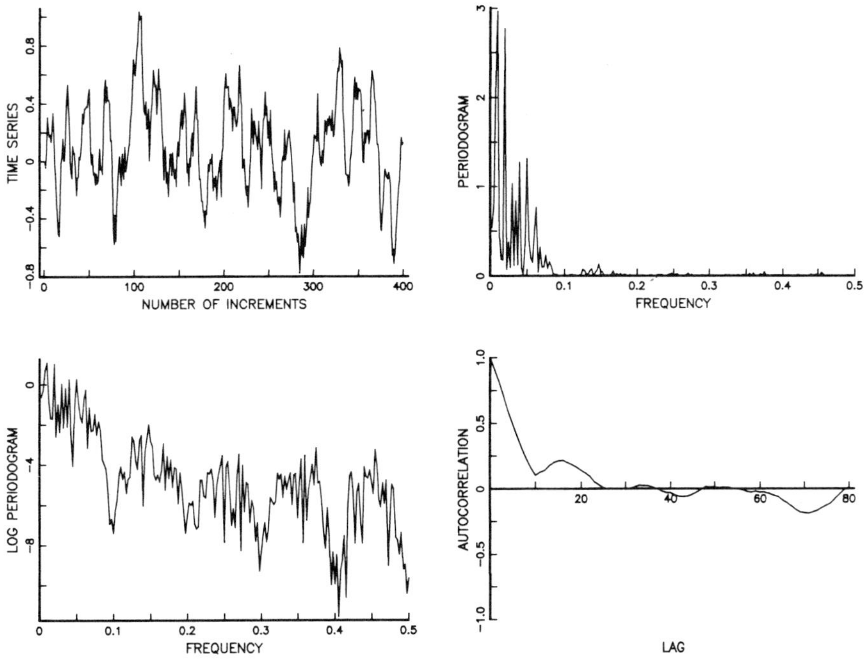

Figure C5: 618 Output of TSERIES Function

GRAPHICAL ANALYSIS OF REGENERATIVE SIMULATIONS

P. Heidelberger
IBM Watson Research Center

P.A.W. Lewis
Naval Postgraduate School

The independent block structure of regenerative processes and the known convergence rates of the means of ratio estimators are exploited to produce bias-reduced regression-adjusted estimates (rare's) for regenerative simulations. Formal and graphical assessments of the evolution of the distributions of the estimates to normality and symmetry are given. Other graphs show the evolution of the bias in the estimates as well as the bias reduction achieved by the rare estimate.

A protocol for guiding the analyst in the interactive and sequential use of the methodology is described. Sample graphs for the output of congested M/G/1 queueing simulations are displayed illustrating the application of the protocol. Empirical sampling tests on the statistical properties of the rare's are also reported.

P. Heidelberger, P.A.W. Lewis, "Regression-Adjusted Estimates for Regenerative Simulations, with Graphics" <u>Communications of the ACM</u>, 24(1981) 260-273.

Probabilistic Analysis of Algorithms

Chair: Jon L. Bentley, Carnegie–Mellon University

Probabilistic Issues in Data Structures

J. Ian Munro and Patricio V. Poblete, University of Waterloo

When is 'Average Case' Reliable: Variance Bounds in Algorithms (Abstract)

J. Michael Steele, Stanford University

Mapping to Cells: Extension of a Data Structure for Fast Storage and Retrieval

Bruce W. Weide, Ohio State University
David J. Hogan, Ohio State University and Bell Laboratories

Probabilistic Issues in Data Structures+

J. Ian Munro

Patricio V. Poblete •

Department of Computer Science
University of Waterloo
Waterloo, Ontario, Canada
N2L 3G1

ABSTRACT

This paper focuses on a number of problems dealing with the expected behaviour of various data structures. It includes both recent results and some open problems. Among the problems discussed will be the behaviour of a tree balancing heuristic, the determination of the expected height of a binary search tree and the expected behaviour of a search and update structure which avoids the use of pointers.

1. Introduction

In this paper we present an overview of some recent (and ongoing) work on the analysis of data structures. Rather than presenting the work in full detail, we simply outline the results and approaches and refer the interested reader to more detailed papers. The basic area of interest is that of structures for search and update including "proximity searches" (find closest value etc.). Hence the general topic of hashing is omitted and attention is primarily focused on search trees and other partial ordering schemes.

2. A Balancing Heuristic for Binary Search Trees

If a binary search tree is kept perfectly balanced then $\log_2 n$ comparisons suffice for a search. The difficulty is that if elements are inserted by simply appending them to the leaves at which their unsuccessful searches terminate a binary search tree can degenerate to a linear linked list. The danger of such a catastrophe can lead one to implement a balancing scheme such as AVL or weight balancing. In this way $O(\log n)$ search and update costs can be guaranteed. The cost of such schemes is the extra storage required for tags or counters and the program complication. This program complication affects both the cost of developing the system and the (constant factor in) run time of the update algorithms.

It is, however, well known that if we can assume the tree is created by inserting elements which have been presented in random order (all $n!$ permutations equally likely), we can expect the resulting tree to be rather well balanced. The average search time for an unsuccessful search in such a tree is $2(H_n - 1) \simeq 1.38 \log_2 n$ and its variance is roughly the same.

Given this rather encouraging information there are a few other questions which spring to mind:

(1) What is the expected height of such trees? (i.e., length of longest path). In other words, are most trees "good" or just most searches "good"?

(2) Are there any *simple* heuristics which can further reduce the expected search cost and, more importantly, the variance, or danger of a costly search?

Recently both questions have been answered positively. Robson [12] has shown that the expected height of a randomly

+ This work was supported in part by NSERC grant A8237.

• On leave from University of Chile

formed binary search tree is $\leq 4.31107 \ln n + o(\ln n)$ where the constant is $-1/w(-e^{-1}/2)$ and $w(x)$ is given by $w(x)e^{w(x)} = x$.

Gonnet [4] has now shown this bound to be accurate (in the lead term). The first step in the proof is to show the expected number of nodes at a depth significantly less than the bound is more than 1 and indeed that at greater depths it is less than 1. This fact is interesting in its own right but does not solve the problem alone. Could it be that most trees are of height far less than $4.3 \cdots \log_2 n$ but that the few which are this tall have many leaves at their lowest levels? Of course this doesn't happen, nature is not that perverse. But proving it is not easy. Gonnet's proof involves going to a continuous model and then developing a class of transforms which allow an accurate return to the discrete case through some analysis proposed by the second author.

The state of the art for such randomly formed trees is, then, rather good. However, one might like to reduce the average search cost and its variance. The following approach has been suggested by several authors [1,5,11,13]. When a new element is inserted, if in following the "usual" insertion scheme its father is the only son of its grandfather, a rotation is performed so that the middle of the 3-values is the father of the other 2 (Figure 1).

This simple "fringe heuristic" had been observed to reduce the average search cost. The authors [11] have recently analyzed the behaviour of this scheme obtaining the generating function and hence any moment of interest. The essence of the analysis is the classification of the types of external nodes or positions in which new elements could be inserted, before applying the heuristic, which are effected by an insertion (Figure 2). We say an external node is of type B if it is attached to the bottom of a pair, C if attached to the top of a pair and A otherwise

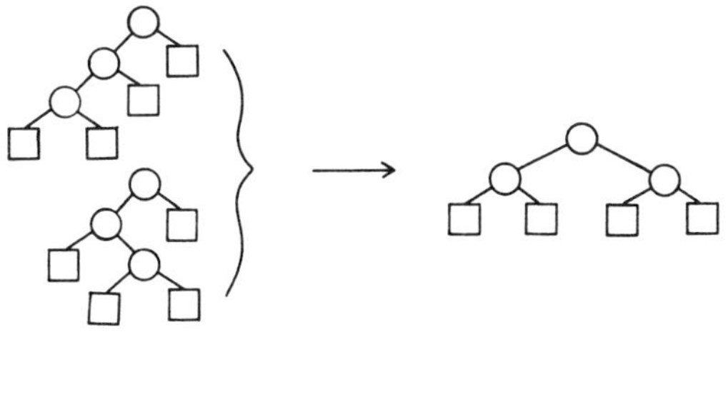

Figure 1
Basic fringe heuristic
○ denotes an internal node or data value
□ denotes an external node or missing element

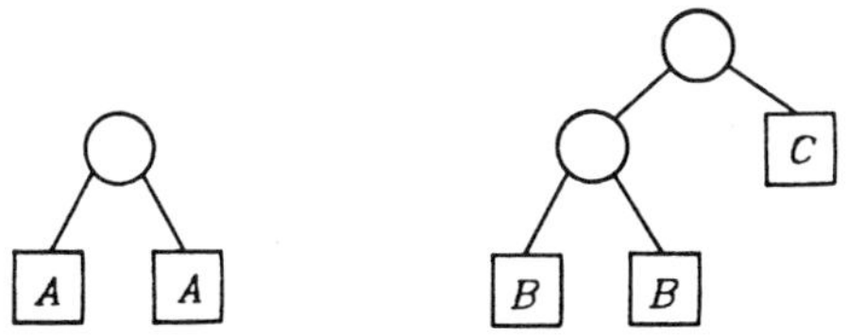

Figure 2
Types of external nodes

If a new internal node is to be inserted in the position of one of these external nodes then the transformation is described by (Figure 3). From this, one can derive "growth equations". Let $A_{n,k}$ be as defined as (expected # of A nodes at level k in the tree)$/n$, and $B_{n,k}$ and $C_{n,k}$ are similarly defined. Then we have the $A_{n+1,k}$ can be determined as

$$A_{n+1,k} = \frac{1}{n+1}(n\, A_{n,k} + 4(B_{n,k} + C_{n,k-1}) - 2A_{n,k})$$

indicating that an A node remains at level k if it was there in the tree on n nodes and the insertion is not made at that point or its brother. 4 new A nodes are created if the insertion occurs at a B or node or at a C node at level $k-1$ and 2 A nodes are "lost" if the insert occurs at the given position or its brother.

Based on this one can derive generating functions for A, B and C and hence the expected number of external nodes at any level. This gives us the generating function for the expected length of a search and indeed a mean of $\frac{12}{7}H_{n+1} - \frac{75}{49} \cdots$ and variance of $\frac{300}{343}H_{n+1} \simeq .61 \log_2 n$.

The most interesting feature is that the variance is reduced by more than a factor of 2. One can clearly extend this scheme to retaining at a node the median of the first k

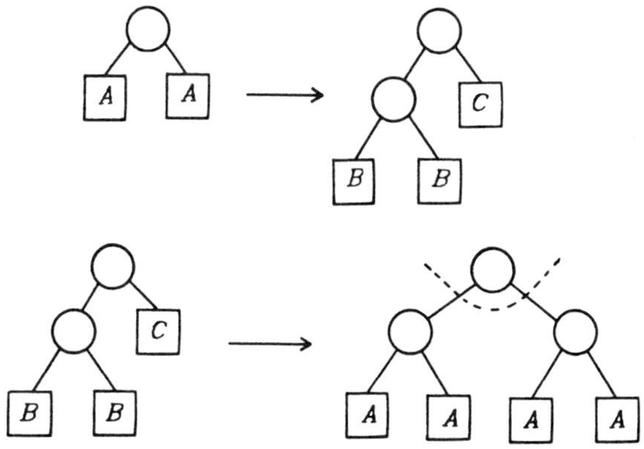

Figure 3
Transformation rules

values to reach that point. The general analysis is complicated by the fact that it involves an awkward eigenvalue problem. However we can derive the mean and variance in the general case.

The state of the art in analyzing the behaviour of "randomly formed" binary search trees is, as our examples show, rapidly becoming a rather solid area. Unfortunately a randomly formed tree which has had an element randomly removed and one randomly added is no longer "randomly formed" [7]. Although such trees seem even better balanced than their random counterparts, results in their analysis are very hard indeed. The analysis of even trees of 3 nodes is amazingly complex involving nontrivial manipulation of Bessel functions [6,8].

3. An Update Technique for a Pointer-free Structure

Binary search trees provide the flexibility of being able to perform updates efficiently as well as searches. The cost is the space required for pointers. The notion of developing structures in which searches and updates are performed efficiently, but no extra storage is required for pointers, has been investigated in the past few years [3,10]. In these structures the structural information must be implicit in the ordering of data rather than explicit in pointers. Bentley et al [2] suggested using $\log_2 n$ sorted lists of lengths 2^i $(i = 0, \cdots (\log n) - 1)$. This clearly permits searches in $\frac{1}{2}\log_2^2 n$ comparisons in the worst case and $2\log_2 n$ on the average. Insertions are made by adding a new list of length $2^0 = 1$. When more than 1 list of the same length exists, they are merged, giving an amortized insertion cost of $O(\log n)$. The authors [9] have shown how this amortized cost can be made a worst case bound with no increase of storage requirements. Deletions, as in the case of binary trees, are a problem. An apparently reasonable approach for the replace operation (an insertion and a deletion) outlined below. In [9] it is also shown that such a method can be extended to the case in which individual insertions and deletions are made and so n changes.

```
Update: remove x, insert y
  Find x in list i ;
  For j:=i-1 step -1 to 0 do
  begin
    Find a(k)<x<a(k+1) in list j ;
    Replace x by a(k) {or a(k+1)}
      and reorder list j ;
    x:=a(k) {or a(k+1)}
  end;
  a(1) of list 0:=y
```

The number of comparisons required for such an update is roughly $\frac{1}{2}\log^2 n$. The number of moves is the interesting term. Clearly the worst case is $\Theta(n)$, but the average looks more like $\Theta(\log n)$. Unfortunately it is not even clear whether the system is ergodic and no reasonable analysis is known. As more elements are changed the system seems to become slowly worse. For example in an experiment with 2047 elements $(2^{11}-1)$ the average number of moves required in the first 1000 updates was about 13, by the time 100,000 updates had been made the average number of moves was over 40. The difficulty of analyzing this technique seems analogous to that of handling deletions in binary search trees. Unfortunately, the experimental evidence is that the system degenerates rather than improving as binary trees seem to. We are inclined to hope that techniques for solving one of these classes of problems may be applied to solve the other.

4. References

[1] Bell, C.J., "An Investigation into the Principles of the Classification and Analysis of Data on an Automatic Digital Computer", Doctoral Dissertation, Leeds University, 1965.

[2] Bentley, J.L., D. Detig, L. Guibas, and J.B. Saxe, "An Optimal Data Structure for Minimal Storage Dynamic Member Searching", unpublished, Dept. of Computer Science, Carnegie-Mellon University, 1978.

[3] Frederickson, G.N., "Implicit Data Structures for the Dictionary Problem", to appear JACM.

[4] Gonnet, G.H., unpublished manuscript, Dept. of Computer Science, University of Waterloo, 1982.

[5] Itai, A. and M. Rodeh, "Modified Binary Search Trees", Tech. Report 182, Dept. of Computer Science, Technion-IIT, Haifa Israel, August 1980.

[6] Jonassen, A.T., and D.E. Knuth, "A Trivial Algorithm whose Analysis Isn't", JCSS 16 (301-322), (1978).

[7] Knott, G.D., "Deletion in Binary Storage Trees", Report STAN-CS-75-491, Dept. of Computer Science, Stanford University, May 1975.

[8] Knuth, D.E., "Deletions that Preserve Randomness", IEEE Trans. on Software Engineering, Vol. SE-3, No. 5 (Sept. 1972), 351-359.

[9] Munro, J.I. and P.V. Poblete, "Searchability in Merging", unpublished, Dept. of Computer Science, University of Waterloo, 1981.

[10]Munro, J.I. and H. Suwanda, "Implicit Data Structures for Fast Search and Update", JCSS 21 (1980), 236-250.

[11]Poblete, P.V. and J.I. Munro, "The Analysis of a Fringe Heuristic for Binary Search Trees", Research Report CS-82-22, Dept. of Computer Science, University of Waterloo, July 1982.

[12]Robson, J.M., "The Height of Binary Search Trees", The Australian Computer Journal", 4 (Nov. 1979), 151-153.

[13]Walker, A. and D. Wood, "Locally Balanced Trees", The Computer Journal 19, 4 (Nov. 1967), 322-325.

WHEN IS 'AVERAGE CASE' RELIABLE: VARIANCE BOUNDS IN ALGORITHMS

J. Michael Steele
Stanford University

Several algorithms are examined to see if expected running time is a reliable measure of performance even if one supposes a fixed model for the input data. It is shown that the Jackknife estimate of variance and the Efron-Stein inequality can be very handy tools for estimating the variance of running times. Some consideration is given to the long-tailed nature of some backtrack and branch and bound procedures.

MAPPING TO CELLS: EXTENSION OF A DATA STRUCTURE FOR FAST STORAGE AND RETRIEVAL

Bruce W. Weide, The Ohio State University
David J. Hogan, The Ohio State University and Bell Laboratories

Abstract - The well-known fast data storage and retrieval technique known as hashing has previously been modified to permit the hashing function to be monotonic, and to adapt to different distributions of the data values. The resulting structure, which we call a cell structure, is based on the statistical technique of sampling. In this work, we show how a dynamic programming algorithm can be used to construct a good mapping from sample values to cells. We also discuss applications of the algorithm (and the mapping) to traditional data storage and retrieval operations, show how a special case of the mapping, which is one-to-one, can be used for data compression and coding, and present an apparent time-space trade-off in using the technique. Finally, we present some open problems that might best be tackled by statisticians.

Keywords - hashing, dynamic programming, data compression and compaction, time-space tradeoff, sampling.

I. INTRODUCTION: HASHING AND CELL STRUCTURES

The technique of hashing is well-known and well-studied as a method for data storage and retrieval [Knuth73, Horowitz76]. Consider the task of maintaining a set of data items with the following operations:

- INSERT (x), which adds item "x" to the set;
- DELETE (x), which removes "x" from the set;
- FIND (x), which determines whether "x" is in the set, and if so, returns some information associated with it.

In theory, if the items of the set are from a linear ordering, and algorithms for performing the operations are only permitted to compare items, then in the worst case, at least one of the above three operations requires a number of comparisons at least proportional to log n, where n is the number of items in the set. In fact, using sophisticated balanced tree structures, this performance can be achieved; each operation requires time proportional to log n in the worst case.

Hashing is a scheme that is not "allowed" in the model of computation described above. In hashing, algorithms for performing the operations may do more than compare items of the set. In particular, they may make use of the following facts:

- Data items in a real digital computer are represented by strings of bits.
- The floor operation can be computed in constant time. The floor of x, where x is a real number, is denoted $\lfloor x \rfloor$, and is the greatest integer less than or equal to x.

The first observation permits the bits in any data item to be manipulated and re-interpreted, perhaps as floating point numbers. The second allows the "conversion" of such a number into an integer in constant time.

Of course, since these additional primitive operations are allowed, the above lower bounds on the running times of INSERT, DELETE, and FIND no longer apply. In practice, there are no known methods that perform in the worst case better than balanced trees. However, it is possible to improve on the expected running times, which is what hashing does. There are two parts to a hashing scheme. The first is the hash table, a vector of size m indexed, say, from 0 to m-1. Each position of this table contains a pointer to a data structure containing some of the data items in the set. This structure may be a balanced tree, for instance, but is usually just an ordinary linked list. The second aspect is a hashing function that maps data item "x" to an integer between 0 and m-1.

To perform FIND (x), for instance, we compute the hash function for "x", and follow the pointer in that position of the hash table to an ordinary data structure, where we FIND (x) as we would for that type of data structure. To INSERT or DELETE, we first compute the hash function, and then follow the pointer in the resulting position to a data structure where we perform the appropriate operation. In a sense, the hash table is a higher-level index into a group of data structures, each of which contains only a portion of the entire set of data items; see Figure 1.

In order for hashing to be valuable, computation of the hashing function must be very fast; in fact, it is usually taken to be a requirement that the hashing function be computed in constant time, independent of the number of items in the set. Suppose we assume this. Furthermore, suppose that the hashing function is equally likely to return each integer from 0 to m-1 as its result. (This assumption is usually justified by constructing a function that sufficiently "messes up" the bits in the representation of a data item so that the result bears no apparent relationship to the

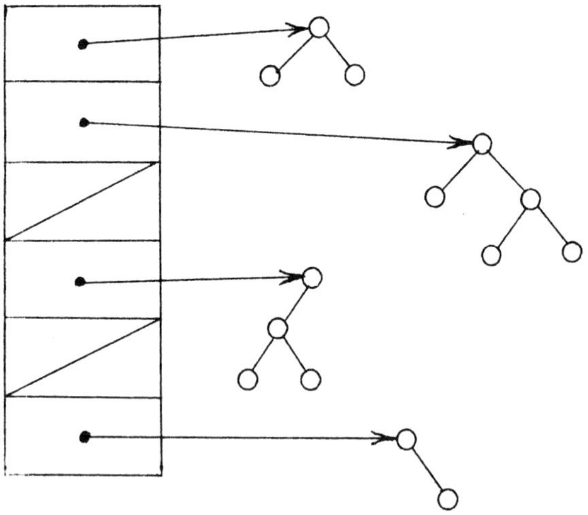

Figure 1: Hashing with binary search trees for each position.

argument, although there is of course quite a direct relationship!) Then the expected number of items that hash to each position of the table is n/m. If n/m is bounded above by a constant, then on the average there will be only a constant number of data items in each ordinary data structure, and doing INSERT, DELETE, or FIND on such a structure will take on the average constant time. Thus hashing can achieve constant expected time for each operation, and maintain good worst-case performance by making the smaller structures balanced trees.

In a previous paper [Weide79], we showed how the notion of hashing can be extended to permit fast execution of operations that depend on a proximity relationship among data items. Included are NEAR-NEIGHBOR and RANGE queries, and printing the data items in sorted order. The key ingredient is a monotonic hashing function. In ordinary hashing, the idea is to organize that data items for fast storage and retrieval by completely <u>dis</u>organizing the bits of the representation of the data item in the process of computing the hashing function. With our structure, called a <u>cell</u> structure, the mapping from data items to cell positions is based upon the <u>empirical cumulative distribution function</u> (ECDF) of a sample of data items. The idea is to organize the data items for fast storage and retrieval by partially sorting the items using the ECDF mapping, and by completing the sort using ordinary comparison-based methods. The details of the resulting data structure and its performance characteristics can be found in [Weide79].

Our concern here is with a special kind of hashing called <u>perfect hashing</u>, which was studied in [Sprugnoli77]. In perfect hashing, the (potential) set of data items is known in advance, and it is required to construct a mapping from this set to the integers from 0 to m-1 that is one-to-one. The problem has also recently been approached from a geometrical standpoint by [Comer82].

Our problem is motivated by an attempt to extend perfect hashing to cell structures. An abstraction and generalization of the problem we discuss here is to find a monotonic function that can be computed very fast that maps a set of n real numbers from [0,1) to the integers between 0 and m-1 in such a way that no more than k numbers from the domain map to any integer in the range. Perfect hashing adapted to cell structures is the problem when k = 1. Even with larger but still fixed k, if the solution to the problem were used as a mapping to cells, we would be guaranteed that not more than k data items could ever map to any cell, and therefore that all the above operations could be done in constant time. The only problem is that it may not be possible to compute the mapping in constant time! Our objective here is to investigate how such a mapping can be found and used, and to determine how quickly it can be computed.

In section II, we present a statement of the problem to be solved. Section III develops a dynamic programming algorithm for its solution, and section IV discusses some experimental results obtained from using the algorithm. Finally, in section V, we summarize our findings and present some open problems.

II. PROBLEM STATEMENT

As mentioned above, the most general version of the problem is the following: Given a set $D = \{x_i, 1 \le i \le n\}$, with $x_i \in [0,1)$, and the set $R = \{0, 1, ..., m-1\}$, find a monotonically increasing function $C: D \rightarrow R$ that maps at most k elements of D into each element of R, and that has minimum computational complexity. Of course, this problem leaves room for considerable interpretation of the last phrase. In order to make things tractable, we limit ourselves to a model of computation normally assumed for hashing, in which the usual arithmetic operations on real numbers, and the floor function, can be computed in constant time. But this restricts the problem only slightly, since the form of the function C could still involve trigonometric functions and the like, leaving open questions more properly considered in numerical analysis, which is not our field.

In order to make the problem discrete and reasonable, we restrict C to be of the form $C(x) = \lfloor F(x) \rfloor$, where F is piecewise-linear, and the pieces to start and end at points of D. Furthermore, if p is the number of pieces used in F, we assign log p as the complexity of computing C(x). The justification for this is that it is possible to use binary search on the end-points of the pieces to determine which piece is required for the particular value x, and constant time to compute C(x) given the slope and intercept for that piece. We ignore the possibility that the end-points themselves might be organized using a cell structure in a recursive fashion, or that some new scheme might be invented that permits faster searching in this extended model of computation.

Finally, then, the problem is to find a piecewise-linear, monotonically increasing function $F: D \rightarrow [0,m)$, such that $C(x) = \lfloor F(x) \rfloor$ maps at most k elements of D into each element of R, and such that F has the minimum number of pieces. Although the algorithm we suggest for this problem is easily extended to work for any value of k, we will discuss only the case $k = 1$. Clearly, in this case, $m \geq n$ in order that there is a solution.

We note that at most n pieces are required, with corresponding complexity log n for computing C, and that this corresponds to sorting the elements of D and doing binary search on them to compute C. The value of C(x) is then one less than the rank of x among the elements of D, so that the smallest element of D maps to 0, the second smallest to 1, and so on. Furthermore, if the items of D are regularly spaced, only one piece of F is required, and the complexity of computing C is constant. Each of these works even when $m = n$. In fact, even if the elements of D are not quite evenly spaced, it still may be possible to get by with only one piece, even if $m = n$, as shown in Figure 2. It is obvious that the number of pieces required for fixed D is a non-increasing function of m, as illustrated in Figure 3.

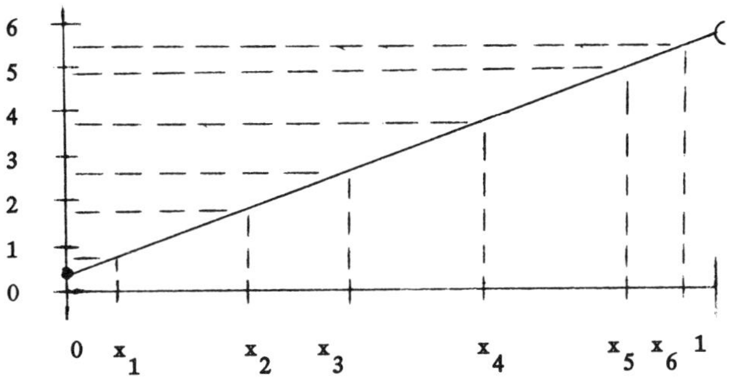

Figure 2: A lucky case requiring one piece.

III. FINDING THE MAPPING

In this section, we give an algorithm for solving the final problem stated in section II: Given D and m, find F with the fewest pieces. To do this, we use dynamic programming. Let $x_{(i)}$ be the i-th smallest element of D, and let $p_{i,j}$ be the minimum number of pieces of F required to go from the point $(x_{(i)},j)$ to the point $(1,m)$. For instance, $p_{n,m-1}$ is always 1. As shown in Figure 4, $p_{n-1,m-2}$ may be either 1 or 2, depending on the values of $x_{(n-1)}$ and $x_{(n)}$, and so on. If $n-i+1$, the number of points involved in computing $p_{i,j}$, exceeds $m-j+1$, the number of cells available to accommodate them, then it is impossible for the function F to pass through the point $(x_{(i)},j)$, so $p_{i,j}$ would not need to be computed. Similarly, if $i > j$, then $p_{i,j}$ is not defined. In any other case, though, it is possible to find a function F passing through $(x_{(i)},j)$ that is a feasible solution to our problem, and $p_{i,j}$ gives the minimum number of pieces required to get from that point to $(1,m)$.

Now $p_{i,j}$ can be calculated from $p_{k,l}$, where $k > i$ and $l > j$, by trying all such $(x_{(k)},l)$ as possible endpoints of pieces starting at $(x_{(i)},j)$. If it is possible to place a piece between $(x_{(i)},j)$ and $(x_{(k)},l)$ without intervening points mapping to the same cell, and $p_{k,l}$ is minimum for all such pairs (k,l), then $p_{i,j}$ is set to $p_{k,l}+1$. The final number of pieces required is given by $p_{1,0}$.

As with most other dynamic programming algorithms, this one can be implemented by considering $p_{i,j}$ to be an entry in an array, which is filled in after all the other values it depends on have already been calculated. By also keeping track of some audit information, it is easy to construct the actual pieces required in F once the entire array has been filled in. In our case, the array has $m-n+1$ rows and $n+1$ columns, and takes time at worst proportional to $n^3(m-n+1)^2$ to fill in. In practice, we observed running times of perhaps $n^{2.5}(m-n+1)^{1.5}$ on the average, since our code has some rules built into it that allow early stopping in the computation of $p_{i,j}$ when certain conditions are met. Still, this running time is horribly bad, and we have worked briefly on other algorithms that are designed to get good approximate solutions. However, we know of no

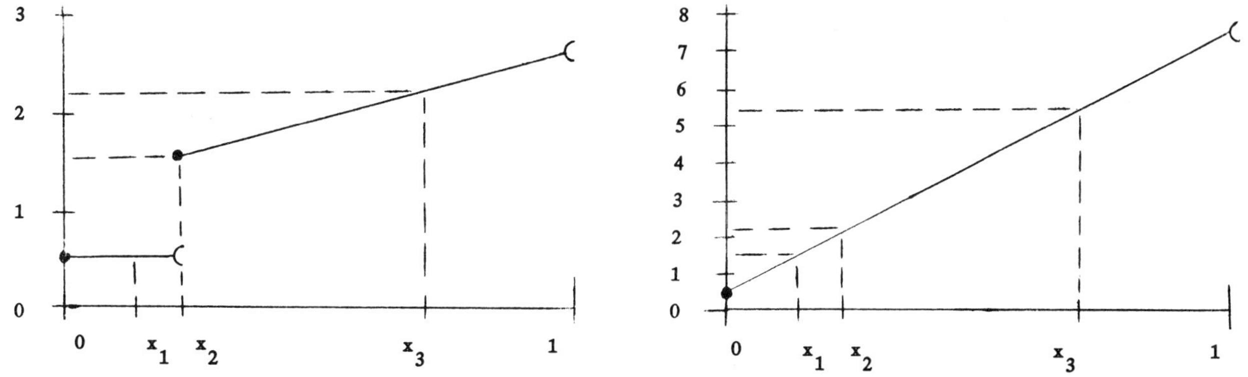

Figure 3: The effect of increasing m.

other algorithms that run even in polynomial time and get the exact answer.

IV. EXPERIMENTS

We implemented the above algorithm in Fortran and ran it on our DECsystem-2060 (KL processor) on ten sets of randomly generated data (uniform on [0,1)) of each size n = 10, 20, ..., 70. For each value of n, we used several values of m in the range $1 \leq m/n \leq 2$, and found p, the average number of pieces used in the best function F. Computation times were reasonable (less than about two seconds per data set) until n reached about 60, at which point the cases with larger values of m began to get rather time-consuming. This was expected, since we had analyzed the worst-case running time, as mentioned in section III, and found the algorithm to be rather inefficient.

After transforming the data and plotting log(n/p) against log(m/n), we got Figure 5. Here, it seems that we might conclude that a plausible relationship is

$$\log (n/p) \approx 1 + 1.7 \log (m/n).$$

This formula has an interesting interpretation. Imagine the following use of the cell structure with the mapping function found by this algorithm. We have a static set of data items, each of which uses a very large number of bits in its representation, and we wish to replace each data item by a shorter representation in the course of computation. Of course, we would like to be able to compare the short representations and have the results turn out as if we had compared the original data items. This could save considerable space, since we might need to store the long representations only externally. Simply replacing the long representation of x by the (presumably shorter) representation of C(x) would suffice, since C(x) is monotonic and one-to-one.

Under this transformation, C(x) would require log m bits, since it can have any value between 0 and m-1. Furthermore, if there are n data items, the shortest possible representation would use log n bits, and this could be achieved by replacing each data item by its rank in sorted order. On the other hand, the number of comparisons between long representations to compute the short representation of a data item would be log n in the latter case, but only log p in the former.

Now we can interpret the formula induced from the experimental data as follows. The term log(m/n) is the number of extra bits used by making the range of C larger than the domain, or equivalently, the number of extra bits used over the shortest possible representation. The term log(n/p) is the number of comparisons saved by using the mapping C in place of the naive sorting-with-binary search approach. Thus, the formula expresses a time-space trade-off. The additive constant 1 indicates that, by using the mapping even without any extra bits, we could expect to save about one comparison over the naive method of computing the short representation. The factor 1.7 says that for each additional bit allocated to the short representation, we can save about 1.7 comparisons in computing it.

Whether this trade-off is valid for larger ratios m/n is an open question whose answer awaits a more efficient algorithm than our dynamic programming solution. When m exceeds n by a large amount, the computation time of the algorithm becomes unbearably large. Also, the algorithm is essentially useless if n is very large. In order to explore these problems further, we continue our development of fast approximation algorithms for finding a mapping with the fewest possible pieces.

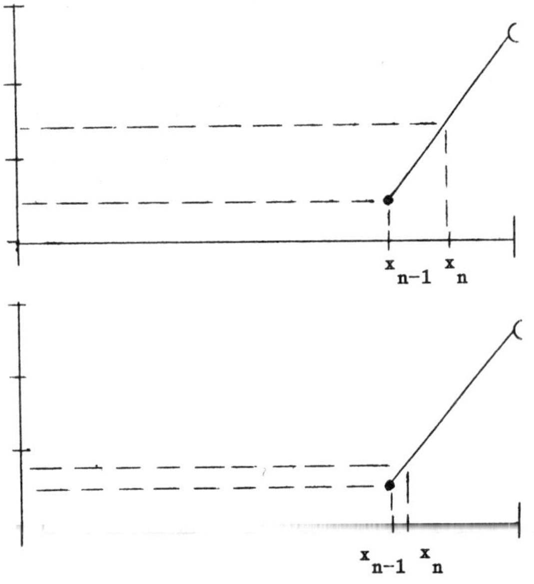

Figure 4: Effect of spacing of data values.

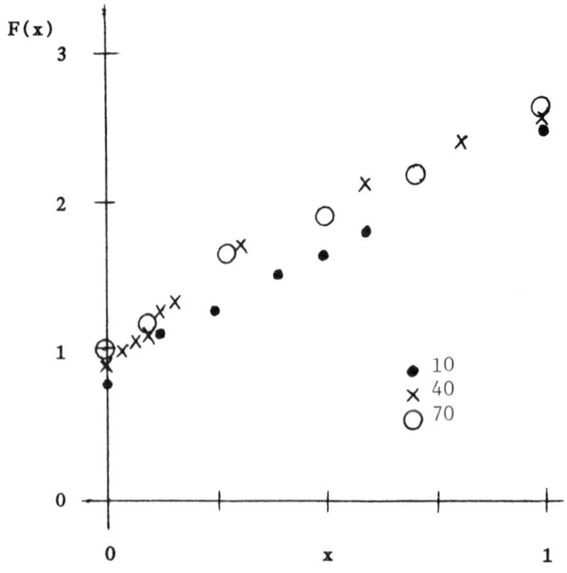

Figure 5: Experimental data.

V. SUMMARY AND CONCLUSIONS

We have presented an abstract optimization problem, and a dynamic programming algorithm for its solution, that has applications in the area of data storage and retrieval. In particular, it may be used to construct data structures with very good expected and worst-case performance for such problems, and to permit data compaction in applications requiring efficient use of storage. We have also attempted to characterize a time-space trade-off in the latter application.

Several problems remain unsolved, or unexplored. One is to find a faster algorithm, perhaps an approximation algorithm, to solve the problem in section II. This would probably be essential to any practical application. Some other similar problems are obvious.

There are, in addition to these, some problems that might best be approached by statisticians. For instance, we have examined only the case of uniformly distributed data items. What is the effect of non-uniformity? If it is great, the statistic p might be useful in a test for uniformity, especially to distinguish uniform but random data from somewhat structured or periodic data. From our experiments we found that the value of p falls off rapidly when the data items are very evenly distributed. A related question concerns the distribution of p, given n and m, and assuming a uniform distribution.

Finally, it may be that the distribution of end-points of the pieces is not uniform. If it turns out that the end-points are more evenly distributed than if they were completely random, recursive application of a cell structure in the search through the end-points could result in substantial improvement over binary search, complicating the problem still further.

It remains to be seen whether the suggested practical applications turn out to be so. In any event, there are many interesting questions raised by the problem, and potentially much work to be done to solve them.

REFERENCES

[Comer82] Comer, D., and O'Donnell, M.J. "Geometric problems with application to hashing", SIAM Journal on Computing 11, 2 (May 1982), 217-226.

[Horowitz76] Horowitz, E., and Sahni, S. Fundamentals of Data Structures, Computer Science Press, Rockville, MD, 1976.

[Knuth73] Knuth, D.E. The Art of Computer Programming, Vol. III: Sorting and Searching, Addison-Wesley, Reading, MA, 1973.

[Sprugnoli77] Sprugnoli, R. "Perfect hashing functions: a single probe retrieving method for static sets", Communications of the ACM 20, (1977), 841-850.

[Weide79] Weide, B.W. "Very fast information update and retrieval using cells", Proc. 17th Annual Allerton Conf. on Comm., Control, and Computing, Univ. of Ill., Oct. 1979, 245-254.

Computational Aspects Associated with Robustness in Statistics

Chair: Albert S. Paulson, Rensselaer Polytechnic Institute

The Computation and Use of Robust Smoothers and Data Cleaners for Time Series (Abstract)
R. Douglas Martin, University of Washington

The Use of Bounded-Influence Regression in Data Analysis: Theory, Computation, and Graphics
William S. Krasker, Harvard University
Roy E. Welsch, Massachusetts Institute of Technology

Sensitivity Analysis in Experimental Design
A. S. Paulson and T. A. Delehanty, Rensselaer Polytechnic Institute

THE COMPUTATION AND USE OF ROBUST SMOOTHERS AND DATA CLEANERS FOR TIME SERIES

R. Douglas Martin
University of Washington

This talk describes several aspects of a class of recursive robust smoothers and data cleaners for time series problems. Computational algorithms are described, and robustness properties are discussed. The latter are partly supported by computing the "linear part" decompositions (Mallows, Annals Stat., 1980, 8, 695-715) for the smoothers and data cleaners. The robust smoother may be used for either exploratory data analysis, or for certain smoothing problems arising in communications and control engineering. When robust smoothing for exploratory purposes is the desired end, cross-validation may be used to choose the smoothness parameter. The data-cleaner version of the algorithm is a basic ingredient of robust procedures for fitting ARMA models and estimating spectral densities. The algorithms have been implemented as functions in the S system (Becker and Chambers, 1981). Several examples are provided illustrating use of the algorithms.

THE USE OF BOUNDED-INFLUENCE REGRESSION IN DATA ANALYSIS: THEORY, COMPUTATION, AND GRAPHICS

William S. Krasker, Harvard University
Roy E. Welsch, Massachusetts Institute of Technology

ABSTRACT

Ordinary least squares is very sensitive to aberrant data, heavy-tailed errors, and certain other violations of the standard assumptions in linear regression. In this paper we will discuss a weighted-least-squares alternative that limits the influence of any small fraction of the data. This estimator has a certain efficiency property among all weighted-least-squares estimators with the same sensitivity to anomalous data. We will discuss the theoretical and computational aspects of this bounded-influence estimator, as well as some related graphics, and illustrate its use as a tool for data analysis with an empirical example.

In this paper we discuss some current research concerning a particular approach to bounded-influence regression. The theory is set out in the first two sections. Section III examines the problem of breakdown. In Section IV we describe the computation of our estimator, and in Section V we illustrate with an empirical example the use of the estimator and some related graphics.

I. Influence and Sensitivity

The linear regression model can be written as

$$y_i = x_i\beta + \varepsilon_i \qquad i=1,\ldots,n$$

where y_i is the ith observation on the dependent variable, x_i is the p-dimensional row vector containing the ith observation on the explanatory variables, β is a p-vector of parameters, and the ε_i are independent disturbances. We assume that the model has an intercept term, so that the first component of x_i equals one.

In robustness one is concerned with how the behavior of an estimator for β changes when the underlying distribution of the data departs from an idealized "central model". For our central model, we will assume that the observations (y_i,x_i) are independent drawings from a distribution P on $\mathbb{R}\times\mathbb{R}^p$ satisfying $(y_i|x_i) \sim N(x_i\beta,\sigma^2)$.

An estimator $\hat\beta$ for β can be thought of as a function of the empirical distribution P_n for the sample $\{(y_i,x_i)\}_{i=1}^n$. In most cases the definition of $\hat\beta$ extends naturally to a function defined on the set of all distributions on $\mathbb{R}\times\mathbb{R}^p$. One can then define the Influence Function for $\hat\beta$ as follows: For any vector (y,x) in $\mathbb{R}\times\mathbb{R}^p$, let $\delta_{(y,x)}$ denote the probability distribution that is degenerate on (y,x). Then the Influence Function Ω: $\mathbb{R}\times\mathbb{R}^p\to\mathbb{R}^p$ is defined by

$$\Omega(y,x) = \lim_{h\to 0} \frac{\hat\beta((1-h)P + h\delta_{(y,x)}) - \hat\beta(P)}{h} \qquad (1.1)$$

(see Hampel (1974)). Ω measures the effect on $\hat\beta$ of "infinitesimal" perturbations of the underlying distribution. If Ω is bounded, $\hat\beta$ is called a bounded-influence estimator.

Under regularity conditions, Ω will satisfy

$$\sqrt{n}\left[\hat\beta_n - \beta - \frac{1}{n}\sum_{i=1}^n \Omega(y_i,x_i)\right] \to 0 \text{ in probability.} \qquad (1.2)$$

Condition (1.2) actually determines Ω almost surely (this follows from Loeve (1977, p. 329)), so that this property could be taken as the definition of Ω. Condition (1.2) shows the sense in which $\Omega(y_i, x_i)$ approximates the effect of the ith observation on $\hat\beta_n$. From (1.2) we see also that if $E\Omega = 0$ and $E|\Omega|^2 < \infty$, then $\hat\beta$ is consistent and asymptotically normal, with asymptotic covariance matrix

$$V = E\Omega\Omega^t. \qquad (1.3)$$

Following Krasker and Welsch (1982), we will define the sensitivity of $\hat\beta$ to be

$$\gamma = \sup_{y,x}\sup_{\lambda} \frac{|\lambda^t\Omega(y,x)|}{\sqrt{\lambda^t V\lambda}} \qquad (1.4)$$

$$= \sup_{y,x} \{\Omega(y,x)^t V^{-1}\Omega(y,x)\}^{\frac{1}{2}}. \qquad (1.5)$$

This is essentially the maximum possible influence of a single observation on a linear combination of the parameters, relative to the standard error of that linear combination.

II. Weighted Least-Squares Estimators

We will restrict attention to weighted least-squares (WLS) estimators for β, which are estimators of the form

$$0 = \sum_{i=1}^n w(y_i,x_i,\hat\beta)\,(y_i-x_i\hat\beta)\,x_i^t \qquad (2.1)$$

for some non-negative, bounded, continuous weight function w. For a WLS estimator, the Influence Function is

$$\Omega(y,x) = w(y,x,\beta)\,(y-x\beta)B^{-1}x^t, \qquad (2.2)$$

where

$$B = -E\{\frac{\partial}{\partial\theta}\left[w(y,x,\theta)(y-x\theta)x^t\right]_{\theta=\beta}\}. \qquad (2.3)$$

According to (1.3), the asymptotic covariance matrix is

$$V = \sigma^2 B^{-1}A(B^{-1})^t, \qquad (2.4)$$

where

$$A = E\, w(y,x,\beta)^2 \left(\frac{y-x\beta}{\sigma}\right)^2 x^t x. \qquad (2.5)$$

From (1.5), the sensitivity is then

$$\gamma = \sup_{y,x} w(y,x,\beta)\left|\frac{y-x\beta}{\sigma}\right|\{xA^{-1}x^t\}^{\frac{1}{2}}. \qquad (2.6)$$

In addition to the weight $w(y,x,\beta)$, (2.6) shows that the influence of an observation (y,x) depends on the product of two components: the scaled residual $|y-x\beta|/\sigma$, and the quadratic expression $\{xA^{-1}x^t\}^{\frac{1}{2}}$ which we call the leverage of the x row.

Krasker and Welsch (1982) have proposed a one-parameter family of WLS estimators for β, indexed by $a > \sqrt{p}$ and defined by

$$0 = \sum_{i=1}^{n} \min\left\{1, \frac{a}{\left|\frac{y_i - x_i\hat{\beta}}{\hat{\sigma}}\right| \{x_i\hat{A}^{-1}x_i^t\}^{\frac{1}{2}}}\right\}(y_i - x_i\hat{\beta})x_i^t \tag{2.7}$$

where

$$\hat{A} = \frac{1}{n}\sum_{i=1}^{n} g\left(\frac{a}{\{x_i\hat{A}^{-1}x_i^t\}^{\frac{1}{2}}}\right) x_i^t x_i , \tag{2.8}$$

$$g(t) = \int_{-\infty}^{\infty} \min\{z^2,t^2\} \, (2\pi)^{-\frac{1}{2}} \exp\{-z^2/2\} \, dz, \tag{2.9}$$

and $\hat{\sigma}$ is a robust estimate of σ. $\hat{A}$ is a consistent estimate of the matrix A defined by (2.5). The Krasker-Welsch (KW) estimator is a bounded-influence estimator, with sensitivity a. It also satisfies a certain first-order condition for efficiency (in the strong sense of minimizing the asymptotic variance of all linear combinations $\mu^t\hat{\beta}$) subject to the constraint $\gamma \leq a$. However, it is possible that no strongly-efficient weight function exists. Instead, the optimal weight function might depend on the particular linear combination μ that one wants to estimate. However, one can show that in this case, the efficient weight function w_μ cannot be coordinate equivariant for each μ. To see this, write the weight associated with a point (y,x) as $w_\mu(y,x,G)$, where G is the marginal distribution for x. For any pxp nonsingular matrix T, let GT be the distribution for xT. Then if w_μ were coordinate equivariant, we would have

$$w_\mu(y,xT,GT) = w_\mu(y,x,G) \quad \text{for all T.} \tag{2.10}$$

On the other hand, suppose we transform each x to xT (thereby redefining the parameters to be $T^{-1}\beta$) and then decide to estimate the linear combination $(T^t\mu)^t(T^{-1}\beta)$ of the new parameters. We must have

$$w_{T^t\mu}(y,xT,GT) = w_\mu(y,x,G) \tag{2.11}$$

because the quantity being estimated is identical in the two cases. From (2.10), we conclude

$$w_{T^t\mu}(y,xT,GT) = w_\mu(y,xT,GT) \tag{2.12}$$

for all T. If we replace x by xT^{-1} and G by GT^{-1} in (2.12), we find

$$w_{T^t\mu}(y,x,G) = w_\mu(y,x,G) \tag{2.13}$$

for all T. Therefore, if w_μ is equivariant it cannot depend on μ. This suggests that even if no strongly efficient weight function exists, the KW estimate might still be efficient in the class of equivariant estimators.

III. Breakdown

The KW estimator is qualitatively robust (Hampel (1971)), meaning that as the fraction of aberrant data in the sample approaches zero, the maximum possible asymptotic bias in $\hat{\beta}$ also approaches zero. Though this limiting property is important, it does not tell us how $\hat{\beta}$ will behave if the aberrant data are, say, 5% or 10% of the data. To answer this question one wants to know the breakdown point of $\hat{\beta}$, which, roughly speaking, is the smallest fraction of aberrant data in the sample that could make the asymptotic bias in $\hat{\beta}$ arbitrarily large.

With respect to breakdown, the weakness in the KW estimator is the matrix $\hat{A}$, whose breakdown point is no larger than $1/(p+1)$. At least in artificial examples, we have found that this can impair the diagnostic value of the estimator. Specifically, we have found that after adding to a fifty-observation data set four replicates of an outlier, the outlier and its replicates did not have large leverages. Moreover, those points were not downweighted by the KW estimator. This shows that it is possible for a group of outliers to escape detection and have a disproportionate effect on the estimates, and suggests that we should replace the matrix A by some alternative expression that can be estimated by a high-breakdown estimator. One alternative approach has been suggested by Donoho and Huber (1982). For each i, let

$$\alpha_i = \sup_{|\lambda|=1} \frac{|x_i\lambda - \text{MED}\{x_j\lambda\}|}{\text{MAD}\{x_j\lambda\}} \tag{3.1}$$

MED stands for the median and MAD is the median absolute deviation from the median. Intuitively, the λ at which the supremum occurs is the direction in which x_i is most outlying, and α_i measures its outlyingness in that direction.

A sensible way to incorporate the α's into KW is to replace $\hat{A}$ in (2.7) by

$$\tilde{A} = \frac{1}{n}\sum_{i=1}^{n} g\left(\frac{a}{\alpha_i}\right) x_i^t x_i . \tag{3.2}$$

One would first re-scale the α's so that they have, say, the same minimum and median as the leverages $\{x_i\hat{A}^{-1}x_i^t\}^{\frac{1}{2}}$. $\tilde{A}$ obtained in this way would have a breakdown point of 1/2. Unfortunately, it seems computationally infeasible to compute the α's in general. Gasko and Donoho (1982) have suggested modifying (3.1) to look only in the n directions $\lambda_i = x_i^t - M(X)$, where $M(X)$ is the coordinatewise median vector for the x's. The resulting modified α's are relatively easy to compute, and, when incorporated into KW, they ameliorated the breakdown problem in the artificial example cited earlier. However, it is not clear how well they approximate the α's derived from (3.1). Also, they are not coordinate invariant.

IV. Computation

One approach to computing the bounded-influence estimator developed in Sections I and II is sketched in Krasker and Welsch (1982). More details can be found in Peters, Samarov, and Welsch (1982). We present here another method which is simpler and generally less expensive. It avoids a separate iterative computation for the leverages $\{x_i A^{-1} x_i^t\}^{1/2}$, and makes no use of the central-model assumption of Gaussian residuals. However, it will occasionally fail to converge.

We need to solve the equations

$$0 = \sum_{i=1}^{n} w_i \cdot (y_i - x_i\beta)x_i^t \tag{4.1}$$

where

$$w_i = \min\left\{1, \frac{a}{\left|\frac{y_i - x_i\beta}{\sigma}\right| \{x_i A^{-1} x_i^t\}^{1/2}}\right\} \tag{4.2}$$

and A is given by (2.5). Let $z = (y - x\beta)x$. Then

$$w_i = \min\left\{1, \frac{a}{\{zQ^{-1}z^t\}^{1/2}}\right\}, \tag{4.3}$$

where

$$Q = E\, w^2 z^t z \tag{4.4}$$

and we have cancelled out σ in (4.2): an advantage of this computational scheme is that there is no need to compute σ during the iterative process.

Iteration proceeds as follows: Assume we have finished an iteration, and weights $w^{(k)}$ are available. To compute $b^{(k)}$ we use either weighted least squares with weights $w^{(k)}$ or a simpler approach based on Huber's algorithm H (Huber 1981), namely,

$$b^{(k)} = b^{(k-1)} + (X^tX)^{-1}X^tW^{(k)}(y - Xb^{(k-1)}) \tag{4.5}$$

where $W^{(k)}$ is the diagonal matrix of weights. Note that with this algorithm, $(X^tX)^{-1}X^t$ can be computed once and saved.

Given $b^{(k)}$ we find $z^{(k)} = (y - xb^{(k)})x$,

$$Q^{(k)} = \frac{1}{n}\sum_{i=1}^{n} w_i^{(k)} (z_i^{(k)})^t z_i^{(k)}, \tag{4.6}$$

and

$$w^{(k+1)} = \min\left\{1, \frac{a}{\{z^{(k)}(Q^{(k)})^{-1}(z^{(k)})^t\}^{1/2}}\right\}. \tag{4.7}$$

Convergence is then checked and if the convergence test fails, we put $k = k+1$ and go back to (4.5).

Usually the starting weights are all ones and $b^{(0)}$ is the least-squares estimate. It is sometimes useful (especially if there are convergence problems) to downweight or omit observations for which $x_i(X^tX)^{-1}x_i^t$ is large. In this case $b^{(0)}$ is obtained by weighted least squares using these weights.

V. Example

Our example is based on data collected by Lave and Seskin (1977) and given in a technical report by Gibbons and McDonald (1980). This data base consists of cross-sectional data on 117 Standard Metropolitan Statistical Areas (SMSAs) for the year 1960.

The eleven explanatory variables in their basic model include the following air pollution indices and socioeconomic factors thought to affect the mortality pattern of a community:

1	SMIN	-	Smallest biweekly sulfate reading ($\mu g/m^3$ x 10)
2	SMEAN	-	Arithmetic mean of biweekly sulfate readings ($\mu g/m^3$ x 10)
3	SMAX	-	Largest biweekly sulfate reading ($\mu g/m^3$ x 10)
4	PMIN	-	Smallest biweekly suspended particulate reading ($\mu g/m^3$)
5	PMEAN	-	Arithmetic mean of biweekly suspended particulate readings ($\mu g/m^3$)
6	PMAX	-	Largest biweekly suspended particulate reading ($\mu g/m^3$)
7	PM2	-	SMSA population density (per square mile x .1)
8	GE65	-	Percent of SMSA population at least 65 years old (x 10)
9	PNOW	-	Percent of non-whites in SMSA population (x 10)
10	POOR	-	Percent of SMSA families with income below the poverty level (x 10)
11	LPOP	-	The logarithm (base 10) of SMSA population (x 10)
12	CONST	-	Intercept

The dependent variable is total morality rate (TMR) expressed as deaths per 100,000 population.

We use two types of plots to summarize this example. The BIFWT contour plot places the final scaled residuals $|y_i - x_i\hat{\beta}|/\hat{\sigma}$ on the vertical axis and the leverages $\{x_i\hat{A}^{-1}x_i^t\}^{1/2}$ on the horizontal axis. Since the final weights depend on the product of these two quantities, the contours show various levels of downweighting. Observations with positive residuals are marked by +, while those with negative residuals are indicated by Δ. The sensitivity a was chosen so that the average of the final weights was .95.

There are several interesting features in this plot. Point 60 (Jersey City) has the largest leverage but still receives a weight of one. It is an outlier that is consistent with the model fit to the rest of the data, and hence not influential.

SMSA number 21 (Charleston, VW) has a large residual and a small weight. SMSA number 112 combines a moderate residual with a fairly large leverage, and is heavily downweighted.

Observations 85 and 86 - Scranton, PA and Wilkes-Barre, PA - both have positive residuals that are sufficiently large that they are downweighted substantially, despite having small leverages. These cities are close geographically, so it would be reasonable to seek some additional regional characteristic that could explain the unexpectedly high mortality rate in those cities.

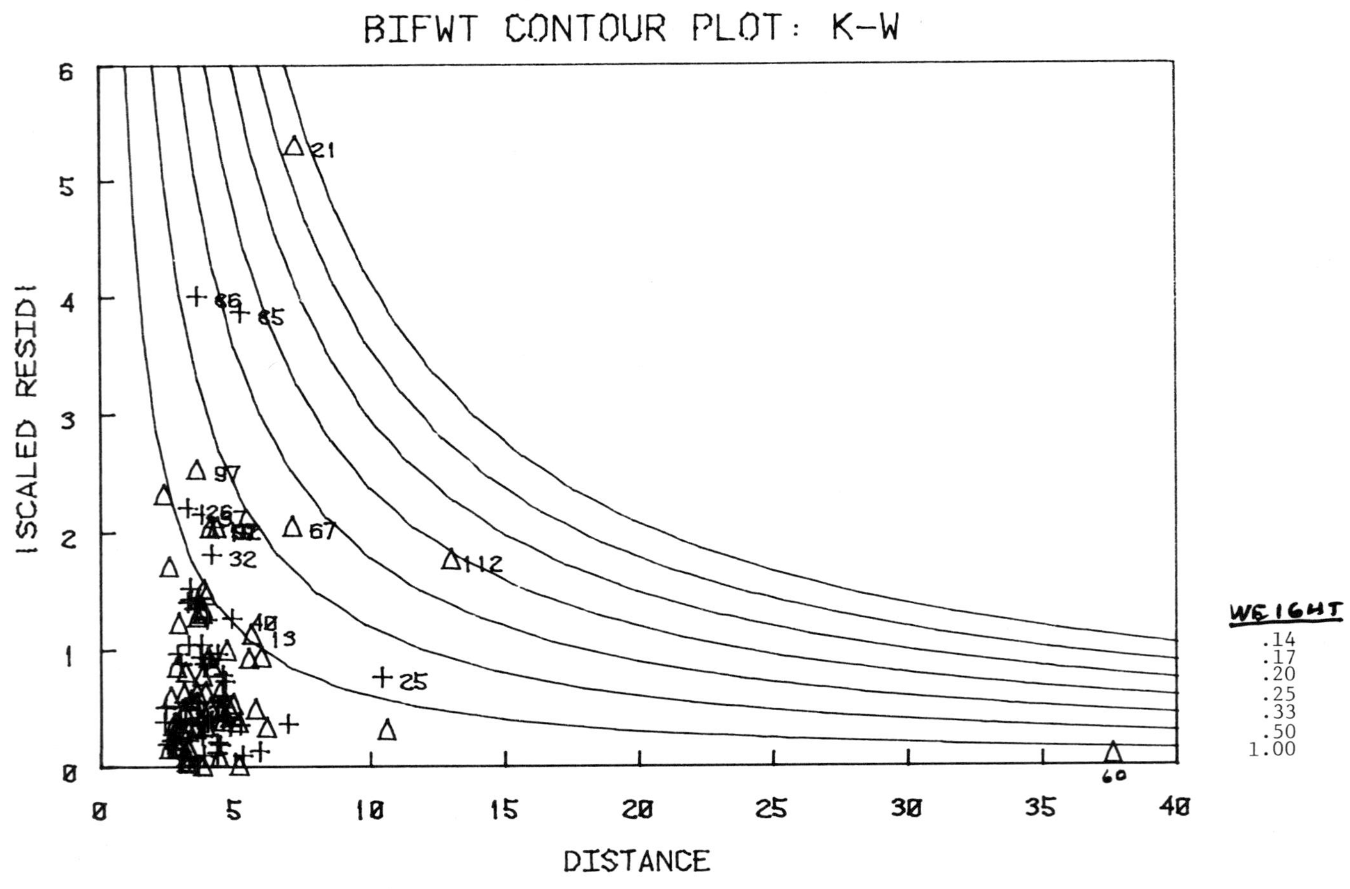
BIFWT CONTOUR PLOT: K-W
|SCALED RESID|
DISTANCE
WEIGHT
.14
.17
.20
.25
.33
.50
1.00
21
86
85
97
126
67
32
112
40
13
25
60

$\bar{\omega} = .95$

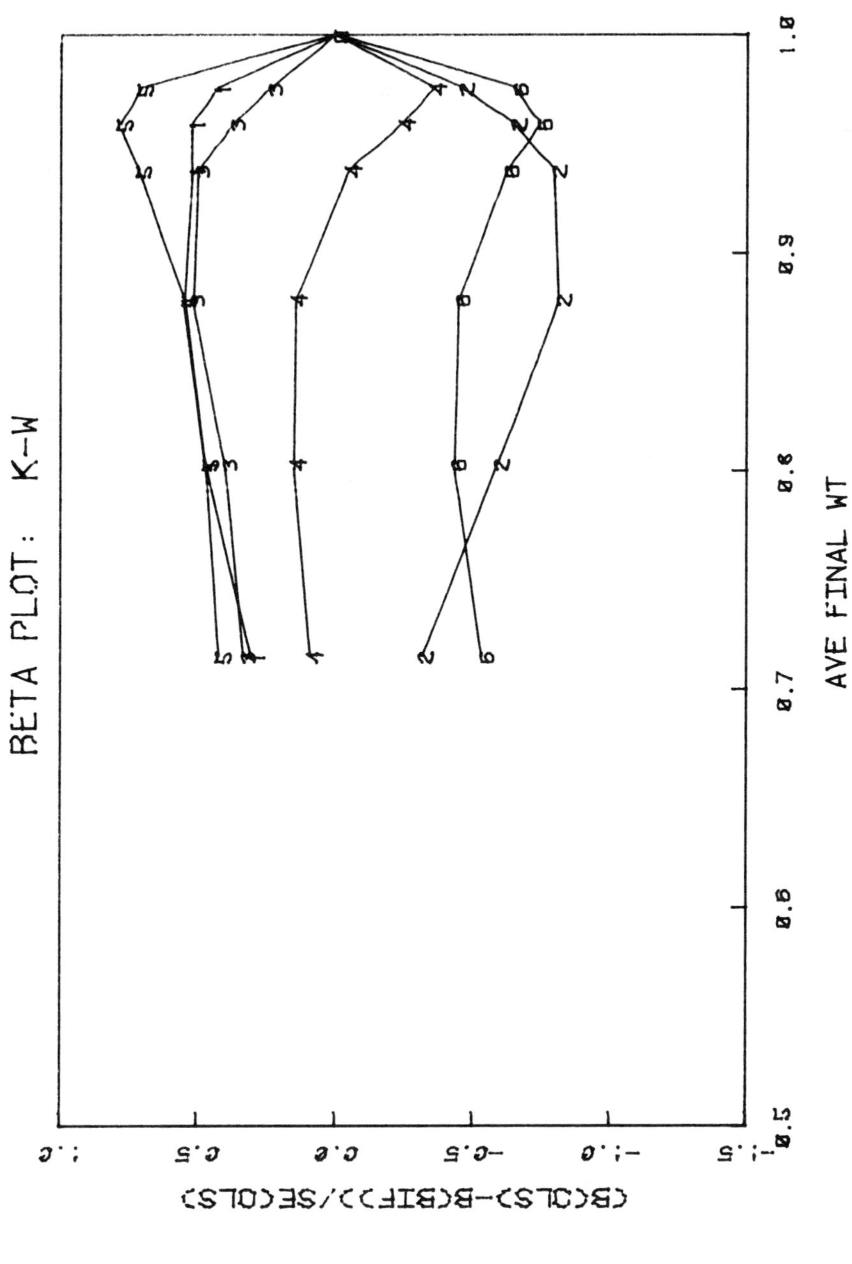
BETA PLOT: K-W
AVE FINAL WT
0.5
0.6
0.7
0.8
0.9
1.0
(B(OLS)-B(BIF))/SE(OLS)
-1.5
-1.0
-0.5
0.0
0.5
1.0

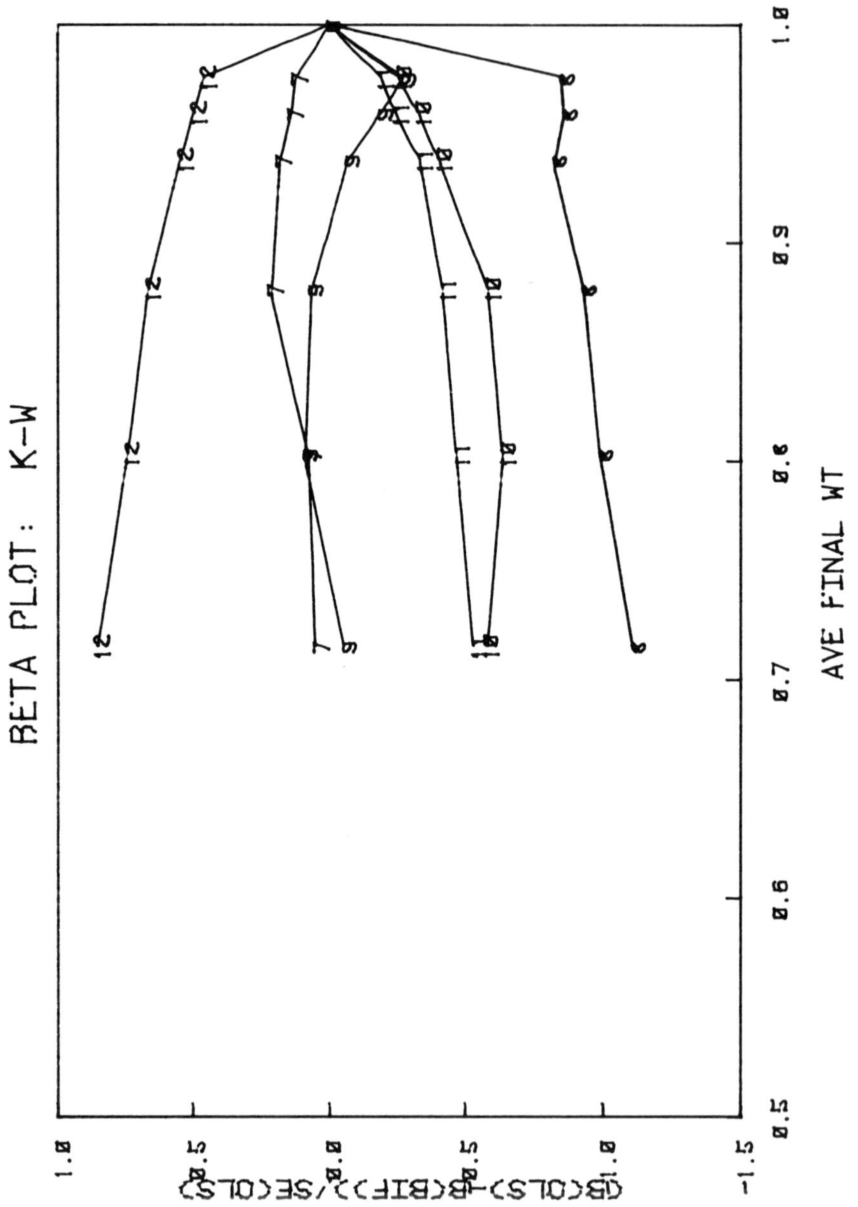
BETA PLOT: K-W
AVE FINAL WT
(B(OLS)-B(BIF))/SE(OLS)
0.5
0.6
0.7
0.8
0.9
1.0
1.0
0.5
0.0
-0.5
-1.0
-1.5

The next two plots (Beta Plots) show what happens to the coefficients as the average of the final weights is varied from .7 to 1.0. Here we plot $(b_j-\hat{\beta}_j)/s(b_j)$ $j=1,\ldots,12$ where b_j is the least-squares estimate, $\hat{\beta}_j$ the KW estimate for a given $\overline{w}$ and $s(b_j)$ is the least squares standard error for b_j. The numbers correspond to the numbers of the variables as listed. There is substantial change in many of the coefficients, especially 8 and 12 (the intercept). The $\overline{w}$ values used were .72, .80, .88, .94, .96, and .98. Note that even a small amount of downweighting has a substantial effect.

We think these plots provide useful summaries of the major diagnostic components of a bounded-influence regression.

Acknowledgements

We would like to acknowledge support from NSF grants SES-8112498 and SES-8112009, and the help of Alan Minkoff in preparing the plots and graphs.

References

Donoho, D.L. and Huber, P.J. (1982). The notion of breakdown point. To appear in: *Festschrift for Erich L. Lehmann*. Kjell Doksum and J.L. Hodges, Jr., eds. Wadsworth Press.

Gasko, M. and Donoho D. (1982), "Influential Observations in Data Analysis," *Proceedings of the 1982 ASA Meetings*.

Gibbons, D.I. and McDonald, G.C. (1980), "Examining Regression Relationships Between Air Pollution and Mortality," General Motors Research Publication GMR-3278, General Motors Research Laboratories, Warren, MI 48090.

Hampel, F.R. (1971), "A General Qualitative Definition of Robustness," *Ann. Math. Statist.*, 42, pp. 1887-1896.

Hampel, F.R. (1974), "The Influence Curve and Its Role in Robust Estimation, *J. Amer. Statist. Ass.*, 62, pp. 1179-1186.

Huber, P.J. (1981), *Robust Statistics*, Wiley, N.Y.

Krasker, W.S. and Welsch, R.E. (1982), "Efficient Bounded-Influence Regression Estimation," *Journal of the American Statistical Association*.

Lave, L.B. and Seskin, E.P. (1977), *Air Pollution and Human Health*, The Johns Hopkins University Press.

Loeve, M. (1977), *Probability Theory I*, 4th edition Springer-Verlag, N.Y.

Peters, S.C., Samarov, A.M. and Welsch, R.E. (1982), "Computational Procedures for Bounded-Influence and Robust Regression, MIT/CCREMS Technical Report No. TR-30.

SENSITIVITY ANALYSIS IN EXPERIMENTAL DESIGN

A. S. Paulson
T. A. Delehanty

Rensselaer Polytechnic Institute
Troy, New York 12181

ABSTRACT

A procedure for the critical analysis of planned experimental layouts is presented. It is illustrated on a univariate and on a bivariate two way layout.

1. INTRODUCTION

It is our opinion that one of the principal uses of robust estimation methods is that they generate, when considered in a fashion complementary to maximum likelihood, a sensitivity analysis. That is, first use the method of maximum likelihood to generate a summary of the data through estimation of the parameters of a parametric model. Next, use a robust estimation method to generate a second summary of the data through estimation of the parameters of the same model. If the results agree in accordance with some pre-defined measure of agreement, than this indicates (possibly non-statistically) some degree of consistency between data and model. The two estimation or summarization methods define two ways of processing the information contained in the data vis-a-vis the model. It is assumed that the two methods estimate the same things. If the two methods of processing information produce different results, then we must be concerned with understanding the data-model structure. This may involve determining which, if any, data are not consistent with the model and then determining whether the model needs to be changed or the data is not representative for the summarization, or both.

We present in this paper a procedure for producing sensitivity analyses for planned experimental layouts. The sensitivity analysis is generated by consideration of a measure of sample information which reduces as a special case to that of Shannon (the negative of the log likelihood).

2. AN INFORMATION MEASURE

Suppose that the p×1 vectors $x_1, x_2, \ldots, x_n$ are a random sample from the multivariate normal distribution with density

$$f(x) = |2\pi D|^{-\frac{1}{2}} \exp(-\tfrac{1}{2}(x-\mu)^T D^{-1}(x-\mu)), \tag{2.1}$$

where μ is the p×1 vector of means and D is the p×p variance-covariance matrix. Define

$$Q(\mu,D,c) = \int_{R_p} f^c(x) f(x)\,dx$$

$$= \int_{R_p} f^{1+c}(x)\,dx$$

$$= (|2\pi D|^c (1+c)^p)^{-\frac{1}{2}}. \tag{2.2}$$

The function $Q(\mu,D,c)$ is the information generating function of the density (2.1); see Golomb (1966). For example,

$$-Q'(\mu,D,0) = -\frac{\partial}{\partial c} Q(\mu,D,c)\Big|_{c=0}$$

$$= -\int_{R_p} f(x)\log f(x)\,dx$$

the entropy of f(x); in general, the rth derivative

$$Q^{(r)}(\mu,D,0) = \int_{R_p} f(x)\log^r f(x)\,dx$$

is, apart from the factor $(-1)^r$, the rth moment of the self-information of f(x). It is easy to see that

$$\int_{R_p} \frac{f^{1+c}(x)}{Q(\mu,D,c)}\,dx = 1,\ c \geq 0. \tag{2.3}$$

If we differentiate under the integral sign with respect to θ, $\theta=\mu$ or D, we find

$$\int_{R_p} f\left\{\frac{f^c}{Q}\left[(1+c)\frac{\partial \log f}{\partial\theta} - \frac{\partial \log Q}{\partial\theta}\right]\right\} dx = 0 \tag{2.4}$$

where the arguments of f and Q have been suppressed for notational convenience. Equation (2.4) implies that

$$E\left\{\frac{f^c}{Q}\left[(1+c)\frac{\partial \log f}{\partial\theta} - \frac{\partial \log Q}{\partial\theta}\right]\right\} = 0,$$

that is,

$$s_c = \frac{f^c}{Q}\left[(1+c)\frac{\partial \log f}{\partial\theta} - \frac{\partial \log Q}{\partial\theta}\right] \tag{2.5}$$

is a score function for estimating the parameters μ and D of (2.1). Accordingly, estimating equations for μ and D are given by

$$\sum_{i=1}^{n} f_i^c \left[(1+c) \frac{\partial \log f_i}{\partial \theta} - \frac{\partial \log Q}{\partial \theta} \right] = 0, \qquad (2.6)$$

where $f_i = f(x_i)$.

If we regard (2.6) as a differential equation in θ we determine that the system (2.6) can be developed from maximization of the objective function

$$O_c = \frac{1}{c} \sum_{i=1}^{n} \left\{ \frac{f_i^c}{Q^a} - 1 \right\}, \qquad (2.7)$$

where $a=c/(1+c)$. There are two special cases of interest: when $c=0$ the objective function O_c in (2.7) reduces to the usual log likelihood; when $c=1$, this objective function is related to the average likelihood. The univariate average likelihood was discussed by Andrews et al. (1972, p. 16) as a vehicle for producing estimates of the location parameter. The average likelihood as presented by Andrews et al. is of no use in obtaining estimates of the scale parameter whereas (2.7) is.

The estimators $\hat{\mu}_c$ and $\hat{D}_c$ are determined as the solutions of the implicit equations

$$\mu = \frac{\sum_{i=1}^{n} x_i v_{ic}}{\sum_{i=1}^{n} v_{ic}}, \qquad (2.8)$$

$$D = (1+c) \frac{\sum_{i=1}^{n} (x_i-\mu)(x_i-\mu)^T v_{ic}}{\sum_{i=1}^{n} v_{ic}}, \qquad (2.9)$$

where

$$v_{ic} = \exp\{-\frac{c}{2} (x_i-\mu)^T D^{-1} (x_i-\mu)\}. \qquad (2.10)$$

Clearly, (2.8) and (2.9) become the usual maximum likelihood estimators when $c=0$. When $c>0$ the weighting structure v_{ic} is determined from the assumed multivariate normal density itself in combination with the data $x_1, x_2, \ldots, x_n$. Data which are not internally consistent with the multivariate Gaussian assumption will receive low values of $v_{ic}|_{\theta=\hat{\theta}}$, say $\hat{v}_{ic}$. Since this mode of estimation with $c>0$ leads to self-criticism of the model vis-a-vis the data we term the estimation procedure self-critical. We will subsequently present an example to illustrate estimation in the absence of structure.

The influence functions of the estimators $\hat{\theta}_c$ determined from (2.6) or from maximization of (2.7) are proportional to the score functions $s_{c\theta}$ of (2.5) (Huber, 1981, p. 45) and are thus re-descendant to (the vector or matrix) zero for $c>0$. The estimators $\hat{\theta}_c$ are (strongly) consistent for θ for $c \geq 0$ and are asymptotically normal.

Shannon's measure of information is $-I(f)=\log f(x)$ for a density $f(x)$. Accordingly the information in a random sample $x_1, x_2, \ldots, x_n$ of n observations is given by

$$-\sum_{i=1}^{n} \log f(x_i)$$

which is a limiting case (as $c \to 0$) of

$$-\frac{1}{c} \sum_{i=1}^{n} \left\{ \frac{f_i^c}{Q^a} - 1 \right\} \qquad (2.11)$$

given in (2.7). Thus the self-critical estimation procedure revolves about determining, from a random sample of observations $x_1, x_2, \ldots, x_n$ with assumed density $f(x)$, the parameter values which minimize the information (in the sense of Shannon) measure (2.11) for given values of c. If for distinct values of c, the parameter estimates differ in an important way, then we must be concerned with a potential lack of internal consistency of the data and the assumed model.

3. A BIVARIATE NORMAL EXAMPLE

The first 25 pairs (x_{1j}, x_{2j}) in Table 1 are taken from Anderson (1958, p. 58). To these 25 pairs are appended an additional 5 outliers. The data are summarized in Figure 1: an X signifies one of the original 25 observations while a Y signifies one of the appended outliers. The estimators $\hat{\mu}_c$ and $\hat{D}_c=(\hat{D}_{cij})$ are presented in Table 2 for $c=0$ (maximum likelihood), .1, .2, .3, .5. The first two entries in each column are the components of the mean vector, the second two are the estimated standard deviations $\hat{\sigma}_1 = \hat{D}_{11}^{1/2}$, $\hat{\sigma}_2 = \hat{D}_{22}^{1/2}$, and the last entry is the estimated correlation $\hat{\rho}_{12}$. As c varies from 0 to .5, the estimated correlation increases from .45 to .88, a value much more consistent with the uncontaminated data. As c varies from 0 to .5, $\hat{\sigma}_2$ decreases from 9.3 to 5.5. The latter value is again much more typical of the uncontaminated data. The estimates of the location parameters change very little with increase of c. Figure 1 shows that this is reasonable behavior for the estimates of location parameters as c increases.

Table 1 provides values of the final weights $\hat{v}_{ic}$. The final weights for $c=0$ would be 100. As c increases from zero, there is a dramatic drop in the $\hat{v}_{ic}$ for observations 25-30. At $c=.3$, only observations 29 and 30 have weights $\hat{v}_{ic}$ different from 0. The five added outliers are thus perceived as not being consistent with the remainder of the data and the single Gaussian population. The estimation procedure is effectively clustering the data in the sense that it retains the original 25 data points as a single population and more or less ignores the remaining five points. An illustration of this is provided by plotting

$$\sum_{i=1}^{30} \frac{f_i^c}{Q} = \sum_{i=1}^{30} \exp(-\frac{c}{2} (x_i-\mu)^T \hat{D}_c^{-1} (x_i-\mu)) \qquad (3.1)$$

Table 1

SENSITIVITY OF OBSERVATION WEIGHTS v_{ic} (x100) TO CHANGES IN c

	X_1	X_2	c: 0.1	0.2	0.3	0.4
1	179	145	98	95	92	84
2	201	152	91	64	38	12
3	185	149	100	99	99	99
4	188	149	99	96	91	83
5	171	142	92	85	76	56
6	192	152	99	94	90	82
7	190	149	99	91	81	64
8	189	152	100	99	98	95
9	197	159	94	87	74	46
10	187	151	100	100	99	98
11	186	148	100	96	92	86
12	174	147	95	87	74	46
13	185	152	100	98	94	80
14	195	157	96	91	83	63
15	187	158	95	79	50	13
16	161	130	73	48	24	4
17	183	158	93	67	30	4
18	173	148	94	81	60	27
19	182	146	99	96	93	85
20	165	137	84	70	55	27
21	185	152	100	98	94	80
22	178	147	98	96	92	82
23	176	143	96	91	85	71
24	200	158	92	83	73	51
25	187	150	100	99	98	98
26	200	130	52	2	0	0
27	200	135	64	6	0	0
28	165	160	66	9	0	0
29	195	170	77	33	4	0
30	220	170	63	37	17	2

Table 2

SENSITIVITY OF PARAMETER ESTIMATES TO VARIATION IN c

Parameter	0	0.1	0.2	0.3	0.5
$\hat{\mu}_1$	185.9	185.5	185.0	184.9	185.0
$\hat{\mu}_2$	149.9	150.1	150.2	149.8	149.5
$\hat{\sigma}_1$	12.4	12.0	11.1	10.3	9.1
$\hat{\sigma}_2$	9.3	8.8	7.5	6.5	5.5
$\hat{\rho}_{12}$	0.45	0.52	0.80	0.86	0.88

as a function of μ_1 and μ_2 for several values of c. The right hand side of (3.1) is essentially a density estimator with arguments μ_1 and μ_2. The expression (3.1) is plotted for the data of Table 1 with c=.4 in Figure 2. The 5 outlying observations are identified in terms of the four minor bumps on the surface. The bump nearest the reader has two data points associated with it. The appearance of this plot will be stable for a wide range of values of c≥.4 and the parameter c has an interpretation similar to that of the window width in density estimation.

Variation of the parameter c through a range of values of c, including c=0, will effectively generate a sensitivity analysis. If the parameter

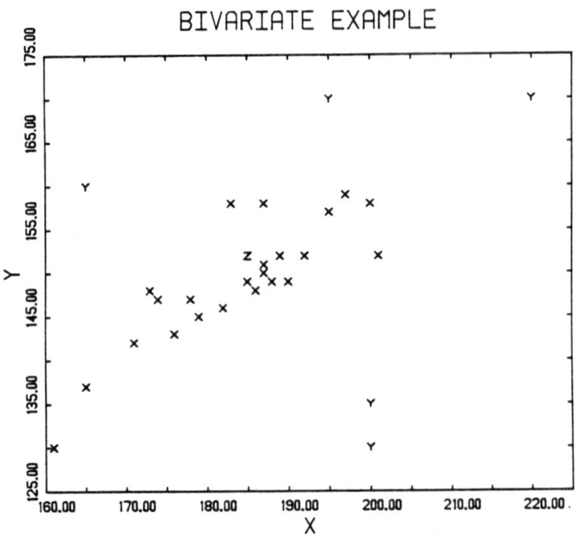

Figure 1

SCATTERPLOT OF DATA OF TABLE 1

estimates agree, say for c=0 and c=.3, then the data and the model will generally be internally consistent. It is difficult to specify in advance a precise range of variation of c which will ensure that the declaration "the data and model are internally consistent" is a correct one since the range over which c can be usefully varied will be a function of sample size and dimension p. While some guidelines can be established from practical empirical experience, it is not essential to know this range since exploration of the response surface of the solutions and final weights to variation in c provides the information that we find most interesting. If one is interested in asking the question "How much of a change in the parameter estimates for a given range of variations in c results in statistical significance", one must be content with fragmentary answers at best. The problems of statistical inference which must be solved for even the simplest cases are formidable. Furthermore, when structure is involved, e.g. regression or experimental design, inappropriateness of model becomes confounded with inappropriateness of distribution and a resolution of

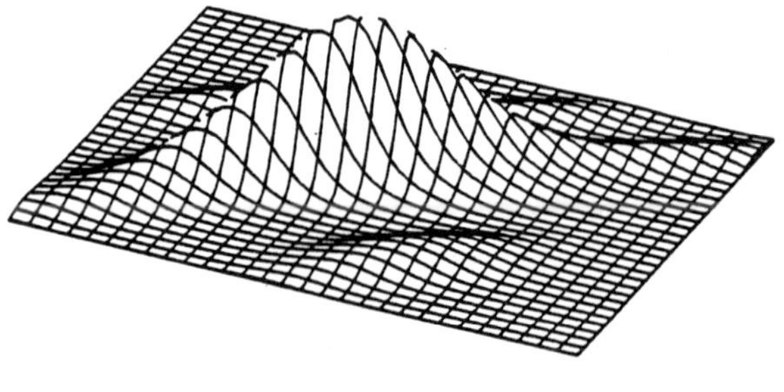

Figure 2

PLOT OF EXPRESSION (3.1), c=.4, FOR DATA OF TABLE 1

"Is the change statistically significant" becomes impossible without extra-statistical information. In the simple multivariate Gaussian situation, simulation may be used to establish statistical criteria for how much is too much; this is related to goodness-of-fit questions. The statistic

$$\sum_{i=1}^{n} \frac{f_i^c}{Q}\bigg|_{\hat{\theta}_c=\theta}, \quad c>0$$

would be used for testing a hypothesis of goodness-of-fit.

4. ANALYSIS OF VARIANCE

As shown in the previous section, the sensitivity analysis induced by the self-critical estimation procedure can be useful in identifying outliers. It can further be useful in evolving structural models since if data and model are not internally consistent, then it may be the model which is inappropriate rather than the data vis-a-vis the model. (It is well to remember that an outlier is only well-defined in terms of a well-defined model.) Since it is often very difficult to isolate problems, or even to ascertain that they exist, in planned experimental layouts, it would seem that this would be a natural area for use of the sensitivity analysis induced by the self-critical estimation procedure. We consider for brevity only the case of two-way layouts. The response data will be of dimension p, $p\geq 1$.

We assume that

$$x_{jk\ell} = \mu + \alpha_j + \beta_k + \gamma_{jk} + e_{jk\ell}, \tag{4.1}$$

$j=1,2,\ldots,J$, $k=1,2,\ldots,K$, $\ell=1,2,\ldots,n_{jk}$. The errors $e_{jk\ell}$ are assumed to be independently, identically distributed $N_p(0,D)$. The density for the $x_{jk\ell}$ is thus

$$f(x_{jk\ell}) = |2\pi D|^{-\frac{1}{2}} \exp\{-\tfrac{1}{2}\, u_{jk\ell}^T\, D^{-1}\, u_{jk\ell}\} \tag{4.2}$$

where

$$u_{jk\ell} = x_{jk\ell} - \mu - \alpha_j - \beta_k - \gamma_{jk}.$$

Substitution of (4.2) in (2.7) gives us the objective function

$$\ell_c(\mu,\alpha_j,\beta_k,\gamma_{jk},D) = \frac{1}{c}\sum_j\sum_k\sum_\ell \left\{\frac{f_{jk\ell}^c}{Q^a} - 1\right\} \tag{4.3}$$

which is to be maximized. Differentiation of (4.3) leads to the implicit system of equations

$$\begin{aligned}
&\sum_j\sum_k\sum_\ell (x_{jk\ell}-\mu-\alpha_j-\beta_k-\gamma_{jk})v_{jk\ell c}=0\\
&\sum_k\sum_\ell (x_{jk\ell}-\mu-\alpha_j-\beta_k-\gamma_{jk})v_{jk\ell c}=0,\ j=1,2,\ldots,J\\
&\sum_j\sum_\ell (x_{jk\ell}-\mu-\alpha_j-\beta_k-\gamma_{jk})v_{jk\ell c}=0,\ k=1,2,\ldots,K\\
&\sum_\ell (x_{jk\ell}-\mu-\alpha_j-\beta_k-\gamma_{jk})v_{jk\ell c}=0,\ j=1,2,\ldots,J,\ k=1,2,\ldots,K
\end{aligned} \tag{4.4}$$

$$D = (1+c)\,\frac{\sum_j\sum_k\sum_\ell u_{jk\ell}\, u_{jk\ell}^T\, v_{jk\ell c}}{\sum_j\sum_k\sum_\ell v_{jk\ell c}}, \tag{4.5}$$

and

$$v_{jk\ell c} = \exp\{-\tfrac{c}{2}\, u_{jk\ell}^T\, D^{-1}\, u_{jk\ell}\}. \tag{4.6}$$

The rank of the system is not full; we thus append the r+c+1 side conditions to remove the singularities

$$\sum_j\sum_k\sum_\ell \alpha_j v_{jk\ell c} = \sum_j\sum_k\sum_\ell \beta_k v_{jk\ell c} = 0, \tag{4.7}$$

$$\sum_k\sum_\ell \gamma_{jk} v_{jk\ell c} = 0,\ j=1,2,\ldots,J \tag{4.8}$$

$$\sum_j\sum_\ell \gamma_{jk} v_{jk\ell c} = 0,\ k=1,2,\ldots,K. \tag{4.9}$$

These equations reduce to the standard maximum likelihood (least squares) system when c=0.

It is easy to write down an analogue to (4.3) for virtually any type of layout. Numerical parameter estimates can be obtained in every case by fixed point iteration.

5. TWO EXAMPLES

We examine two layouts in this section, one a univariate two-way layout with interaction, the second a bivariate two-way layout without interaction.

The survival time data in Table 3 are taken from Box and Cox (1964). Parameter estimates for the model (4.1) with dimension p=1 are determined by maximizing (4.3) for c=0, .1, .2, and .3. The weights $v_{jk\ell c}=v_{jk\ell c}|_{\theta=\hat{\theta}}$ for c=.3 are given in Table 4. Especially low weights are found in cells (1,2,2) (i.e., for poison 1, treatment 2, and replication 2), (1,3,4), (1,4,1), (2,2,1), (2,2,4), (2,4,2), (2,4,4). These observations and the two-way layout with interaction on the assumption of a Gaussian error distribution do not appear to be consistent. There are a few more cells with relatively low weights, namely cells (1,3,3) and (2,4,3) while all the cells for poison 3 have high weights. This particular pattern suggests that some facet of the model may not be appropriate.

Table 3

SURVIVAL TIMES

		TREATMENT			
		1	2	3	4
POISON	1	.31	.82	.43	.45
		.45	1.10	.45	.71
		.46	.88	.63	.66
		.43	.72	.76	.62
	2	.36	.92	.44	.56
		.29	.61	.35	1.02
		.40	.49	.31	.71
		.23	1.24	.40	.38
	3	.22	.30	.23	.30
		.21	.37	.25	.36
		.18	.38	.24	.31
		.23	.29	.22	.33

Table 4

WEIGHTS $\hat{v}_{jk\ell.3}$ FOR SURVIVAL TIME DATA

		TREATMENT			
		1	2	3	4
POISON	1	.59	1	.91	.21
		.97	.04	.97	.85
		.95	.85	.39	.99
		1	.68	.04	.97
	2	.95	.004	.84	.98
		.96	.87	.97	.0004
		.78	.86	.84	.53
		.70	.4(-8)	.97	.18
	3	1	.95	1	.97
		1	.95	.99	.95
		.96	.92	1	.99
		.98	.92	.99	1

In fact, the pattern of the weights suggests a short tailed distribution to the left and a longer tailed distribution to the right and that a transformation of the data may be helpful. This is in fact what Box and Cox concluded. When the inverse transformation is made, only one of the cells possesses a relatively low value of $\hat{v}'_{jk\ell c}$, the prime indicating the weights for the transformed responses. Figure 3 contains interaction plots for c=0,.1, .2, .3. At c=0 one would declare the existence of a strong interaction. However as c moves through .1 to .3 the evidence for interaction is much diminished. The overall interaction pattern is thus a sensitive function of the way the information is processed. This sensitivity calls for a more careful study of the data and the model.

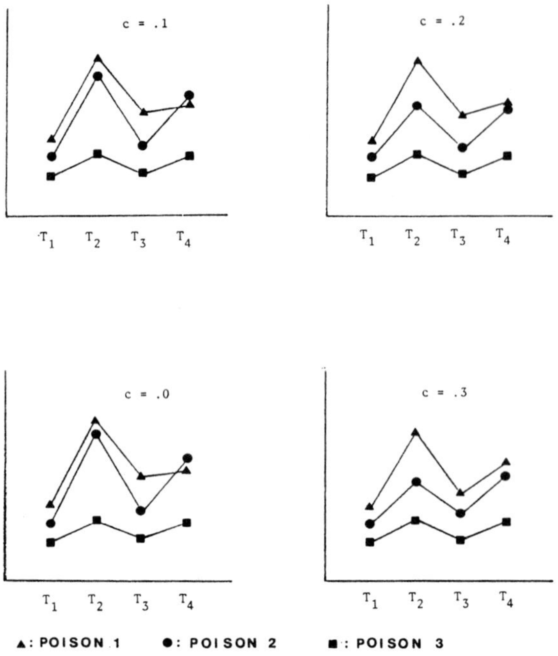

Figure 3

INTERACTION PLOTS, c=0(.1).3, FOR SURVIVAL TIME DATA.

The crop yield data in Table 5 is taken from Anderson (1958, p. 218). We use equation (4.3) to generate parameter estimates for the model (4.1) with $n_{jk}=1$, $\gamma_{jk}=0$, p=2. These estimates are given in Table 6. We have used c=.2 for the self-critical analysis. For c much greater than .2 the procedure begins to experience convergence difficulties. Among the α's and β's, only the estimate of the vector α_5 changes to any appreciable degree when c varies from 0 to .2. The estimated correlation coefficient increases from .22 to .39. An examination of the weights $\hat{v}_{jkc}$ of Table 7 indicates that observations (5,3), (5,4), and (1,3) receive the lowest weights and thus indicate where we should look for problems with either the data or the model. On referring back to Table 5, we are led to suspect that the coordinates (69,97) have been changed from (97, 69). This single data point would have produced a dramatic effect on the estimate of correlation. The observation in cell (5,4) seems somewhat out of place with respect to the high yielding variety 4. The observation in cell (1,3) appears to have a somewhat high yield in the first component.

6. DISCUSSION

The sensitivity analysis procedure we have proposed seems to be extremely useful for informal exploratory analysis of structured statistical data. For fixed c>0, the maximization of (2.7) (for any density or discrete distribution, univariate or multivariate) produces joint robust estimators for arbitrary types of parameters, e.g.

Table 5

CROP YIELDS FOR TWO CONSECUTIVE YEARS

LOCATION	VARIETIES 1	2	3	4	5
1	81 81	105 82	120 80	110 87	98 84
2	147 100	142 116	151 112	192 148	146 108
3	82 103	77 105	78 117	131 140	90 130
4	120 99	121 62	124 96	141 126	125 76
5	99 66	89 50	69 97	89 62	104 80
6	87 68	77 67	79 67	102 92	96 94

Table 6

MAXIMUM LIKELIHOOD (ML) AND SELF-CRITICAL (c=0.2) PARAMETER ESTIMATES

	μ	β_1	β_2	β_3	β_4	β_5
ML	109.1 93.2	-6.4 -7.0	- 7.2 -12.8	- 5.6 1.7	18.4 16.0	0.8 2.2
c = 0.2	108.7 92.7	-5.6 -6.1	- 7.3 -11.0	- 3.3 - 1.9	18.5 18.0	1.0 4.5

	α_1	α_2	α_3	α_4	α_5	α_6
ML	- 6.3 -10.4	46.5 23.6	-17.5 25.8	-17.1 - 1.4	-19.1 -22.2	-20.9 -15.6
c = 0.2	- 7.9 -10.9	45.3 22.2	-19.8 25.2	16.9 0.3	-12.1 -25.7	-21.3 -16.1

Estimated $\begin{pmatrix} \sigma_1 & \rho_{12} \\ \rho_{12} & \sigma_2 \end{pmatrix}$: ML $\begin{pmatrix} 10.5 & 0.22 \\ 0.22 & 11.6 \end{pmatrix}$ c = 0.2 $\begin{pmatrix} 9.6 & 0.39 \\ 0.39 & 10.8 \end{pmatrix}$

Table 7

WEIGHTS $\hat{v}_{jkc}$ (×100) WITH c=0.2

71	83	52	84	98
93	80	100	63	87
93	98	92	52	94
86	63	98	76	64
93	97	9	42	93
95	98	94	98	86

location, scale, shape, orientation. Moreover, the procedure may be extended to cover censored and binary data.

ACKNOWLEDGMENTS

This research was supported by the U.S. Army Research Office under contract DAA G29-81-K-0110.

REFERENCES

Anderson, T.W. (1958). An Introduction to Multivariate Statistical Analysis. New York: Wiley.

Andrews, D.F., Bickel, P.J., Hampel, F.R., Huber, P.J., Rogers, W.H., Tukey, J.W. (1972). Robust Estimators of Location. Princeton: Princeton University Press.

Box, G.E.P. and Cox, D.R. (1964). An analysis of transformations. Journal of the Royal Statistical Society, B, pp. 211-252.

Golomb, S.W. (1966). The information generating function of a probability distribution. IEEE Transactions on Information Theory, pp. 75-77.

Huber, P.J. (1981). Robust Statistics. New York: Wiley.

Graphical Data Analysis and its Applications

Chair: Ingram Olkin, Stanford University

Some Graphics for Studying Four-Dimensional Data
John W. Tukey, Princeton University and Bell Laboratories
Paul A. Tukey, Bell Laboratories

The Need of Real Time Graphics and The Example of Multidimensional Scaling (Abstract)
Andreas Buja, University of Washington and Stanford University

On the Role of Computers and Mathematical Statistics in Tomography (Abstract)
Larry A. Shepp, Yehuda Vardi, and Linda Kaufman, Bell Laboratories

Some Graphics for Studying Four-Dimensional Data

John W. Tukey

Princeton University* and Bell Laboratories

Paul A. Tukey

Bell Laboratories

ABSTRACT

Four-dimensional data can be visualized quite effectively with a variety of computer-generated static graphical displays. While many techniques useful for four-dimensional data have useful extensions to higher dimensions, this paper deals only with four dimensions. It describes and contrasts draftsman's views, draftsman's casements, and window plots, and it considers the vital role of re-expression for making these displays informative.

Keywords: *data analysis, statistical computing.*

* Research supported in part by DOE and ARO(D).

1. Introduction

Using computers to help look at data will be of increasing importance for statisticians and their clients. While dynamic displays remain more powerful, static displays can be very helpful. Both are likely to be computer-driven.

Four-dimensional data can be visualized quite effectively with a variety of static graphical displays. Many of the techniques useful for four-dimensional data have useful extensions to higher dimensions. But since it is important to learn to deal with four-dimensional data before moving on to higher dimensions, our examples in this paper are all four-dimensional. We show, describe, and contrast examples of generalized draftsman's views, draftsman's casements, and window plots.

The simplest serious trap one can fall into in data display is to neglect desirable or vital re-expression. Naming a variable does not fix how it is displayed — applying logarithms, reciprocals and square roots can often be important — wholly changing both appearance and natural conclusions. Our examples will demonstrate the interplay between re-expression and graphical display.

2. Draftsman's Views

Draftsmen routinely draw "front", "top" and "side" views of objects, as suggested by Exhibit 1. By doing the same thing for a three-dimensional cloud of data points, we obtain the three two-coordinates-at-a-time scatter plots arranged so that adjacent pairs of plots share a common axis.

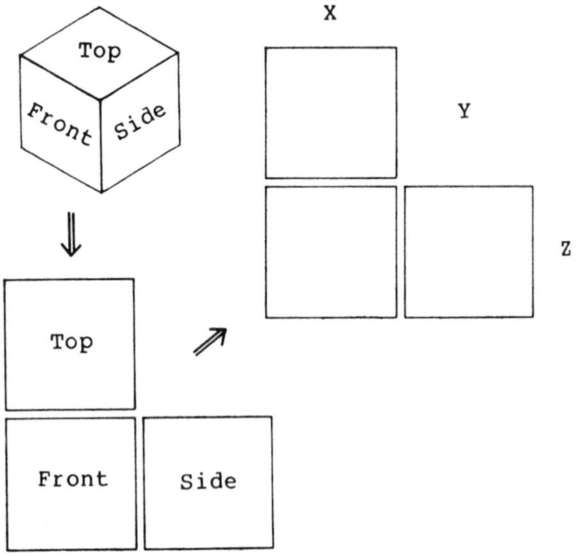

Exhibit 1

Evolution of a draftsman's view

The idea extends easily to four and more dimensions by adding extra rows to the array of plots to produce a *generalized draftsman's view*, as suggested by Exhibit 2 (Tukey and Tukey, 1981).

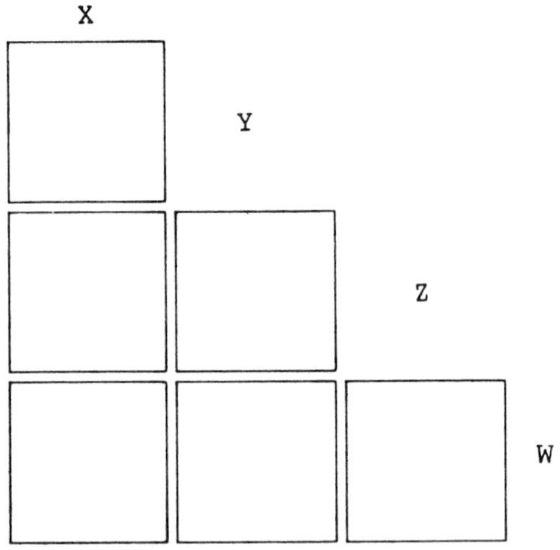

Exhibit 2

Generalized draftsman's view

This arrangement of the plots makes it easy to match up individual points from one plot to the next. For large numbers of variables, either the plots must be made small, or the array of plots must be pasted together from several sheets and hung on the wall. Some of our colleagues have found the twenty-dimensional version useful!

Exhibit 3 is a generalized draftsman's view of a set of four-dimensional data from a particle physics experiment.

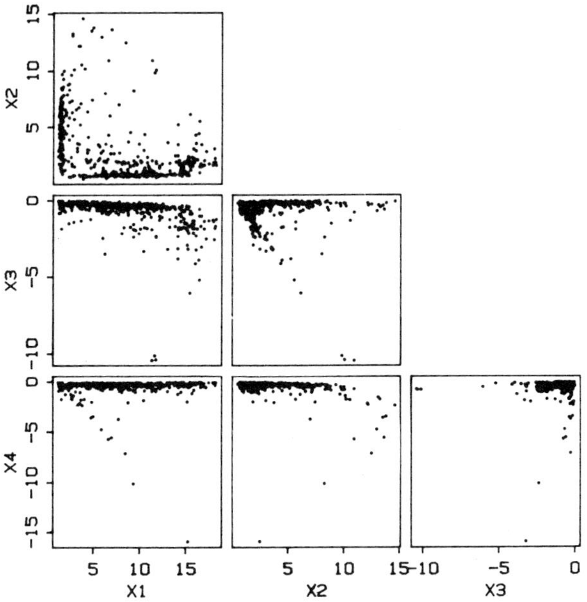

Exhibit 3

Generalized draftsman's view of
the raw particle physics data

Each of the 500 data points depicts one instance of a reaction in which an elementary particle of a specific kind with about 12 billion volts of energy hits another particle of a specific kind and produces three particular resultant particles.

Looking at Exhibit 3, we might feel that the generalized draftsman's view of the particle physics data

- shows things are highly structured
- hints at some of aspects of the structure
- doesn't do nearly as well as a dynamic display can — and did in the PRIM-9 system — for this data set (see Tukey, Friedman and Fisherkeller, 1979).

3. Casement Displays

As an introduction to handling dimensions by quantization, Exhibit 4 suggests how a *casement display* of a three-dimensional point cloud is constructed. A three-dimensional region of space surrounding the point cloud is "sliced" into cells with planes parallel to one of the coordinate axis planes. Each cell is then "flattened" into a two-dimensional scatter plot, and the several scatter plots are arranged side-by-side. Note that the slicing is really a matter of quantizing according to the value of one variable or coordinate. The mnemonic comes from imagining a series of side-by-side casement windows being cranked open, each data point being drawn to the nearest window, and the set of windows being swung shut again.

To deal analogously with four-dimensional data, we can make a *draftsman's casement display* by slicing on one

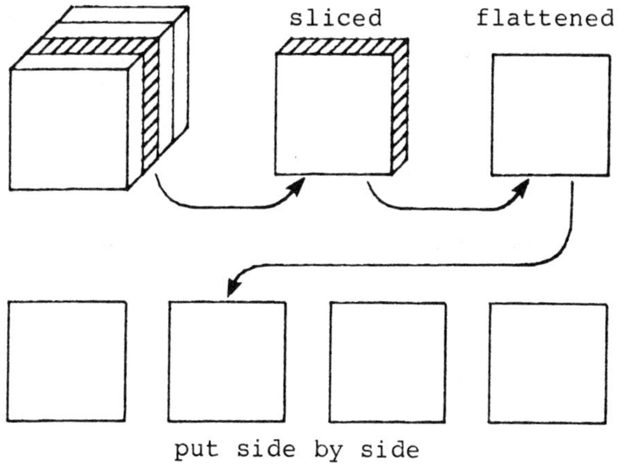

Exhibit 4

Evolution of a casement display

variable, taking the points in each slice and making a draftsman's view of them for the other three variables, then displaying the several draftsman's views side-by-side.

This is done in Exhibit 5 for the particle physics data. The data were quantized into three groups according to whether X_1 had a low, middle, or high value. One interesting feature of this data set that can be seen in the display is the "arm" of points parallel to the X_2,X_3 plane visible in the X_2,X_3 plot on the left, and another arm of points in the X_2,X_3 plot on the right. In the four-dimensional configuration, these two arms are not parallel, and do not intersect, but rather they are connected by a column of points parallel to the X_1 axis which shows up as a concentration of points in the north-west corner of the middle draftsman's view.

4. Casements, Jalousies, and Window Plots

Exhibit 6 suggests another way of applying these same ideas to viewing four-dimensional data. If we restrict ourselves to looking only at X_3,X_4 scatter plots, we can make a casement display of X_3,X_4 in X_1, or we can make a jalousie display of X_3,X_4 in X_2. (A jalousie is, in effect, a set of casement windows stacked vertically and hinged horizontally, so a jalousie display is naturally a casement display with the scatter plots arranged above each other instead of side-by-side.) Since we can do each of these separately, we can do both together. That is, we can take the top jalousie plot of X_3,X_4 in X_2, make a casement display for the points in that plot by quantizing on X_1, and place it to the right of the top jalousie plot. Then we can do the same for the next jalousie plot. And so on. Equivalently, we could make a jalousie display under each of the casement plots of X_3,X_4 in X_1. We call the result a *window plot* (Tukey and Tukey, 1981).

The process of quantizing first on X_2 and then on X_1 (or vice versa) can be thought of in a single step in which the X_1,X_2 plane is "cellulated" by a square grid of cells.

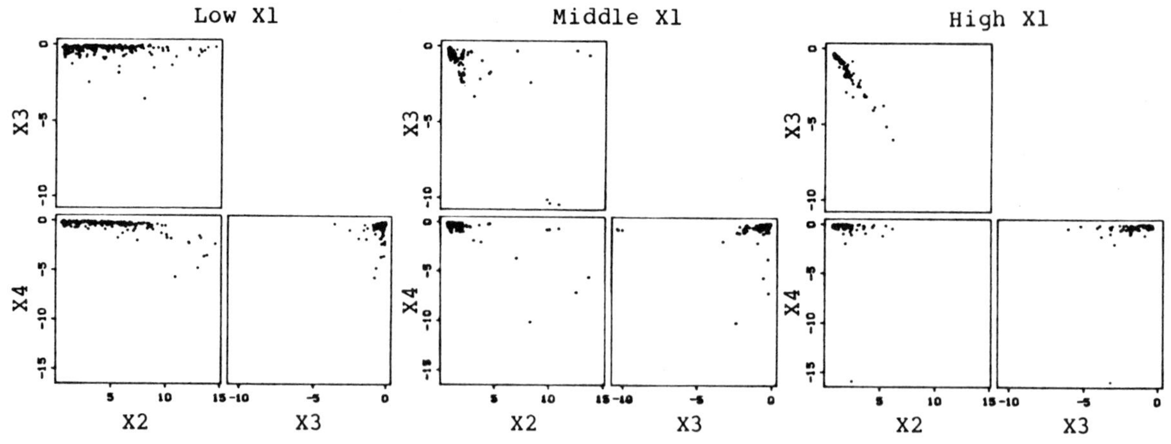

Exhibit 5

Draftsman's casement display
of the particle physics data

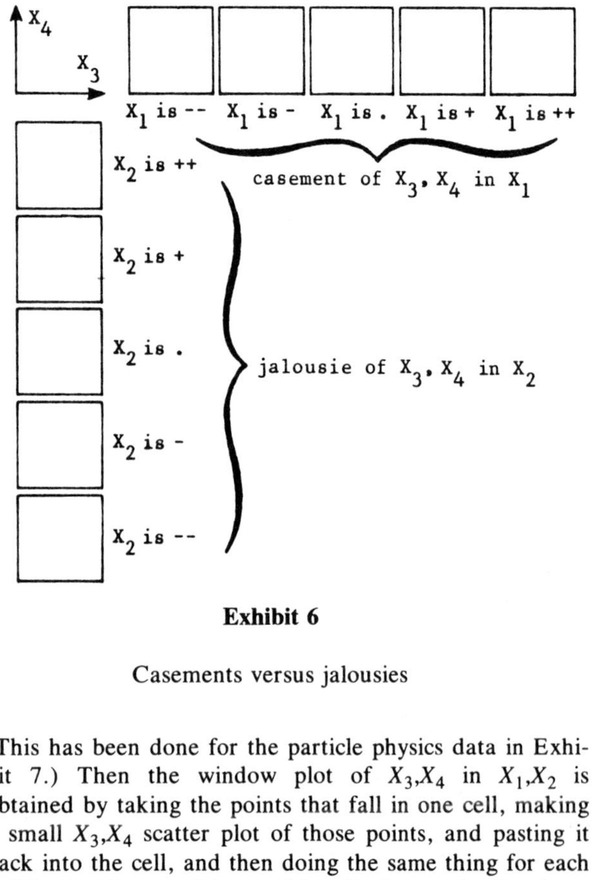

Exhibit 6

Casements versus jalousies

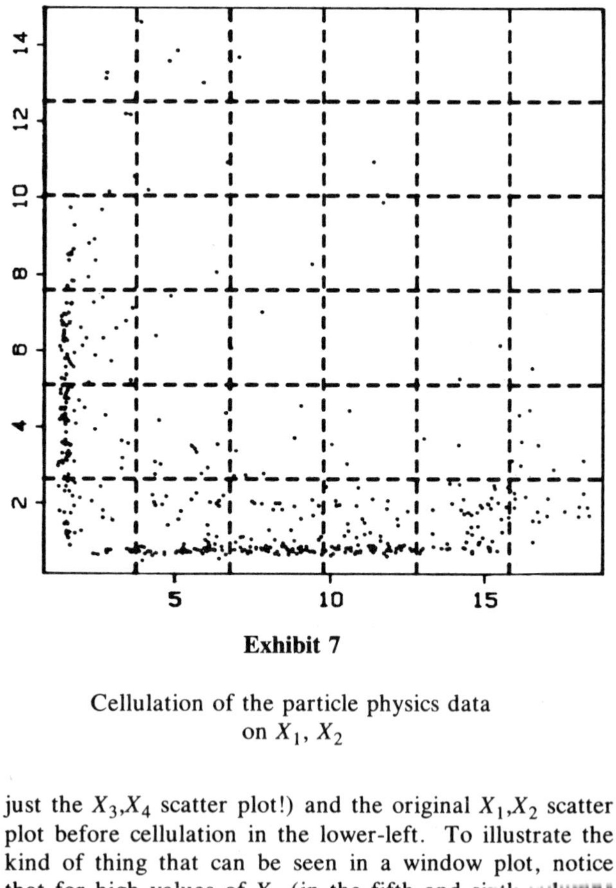

Exhibit 7

Cellulation of the particle physics data
on X_1, X_2

(This has been done for the particle physics data in Exhibit 7.) Then the window plot of X_3,X_4 in X_1,X_2 is obtained by taking the points that fall in one cell, making a small X_3,X_4 scatter plot of those points, and pasting it back into the cell, and then doing the same thing for each cell in the picture. The resulting display can be fitted out with row and column aggregate plots positioned along the edges.

One way or the other, the result for the particle physics data is Exhibit 8. This exhibit also includes an overall aggregate plot in the upper-right corner (It's really just the X_3,X_4 scatter plot!) and the original X_1,X_2 scatter plot before cellulation in the lower-left. To illustrate the kind of thing that can be seen in a window plot, notice that for high values of X_1 (in the fifth and sixth columns of the array of plots), increasing X_2 (that is, moving from the bottom plot up) corresponds to decreasing values of X_3 (that is, the points move to the left). But in the first few columns, where X_1 has low values, X_3 does not decrease with increasing X_2.

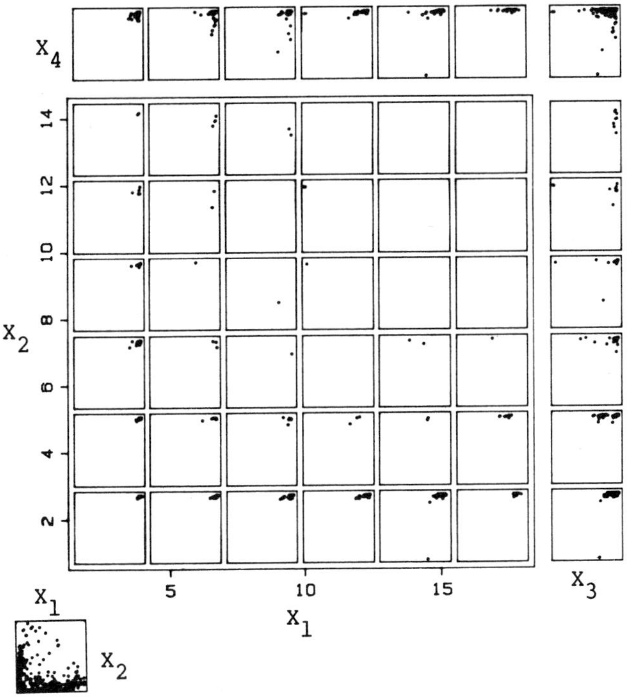

Exhibit 8

Window plot of the particle physics data;
plots of X_3, X_4 windowed by X_1, X_2

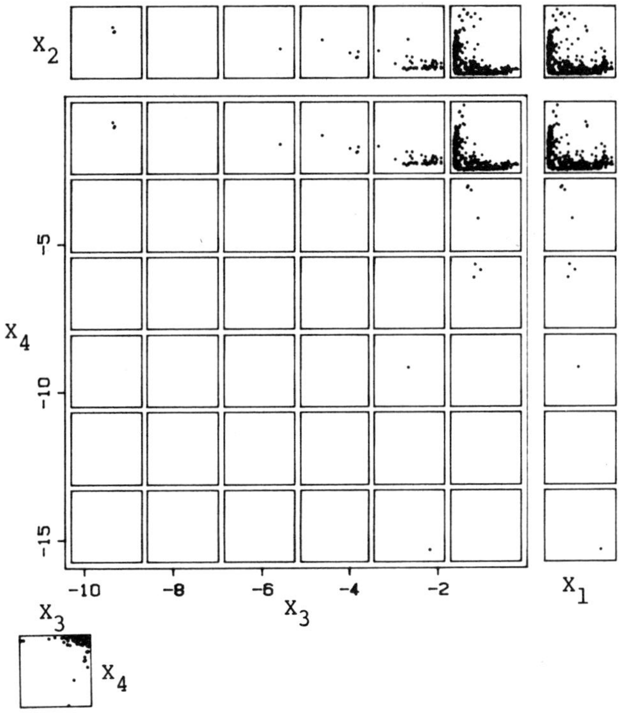

Exhibit 9

Window plot of the particle physics data;
plots of X_1, X_2 windowed by X_3, X_4

It is useful to study the window plot both alone and in comparison with the generalized draftsman's view of Exhibit 3. One shouldn't be surprised if any four-dimensional representation takes a while to be fully meaningful.

If we have four variables to study, we can pick one of the $\binom{4}{2} = 6$ pairs of variables on which to do the cellulating, and we will have four closely related pictures for each choice, depending upon which variables are plotted horizontally and which vertically. The full transpose is obtained by interchanging the outside (quantized) variables with the inside (intracell) variables while keeping the same variables horizontal and the same vertical. Exhibit 9 is the full transpose of Exhibit 8.

5. Rotations

One natural thing to do — in any number of dimensions — is to rotate the configuration and see what happens to the appearance of structure. Exhibit 10 is the generalized draftsman's view of a particular rotation of the particle physics data.

We can see that there still appears to be a lot of structure. At the very least, it surely does not look anything like a collection of elliptical blurs! However it is somewhat harder than before to see what is going on and to characterize the structure.

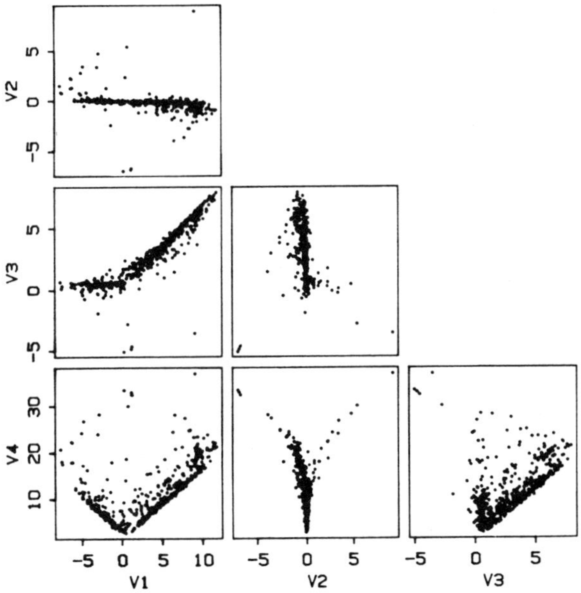

Exhibit 10

Draftsman's view of the rotated
particle physics data

6. A Second Data Set

Now that we have a few ways to look at data in four dimensions — each statically and incompletely — we will go on to a new four-dimensional data set which we will call the "hypo-data", and its structure will gradually emerge.

The hypo-data is shown first in Exhibit 11 in a generalized

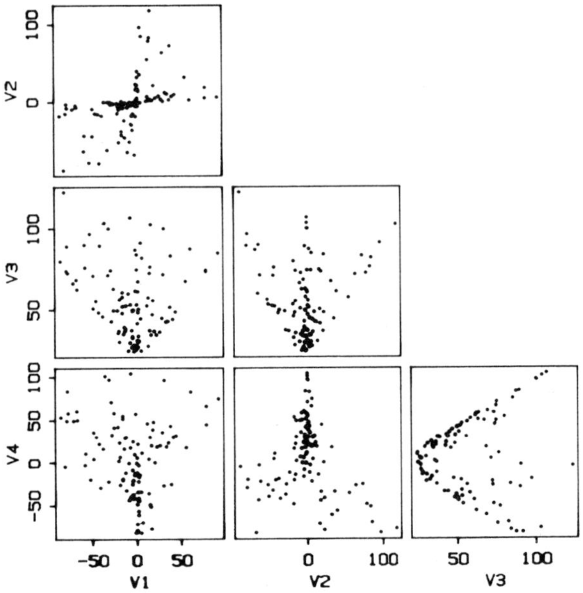

Exhibit 11

Draftsman's view of the rotated hypo-data

draftsman's view under the same rotation that was used for the particle physics data in Exhibit 10. Allowing for the decrease from 500 to 100 data points, we have to say that the intensity and complexity of the structure seems about the same in the two data sets.

When we de-rotate the hypo-data, as in Exhibit 12, we see something much simpler. For two of the scatter plots, Y_1,Y_4 and Y_2,Y_3, the points are close to vaguely hyperbolic curves, while every coordinate shows a squeezing toward zero. This is still strong structure, but the apparent need to break the data up into "hunks" to be described separately has gone away.

The natural way to deal with the "squeezing toward zero" is to take logs throughout, which produces Exhibit 13. We now see that the structure of the hypo-data, when de-rotated and logged, can be described very simply as

$$X_1 + X_4 \approx \text{a constant}$$

$$X_2 + X_3 \approx \text{a constant}$$

otherwise random

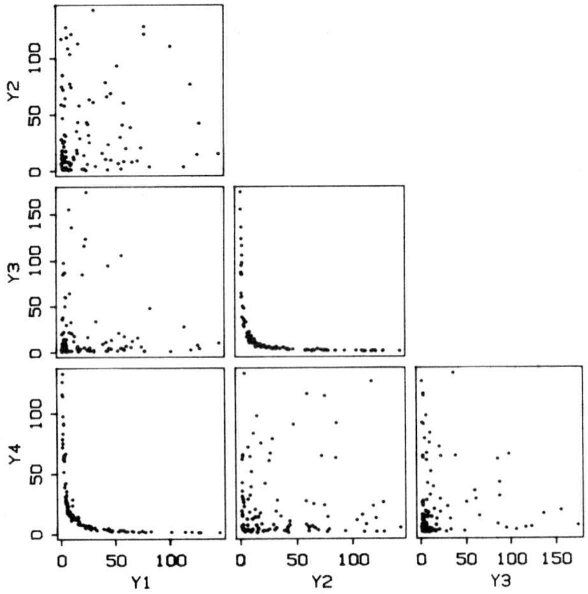

Exhibit 12

Draftsman's view of the de-rotated hypo-data

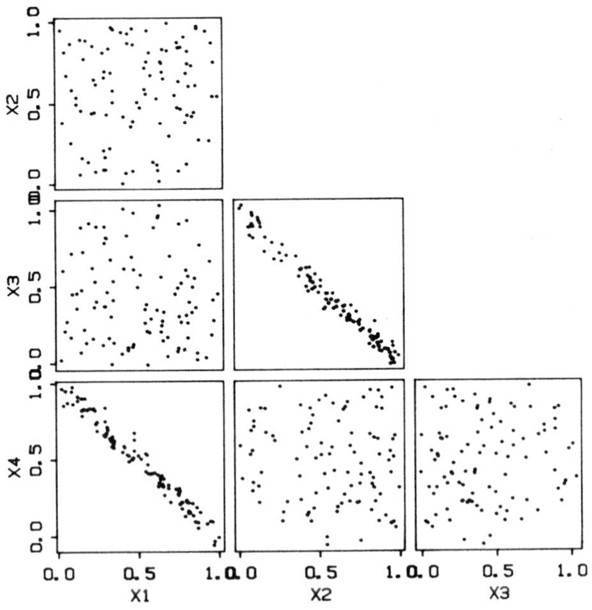

Exhibit 13

Draftsman's view of the logged, de-rotated hypo-data

We are down to two pairs of closely related variables.

The X_3,X_4 in X_1,X_2 window plot of this data in Exhibit 14 shows a lot about what

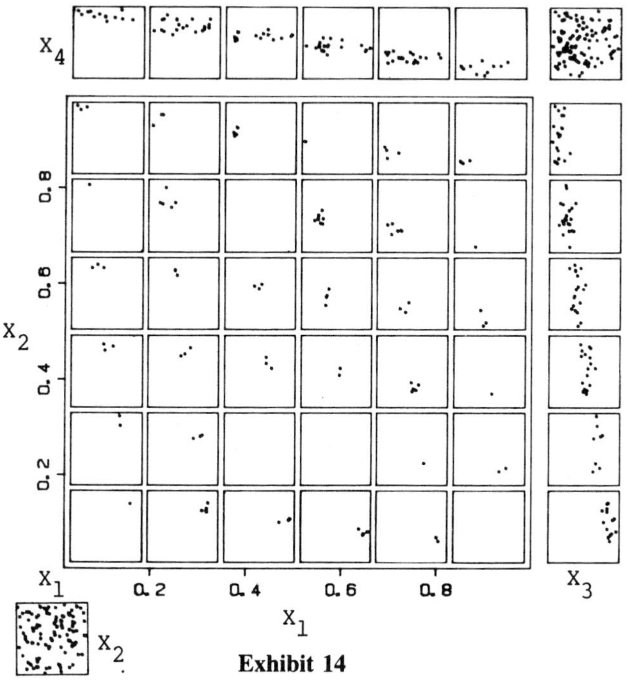

Exhibit 14

Window plot of the logged, de-rotated hypo-data; plots of X_3, X_4 windowed by X_1, X_2

is going on, even though this plot, with each pair of closely related variables split between the outside pair and the inside pair, might plausibly be the *least* effective of the six kinds of window plots for this particular set of data. (In some of the others, the structure would hit us in the eye.) The marginal plots in Exhibit 14 are particularly revealing.

Statisticians might naturally ask what would happen if we were to remove the "dependencies" that are so obvious in the last two pictures. One way to do this is to put

$$U_1 = X_1$$

$$U_2 = X_2$$

$$U_3 = X_2 + X_3$$

$$U_4 = X_1 + X_4$$

and then work with (U_1, U_2, U_3, U_4), or actually (in our plots) with $(U_1, U_2, 10{\times}U_3, 10{\times}U_4)$, since $X_1{+}X_4$ and $X_2{+}X_3$ are nearly constants. The resulting generalized draftsman's view is Exhibit 15 and the window plot is Exhibit 16.

In fact, the (de-rotated, logged) hypo-data were generated as a sample from a uniform distribution on a square, randomly matched with a sample from a circular

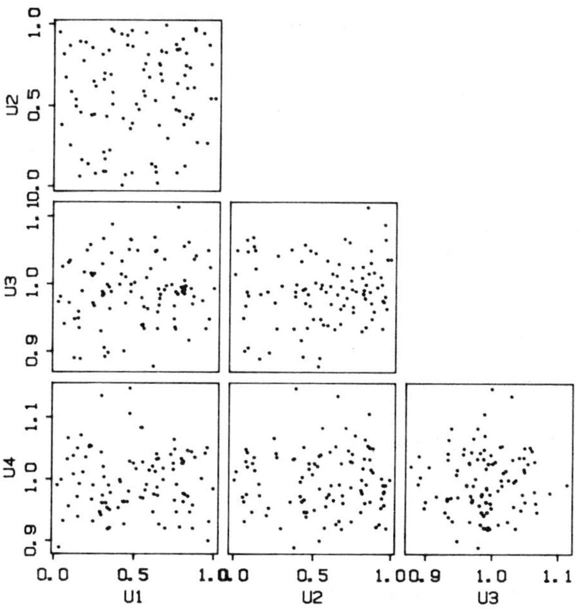

Exhibit 15

Draftsman's view of the logged, de-rotated hypo-data with dependencies removed

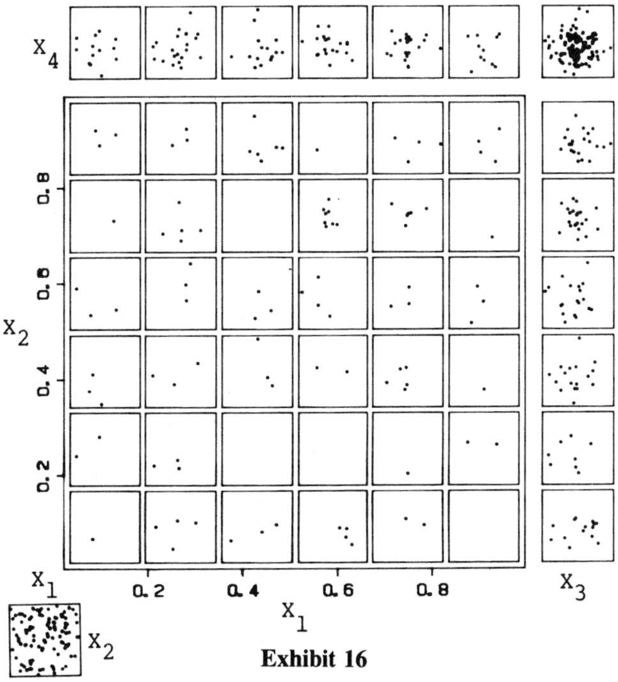

Exhibit 16

Window plot of the data in Exhibit 15; plots of X_3, X_4 windowed by X_1, X_2

Gaussian distribution. The first sample produced U_1 and U_2, while the second produced U_3 and U_4.

7. Particle Physics Data Revisited

Before stopping, we should show the result of taking logs of the (unrotated) particle physics data, since it too showed squeezing toward zero in all variables. To allow for negative numbers, we took $\text{sgn}(X) \times \log|X|$, and obtained Exhibit 17.

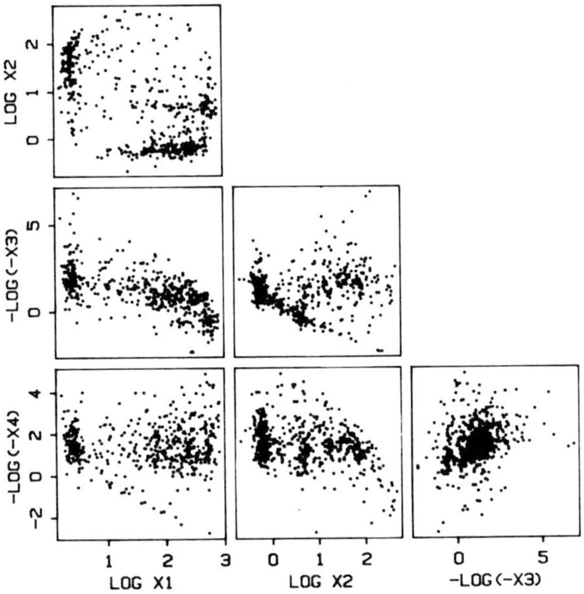

Exhibit 17

Draftsman's view of the logged particle physics data

This has spread things out, and although we do not see the linear-arms structure as clearly as we did in Exhibit 3, we can see some things that were obscured before, such as a faint arm extending to the north-east in the $-\log(-X_3), \log X_2$ plot. Neither Exhibit 3 nor Exhibit 17 seems to dominate the other.

Exhibit 18 is one of the companion window plots of the logged particle physics data. Compared to Exhibit 8, the spreading out of the points brings out considerably more structure in the point cloud. We invite the reader to trace through the intracacies of this plot.

8. Conclusions

There are several conclusions:

- Static displays can be constructed that tell a lot about four dimensional data. (But don't expect them to do everything!)
- Both generalized draftsman's views and window plots have merits (but choosing a good one of the $4 \times \binom{4}{2} = 24$ window plots may be important).

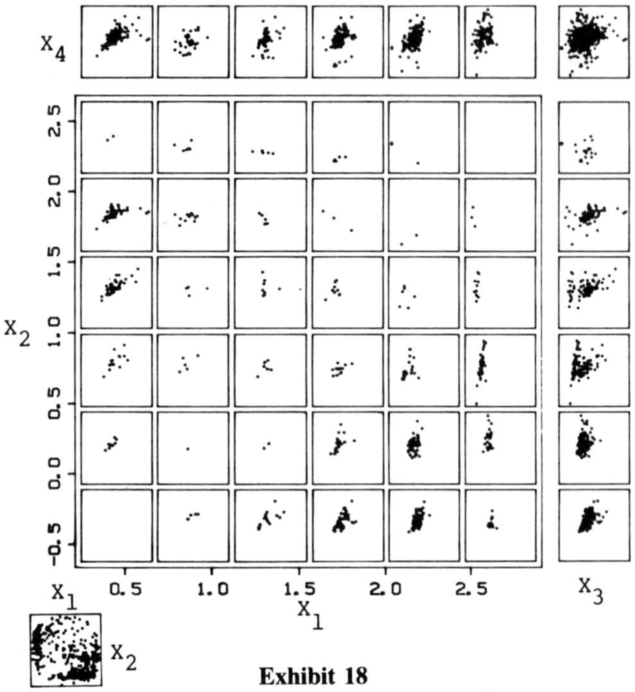

Exhibit 18

Window plot of the logged particle physics data; plots of X_3, X_4 windowed by X_1, X_2

- Sometimes, apparently complicated structure can mean that the best real-world description is itself complicated (as with the particle physics data) — but sometimes it can mean nothing of the sort (as with the hypo-data).
- Just because we have good graphic displays, we are *not* allowed to forget about the possible importance of re-expression.
- We should try a variety of re-expressions and not expect any one of them to tell us everything that all of them together can tell.
- To get hold of what a particular kind of picture can tell about a single set of data (even for a fixed set of underlying variables), it may take pictures using more than one set of expressions for these variables.

9. References

Tukey, J. W., Friedman, J. H., and Fisherkeller, M. A. (1976). PRIM-9, an interactive multidimensional data display and analysis system. In *Proc. 4th International Congress for Stereology*, Sept. 4-9, 1975, Gaithersburg, Maryland.

Tukey, P. A. and Tukey, J. W. (1981). Graphical display of data sets in 3 or more dimensions. Chapters 10, 11 and 12 in *Interpreting Multivariate Data* (Ed., V, Barnett) Wiley, London.

THE NEED OF REAL TIME GRAPHICS AND THE EXAMPLE OF MULTIDIMENSIONAL SCALING

Andreas Buja
University of Washington and Stanford University

Real time graphics can be provided by a CRT connected to suitable hardware. For statistical purposes, desirable real time operations comprise rotations of 3-D scatterplots, interactive grouping and identification of data, and minimization of data dependent functions. A real time graphics configuration was designed by J.H. Friedman and W. Stuetzle at the Stanford Linear Accelerator Center. It will be briefly described. Its power will be demonstrated with the example of multideminsional scaling.

ON THE ROLE OF COMPUTERS AND MATHEMATICAL STATISTICS IN TOMOGRAPHY

Larry A. Shepp
Yehuda Vardi
and
Linda Kaufman
Bell Laboratories

Computer tomography (CT) benefits tens of thousands of patients annually. Special purpose computer hardware now implements the mathematical algorithm which reconstructs the X-ray density of the body from its X-transmission attenuation measurements in order to achieve prompt reconstructions.

Emission tomography is a newer direction of CT with much promise and sits exactly on the interface between computer science and statistics. A radionuclide whose chemical affinity under metabolic action causes it to be deposited preferentially in various body tissues forms an unknown emission density $\lambda=\lambda(x,y,z)$. Thereafter positrons are emitted as in a Poisson process with variable rate λ. Each positron emitted finds a nearby electron and annihilates with it to form two X-ray photons which fly off in opposite directions at the speed of light along a line with random uniform orientation through the point of annihilation. A bank of detectors surrounding the body and wired for coincidence detects each line, but does not detect where along the line the annihilation took place. The problem then is to reconstruct λ from a knowledge of the set of lines observed (typically there are about 10^7 lines).

Although conventional algorithms for X-ray transmission CT are now used in this emission CT case, we show that mathematical statistics provides us with a much more accurate algorithm, the E-M algorithm, which gives a λ for which the given set of observed lines has maximum probability (likelihood).

A major problem with using the E-M algorithm in practice, however, is that it is nonlinear and iterative and intrinsically slower than the conventional transmission algorithms. Here much work is required to implement the E-M algorithm to run on general purpose minicomputers to achieve reasonable reconstruction times, for each given detector array geometry.

Symbolic Computing and Statistics

Chair: Joseph Deken, University of Texas at Austin

SYMBOLIC COMPUTING AND STATISTICS

Joseph Deken
The University of Texas at Austin

Abstract: Computer software and hardware systems for doing symbolic, rather than numeric computation are becoming widely available and moderate in cost. A wide variety of mathematical and programming capabilities are available interactively on such systems. An annotated session of interaction with the MACSYMA algebraic manipulation system developed at M.I.T. is given here, with emphasis on functions familiar to statisticians.

Key Words: algebraic manipulation, symbolic integration, LISP, MACSYMA, symbolic computation, Taylor series

In this session, we covered the background of symbolic computation, starting from its origins in artificial intelligence research, to its present development and prospects. These developments include large and powerful symbolic manipulation systems such as M.I.T.'s MACSYMA, which has been recently transported and revised for use with the VAX minicomputer and smaller systems at Berkeley. In addition special purpose hardware such as the Symbolics, Inc. LISP machine is now available. The LISP machine is by design a symbolic processing engine which can execute the most advanced M.I.T. MACSYMA system, and is competitive in price with conventional minicomputers.

The upshot of the current progress in symbolic processing programs and hardware is that symbolic processing, particularly algebraic manipulation such as that provided by MACSYMA, can soon be expected to be part of the tool kit of the theoretical and applied statistician. The session provided two demonstrations of MACSYMA capabilities and interactive style. The first demonstration is reproduced here in the form of an annotated transcript. The interaction is with the MACSYMA program running on a DEC KL-10 at M.I.T.'s Laboratory for Computer Science. A second, more inspirational demonstration, was provided at the session via a videotape showing Bill Gosper putting the Symbolics Lisp Machine, MACSYMA, and several branches of applied mathematics and computer graphics through their paces to explore and solve a problem in coding theory.

(In the following MACSYMA transcript, comments will be delimited by double brackets, e.g. <<this is a comment>>. Commands typed to the MACSYMA program are generally in lower case and (automatically) numbered C1, C2, ... by a prompt from the program after it displays each result. Results produced by the program are generally in upper case, and numbered D1, D2, ... After each command, the time to produce the result, in milliseconds, is shown.)

```
        <<The session starts>>

This is MACSYMA 302

FIX302 1 DSK MACSYM being loaded
Loading done


        <<The input format ala FORTRAN>>
(C1) (a+b*x+c*x¬2)¬3;
Time= 15 msec.

        <<But a nicer display output>>
                 2           3
(D1)        (C X  + B X + A)


        <<The expression D1 is saved for
          any future reference.  In any
          command "%" is shorthand for
          "the last expression."  Here,
          % = D1. >>

(C2) expand(%);
Time= 130 msec.
      3  6          2  5          2  4
(D2) C  X  + 3 B C  X  + 3 A C  X

      2    4             3    3  3
 + 3 B  C X  + 6 A B C X  + B  X

      2    2          2  2        2          3
 + 3 A  C X  + 3 A B  X  + 3 A  B X + A

        <<There's a little algebra in
        expanding that expression. More,
        in factoring the expanded
        version.>>

(C3) factor(%);
Time= 1259 msec.
                 2           3
(D3)        (C X  + B X + A)

        <<Following the symbolic
        manipulation philosophy, an
        expression can be almost
        anything. Below, C4 and D4 are
        not polynomials, but
        equations. Also, %E denotes
        the base of the Naperian
        logarithms, as distinct from
        some arbitrary variable E. >>

(C4) sin(x/(x¬2+x))=%e¬((log(x)+1)¬2-
        log(x)¬2);
Time= 136 msec.
```

```
              X
(D4) SIN(------) =
             2
            X  + X

                              2        2
                   (LOG(X) + 1)  - LOG (X)
                 %E
```

<<We're not really interested in solving these equations, but they can be simplified considerably.>>

```
(C5) ratsimp(%);
Time= 578 msec.
                    1            2
(D5)          SIN(-----) = %E X
                  X + 1
```

<<A gaggle of other algebraic capabilities are provided by means of an ever expanding library of functions. If it's commonly (or even occasionally) used, chances are there is a function built in to do it. Here, we find a partial fraction decomposition.>>

```
(C6) x/(x¬3+4*x¬2+5*x+2);
Time= 16 msec.
                       X
(D6)        -------------------
             3      2
            X  + 4 X  + 5 X + 2

(C7) partfrac(%,x);

PFRAC FASL DSK MAXOUT being loaded
Loading done
Time= 146 msec.
            2       2         1
(D7)    - ----- + ----- - --------
          X + 2   X + 1          2
                          (X + 1)
```

<<In all calculations involving integers and rational numbers, all digits of the result are kept, allocating memory as needed: "infinite precision arithmetic." >>

```
(C8) 128047*7177551263;
Time= 3 msec.
(D8)         919063906573361
```

<<MACSYMA has a large data base of prime numbers, used by several functions, in particular, FACTOR will find the prime factors of an integer.>>

```
(C9) factor(%);
Time= 17888 msec.
(D9)        128047 7177551263
```

<<Here we define a function for future use, with ":=". The LAMBDA notation of LISP may also be used.>>

```
(C10) f(k):=sum(2¬n/(n+1),n,0,k);
Time= 5 msec.
                             N
                            2
(D10) F(K) := SUM(-----, N, 0, K)
                           N + 1
```

<<Since this is a symbolic manipulation system, we may apply f(m) even though m has no numerical value. The result returned will be a "quoted" form, displayed in standard format.>>

```
(C11) f(m);
Time= 139 msec.
                M
               ====     N
               \       2
(D11)           >     -----
               /      N + 1
               ====
               N = 0
```

<<Of course, if we apply f to a numerical argument, we get a numerical result.>>

```
(C12) f(12);
Time= 232 msec.
                  31418368
(D12)             --------
                   45045
```

<<A key feature of MACSYMA is the ability of users to SHARE functions and routines which they have developed. The example below is a function NUSUM written by Gosper to find closed form expressions for a wide class of indefinite sums. As with the function SUM, the syntax is: NUSUM(expression, summation index, lower limit, upper limit) . >>

```
(C14) nusum(2¬n,n,0,m);

NUSUM 48 DSK SHARE being loaded
Loading done

Time= 1286 msec.
                       M
(D14)             2 2   - 1
```

<<That sum is familiar. Below, a more challenging one:>>

```
(C17) nusum(n¬4*4¬n/binomial(2*n,n),
        n,0,m);

BINOML FASL DSK MAXOUT being loaded
Loading done

XRTOUT FASL DSK MAXOUT being loaded
Loading done
Time= 7278 msec.
                           4          3         2
(D17) 2 (M + 1) (63 M  + 112 M  + 18 M

                   M
 - 22 M + 3) 4 /(693 BINOMIAL(2 M, M))

     2
 - ---
   231
```

<<Below are some examples of indefinite and definite integration, which is the first success of MACSYMA, and perhaps still the workhorse type of application. >>

```
(C1) (x¬2-3*x)/(3+x);
Time= 16 msec.
                    2
                   X  - 3 X
(D1)               --------
                    X + 3

(C2) integrate(%,x);
Time= 96 msec.
                            2
                           X  - 12 X
(D2)    18 LOG(X + 3) + ---------
                               2

(C3) 'integrate(f(x,y),y,g(x),h(x));
Time= 72 msec.
              H(X)
             /
             [
(D3)         I      F(X, Y) dY
             ]
             /
              G(X)
```

<<The above expression is not much more than a pretty form of the input C3. We could be interested in taking its derivative: >>

```
(C4) diff(%,x);

DIFF2 FASL DSK MAXOUT being loaded
Loading done
Time= 776 msec.

       H(X)
      /
      [         d
(D4)  I      (-- (F(X, Y))) dY
      ]       dX
      /
       G(X)

                       d
 + F(X, H(X)) (-- (H(X)))
                      dX

                       d
 - F(X, G(X)) (-- (G(X)))
                      dX

(C1) x¬a/(x+1)¬(5/2);
Time= 13 msec.
                       A
                      X
(D1)               ---------
                            5/2
                     (X + 1)

(C2) integrate(%,x,0,inf);
```

<<In order to do this definite integral, some information about the variable A is necessary. The INTEGRATE function asks for it: >>

```
Is  A + 1  positive, negative, or zero?

pos;
     2 A + 2
Is   -------   an integer?
        5

no;
Is  2 A - 3

            positive, negative, or zero?

neg;

GAMMA FASL DSK MAXOUT being loaded
Loading done
Time= 3555 msec.
                                  3
(D2)        BETA(A + 1,  - - A)
                                  2
```

<<The variables in the above expression, as in any other, can be given new values, and the expression re-EValuated:>>

```
(C3) ev(%,a=1/2);

Time= 64 msec.
                           2
(D3)
                           3
```

```
(C4) ev(d2,a=4/5);
Time= 22 msec.
                       9  7
(D4)            BETA(-, --)
                       5  10

(C5) ev(%,numer);

Time= 61 msec.
(D5)              0.90946402
```

<<Limits are also calculable. A package for "little o, big O" calculus has been assembled.>>

```
(C1) limit(sin(x/a)/x,x,0,plus);
Is  A  positive or negative?

pos;

Time= 1749 msec.
                         1
(D1)                     -
                         A
```

<<With limits and derivatives available, you might expect to have Taylor series built in as well. Below, we construct two Taylor approximations of different degree (D2 and D4) to the same function. Then we compare the true value of the function with the two approximations, using the built-in graphics routines.>>

```
(C1) log((1+x)/(1+x¬2));
Time= 12 msec.
                      X + 1
(D1)             LOG(------)
                       2
                      X  + 1

(C2) taylor(%,x,0,3);
Time= 49 msec.
                  2     3
               3 X     X
(D2)/T/  X - ---- + -- + . . .
               2     3

(C3) ratsimp(%);
Time= 34 msec.
                3      2
             2 X  - 9 X  + 6 X
(D3)         -----------------
                     6

(C4) taylor(d1,x,0,6);
Time= 93 msec.
              2    3    4    5    6
           3 X    X    X    X    X
(D4)/T/ X - ---- + -- + -- + -- - --
             2     3    4    5    2

                                    + . . .

(C5) ratsimp(%);
Time= 65 msec.
              6        5        4        3
(D5) - (30 X  - 12 X  - 15 X  - 20 X

                                 2
                          + 90 X  - 60 X)/60


(C9) plot([d1,d3,d5],x,0,.75,[t,3,6]);

GRAPH FASL DSK MAXOUT being loaded
Loading done


 8[
  [                TTTTTTTT
 6[              TT33 3333 TTT
  [            TT         33  TT
 4[           T3            33 6TT
  [          T               3  6TT
 2[         T                 3  6 T
  [        T                   3  6 T
 0[       T                     3  6 T
  [                               3  6
 8[      T                         3  6
  [     T                           3
 6[                                  3
  [    T
 4[   T                               3
  [
 2[ T
  [
 0[T
  -------------------------------------
   0 2 4 6 8 0 2 4 6 8 0 2 4 6 8 0 2 4
XORG=0.0 YORG=0.0
XMAX=0.747999996 YMAX=0.1882142

Time= 3218 msec.
```

==

This "walking tour" can only provide a small glimpse of the present capabilities and future possibilities of MACSYMA and its successors, and of symbolic computation systems in general. Besides the original MACSYMA project at M.I.T.'s Laboratory for Computer Science, further information may be obtained from Professor Richard Fateman at the University of California, Berkeley. Professor Fateman is the director of a newly organized Mathematical Representation and Manipulation Project at Berkeley's Center for Pure and Applied Mathematics. Information about symbolic processing and MACSYMA on the LISP machine may be obtained from Symbolics, Inc.; 21150 Califa Street; Woodland Hills, Ca. 91367.

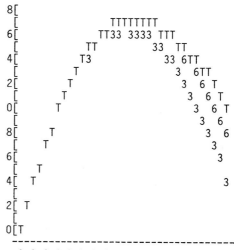

Software for Microcomputers

Chair: David M. Allen, University of Kentucky (on leave at Pennsylvania State University)

A Linear Models Package in UCSD Pascal
David M. Allen, University of Kentucky (on leave at Pennsylvania State University)

Minitab on Microcomputers
Barbara F. Ryan and Thomas A. Ryan, Jr., Pennsylvania State University

Where to Find the Nuts and Bolts: Sources of Software
John Nash, University of Ottawa

A LINEAR MODELS PACKAGE IN UCSD PASCAL

David M. Allen, University of Kentucky

UCSD Pascal is a dialect of the Pascal language originally developed at the University of California, San Diego and subsequently distributed by SofTech Microsystems. Clark and Koehler (1982) give the details of the language. This paper presents information on the capabilities of a linear models package written in UCSD Pascal. The good and bad features of the UCSD Pascal System, with respect to statistical system development, are also discussed. The package is named STAN for STatistical ANalysis. STAN is interactive and is exceedingly easy to use. Extensive error checking is done to make sure the input is of the proper form. A data set is analyzed using STAN.

FEATURES OF PASCAL

The data structures and other features of Pascal are very convenient for writing statistical software. In this section we note how pointers, recursion, sets, and strings can be used in statistical programming.

Models may be quite complex consisting of a sum of several terms with each term containing a variable or a product of two or more variables. Because of their ability to represent non-rectangular data structures, pointer variables are very useful for representing models.

It is frequently desirable to form new variables that are functions of original variables (a process called transformation of variables). A good statistical analysis program will have the ablility to interpret expressions defining transformations. It might seem difficult to write a procedure to handle expressions with lots of nested parentheses, but with Pascal's recursion feature it is easy. Suppose a procedure to build a stack of instructions from an algebraic expression has an array of characters and two integers as arguments. The array of characters contains the expression to be evaluated, and the two integers identify the first and last positions of a sub-expression. The first call of the procedure uses the first and last significant characters in the array. If during the evaluation process a left parenthesis is encountered, a scan is made to locate the matching right parenthesis. The procedure then calls itself to evaluate the expression between these parentheses. Remarkably, nested parentheses cause no difficulty.

Graphs are very valuable for displaying the relationship between variables. If the data points are to be connected with a solid line the data must first be sorted with respect to the variable to be on the horizional axis. Recursion provides a very quick and eloquent method for sorting. For details, see the Pascal procedure for quicksort given by Kernighan and Plauger (1981).

Experimental data often contain a large number of variables, and a statistical analysis may involve only a few at a time. The Pascal set structure is a very handy way to identify the active set of variables.

A string is a data type, similar to a packed array of characters, that is present in most dialects of Pascal but not in standard Pascal. Strings provide convenient means for having mnemonic variable labels. For example, LOGPPM can be used to reference the logarithm of parts per million. This is easier than remembering the column number of a particular variable in a table. Many other features of Pascal make statistical programming easier than with FORTRAN or BASIC.

The disadvantages of Pascal are relatively few. The size of an array is part of its type which may cause difficulty when arrays are arguments of procedures. It would be nice if the user could use the abilities of the compiler in applications programs. For example, STAN has procedures for compiling limited amounts of Pascal code. These duplicate the functions procedures in the compiler that are not available to the programmer.

A STATISTICAL ANALYSIS SYSTEM IN PASCAL

We now give an overview of STAN. Use of STAN requires the UCSD Pascal system. STAN is an interactive statistical analysis system for microcomputers. Considerable effort was made to make STAN easy to use. Prompts are given at every stage to show possible options. Variables are referenced by mnemonic names given by the user and not by their positions in the data set or a model. STAN tries to recover from input errors. Should a variable be specified that is not in a data set, then the names of the legal variables are displayed so that a substitute may be entered. Illegal characters in numerical input are detected, and the user may then enter the proper value. Since the result of a statistical analysis is usually presented in report or paper, STAN has a text formatting procedure to merge discussion and selected tables and graphs.

STAN is modular with related procedures grouped together to make an efficient system. The first version has four modules:

DATA MANAGEMENT. Data sets are created, corrected, and updated using the system editor. STAN has procedures for summarizing, transforming, sorting, and neatly printing selected rows and columns of the data set.

LINEAR MODELS. Qualitative variables are automatically expanded into indicator variables. Models with restrictions can be fit. Products of variables can be used in the model specification. Analysis of variance, regression coefficients, linear combinations of parameters, and calculation of predicted values, residuals, and related variances are some of the procedures available. Models may be fit to selected portions of the data.

GRAPHICS. Graphic procedures are very flexible. Different patterns of dotted lines and different symbols are selected by the user. Graphs may go over the entire data or selected portions of the data. Multiple variables may be placed on the same graph.

TEXT FORMATTING. A paper or report is created using the system editor. Simple commands control margins, indentations, centering, underlining, spacing, top and bottom running titles, page numbering, justification, and several other features. A simple code indicates where the tables and figures produced by the other modules are to be inserted.

Except for transformations, a STAN user needs no knowledge of Pascal or of any other programming language. Transformations are made using Pascal statements.

A DATA SET

We consider the environmental study of Bencko and Symon (1977) in which they reported arsenic determinations on hair samples from people residing near a power plant that burned coal with a high arsenic content. Only part of the data given by the authors will be used here. This data is also discussed by Allen and Cady (1982). Groups of 10-year-olds, each with 20 to 27 boys, were selected from ten communities located generally southwest of the plant. The response variable is the concentration of arsenic (in parts per million, ppm), and the measurement of this variable is the group average determination. The explanatory variable is the distance (in miles) of the community from the plant. Our interest lies in the relationship between these variables. The assumed model is

logarithm of arsenic concentration =

$$b_0 + b_1 \text{ (distance from plant)} + e.$$

The data from the study are

ppm	miles
2.05	15
3.26	4
1.82	8
0.79	23
1.02	10
1.85	12
0.66	30
3.19	2
0.30	36
1.34	21

Our objectives for an analysis of this data are to estimate the regression coeifficients, estimate arsenic concentrations for selected distances, and to graph the data superimposed with the values predicted by the fitted model. The next section and the Appendix give an analysis of this data.

ANALYSIS OF THE ARSENIC DATA USING STAN

We conclude by analyzing the Arsenic data using STAN. This section gives an overview of steps involved. The Appendix is a log of a session using STAN. It is best to read this section and the Appendix side by side.

To follow the log it is helpful to know there are two types of prompts. One type is a verbal instruction or question which has an obvious response provided the statistical objective is well in mind. A single character Y or N is used in response to questions with a yes or no answer. Upper or lower case may be used. The second type of prompt is a key word followed by list of characters. One of the characters is always an H (for help) and responding with an H will provide information regarding the other responses.

The session begins by executing the data management module. The first step is to inspect the file ARSENIC which has been prepared for input into STAN. The file ARSENIC is displayed on the console. This step is strictly optional but is useful for last second checks.

The next operation converts the numbers to their internal binary representation. Since STAN repeatedly accesses the data on the disk, making this conversion once and only once saves considerable time. This conversion must be done before the data is used in any other way.

The data is sorted on MILES.

A new data set is created that contains the original variables and the natural logarithm of concentration (LOGPPM). The old data set is removed to save space on the disk.

We now execute the linear models module. Since this is a simple model, we continue past the options. We list the expanatory variables. CONSTANT is the built-in name for the intercept which could have been changed using one of the options. The response variable is specified and the major computations are done. The response B gives estimates of the regression coefficients and related information. The fitted model is

estimated logarithm of
arsenic concentration =

1.2570 - 0.0611 (distance from plant).

The next analysis we do is to calculate linear combinations that represent estimated values at 10, 20, and 30 miles from the plant which are 0.6459, 0.0348, and -0.5764 respectively. The last analysis is to pass through the data and to calculate an estimated value for every observation. The results are not shown yet, but are saved in the data set arsenic.

We now again execute the data management module. Exponentials of estimated values are calculated so they are in the original units. A table is prepared containing the distances, original determinations, and estimated values.

For the last step we use the graphic module. The values in the table produced above are graphed. This type of graph, containing superimposed observed and fitted values, is excellent for assessing the validity of the model.

We have now demonstrated the use of three of the four modules (but not all their capabilities). All the tables and figures that have been produced are saved on a disk for inclusion into a report. The text formatting module is demonstrated in Allen and Cady (1982).

REFERENCES

Allen, David M. and Foster B. Cady. 1982. Analyzing Experimental Data by Regression. Lifetime Learning Publications : Belmont, California.

Bencko, Vladimir and Karel Symon. 1977. "Health Aspects of Burning Coal with a High Arsenic Content. Part I: Arsenic in Hair, Urine and Blood in Children Residing in a Polluted Area." Environmental Research 13: 378-385.

Clark, Randy and Stephen Koehler. 1982 The UCSD Pascal Handbook. Prentice-Hall, INC : Englewood Cliffs, New Jersey.

Kernighan, Brian W. and P. J. Plauger. 1981. Software Tools in Pascal. Addison-Wesley Publishing Company : Reading, Massachuetts.

APPENDIX: LOG OF SESSION USING STAN

```
{Execute the data management module.}

DATA C, H, I, P, S, T, Q? H
C: Convert file to binary data set.
H: Help, display this key.
I: Inspect a text file.
P: Print a data set.
S: Sort a data set.
T: Transform variables.
Q: Quit.
DATA C, H, I, P, S, T, Q? I
Name of file?
ARSENIC
PPM MILES;
2.05 15
3.26 4
1.82 8
 .79 23
1.02 10
1.85 12
 .66 30
3.19 2
 .30 36
1.34 21

DATA C, H, I, P, S, T, Q? C
Enter name of data set.
ARSENIC
ARSENIC is converted to binary data set.
Save summary statistics? N
DATA C, H, I, P, S, T, Q? S
Enter name of data set to be sorted.
ARSENIC
List key variables followed by ";".
MILES;
Reading data.
Saving data.
ARSENIC is sorted.
DATA C, H, I, P, S, T, Q? T
Input data set (Y or N)? Y
Enter name of input data set.
ARSENIC
Enter name of output data set.
ARSENIC2
Will GAU or UNF be used? N
Enter statement.
LOGPPM:=LN(PPM);
Another new variable? N
Drop some variables? N
Data set ARSENIC2 has been created.
Remove ARSENIC? Y
DATA C, H, I, P, S, T, Q? Q

{Execute the linear models module}

Inspect a text file? N
Enter name of data set to be used.
ARSENIC2
OPTION C, H, O, R, S, W, Q? H
C: Continue.
H: Help, display this key.
O: Omit observations.
R: Rename column of ones.
S: Set values of constants.
W: Weight observations.
Q: Quit.
```

```
OPTION C, H, O, R, S, W, Q? C
Enter names of explanatory variables
in the model.  Follow list by ";".
CONSTANT MILES;
Enter name of response variable.
LOGPPM
Model is fit.
Error degrees of freedom: 8.
Standard deviation:      0.3170
ANALYSIS A, B, C, F, H, L, P, R, Q? H
A: Analysis of variance.
B: Estimates of Beta.
C: Add an observation from Console.
H: Help, display this key.
F: Fit another model.
L: Linear combination of Beta's.
P: Print counterpart to ABDO.
R: Residuals, predicted values, etc..
Q: Quit.
ANALYSIS A, B, C, F, H, L, P, R, Q? B
Name file where table is to be stored:
BETA
```

REGRESSION COEFFICIENTS

VARIABLE	ESTIMATE	Vc	STANDARD ERROR	P-VALUE
CONSTANT	1.2570	0.3300	0.1821	0.0001
MILES	-0.0611	0.0009	0.0094	0.0002

```
Save? Y
ANALYSIS A, B, C, F, H, L, P, R, Q? L
Name file where table is to be stored:
LC
Enter title.
TEN MILES
          CONSTANT: 1
             MILES: 10
            LOGPPM: 0
Another linear combination? Y
Enter title.
TWENTY MILES
          CONSTANT: 1
             MILES: 20
            LOGPPM: 0
Another linear combination? Y
Enter title.
THIRTY MILES
          CONSTANT: 1
             MILES: 30
            LOGPPM: 0.0
Another linear combination? N
```

LINEAR COMBINATIONS

TITLE	ESTIMATE	Vc	STANDARD ERROR	P-VALUE
TEN MILES	0.6459	0.1330	0.1156	0.0005
TWENTY MILES	0.0348	0.1135	0.1068	0.7532
THIRTY MILES	-0.5764	0.2715	0.1652	0.0082

```
Save? Y
ANALYSIS A, B, C, F, H, L, P, R, Q? R
A new data set consisting of ARSENIC2
with selected other variables appended
will be created.  Name this data set.
ARSENIC3
VARIABLE C, E, H, L, P, R, S, U, V? H
C: Continue.
E: Estimated or predicted values.
H: Help, display this key.
L: Lower confidence limits.
```

```
P: PRESS residuals.
R: Residuals.
S: Studentized residuals.
U: Upper confidence limits.
V: Variance constants.
VARIABLE C, E, H, L, P, R, S, U, V? E
Name this variable.
ESTIMATE
VARIABLE C, E, H, L, P, R, S, U, V? C
ARSENIC3 has been created.
Remove ARSENIC2? Y
ANALYSIS A, B, C, F, H, L, P, R, Q? Q

{Execute the data management module.}

DATA C, H, I, P, S, T, Q? T
Input data set (Y or N)? Y
Enter name of input data set.
ARSENIC3
Enter name of output data set.
ARSENIC
Will GAU or UNF be used? N
Enter statement.
ESTPPM:=EXP(ESTIMATE);
Another new variable? N
Drop some variables? N
Data set ARSENIC has been created.
Remove ARSENIC3? Y
DATA C, H, I, P, S, T, Q? P
Enter name of data set.
ARSENIC
Print all variables? N
Enter names of variables to be printed.
Follow list by ";".
MILES PPM ESTPPM;
Use default format? Y
Print all rows? Y
Enter title for table.
ACTUAL AND ESTIMATED ARSENIC CONCENTRATIONS
Enter name of output file.
TABLE
ACTUAL AND ESTIMATED ARSENIC CONCENTRATIONS

     MILES        PPM     ESTPPM

      2.00       3.19       3.11
      4.00       3.26       2.75
      8.00       1.82       2.16
     10.00       1.02       1.91
     12.00       1.85       1.69
     15.00       2.05       1.41
     21.00       1.34       0.97
     23.00       0.79       0.86
     30.00       0.66       0.56
     36.00       0.30       0.39
DATA C, H, I, P, S, T, Q? Q

{Execute the graphic module.}

GRAPHIC G, H, I, Q? H
G: Graph.
H: Help, display this key.
I: Inspect a text file.
Q: Quit.
GRAPHIC G, H, I, Q? G
Name file where plot is to be stored:
PLOT
Enter name of data set to be used.
```

```
ARSENIC
Enter height of graph.
3
Enter width of graph.
5
Enter title.
ACTUAL AND ESTIMATED ARSENIC CONCENTRATIONS
Variable on horizonal axis?
MILES
Variables on the vertical axis?
Follow list by ";".
PPM ESTPPM;
Graph PPM over
E  entire data set, S segmented? E
How is PPM to be graphed
L line, S symbol, K skip? S
Enter symbol. o
Make legend entry? N
Graph ESTPPM over
E  entire data set, S segmented? E
How is ESTPPM to be graphed
L line, S symbol, K skip? L
Enter line density.
Ø
Make legend entry? N
Horizonal axis? Y
Vertical axis? Y
OUTPUT C, P, R, H? H
C: To CONSOLE:.
P: To PRINTER:.
R: To REMOUT:.
H: Help, display this key.
OUTPUT C, P, R, H? C
```

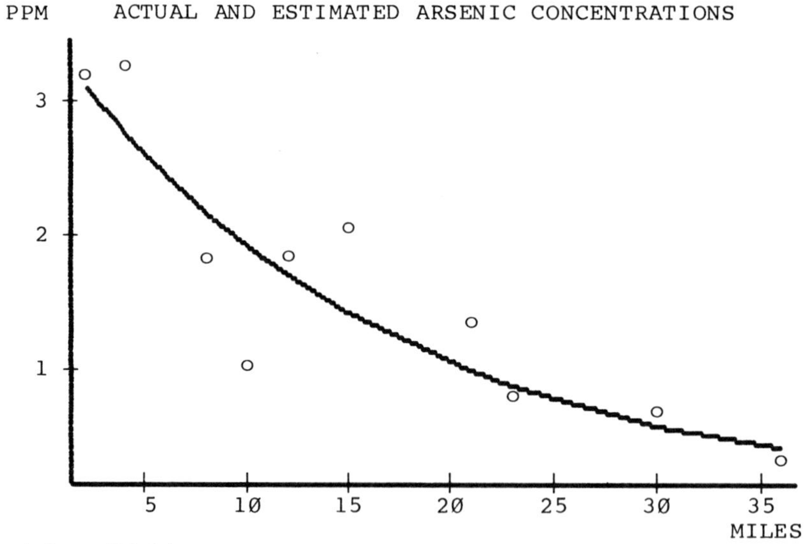


```
Graph takes 22 lines.
Save? Y
GRAPHIC G, H, I, Q? Q
```

MINITAB ON MICROCOMPUTERS

Barbara F. Ryan
Thomas A. Ryan, Jr.
The Pennsylvania State University

ABSTRACT

This paper describes our experiences in implementing Minitab on microcomputers, including the major difficulties and our successes. Most of this experience is relevant to other large, integrated Fortran systems. The principal difficulties are (a) limited main memory, (b) limited disk space, and (c) problems of overlaying.

Keywords: Statistical packages, microcomputers, Fortran, software

I. INTRODUCTION

Minitab is a general purpose interactive statistics package. It is written in "portable" Fortran, and runs on most minicomputers and mainframes. It consists of about 30,000 lines of code (excluding comments) and about 350 subroutines. Data are stored in an array in main memory. User input is in the form of commands; on-line HELP is available in case the user cannot remember a command or has a problem. The system is fully integrated - i.e., all facilities of Minitab are available at all times without leaving Minitab.

Example

The following example retrieves data from a Minitab save file named PULSE. The data set has 42 observations on 8 variables. (In interactive use, the output for a command appears immediately after the command is typed. In the example, input is shown in upper case letters, and the position of the output is indicated.)

```
RETRIEVE 'PULSE'
PLOT 'WEIGHT' VS 'HEIGHT'
  (plot output here)
HISTOGRAM 'WEIGHT'
  (histogram output here)
TABLE 'SMOKES' BY 'SEX';
  MEAN 'WEIGHT';
  MEDIAN 'WEIGHT'.
    (table output here)
```

II. LSI-11 BASED MICROCOMPUTERS

At Penn State we use Minitab on a Terak micro. The characteristics of this system are:

- LSI-11 based (essentially a PDP-11/03)
- 16 bit addressing
- 64K bytes of memory (56K available)
- RT-11 operating system
- Two double density, single sided 8" floppy disk drives (500K bytes of storage per drive)
- Monitor is a CRT displaying 24 lines, 80 spaces wide
- Full ASCII keyboard
- Paper printer

Performance of Minitab on this computer is very satisfactory, especially on small data sets (e.g., n=100). Response is generally faster than on moderately loaded large time-sharing systems. While this is a relatively deluxe microcomputer, many of its characteristics are similar to other microcomputers. Of course, performance is significantly better on LSI-11/23 based microcomputers, such as the new DEC Professional personal computers.

III. IMPLEMENTATION PROBLEMS

Size of Disk Memory

Since Minitab is an integrated system (rather than a collection of separate programs), the entire system must be available, in some sense, to the user. Under most operating systems, this means that the entire load module must be on one disk. The approximate size of commonly available disks are:

disk	density	sides	bytes
5 1/4"	single	1	85K
5 1/4"	double	1	170K
5 1/4"	double	2	340K
8"	single	1	250K
8"	double	1	500K
8"	double	2	1M
Winchester			5M and up

We need space for (a) load module, (b) operating system, (c) HELP file, and (d) data files. The load module is 400K bytes on LSI-11 and 1M bytes on IBM mainframes. The needed space can be provided by an 8" double density disk with 500K or 1M bytes, by a Winchester disk, or by several small disks if we can split the load module. In general, we cannot expect to put Minitab on a system with one or two 5 1/4" floppies without a significant change in structure of Minitab.

Size of Main Memory

Microcomputers typically have up to 64K bytes of memory, and an address space of 64K bytes, which means that they could not make effective use of a larger memory. Since the load module is many times as large as the available memory, something has to be done. The solution is to overlay. The programmer divides the code up into collections of subroutines called overlay segments. The linkage editor organizes the code so that the overlay segments can be brought into main memory as needed at run time.

A second problem with the size of main memory is that Minitab stores data in main memory. On large virtual memory computers, this is no problem. On microcomputers, it can be. If all 64K could be given to data, we would be limited to 16,000 total data items. In practice, the limit is much smaller, about 2,500 data items currently on the Terak.

The Linkage Editor

As mentioned above, Minitab must be broken up into overlay segments. Some individual commands (e.g., TABLE, ARIMA, REGRESS) are sufficiently large that they cannot fit into memory without themselves being broken up.

On the Terak, we use a multiregion overlay. This means that the memory allocated to Minitab code is divided into 9 regions. The code itself is divided up into 167 segments. Each of these segments can be loaded into only one of the 9 regions; they are loaded as needed at run time. Dividing Minitab into overlay segments was by far the most difficult part of installing Minitab on the Terak. The linkage editing itself cannot be done on the Terak, since there is not enough room on the disk for the necessary scratch files. The overlaying was done (by the PDP-11 converter for Minitab, Brian Nelson of the University of Toledo) on a PDP-11/70, and then copied onto floppy disk and installed on the Terak.

Some linkage editors for microcomputers are not sophisticated enough for Minitab. For example, the UCSD P-system version II allows only 12 segments -- far fewer than the 160 or so Minitab requires. The LYNX linkage editor program appears to be capable of handling Minitab, using a tree-structured overlay, but it requires the source code to contain calls to the overlay program for most subroutine calls. This would require inserting and maintaining a thousand or more calls to the overlay program, which would need to be changed for every modification of the overlay structure.

Another linkage editor that does work is PLINK II, which was used by the University of Glasgow to put Minitab on a Superbrain computer. A disadvantage of this is that a run-time support portion of PLINK II needs to be available to run Minitab, so that the user must purchase PLINK II (or a portion of it) to run Minitab.

The UCSD P-system version IV appears to allow the overlay structure that Minitab needs (including up to 255 segments). However, Minitab will probably run slowly on this system, since each overlay swap will require two disk accesses (one to look up the location of the segment in a table stored on disk, the other to bring in the segment itself). Also, in the current implementation of the P-system, the compiler produces "p-code", which must be integrated. This also means that Minitab would run slowly.

Speed

The response time on our Terak is usually good - generally better than moderately loaded large time-sharing systems. The only time that speed seems to be a problem is on non-linear fitting problems (in Minitab, this occurs for ARIMA models), and for large (n=1000) data sets. For small problems, the time is dominated by the disk accesses on the floppy disk system to do overlay swapping. For large problems, the CPU time dominates. Of course, on a system with a Winchester technology disk drive, response would be much faster, since disk access is greatly improved. A faster CPU, such as the LSI 11/23 with floating point hardware, would decrease CPU time by a factor of 4 to 10. With our configuration, some typical times are:

Regression	n = 100	1 predictor	10 seconds
Regression	n = 100	5 predictors	20 seconds
Histogram	n = 100		4 seconds
Histogram	n = 1000		8 seconds

IV. A SECOND IMPLEMENTATION ON A MICROCOMPUTER

A second implementation on a microcomputer was done at the University of Glasgow (Scotland) by Rod Aukland. The computer is a Superbrain (Intertec). The characteristics of this computer are:

8-bit CPU
52K bytes of memory
CP/M operating system (version 2.2)
Microsoft Fortran 80
PLINK II linkage editor
5 1/4" floppy disks with 160K bytes per disk

This implementation is still undergoing development. It currently has most of the capacilities of Minitab. The principal limitations are:

(a) Up to 25 variables (columns).
(b) Up to 2200 data items.
(c) No variable names.
(d) No matrices.
(e) The TABLE, ARIMA, and EDA commands have not been implemented.

For the problems typically run on this computer, the lack of variable names is probably the most annoying limitation, and Aukland expects to correct this soon. This version is heavily overlaid, but the primary limitation in speed is CPU computation.

The disk space limitation forced some restructuring of Minitab. On this computer, the entire load module must be on one disk. The available disks, however, are too small to hold Minitab. To get around this difficulty, three versions of Minitab were created. All three contain the same collection of basic routines -- main control routines, I/O commands, arithmetic and manipulation commands, plotting, etc. Then one version contains these basic routines plus regression; one contains the basic routines plus some time series commands (ACF, PACF, CCF, LAG, TSPLOT), and the MANN-WHITNEY command; and one version contains basic routines plus analysis of variance and chisquare commands. To go from one version to another, you SAVE the worksheet, change disks, then RETRIEVE the worksheet in the other version.

V. OTHER MICROCOMPUTERS

We have discussed primarily floppy disk based microcomputers with memory or address space limited to 64K bytes, which is typical of current 8-bit microcomputers, and also of small LSI-11 based computers (which are 16 bit, but have an architecture limited to an address space of 64K bytes). Microcomputers with fewer limitations are being introduced rapidly, and are rapidly decreasing in price.

Hard disks (Winchester technology) are becoming much more widely available, and the price is dropping toward $2000. Since these have a capacity of 5M bytes or more, and since they are much faster than floppy disks, the problems of disk space and speed will disappear for many users.

The IBM Personal Computer, the Apple III, and the Zilog Z8000 are examples of micros which have some limitations, but should be much more suitable to install Minitab than smaller computers. All of these can address 128K bytes of memory or more, so overlaying is much easier. (Our experience on minicomputers indicates that only 25 or so segments will be needed, the overlay structure will be much simpler, and a worksheet of over 10,000 data items will be possible.

A new generation of "super micros" is also appearing. These include the WICAT, PERQ, the new Cromenco, the new Radio Shack, etc. These are based on the Motorola 68000 CPU, are 16/32 bit machines with 16M byte address space, have 250K bytes of memory and up, and have Winchester disks available. Prices are $7000 to $14,000.

Most problems with the newer generations involve software. Some do not have a Fortran compiler at all. Others do not yet have a "debugged" Fortran compiler. Linkage editors which allow the necessary overlaying seem not to be available yet. Virtual memory, which would eliminate the need for overlaying, is not yet available either.

VI. PROBLEMS OF DISTRIBUTING MINITAB FOR MICROS

Our organization is set up to provide Minitab to a computer with many users, with telephone consultation for each site. It is licensed for an annual fee, at a price which would be very high for a microcomputer. Updating to new versions is done automatically.

For microcomputers, software is normally purchased, rather than leased. This raises questions about updates, out-of-date versions, and service (e.g., telephone consultation).

Price is also an issue. Minitab is over four times as large as VISICALC, and has a smaller potential audience. To pay for ongoing development, distribution, and service, clearly the price will have to be much higher than VISICALC. Users will have to get used to paying a much higher portion of their budget for software than they did in the past, since the factors that are bringing down the price of hardware do not apply, or apply in only a limited way, to software. It still may be a shock to pay $1500 for statistical software to run on a $2000 computer.

WHERE TO FIND THE NUTS & BOLTS: SOURCES OF SOFTWARE

John C. Nash, Faculty of Administration, University of Ottawa, Ottawa K1N 9B5, Canada

Abstract: The widespread introduction of personal computers has stimulated interest in their use for statistical computations. However, prospective users may be hard pressed to find appropriate software to carry out such calculations. This paper considers where users of small or special computers may find suitable software, in particular, building blocks for application programs rather than complete packages.

Keywords: statistical computing, software sources, microcomputers, parallel processors

Purpose

The purpose of this paper is to assist users of small or special computers to carry out statistical computations on their machines. To this end, the primary goal is to suggest where software may be found. However, it is important to recognize the manner in which small or special computers may be used in statistical computations. It is clearly foolish to misuse tools and our computers are neither more nor less than tools to help us get our jobs done. Just as attempts to use a fine chisel as a screwdriver should upset our sense of propriety, so should attempts to misuse or abuse our computers. Therefore, a discussion of how small or special computers may be used by statisticians and data analysts is germane to consideration of the software needed.

It is also worthwhile to consider the kinds of building blocks for application programs and what such programs should aim to accomplish, since such goals colour the software requirements. This will be treated briefly.

Target audience

The people who will be interested in this paper are users of small computers or systems with unusual architectures - special computers. Such users have a number of common problems:

1) They are usually the only user, or one of a small group of users.

2) There may be little or no programming help and often no systems help for operating and maintaining the hardware, software and data. Such tasks fall upon the user.

3) The programming languages and programming environment may be limited, unusual or even unique.

4) The configuration of the system, that is, its architecture, input/output devices, memory, address assignment, and general or special features, may be unusual and frequently unique.

5) Any and all resources such as memory, backing store, processor speed or input/output channels, may be very limited in number or power.

6) The utility and support programs which assist in file handling, disk reorganization, and similar tasks may be extremely limited in number and scope.

To particularize the systems of interest, we can cite some examples. From the realm of microcomputers come the Radio Shack Models I, II or III, the North Star Horizon or Advantage, the Commodore PET or VIC-20, the Apple, the Acorn Atom, the Osborne I, various generic S-100 and/or CP/M computers, the IBM and Digital Equipment personal computers, and even the Sinclair ZX81. This last machine is so inexpensive that it has even been referred to as the disposable computer. Its power is sufficient, however, to make it a viable tool for statistical computation.

At the other end of the scale of calculating power are special parallel processors such as the Illiac IV, Cray 1 and new systolic and other non-Von Neumann architectures. The situation facing the user of these processors who wishes to carry out statistical calculations resembles that of the microcomputer user quite closely. Recently, I have had requests from several special processor users for information on my own algorithms for the above supercomputers, with one such implementation already reported (Luk, 1980)

Why bother?

Clearly, if the user has to implement his own statistical programs, when there are eminently satisfactory routines available in major packages for common mainframe computers, one may question the value of performing calculations on machines which lack such software.

The first argument is time. The special computers offer a speed of processing otherwise unavailable, and permit very large or complicated problems to be solved in a reasonable elapsed time. Speed of response - elapsed time to a successful solution to a problem - may also be a consideration. On one occasion I have solved an order 100 linear equation problem on my North Star Horizon in approximately 90 minutes, while a time-shared IBM 3033 took longer than this to begin executing a batch job remotely initiated to carry out the same problem. The limit of such considerations is found in real-time applications, which demand that an ansver be obtained within a specific time period. The final time reason comes from human time (and effort). It may be quicker to program a statistical procedure than to move and reformat data or to learn another operating system and applications package.

Money is another motivation. Even in the western world, one may be unable to afford to use the machine and software of choice. In developing countries the need to stretch resources is painfully obvious. However, budget controls and bureaucratic red tape may imply that the perceived cost of using the small or special computer is lower even for affluent workers.

The application may dictate the use of a particular machine. To maintain the security of data or results, one may be required to avoid the use of any multi-user computing system. For systems dedicated to special tasks such as automated manufacturing, communications, control of experiments or monitoring of other computers, the processor and system configuration may have to be decided on the basis of priorities unrelated to computation.

Finally, there is always personal taste or preference. Most of us like to have control of our own empire, however small, and to be able to exercise the freedoms which accompany such effective ownership. Anyone who has used microcomputers is sure to have found the response from even a lightly used time-sharing system quite slow by comparison. The ability to interact with the machine and data is for many users a powerful pull towards personal computers.

Statistical computations

The types of calculations which are performed in statistics and data analysis span most areas of numerical mathematics. Not all calculations can be easily handled on small or special computers, due to the lack of resources or suitable software. Following is a classification of computational problems and a brief appraisal of the likely success small computers may achieve in tackling them. (Special computers are set aside in this section.)

1) Data handling, edit, checking and transformation: Small computers excel at these tasks, for which they are easily programmed. The only limitations come from small memory or backing store capacity.

2) Distributions, special functions and quadrature: In both mathematical statistics and data analysis one frequently needs to calculate critical values of statistics or probabilities that a statistic exceeds some value. This requires that a special function be computed or an integration performed. Quadrature (numerical integration) is the final resort when the special functions are difficult or impossible to derive as algebraic forms. While automatic integrators may be large programs, most special function and conventional numerical integration routines are small. The only obstacle to a successful implementation on a small computer may be the limited floating-point arithmetic precision in some systems or languages.

3) Random numbers and combinatorics: Useful in simulation,pseudo-random number generators are relatively small programs. Some slight difficulties may be experienced in implementation of certain methods on small machines due to word length considerations but generally small computers can handle these tasks easily and efficiently. Related combinatoric problems, apart from huge enumeration tasks, present the user with similar questions during implementation.

4) Summation and tabulation: Small computers have become day to day tabulation machines thanks to software such as Visicalc and its copiers. Statisticians are more likely to want to code their own routines in order to take care of rounding and issues such as percentages summing to 100. Small computers will only be inappropriate for these tasks when the data set is too huge to store. Even then, for calculation of the mean and variance it is possible to make a single sequential pass through the data without compromising accuracy (Nash, 1981a).

5) Linear Algebra: Linear algebraic calculations are at the center of many, perhaps most, statistical analyses. Small computers can handle most types of linear algebraic computations, whether the matrix is explicitly stored or used via an iterative method in which it appears only implicitly. Any limitations are the usual ones imposed by memory or disk capacity but most small computers can handle a large proportion of real world linear calculations. Most methods for linear equations, least squares, eigenvalue problems and matrix decompositions have been implemented on a microcomputer. Matrix inverses can be all too easily calculated, to the chagrin of numerical analysts who wish that methods expressed in terms of inverses rather than matrix decompositions would quickly lose their popularity, especially among those who are unaware of the properties of the different techniques.

6) Nonlinear least squares: Small computers are surprisingly good tools for nonlinear least squares. Their interactive use is a great help in avoiding the common pitfalls of a poor starting point or errors in the derivative routines. Methods similar to those used on large machines are easy to implement and use (Nash, 1977,1981b).

7) Nonlinear function minimization: When more sophisticated estimation methods are applied, one may wish to minimize a nonlinear function which is not in the form of a sum of squares. This may or may not be subject to constraints and derivatives may or may not be easy to calculate. As with nonlinear least squares, small computers can handle such problems without difficulty except for very complicated problems. Even on a very small machine such as the Sharp PC1211 (Radio Shack Pocket Compu-

ter 1), the Hooke and Jeeves method may be applied to solve function minimization problems in seven parameters using only 40% of the available memory.

8) Mathematical programming: Some approximation problems - minimax or minimum sum of absolute deviations fits or constrained least squares may be solved using mathematical programming methods. This is constrained function minimization viewed from the constraints rather than the function. Because most MP methods generate large working tableaus, they have not been easily adapted to small computers. The development of compact mathematical programming methods remains an outstanding issue. Small problems may, of course, be solved without difficulty.

9) Differential equations: Statistical computations do not frequently require the solution of ordinary or partial differential equations. However, some modelling problems are best expressed as differential equations where parameters may be varied and some distributions may be defined in terms of differential equations. These can be integrated as easily on small computers as on large ones. Large systems of ordinary differential equations and most partial differential equations are, however, too demanding of storage to be solved on small machines. Adaptive packages such as that of Gear(1971) are too big also, but their component parts have been adapted successfully.

10) Symbolic manipulation: In mathematical statistics or for computing partial derivatives for nonlinear models, it is useful to be able to obtain analytic expressions automatically. Similarly algebraic manipulation or integration are useful in verifying theorems. Until relatively recently, symbolic manipulation packages required large amounts of memory on large computers. However, David Stoutmeyer's MuMath for Intel 8080 and Zilog Z80 based microcomputers has shown that considerable power and speed need not demand a large memory capacity. Since symbolic manipulation is close to the periphery of statistical computation and MuMath is a unique product, it is worth mentioning that it is marketed by Microsoft through a number of software outlets.

Software styles

Software may be obtained in basically three ways: as an integrated package for essentially all the tasks we wish to perform; as subroutines or bare bones programs for one or more problem types only; or as algorithms which describe a method for a problem.

On larger machines integrated packages have been popular for statistical work. The user does not have to learn to program and, if the package is well done, can easily accomplish desired tasks in a short period of time. The disavantages are that the package may not fit on the particular system, may not fit the problem and is difficult to modify.

Examples of packages are not yet common on microcomputers (Minitab is considered in the large machine category, though it works on machines hardly bigger than many micros.) There have been several packages advertised; of these I am familiar only with Microstat by Ecosoft for North Star and CP/M systems, which appears to be well programmed and structured. However, as this paper is directed to sources of building block software, I do not propose to present details.

For the builder of application programs, subroutines are a more useful style of software to seek as a starting point for development. Here we presumably have working code to solve a specific problem or sub-problem, for example,nonlinear least squares. In some programming languages, such as BASIC, a bare-bones program may be more appropriate and will be considered as equivalent to a separately compiled FORTRAN subroutine. The advantages of subroutines are that they are clearly adaptable without great difficulty to any system configuration or problem. The main drawback is that the user must do the adapting. Furthermore, the resulting program must be integrated with data entry and edit routines and with report writing programs. These integration tasks are frequently very time consuming and involve two to three times the effort required for just solving the statistical problem alone.

Finally, if no suitable machine executable method is available, we must resort to algorithms - written reports of methods to solve various problems. We may include a program in a language not available on our system in this category. Obviously, by searching through the literature, methods highly specific to the problem at hand may be found. However, the user must do most of the work, including perhaps finding the errors in the algorithm as published.

Software strategy

The rest of this paper is concerned with subroutines or algorithms and where to find them, based on my own experience over the past decade in using such nuts and bolts to build application programs for statistical and other computations.

It is important, however, that users do not rush headlong to develop statistical software for small computers but decide their goals and how to achieve them within the cont xt of their needs and resources. Three questions which may be posed:

1) Do I want to solve every possible problem on this particular computer?

2) What are my options for achieving the results desired?

3) How many features should be included in the program?

Some guidelines I try to follow in developing programs are:

- keep software as simple as possible
- document all work, however crudely
- throw away any program code which is not properly documented or fully understood
- restrict the aims of the software to a manageable set of tasks
- control subsequent development to essentials

Where to find programs

In this section are presented some sources of machine executable programs suitable for small computers. The opinions expressed here and in the next section are my own.

1) C. Abaci, P.O. Box 5715, Raleigh NC 27650 tel. (919) 832-4847
This company was founded by Ed Battiste who was instrumental in the formation of IMSL. C. Abaci offers mainly application modules for different problems. Each module consists of subroutines, driver programs, a tutorial and documentation. These modules are designed to fit on a single floppy disk which can simply be inserted and run to learn about the programs it contains. The emphasis on quality in the C. Abaci products implies that development is relatively slow. However, a number of products are already available for real and complex elementary functions, random number generation and testing, linear algebra (especially linear equations) and quadrature. These have been implemented on a range of popular microcomputer systems.

2) The Collected Algorithms of the Association for Computing Machinery, drawn from the ACM Communications and ACM Transactions on Mathematical Software, contains a great variety of mathematical software. For small computer users, the earlier, smaller codes are more useful, along with any comments and corrections. There is also a subject index which lists programs published in related journals. Programs in the ACM collection may be ordered through the distribution service, unfortunately on media suited mainly to large machines.

3) Computer magazines such as Byte, Interface Age, Microcomputing and Micro-Systèmes have frequently included mathematical articles. For the past eighteen months I have written a regular column for Interface Age. Unfortunately, the quality and utility of programs published in these sources is very variable. My own columns have aimed to include didactic rather than efficient programs. Clearly magazine sources should be used with discretion but may contain useful material, particularly if the author's credentials can be verified.

4) The software from the book by F.R. Ruckdeschel (1981) by title and list of contents would appear to offer the answer to many scientific computing needs on North Star and CP/M machines. While the programming style and structure is to be admired, the methods employed are dated and relatively weak, so caution is advised in their use.

5) For exploratory data analysis tools in FORTRAN and BASIC, the work of Velleman and Hoaglin (1980) is a good source.

6) The forthcoming book Linear Statistical Computations by John Maindonald of the New Zealand Department of Scientific and Industrial Research contains programs in BASIC which use modern numerical methods for the problems considered.

7) For those fortunate enough to have the right system, the manufacturer may have produced suitable software. This usually concerns more expensive systems, in particular Tektronix and Hewlett Packard. Clearly such software is of little use to those with different machines. However, the lack of software for statistical computations on small computers is made clear in the absence of mention of other software sources by Boardman(1982).

8) The Statistical Computing section of The American Statistician contains product announcements for programs useful in statistics. Because these are announcements, the software should be considered unproven.

Where to find algorithms

Algorithms are considerably easier to track down. The following are some suggested sources:

1) My own book (Nash, 1979) contains step-description algorithms for solving linear algebraic and function minimization problems. Users have found the algorithms easy to implement in whatever language was available. A list of the few typographical errors which have been found is available from the author.

2) Numerical analysis texts, particularly recent ones, are good primary sources. Two of my most used ones are Dahlquist and Björck(1974). and Lawson and Hanson (1974).

3) Several statistical computing texts have appeared recently. Examples are Belsley, Kuh and Welsch(1980), Chambers(1977) and Bard (1974).

4) Frequently, journal articles discuss methods for statistical problems. Use can be made of these articles, especially if their author can be contacted. Journals I consult in this fashion include Mathematics of Computation, SIAM journals on Numerical Analysis and on Scientific and Statistical Computing, as well as the statistical journals. As an example, a compact method recently discussed is the use of the conjugate gradients method for certain analysis of variance problems (Golub and Nash, 1981).

5) Colleagues are an invaluable source of information. I had reason to be grateful recently to two colleagues who supplied me with programs and methods I would not otherwise have found.

6) Finally, it is an unfortunate reality that many small machine users are drawing their inspiration from the source codes of proprietary packages such as IMSL. Because there are no formal mechanisms which adequately handle the licencing of the translated program code and because of the general legal confusion concerning software protection, this borrowing of ideas raises a number of legal and ethical questions which to date are unresolved.

Conclusions and forecasts

The field of statistical computing is a rapidly developing one, with the small computer area being particularly disorderly. Small machine users continue to spend a considerable portion of their time programming for tasks which are routine on large computers. Thus it is to be expected that as small computers become powerful enough to execute popular statistical packages, users will migrate to these more powerful but still small machines. At the same time, the price and availability of microcomputers with capabilities equal to contemporary popular systems is likely to make them extremely popular and to entice statisticians to use them in their work. Software will therefore become more widely available, both through informal use of small computers and through the efforts of workers like the author. The quality of software marketed is likely to remain uneven, so buyers should be cautious.

References

Bard, Y. (1974) Nonlinear parameter estimation, Academic Press, New York.

Belsley, D.A., E. Kuh and R.E. Welsch (1980) Regression diagnostics, Wiley, New York.

Boardman, T.J. (1982) "The future of statistical computing on desktop computers", American Statistician, v. 36, no. 1, 49-58.

Chambers, J.M. (1977) Computational methods for data analysis, Wiley, New York.

Dahlquist, G. and A. Björck (1974) Numerical methods, (tr. N. Anderson), Prentice-Hall, Englewood Cliffs.

Gear, C.W. (1971) Numerical initial value problems in ordinary differential equations, Prentice-Hall, Englewood Cliffs.

Golub, G. and S.G. Nash (1982) "Nonorthogonal analysis of variance using a generalized conjugate-gradient algorithm", J. Amer. Stat. Assoc., v. 77, no. 377, 109-116.

Lawson, C.L. and R.J. Hanson (1974) Solving least squares problems, Prentice Hall, Englewood Cliffs.

Luk, F.T. (1980) "Computing the singular-value decomposition on the Illiac IV", ACM Trans. Math. Software, v. 6, no. 4, 524-539.

Nash, J.C. (1977) "Minimizing a nonlinear sum of squares function on a small computer", J. Inst. Maths Applics., v. 19, 231-237.

Nash, J.C. (1979) Compact numerical methods for computer: linear algebra and function minimi a-tion Adam Hilger, Bristol, UK . (Halsted Press, New York in USA).

Nash, J.C. (1981a) "Fundamental statistical calculations", Interface Age, September, 1981, 40-42.

Nash, J.C. (1981b) "Nonlinear estimation using a microcomputer", in Computer science and statistics: proceedings of the 13th symposium on the interface. (ed. W.F. Eddy), Springer Verlag, New York, 363-366.

Ruckdeschel, F.R. (1981) BASIC scientific subroutines, Vols. 1 & 2, Byte/McGraw-Hill, Peterborough, NH.

Velleman, P.F. and D.C. Hoaglin (1980) Applications, basics and computing for exploratory data analysis, Duxbury Press, Boston.

Nonparametric Statistics

Chair: Myles Hollander, Florida State University (on leave at Stanford University)

Implementation and Computational Considerations of the Cox Partial Likelihood Analysis

Arthur V. Peterson Jr., Ross L. Prentice, and Patrick M. Marek, Fred Hutchinson Cancer Research Center and University of Washington

The Bootstrap for Robust Bayesian Analysis: An Adventure in Computing

Dennis D. Boos and John F. Monahan, North Carolina State University

IMPLEMENTATION AND COMPUTATIONAL CONSIDERATIONS OF THE COX PARTIAL LIKELIHOOD ANALYSIS

Arthur V. Peterson, Jr.*, Ross L. Prentice* and Patrick M. Marek
Fred Hutchinson Cancer Research Center and the University of Washington*

Abstract

The Cox (1972) proportional hazards regression model is a widely-utilized semi-nonparametric model for the analysis of failure time data with covariates. An implementation of the partial likelihood analysis is presented. Emphasized are generalizations of the model, and their uses, including (1) stratification, (2) time-dependent covariates, (3) competing risks, (4) multiple events, and (5) time-dependent strata. The implementation is analyzed in terms of number and type of operations, and CPU time.

Keywords: Cox proportional hazards model; partial likelihood analysis; failure time data; computer implementation (RCOX); computation efficiency; time-dependent covariates, stratification; competing risks; multiple events.

1. Introduction

The statistical analysis of survival time data is enjoying widespread application, particularly in clinical trials and epidemiologic follow-up studies in medical settings, and in failure testing of machines and components in industrial settings. The proportional hazards model, a semi-nonparametric model first introduced by Cox (1972), is the most widely-used model for the analysis of survival time data in the presence of covariates. We present here a computer implementation of the Cox (1972,1975) partial likelihood analysis of the proportional hazards model, with emphasis on various useful generalizations. We also consider for various combinations of study parameters the efficiency of the implementation in terms of number and type of individual operations, and CPU time.

The proportional hazards model, and its partial likelihood analysis, are reviewed in Section 2. Emphasized are the nonparametric features of the model, and several useful generalizations under which the partial likelihood analysis remains appropriate. Section 3 describes a FORTRAN implementation of this analysis, and illustrates its use and special features. Section 4 considers the efficiency of the implementation with respect to number and type of operations and CPU time, and discusses how various generalizations of the model affect the efficiency of computation. Investigation into methods for reducing the computation time is ongoing, and will be reported elsewhere.

2. Proportional Hazards Model and the Partial Likelihood Analysis

2.1 Model

Survival data methodology applies to situations where interest is focused on the time T from entry into the study until the occurrence of an event of interest. The event may be death, as in a population mortality study; or the recurrence of disease, as in a clinical trial; or the failure of a machine, as in an industrial life test. A feature that distinguishes survival methods from other methodologies is that data on the (failure) time T may be censored; that is, T may be known only to exceed some known censoring time t_0. Such censored times are common, for example, in follow-up studies that are analyzed before all individuals encounter the event; only the experience up to the date of analysis is available. Censoring due to loss of some individuals to follow-up may also occur. We make the usual assumption in what follows that censoring is not predictive of the (unobserved) failure time.

Of interest here are regression situations where information on other variables $\underline{x} = (x_1,\dots,x_q)$ is also available, and primary interest focuses on the relationship between one (or more) of these variables (or functions of them) and the distribution of the survival time T. Cox (1972) proposed a model for the distribution of T given $\underline{x}$ in terms of the hazard rate

$$\lambda(t) \equiv \lim_{\Delta t \to 0} P(t \le T < t+\Delta t \mid T \ge t)/\Delta t$$

for T, here assumed continuous. The hazard rate is just the instantaneous rate of occurrence of events at follow-up time t for individuals still alive at time t. When the event is death, the hazard rate is readily recognized as the familiar mortality rate.

Cox's proportional hazards model specifies that the hazard rate $\lambda(t;\underline{z})$ of an individual with covariate $\underline{z}$ is of a multiplicative form:

$$(1) \qquad \lambda(t;\underline{z}) = \lambda_0(t) \cdot \exp(\underline{\beta}'\underline{z}) ,$$

where $\lambda_0(\cdot) \ge 0$ is a completely arbitrary function of time, $\underline{z}' = (z_1,\dots,z_p)$ is a regression vector whose components are functions of the variables $\underline{x}' = (x_1,\dots,x_q)$, and $\underline{\beta}' = (\beta_1,\dots,\beta_p)$ is a vector of regression coefficients that are usually the aim of the inference.

Model (1) specifies the ratio of hazard rates at any two values $\underline{z}_1$, $\underline{z}_2$ of the covariate, $\lambda(t;\underline{z}_1)/\lambda(t;\underline{z}_2) = \exp\{\underline{\beta}'(\underline{z}_1 - \underline{z}_2)\}$, to not depend on time. The coefficients $\underline{\beta}$ are seen to have a meaningful interpretation: $\exp\{\underline{\beta}'(\underline{z}_1 - \underline{z}_2)\}$ is the relative hazard rate, or relative risk, between an individual with covariate value $\underline{z}_1$ and one with $\underline{z}_2$. Although we restrict consideration here to the particular exponential form $\exp(\underline{\beta}'\underline{z})$ of the covariate factor in (1), the exponential form is not crucial to the method of analysis. Other parametric forms for $g(\underline{\beta}'\underline{z}) \geq 0$ can be specified without unduly complicating the inference.

The covariates $\underline{z}' = (z_1,\ldots,z_p)$ are functions of the available variables $\underline{x}' = (x_1,\ldots,x_q)$. As in most regression methods, there is considerable flexibility in their definition. They may include the variables themselves, functions of them, and 'interactions' among them. Furthermore, a useful feature of the partial likelihood analysis is that it can easily accommodate covariates $\underline{z}' = (z_1,\ldots,z_p)$ whose components may depend on time. In this case model (1) specifies that the hazard rate $\lambda(t;\underline{z})$ for T at any follow-up time t depends on the covariate $\underline{z} = \underline{z}(t)$ evaluated at that time t. The use of time-dependent covariates in the model is quite useful for two different applications. First, there is an assumption inherent in (1) that the relationship between a covariate $z_1 = x_1$ and the survival time T can be described as a constant (independent of time) effect on the hazard rate. This assumption can be relaxed and investigated by including in the model 'interaction' terms between x_1 and t such as the product $z_2 = x_1 \cdot t$. The relative risk at t per unit of x_1 is then $\exp[(\beta_1 + \beta_2 t)]$, and the dependence of the relative risk on time can be investigated through inference on β_2. A second application is in investigating the relationship between survival time and (stochastic) variables that may change during the course of follow-up. For example, a time-dependent covariate may indicate whether a treatment (e.g., heart transplant) has yet been performed. Alternatively, a sequence of measurements $x_1(t_1)$, $x_2(t_2)\ldots$ (for example, several blood pressure measurements) may be obtained periodically on each individual during follow-up, and a covariate of interest may be defined to change with time as a function of these periodic measurements. Both types of time-dependent covariates have proved useful in a variety of settings.

2.2 Partial Likelihood Analysis

Cox (1972) noted that the arbitrary (nonparametric) nature of the underlying hazard function $\lambda_0(\cdot)$ in (1) suggests the use of a partial likelihood for inference on the regression parameter $\underline{\beta}$. Let $t_1 < t_2 < \cdots < t_r$ denote the ordered uncensored failure times, assumed for the moment to be distinct, and by $R_i = R(t_i)$, called the risk set at t_i, the set of individuals still surviving at time t_i^-. Then the partial likelihood is a product over all failed individuals:

$$(2) \quad L(\underline{\beta}) = \prod_{i=1}^{r} \left\{ \frac{\exp\{\underline{\beta}'\underline{z}_i(t_i)\}}{\sum_{j\in R_i} \exp\{\underline{\beta}'\underline{z}_j(t_i)\}} \right\} .$$

Here the common argument t_i of the covariates $\underline{z}_i$ in the numerator and the covariates $\underline{z}_j$, $j\in R_i$, in the denominator is written out explicitly to emphasize that for the ith factor of $L(\underline{\beta})$ any time-dependent covariates are evaluated at the failure time t_i of the failed individual i.

A remarkable feature of the proportional hazards model (1) is that inference on $\underline{\beta}$ is conveniently performed via (2), which does not depend on the nuisance function $\lambda_0(\cdot)$. Other attractive features are that (2) conveniently accommodates censoring, and that it conveniently accommodates time-dependent covariates.

That the partial likelihood (2) can be used for asymptotic inference just as a full likelihood was suggested by Cox (1975), and more recently justified by Andersen and Gill (1981), and Prentice and Self (1982) using martingale arguments. That the maximum partial likelihood estimator of $\underline{\beta}$ might be fully efficient (assuming $\lambda_0(\cdot)$ completely unknown) was suggested by Cox's (1972) original argument, and also by its characterization as a marginal likelihood (Kalbfleisch and Prentice (1973)) of the rank vector of survival times in the special case of no time-dependent covariates. Efron (1977) and Oakes (1977) provide explicit computations suggesting the full efficiency of the partial likelihood.

When ties occur among the uncensored failure times, modification to (2) is needed. A modification that is motivated by the partial likelihood nature of (2) is:

$$(3) \quad L(\underline{\beta}) = \prod_{i=1}^{r} \left\{ \frac{\exp(\underline{\beta}'\underline{s}_i)}{\sum_{\psi} \prod_{k=1}^{d_i} \exp(\underline{\beta}'\underline{z}_{\psi_k})} \right\} ,$$

where r denotes the number of distinct uncensored failures times, d_i denotes the number of uncensored failures at t_i, $\underline{s}_i = \sum_{k=1}^{d_i} \underline{z}_k$ is the sum of covariate vectors of those failing at t_i, and ψ denotes the set of all subsets $(\psi_1,\ldots,\psi_{d_i})$ of size d_i from $\{1,2,\ldots,n_i\}$, where n_i denotes the size of the risk set R_i. Direct computation of the denominators of (3) for non-zero $\underline{\beta}$ is extremely cumbersome if the number of ties is large at any failure time. Gail, Lubin and Rubenstein (1981) discuss a computational procedure for the denominator of (3) that evidently yields feasible computations for moderate values of d_i and n_i, $i = 1,2,\ldots,r$. Such a procedure is not considered here partially because (3) estimates the odds ratio parameter in a closely-related logistic regression model, rather than the relative risk parameter in (1). The tied data likelihood function developed from marginal likelihood considerations (e.g., Kalbfleisch and Prentice, 1973) avoids this latter problem but also involves very extensive calculations. The implementation described here therefore uses a very simple approximation to these other likelihood functions. This approximation (Peto, 1972; Breslow, 1974) is adequate when d_i/n_i is small at most failure times. It is given by

$$(4) \quad L(\underline{\beta}) = \prod_{i=1}^{r} \left\{ \frac{\exp(\underline{\beta}'\underline{s}_i)}{[\sum_{j\in R_i} \exp(\underline{\beta}'\underline{z}_j)]^{d_i}} \right\} .$$

2.3 Generalizations

A useful generalization of (1) that still admits a partial likelihood of the form (2) is model (1) with stratification. For an individual in stratum s, s = 1,2,...,NS, where the stratum s is specified for each individual in terms of the available variables $\underline{x} = (x_1,\ldots,x_q)$, the Cox proportional hazards model (1) generalizes to

$$(5) \quad \lambda(t;\underline{z},s) = \lambda_{0s}(t) \cdot \exp(\underline{\beta}'\underline{z}) \quad ,$$

where each of the underlying stratum-specific hazard rates $\lambda_{0s}(\cdot)$, s = 1,2,...,NS is arbitrary. In particular, no relationship is imposed among the $\lambda_{0s}(\cdot)$, s = 1,2,...,NS. Stratification allows for unrestricted (except perhaps for the discrete nature of s) control of some variables in $\underline{x} = (x_1,\ldots,x_q)$, and offers a useful alternative to controlling by means of regression modelling. The partial likelihood (4) generalizes with stratification to

$$L(\underline{\beta}) = \prod_{\ell=1}^{NS} L_\ell(\underline{\beta}) \quad ,$$

where the contribution L_ℓ from the ℓth stratum to the partial likelihood L is just the partial likelihood (2) for a hypothetical study that includes only those individuals in stratum s.

Another useful generalization of (1), or of (5), occurs when data on the type of failure (competing risks) are also available. When data are available not only on the time T of event occurrence, but also on the type $J\varepsilon\{1,2,\ldots,v\}$ of event, then a proportional hazards model of the type (5) can be specified for any or all of the v type-specific hazard rates $\lambda_j(t) = \lim_{\Delta t \to 0} P(t \leq T < t+\Delta t;\ J = j \mid T \geq t)/\Delta t$, j = 1,2,...,v. For example, for failure type j a model of the same form as (5) may be specified:

$$(6) \quad \lambda_j(t;\underline{z},s) = \lambda^j_{0s}(t) \cdot \exp(\underline{\beta}_j'\underline{z}) \quad ,$$

where now the coefficient $\underline{\beta}_j$ is specific to the jth failure type, and is interpreted as a measure of the relationship between $\underline{z}$ and the type-j hazard rate $\lambda_j(t;\underline{z},s)$. A partial likelihood of the form (2) is appropriate for this situation also, provided that events of type other than j are included in (4) as censored observations. No assumption about the relationships between the different types of failure (e.g., no "independence" assumption) is needed (Prentice, et al. (1978)).

A final generalization is time-dependent strata. Time-dependent strata are useful for two different applications:
(1) nonparametric control for variables that depend on time (e.g., that are measured periodically during follow-up);
(2) including and excluding individuals from the risk set R_i, at follow-up time t_i. A useful feature of the RCOX implementation, discussed in the next section, is that it deletes from the analysis any individual whose stratum is specified to be zero. The most common use of this feature is to allow analysis of (fixed) subsets of the data (e.g., those for whom certain covariates all have known values) without having to delete records from the data set. This feature also permits the inclusion or exclusion of individuals on a time-dependent basis. This can be useful, for example, when time-dependent strata are used to control for periodically-measured variables for which some measurements are missing.

Including and excluding individuals from the risk set in a time-dependent fashion is also useful for the analysis of survival-type data that includes multiple event times on the same individual (for example, multiple episodes of infection). In such an application (Prentice, Williams, Peterson (1981)) the use of time-dependent strata is a trick that allows the use of a survival analysis (single-event) program for a multiple-event application. For example, consider a Cox-type model for the intensity $\lambda\{t;\underline{z}\}$ of a nonhomogeneous Poisson process that governs the occurrence of multiple events:

$$\lambda(t;\underline{z}) = \lambda_0(t) \cdot \exp(\underline{\beta}'\underline{z}) \quad .$$

The partial likelihood is just (2), where it is understood that more than one "failure" time t_i may belong to one individual, and where the risk set R_i includes all those individuals still under observation at t_i even if some of such individuals have already experienced one or more event. This partial likelihood analysis can be implemented using a survival analysis (single-event) program by (1) replicating each of the data items for each individual, as many times as events, and (2) modifying the replicated data for each individual by specifying the survival time to be the time of one of the events, and specifying a time-dependent stratum indicator to be zero for the entire follow-up period except the interval between the event and the previous event.

Similar tricks allow the use of single-event methods to analyze multiple-event data from other and more general Cox-type intensity models. See Prentice, Williams and Peterson (1981) for further discussion of these models and their analysis.

Omitted here is any discussion of the estimation of the underlying hazard rate $\hat{\lambda}_0(\cdot)$, and associated survival functions $\hat{S}(t;z) = \hat{S}_0(t)^{\exp(\underline{\beta}'\underline{z})}$. An account of this subject, as well as additional details about the proportional hazards model, its generalizations and analysis, can be found in Kalbfleisch and Prentice (1980).

3. An Implementation

3.1 Features and Capabilities

A FORTRAN implementation of the partial likelihood analysis is described. This implementation (RCOX) is based on work done by one of us (Marek) to rewrite and generalize an existing program developed by J.D. Kalbfleisch and A. McIntosh (see Appendix 3 of Kalbfleisch and Prentice, 1980).

The RCOX implementation consists of a small user-modifiable main program and 45 subroutines that handle the input and checking of data, input of analysis specifications, error checking, analyses and summary outputs. It is designed to be as portable as possible, and is written in FORTRAN-66 standard code, with some minor departures dictated by the implementation of FORTRAN on the Hewlett-Packard HP3000. It is designed for batch-mode operation (the CPU requirements are generally too great for interactive use on most minicomputers) with no intrinsic limit on data file size.

Except for the small main program, the RCOX code is fixed and can reside in object-code libraries. To permit flexibility in setting study parameters, a very small main program can be changed as needed to allow a user to set some data statement constants (and hence array dimensions which depend upon these constants). An interactive front-end program (MAKE-RCOX) is available that produces an appropriate main program for the user. But for computers with less restrictive memory management than the HP3000, (i.e., most other computers) it would be advisable to set the array dimensions to suitably large values and transfer the data statement inputs to the "command file", which includes all other analysis specifications.

The user may write his or her own subprograms for defining covariates, strata, survival times or failure indicators. This is particularly useful for defining time-dependent covariates and time-dependent strata. It can also be used to define fixed covariates or strata through transformations of the input variables.

The RCOX program performs a partial likelihood analysis of censored survival data with covariates, and includes features to allow for:

1. time-dependent covariates,
2. stratification,
3. competing risks, and
4. time-dependent strata.

3.2 Analyses and Output

The RCOX implementation uses the partial likelihood to perform inference on the regression coefficients $\underline{\beta}$. Computed and printed are:
(a) the maximum (partial) likelihood estimator $\hat{\beta}$ from an iterative Newton-Raphson search,
(b) the estimated covariance matrix for $\hat{\beta}$,
(c) test statistics, and p-values, of hypotheses that one regression component is zero [using the asymptotic normal approximation for the distribution of the maximum likelihood estimator],
(d) approximate 95% confidence intervals for the regression parameters β_i, as well as 95% confidence intervals for the corresponding relative risks $\exp(\beta_i)$ per unit change in z_i,
(e) the score test statistic, and p-value, of the global hypothesis that all coefficients are zero, and
(f) the value of the maximized log partial likelihood.

In addition, but not discussed further here, estimates and plots of the underlying hazard function $\lambda_0(\cdot)$ and related survival, failure and cumulative hazard functions may be computed.

The output of the RCOX program includes (each at the user's option):

1. Echo of data parameters specified by the user,
2. Echo of the analysis features specified by the user,
3. Echo of the input data records,
4. Tabulations of number of data items by stratum number and by competing risks,
5. Listing of all included data records (survival times, failure indicator, stratum number and input variables), in order of increasing survival time,
6. Listing of all distinct uncensored survival times (with number of uncensored failures and number of individuals at risk at that time), in order of increasing time,
7. The results (listed above) of the partial likelihood analysis for the regression coefficients,
8. Listing and/or plots of various survival functions.

3.3 Specification of Program Runs and Special Options

Flexibility is designed into specifying program runs in order to allow multiple runs with varying features to be conveniently run on the same data set. To specify information on data to be input and the analysis specification, the following may be specified by the user (starred(*) items must be specified):

* a. Purpose of the run. The value "1", the usual case, indicates that the MPLE is sought,
b. (optional) Number of data records. This is useful if only part of a data set is to be analyzed.
* c. Name of each potential covariate, and whether or not it is time-dependent.
* d. How the parameter of each potential covariate is to be treated: either (i) to be estimated, or (ii) fixed at a specified value, or (iii) set to zero (covariate eliminated from the analysis).
e. (optional) Names for strata.
f. (optional) Names for failure types (competing risks).
g. (optional) Grouping of failure types.
h. (optional) Initial values of coefficients $\underline{\beta}$ for the iterative search for MPLE $\hat{\beta}$. The default initial value is zero.
* i. Format for reading the data.
j. (optional) Specification of the degree of detail desired for output.

The format for these and other commands is given in the user's manual for the RCOX program (RCOX Manual).

As previously noted, RCOX was written to be as portable as possible. But in order to create a program that could handle very large studies on the HP3000 this goal was relaxed somewhat. Diverging from standard FORTRAN is the use of special "direct access" scratch files into which the input data is transferred for use by the analysis routines. Fortunately, most other implementations of FORTRAN have similar statements for setting up and using such files. (In particular, the conversion to most DEC and IBM FORTRANS should not be difficult.) Another feature of RCOX that would require changing for use on another machine is the use of HP3000 Library routines to sort the data file. Calls to similar SORT/MERGE routines may be substituted, or alternatively, a pre-sorted data file may be used. Details concerning these and other modifications are included in the RCOX User's Manual, Section IX, Conversion Notes.

In summary, RCOX has been designed to be a flexible implementation of Cox's (1972) partial likelihood analysis of survival data that allows a considerable number of generalizations and special features, especially useful for specially-tailored analyses and for multiple exploratory runs on the same data.

4. Implementation of Partial Likelihood Analysis, and Determination of Number of Operations and Computer Storage

The subroutine COXMPL performs the partial likelihood analysis. Specifically, this subroutine:
1. finds the maximum (partial) likelihood estimator $\hat{\beta}$, by finding the zero (vector) of the vector of first partial derivatives (with respect to components of $\underline{\beta}$) of the log partial likelihood. The zero vector is attained by a Newton-Raphson iteration, for which all second partial derivatives of the log partial likelihood are also needed.
2. computes the estimated covariance matrix for $\hat{\beta}$.
3. manipulates the results from 1 and 2 above to obtain test statistics and confidence intervals for the regression coefficients $\underline{\beta}$.

The partial likelihood for the Cox proportional hazards model (1) with stratification is $L = \prod_{s=1}^{NS} L_s$, where each of the stratum-specific factors L_s is of the form (4):

$$L_s = \prod_{i=1}^{r} \frac{\exp(\underline{\beta}'\underline{s}_i)}{\left[\sum_{j\in R_i} \exp(\underline{\beta}'\underline{z}_j)\right]^{d_i}} ,$$

where for conciseness all the notations above ($r = r(s)$, $\underline{s}_i = \underline{s}_i(s)$, $R_i = R_i(s)$ and $d_i = d_i(s)$) suppress the important fact that they refer only to the subset of individuals in stratum s. The product $\prod_{i=1}^{r}$ is over the $r = r(s)$ distinct uncensored failure times in stratum s.

For each iteration the COXMPL subroutine computes for each stratum s:

$$1.\quad \ell n\, L_{(s)} = \sum_{i=1}^{r} [\underline{\beta}'\underline{s}_i - d_i \cdot \ell n(SI_i)] ,$$

$$2.\quad \frac{\partial \ell n\, L_{(s)}}{\partial \beta_k} = \sum_{i=1}^{r} \left[s_{ik} - d_i \cdot \frac{SI1_i(k)}{SI_i} \right] ,k=1,2,\ldots,p,$$

and

$$3.\quad \frac{-\partial^2 \ell n\, L_{(s)}}{\partial \beta_k\, \partial \beta_\ell} = \sum_{i=1}^{r} d_i \cdot \left[\frac{SI2_i(k,\ell)}{SI_i} - \frac{SI1_i(k) \cdot SI1_i(\ell)}{(SI_i)^2} \right] ,$$

$k = 1,2,\ldots,p,$

$\ell = k,k+1,\ldots,p,$

where (for each s):

$$SI_i = \sum_{j\in R_i} \exp(\underline{\beta}'\underline{z}_j) , \quad i = 1,2,\ldots,r ,$$

$$SI1_i(k) = \sum_{j\in R_i} z_{jk} \cdot \exp(\underline{\beta}'\underline{z}_j) , \quad i = 1,2,\ldots,r, \quad k = 1,\ldots,p ,$$

$$SI2_i(k,\ell) = \sum_{j\in R_i} z_{jk} \cdot z_{j\ell} \cdot \exp(\underline{\beta}'\underline{z}_j), \quad i = 1,2,\ldots,r, \quad k = 1,2,\ldots,p, \quad \ell = k,k+1,\ldots,p.$$

CASE 1: Covariates are not time-dependent.

In this case, the SI_i, $SI1_i(\cdot)$, and $SI2_i(\cdot,\cdot)$ need not be entirely recomputed for each i. Rather, because the r distinct survival times $t_1 < t_2 < \cdots < t_r$ are ordered, we have $R_i \supset R_{i+1}$ for all i by the definition of risk set, and consequently the SI_i, $SI1_i(\cdot)$, and $SI2_i(\cdot,\cdot)$ can be computed by accumulation:

$$SI_r = \sum_{j\in R_r} \exp(\underline{\beta}'\underline{z}_j)$$

$$SI_{r-1} = SI_r + \sum_{j\in[R_{r-1} - R_r]} \exp(\underline{\beta}'\underline{z}_j)$$

$\vdots$

and similarly for $SI1_i(\cdot)$ and for $SI2_i(\cdot,\cdot)$, $i = r, r-1, \ldots, 1$. The computation by accumulation, well-known for this application, avoids a considerable number of unneeded steps.

Table 1 shows for various combinations of study parameters the number of floating-point operations per iteration of a partial likelihood analysis with no time-dependent covariates. We make the conservative assumption of no ties. The number of operations is computed for the main computation loop of the COXMPL subroutine that computes the log partial likelihood and its first and second partial derivatives according to the expressions given above. It is apparent that the number of operations is (a) $O(n \cdot p^2)$ for additions and multiplications, and (b) $O(r \cdot p^2)$ for additions, multiplications and divisions. Note that the number of operations does not depend on the number of strata.

The right-most column of Table 1 shows the CPU time required on an HP3000 to execute all the indicated operations. The main conclusion is that the numbers of operations, and CPU time, are computationally feasible for analysis at least up to 10,000 individuals all of whom have uncensored times with 10 covariates (7.9 minutes CPU time per iteration). Also feasible would be an analysis of 100,000 individuals with 10,000 events and 5 covariates (11.0 minutes CPU time per iteration).

CASE 2: Covariates are Time-Dependent

In this case, the values of all covariates in the ith factor of the partial likelihood depend on the failure time t_i. This includes the covariates of individuals failing at t_i and those of individuals in the risk set at t_i. Thus, the quantities SI_i, $SI1_i(\cdot)$, $SI2_i(\cdot,\cdot)$ cannot be accumulated, but rather in general must be recomputed from scratch at each distinct failure time t_i, $i = 1, 2, \ldots, r$. Table 2 shows for various combinations of study parameters the number of floating-point operations per iteration of a partial likelihood analysis with time-dependent covariates. Of particular note is that the number of operations is proportional to $n^* = \sum_s \sum_{i=1}^{r} n_i(s)$, where $n_i = \#\{R_i\}$, instead of merely n. The number of operations is (a) $O(n^* \cdot p^2)$ for additions and multiplications, and (b) $O(r \cdot p^2)$, as before, for additions, multiplications, and divisions.

Unfortunately, n^* can be considerably larger than n. In the worse case, where all times are uncensored and distinct, $n^* = \sum_{i=1}^{n} i = \frac{n(n+1)}{2}$ for the case of no stratification. In the case where r ($<n$) of the times are uncensored (and they are distinct and uniformly distributed among the censored times) n^* is equal to $\sum_{i=1}^{r} n_i = \sum_{i=1}^{r} \left(\frac{n}{r}\right) i = \frac{n(r+1)}{2}$, which is typically ($10<r<1{,}000$) still considerably larger than n. Shown in the right-most column of Table 2 are the CPU times required to execute all the indicated operations on an HP3000 computer. It is clear that the study parameters (size of study (n), number of events (d), and number of covariates (p)) do not have to be very large at all before the computation becomes impractical. Analyses with 1,000 individuals, 100 events, and 10 time-dependent covariates (14.0 minutes per iteration), or with 10,000 individuals, 10 events, and 10 time-dependent covariates (15.2 minutes per iteration) are still computationally feasible. But analyses with 1,000 individuals, all having uncensored events, with only 5 covariates (47.1 minutes per iteration), or with 10,000 individuals with 100 events and 5 covariates (47.4 minutes per iteration) already begin to take considerable time. The most ambitious run that we attempted was an analysis of over 16,000 cases with about 1,000 distinct failure times with one time-dependent covariate. The CPU time per iteration was over 2 hours, clearly impractical as a routine procedure.

Data sets of over 10,000 individuals and over 1,000 events are not uncommon, and typically at least several covariates are desired in the analyses. We have encountered three very large data sets in the last two years for which proportional hazards regression analysis with time-dependent covariates are appropriate. One is the data set mentioned above with 16,000 items and 1,000 distinct uncensored failures. Another is the mortality follow-up data (over 4,000 cancer deaths) of the cohort of 80,000 Hiroshima and Nagasaki A-bomb survivors (Life Span Study (LSS)) of the Radiation Effects Research Foundation. In both of these studies time-dependent covariates are useful for establishing the trend with follow-up time of the relative cancer mortality. A third study is the clinical follow-up cohort, a 16,000 subset of the LSS. In this study proportional hazards analyses with time-dependent covariates have been useful for studying the relationship between various clinical outcomes (e.g., cardiovascular disease) and clinical measurements (e.g., blood pressure, serum cholesterol, and others) taken periodically (every two years) during follow-up.

Methods that are computationally less cumbersome are clearly needed to analyze such large data sets, particularly when time-dependent covariates are used. Investigations are underway into several possible methods for reducing computation time. Results of these investigations will be reported elsewhere.

References

Andersen, P.K. and Gill, R.D. (1982). Cox regression model for counting processes: a large sample study. To appear, Annals of Statistics.

Breslow, N.E. (1974). Covariance analysis of censored survival data. Biometrics 30, 89-99.

Cox, D.R. (1972). Regression models with life tables (with discussion). J.R. Stat. Soc. B. 34, 187-220.

References (continued)

Cox, D.R. (1973). The statistical analysis of dependencies in point processes. In Stochastic Point Processes, Ed. P.A.W. Lewis, pp. 55-66, New York: Wiley.

Cox, D.R. (1975). Partial likelihood. Biometrika 62, 269-279.

Efron, B. (1977). The efficiency of Cox's likelihood function for censored data. J. Am. Statist. Assoc. 72, 557-565.

Gail, M.H., Lubin, J.H. and Rubenstein, L.V. (1981). Likelihood calculations for matched case-control studies and survival studies with matched death times. Biometrika 68, 703-707.

Kalbfleisch, J.D. and Prentice, R.L. (1973). Marginal likelihoods based on Cox's regression and life model. Biometrika 60, 267-278.

Kalbfleisch, J.D. and Prentice, R.L. (1980). The Analysis of Failure Time Data. New York: Wiley.

Oakes, D. (1977). The asymptotic information in censored survival data. Biometrika 64, 441-448.

Peto, R. (1972). Contribution to discussion of paper by D.R. Cox. J.R. Statist. Soc. B 34, 205-207.

Prentice, R.L., Kalbfleisch, J.D., Peterson, A.V., Flournoy, N., Farewell, V.T. and Breslow, N.E. (1978). The analysis of failure time data in the presence of competing risks. Biometrics 34, 541-554.

Prentice, R.L. and Self, S.G. (1982). Asymptotic distribution theory for Cox-type regression models with general relative risk form. Submitted to Ann. Statist.

Prentice, R.L., Williams, B.J. and Peterson, A.V. (1981). On the regression analysis of multivariate failure time data. Biometrika 68, 373-379.

Williams, B.J. (1980). Proportional intensity models for multiple event times. Ph.D. Thesis. University of Washington.

Acknowledgement

This work was supported in part by Contract N01-ES-8-2125 from the National Institute of Environmental Health Sciences and by Grants CA-15704 and GM-28314 from the National Institutes of Health.

TABLE 1. Number of Operations per Iteration of a Partial Likelihood Analysis With No Time-Dependent Covariates (and no ties)

Study Parameters			Number of Operations					
n= number of individuals	d= number of events (r=)	p= number of covariates	$n\cdot(1+\frac{5}{2}p+\frac{1}{2}p^2)+(d\cdot p)+r(2+4p+p^2)$ Add	$n\cdot(3p+p^2)+r\cdot(1+\frac{7}{2}p+\frac{3}{2}p^2)$ Multiply	n Exp	$r\cdot(p^2+2p)$ Divide	r Logarithm	CPU time (min) on HP3000
100	10	5	3,120	4,560	100	350	10	.011
	10	10	9,120	14,860	100	1,200	10	.033
	100	5	7,800	9,600	100	3,500	100	.026
	100	10	22,800	31,600	100	12,000	100	.079
1,000	100	5	31,200	45,600	1,000	3,500	100	.11
	100	10	91,200	148,600	1,000	12,000	100	.33
	1,000	5	78,000	96,000	1,000	35,000	1,000	.26
	1,000	10	228,000	316,000	1,000	120,000	1,000	.79
10,000	1,000	5	312,000	456,000	10,000	35,000	1,000	1.1
	1,000	10	912,000	1,486,000	10,000	120,000	1,000	3.3
	10,000	5	780,000	960,000	10,000	350,000	10,000	2.6
	10,000	10	2,280,000	3,160,000	10,000	1,200,000	10,000	7.9
100,000	10,000	5	3,120,000	4,560,000	100,000	350,000	10,000	11.0
	10,000	10	9,120,000	14,860,000	100,000	1,200,000	10,000	32.7
	100,000	5	7,800,000	9,600,000	100,000	3,500,000	100,000	25.8
	100,000	10	22,800,000	31,600,000	100,000	12,000,000	100,000	78.7

TABLE 2. Number of Operations per Iteration of a Partial Likelihood Analysis with Time-Dependent Covariates, With No Stratification and No Ties

Study Parameters			Number of Operations					
n= number of individuals	d= number of events (=r)	p= number of covariates	$n^* \cdot (1+\frac{5}{2}p+\frac{1}{2}p^2) + (d \cdot p) + r(2+4p+p^2)$ Add	$n^* \cdot (3p+p^2) + r(1+\frac{7}{2}p+\frac{3}{2}p^2)$ Multiply	n^* Subroutine call (to compute time-dependent covariate) & Exponential	$r \cdot (2p+p^2)$ Divide	r Logarithm	CPU Time (min) on HP 3000
100	100	1	21,000	20,800	5,050	300	100	.10
	100	5	136,500	207,600	5,050	3,500	100	.49
	100	10	399,000	675,100	5,050	12,000	100	1.45
1,000	10	1	22,080	22,060	5,500	30	10	.10
	10	5	143,520	220,560	5,500	350	10	.52
	10	10	419,520	716,860	5,500	1,200	10	1.52
	100	1	202,800	202,600	50,500	300	100	.96
	100	5	1,318,200	2,025,600	50,500	3,500	100	4.75
	100	10	3,853,200	6,583,600	50,500	12,000	100	14.0
	1,000	1	2,010,000	2,008,000	500,500	3,000	1,000	9.5
	1,000	5	13,065,000	20,076,000	500,500	35,000	1,000	47.1
	1,000	10	38,190,000	65,251,000	500,500	120,000	1,000	138.8
10,000	10	1	220,080	220,060	55,000	30	10	1.0
	10	5	1,430,520	2,200,560	55,000	350	10	5.2
	10	10	4,181,520	7,151,860	55,000	1,200	10	15.2
	100	1	2,020,800	2,020,600	505,000	300	100	9.6
	100	5	13,135,200	20,205,600	505,000	3,500	100	47.4
	100	10	38,395,200	65,668,600	505,000	12,000	100	139.6
	1,000	1	20,028,000	20,026,000	5,005,000	3,000	1,000	95
	1,000	5	130,182,000	200,256,000	5,005,000	35,000	1,000	470
	1,000	10	380,532,000	650,836,000	5,005,000	120,000	1,000	1,384
	10,000	1	200,100,000	200,080,000	50,005,000	30,000	10,000	947
	10,000	5	1,300,650,000	2,000,760,000	50,005,000	350,000	10,000	4,694
	10,000	10	3,801,900,000	6,502,510,000	50,005,000	1,200,000	10,000	13,823
100,000	100	10	383,815,200	656,518,600	5,050,000	12,000	100	1,396
	1,000	10	3,803,952,000	6,506,686,000	50,050,000	120,000	1,000	13,831
	10,000	10	38,005,320,000	65,008,360,000	500,050,000	1,200,000	10,000	138,186

THE BOOTSTRAP FOR ROBUST BAYESIAN ANALYSIS: AN ADVENTURE IN COMPUTING

Dennis D. Boos and John F. Monahan
North Carolina State University

ABSTRACT

One step in Bayesian analysis seldom questioned is the selection of the model $f(x|\theta)$. A simple approach is presented to robustify Bayesian analysis in the location parameter case through use of robust estimators $\hat{\theta}$ (e.g., a trimmed mean). The likelihood is replaced by a bootstrap approximation to the distribution of $\hat{\theta}|\theta$ and a normal prior is assumed. Implementation of this procedure and evaluation of its performance require the use of a wide variety of computational techniques: numerical integration, interpolation, Monte Carlo methods (including swindle), fast fourier transforms, spline approximation, fast selection, and binary search. We discuss both the statistical motivation and the use of these computational techniques.

KEY WORDS: Bayesian, robust, bootstrap, Monte Carlo, spline approximation.

1. Introduction

Model assumptions of the form $f(x|\theta)$ are often the most crucial aspect of a Bayesian statistical analysis. Recently, researchers have begun to make suggestions about how to lessen the impact of such assumptions (e.g., Box and Tiao, 1973, Ch. 3, Novick and Ramsay, 1980, and Box, 1980). We would like to present one such suggestion based on robust parameter estimates and the bootstrap estimate of their sampling distribution.

Consider $X_1,\ldots,X_n$ from the simple location model $f(x|\theta) = f_0(x-\theta)$, where f_0 is unknown but symmetric so that θ may be estimated by $\hat{\theta}$, e.g., a trimmed mean. Suppose that we have prior information about θ which can be expressed as a normal density $\pi(\theta)$ with mean θ_0 and precision τ_0 $(= \sigma_0^{-2})$. Typically, $\hat{\theta}$ will be approximately normal in *large* samples with mean θ and some precision τ_n, so that an approximate posterior (after reducing to $\hat{\theta}$) is the normal density with mean $(\tau_n\hat{\theta} + \tau_0\theta_0)/(\tau_n + \tau_0)$ and precision $\tau_n + \tau_0$. However, prior information is of little importance in large samples since the data will dominate the prior. Therefore, we concentrate on small samples (say $n \le 20$) and propose use of the bootstrap (Efron, 1979) to estimate the distribution of $\hat{\theta} - \theta$ as a replacement for the normal approximation.

The paper is organized as follows. Bootstrap details are given in Section 2 and the performance of the approach is discussed in Section 3. Section 4 explains use of a Monte Carlo swindle as well as a new algorithm for fast computation of the Hodges-Lehmann estimator. Section 5 illustrates the approach with some examples.

2. Implementing the Bootstrap

Our use of the bootstrap method is to artificially generate B random samples of size n chosen *with* replacement from the observed sample values $x_1,\ldots x_n$ (taken as fixed), calculate $\hat{\theta}_1^*,\ldots,\hat{\theta}_B^*$ from each of these samples, and then use the kernel estimator

$$\hat{g}_{n,B}(u) = \frac{1}{Bh_B}\sum_{i=1}^{B} k\left(\frac{u-(\hat{\theta}_i^*-\hat{\theta})}{h_B}\right) \qquad (2.1)$$

as an estimate of the density of $\hat{\theta} - \theta$. If we put $u = x - \theta$ in (2.1), then $\hat{g}_{n,B}(x-\theta)$ is an estimate of the density of $\hat{\theta}|\theta$, and at $x = \hat{\theta}$ this function of θ is our bootstrapped likelihood

$$\hat{L}_{n,B}(\theta;\hat{\theta}) = \frac{1}{Bh_B}\sum_{i=1}^{B} k\left(\frac{2\hat{\theta}-\theta-\hat{\theta}_i^*}{h_B}\right) . \qquad (2.2)$$

The first computational problems arise in expressing the estimated posterior of θ

$$\hat{\pi}(\theta|\underline{x}) \propto \pi(\theta)\hat{L}_{n,B}(\theta;\hat{\theta}(\underline{x})) . \qquad (2.3)$$

We require $\hat{\pi}$ (and thus $\hat{L}$) evaluated at many values of θ as well as the normalizing constant

$$\int\pi(\theta)\hat{L}_{n,B}(\theta;\hat{\theta})d\theta . \qquad (2.4)$$

Let us first consider the integral (2.4). Given a smooth kernel k, the integrand in (2.4) should be locally very smooth, but globally it may have many wiggles due to "undersmoothing" in L (choosing h_B too small). Thus, simplicity, stability, and ease of extension are important as well as efficiency. The method selected was an extended Simpson's rule with varying interval sizes so that more points could be placed in the middle, "where the action is." The prior was used to adjust the location and spread of the grid. A problem can arise with a badly mislocated prior; however, a warning is available if the computed integral of $\hat{L}$ alone (which has mass one) is too small.

The second problem concerns efficient evaluation of (2.2). Notice that other nonparametric density estimates based on the $\hat{\theta}_i^*$ could have been used, but none guarantee non-negativity like the kernel estimate. Although evaluating (2.2) for each θ requires $O(B)$ operations when computed directly, if a kernel k with finite support is used and the $\hat{\theta}_i^*$ are sorted initially $(O(B\log B))$, then each evaluation costs only $O(Bh_B) + O(\log B)$. The procedure to find which of the $O(Bh_B)$ $\hat{\theta}_i^*$'s contribute to the sum consists of two searches of an ordered list and takes $O(\log B)$ operations using a discrete bisection search (see Kao and Monahan, 1977). This procedure works well in practice but has the disadvantage that $\hat{L}_{n,B}(\theta;\hat{\theta})$ can be zero for extreme values of θ , whereas the true $L_n(\theta;\hat{\theta})$ may never be zero. Such values can be a computational problem when considering information measures.

3. Evaluating Performance

We focused on the following simple inference situation:

1) The observations $X_1,\ldots,X_n$ are i.i.d., each with density $f(x|\theta) = f_0(x-\theta)$.

2) The given prior is normal with mean θ_0 and variance σ_0^2 $(= \tau_0^{-1})$.

A third assumption we might make is

3) $f_0(x) = \phi(x)$, the standard normal density.

If 1)-3) is assumed, the usual analysis yields a normal posterior with mean $(n\bar{X} + \tau_0\theta_0)/(n + \tau_0)$ and precision $n + \tau_0$. When 3) is true, we are interested in the cost of using the scheme outlined in Section 2 compared to the usual analysis. This cost may be broken into two parts: a) the cost due to reducing to the (not fully efficient) estimator $\hat{\theta}$ and b) the cost of estimating the density of $\hat{\theta}|\theta$. These topics are discussed in the following two subsections. The gains to be made by our approach when 3) is false can be large and are investigated in Boos and Monahan (1982).

In both the following subsections, we required the exact sampling distributions for a set of robust estimators. The task of obtaining accurate estimates using Monte Carlo methods required considerable effort and is discussed in Section 4.

3A. Cost of Reducing to $\hat{\theta}$

Lindley (1956) proposed

$$I(E,\pi(\theta)) = \iint f(x|\theta)\pi(\theta)\log(f(\theta|x)/\pi(\theta))dxd\theta \quad (3.1)$$

as a measure of the expected information contained in an experiment E having likelihood $f(x|\theta)$ and prior $\pi(\theta)$. This measure has been used by numerous authors and Bernardo (1979) gives added support for I via an analysis of utility functions. The use of I may be appropriate when inference about θ is desired but no specific decisions have been formulated.

Lindley (1956) gives the following example. If E consists of n independent observations from a normal distribution with mean θ and known precision τ and $\pi(\theta)$ is normal with mean θ_0 and precision π_0 , then $I(E,\pi(\theta)) = \frac{1}{2}\log(1+n\tau/\tau_0)$.

In general, if we reduce to a statistic $\hat{\theta} = T(X)$, then the expected information contained in $\hat{\theta}$ relative to $\pi(\theta)$ is

$$I(\hat{\theta},\pi(\theta)) = \iint f(x|\theta)\pi(\theta) \log(f(\theta|T(x))/\pi(\theta))dxd\theta \quad (3.2)$$

$$- \iint f(T|\theta)\pi(\theta) \log(f(0|T)/\pi(0))dTd0 .$$

When (3.2) is compared to (3.1), one can judge the information lost due to reducing to $\hat{\theta}$.

We have considered the situation mentioned in 1)-3) above: n observations are each normal $(\theta,1)$ and $\pi(\theta)$ is normal (θ_0,τ_0^{-1}) . Note that in this simple location model I is invariant with respect to changes in θ_0 . The estimators $\hat{\theta}$ studied were 10% and 20% trimmed means, the median, and the Hodges-Lehmann (H-L) estimator: $\text{median}\{(X_i+X_j)/2,\ 1 \le i \le j \le n\}$. Table 1 reports the quantity $\exp\{2(I(E,\pi(\theta)) - I(\hat{\theta},\pi(\theta)))\}$ because for the estimators $\hat{\theta}$ considered, the true distributions of $\hat{\theta}$ are *very closely* approximated by normal distributions. In fact, the entries in Table 1 can be almost reproduced by using $(\tau_0+n)/(\tau_0+\tau_n)$, where n/τ_n is given in the last row of each estimator's results. As one would expect, the loss of information increases as the variance of the prior increases. Note that the variance of the median has a curious dip as one goes from $n = 5$ to $n = 10$ due to the definition median $= X_{(3)}$ for $n = 5$ and median $= [X_{(5)} + X_{(6)}]/2$ for $n = 10$.

Table 1. Loss of Information Due to Use of $\hat{\theta}$ Instead of $\bar{X}$.

$\hat{\theta}$	Variance of Prior	n = 5	n = 10	n = 20	n = 40
10% trim	0.1		1.026	1.036	1.045
	0.5		1.044	1.050	1.054
	2.0		1.051	1.054	1.057
	n·Var $\hat{\theta}$		1.052	1.055	1.057
20% trim	0.1	1.041	1.062	1.087	1.109
	0.5	1.093	1.108	1.123	1.133
	2.0	1.121	1.125	1.133	1.139
	n·Var $\hat{\theta}$	1.135	1.133	1.137	1.141
Median	0.1	1.112	1.161	1.269	1.375
	0.5	1.275	1.301	1.407	1.480
	2.0	1.379	1.360	1.450	1.507
	n·Var $\hat{\theta}$	1.433	1.385	1.466	1.517
H-L	0.1	1.024	1.036	1.040	1.043
	0.5	1.053	1.061	1.055	1.052
	2.0	1.068	1.070	1.060	1.054
	n·Var $\hat{\theta}$	1.075	1.074	1.061	1.055

Entries are $\exp\{2(I(E,\pi(\theta)) - I(\hat{\theta},\pi(\theta)))\}$, where E consists of a sample of n normal $(\theta,1)$ random variables with normal prior.

Evaluation of (3.2) provides an interesting application of the Fast Fourier Transform (FFT). Notice that for location estimators, the density $f(T|\theta)$ in (3.2) can be rewritten as $f_0(T-\theta)$, where f_0 is $f(T|\theta = 0)$. Thus, substituting $f(t|\theta)/\int f(t|0)\pi(0)d0$ for $f(0|t)/\pi(0)$ and then $f_0(t-\theta)$ for $f(t|\theta)$ we have

$$I(\hat{\theta},\pi(\theta)) = \iint f_0(t-\theta)\pi(\theta)\log\left[\frac{f_0(t-\theta)}{\int f_0(t-\theta)\pi(\theta)d\theta}\right] d\theta dt$$

$$= \iint f_0(t-\theta)\pi(\theta) \log f_0(t-\theta)d\theta dt \qquad (3.3)$$

$$- \iint f_0(t-\theta)\pi(\theta)\log[\int f_0(t-\theta)\pi(\theta)d\theta]d\theta dt .$$

The first integral in (3.3) can be reduced to $\int f_0(u)\log f_0(u)du$ through the change of variable $u = t - \theta$. Now, let $g(t) = \int f_0(t-\theta)\pi(\theta)d\theta$ so that the second integral of (3.3) becomes

$$\iint f_0(t-\theta)\pi(\theta)\log g(t)d\theta dt$$

$$= \int \log g(t)\{\int f_0(t-\theta)\pi(\theta)d\theta\}dt$$

$$= \int g(t)\log g(t)dt .$$

The first integral $\int f_0(u)\log f_0(u)du$ can be computed simply by a number of methods. However, this second integral $\int g(t)\log g(t)dt$ appears to be a double integral requiring "squared" as much work as the first. Suppose that we evaluate $g(t)$ using the midpoint rule over its support (or over most of it). Then

$$g(t_k) = \sum_j f_0(t_k-\theta_j)\pi(\theta_j) w_j .$$

If we put t and θ on the same scale so that $t_k = kh$ and $\theta_j = jh$, then

$$g(kh) = \sum_j f_0(h(k-j))\pi(jh)w_j$$

$$= \sum_j f_{k-j}\pi_j w_j ,$$

which is a convolution of f_k and $\pi_j w_j$. Thus, if M points are evaluated, the value of g at M points can be found using three FFT's requiring only $O(M\log M)$ work instead of $O(M^2)$. Once $g(kh)$ is available for $k = 1,\ldots,M$, computing $\int g(t)\log g(t)dt$ is then a simple task.

3B. The cost of Using an Estimated Posterior

We wanted to compare the posterior obtained by using the true distribution of $\hat{\theta}|\theta$ with that obtained from the bootstrap. Several particular items of interest are the posterior median and variance. A more global comparson of posteriors is the L_1 distance $d_{L_1}(f,g) = \int|f(x)-g(x)|dx$. Table 2 reports some of these results based on 200 Monte Carlo replications. (More complete

Table 2. Monte Carlo Estimates of L_1 Distances Between Posterior Densities.

			n = 5			n = 10			n = 20			n = 40		
Estimator	Mean	Variance	(P,T)*	(S,T)*	(P,S)*	(P,T)	(S,T)	(P,S)	(P,T)	(S,T)	(P,S)	(P,T)	(S,T)	(P,S)
$\bar{X}$	0.0	0.2	.25	.22	.111	.18	.17	.100	.15	.14	.096	.109	.114	.102
	1.0	5.0	.33	.29	.140	.22	.21	.115	.17	.17	.107	.119	.124	.109
20% trim	0.0	0.2	.29	.23	.14	.20	.19	.101	.17	.16	.094	.13	.13	.099
	1.0	5.0	.36	.31	.17	.25	.24	.118	.21	.20	.106	.14	.14	.106
Median	0.0	0.2	.51	.28	.38	.36	.24	.24	.37	.25	.25	.36	.23	.25
	1.0	5.0	.62	.39	.45	.41	.30	.26	.42	.30	.27	.40	.27	.26
H-L	0.0	0.2	.37	.23	.25	.26	.19	.17	.20	.16	.125	.139	.123	.113
	1.0	5.0	.43	.32	.27	.31	.24	.19	.22	.19	.136	.151	.136	.120

*(P,T) = d_{L_1} (Pristine,True), (S,T) = d_{L_1} (Smooth,True), (P,S) = d_{L_1} (Pristine,Smooth).

Note: Standard errors are from .006 to .05 if two decimals are given and from .001 to .005 if three decimals are included. Data and prior are normally distributed.

results may be found in Boos and Monahan, 1982.) Here, the number of bootstrap replications was $B = 400$ and the standard errors of the entries range from .001 to .05 . We actually used two versions of the bootstrap - the "Pristine" is Efron's original suggestion and the "Smooth" gives bootstrap samples from a smoothed empirical distribution function having mean $\bar{X}$ and variance $(n-1)^{-1}\Sigma(X_i-\bar{X})^2$. We note that the Smooth is much closer to the true posterior for the median and the H-L and only a small improvement for $\bar{X}$ and the 20% trimmed mean. The fact that the H-L is actually a median accounts for its similarity to the median for small samples. At $n = 80$ the first row for $\bar{X}$ is .091, .094, and .101 .

Some computational details are appropriate here. The accuracy that would be desired for computing the normalization constant (2.4) for a single problem had to be modified in light of the fact that this task was surrounded by the main Monte Carlo replication loop of size 200. Thus less accuracy in computing (2.4) and

$$d_{L_1}(\pi(\theta|x),\hat{\pi}(\theta|x)) = \int|\pi(\theta|x) - \hat{\pi}(\theta|x)|d\theta$$

was tolerated but the error was kept an order of magnitude below the final Monte Carlo standard errors using the extended Simpson's rule mentioned previously. The posterior median was computed using quadratic interpolation appropriate for a function integrated by Simpson's rule. However, constant interpolation was used if the quadratic interpolant was not nonnegative.

4. Additional Computational Techniques

4A. The True Distribution of $\hat{\theta} - \theta$ Using a Monte Carlo Swindle

We needed to table very accurately (but in an easily retrievable form) the sampling distribution under normality of our four robust estimators. The method used is an interpolation by cubic splines of the sampling density estimated via a location swindle (see Andrews, et al., 1972, or Gross, 1973).

Let $T_{k,n}(Z)$ represent the value of estimator k (e.g., a 10% trimmed mean) for sample size n and data vector Z. Notice that all of the estimators here are location invariant:

$$T_{k,n}(Z+\gamma 1) = \gamma + T_{k,n}(Z)$$

for any scalar γ and where 1 is a column vector with all entries one. For all of this work, the vectors Z_i are i.i.d. multivariate normal with mean vector 0 and identity covariance matrix. Let $F_{k,n}(x)$ represent the distribution function of $\sqrt{n}\,T_{k,n}(Z_i)$ and $\bar{z}_i = 1^T Z_i/n$. Then the location swindle is applied as follows:

$$\begin{aligned}
F_{k,n}(x) &= \Pr(\sqrt{n}\,T_{k,n}(Z_i) \le x) && (4.1a)\\
&= \Pr(\sqrt{n}\,T_{k,n}(Z_i-\bar{z}_i1 + \bar{z}_i1) \le x) && (4.1b)\\
&= \Pr(\sqrt{n}\,T_{k,n}(Z_i-\bar{z}_i1) + \sqrt{n}\,\bar{z}_i \le x) && (4.1c)\\
&= E(E(I(\sqrt{n}\,T_{k,n}(Z_i-\bar{z}_i1) - x \le -\sqrt{n}\,\bar{z}_i)|Z_i-\bar{z}_i1 = Z^*)) && (4.1d)\\
&= E(\Phi(x-\sqrt{n}\,T_{k,n}(Z_i-\bar{z}_i1)) && (4.1e)\\
&= E[\Phi(x-\sqrt{n}\,(T_{k,n}(Z_i)-\bar{z}_i))] . && (4.1f)
\end{aligned}$$

Notice that $\bar{z}_i$ is independent of the vector $Z_i - \bar{z}_i1$ so that the inner expectation of line (4.1d) above is just $\Phi(x-\sqrt{n}\,T_{k,n}(Z^*))$, where Φ is the standard normal df. Thus an estimate of $F_{k,n}(x)$ is constructed by

$$\hat{F}_{k,n}(x) = \frac{1}{N_r}\sum_{i=1}^{N_r} \Phi(x-\sqrt{n}\,\{T_{k,n}(Z_i) - \bar{z}_i\}), \quad (4.2)$$

where N_r is the number of replications of the vectors Z_i of length n . An estimate of the density is easily obtained by differentiation:

$$\hat{f}_{k,n}(x) = \frac{1}{N_r}\sum_{i=1}^{N_r} \phi(x-\sqrt{n}\,\{T_{k,n}(Z_i) - \bar{z}_i\}). \quad (4.3)$$

The expression (4.3) gives merely some points where the density is evaluated. Because N_r is so large (10000 or more), $\hat{f}_{k,n}(x)$ is not a practical estimate of the density. Instead, a set of points $\{x_i,\ i = 1,33\}$ were chosen equally spaced on the interval $(-6,+6)$, i.e., $x_i = 3(i-17)/8$. Expression (4.3) was then evaluated at $\{x_i\}$ to obtain $\hat{f}_i = \hat{f}_{k,n}(x_i)$. These pairs of values $\{(x_i,\hat{f}_i),\ i = 1,33\}$ can then be interpolated to obtain an estimate of the density of $\sqrt{n}\,T_{k,n}$ at every $x \in [-6,+6]$. The interpolation technique chosen here was cubic splines; the "extra" condition on the splines was chosen to be the derivative condition at the endpoints, for which estimates f_1 and f_{33} were obtained by evaluating the derivative of $\hat{f}_{k,n}$ at $x = \pm 6$ (x_1 and x_{33}) from (4.3). Let $\hat{f}^*_{k,n}$ denote the final estimate, with $\hat{f}^*_{k,n} \equiv 0$ outside $|x| \le 6$. Some remarks are in order:

1) The advantage of the swindle is the reduction in variance due to the high correlation between $T_{k,n}(Z_i)$ and $\bar{z}_i$.

2) There is a choice of whether to interpolate $\{\hat{F}_{k,n}(x_i)\}$ or $\{\hat{f}_{k,n}(x_i)\}$; the latter carries more information.

3) There is no guarantee that $\hat{f}^*_{k,n}$ will be non negative.

4) Equally spaced knots $\{x_i\}$ yielded a better estimate in preliminary work than unequally spaced.

5) The range $[-6,6]$ was chosen somewhat arbitrarily. The hope was that it would be large enough to contain most of the probability mass, yet not so large that the interpolant might turn negative in trying to fit an exponential function in the tails with a cubic polynomial.

6) Symmetry is imposed by averaging; replace $\hat{f}_i$ by

$$\hat{f}_i = \hat{f}_{34-i} = \tfrac{1}{2}[\hat{f}_{k,n}(x_i) + \hat{f}_{k,n}(x_{34}-x_i)] \quad (4.4a)$$

and also

$$\hat{f}'_i = -\hat{f}'_{34-1}$$

$$= \tfrac{1}{2}\left[\frac{d}{dx}\hat{f}_{k,n}(x)\Big|_{x=x_1} - \frac{d}{dx}\hat{f}_{k,n}(x)\Big|_{x=x_{33}}\right]. \quad (4.4b)$$

7) The support of the estimate could be extended beyond the interval $[-6,6]$ by fitting a decreasing curve to $\hat{f}_1$ and $\hat{f}'_1$ at x_1 and similarly for x_{33}. An exponential curve was used in some preliminary tests but this appears to be unnecessary.

The replication size for this task was $N_r = 250{,}000$ and the accuracy is difficult to assess but appears to be remarkably good. The estimates are nonnegative over $[-6,6]$ and their integrals differ from one by no more than 2×10^{-6}. The interpolated values have a relative standard error of about 10^{-3}. Comparisons with results in Andrews, et al. (1972) yield no contradictions. Comparisons with two cases where the sampling distribution is known (1) the median with $n = 5$ and (2) the mean can be seen in Table 3.

Table 3. Distances Between Exact and Swindle-Spline Density Estimates.

Criterion	Median, n = 5	Mean, any n
L_1	1.7×10^{-4}	9.6×10^{-5}
L_2	6.4×10^{-5}	5.4×10^{-5}
Weighted L_2	2.3×10^{-5}	2.8×10^{-5}
Kolmogorov-Smirnov	9.7×10^{-5}	1.3×10^{-4}

Note: For F and G with densities f and g $L_1 = \int|f-g|$, $L_2^2 = \int|f-g|^2$, weighted $L_2^2 = \int|f-g|^2 dG$, Kolmogorov-Smirnov $= \sup_x|F(x)-G(x)|$.

4B. Fast Computation of the H-L Estimator

A major computational problem arose with the decision to include the Hodges-Lehmann location estimator

$$\hat{\theta} = \text{median}\{(X_i+X_j)/2\ ,\ 1 \le i \le j \le n\} \quad (4.6)$$

among the other estimators. Sorting of the X_i's is an acceptable cost but computing $\hat{\theta}$ directly requires $O(n^2 \log n)$ work. Inverting the Wilcoxon statistic is faster $O(n \log n)$ but yields only an approximation to $\hat{\theta}$ (see McKean and Ryan, 1977). Fast methods for *exact* computation of $\hat{\theta}$ can be found in Johnson and Kashdan (1978) and Johnson and Mizoguchi (1978). With no code known to be extant, the first task was to implement an algorithm by Johnson and Kashdan (1978). Their method follows the "divide-and-conquer" theme:

$S_0 = \{(X_i+X_j),\ 1 \le i \le j \le n\}$; $m = 0$;

while it's a good idea *do*

Find a partition element a_m ;

Let L_m be the elements of S_0 that are less than a_m ;

if $|L_m| > k$ *then* $S_{m+1} = S_m \cap L_m$

else $S_{m+1} = S_m \cap L_m^c$

end while;

Here "it's a good idea" means $|S_m| > n$; otherwise finish by sorting S_m. Also, a_m is chosen to be the weighted median of row medians and will cut off at least ¼ of S_m at every step. This implementation HLFEST was used in the Monte Carlo swindle work (Section 4A), but improvements were sought; too much time was spent finding a_m. Improvements were

1) Choose a_m randomly (random row median) from S_m (á là QUICKSORT).

2) $a_0 = 2 \cdot \text{median of } \{X_1,\ldots,X_n\}$.

3) If $a_m = a_{m-1}$, choose a_m = midrange of S_m (tiebreaker).

The resultant algorithm HLQEST is superior to any other exact method, faster than the approximate method in small samples $(n \le 10)$ and only slower in large samples $(n \ge 100)$ by less than a factor of 3.

In both HLFEST and HLQEST, the expected number of partitions is $O(\log n)$ and each partition step requires $O(n)$ work. Thus, the expected computational complexity of both is $O(n \log n)$.

5. Examples

"Stylized sensitivity curves" were introduced in Andrews, et al. (1972) to study the effect of outliers on parameter estimates. Basically, a "sample" consists of the expected values of the order statistics from a random sample of size $n - 1$ from the standard normal distribution and the nth observation is x. Then one plots the parameter estimate versus x to get an idea of how the estimate changes with different x values. In our case each x value generates a posterior distribution, so we considered $x = 0, 1, 2, 5,$ and 10 with $n = 10$ and a flat prior on the location parameter θ. Figure 1 displays these five curves for the 20% trimmed mean using what we call the Symmetric Pristine bootstrap. This latter bootstrap draws samples from the distribution which places mass $(2n)^{-1}$ at the sample points $x_1,\ldots,x_n$ and also at $2\hat{\theta}-x_1,\ldots,2\hat{\theta}-x$. This bootstrap ensures that the estimated likelihood (bootlihood) is centered over $\hat{\theta}$ and makes sense if one really believes that the data is from a symmetric distribution. The related five curves from the usual Pristine bootstrap look very similar to Figure 1 but are somewhat different in the tails for $|x|>1$. Table 4 illustrates this fact by reporting the quantiles of the two sets of posteriors. Note how the left tail of the Pristine posterior thickens as x gets large.

Figure 1

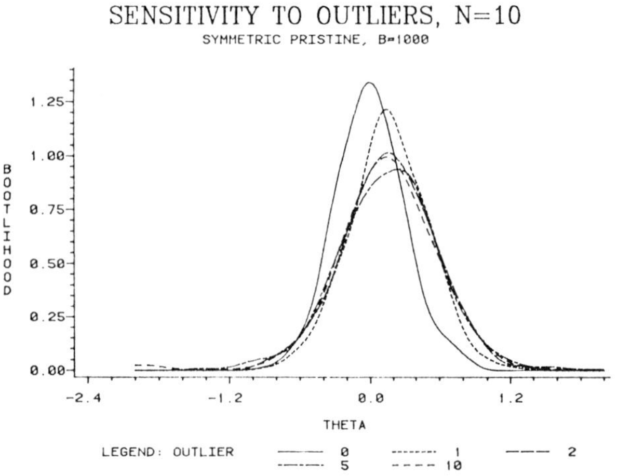

The second example concerns Darwin's data on the differences in height of 15 self- and cross-fertilized plants found in Fisher (1960, p. 37) and reanalyzed by Box and Tiao (1973, Ch. 3). Figure 2 gives results for $\bar{X}$ and the 20% trimmed mean using a flat prior. The reference curve (unbroken line) is a t distribution with 14 degrees of freedom centered at $\bar{X} = 20.933$, with scale factor $s/\sqrt{n} = 9.746$. This is the posterior we get when assuming normality and using $\sigma^{-1}d\theta d\sigma$ as a prior. The Pristine bootstrap of $\bar{X}$ is very close to this t distribution. The other two curves are the posteriors obtained by using the Pristine and Symmetric Pristine bootstrap on the 20% trimmed mean. Because the data is skewed

Table 4. Posterior Quantiles from 20% Trimmed Mean for Sensitivity "Samples."

x	Bootstrap	.025	.05	.50	.95	.975
0	Pristine	-.63	-.52	-.01	.50	.61
	Symmetric	-.59	-.49	.00	.53	.65
1	Pristine	-.50	-.40	.16	.77	.90
	Symmetric	-.54	-.42	.16	.72	.83
2	Pristine	-.66	-.53	.19	.81	.93
	Symmetric	-.65	-.51	.17	.81	.93
5	Pristine	-.99	-.74	.14	.80	.92
	Symmetric	-.76	-.56	.17	.86	1.03
10	Pristine	-1.85	-1.44	.17	.82	.94
	Symmetric	-.80	- .58	.15	.86	1.02

Note: The sample values are $\pm$ 1.485, $\pm$ .932, $\pm$ .572, $\pm$ .275, 0.0, and x. At $x = 0$, $\hat{\theta} = 0$, and at $x \geq 1$, $\hat{\theta} = .155$. $B = 1000$ and standard errors of the median are of the order $\pm$ .01 to $\pm$ .02 and for the more extreme quantiles $\pm$ .03 to $\pm$ .1.

to the left, the Pristine posterior is moved to the right of $\hat{\theta} = 25.8$ with median 29.5 (recall the reflection about $\hat{\theta}$ in (2.2)). We feel the Symmetric Pristine is more appropriate here because differences have a tendency to be symmetrically distributed. Although the data (-67, -48, 6, 8, 14, 16, 23, 24, 28, 29, 41, 49, 56, 60, 75) appears to have two outliers, Figure 2 indicates that the data is more normal than one might think and $\bar{X}$ may be the preferred estimator.

Figure 2

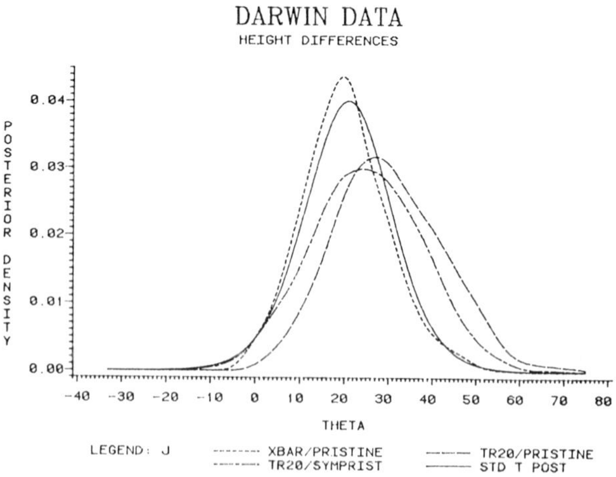

References

Andrews, D. F., Bickel, P. J., Hampel, F. R., Huber, P. J., Rogers, W. H., and Tukey, J. W. (1972). *Robust Estimates of Location: Survey and Advances*. Princeton University Press, Princeton, NJ.

Bernardo, J. M. (1979). Expected information as expected utility. *Ann. Statist.* 7, 686-690.

Boos, D. D., and Monahan, J. F. (1982). A robust Bayesian approach using bootstrapped likelihoods. In preparation.

Box, G.E.P., and Tiao, G. C. (1973). *Bayesian Inference in Statistical Analysis*. Addison-Wesley, Reading, Mass.

Box, G.E.P. (1980). Sampling and Bayes' inference in scientific modelling and robustness. *J. R. Statist. Soc.* A 143, 383-430.

Efron, B. (1979). Bootstrap methods: Another look at the jackknife. *Ann. Statist.* 7, 1-26.

Fisher, R. A. (1960). *The Design of Experiments*. Hafner, New York.

Gross, A. M. (1973). A Monte Carlo swindle for estimators of location. *Appl. Statist.* 22, 347-353.

Johnson, D. B., and Kashdan, S. D. (1978). Lower bounds for selection in $X + Y$ and other multisets. *J. Assoc. Computing Machinery* 25, 556-570.

Johnson, D. B. and Mizoguchi, T. (1978). Selecting the k-th element in $X + Y$ and $X_1 + X_2 + \ldots X_m$. *SIAM J. Computing* 7, 147-153.

Kao, S., and Monahan, J. F. (1977). Comparison of density estimators. *Proc. 1977 Stat. Comp. Sect., Amer. Statist. Assoc.*, 266-271.

Lindley, D. V. (1956). On a measure of the information provided by an experiment. *Ann. Math. Statist.* 27, 986-1005.

McKean, J. W., and Ryan, T. A. (1977). An algorithm for obtaining confidence intervals and point estimates based on ranks in a two-sample location problem. *ACM Trans. Math. Software* 2, 183-185.

Novick, M. R., and Ramsay, J. O. (1980). PLU robust Bayesian decision theory: Point estimation. *J. Amer. Statist. Assoc.* 75, 901-907.

User Interfaces to Data Analysis Systems

Chair: James J. Thomas, Pacific Northwest Laboratory
Chair: John Chambers, Bell Laboratories

AN EXPERT SYSTEM FOR REGRESSION ANALYSIS

William A. Gale and Daryl Pregibon
Bell Laboratories, Murray Hill, NJ 07974

ABSTRACT

Powerful tools for statistical data analysis are now widespread and are in use by non-statisticians. While the computational processes of data analysis have thus been made available, without statistical expertise to guide the analysis, these tools are subject to misuse. In response to this danger, we have attempted to put some statistical expertise into software.

This paper reports work in progress in expert software for regression analysis; that is, software which emulates some of the interaction between a client and an expert statistical consultant. It is anticipated that the software will also operate in learning mode to acquire information from human experts, and in tutorial mode to teach about regression analysis.

Keywords: *automated consultation, frame-based systems, production rules, knowledge-based programming, statistical software, statistical strategy.*

1. INTRODUCTION

Current statistical software provides the user with the mechanics of doing data analysis. This consists of subroutines for calculating summaries, graphical display facilities, and an environment for data manipulation and management. Such a system does little for those not well versed in the strategy of doing data analysis. Questions such as

> What do I look for?
>
> When do I look for it?
>
> How do I look for it?
>
> Why do I look for it?
>
> What do I do when I find it?

are not addressed by current software. Answers to these questions make up what we call the strategy of doing data analysis. The need for software which incorporates strategy has been stated quite forcefully by Chambers (1981).

Strategy is a result of statistical training and experience; it has both rigorous and heuristic aspects. Currently available languages to express strategy are either too vague for use on a computer (English), or too specific to match the heuristic components of strategy (procedural computer languages). Therefore, providing software to give strategic guidance requires developing a suitable means of expression, as well as developing an expression of statistical knowledge. Expert systems have provided high level languages suited to knowledge-based programming in several application areas (Duda and Gashnig, 1981) and look promising for our statistical domain (Chambers, Pregibon, and Zayas, 1981). Where developed, they have usually been used for consultation by human experts but sometimes for teaching. We hope to provide both functions.

We are building a prototype expert system for linear regression analysis. Currently, the system handles only simple linear regression, but some groundwork for multiple linear regression is in place. Linear regression is a well enough understood area of statistics that we can focus on expressing its strategy in a form suitable for computers. It is also a widely used statistical technique, so that the practical utility of software strategic guidance should be assessable. The strategy being developed for regression analysis is described in section 3.

In developing the means for expressing statistical strategy, we have begun building a set of tools which can be used in various ways. One tool for this work manages "production rules" (if *premise* then *conclusion*). Production rules are used to represent explicitly heuristics and small pieces of statistical knowledge. The conclusions drawn by the production rules are recorded using a specialized data base manager. By deliberately choosing an English-like appearance for the data base language, the rules become readily intelligible to a nonprogramming domain expert. Invocation of rules is guided by a tree-like structure representing broader aspects of statistical knowledge. These tools and others used in building the current prototype are discussed in section 4.

The prototype system consists of two main parts:

- a statistical computing system to do the mechanics of the analysis, and
- an interpreter which guides the strategy of the analysis.

The statistical system we use is the **S** system and language for data analysis (Becker and Chambers, 1981). It requires no further development apart from specialized procedures that we are supplying for implementing tests required by the production rules. We are primarily concerned with the development of the interpreter and the necessary code for interpreting. We chose to write the interpreter in LISP (Winston and Horn, 1980).

The user interacts with the interpreter which spawns requests to the statistical computing system. Results of inferences made by the interpreter are presented to the user and a menu of possible responses is provided. The interpreter processes this response and continues the analysis until successfully satisfying all the rules, or reaching a stage in the analysis where expert human intervention is required. The user's interaction with the system is described further in the next section.

2. APPEARANCE OF THE EXPERT SYSTEM TO THE USER

This section compares the user interface of the expert system with the underlying S system. The S system is typical of current advanced statistical software systems in providing many possible computations, but little or no interpretation and guidance. The expert system, sitting on top of **S**, is designed to provide these functions.

The basic request in **S** is

regress(x,y,w)

meaning to regress y on x with weights w. When this command is given to **S**, the system replies (assuming that x, y, and w are defined) with the results of the computation :

- An intercept, standard error, and t-value for each variable and the intercept;
- The residual standard error, the multiple r-squared, the number of points, and an aggregate F test with its degrees of freedom;
- The covariance matrix of the coefficients; and
- The correlation matrix of the coefficients.

The user is expected to make interpretations based on the t-values, the multiple r-squared, the F test, etc. This in itself assumes a considerable amount of knowledge on the part of the user. For the user who is even more sophisticated, the **S** system provides ample opportunity to make plots of residuals, to make further calculations, to change weights, etc. However, notice that the basic command did not even mention other possibly interesting commands. The user must know what the other interesting things to do are, how to do them, and how to draw appropriate conclusions.

The basic command for the expert system is

(regress y on x with w).

The extra "on" and "with" clarify the positional roles. The "with w" is optional. The interpreter then begins by asking how much the user wants to hear from the system. The user's response determines how much the system explains of what it does as it does it. The more experienced users will presumably want less explanation. Other queries to personalize the system's responses are planned, including queries about the thoroughness of the analysis and the expertise of the user. These facilities will permit a variety of people to use the system productively.

Assuming that the specified data sets are known to the **S** system when called by the interpreter, the analysis begins by making tests. So long as each test succeeds, another test is made. In the (rare) case that all tests succeed, *i.e.* no problem is found, the system reports the results of the regression. Under greater verbosity conditions, the results of the individual test statistics are reported with an interpretation of its severity as large, moderate, or small. Under maximum verbosity, the user is given a chance to ask about the meaning of the tests.

In the more common case that some test fails, the expert system attempts to diagnose the problem and suggests a way to fix it. The user is always asked whether the proposed change is acceptable, and may at this time ask what the proposed change means, and why it is suggested. When asked why, the system reviews the conclusions and rules which led to the suggested action.

The explanation mechanism is an on-line lexicon, a simplification of a suggestion by Greg Edwards (personal communication). The user needs only know that technical words and phrases in an explanation, rule, or other output is defined in the lexicon. The lexicon items refer to other lexicon items by this same mechanism. The system notes when an item the user wanted explained is not available. As a fall back, references into standard tutorial texts and to journal articles are available.

If the user accepts a suggested change, the change is made and the resulting regression is reexamined from the start. If the user rejects the change suggested, other possible changes are suggested. If all suggestions are turned down, the expert system suggests that the user get expert human help. It does not provide the results of the regression in this case but instead, a summary of the findings, suggestions, and interactions with the user is available. In most cases this will give the resident human expert a head start in straightening out the problem.

The expert system only knows about a fixed set of tests and fix-up procedures. It will never make tests, nor suggest changes outside its repertory. The system imposes a structure on these tests and changes which reflect current trends in data analysis. We call this structure *strategy,* and it is the topic of the next section.

3. A STRATEGY FOR REGRESSION ANALYSIS

The strategy we have implemented has been and continues to be developed by analyzing actual data analysis sessions. Dozens of regression problems have been used in this study. For each problem, special attention was given to why a particular test was being applied, why a particular plot was being displayed, how a particular conclusion was obtained, and what user-supplied information would have helped in guiding inferences. From an initial study of the diaries from these sessions, a tentative strategy was formulated. This has been successively refined by doing more sessions and redoing earlier ones with this tentative strategy in mind. Iteration has left us with the current strategy outlined below.

A regression problem can be represented as a triple {data; model; fitting method}. The model and fitting method specifications require the data to satisfy certain assumptions. Failure to meet these requirements is often the cause of poor analyses.

The user presents the system with his triple via a regression request which nearly always specifies a linear model and fitting by least squares. The system's goal is to derive, in consultation with the user, an associated triple {data*; model*; fitting method*} which better satisfies the assumptions underlying an analysis by linear models. Strategy is the explicit formulation of the mapping from {data; model; fitting method} to {data*; model*; fitting method*}.

Our strategy begins with an initial model-independent scrutiny of the data. This is done partly to protect against a poor choice of model, but also serves to draw the user's attention to peculiarities in the data (*e.g.* if the values of y are equally spaced). In addition, some of the information which is elicited from the user at this stage may also be needed in later stages (*e.g.* the units that y is recorded in).

The next stage consists of an assessment of model adequacy. This is primarily concerned with the linearity of the relationship between y and x. If non-linearity is detected, then parametric and non-parametric transformations of the data are used to achieve or enhance linearity. This stage poses perhaps the most serious challenge to the system since assessing linearity from a plot is something that human experts do better than their software counterparts. In addition, automated correction of an observed non-linearity is a non-trivial, complex, and controversial task.

The final stage of the analysis consists of an examination of the fitting method. This includes methods of detecting and correcting variance heterogeneity, violations of independence, and outlying and influential data points. The presence of any of these problems should not dramatically affect the choice of model made in the previous stage, especially since robust/resistant methods are used quite liberally there. The real importance of the last stage is to fine tune inferences.

The {data; model; fitting method} triple serves to define major stages of data analysis. Within each of these, substages are also present. The detailed picture of the substages in the model assessment (linearity) stage is displayed as a hierarchial tree structure in Figure 3.1. The internal nodes in the figure represent specific possible problems given that non-linearity is a problem. The terminal nodes (leaves) of the tree of nodes represent possible suggestions for modifying the model.

FIGURE 3.1. A partial diagram of the currently implemented statistics strategy.

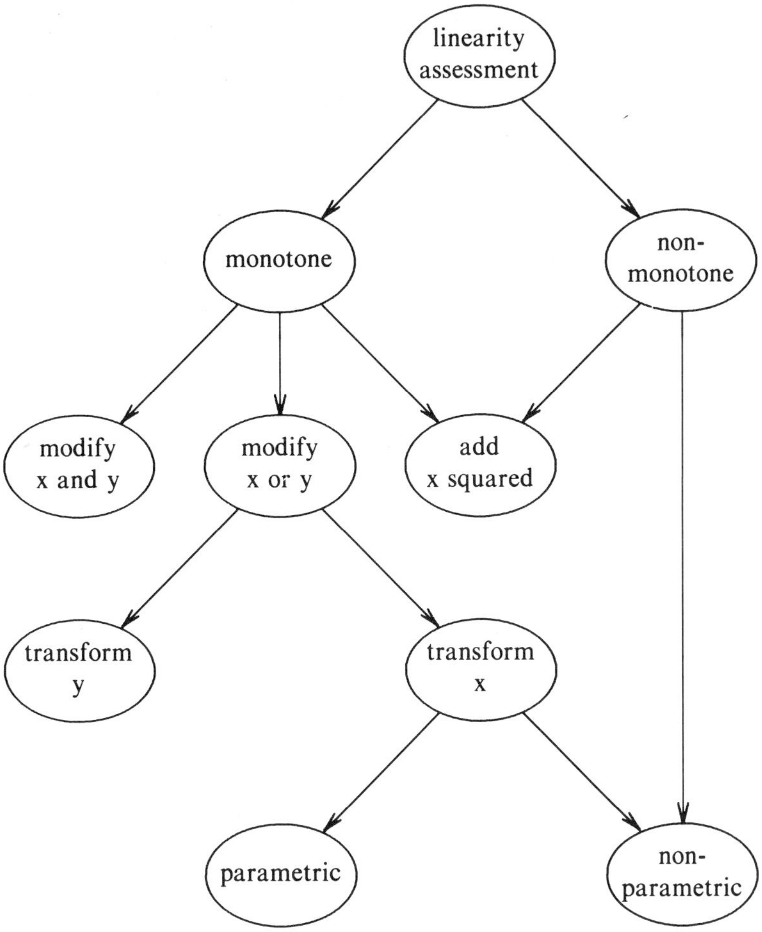

FIGURE 3.2. Examples of some production rules relevant in the context of assessing an observed nonlinearity. Note that these rules are not applicable outside this context.

RULE trigger.modifyxory.6:
if the distribution of x is severely skewed to the right,
then revise the plausibility index for transforming x by adding 15.

RULE confirm.ptransx.1:
if the F-test for parametrically transforming x is significantly large,
then assert that we can parametrically transform x.

RULE refine.ptransx.4:
if 0.5 lies between the upper and lower limits on the power for transforming x
and if the units of x are counts,
then revise the plausibility index for the square root transformation of x by adding 10.

The nodes of the tree represent macro units of knowledge which we call frames. Associated with each node or frame, is a collection of tests, facts, and heuristics. If there is a definitive test for a problem, then the node and its descendents will only be considered if the test is passed. Otherwise the node represents a tentative hypothesis and an exploration of its descendents is undertaken. Usually heuristics applicable to the data set will guide the search, but if none are applicable, the search is depth first (taking the leftmost child node rather than an adjacent sibling node).

Heuristics and other micro units of knowledge are expressed in production rules. In our prototype system, we use production rules in three different ways. "Trigger" rules are used to rank competing hypotheses. For each hypothesis a plausibility index is maintained. Trigger rules increment or decrement the plausibility indices of competing hypotheses. The trigger rule in Example 3.2 is invoked in the frame "modify x or y". The rule is one which increases the plausibility index of transforming x (as opposed to transforming y) by 15 units, this value being chosen heuristically. "Confirmation" rules are used to decide if a particular frame and its descendants should be pursued in more detail. The confirmation rule in Figure 3.2 is invoked in the "parametric" frame. If the premise of this rule is true, an active attempt will be made to parametrically transform x. "Refinement" rules are used to fine tune changes that the system has found to be necessary. The refinement rule in Figure 3.2 is used in selecting a power for transforming x. We consider powers in a data-dependent portion of the range from 1 to -1. For particular values of the power, a plausibility index is maintained. Refinement rules increment or decrement the plausibility indices of competing powers.

The data analysis strategy outlied above has been implemented in our prototype system. The details of this implementation are the topic of the next section.

4. HOW IT IS BUILT

This section discusses the internal structure that supports the strategy described in the previous section. This internal structure is displayed in Figure 4.1, which is discussed below. The intent of the structure is to be a flexible research tool allowing changes to any part of the system.

Figure 4.1 shows modules of the system as rectangles, or in one case as a blob. The arrows in the figure show calls to functions of other modules. The modules shown by rectangles are written to provide some limited service, with a few functions to access the service. The module shown by a blob is written to glue the others together.

At the top of the figure are the modules which are specific to the statistics application. These consist of the modules with the statistics rules and the statistics frames, and because it deals with them, the tasks module. Those lower down do not know that they are working in a statistics expert system, and could be used in other systems.

The system starts with a call to the *control module*. This module mainly provides a stack of tasks that need to be done.

The *frame processing* module manages storage and retrieval in frames. Winston and Horn (Chapter 22, 1981) provide a good introductory description of frames and useful functions for managing them. A frame allows storage of any kind of object under a named slot of a named frame. It has been used here to collect similar kinds of information about problems, tests, and changes that might be made. In particular, slots can be used to store lists of rules which are relevant in detecting problems and suggesting changes. The use of frames to guide the invocation of rules was suggested by Aikens (1980).

The *rule processing* module provides the inference mechanism used by the system. Winston and Horn (Chapter 18, 1981) provide a good introduction to rules and functions for managing them. We have implemented two basic means of using rules in our system, called "forward inference" and "backward chaining".

Under backward chaining, the system is given a set of rules and a proposition to verify or disprove. If the proposition is known (by the data base) to be true or false, the question is settled. Otherwise, the backward chaining mechanism looks for a rule that asserts the desired proposition in its conclusions. If it finds such a rule, then it attempts to establish the truth of each condition of that rule. This can be done either directly or by further recursion through rules. The recursion is sharply controlled in our application by handing the backward chainer a limited set of possibly relevant rules. The backward inference mechanism is used to establish hypotheses that certain problems exist or that a certain change would be useful. Backward inference operates on confirmation rules.

FIGURE 4.1. Schematic diagram of the internal structure of the system.

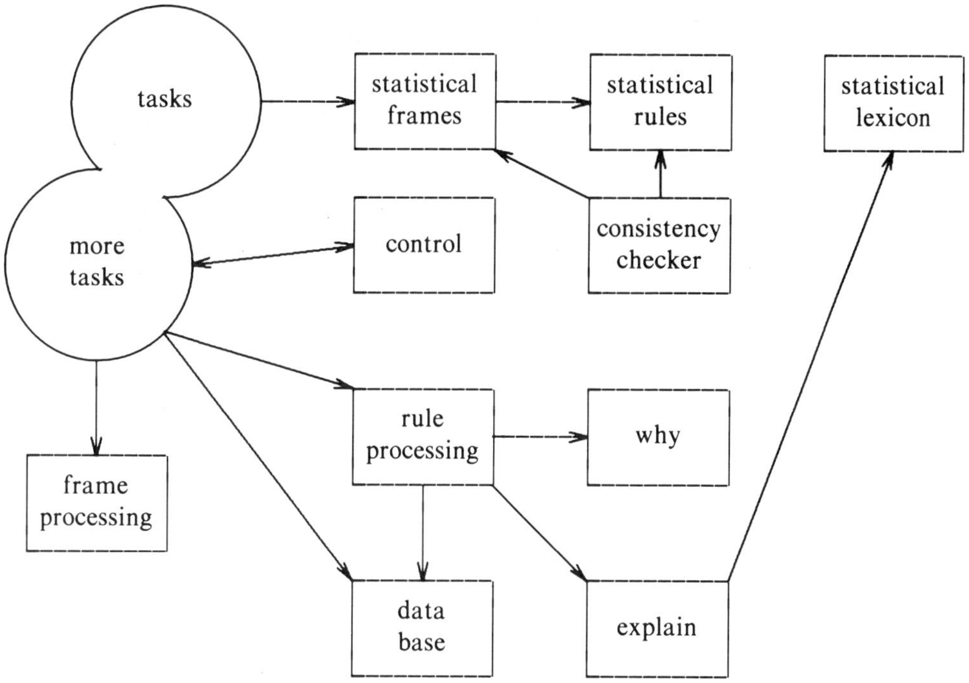

FIGURE 4.2. Internal (LISP) representation of production rules listed in FIGURE 3.2.

```
(rule trigger.modifyxory.6
  (if (right skew of x is large))
  (then (modify: do consider transform x with revised plausibility = plausibility + 15)))

(rule confirm.ptransx.1
  (if (F-test for parametrically transforming x is large))
  (then (assert: can parametrically transform x)))

(rule refine.ptransx.4
  (if (lower limit on power for transforming x does equal <= 0.5)
      (upper limit on power for transforming x does equal >= 0.5)
      (units of x are counts))
  (then (modify: power for transform x does equal 0.5
```

Under forward inference, the system is handed a set of rules which it examines sequentially. If it establishes that the hypotheses of any such rule are met, then it takes the action indicated. Forward inference is used to highlight particularly likely problems or changes, and to refine the suggestion that a particular change will be useful. Forward inference operates on trigger and refinement rules.

The *why* module administers a stack and a log. The stack contains currently uncertain propositions in a dynamic upper part, and established facts in a frozen lower portion. A why request reads the entries from the stack. The log provides a complete record of actions taken. It now provides debugging help, but may augment the entries on the stack in the future.

The *explain* module administers an on-line lexicon. If a request matches an entry exactly, the entry is located and printed. Otherwise it matches the longest initial substring from the user's request, and asks if the user wants to see the corresponding entry. If the user declines, the request is saved for the designers to study.

The *data base* stores labeled N-ary relations known to be true or false. It provides storage for constant symbols and constant numbers. (That is, it does not provide storage for variables, sets, or numerical ranges.) It can be queried by constant or variable symbols, by constant numbers, ranges of numbers, numerical variables, or numerical operations such as maximum and total.

The data base also provides a query language which can be written so that it resembles English. This idea was taken from ROSIE (Fain *et al.*, 1981). An English-like query language allows rules to be written in such a way that they can be shown to users in explanation of actions being suggested. The internal form of the rules paraphrased in Figure 3.2 is shown in Figure 4.2. Comparison shows the relatively small differences between the English version and the pseudo-English version.

The *consistency checker* module is a debugging tool comprised of a separately invoked set of functions. It can make certain static tests on sets of rules and frames. For instance, slots in frames which represent child nodes should hold only names of other frames.

5. FUTURE DIRECTIONS

This paper has described our prototype system for guided regression analysis. It is a working system currently running on a VAX 11/780 under the UNIX™ operating system. We feel that we have come a long way though we fully acknowledge that we still have a long way to go.

The system does not know about any of the useful plots that are associated with various statistical tests. We would like the system to provide graphical output to the user, and accept graphical input as well. The organization of this aspect of the system will require more work on the interface between the S system and the LISP interpreter.

We have obtained input from other statisticians on our work, but the majority of this has been concerned with quite general issues. We hope to involve other statisticians in further development and fine tuning of the regression strategy.

Benchmarks should be formulated that will show what the statistical limits of the system are. We hope our work will stimulate research in such areas.

The set of rules and frames for data editing and fitting method assessment require more work. The lexicon entries are only a demonstration of feasibility now. The automatic checking of input, or debugging aids in general, are currently very primitive.

All other areas need extensive polishing of function and efficiency. It should be possible to revise the system's knowledge rather than destroying it all after a change is made. There may need to be some option for backtracking on the part of the user. The explanations leave much to be desired in readability, and the data base is quite inefficient.

REFERENCES

Aikens, J.S. (1980). *Prototypes and Production Rules,* Stanford Heuristic Programming Project Memo HPP-80-17: Stanford University, CA.

Becker, R.A. and Chambers, J.M. (1981). *S --- A Language and System for Data Analysis,* Computer Information Service, Bell Laboratories: Murray Hill, NJ.

Chambers, J.M. (1981). "Some Thoughts on Expert Software," Proc. 13th Symposium on the Interface: Pittsburgh, PA.

Chambers, J.M., Pregibon, D., and Zayas, E. (1981). "Expert Software for Data Analysis: An Initial Experiment," Proc. 43rd Session ISI : Buenos Aires, Argentina.

Duda, R.O. and Gashnig, J.G. (1981). "Knowledge Based Expert Systems Come of Age," *Byte,* **September,** 238-247.

Fain, J., Gorlin, D., Hayes-Roth, F., Rosenchein, S., Sowizral, H., and Waterman, D. (1981). *The ROSIE Language Reference Manual,* The Rand Corporation: Santa Monica, CA.

Winston, P.H. and Horn, B.K.P. (1980). *Lisp,* Addison Wesley: New York, NY.

A USER INTERACTION MODEL FOR MANIPULATION OF LARGE DATA SETS*

James J. Thomas
Pacific Northwest Laboratory

ABSTRACT:

The process of interactive data analysis on large data sets can be inhibited if not made impossible by a poorly designed interactive operating environment. This paper describes a two-way interaction model to illustrate the impact of large data sets on interactive data analysis with particular emphasis on the data manipulation language. This interaction model takes into account many of the principles in human factors and cognitive psychology. The model illustrates parallel as well as sequential environments for data manipulation with a high degree of control for the data analysis process. Examples of interaction sequences to illustrate the presented concepts are provided from an interactive data editor specifically designed for editing and subsetting large data sets. Experience gained in implementing a system tailored to analyze large data sets shows that the data set size has a direct impact on the human interface to a data management and analysis system.

Keywords: Data Management, Data Manipulation Languages, Large Data Sets, Interaction Style, Human Factors

INTRODUCTION:

The methods of interaction form the bridge between the problem solver and the computer during interactive statistical data analysis. In the 1970's the methods of this interaction had been considered of secondary importance [1]. Because of the development of desktop computing and professional workstations that combine capabilities in data analysis, graphics, and data base management into interactive systems, there is a new emphasis on the interaction methods. There has been a clear trend towards emphasizing human factors and interaction style on data base systems [2]. With large data sets the methods of interaction are critical because the initial steps in data analysis of large data sets are exploratory [3]. This unstructured, iterative process requires a highly interactive interface that allows the user to concentrate on the problem rather than the interaction language.

The exploratory data analysis process is partly characterized by extensive data manipulation requirements involving multiple operating and temporary data analysis environments. These temporary environments, along with a greater emphasis on interaction to reduce catastrophic errors with large data sets, prompted the development of an interaction model for data manipulation. For global operations involving access to all or a large portion of a data file, the consequences of erroneous handling of the file increase exponentially as the size of the file increases [4]. Use of an interactive data editor [5] in the Analysis of Large Data Sets (ALDS) project at PNL [6-8] also indicates that data analysts are very much aware of these consequences and, therefore, seek a higher degree of interaction, accuracy, control, and verification in the interface between the data analyst and the data management software.

Another motivation for developing the model was to express the impact of large data sets on a data manipulation language. In the future, data analysis systems will include extensive data manipulation facilities commonly found in DMBS packages. Also there will be a breadth of other support, like report quality presentation aids, interactive graphics, and banks of library tools for statistical data analysis. These tools, and others will be prohibitively expensive to develop by a single source. Therefore the use of standard software modules will be common practice. This will place a greater emphasis on the glue (method for module-to-module communication) and the interaction techniques (human-to-module communication).

Interaction style plays an important part in the human-to-module interaction. The impact of varying interaction styles for data manipulation languages has been addressed in several disciplines including cognitive psychology, human factors, and computer science [9-17]. Also several sets of guidelines have been developed from these disciplines [2,18-25]. Most address interaction style in general with only a few comments

* This work was performed for the U.S. Dept. of Energy under contract #DE-AC-06-76-RLO-1830

regarding the impact of large data sets. The interaction model presented here is mostly independent of interaction style. This model applies equally well to interfaces involving voice or graphical interaction.

The remainder of this paper presents the terms used to describe the model, the interaction model and underlying concepts, the impact of large data sets on the interaction model, examples of interaction sequences, and conclusions.

DESCRIPTIVE TERMS USED IN MODEL DEFINITION

The model presented here uses terms that often have different meanings in the technical community based on their context. To help define and clarify the scope of the model as well as the terms being used, the following definitions are included:

Interaction Model - An interaction model represents all human-computer interactions. These interactions can be at varying levels from simple keystrokes to phrases or commands. For the purpose of this paper the syntax- or style-dependent levels are not addressed. Only the semantic interaction concepts are discussed to lead towards a goal of interaction style independence.

Data Manipulation Language - The data manipulation language is both the semantic and syntactic interaction between the human and the data management modules. This interaction could be voice, graphic (e.g. menu), or normal command strings entered from a keyboard. The presented model will address only the semantic interpretation of commands.

Data Manipulation Environment - Data manipulation in the analysis of large data sets relies heavily on exploratory techniques requiring both confirmation and exploratory analysis environments to proceed in parallel [3]. These analysis environments directly result in multiple data manipulation environments. An example is analyzing a data set in one environment on one device and another related data set in a second environment on a second device where one would be the exploratory and the other would be the confirmatory analysis environment.

Data Model - The user's view of the data structure is the data model. In the examples discussed in this paper, a relational model was chosen with the user's model being a two-dimensional table of cases by variables, with cases being represented by the rows in the table, and variables being represented by the columns.

Phrase-Structured Commands - Phrase-structured commands are developed from a logical grouping of English phrases into commands. These phrases are similar to those used in SEQUEL [13] except the logical phrases themselves may be used as commands, thus providing phrase-like commands. An example of such a command would be setting specifications for subsequent commands as in a "where" clause:

```
WHERE height > 25
```

In phrase-structured commands this WHERE clause is itself a command that can be specified separately or combined with other clauses to form what is normally seen in data base management languages. The following command contains three phrases:

```
SUBSET FROM file2 WHERE volume > 3.14
```

The three clause key words are SUBSET, FROM, and WHERE. The included interaction model allows individual use of phrases or combined uses for those desiring lengthy commands. This takes into account two important human factors guidelines: short commands and consistent interaction tempo [23]. This tempo and quick feedback [22] are important factors in a two-way interactive data manipulation system.

Temporary Data Manipulation Environments - A temporary data manipulation environment is a technique to temporarily define the scope of an environment for hypothesis testing in the scientific process. This is much like the environments established by block structured languages allowing automatic storage allocation. These environments are an integral part of exploratory analysis, as data manipulation is the dominant activity in formulating the hypothesis. These environments must provide dynamic scope definitions and versatile data management capabilities. It is quite desirable to be able to traverse a tree structure of these temporary environments, allowing restart of the analytical process when a null path has been discovered by a data analyst.

Command Environment - The command environment is established to include all specifications that affect or control the command, including case, variable, and value selections.

Virtual Subset - A virtual subset (V-set) [5] is a definition of a logical grouping of data. A virtual subset provides all the information necessary to have access to data that satisfy the condition or relation that defines the virtual subset. The virtual subset itself contains no data, although the perceived view from the user is as if a true data set exists. The opposite of a V-set is a physical subset or P-set. The P-set physically contains all records defining the subset plus a mapping to the original master file and the relational expression which created the P-set. V-sets are intended to be dynamically created containing a temporary referencing structure through the master data set.

INTERACTION MODEL

The interaction model will be described as a bi-level model representing the data manipulation environments, the interaction events, the feedback locations, and interaction control. The interaction model focuses on the interactive exploratory data analysis environment. In particular the major emphasis will be on the data manipulation portion of the data analysis process. The model was derived from observations of statisticians at PNL using a system designed for the analysis of large data sets.

To describe the data manipulation interaction model, five symbols will be used as defined in Figure 1. The first level of the model is the data manipulation environment level. This is illustrated in Figure 2. It is common for the user to operate in the global data manipulation environment for a short time to identify the general characteristics of the master large data set or cluster of data sets. Then through a series of interactions the user creates several testable subgroups (V-sets) to determine the feasibility of the hypothesis. These subgroups are formed in temporary data manipulation environments and are local to the master data manipulation environment. They are only active when the master file is active. An example of a set of testable subgroups could be created by classifying cases by unique type of missing values. A single pass through the data set can define all the virtual subsets classified by different types of missing values, allowing each to be tested for significance. A detailed example is given later to illustrate a sample session. The temporary definitions (V sets) are an integral part of the manipulation of large data sets. They provide fast retrieval and efficient storage for exploratory analysis. Data analysts go back and forth from the master environment to the virtual environment. Several temporary environments can be active at any time, providing parallel analysis paths. It is then straightforward to perform similar operations on different subsets and produce comparative statistics. It is conceivable that these operations would be performed in a logically or physically parallel manner and implemented in a multiprocessor system. Each of these environments should be dynamically interruptible with the complete data manipulation environments being restored on reentry.

The second level of the interaction model is more detailed. This level presents most of the usual interaction sequences found in common data manipulation languages.

The command environments established within the data manipulation environment are modeled in Figure 3. To describe this level, the commands typically found in data manipulation languages have been divided into four classes:

A) <u>Specification commands</u> - These commands establish environments for subsequent operations. Examples include commands such as WHERE clauses or case and variable selection clauses.

B) <u>Information commands</u> - These commands present information about the status of specification commands or list data as requested.

C) <u>Manipulation commands</u> - These commands perform all selections and transformations on the data, including deletions, insertions, and replacements of individual values.

D) <u>Control commands</u> - These commands control the flow of grouped commands such as block structure in programming languages. An example of such a command might be one which executes a command file.

We assume a startup condition for entry to the top-level environment which will provide a complete status of which file and variables are available for data manipulation during any of the operating environments. These should be available to the user at any time, although only on request because of the possibility of a large number of variable names. If one were using a menu interaction style, a set of menus would be presented at this time. If a command style were being used, a prompt would be issued. It is important that the status information be present, not just the typical prompt of

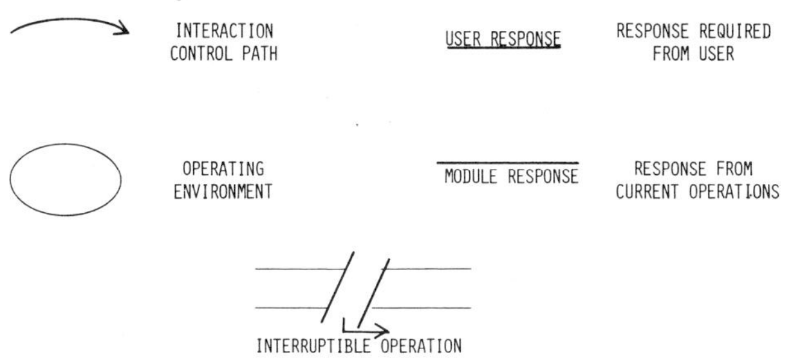

FIGURE 1 Interaction Model Notation

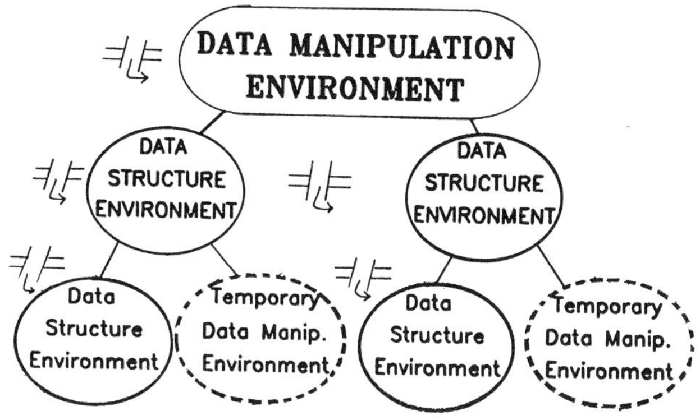

FIGURE 2 Level 1 DM Interaction Model

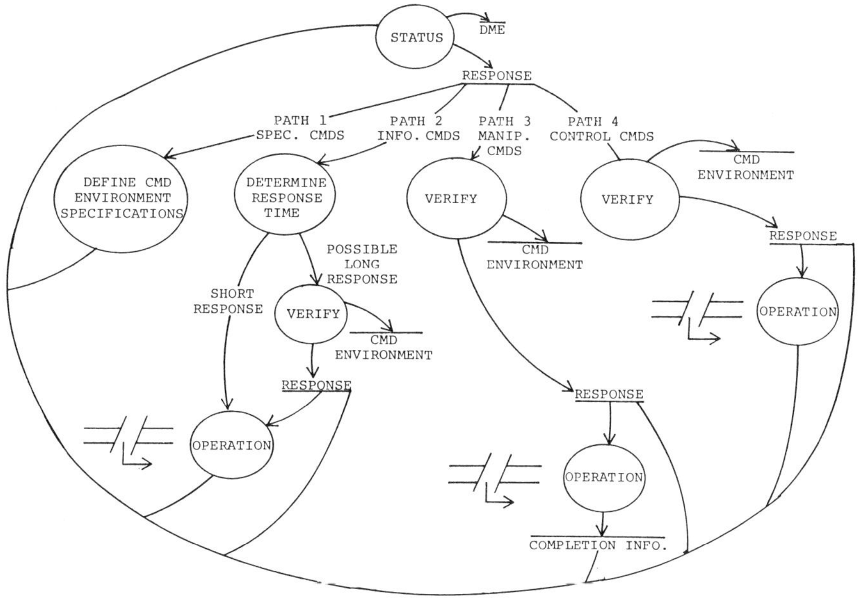

FIGURE 3 Level 2 DM Interaction Model

':', ';', etc. Let's assume the user has made a response at the top of our interaction model. From here there are four interaction paths that may be traversed.

Path 1
For specification commands the environment is established and the command is executed. Then the status is reset, if necessary to indicate the proper operating environment, and the user is prompted for the next command. An interesting technique that has proved quite useful is to include in the prompt the general operating status at all points of interaction. This will be illustrated in later examples.

Path 2
On traversal of path 2 an internal check is made to determine the estimated length of command execution. If the response is expected to be lengthy, then the user is asked to verify or review the condition under which this path is to be executed. This verify or review facility indicates to the user how the computer interpreted the commands and conditions for continuing. This is an integral part of two-way communication in a data manipulation language dialogue between the user and the data manipulation modules. Examples of specifications that would be included for verification are variable or case selection or the relational selection criteria. After response to the verification option the operation will continue (or be bypassed if the response is negative). The verification process was installed as an option that could be turned off in the data manipulation language described later in this paper. However, in approximately one year of operation, the verification option has only rarely been turned off, which demonstrates the critical importance of two-way communication between the user and the data manipulation modules.

An important concept noticeable in several places in this model is that of a context-sensitive interrupt. These interrupts are user invoked, with responses that indicate the operations taking place, the status of that operation, and a request for a response from a user to continue or abort. While many systems offer dynamic interrupt capabilities, few offer the critical characteristics of being context sensitive and allowing users the option of re establishing the environment at the interrupt point.

Path 3
Data manipulation commands are the most heavily used commands. They modify or group data. The verification process is again optional. This two-way communication has been a vital component to ensure the level of confidence and control in exploratory data analysis. After a positive response, the operation is initiated. Note that all operations are dynamically interruptible. An example would be a REPLACE operation on 100,000 cases. During the REPLACE operation the user could interrupt, yielding a context-sensitive response of an operation in progress, the position of the operation in the file, and the number of values replaced. The user would then be given the option to abort or continue. On completion the operation would then respond and indicate the total number of values modified.

Path 4
Control commands provide block structure for other commands in the other three categories. These control commands have all the characteristics of the individual commands being executed. This includes dynamic interruption of an executing command file, giving the user the ability to stop the processing in the block structure.

THE IMPACT OF LARGE DATA SETS ON THE INTERACTION MODEL

The Data Manipulation Interaction Model and resultant DM capabilities have been directly affected by the goals of being able to comfortably manipulate large data sets interactively. Some of the model features noted below are loosely coupled to the largeness of data sets, and work equally well on small-to-medium-size data sets. Others, however, were only conceived based on the opportunities offered by large data sets.

The use of temporary data manipulation environments and temporary virtual subsets is a direct result of working in an exploratory data analysis environment on large data sets. Multiple copies of files or even subsets of files are often impractical. Therefore storing only the definitions of subsets is a viable concept in the large data set environment. V-set definitions can be used for both referencing and manipulating groups of data from the user's data model. The user perceives the availability of the entire subset. This reduces the number of working files and storage requirements.

Phrase-structured commands are a result of the efforts to incorporate good human factors principles, using short commands with consistent tempo of interactions. Also an effort has been made to reduce the complexity and length of the commands prior to obtaining feedback from the system. In working with large data sets the commands tend to get complicated, particularly when multiple operations and command environments are specified on a single pass on a data set.

The auto-verify and review concept is a result of efforts to obtain two-way communication in a data manipulation language dialogue. The largeness of data sets encouraged the desire to reduce catastrophic errors.

Dynamic user control is required to provide complete control and status of operations in progress. On large data sets operations will take longer than a few seconds. Those longer operations should be interruptible for providing the status at any point.

Continual awareness of status is provided by means of several concepts: the auto verify, dynamic interrupts, command completion status, and status in the prompt. This continual user orientation information has been stated as being an important factor in man/display interfaces [21]. Having the computer keep the user aware of its status reduces the entropy in data manipulation interactions and allows better concentration on the operations to be performed.

EXAMPLES OF INTERACTION SEQUENCES:

The concepts presented can be demonstrated through the ALDS Data Analysis Laboratory currently implemented at PNL on a VAX 11/780 computer. This laboratory was created to meet specific needs, including manipulating and subsetting large data sets. To meet these needs an interactive data editor was developed [5]. The ALDS data editor (ADE) was designed specifically to aid the exploratory data manipulation operations required to analyze large data sets. The following are annotated examples illustrating interaction concepts.

CONCLUSIONS

Several conclusions can be drawn from the definition of this interaction model and the implementation to demonstrate the concepts. The goal of being able to interactively manipulate large data sets has a direct impact on the interaction between the human and the data base management modules. This impact will become greater as more data analysts become accustomed to working in highly interactive environments.

The data model gives a user the top-level view of the data, and the interaction model provides the techniques to interact with the data model. The interaction model concept helps define the top-level view of the data manipulation modules. Modeling this process has a significant effect on the design of a data manipulation system, including module construction, intermodule communication, interface of the data manipulation module to the operating system, and the human-to-module interactions. Any new system under consideration should use an interaction model as the first phase of the top-down design process. This provides a user's view of the entire system and has a substantial impact on the structure of the newly considered system. This interaction model has been useful in expressing the impact of large data sets on data manipulation languages.

ACKNOWLEDGEMENTS

The author wishes to thank the statisticians at PNL, guided by Wes Nicholson and Dave Hall, for their help and close relationship that provided the joint atmosphere where talents and experience in computer science and statistics can complement each other. Bob Burnett, Rik Littlefield, and Dan Carr have also provided valuable assistance in developing the presented concepts.

```
     *****ALDS Data Editor Selected*****

   | Enter edit filename
   |
   | SAMPLEFILE.SDB
   |
 1 | Do you want to backup the data file Y/N?  N
   |
   | SAMPLEFILE opened for edit with 21,682 cases with 42 variables
   | per case
   |
   | THE VARIABLES ON THE FILE YOU ARE EDITING ARE:
```

```
   CASE_ID, SEQNO, DATE, TIME, TEST1, TEST2, CLASS1, CLASS2, SM1,
   SM2, SM3, SM4, SM5, SM6, SM7, SM8, SM9, SM10, SM11, SM12, SM13,
1  SM14, SM15, SM16, SM17, SM18, SM19, SM20, SM21, SM22, SM23, SM24,
   SM25, SM26, SM27, SM28, SM29, SM30, SM31, SM32, SM33, SM34,

   ADE:M1>>VARSEL SM4:SM8

   ADE:M1>>LIST 10
   CONDITION : NONE
   TRANSFORM : NONE
   VARIABLES SELECTED:  SM4, SM5, SM6, SM7, SM8,
   CASE SELECTIONS:  NONE
   DO YOU WANT TO CONTINUE Y/N?  Y

2  SEQ NO        SM4         SM5           SM6          SM7          SM8
        1    7.00000    23.00000      19.00000     16.00000      2.00000
        2    3.00000    29.0000       32.00000     21.00000      8.00000
        3    3.00000    26.00000      24.00000     18.00000      6.00000
        4   13.00000    38.00000      36.00000     33.00000     20.00000
        5    8.00000    14.00000      10.00000      6.00000      3.00000
        6   15.00000    22.00000      18.00000     13.00000      1.00000
        7    8.00000    16.00000      12.00000      8.00000      3.00000
        8   13.00000    19.00000      15.00000     10.00000      6.00000
        9    0.00000     0.00000       0.00000      0.00000      0.00000
       10   15.00000    27.00000      24.00000     20.00000      8.00000

   ADE:M1>>CASSEL 1,10,15,20:25

   ADE:M1>>LIST 10
   CONDITION : NONE
   TRANSFORM : NONE
   VARIABLES SELECTED:  SM4, SM5, SM6, SM7, SM8,
   CASE SELECTIONS : 1, 10, 15, 20 : 25
   DO YOU WANT TO CONTINUE Y/N?  Y
3
   SEQ NO        SM4         SM5         SM6          SM7          SM8
        1    7.00000    23.00000    19.00000     16.00000      2.00000
       10   15.00000    27.00000    24.00000     20.00000      8.00000
       15   15.00000    21.00000    16.00000     12.00000      0.00000
       20   18.00000    24.00000    20.00000     16.00000      4.00000
       21    7.00000    31.00000    28.00000     24.00000     11.00000
       22   14.00000    24.00000    21.00000     16.00000      3.00000
       23   15.00000    23.00000    19.00000     16.00000      0.00000
       24   22.00000    28.00000    24.00000     19.00000      5.00000
       25   11.00000    24.00000    26.00000     27.00000     27.00000

   ADE:M1>>CONDITION SM6 > 20

   ADE:M1>>LIST ALL
   CONDITION : SM6 > 20.00000

   TRANSFORM : NONE
4  VARIABLES SELECTED:  SM4, SM5, SM6, SM7, SM8,
   CASE SELECTIONS : 1, 10, 15, 20 : 25
   DO YOU WANT TO CONTINUE Y/N?  Y

   SEQ NO        SM4         SM5         SM6          SM7          SM8
       10   15.00000    27.00000    24.00000     20.00000      8.00000
       21    7.00000    31.00000    28.00000     24.00000     11.00000
       22   14.00000    24.00000    21.00000     16.00000      3.00000
       24   22.00000    28.00000    24.00000     19.00000      5.00000
       25   11.00000    24.00000    26.00000     27.00000     27.00000

5  ADE:M1>>RESET

   ADE:M1>>CONDITION SM6 > 25
6
   ADE:M1>>SELECT ALL
   CONDITION : SM6 > 25.0000
```

```
TRANSFORM : NONE
VARIABLES SELECTED: NONE
CASE SELECTIONS:  NONE
DO YOU WANT TO CONTINUE Y/N?  Y

6    SELECTION PROCEEDING FROM 21,682 CASES

     ---INTERRUPT DURING SELECTION AT CASE 4329
     DO YOU WANT TO CONTINUE Y/N?  Y

     ---INTERRUPT DURING SELECT AT CASE 18,314
     DO YOU WANT TO CONTINUE Y/N?  Y

     11,452 CASES SELECTED

ADE:S1>>VARSEL SM4:SM8

ADE:S1>>LIST 10

CONDITION : SM6 > 25.00000
TRANSFORM : NONE
VARIABLES SELECTED:  SM4, SM5, SM6, SM7, SM8,
CASE SELECTIONS:  NONE
DO YOU WANT TO CONTINUE Y/N?  Y
7
SEQ NO        SM4         SM5         SM6         SM7         SM8
     2    3.00000    29.00000    32.00000    21.00000     8.00000
     4   13.00000    38.00000    36.00000    33.00000    20.00000
    12   15.00000    23.00000    26.00000    27.00000    26.00000
    21    7.00000    31.00000    28.00000    24.00000    11.00000
    25   11.00000    24.00000    26.00000    27.00000    27.00000
    26   15.00000    24.00000    26.00000    27.00000    27.00000
    28    8.00000    36.00000    33.00000    29.00000    16.00000
    29   11.00000    24.00000    27.00000    27.00000    27.00000
    41   15.00000    37.00000    34.00000    31.00000    17.00000
    58   15.00000    37.00000    52.00000    31.00000    17.00000

ADE:S1>>RAND 200

ADE:S1>>SELECT
RANDOM SPECIFICATION:200
8 CONDITION : SM6 > 25.0000
TRANSFORM : NONE
VARIABLES SELECTED:  SM4, SM5, SM6, SM7, SM8,
CASE SELECTIONS : NONE
DO YOU WANT TO CONTINUE Y/N?  Y
200 CASES SELECTED FROM 11452

ADE:S1>>NWVAR
***ADD A NEW DEPENDENT VARIABLE*****
Enter a label (16 chars. or less): TOTALS

Enter a verbal description of the new variable:
  TOTALS OF SOME SAMPLE VARIABLES

Data type:  (R)eal, (I)nteger, or (C)haracter string?  I

9 Maximum value limit?  (Y or N)  N

Minimum value limit?  (Y or N)  N

How many values (cases) will be entered?  0

ADE:S1>>VARSEL SM4:SM7, TOTALS

ADE:S1>>LIST 10
CONDITION : SM6 > 25.0000
TRANSFORM : NONE
VARIABLES SELECTED:  SM4, SM5, SM6, SM7, TOTALS,
```

```
CASE SELECTIONS : NONE
DO YOU WANT TO CONTINUE Y/N?  Y

SEQ NO         SM4          SM5          SM6          SM7     TOTALS
     2     3.00000     29.00000     32.00000     21.00000         ##
    29    11.00000     24.00000     27.00000     27.00000         ##
9   128    15.00000     24.00000     26.00000     27.00000         ##
   313     7.00000     63.00000     63.00000     63.00000         ##
   321     3.00000     59.00000     59.00000     59.00000         ##
   357     8.00000     40.00000     40.00000     40.00000         ##
   372     6.00000     62.00000     62.00000     62.00000         ##
   512     7.00000     63.00000     63.00000     63.00000         ##
   514     7.00000     63.00000     63.00000     63.00000         ##
   546     7.00000     63.00000     63.00000     63.00000         ##
```

```
ADE:S1>>XFORM TOTALS = SM4 + SM5 + SM6 + SM7

ADE:S1>>CONDITION SM4 < 10

ADE:S1>>REPLACE ALL
CONDITION : SM4 < 10.0000
TRANSFORM : TOTALS = SM4 + SM5 + SM6 + SM7
VARIABLES SELECTED:  SM4, SM5, SM6, SM7, TOTALS,
CASE SELECTIONS: NONE
DO YOU WANT TO CONTINUE Y/N?  Y

        136 values replaced

ADE:S1>>CON

ADE:S1>>LIST 10
CONDITION : NONE
10
TRANSFORM : TOTALS = SM4 + SM5 + SM6 + SM7
VARIABLES SELECTED:  SM4, SM5, SM6, SM7, TOTALS,
CASE SELECTIONS: NONE
DO YOU WANT TO CONTINUE Y/N?

SEQ NO         SM4          SM5          SM6          SM7     TOTALS
     2     3.00000     29.00000     32.00000     21.00000         85
    29    11.00000     24.00000     27.00000     27.00000        ##
   128    15.00000     24.00000     26.00000     27.00000        ##
   313     7.00000     63.00000     63.00000     63.00000        196
   321     3.00000     59.00000     59.00000     59.00000        180
   357     8.00000     40.00000     40.00000     40.00000        128
   372     6.00000     62.00000     62.00000     62.00000        192
   512     7.00000     63.00000     63.00000     63.00000        196
   514     7.00000     63.00000     63.00000     63.00000        196
   546     7.00000     63.00000     63.00000     63.00000        196
```

1. Entry into the data editor includes the file descriptive information. Note that the prompt ADE:M1>> includes an M, indicating master file environment, and the number 1, indicating the positioning at the starting case (case sequence #1).

2. Selection and listing of variables SM4 through SM8. The verification information includes all lines from the CONDITION status through the required Y/N response.

3. Selection of specific cases is illustrated. Note the grouping of case numbers similar to the grouping of variables in the previous command. Also note the retention of previously specified variable selection criteria.

4. This illustrates selection by data value through use of the CONDITION command combined with selection criteria from earlier commands.

5. Reset all command environment specifications to default conditions.

6. This sequence illustrates forming a temporary data manipulation environment. Also illustrated are two dynamic interrupts invoked by typing a special control key during operation execution. The operation being performed is acknowledged and the specific case number currently

under consideration is shown. On completion the response indicates the number of cases selected.

7. Note the change in the edit mode from `M' to `S' in the prompt. This indicates a temporary DM environment (subset of the original file). A selection of variables and the first ten cases is performed.
8. This illustrates taking a 200-case sample from the 11,452 cases in the previously formed V-SET.

9. This illustrates creation of a new variable. Note that missing values fill cases which are not entered.

10. This illustrates specification of a transformation on the V-SET under a specified condition. Note the values replaced; the non-replaced values still contain the missing value symbol.

REFERENCES

1. Chambers, J. M., Computers in Statistical Research: Simulation and Computer-Aided Mathematics, Technometrics, Vol. 12, No. 1, Feb. 1970

2. Schneiderman, B., Improving the Human Factors Aspect of Data Base Interactions, ACM Trans. Database Syst. 3,4, Dec. 1978, pp.417-439

3. Tukey, J.W., Exploratory Data Analysis, Addison-Wesley Co., Reading Mass., 1977

4. Muller, M.E., Computers as an Instrument for Data Analysis, Technometrics, Vol. 12, No. 2, May 1970

5. Thomas, J.J., et al., "Data Editing on Large Data Sets", Computer Science and Statistics: 13th Symposium on the Interface, Pittsburgh, Pa., 1981

6. Nicholson, W.L., Analysis of Large Data Sets, Proceedings of the 1979 DOE Statistical Symp., Oak Ridge, Tn., Sept. 1980

7. Thomas, J.J., et al., "Analysis of Large Data Sets on a Minicomputer", Computer Science and Statistics: 12th Symposium on the Interface, Univ. of Waterloo, Waterloo, Ontario, Canada, May 10-11, 1975, pp.442-426

8. Burnett, R.A., "The Analysis of Large Data Sets Project -- Computer Science Research Areas", Proceedings of the 1979 DOE Statistical Symposium, Oak Ridge, Tn., September 1980, pp.205-208

9. Thomas, J.C., J.D. Gould, A Psychological Study of Query By Example, Proceedings of th AFIPS National Computer Conference. 1975, PP. 434-445

10. Lough, D.E., A.D. Burns, An Analysis of Data Base Query Languages, NTIS, U.S. Dept. of Commerce, AD/A-039 783, 1977

11. Boyce, R.F., and others, Specifying Queries as Relational Expressions, Proceedings of the IFIP Working Conference on Data Base Management, 1974

12. Reisner, P., Human Factors Studies of Database Query Languages: A Survey and Assessment, ACM Computing Surveys, Vol. 13, No. 1 March 1981

13. Reisner, P., Boyce, R.F., and Chamberlin, D.D., Human Factors Evaluation of Two Data Base Query Languages- Square and Sequel, Proc. Nat. Computer Conf. AFIPS Press, Arlington, Va, 1975, pp.447-452

14. Reisner, P., Use of Psychological Experimentation as an Aid to Development of a Query Language, IEEE Trans. Softw. Eng. SE-3(May 1977), pp.218-229

15. Thomas, J.C., Psychological Issues in Data Base Management, Proc. Third Int. Conference on Very Large Data bases, Tokyo, Oct 1977, pp.169-185

16. Welty, C., and Stemple, D.W., Human Factors Comparison of a Procedural and a Nonprocedural Query Language, ACM Trans. Database Syst. 1981

17. Treu, S., Interactive Command Language Design Based on Required Mental Work, Int. Journal Man-Machine Studies,Vol.7, 1975, pp. 135-149

18. Box, G.E.P., Science and Statistics, Journal of the American Statistical Association, December 1976, Vol. 71, No. 356, pp. 791-799

19. Ling, R.F., General Considerations on the Design on an Interactive System for Data Analysis, CACM, Vol. 23, No. 3, March 1980

20. Stonebracker, M., Rowe L.A., Observations on Data Manipulation Languages and Their Embedding in General Purpose Programming Languages, 3-rd VLDB, 1977

21. Engel, S.E., and Granda, R.E, Guidelines for Man/Dsiplay Interfaces, IBM Tech. Report, TR 00.2720, December 1975

22. Sterling, T.D., Guidelines for Humanizing Computerized Information Systems: A Report from Stanley House, CACM, Vol. 17, No. 11, Nov. 1974

23. Kennedy, T.C.S., The Design of Interactive Procedures for Man-Machine Communication, Int. Journal Man-Machine Studies Vol. 6, 1974, pp. 309-334

24. Sackman, H., Computer Systems Science and Evolving Society, New York: Wiley 1967

25. Martin, J., Design of Man-Computer Dialogues, England Cliffs, N.J.: Prentice Hall, 1973

RESTRUCTURING THE USER INTERFACE TO SEEDIS

Harvard Holmes
Lawrence Berkeley Laboratory

The Socio-Economic Environmental Demographic Information System (SEEDIS) is a large system of software and databases for the retrieval, analysis and display of geographically related information. In restructuring the interface to SEEDIS, we found the assistance of a graphic arts designer to be invaluable. Our users are almost entirely novice users. It is important that the user interface be a consistent conceptual model in itself, not a set of clues to what is "really happening". Above all, this consistency forms a stable background against which relevant changes can be perceived, rather than forcing the user to pick them out of the "noise" of cluttered, inconsistent user interfaces. Acquiring this new awareness of user interfaces is a difficult, yet rewarding, transition for programmers. Achieving a consensus on the "new look" of the user interface requires a fair amount of work. After this, the amount of actual coding required is surprisingly small.

DATA ANALYSIS IN THE UNIX ENVIRONMENT

Gary Perlman, University of California, San Diego

ABSTRACT

In this paper I discuss data analysis on the UNIX operating system and how the UNIX environment affect both the design and use of programs. UNIX is a highly interactive operating system and as such, is ideal for data analysis, allowing analysts to make immediate decisions based on intermediate results. UNIX provides facilities for directing the output of one program as the input to another and this has resulted in a program design philosophy unique to and ubiquitous in UNIX: to build modular programs that do one task well and that can be combined in many ways to form complex ones. The application of this philosophy to the design of data analysis programs in UNIX has resulted in the development of separate programs to validate, transform and re-format, enter and edit, print, and do calculations on data. From the user's point of view, programs are smaller and hence more portable to small systems, and can be used in a wide variety of contexts. I give examples of programs developed under the UNIX philosophy, and show how it leads to the development of automated interfaces for experimental design specification.

KEYWORDS: Interactive User Interface Design, Computer Statistical Packages.

In this article, I will discuss how the UNIX (TM Bell Telephone Laboratories) operating system (Richie & Thompson, 1974) supports data analysis, and how some of my data analysis programs (Perlman, 1980) developed under the influence of the UNIX environment. I begin with an overview of UNIX, and how its support of process control affects data analysis. Then I describe some programs developed for data analysis on the UNIX operating system. Finally, I discuss how many aspects of data analysis, particularly the specification of experimental designs, can be automated.

UNIX is an interactive operating system and as such is ideal for data analysis. Users generally sit in front of a terminal and repeatedly specify a program, its input, and to where its output should be directed. Users can immediately observe intermediate results of programs, and can make decisions based on them. One common decision is to use another program on such results.

It is possible to combine simple UNIX programs into more complicated ones. The implementors of UNIX made it possible to direct the output of one program into the input of another program. This linking of outputs to inputs is called "pipelining." Programs in a pipeline are connected with the pipe symbol, the vertical bar. For example, several programs can be joined together with a command like:

```
IO DATA | PROGRAM1 | PROGRAM2 | PROGRAM3
```

Here, a series of transformations of the file DATA is initiated by an input/output program called IO. (I will use the convention of capitalizing the names of programs and files, though in actual use, they would probably be lower case.) The output from IO is used as input to PROGRAM1 whose output is used as input (piped) to PROGRAM2 whose output is piped finally to PROGRAM3. In effect, PROGRAM1, PROGRAM2, and PROGRAM3 are combined to make a more complex program.

The ability to pipeline programs has led to a philosophy of modular program design unique to and ubiquitous in UNIX: to build program tools that accomplish one task well that produce outputs convenient for input to other programs. Convenience here means output stripped of unnecessary labeling information, and that is easily parsed by other programs. In UNIX, there are dozens of programs with general uses such as ones to search though or sort files, count lines, words, and characters in files, and so on. The philosophy is to have programs that can be used in a variety of contexts. This philosophy has been followed in the design of data analysis programs I will describe later, especially those for applying pre-analysis transformations.

Doing data analysis in a general programming environment overcomes some problems associated with many statistical packages. In a general environment like UNIX, users have easy access to all the programs that come with the system, as well as those locally developed. That means people doing data analysis in UNIX can use system editors, printing programs, and perhaps most importantly, they can control data analysis with the general command language used to control all program execution in UNIX. The UNIX command line interpreter is called the <u>shell</u> and it simplifies file input and output. It also provides the pipelining facilities mentioned earlier. The UNIX shell is a high level programming language in which users can write shell "scripts" that allow program control with primitives for condition testing and iteration. In short, doing data analysis in a general programming environment provides many resources lacking or weak in statistical packages.

While UNIX allows easy access to a wide variety of programs peripherally related to data analysis, such is not the case with most statistical packages. These usually have individual programs have many general utilities, such as data transformation, editing, and printing subroutines built in, making them larger than necessary, and hence less portable to small computers. This is necessary for statistical packages expected to run on a variety of operating systems where it is not clear what utilities are available. It is also a remnant of the 1960's batch processing philosophy when the major statistical packages were first developed.

Under the UNIX philosophy of modular design, data are transformed by specialized programs before being input to specific data analysis programs. The result is that data transforming functions are independent of analysis programs and are applicable in a wider variety of contexts.

Recall that the UNIX design philosophy of modularity is in support of pipelines of simple uni-purpose tools. An application of this philosophy to data analysis is to first transform data and pipe the transformed data to specific analysis programs. The following represents an example of just such a use.

IO DATA | TRANSFORM | ANALYZE

Writing programs to be used in pipelines require that their outputs be uncluttered and easily parsed by programs down stream. This requirement is satisfied by having all programs process data as human readable character files with fields separated by white space (blanks or tabs). While such free format slows processing, the slowdown is negligible compared to the time required for complex analyses. Free format also costs storage space, but space limitations do not affect the majority of users, and as the cost of storage goes down, this factor is even less of a problem. The requirement of putting data in plain files rather than binary code, or even the traditional fixed column FORTRAN formats makes the files easier for people to read, and increases their acceptability to all UNIX programs, such as system wide programs like editors and printing programs.

To be able to efficiently construct pipelines of programs requires that much of the task of the user be automated. If a special control language file were needed for each program in a pipeline, constructing analysis commands would be prohibitively time consuming, and error prone. It would also obliterate the advantage UNIX offers as an interactive system. In many cases, there is no need for a control language when programs are made intelligent enough to determine mundane properties of their inputs automatically. Delimiting fields with white space allows programs to count the number of fields per line, and UNIX file handling makes it easy to tell when the end of a file has been reached, which makes it easy to count lines as well as columns.

DESCRIPTIONS OF DATA ANALYSIS PROGRAMS

The best way to appreciate how data are analyzed in a UNIX environment is to see examples of their use. In this section, I describe some of the programs I developed for data analysis (Perlman, 1980). My major concern in designing them was to allow data analysis to be automated to such an extent that users had to interact with them minimally. This is desirable because people make errors, and the more chances they have to make them, the more they will. My goal was to reduce errors by removing opportunities to make them.

The programs have been designed to be easy to use, and small enough to fit on mini computers such as DEC PDP 11/45's, 11/34's, and 11/23's. I will first describe the format prescribed for the programs, and how people use the programs in the UNIX environment. The programs are of several different types:

Data Transformation. These programs are useful for changing the format of data files, for transforming data, and for filtering unwanted data. In addition, one program is useful for monitoring the progress of the data transformations.

Data Validation. These include programs for checking the number of lines and columns in data files, their types (e.g., alphanumeric, integer), and their ranges.

Descriptive Statistics. These procedures include both numerical statistics, and simple graphical displays. There are procedures for single distributions, paired data, and multivariate cases.

Inferential Statistics. These include multivariate linear regression and analysis of variance. Some simple inferential statistics are also incorporated into the descriptive statistics programs, but are used less often.

Table of Programs Described

Pre-Processing Programs	
ABUT	abut files
DM	conditional transformations of data
IO	control/monitor file input/output
TRANSPOSE	transpose matrix type file
VALIDATA	verify data file consistency
Analysis Programs	
ANOVA	anova with repeated measures
BIPLOT	bivariate plotting + summary statistics
CORR	linear correlation + summary statistics
DESC	statistics, frequency tables, histograms
PAIR	bivariate statistics + scatterplots
REGRESS	multivariate linear regression

Using UNIX

This section describes the typical use of UNIX and is meant to give non-users a brief introduction to its use. It may also provide a useful summary for somewhat experienced users who have little experience with constructing complex commands with pipelines. UNIX users generally sit in front of a terminal at which they repeatedly specify a program, the input to that program, and to where the output from the program should be directed. They specify this program, input, and output to a program called a "shell." The shell is most users primary way of interacting with UNIX. If the user does not specify from where the input to a program is to be read, the default "standard input" is the user's terminal keyboard. (For data analysis programs, this often is a mistake.) Similarly, if unspecified, the default "standard output" is the terminal screen. To override these default standard input and outputs, UNIX shells provide simple mechanisms called "redirection" and "pipelining." To indicate that a program should read its input from a file rather than the terminal keyboard, a user can "redirect" the input from a file with the "<" symbol. Thus,

```
PROGRAM < FILE
```

indicates to UNIX (really it indicates to the shell which controls input and output) that the input to the program named PROGRAM should be read from the file named FILE rather than the terminal keyboard. Analogously, the output from a program can be saved in a file be redirecting it to a file with the ">" symbol. Thus,

```
PROGRAM < INPUT > OUTPUT
```

indicates that the program PROGRAM should read its input from the file INPUT and put its output into a new file called OUTPUT. If the file INPUT does not exist, an error message will be printed. If the file OUTPUT exists, then whatever was in that file before will get destroyed. A mistake novices and experts alike should avoid is a command like:

```
PROGRAM < DATA > DATA
```

which might be used to replace the contents of data with whatever PROGRAM does to it. The effect of such a command is to destroy the contents of DATA before PROGRAM has a chance to read it. For a safer method of input and output, see the later discussion of the IO program.

The output from one program can be made the input to another program without the need for temporary files. This action is called "pipelining" or "piping" and is used to create one complex function from a series of simple ones. The vertical bar, or "pipe" symbol, ´|´, is placed between programs to pass the output from one into the other. Thus,

```
PROGRAM1 < INPUT | PROGRAM2
```

tells UNIX to run the program PROGRAM1 on the file INPUT and feed the output to PROGRAM2. In this case, the final output would be printed on the terminal screen because the final output from PROGRAM2 is not redirected. Redirection could be accomplished with a command line like:

```
PROGRAM1 < INPUT | PROGRAM2 > OUTPUT
```

In general, only one input redirection is allowed, and only one output redirection is allowed, and the latter must follow the former. Any number of programs can be joined with piping.

In general, UNIX programs do not know if their input is coming from a terminal keyboard or from a file or pipeline. Nor do they generally know where their output is destined. One of the features of UNIX is that the output from one program can be used as input to another via a pipeline making it possible to make complex programs from simple ones without touching their program code. Pipelining makes it desirable to keep the outputs of programs clean of annotations so that they can be read by other programs. This has the unfortunate result that the outputs of many UNIX programs are cryptic and have to be read with a legend. The advantages of pipelining will be made clear in the examples of later sections.

Data are most easily manipulated and analyzed if they are in what I will call the master data file format. The key ideas of the format of the master data file are simplicity and self documentation, and are derived from relational databases. The reason for this is to make transformation of data easy, and to be able to use a wide variety of programs to operate on a master data file. Each line of a master data has the same number of alphanumeric fields. For readability, the fields can be separated by any amount of white space (blank spaces or tabs), and, in general, blank lines are ignored. Each line of a master data file corresponds to the data collected on one trial or series of trials of an experiment. Along with the data, a set of fields describe the conditions under which those data were obtained. Usually, a master data file contains all the data for an experiment. However, in many cases, a user would not want all the data from an experiment from this file to be input to a program. Some parts may be of particular interest for a specific statistical test, or some data may need to be transformed before input to a data analysis program. In a later section, I will expand on the notion of a master data file, and show how it can be used to convey experimental design information implicitly.

PROGRAM DESCRIPTIONS

The programs described here were designed with the philosophy that data, in a simple format, can convey all or most of the information a program needs to analyze them. With data transforming utilities, the need for a special language to specify design information all but disappears. Users can implicitly specify design information by putting their data into specific formats.

The strategy I will use here is to describe the programs and give examples of how they are used. This is meant only to make the ideas of analysis with these programs familiar and should not be used as a substitute for the manual entries on individual programs. Only a few of the capabilities of the programs are described.

Transforming Data

In this section, I will describe programs for transforming data. The reason for describing these before statistical programs is that in most cases, user will want to transform their data before analyzing them. The general form of a command would thus be:

```
TRANSFORM < DATA | ANALYZE > OUTPUT
```

where TRANSFORM is some program to transform data from an input file DATA and the output from TRANSFORM is piped to an analysis program, ANALYZE, whose output is directed to an output file, OUTPUT.

ABUT: Abut Files

ABUT is a program to take several files, each with N lines, and make one file with N lines. This is useful when data from repeated measures experiments, such as paired data, are in separate files and need to be placed into one file for analysis (see PAIR and REGRESS). For example, the command:

```
ABUT FILE1 FILE2 FILE3 > FILE123
```

would create FILE123 with its first line the first lines of FILE1, FILE2, and FILE3, in order. Successive lines of FILE123 would have the data from the corresponding lines of the named files joined together.

IO: Control and Monitor Input/Output

IO is a general program for controlling input and output of files. It can be used instead of the standard shell redirection mechanisms and is in some cases safer. It can also be used to monitor the progress of data analysis commands, some of which can take a long time.

Catenate Files. IO has a similar function to ABUT. Instead of, in effect, placing the files named *beside* each other, IO places them one after another. A user may want to analyze the data from several files, and this can be accomplished with a command like:

```
IO FILE1 FILE2 FILE3 | PROGRAM
```

Monitoring Input and Output. IO also can be used to monitor the flow of data between programs. When called with the -m flag, it acts as a meter of input and output flow, printing the percentage of its input that has been processed. (In UNIX, it is common for options to be specified to programs by preceding letters by a dash to distinguish them from file names.) The program can also be used in the middle and end of a pipeline to monitor the absolute flow of data, printing a special character for every block of data processed.

Input and Output Control. Finally, it can be used as a safe form of controlling i/o to files, creating temporary files and copying rather than automatically overwriting output files. For example, IO can be used to sort a file onto itself with one pipeline using the standard UNIX SORT program:

```
IO -m FILE | SORT | IO -m FILE
```

The above command would replace FILE with a sorted version of itself. Because the monitor (-m) flag is used, the user would see an output like:

```
10% 20% 30% 40% 50% 60% 70% 80% 90% 100%
==========
```

The percentages show the flow from FILE into the SORT program (percentages are possible because IO knows the length of FILE), and the equal signs indicate a flow of about a thousand bytes each coming out of the SORT program. The command:

```
SORT FILE > FILE
```

would destroy the contents of FILE before SORT had a chance to read it. The command with IO, is both safer and acts as a meter showing input and output progress.

Saving Intermediate Transformations. In a command like:

```
IO FILE1 FILE2 | PGM1 | PGM2 | IO OUT
```

the intermediate results before PGM1 and before PGM2 are lost. IO can be used to save them by diverting a copy of its input to a file before continuing a pipeline:

```
IO FILE1 FILE2 | PGM1 | IO SAVE | PGM2 | IO OUT
```

Any of these calls to IO could be made metering versions by using the -m option flag.

TRANSPOSE: Transpose Matrix-Type Files

TRANSPOSE is a program to transpose a matrix-like file. That is, it flips the rows and columns of the file. For example, if FILE looks like:

```
1 2 3 4
5 6 7 8
9 10 11 12
```

then the command:

```
TRANSPOSE FILE
```

will print:

1	5	9
2	6	10
3	7	11
4	8	12

TRANSPOSE is useful as a pre/post-processor for the data manipulator, DM, as it reads from the standard input stream when no files are supplied.

DM: A Data Manipulator

DM is a data manipulating program that allows its user to extract columns (delimited by white space) from a file, possibly based on conditions, and produce algebraic combinations of columns. DM is probably the most used of all the programs described in this paper. To use DM, a user writes a series of expressions, and, for each line of its input, DM reevaluates and prints the values of those expressions in order.

DM allows users to access the columns of each line of its input. Numerical values of fields on a line can be accessed by the letter "x" followed by the column number. Character strings can be accessed by the letter "s" followed by the column number. Consider for example the following contents of the file EX1:

12	45.2	red	***
10	42	blue	---
8	39	green	---
6	22	orange	***

The first line of EX1 has four columns, or fields. In this line, x1 is the number 12, and s1 is the string ´12´. DM distinguishes between numbers and strings (the latter are enclosed in quotes) and only numbers can be involved in algebraic expressions.

Column extraction. Simple column extraction can be accomplished by typing the strings in the columns desired. To print, in order, the second, third, and first columns from the file EX1, one would use the call to DM:

```
DM s2 s3 s1 < EX1
```

This would have the effect of reordering the columns and removing column 4.

Algebraic Expressions. DM can be used to produce algebraic combinations of columns. For example, the following call to DM will print the first column, the sum of the first two columns, and the square root of the second column.

```
DM x1 x1+x2 "sqrt(x2)" < EX1
```

Note that the parentheses in the third expression requires quotes around the whole expression. This is because parentheses are special characters in the shell. If a string in either of the columns was not a number, DM would print and error message and stop.

Conditional Operations. DM can be used to filter out lines that are not wanted. A simple example would be to print only those lines with stars in them.

```
DM "if '*' C INPUT then INPUT else NEXT" < EX1
```

The above call to DM has one expression (in quotes to overcome problems with special characters and spaces inserted for readability). The conditional has the syntax "if-then-else." Between the "if" and "then" is a condition that is tested, in this case, testing if the one-character string '*' is in INPUT, a special string holding the input line. If the condition is true, the expression between the "then" and "else" parts is printed, in this example, the input line, INPUT. If the condition is not true, then the expression after the "else" part is printed, in this case, NEXT is a special control variable that is not printed and causes the next line to be read.

Data Validation

Before analysis begins, it is a good idea to make sure data are entered correctly. The programs described in this sub-section are useful for verifying the consistency of data files. Individual analysis programs do their own verification, so the programs described are, in practice, used to help find errors picked up by specific analysis programs.

VALIDATA: Check Data Validity

A master data file is assumed to have an equal number of fields per line. VALIDATA checks its input from the standard input or argument file and complains if the number of fields per line changes. After reading all its input, VALIDATA reports the number of entries of various data types for each column. The data types VALIDATA knows about include integer and real numbers, alphabetic, and alphanumeric fields, and some others. VALIDATA can be used to spot incorrect entries such as columns expected to be numerical that are not, and accidently entered invisible control characters.

DM: Range Checking on Columns

DM can be used to verify data as well as transform it. For example, to check that all numbers in column three of a file are greater than zero and less than 100, the following call to DM would print all lines that did not display that property.

```
DM "if !(x3>0 & x3<100) then INPUT else NEXT"
```

If non-numerical data appeared in column three, DM would report an error.

Descriptive Statistics

DESC: Describing a Single Distribution

DESC can be used to analyze a single distribution of data. Its input is a series of numbers, in any format, so that numbers are separated by spaces, tabs, or newlines. Like most of these programs, DESC reads from the standard input.

Summary Statistics. DESC prints a variety of statistics, including order statistics. Under option, DESC will print a t-test for any specified null mean.

Frequency Tables. DESC can print frequency tables, or tables of proportions, with cumulative entries if requested. These tables will be formed based on the data so they are a reasonable size, or they can be formatted by the user who can specify the minimum value of the first interval, and the interval width. For example, the following command would print a table of cumulative frequencies and proportions (cfp) in a table with a minumum interval value of zero (m0) and an interval width of ten (i10).

```
DESC i10 m0 cfp < DATA
```

Histograms. If requested, DESC will print a histogram with the same format as would be obtained with options used to control frequency tables. For example, the following command would print a histogram of its input by choosing an appropriate interval width for bins.

```
DESC h < DATA
```

The format of the histogram, as well as tables, can be controlled by setting options. The following line sets the minimum of the first bin to zero, and the interval width to ten, an appropriate histogram for grading exams.

```
DESC h i10 m0 < GRADES
```

PAIR: Paired Data Analysis

PAIR can be used to analyze paired data. Its input is a series of lines, two numbers per line, which it reads from the standard input. Options are available for printing a bivariate plot, which is the default when the program is called by its alias, BIPLOT. Other options control the type of output.

Summary Statistics. From PAIR's input, minimums, maximums, means, and standard deviations are printed for both columns as well as their difference. Also printed is the correlation of the two columns and the regression equation relating them. The simplest use of PAIR is with no arguments. To analyze a data file of lines of X-Y pairs, the following command will in most cases be satisfactory:

```
PAIR < DATA
```

Often the paired data to be analyzed are in two files, each variable occupying a single column. These can be joined with ABUT and input to PAIR via a pipe:

```
ABUT VAR1 VAR2 | PAIR
```

Or perhaps the two variables occupy two columns in a master data file. If the variables of interest are in columns four and six, the following command would produce the paired data analysis:

```
IO DATA | DM s4 s6 | PAIR
```

Scatterplots. With the "p" or "b" options, a scatterplot of the two variables can be printed. Alternatively, PAIR has an alias, called BIPLOT, which lets the user get a bivariate plot of a data file of X-Y pairs:

```
BIPLOT < DATA
```

CORR: Multiple Correlation
CORR can be used to get summary statistics for repeated measures data. Its input is a series of lines, each with an equal number of data. It prints the mean, standard deviation, minimum, and maximum for each column in its input. Then it prints a correlation matrix with all pairwise correlations. Like PAIR, columns from files can be joined with ABUT or extracted from files with DM.

Inferential Statistics

ANOVA: Multivariate Analysis of Variance
ANOVA performs multivariate analysis of variance with repeated measures factors (within subjects), and with unequal cell sizes allowed on grouping factors (between subjects). ANOVA reads in a series of lines from the standard input, each with the same number of alphanumeric fields. Each datum occupies one line and is preceded by a list of levels of independent variables describing the conditions under which that datum was obtained. The first field is some string indicating the level of the random variable in the design, and subsequent fields describe other independent variables. From this input, ANOVA infers which factors are between subjects, and which are within subjects. ANOVA prints cell sizes, means, and standard deviations for all main effects and interactions. Then ANOVA prints a summary of the design of its input, followed by a standard F-table.

Suppose you had a design in which you presented problems to subjects. These problems varied in difficulty (easy/hard), and in length (short/medium/long). The dependent measure is time to solve the problem, with a time limit of five minutes. Your data file would have lines like this:

```
fred    easy    medium  5
ethel   hard    long    2
```

In the first column is a string that identifies the level of the random factor (here, subject name), followed by strings indicating the level of the independent factors, followed by the dependent measure (here, solution time). The data file holding lines like those above would be analyzed with:

```
ANOVA subject difficulty length time < DATA
```

Individual factors can be ignored by excluding their columns from the analysis:

```
DM s1 s2 s4 < DATA | ANOVA subject difficult ti
```

Similarly, different factors can be used as the random factor. This is common in psycholinguistic experiments in which both subjects and items are random variables.

REGRESS: Multivariate Linear Regression
REGRESS reads its input of a series of lines from the standard input, each with the same number of columns of numbers. From this input, REGRESS prints minimums, maximums, means, and standard deviations for each variable in each column. Also printed is the correlation matrix showing the correlations between all pairs of variables. Suppose you had a file called DATA with any number of lines and five columns, respectively called "blood pressure," "age," "height," "risk," and "salary." You could do a multiple regression with:

```
REGRESS bp age height risk salary < DATA
```

If only a few columns were of interest, they could be extracted with DM:

```
DM x1 x3 x5 < DATA | REGRESS bp height salary
```

PAIR: Paired Data Comparisons
PAIR can be used to compare two distributions of paired data. Often, the two columns of interest are pulled out of a master data file with DM. The following command takes columns 5 and 3 from DATA and inputs them to PAIR:

```
DM x5 x3 < DATA | PAIR
```

For its two-column input, PAIR will print a t-test on the differences of the two columns, which is equivalent to a paired t-test. PAIR will also print a regression equation relating the two, along with a significance test on their correlation, which is equivalent to testing the slope against zero.

AUTOMATED INTERFACES FOR DESIGN SPECIFICATION

Now I will turn to automated interfaces for design specification. This section is a natural extension of the ideas introduced in the ANOVA program discussed in the previous section. My claim is that most data can be analyzed automatically, without the need for any special design specification language commonly used in statistical packages. In their stead, data are put in formats that make their structure transparent, often by some preprocessing by data transforming facilities.

Most statistical programs offer similar capabilities, but they differ in how easily they are used. One purpose of this paper is to introduce a system that is both easy to use and highly powerful in the class of designs it can be used to specify. My goal is to motivate the implementation of more easily used statistical programs by presenting a convenient interface between users and programs.

The Master Data File Format

Besides providing a notation for describing the structure of data, the system introduced in this section allows the specification of design information difficult or impossible using schemes used by most packages. It also allows programs to analyze data without any specification other than the format of the data. The system will be introduced by examples showing how designs of increasing complexity are coded. I will first concentrate on designs with one random factor, and assume the data will be subjected to an analysis of variance. Later on, that assumption will be relaxed. Besides coding of the simplest designs, the following special cases will be discussed.

Many independent variables
Different types of factors
Unequal group sizes
Replications
Missing data
Categorical data
Many dependent variables
Covariates
Other than one random factor

In this system, the role of each datum in the overall design is specified so a design interpreter program can infer the design by relationships among data. All design information is implicit in the format of data. Data are kept in a Master Data File, or MDF. Each line of an MDF contains an equal number of alphanumeric fields that code information about an experimental trial. These lines are in free format with fields separated by tabs or spaces for readability and are conceptually divided into two parts: a description of the conditions under which the data are obtained (e.g.,. independent variables), a description of the data (dependent measures) obtained on that trial.

The MDF format provides useful terms in which people can think about their data. Each line corresponds to a trial on which data were collected. Each column corresponds to a variable such as independent or dependent.

Coding Designs with the MDF Format

In the MDF format, design information is implicit in the format of the data, and analysis routines can be designed to remove the task of specification from the user, resulting in efficient and error free analysis. Just how programs can infer design information from data formats will be shown in the following examples.

Examples of Coding Design Information

A Simple Design: One Group's Data. In the simplest case, each level of the random factor has one datum associated with it. The task of a statistical program is to provide a description about the distribution of those scores, and to compare this distribution to some other. In the MDF format, data follow the description of the random variable, as in the following example where a person's score follows his or her name.

```
fred    68
judy    62
bob     67
jane    67
```

One Grouping Factor. To compare data from two groups, there must be some way of distinguishing them. This is done by using strings to indicate levels of factors in a column as in the following example where each person's sex is included as an index to distinguish groups.

```
fred    male      68
judy    female    62
bob     male      67
jane    female    67
```

Factorial Designs. It is a simple generalization to higher order designs. For each factor, a column is added holding levels for that factor. In the following example, there are two factors, sex with {male, female} as levels, and difficulty with {easy, hard} as levels.

```
bob     male      easy    56
bob     male      hard    67
jane    female    easy    63
jane    female    hard    70
```

Different Types of Factors. All types of designs can be coded in the same system, and design information is implicit in the relation of columns holding levels of independent variables to that of the random factor. By assuming that the indexes for the random factor fall in the first column of an MDF, the type of a factor can be inferred to be between groups, within groups, or nested within some other factor. In the previous example, the difficulty factor can be inferred to be a within groups factor because each level of the random factor is paired with all levels of the that factor. Of course, the sex factor is between subjects, and a computer program can infer this because each level of the random variable is paired with exactly one level of the sex factor.

Nested factors can also be easily coded. In the following example, gymnastic event, indexed in column three, is nested in gender.

```
fred    male      rings    9.4
bob     male      horse    8.2
judy    female    vault    8.8
jane    female    bar      9.2
```

Unequal Group Sizes. To code unequal group sizes on between groups factors, all that is needed is more data for one group than an for other. In the following example, the male group has three members compared to two for the female.

```
fred    male      69
bill    male      62
bob     male      78
jane    female    65
judy    female    74
```

Replications. Replications are coded by having more than one line with the same leading indexes. This is shown in the next example. One person has three replications while another has two.

```
john    male      5
john    male      3
john    male      8
jane    female    10
jane    female    12
```

Missing Data. Many statistical programs require fixed column input formats and treat blank fields as zeros and have to handle missing data by requiring special values that the programs recode as missing. This is clumsy and can lead to errors. Missing values are a special case of multiple observations for which zero replications are collected. In the MDF format, a value is missing if there is no line in the MDF containing it.

Categorical Data. Even though the methods of analysis of numerical data and categorical data differ greatly, the sorts of designs from which they are obtained are often similar. It is not uncommon to collect both numerical and categorical data during one experiment. Categorical data are coded in the same way as numerical data, except that categorical dependent measures can be coded by arbitrary strings. These strings, like those specifying levels of variables, can be used in printouts to make outputs more easily interpreted. For example, the following data might have been obtained from a questionnaire.

john	question-1	agree
john	question-2	disagree
jane	question-1	agree
jane	question-2	disagree

Extending the MDF Format

One drawback of the MDF format as so far presented is that it depends heavily on the fact that there is one random factor that is indexed by the first column, and that there is one dependent measure, in the final column. An extension of the MDF format that solves a number of problems is the use of column tags. A column tag holds information about the variable in that column so that columns need not have any fixed type or location. Some column tags that promote ease of use are the **name** of a variable, its **type**, the criterion for **selection** of its levels, its **scale** of measurement, and its allowable **range** of values. If unspecified, reasonable default values often exist. The use of column tags will be shown in a later example and their meanings are described below.

Name. Analysis programs with access to meaningful variable names can use them in messages and outputs so that users can more easily interpret results. Adding names promotes a master data file to a full relational database, making possible powerful database operations. If unspecified, default names can be chosen based on column number and type.

Type. A variable can be of type unit (from which individual scores are collected), independent, dependent, or covariate. Intelligent programs with type information can can determine the desired analysis by the relationships between pairs of columns in an MDF. This allows automated design interpretation and removes the earlier restriction that columns be ordered.

Selection. The levels of unit and independent variables are either selected according to some fixed criterion or by random sampling. Program with information about how levels of these variables are selected can select the correct error terms for significance tests. Most often, a unit variable is random while all independent variables are fixed, and both are useful default assumptions.

Scale. How data are analyzed depends on the scale of measurement of all variables in a design. Variables can have levels defined by name alone (nominal), or there may be an inherent ordering of levels (ordinal), or differences between levels may be meaningful (interval), or the ratio of levels may be meaningful (ratio). Depending on the scale of measurement, data may be analyzed with cross-tabulations, order statistics, or parametric methods. If unspecified, it is reasonable to assume unit and independent variables are nominal while dependent measures are at least on an interval scale if their range is numerical.

Range. The range of allowable values of a variable is useful for checking the validity of inputs. Ranges can be specified by individual values or by implied subranges in the case of variables at least on an ordinal scale.

More Examples of Coding Designs

More Than One Dependent Measure. To code having more than one dependent measure, columns holding the data are added to the MDF. To analyze data with several dependent variables, a separate analysis is computed for each measure, and an analysis routine would only need know to do a separate analysis for each column tagged with type dependent.

Covariates. Similarly, covariates are included as columns in the MDF, and are tagged with type covariate. An analysis of covariance program would then know to first remove any variability on the data attributable to the covariate before performing analyses for dependent measures. Variables labeled covariate can also be coded as independent variables measured on interval or ratio scales.

Other Than One Random Factor. Experimental designs with any number of random factors can be coded by tagging the columns corresponding to those variables random. Designs with no random factors are identified by having no random variables.

Coding A Complicated Design

In this section, the MDF for a complicated design is shown as an example. Students from two classes are compared for their performance on a manual dexterity test. There are five students, two in group A and three in group B. Before taking the dexterity test, a physical skill test score is obtained for each student. Students attempt three dexterity problems of increasing difficulty which they try to complete in a limited recorded time span. Some students try the same problem more than once, so occasionally there are replications. At the top of the MDF in Table 1 are the column tags for the variables.

Final Comments on the MDF Format

Most experimental designs are representable in the same simple notation. What are special cases for many programs are handled naturally in the MDF format. MDFs can be used as input to a large variety of programs because they have a uniform

Table 1. Master Data File with Column Tags

A master data file with column tags for a design with one random factor, two independent variables (one with unequal cell sizes), one covariate and two dependent measures. At the top of the file are column tags for column name, type, selection, scale, and allowable range.

student	class	problem	skill	complete?	time
unit	indep	independ	covar	dependent	depen
random	fixed	fixed			
nominal	nominal	ordinal	interv	nominal	ratio
{1-5}	{A,B}	{1-3}	{1-10}	{yes,no}	{1-5}
1	a	1	4	no	2
1	a	1	4	no	3
1	a	2	4	yes	1
1	a	3	4	yes	4
2	a	1	7	no	4
2	a	2	7	yes	2
2	a	3	7	no	5
3	b	1	2	yes	3
3	b	2	2	yes	1
3	b	3	2	yes	3
4	b	1	10	yes	1
4	b	1	10	yes	2
4	b	2	10	no	2
4	b	3	10	no	3
4	b	3	10	yes	4
5	b	1	8	yes	5
5	b	2	8	no	4

uncluttered structure. Users can think of an MDF as a file with columns corresponding to variables of various types with definable names and allowable ranges. Or they can think of an MDF as a file with data collected for each trial on its own line. The notation has the virtue that the complexity of the design determines the complexity of the data file, making the system easy to learn, and the virtue that similar designs have similar representations, making it possible to transfer what is learned from one analysis to another. Options are often not necessary because the data in an MDF are structured so that programs can analyze them without any specification by the user. Data in MDF format can be transformed easily with data manipulating tools because of the columnar format of variables.

By incorporating column tags, most designs can be represented and allow design information to be interpreted by data analysis routines instead of requiring a person to describe the structure of the input. This last property is perhaps the system's most important virtue because it reduces the probability of design specification errors, and also can be used to force the use of appropriate statistical procedures.

CONCLUSION

In this paper I described how the UNIX environment affects the development of programs which in turn affects the way people view the task of data analysis. UNIX pipelining promotes the view of data analysis as a series of transformations on a relational data base. Using an interactive system like UNIX allows analysts to use many programs peripherally related to data analysis in addition to statistical programs. The same simple command language can be used to control data analysis as is used for system and personally developed programs. Because of UNIX support for combining programs (with pipelines), individual programs tend to be smaller and can be used on small systems, and programs tend to do one task well and so can be used in a relatively wide variety of tasks. All the preceding properties of UNIX--its interactive interface and its capability to combine modular programs--combine to make for fast command execution. In support of this, in the context of data analysis, it became desirable, even necessary, to remove the task of design specification from users by having programs determine mundane properties of data files such as the number of lines and columns. In support of this, data files are best restricted to rectangular ASCII files with fields separated by white space. This also removes the need for format statements. With some assumptions about the data types of columns, data analysis can be automated. Alternatively, auxiliary data structures defining properties of columns holding variables (name, type, selection, scale, and range) make rectangular data files relational databases that allow automatic data validation and design interpretation followed by a suggested data analysis. Such an orientation provides people with considerable freedom in doing data analysis because many of the tedious and error prone tasks are automated. This is most valuable to the majority of users, non-experts, who are often overwhelmed by the user interfaces of data analysis programs which require much more computer sophistication than this paper has shown is necessary.

REFERENCES

Perlman, G. (1980) Data analysis programs for the UNIX operating system. Behavior Research Methods and Instrumentation, 1980, 12:5, 554-558.

Richie, D. M., & Thompson, K. The UNIX time-sharing system. Communications of the ACM, 1974, 17, 365-375.

ACKNOWLEDGMENTS

Jay McClelland has been instrumental in his influence in the user interfaces, particularly DM and ANOVA. He also wrote the original version of ABUT. Mark Wallen has been helpful in being able to convey many of the intricacies of UNIX C programming. Greg Davidson was the force behind most of the error checking facilities. Don Norman wrote the original flow meter on which the IO program is based.

The research reported here was conducted under Contract N00014-79-C-0323, NR 157-437 with the Personnel and Training Research Programs of the Office of Naval Research, and was sponsored by the Office of Naval Research and the Air Force Office of Scientific Research.

Data Analysis in the Presence of Error

Chair: Lynne Billard, University of Georgia

Mapping Contingency Tables
Jonathan Arnold, Rutgers University
Douglas R. Kankel, Yale University

An Interactive Program for Adaptively Analyzing Data
Michael Brannigan, University of Georgia

Solving Integral Equations With Noisy Data: An Application of Smoothing Splines in Pathology
Doug Nychta, University of Wisconsin

MAPPING CONTINGENCY TABLES

Jonathan Arnold, Rutgers University
Douglas R. Kankel, Yale University

ABSTRACT

An interactive package for the collection, exploratory analysis, and modeling of data from experiments in Developmental Genetics and Neurogenetics is described. The experiments aim to map behavioral and developmental phenomena in the fruit fly Drosophila melanogaster to anatomical regions (referenced to an early developmental stage of that organism) which control these phenomena. We focus exclusively on the use of mosaics which are a composite of male and female cells, to address the problem.

Landmarks (e.g. wings) have been mapped to anatomical regions early in development. Bilaterally symmetric landmarks on the fly are scored as (i) both male; (ii) one side, male; or (iii) neither side, male, and the fly is also scored for a clearcut behavior (in the case considered here 'collapsed' or 'standing' under the influence of a mutation known as comatose). As each fly's behavior and landmarks are scored using a voice-activated input device associated with a dissecting microscope and DEC PDP-11/34A, the computer responds with an updated color schematic, showing the scoring of a fly. With L landmarks, the data modeled is a $2{\times}3^L$ table of counts of behavior by landmark scores. From the data the package constructs summary table, histograms, and maps of the tables.

A family of categorical models for the experiments is developed. Hidden categorical variables, called foci, each taking 3 values (like the landmarks) turn the behavior on ('collapsed') or off ('standing'). With F foci hidden, a 3^{L+F} table with many cells observationally indistinguishable is collapsed to the observed $2{\times}3^L$ table, whose cells are linear in the model's parameters. The package fits a model by maximum likelihood using the EM algorithm and summarizes the fitted model using a multi-dimensional scaling subroutine to map associations between the observed variables, the landmarks, and the hidden variables, the foci. This map is interpreted as a physical map of the fly early in development.

Keywords: Fate mapping, mosaics, comatose, Developmental Genetics model, contingency table, indirect observation, multi-dimensional scaling, mapping contingency tables, maximum likelihood estimation, EM algorithm.

INTRODUCTION

The experiments discussed herein aim to map behavioral and developmental phenomena in Drosophila melanogaster to anatomical regions (referenced to an early developmental stage of that organism) which control these phenomena. We focus exclusively on the use of mosaics which are a composite of male and female cells, to address the problem. The work in this area was pioneered by Sturtevant (1929) and Garcia-Bellido and Merriam (1969), and more recently, techniques have been developed to map relatively complex behaviors to a pair of sites defined on the surface of the cellular blastoderm (Hotta and Benzer (1973); Merriam and Lange (1974); Flanagan (1977)), an ellipsoidal surface of cells (200-1500 cell nuclei) formed 9-14 divisions after fertilization. A new procedure is reported here which tests the adequacy of the single site-pair model and allows models involving two or more site-pairs to be developed and tested; it allows us to test how many pairs of sites may be controlling a behavior and further to examine how the sites interact to determine the behavior of interest.

THE DATA

Landmarks, such as the wing, proximal antennal segment, and various hairs and bristles have had their progenitors localized on the surface of the blastoderm (on early embryonic stage) by a combination of convential observational (e.g., Poulson (1950)) and genetic fate mapping (e.g., Garcia-Bellido and Merriam (1969)) procedures; some landmarks and the behavior in mosaic experiments to be discussed here are tabled below in Exhibit 1.

Landmarks and Behavior Used in Mosaic Experiments

Landmark	Abbreviation	Landmark	Abbreviation
Head		Thorax	
arista	ar	humeral bristle	hu
proximal antenna	pan	presutural bristle	pst
medial orbital bristle	mo	posterior dorsocentral bristl	pac
ocellar	oc	posterior scutellar bristle	psc
outer vertical bristle	ov	median sternal pleural bristle	mst
postvertical bristle	pv	posterior sternopleural bristle	psp
dorsal facet of compound eye	e-d	prothoracic coxal seta (anterior leg)	prc
ventral facet of compound eye	e-v	mesothoracic coxal seta (middle leg)	msc
vibrissae	vb	metathoracic coxal seta (posterior leg)	mtc
palp (maxillar)	pa	prothoracic leg	I
postorbital bristle	po	mesothoracic leg	II
proboscis	pr	metathoracic leg	III
Behavior		wing	w
comatose	com	Abdomen	
		3rd abdominal tergite	3t
		5th abdominal sternite	3s
		external genitalia	g

A number of methods exist to generate relatively large numbers of flies that are mosaics of both male and female cells (see review by Hall, Gelbart and Kankel (1976)) and so that the male cells are genetically marked to distinguish them from female cells. For example, on the adult's cuticle cells (on I, II, III in Exhibit 1) may be yellow; bristles (ov or pv) from male cells may be 'singed' in appearance; and facets of the compound eye (e-d or e-v) composed of male cells may be white in color.

The actual identification of the maleness or femaleness of a landmark is carried out by observing a lightly etherized mosaic under a dissecting microscope. The data on each structure are recorded by use of the interactive program GYNSCR. Data are entered into the computer verbally through an Interstate Electronics Corp. VRT-200 voice recognition system. Data are stored directly on magnetic medium and the results of each entry displayed on a color monitor adjacent to the microscope which has a graphic depiction of the fly. This system is driven by a DEC PDP-11/34A computer. Landmarks may be scored in a prescribed sequence or the user may call out each landmark's name (Exhibit 1) and identification in any sequence. As scoring progresses, the computer displays an updated color schematic diagram of a fly (uncolored=female, colored=male, and additional color codes for 'mixed' and 'not scored') on a JVC 5, color monitor, which is a slave to an Advanced Electronics Design (Model AED 512) color graphics terminal, the principal display device of the computer. In Exhibit 2 the schematic of the fly is displayed as entirely female (no color). The computer allows the user to correct his scoring at any stage.

Each fly is also scored for a clearcut behavioral or developmental phenotype; the behavior that we will focus on is a temperature induced paralysis under the control of the mutation 'comatose' (com).

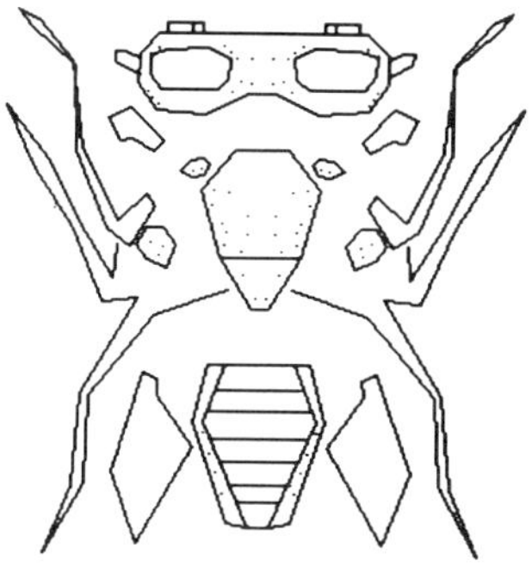

Each mosaic is scored for whether or not the fly has 'collapsed' at an elevated temperature (38°C). The data on 11 mosaic flies is displayed below in Exhibit 3 (Panel A). The first 27 columns in each row code one side (left (L) or right (R)) of 27 landmarks. Each side of a landmark is coded as male (0), female (1), mixed (2), or unscored (3). The last column is the behavioral score coded like the landmarks with 'collapsed' being male (e.g. '0' denotes 'collapsed').

```
1L0000000001111111111111112110
1R0000000001000000000010010000
2L1111111111111110001111112210
2R0000000000000000000000030000
3L0000000000011001101000001110
3R0000000000000000000000000000
4L1111111111100001200110021021
4R1111111111111111111111111111
5L0000000001111110211111112120
5R0000000000000000000011110000
6L0000000000000000220000010001
6R0000000001111111111111111111
7L1111111111111111111111101220
7R1111111111000000000021000000
8L1111111111111111111111101111
8R1111111111000002200000002221
9L0000000000001111111121111111
9R0000000000001001011111112111
10L1111111110001100000000000000
10R1111111111011010101111101020
11L0000000000000000000000000000
11R0000000000010110111000001220
```

Using '*' to denote exponentiation, the data on L (= 27 in Exhibit 3) landmarks are used to construct a 2×(3*L) table in Exhibit 3 - Panel B of behavior score by landmark scores, a table which is modeled in the next two sections. In that flies are bilaterally symmetric, each landmark has a right and left side. Each mosaic's landmark is scored as: (i) both sides, male (2); (ii) one side, male (1); or (iii) neither side, male (0), and tabled in Exhibit 3 - Panel B. In fitting models in the last section of this paper, mixed identifications were randomized to male or female, and unscored mosaics were dropped from the analysis in the last two sections. A more detailed description of the mosaic experiments, which aim to map the comatose behavior, can be found in Arnold and Kankel (1982, p. 218). The discrete variables in these experiments code behavior and the landmarks (Exhibit 3).

The program (FMAP) illustrated below initially performs an exploratory analysis. Various summary tables of maleness by landmark and maleness by mosaic are computed. These two tables are the basis of two histograms. Firstly maleness by landmark (the proportion of mosaics which are male, for each landmark) is histogrammed to determine at what developmental stage (i.e. 1,2,3,... cell divisions after fertilization) the mosaic is created; each count in Exhibit 4 - Panel A (top of next page) in the histogram corresponds to a different landmark. Secondly, a histogram for maleness by mosaic (the proportion of landmarks which are male, per mosaic) is also presented to determine at what division (e.g. 1, 2, or 3) the mosaic is created and to check assumption 1 in 'The Model' section. Each count in Exhibit 4 - Panel B (top of next page) is a different mosaic.

Associations between landmarks in an N-mosaic experiment are also studied. Two sites on the adult mosaic can have one of the following four joint outcomes with counts N(00), N(01), N(10), N(11), summing to N.

		Site 2	
		female (0)	female (1)
Site 1	male (0)	N(00)	N(01)
	female (1)	N(10)	N(11)
			N

Mosaic data on comatose†*

i	*N*(1, *j*)	*N*(2, *j*)	L
0	21	1	000
1	4	0	100
2	0	0	200
3	1	1	010
4	3	1	110
5	1	0	210
6	0	0	020
7	0	0	120
8	0	0	220
9	4	1	001
10	1	0	101
11	0	0	201
12	4	2	011
13	38	59	111
14	1	10	211
15	0	1	021
16	1	5	121
17	0	3	221
18	0	0	002
19	0	0	102
20	0	0	202
21	0	1	012
22	1	5	112
23	0	1	212
24	1	0	022
25	0	5	122
26	0	14	222

* The landmarks and their order along the blastoderm in Table 2 are Leg I–Leg II–Leg III.
† As pointed out in the text, only those cases with complete data were used in any particular analysis. Thus, of the 226 gynandromorphs available, only 191 were used for these particular

The pairwise distance (or lack of association) between sites is commonly measured by D(1,2) = (N(01) + N(10))/N. The package standardly computes all pairwise distances between landmark

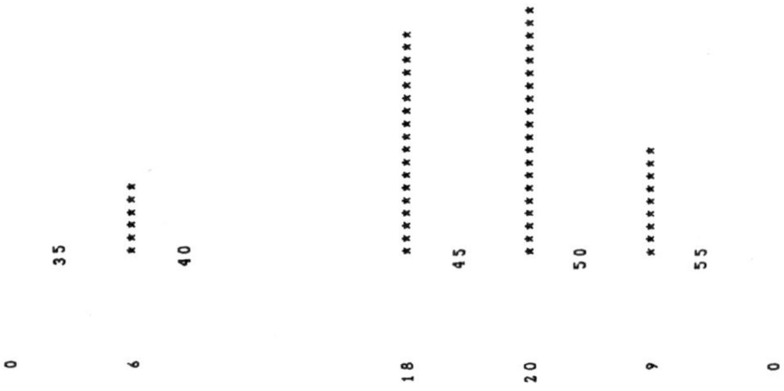

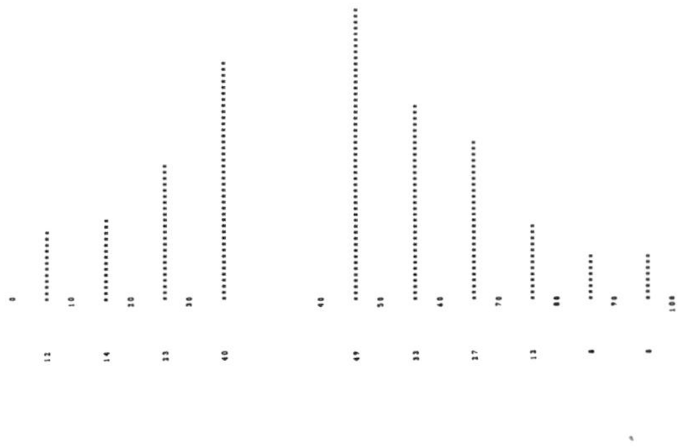

STURT MATRIX FOR LEFT+RIGHT (STURTS)

	PRANT	MDORB	OCELL	PVERT	EYED	EYEV	VBRSA	PALP	PORTB	PRBSC	HUMER	PRSUT	PDOCN	PSCUT	MSTPL	PRCOX	MSCOX	MTCOX	WING	TER3	TER5	STER5	STER7	GNTLA	BLEG1
PRANT	0.0																								
MDORB	14.7	0.0																							
OCELL	14.4	0.9	0.0																						
PVERT	16.8	2.9	3.5	0.0																					
EYED	15.7	2.6	3.1	1.3	0.0																				
EYEV	15.7	2.6	3.1	1.3	0.7	0.0																			
VBRSA	15.7	2.9	3.8	3.8	3.5	2.9	0.0																		
PALP	15.4	3.0	3.7	4.1	3.6	3.2	0.8	0.0																	
PORTB	15.0	2.9	3.4	4.1	3.7	3.2	0.8	0.2	0.0																
PRBSC	27.1	14.3	15.2	13.4	13.8	13.4	12.3	11.9	12.5	0.0															
HUMER	28.0	18.9	20.5	19.1	18.9	18.7	17.3	18.6	19.0	10.7	0.0														
PRSUT	27.3	18.1	19.5	18.5	18.5	18.3	16.8	18.5	18.6	15.4	11.4	0.0													
PDOCN	27.4	17.0	17.9	17.7	18.3	18.1	17.0	18.0	18.4	14.7	12.7	7.7	0.0												
PSCUT	28.1	17.2	18.5	18.3	18.5	18.3	17.0	18.4	18.6	14.9	11.6	7.7	3.3	0.0											
MSTPL	27.0	15.5	17.2	15.9	16.3	16.1	14.6	15.6	15.7	15.6	14.0	8.6	8.6	6.8	0.0										
PRCOX	24.8	16.6	17.3	16.8	17.9	17.4	15.7	16.5	14.9	17.2	19.7	17.0	15.3	15.9	12.8	0.0									
MSCOX	25.8	15.8	17.3	16.6	17.7	17.3	15.1	15.9	16.3	17.7	19.1	16.2	16.0	15.5	11.3	10.5	0.0								
MTCOX	27.7	17.7	19.0	18.1	19.8	19.4	17.2	18.0	18.1	17.6	19.3	15.0	12.1	13.0	10.4	11.5	7.3	0.0							
WING	26.1	16.8	18.4	18.1	18.8	18.5	16.4	17.4	17.5	15.4	16.1	10.2	7.1	7.5	9.1	11.9	8.9	7.6	0.0						
TER3	31.8	21.1	22.2	20.9	22.0	21.6	20.1	21.1	21.4	16.7	16.9	16.1	11.9	11.8	16.5	18.5	18.6	16.9	15.3	0.0					
TER5	34.8	29.6	30.5	29.3	28.9	28.9	27.2	28.1	28.5	21.7	19.7	21.0	22.5	20.5	24.2	27.4	26.8	25.1	23.5	14.4	0.0				
STER5	31.8	26.5	27.7	26.7	26.3	26.3	24.3	26.2	26.4	22.3	19.0	18.1	19.2	17.4	20.1	24.6	22.4	21.9	20.5	17.2	11.3	0.0			
STER7	32.9	26.5	27.1	27.1	26.8	26.8	24.9	25.2	25.4	22.9	21.1	18.6	18.6	17.0	17.9	22.4	19.8	18.6	17.6	15.2	12.7	8.5	0.0		
GNTLA	35.7	29.5	30.2	30.4	29.7	29.5	27.9	28.5	28.2	28.0	25.6	21.6	23.6	22.2	21.3	24.8	22.8	22.6	22.4	21.3	19.6	16.0	10.0	0.0	
BLEG1	21.6	21.8	22.5	23.1	23.4	23.1	21.4	22.6	22.8	22.5	22.1	18.0	19.1	18.7	17.1	17.3	15.4	18.9	16.9	27.1	26.9	24.8	24.9	27.9	0.0
BLEG2	28.2	17.9	19.0	19.7	19.9	19.7	17.7	18.9	19.3	19.6	20.3	14.6	14.4	14.1	12.8	15.7	11.4	13.0	13.6	23.4	30.1	27.5	28.4	32.6	20.6

	BLEG2
BLEG2	0.0

sites as in Exhibit 5. The package then constructs a map from the matrix of distances (or associations) between landmark sites with a modified version of the multi-dimensional scaling routine in Flanagan (1976). The program MAPPNG calculates the map coordinates $\underline{X}_1 = (X_{11}, X_{12})$, $\underline{X}_2 = (X_{21}, X_{22})$, ... by minimizing the error criterion E below. The algorithm is modified steepest descent. Defining an expected euclidean distance $ED(i,j) = (X_{i1}-X_{j1})*2+(X_{i2}-X_{j2})*2$, the error criterion is

$$E = \Sigma(i)\Sigma(j)(D(i,j)-ED(i,j))*2/D(i,j).$$

In that the fly is bilaterally symmetric, each landmark (L1 or L2) has two sites. Distances between landmark sites on the left side, right, or both sides can yield 3 distinct maps. What is usually reported is a map of landmarks in which distances between landmarks are computed from a 2×2×2 table = (L1 = Male or Female) × (L2 = Male or Female) × (Side = L or R) after collapsing on side. Such a map for the landmarks in the comatose-mosaic experiments is shown in Exhibit 6 in the next column and is termed a fate map. Each landmark and its relation to other landmarks in the map is in good agreement with an embryological map of the blastoderm for *Drosophila melanogaster* in Poulson (1950). The landmarks on the map above are physically identified with sites on the blastoderm's surface. The left and right sides (sites) on the surface of the adult mosaic are identified with the blastoderm's dorsal and ventral sides (sites) controlling each landmark. One or more hypothetical pairs of sites, called foci, are postulated to turn the behavior on ('collapsed') or off ('standing').

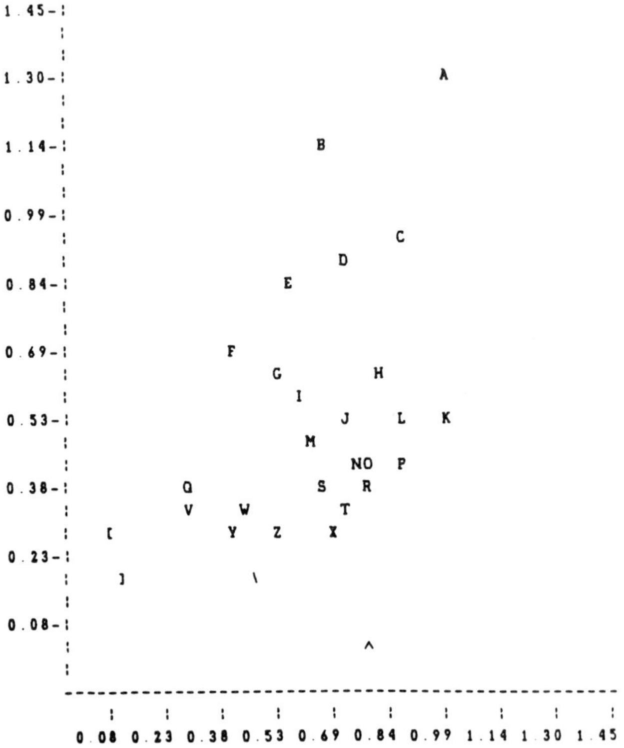

THE MODEL

Assumption 1: Half the blastoderm is covered by male cells. One of the coverings is convex.

A number of methods exist to generate relatively large numbers of mosaics (Hall, Gelbart, and Kankel (1976)), but the procedure developed here concerns itself only with those methods yielding half-male, half-female mosaics. The procedure also assumes that both male and female regions (coverings) of cells on the blastoderm occupy essentially contiguous regions. Zalokar, Erk, and Santamaria (1980) directly monitored the distribution of male cells over the blastoderm. More than one patch of male cells occasionally occurs, but the bulk of male cells seems to be confined to a single connected patch. The boundary between male and female regions tends to be quite irregular.

Assumption 2: All site pairs are symmetrically arranged about the midline (defined below). Each landmark autonomously determines a mosaic's adult phenotype (i.e. male or female). There are F pairs of foci determining the fate of a behavioral phenotype (e.g. 'collapsed' or 'standing'). When k (defined as the behavior's threshold) or more foci are covered by male cells, then the mosaic exhibits the behavior.

In that the blastoderm and adult mosaic are bilaterally symmetric, S site pairs are arranged along the blastoderm, and the members of each pair are symmetrically situated about the midline, a great ellipse separating the dorsal and ventral halves of the blastoderm. The site pairs 1,...,S are ordered by their position along the anterior-posterior axis of the blastoderm. Some site pairs are landmarks and others, foci. Landmarks on the blastoderm give rise to pairs of anatomical features in the adult, such as right and left posterior scutellar bristles (psc in Exhibit 1); foci are hypothetical sites on the blastoderm determining the fate (e.g. 'collapsed' or 'standing') of the adult. The L landmarks and F foci take a position in the ordering 1,...,S of S (= L+F) site pairs along the blastoderm. Site pairs in positions $\lambda(1),\ldots,\lambda(L)$ are landmarks, and site pairs in positions $\phi(1),\ldots,\phi(F)$ are focal pairs. A schematic of the blastoderm is shown below in Exhibit 7.

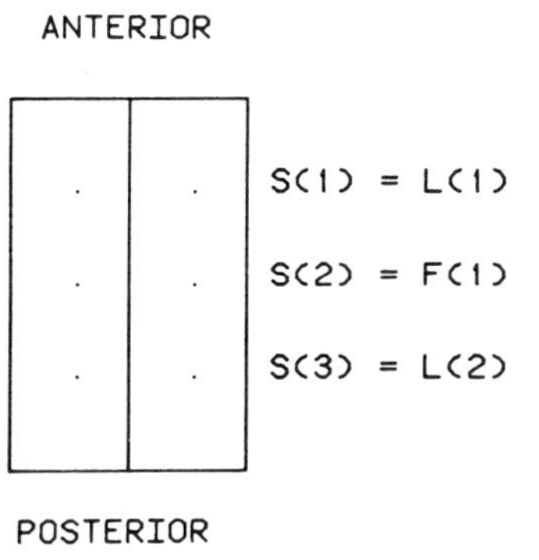

Male cells are genetically marked to distinguish them from female cells. When male cells cover a landmark, the adult feature derived from it is male and marked so. Similarly, when a given number k, $1 \leq k \leq 2F$, or more foci are (not) covered by male cells, then the mosaic is (not) fated to exhibit the mutant behavioral phenotype, i.e. 'collapsed'. In the extreme case in which the behavior's threshold k is 1 or 2F (the total number of foci), the model herein is termed domineering or submissive, respectively.

Different configurations of the blastoderm are displayed in Exhibit 8. A configuration is the total genotype of the mosaic and is specified once the number (0, 1, or 2) of sites covered by male cells in each site pair is known. Configurations 1, 2, 3, and 4 in Exhibit 8 have 6, 3, 3, and 1 site(s) covered, respectively.

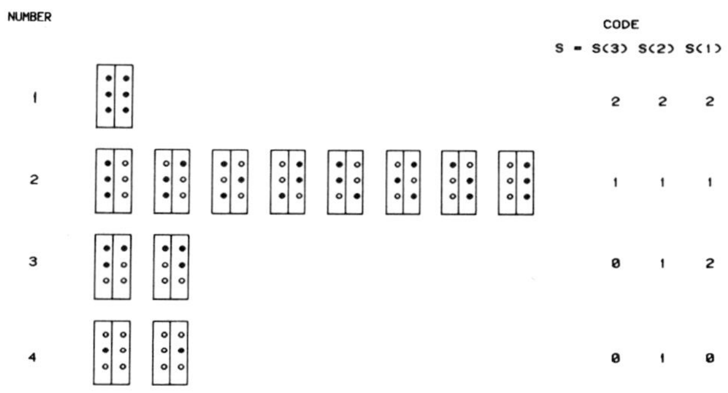

Configurations are the aggregate of one or more covering events, which are not distinguished by the model. For each configuration in Exhibit 8, the simpler events that yield the blastoderm configuration coded on the far right hand side are presented. A blastoderm configuration is then identified with a coding sequence $\underline{S}$ of length S: (i) if both sites of site pair i are covered, then the count S(i) is 2; (ii) if one site of site pair i is covered, then the count S(i) is 1; or (iii) if neither site of site pair i is covered, then the count S(i) is 0. The site pair variables [S(i)] code the cells of a 3*(L+F) = 3*S table, into which a mosaic can belong. The blastoderm configuration is the list of counts $\underline{S} = [S(1),\ldots,S(S)]$.

Similarly, a landmark score is the landmark phenotype of the mosaic and is specified once the number of sides covered is known for each landmark. A landmark score can be coded by a sequence $\underline{L}$ of length L: (i) if both sites of landmark $\lambda(i)$ are covered, then the right and left sides of the adult mosaic's landmark are male, and the count $L[\lambda(i)] = 2$; (ii) if one site of landmark $\lambda(i)$ is covered, then the right or left side of the adult mosaic's landmark is male, and the count $L[\lambda(i)] = 1$; or (iii) if neither site of landmark $\lambda(i)$ is covered, then neither side of the adult mosaic's landmark is male, and the count $L[\lambda(i)] = 0$. The landmark score of an adult mosaic is then the list of counts $\underline{L} = \{L[\lambda(1)],\ldots,L[\lambda(L)]\}$. The landmark scores of 11 mosaics can be obtained from Exhibit 3 - Panel A. Similarly, the counts $\underline{F} = \{F[\phi(1)],\ldots,F[\phi(F)]\}$ code the numbers of each focal pair covered by male cells. If there are three site pairs on the blastoderm (S = 3) being examined, all blastoderm configurations can be enumerated by counting in base 3 from 000 to 222. In Exhibit 9 at the top of the next page the blastoderm configurations can be identified with points in a three-sided lattice.

Definition 3: Noncontiguous configurations have zero probability of occurrence.

Some configurations are highly unlikely. They would require either multiple patches of male cells on the blastoderm or both its covers to be nonconvex, contrary to assumption 1. Two site

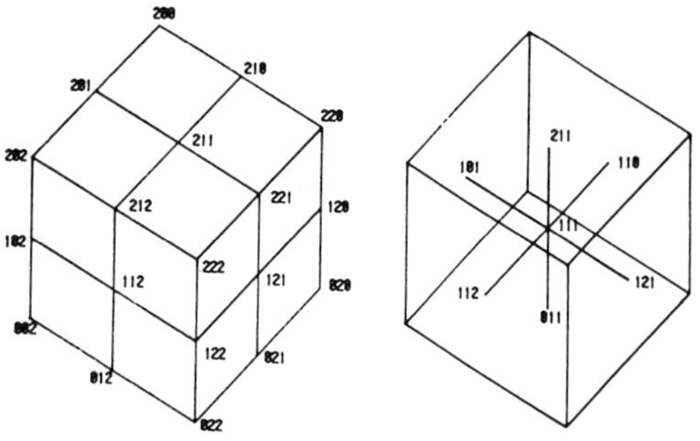

A B

pairs in a configuration are coordinated if there is at least one site from each of common gender. Coordinated site pairs in a configuration are required to be contiguous. For example, all configurations in Exhibit 8 are contiguous. Exhibit 10 below displays a noncontiguous configuration.

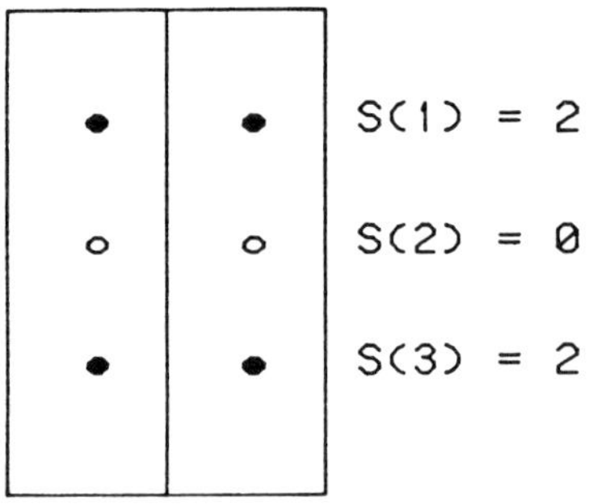

A noncontiguous configuration in the case above contains a 2 surrounded by numbers less than 2 or a 0 surrounded by numbers greater than 0.

There are three types of contiguity requirements on blastoderm configurations. (i) There can be no contiguity requirement. (ii) A configuration can be required to be locally contiguous. A locally contiguous configuration has a code S in which there are no 2's surrounded by numbers less than 2 or 0's surrounded by numbers greater than 0. (iii) A configuration can be required to be globally contiguous. In this case all runs of 0's, 1's, and 2's in the sequence S are replaced by a single 0, 1, or 2, and the resulting shortened sequence without runs is required to be locally contiguous. Checking global contiguity of a configuration is equivalent to determining whether or not a configuration code shortens to one of 12 codes below.

0	01	010	012	02	10
2	21	212	210	20	12

In Exhibit 11 below there is an example of a blastoderm configuration that is locally contiguous, but is not globally contiguous. The model assumes no contiguity, local contiguity, or global contiguity in Definition 3. For example, if the model makes a global contiguity assumption in Definition 3, then all globally noncontiguous

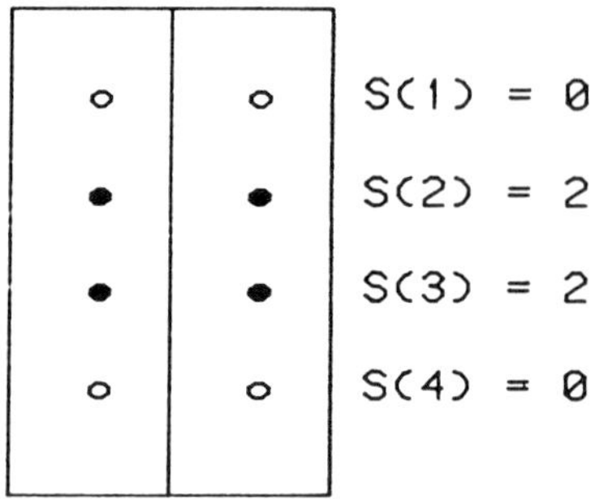

configurations have zero probability. Global contiguity implies local contiguity, and they are equivalent so long as there are three or fewer site pairs. With only two site pairs, all three contiguity assumptions are equivalent.

Definition 3 follows from Assumption 1 and is suggested in the single focal-pair model of Hotta and Benzer (1973, p. 150, caption of Figure 10). Definition 3 is empty if there is no contiguity requirement. The model and the interactive package implementing the fitting of the model allow a choice of contiguity definitions. A number of other notions of contiguity need consideration, and ultimately, the mosaic data themselves (Exhibit 3) will select the correct notion of contiguity.

Assumption 4: Two blastoderm configurations S and S', equivalent under reflection R, are equiprobable.

Letting 1 = (1,...S times ...,1) be the center of the lattice, define the reflection R(S) = 1 - (S-1) of S through the center 1. Two configurations S and S' are equivalent under reflection R if and only if S = R(S'). The reflection changes 2(0) to 0(2) in a configuration and leaves 1 unchanged.

Assumption 4 is employed in the single focal-pair models of Hotta and Benzer (1973). Some equivalent configurations are displayed below in Exhibit 12.

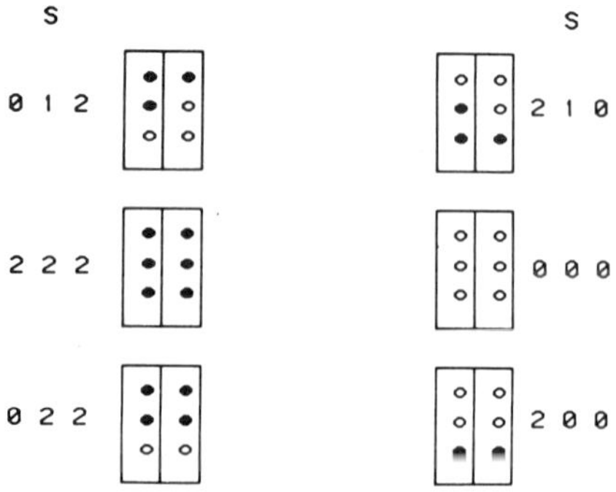

The configuration 1 is its own symmetry partner, and all other configurations have one symmetry partner. By enumerating the configurations

$\underline{0}$ = (0,...S times...,0) up to $\underline{1}$, the remaining configurations can be obtained by reflection R. If a configuration $\underline{S}$ is noncontiguous, then its reflection R($\underline{S}$) is also noncontiguous.

The model's structure is defined by the numbers of landmarks (L) and foci (F), their positions along the blastoderm (λ's and ϕ's), the behavior's phenotypic threshold (k), the landmarks entered in the model, and the contiguity assumption. After the interactive package is supplied with the model's structure and the data structure (number of mosaics, etc.), the package completes the model's description by responding with estimates of the model's parameters and other statistics.

The parameters in the model are the nonzero probabilities of contiguous configurations with codes from $\underline{0}$ to $\underline{1}$. The probability of configuration $\underline{S}$ is denoted $\theta(\underline{S})$. For example, the probability of the center configuration $\underline{1}$ is $\theta(\underline{1})$. The list of configuration probabilities $\theta=[\theta(\underline{0}),\ldots,\theta(\underline{1})]$ are positive and are constrained by Assumption 4 to be positive and satisfy

$$1 = \theta(\underline{1})+2\Sigma[\underline{S}=\underline{0} \text{ up to } (1,\ldots S\text{-}1 \text{ times}\ldots 0)]\theta(\underline{S}).$$

The number of nonzero configuration probabilities of parameters under the global contiguity assumption with varying numbers of site pairs S is tabled.

S	1	2	3	4	5
Parameters	2	5	10	17	26

Each mosaic is scored for the presence or absence of the mutant behavior (e.g. comatose) and the number of male sides for each landmark, yielding the landmark score $\underline{L}$. If the adult fly had a blastoderm configuration $\underline{S}$, then the 0-1 indicator c($\underline{S}$,$\underline{L}$) of the blastoderm configuration having been contiguous and having landmark phenotype $\underline{L}$ is

$$c(\underline{S},\underline{L}) = \begin{cases} 1, & \underline{S} \text{ contiguous}, \; S[\lambda(i)] = L[\lambda(i)], \; i = 1,\ldots,L \\ 0, & \text{otherwise} \end{cases}$$

For the adult mosaic to express the mutant behavior, k or more foci on the blastoderm need to be covered. The fate f($\underline{S}$) of a mosaic as determined by its blastoderm configuration $\underline{S}$ is:

$$f(\underline{S}) = 1, \; \Sigma(i=1,F)F_{\underline{S}}[\phi(i)] \geq k$$
$$= 0, \; \Sigma(i=1,F)F_{\underline{S}}[\phi(i)] < k$$

The probability of the observed behavioral phenotype and landmark score is the sum of the probabilities of contiguous configurations that have the landmark phenotype observed and fate the adult mosaic to have the observed behavioral phenotype. Letting the normal fate $\overline{f(\underline{S})}$ = 1-f($\underline{S}$), the outcome of an experiment yielding a mosaic with previous configuration $\underline{S}$ is: (i) normal behavioral phenotype (e.g. 'standing') and landmark score $\underline{L}$ with probability

$$P(0,\underline{L}|\theta) = \Sigma(\underline{S})[\theta(\underline{S})c(\underline{S},\underline{L})\overline{f(\underline{S})}];$$

or (ii) mutant behavioral phenotype (e.g. 'collapsed') and landmark score $\underline{L}$ with probability

$$P(1,\underline{L}|\theta) = \Sigma(\underline{S})[\theta(\underline{S})c(\underline{S},\underline{L})f(\underline{S})].$$

These are the cell probabilities for Exhibit 3 - Panel B derived from data partly displayed in Exhibit 3 - Panel A.

After N mosaics are generated and scored for the behavior and landmarks, the data are recorded in a 2×(3*L) contingency table $\underline{N}$ = [N(i,$\underline{L}$)], as in Exhibit 3 - Panel B, according to the absence or presence (i = 0 or 1, respectively) of the mutant behavioral phenotype and by landmark score $\underline{L}$. When a fixed number of mosaics are independently generated, then the density of the table of counts given the model, namely P($\underline{N}$|θ), is multinomial and proportional to:

$$P(\underline{N}|\theta)\propto\Pi(i)\Pi(\underline{S})[P(i,\underline{S}|\theta)]*N(i,\underline{S}) \qquad (1)$$

Equation (1) is the model specification for the problem (e.g. Exhibit 3 - Panel B). This model specification is a special case of that in Haberman (1977) and is termed a model specification for a <u>contingency table with indirect observation</u>. The cell probabilities for Exhibit 3 - Panel B are linear in the model parameters θ. With F foci hidden, a 3*(L+F) = 3*S table with many cells observationally indistinguishable is collapsed to the observed 2×(3*L) table, whose cell probabilities are linear in the configuration probabilities θ.

ANALYSIS AND CONVERSATIONS WITH AN INTERACTIVE PACKAGE

The model is estimated by maximum likelihood, and different multi-focus models (e.g. with differing numbers of foci or differing thresholds) are compared and selected on the basis of their likelihood ratios. Once an adequate model is found, the null hypothesis is assessed for goodness-of-fit by the Pearson χ^2 statistic.

The maximum likelihood estimates $\hat{\theta} = [\hat{\theta}(\underline{0}),\ldots,\hat{\theta}(\underline{1})]$ of a multi-focus model can be iteratively computed by the <u>EM algorithm</u>, as in Haberman (1977, p. 1143) and more generally in Dempster, Laird, and Rubin (1977). The algorithm has the advantages of easy programmability, quick convergence for this model specification, numerical stability, and yielding closed-form expressions (in some cases) for the maximum likelihood estimates. Its application to other contingency table models (Haberman (1974), p. 73) also suggests a gain in computational efficiency when large numbers of parameters are involved (as in the case of a multi-focus model).

The application of the EM algorithm to the model specification in (1) <u>in general</u> is described in Arnold and Kankel (1982, p. 221). Here we illustrate the algorithm on the two possible one focal-pair models of Hotta and Benzer (1973). In their models there is one pair of landmarks and one pair of foci. The positions of the foci and landmarks along the blastoderm are $\phi(1)$ = 1 and $\lambda(1)$ = 2. All the contiguous configurations and their probabilities θ are tabled below.

		Number of Male Landmarks 0	1	2
Number of Male Foci	0	$\theta(00)$	$\theta(01)$	$\theta(02)$
	1	$\theta(10)$	$\theta(11)$	$\theta(10)$
	2	$\theta(02)$	$\theta(01)$	$\theta(00)$

S=2; L=F=1
$2[\theta(00)+\theta(01)+\theta(02)+\theta(10)]+\theta(11) = 1$

The threshold k can be k = 1 (Domineering Model) or k = 2 (Submissive Model). Some of the cells in the table above are observationally indistinguishable, depending on the behavior's threshold.

Domineering Model (k = 1)

		0	1	2
Behavior	0	$\theta(00)$	$\theta(01)$	$\theta(02)$
	1	$\theta(10)+\theta(02)$	$\theta(11)+\theta(01)$	$\theta(10)+\theta(00)$

Table of Counts $\underline{N}$

	0	1	2
0	N(0,0)	N(0,1)	N(0,2)
1	N(1,0)	N(1,1)	N(1,2)

Submissive Model (k = 2)

	0	1	2
0	$\theta(00)+\theta(10)$	$\theta(01)+\theta(11)$	$\theta(02)+\theta(10)$
1	$\theta(02)$	$\theta(01)$	$\theta(00)$

For the one focal-pair models (S = 2), the model specification is (as noted in Merriam and Lange (1974, p. 199, equations (21) and (18)) proportional to:

$$\begin{aligned} P(\underline{N}|\theta) &\propto \{[\theta(00)]{*}N(0,0)\}\{[\theta(01)]{*}N(0,1)\}\{[\theta(02)]{*}N(0,2)\}\times \\ &\quad \{[\theta(10)+\theta(02)]{*}N(1,0)\}\{[\theta(11)+\theta(01)]{*}N(1,1)\}\{[\theta(10)+\theta(00)]{*}N(1,2)\}, \quad k = 1 \\ &\propto \{[\theta(00)+\theta(10)]{*}N(0,0)\}\{[\theta(01)+\theta(11)]{*}N(0,1)\}\{[\theta(02)+\theta(10)]{*}N(0,2)\}\times \\ &\quad \{[\theta(02)]{*}N(1,0)\}\{[\theta(01)]{*}N(1,1)\}\{[\theta(00)]{*}N(1,2)\}, \quad k = 2 \end{aligned} \tag{1A}$$

The EM algorithm in these two cases can be described as follows. If the blastoderm has a contiguous configuration $\underline{S}$ (always is for S = 2) and if the whole blastoderm configuration $\underline{S}$ were observable in a developing mosaic, then configuration $\underline{S}$ could be seen $N^*(\underline{S})$ times in a N-mosaic experiment. The counts $\underline{N}^* = [N^*(S)]$ would be multinomial with configuration probabilities θ and sample size N. The maximum likelihood estimates $\hat{\theta}$ could then be computed

$$\underline{\text{(M-Step)}} \qquad \begin{aligned} \hat{\theta}(\underline{S}) &= [N^*(00)+N^*(22)]/2N, & \underline{S} &= 00 \\ &= [N^*(01)+N^*(21)]/2N, & \underline{S} &= 01 \\ &= [N^*(02)+N^*(20)]/2N, & \underline{S} &= 02 \\ &= [N^*(10)+N^*(12)]/2N, & \underline{S} &= 10 \\ &= [N^*(11)]/N, & \underline{S} &= 11 \end{aligned} \tag{2}$$

In fact, the counts of mosaic configurations $\underline{N}^*$ are not observed, but their expected values $\{E[N^*(\underline{S})|\underline{N},\theta]\}$, conditional on the 2×3 table of behavior by landmark scores $\underline{N} = [N(i,\underline{L})]$ and the model θ, can be computed from (1A) via:

<u>E-Step</u>

Domineering Model (k = 1)

	0	1	2
0	$\frac{\theta(00)N(0,0)}{\theta(00)}$	$\frac{\theta(01)N(0,1)}{\theta(01)}$	$\frac{\theta(02)N(0,2)}{\theta(02)}$
1	$\frac{\theta(10)N(1,0)}{\theta(10)+\theta(02)}$	$\frac{\theta(11)N(1,1)}{\theta(11)+\theta(01)}$	$\frac{\theta(10)N(1,2)}{\theta(10)+\theta(00)}$
2	$\frac{\theta(02)N(1,0)}{\theta(10)+\theta(02)}$	$\frac{\theta(01)N(1,1)}{\theta(11)+\theta(01)}$	$\frac{\theta(00)N(1,2)}{\theta(10)+\theta(00)}$

Submissive Model (k = 2)

	0	1	2
0	$\frac{\theta(00)N(0,0)}{\theta(00)+\theta(10)}$	$\frac{\theta(01)N(0,1)}{\theta(01)+\theta(11)}$	$\frac{\theta(02)N(0,2)}{\theta(02)+\theta(10)}$
1	$\frac{\theta(10)N(0,0)}{\theta(00)+\theta(10)}$	$\frac{\theta(11)N(0,1)}{\theta(01)+\theta(11)}$	$\frac{\theta(10)N(0,2)}{\theta(02)+\theta(10)}$
2	$\frac{\theta(02)N(1,0)}{\theta(02)}$	$\frac{\theta(01)N(1,1)}{\theta(01)}$	$\frac{\theta(00)N(1,2)}{\theta(00)}$

(3)

The EM algorithm 'estimates' the unobserved table of mosaic counts $\underline{N}^*$ via the E-Step (3) from provisional estimates of the configuration probabilities $\hat{\theta}$ and from the observed table $\underline{N}$ (e.g. Exhibit 3 - Panel B). Then the algorithm recomputes the provisional estimates of the configuration probabilities $\hat{\theta}$ via the M-Step (2) from the "estimated table" $\{E[N^*(\underline{S})|\underline{N},\hat{\theta}]\}$.

Substituting (3) into (2) gives a system of five difference equations for each of the one focal-pair models, which iterate to the solutions of the likelihood equations (Haberman (1977), Theorem 4, p. 1143), namely equations (4) on the next page.

Closed-form expressions for the maximum likelihood estimates can be obtained by solving equations (4). There are four solutions to each system of 5 equations, corresponding to multiple peaks in the <u>likelihood</u> surface $L(\theta|\underline{N})$, the right hand side of (1) in general or the right hand side of (1A) for the one focal-pair models. Depending on the data $\underline{N}$, one or more of the peaks may fall outside the parameter space ($\theta(\underline{S}) > 0$ and $\Sigma(\underline{S})\theta(\underline{S}) = 1$) and can be dismissed. The four solutions for each of the two single focal-pair models of Hotta and Benzer (1973) are given in equations (4A) on the next page.

	Domineering Model (k = 1)	Submissive Model (k = 2)
$\hat\theta'(00) =$	$[N(0,0) + \frac{\hat\theta(00)}{\hat\theta(10)+\hat\theta(00)} N(1,2)]/2N$	$[\frac{\hat\theta(00)}{\hat\theta(00)+\hat\theta(10)} N(0,0) + N(1,2)]/2N$
$\hat\theta'(01) =$	$[N(0,1) + \frac{\hat\theta(01)}{\hat\theta(11)+\hat\theta(01)} N(1,1)]/2N$	$[\frac{\hat\theta(01)}{\hat\theta(01)+\hat\theta(11)} N(0,1) + N(1,1)]/2N$
$\hat\theta'(02) =$	$[N(0,2) + \frac{\hat\theta(02)}{\hat\theta(10)+\hat\theta(02)} N(1,0)]/2N$	$[\frac{\hat\theta(02)}{\hat\theta(02)+\hat\theta(10)} N(0,2) + N(1,0)]/2N$
$\hat\theta'(10) =$	$[\frac{\hat\theta(10)}{\hat\theta(10)+\hat\theta(02)} N(1,0)+ \frac{\hat\theta(10)}{\hat\theta(10)+\hat\theta(00)} N(1,2)]/2N$	$[\frac{\hat\theta(10)}{\hat\theta(00)+\hat\theta(10)} N(0,0)+ \frac{\hat\theta(10)}{\hat\theta(02)+\hat\theta(10)} N(0,2)]/2N$
$\hat\theta'(11) =$	$[\frac{\hat\theta(11)}{\hat\theta(11)+\hat\theta(01)} N(1,1)]/N$	$[\frac{\hat\theta(11)}{\hat\theta(01)+\hat\theta(11)} N(0,1)]/N$

(4)

$\hat\theta$	Domineering Model (k = 1)	Submissive Model (k = 2)
$\hat\theta(00) =$	$\frac{1}{2}[\frac{N-N(0,1)-N(1,1)}{N}][\frac{N(0,0)}{N(0,0)+N(1,0)}]$	$\frac{1}{2}[\frac{N-N(0,1)-N(1,1)}{N}][\frac{N(1,2)}{N(0,2)+N(1,2)}]$
$\hat\theta(01) =$	$[\frac{N(0,1)}{N}]$	$[\frac{N(1,1)}{N}]$
$\hat\theta(02) =$	$\frac{1}{2}[\frac{N-N(0,1)-N(1,1)}{N}][\frac{N(0,2)}{N(0,2)+N(1,2)}]$	$\frac{1}{2}[\frac{N-N(0,1)-N(1,1)}{N}][\frac{N(1,0)}{N(0,0)+N(1,0)}]$
$\hat\theta(10) =$	$\frac{1}{2}[\frac{N-N(0,1)-N(1,1)}{N}][\frac{N(1,0)}{N(0,0)+N(1,0)} - \frac{N(0,2)}{N(0,2)+N(1,2)}]$	$\frac{1}{2}[\frac{N-N(0,1)-N(1,1)}{N}][\frac{N(0,2)}{N(0,2)+N(1,2)} - \frac{N(1,0)}{N(0,0)+N(1,0)}]$
$\hat\theta(11) =$	$[\frac{N(1,1)-N(0,1)}{N}]$	$[\frac{N(0,1)-N(1,1)}{N}]$
	, Hotta and Benzer Estimates	, Hotta and Benzer Estimates
$\hat\theta(00) =$	$\frac{1}{2}[\frac{N(1,2)+N(0,0)}{N}]$	-
$\hat\theta(01) =$	$[\frac{N(0,1)}{N}]$	$[\frac{N(1,1)}{N}]$
$\hat\theta(02) =$	$\frac{1}{2}[\frac{N(1,0)+N(0,2)}{N}]$	-
$\hat\theta(10) =$	0	-
$\hat\theta(11) =$	$[\frac{N(1,1)-N(0,1)}{N}]$	$[\frac{N(0,1)-N(1,1)}{N}]$
$\hat\theta(00) =$	$\frac{1}{2}[\frac{N-N(0,1)-N(1,1)}{N}][\frac{N(0,0)}{N(0,0)+N(1,0)}]$	$\frac{1}{2}[\frac{N-N(0,1)-N(1,1)}{N}][\frac{N(1,2)}{N(0,2)+N(1,2)}]$
$\hat\theta(01) =$	$\frac{1}{2}[\frac{N(1,1)+N(0,1)}{N}]$	-
$\hat\theta(02) =$	$\frac{1}{2}[\frac{N-N(0,1)-N(1,1)}{N}][\frac{N(0,2)}{N(0,2)+N(1,2)}]$	$\frac{1}{2}[\frac{N-N(0,1)-N(1,1)}{N}][\frac{N(1,0)}{N(0,0)+N(1,0)}]$
$\hat\theta(10) =$	$\frac{1}{2}[\frac{N-N(0,1)-N(1,1)}{N}][\frac{N(1,0)}{N(0,0)+N(1,0)} - \frac{N(0,2)}{N(0,2)+N(1,2)}]$	$\frac{1}{2}[\frac{N-N(0,1)-N(1,1)}{N}][\frac{N(0,2)}{N(0,2)+N(1,2)} - \frac{N(1,0)}{N(0,0)+N(1,0)}]$
$\hat\theta(11) =$	0	-
$\hat\theta(00) =$	$\frac{1}{2}[\frac{N(1,2)+N(0,0)}{N}]$ *	- *
$\hat\theta(01) =$	$\frac{1}{2}[\frac{N(1,1)+N(0,1)}{N}]$	-
$\hat\theta(02) =$	$\frac{1}{2}[\frac{N(1,0)+N(0,2)}{N}]$	-
$\hat\theta(10) =$	0	-
$\hat\theta(11) =$	0	-
	, Koana and Hotta Estimates	, Koana and Hotta Estimates

(4A)

*As the foci approach the midline, the domineering and submissive models approach each other, resulting in the same estimates $\hat\theta$.

A dash '-' in the table of equations (4A) indicates that an estimate $\hat\theta(\underline{S})$ in each model is the same (k = 1 or 2). One of the solutions is that of Hotta and Benzer (1973, p. 49), and another solution is for the midline model (foci on the midline), which yields the map distance estimates in Koana and Hotta (1978, p. 128). The variance-covariance matrix for the maximum likelihood estimates $\hat\theta$ of the single focal-pair models can be obtained by firstly inverting the symmetric matrix below and secondly dividing the inverse by N.

Surprisingly, the <u>information</u> matrix which is N×(matrix (5)), is the same for both the domineering and submissive models (S = 2)! As summarized by (5), the precision of the fit of one focal-pair models is independent of the behavioral threshold k postulated (S > 2)?

$\underline{S}$	00	01	02	10
00	$\frac{1}{\theta(00)} + \frac{4}{\theta(11)+ (01)} + \frac{1}{\theta(10)+ (00)}$	$\frac{2}{\theta(11)+\theta(01)}$	$\frac{4}{\theta(11)+\theta(01)}$	$\frac{4}{\theta(11)+\theta(01)} + \frac{1}{\theta(10)+\theta(00)}$
01	-	$\frac{1}{\theta(01)} + \frac{1}{\theta(11)+\theta(01)}$	$\frac{2}{\theta(11)+\theta(01)}$	$\frac{2}{\theta(11)+\theta(01)}$
02	-	-	$\frac{1}{\theta(02)} + \frac{1}{\theta(10)+\theta(02)} + \frac{4}{\theta(11)+\theta(01)}$	$\frac{1}{\theta(10)+\theta(02)} + \frac{4}{\theta(11)+\theta(01)}$
10	-	-		$\frac{1}{\theta(10)+\theta(02)} + \frac{4}{\theta(01)+\theta(11)} + \frac{1}{\theta(00)+\theta(10)}$

(5)

In addition to the exploratory data analysis performed in a previous section, the program MAXLE in the interactive package asks the user to describe the data to be analyzed and then to choose a model by selecting the number of foci, etc. With the model structure selected, the program fits the model as in (4) and (5) and graphically displays the model's foci and landmarks in a fate map, using the program MAPPNG.

Models θ and θ' with different assumptions (e.g. on number of foci) and fitted to the same table of mosaic counts $\underline{N}$ (e.g. Exhibit 3 - Panel B) can be compared by their likelihood ratio $L(\theta|\underline{N})/L(\theta'|\underline{N})$. The likelihood $L(\theta|\underline{N})$ guides the search for a reasonable model to serve as the null hypothesis.

Having found a model, goodness-of-fit to this null hypothesis is assessed by a significance test using the Pearson χ^2 goodness-of-fit statistic in (6):

$$\chi^2 = \Sigma(i)\Sigma(\underline{L})\{N(i,\underline{L}) - E[N(i,\underline{L})|\hat{\theta}]\}*2/E[N(i,\underline{L})|\hat{\theta}] \quad (6)$$

with the convention 0/0 = 0 and degrees of freedom being the (number of cells) - (number distinct parameters). Conversations with the package are now illustrated in Exhibit 13 firstly using the program MAXLE.

The package reminds the user as to the expected data format (paragraphs (pr.) 1-2). Then the program queries the user about input-output control (pr. 3-9) and reads the data (pr. 10-11). Model structure and data structure (e.g. number of foci and number of mosaics (i.e. gynanders), respectively) are entered (pr. 12-29). At each input step the package checks that input is sensible (such as F < S), and if an entry is not sensible, the package instructs the user.

The package responds with limited details on the fit of the model (pr. 30) or can be asked for more extensive output, such as estimates of all blastoderm configuration probabilities $\hat{\theta}$ (see Table 5, Arnold and Kankel (1981)) and their standard errors. The user can cycle through the package (pr. 31), conveniently selecting a few features of the data and model structure to alter or many features (see Table 4 in Arnold and Kankel (1981) for 31 runs through the package made in one session). Finally the package terminates its session, outputing a distance matrix (pr. 31), which is passed to the fate mapping program MAPPNG (pr. 33).

The program MAPPNG graphically displays associations between the variables, landmarks, and foci, and the fate map is interpreted as a physical map of the blastoderm. Input is provided to MAPPNG (pr. 33-35); the number of iterations is controlled in the modified steepest descent algorithm used to minimize the error criterion E (pr. 36-38). The procedure is initialized (pr. 40-43). Output control is selected by the user (pr.39, 44 and 47).

As the program searches for coordinates $\underline{X}_1, \underline{X}_2, \ldots$

```
   .R MAXLE

1  THE GYNANDER DATA MUST HAVE THE FOLLOWING FORMAT:
   LEFT SIDE:ID,SIDE,DATA[7X,I3,A1,69I1]
   RGHT SIDE:ID,SIDE,DATA[7X,I3,A1,69I1]
   SO, THERE ARE TWO CARD IMAGES PER GYNANDER

2  EACH RECORD MUST CONTAIN 7 BLANK COLUMNS
   FOLLOWED BY A THREE DIGIT INTEGER
   SEQUENCE NUMBER FOLLOWED BY AN "L" OR AN "R" TO
   INDICATE LEFT OR RIGHT SIDE--LEFT SHOULD PRECEDE
   RIGHT.  THE CODES FOR EACH VARIABLE FOLLOW(UP TO
   68 STRUCTURES + 1 GLOBAL BEHAVIOR).  THE GLOBAL
   BEHAVIOR IS ALWAYS IN THE LAST COLUMN OF THE RECORD.
   ALL VARIABLES MUST BE CODED AS "0" FOR MALE,
   "1" FOR FEMALE, "2" FOR MIXED AND "3" FOR UNSCORED.

3  DO YOU WISH DIALOG KEPT IN A LOG FILE? N

4  DO YOU WISH THE PRINTER TO FUNCTION AS THE LOG FILE? N
   WHEN THE DATA IS ENTERED, SCORES OF
   LANDMARKS WHICH ARE MIXED WILL BE RANDOMLY
   ASSIGNED A VALUE OF MALE(0) OR FEMALE(1).

5  THE RANDOM NUMBER GENERATOR USED IN THIS PROCESS
   REQUIRES 2 INTEGER SEED VALUES.  YOU MAY USE THE
   VALUES:       35,  -12519
   OR ANY TWO VALUES BETWEEN -32,000 AND +32,000[2I6] --> 35,-12519

6  IF YOU DO NOT EXIT FROM THE PROGRAM, THE
   PROGRAM ON EACH SUCCESSIVE RUN WILL CHOOSE NEW SEED
   VALUES;HOWEVER, IF YOU DO EXIT FROM THE PROGRAM, THEN
   ON THE NEXT RUN USE THE SEED VALUES OUTPUTED BELOW.

7  DO YOU WISH TO RESTART THE PROGRAM BASED ON
    THE INPUT OF A PREVIOUS RUN?
   YOU MUST ENTER Y FOR YES AND N FOR NO.
   YOU MUST ENTER "N" FOR NO IF THIS IS YOUR FIRST RUN: N

8  DO YOU WISH THE EXPANDED FORM OF THE OUTPUT TO
   BE PRINTED ON THE LINE PRINTER?  IF YOU ANSWER "NO" TO
   THIS QUESTION, YOU WILL STILL RECEIVE LINE PRINTER
   OUTPUT OF THE MOST RELEVANT PORTIONS OF THE ANALYSIS,
   BUT CERTAIN LONG TABLES WILL BE DELETED IN ORDER TO
   SAVE TIME AND PAPER --> N

9  DO YOU WANT THE RAW DATA PRINTED?
   ENTER Y FOR YES OR N FOR NO; ALL YES-NO QUESTIONS IN
   THIS PROGRAM ARE TO BE ANSWERED IN THIS WAY: N

10 WHAT IS THE NAME OF THE DATA FILE?
   ENTER IN THE FORM "DDn:NNNNNN.XXX": DL0:COMADU.DAT
   DO YOU WISH THIS FILE SCANNED TO DETERMINE
   THE NUMBER OF GYNANDERS AND VARIABLES(SITES) AVAILABLE
   AND TO CHECK ON THE DATA FORMAT? Y

11  454 RECORDS HAVE BEEN COUNTED= 227 GYNANDERS.
    39 COLUMNS WERE COUNTED.
   ASSUMING THE STANDARD CONVENTION, THERE ARE 28
   VARIABLES OF WHICH 1 IS A GLOBAL BEHAVIOR.
      0BAD RECORDS WERE ENCOUNTERED.

12 HOW MANY SITE-PAIRS ARE AVAILABLE?[I4]] 27
13 HOW MANY SITE-PAIRS ARE TO BE ENTERED?[I4] 4
14 HOW MANY LANDMARKS ARE TO BE ENTERED?[I4] 2
15 WHAT IS THE BLASTODERM?
16 IF A SITE IS A LANDMARK, ENTER A 0
   IF A SITE IS A FOCUS, ENTER A 1
17 SITE   1?[I1] 0
18 SITE   2?[I1] 1
19 SITE   3?[I1] 1
20 SITE   4?[I1] 0
21 WHAT IS THE CHARACTER THRESHOLD?[I4] 4
22 WHAT IS THE CONTIGUITY REQUIREMENT?
   ENTER 0 FOR NO CONTIGUITY REQUIREMENT;
   ENTER 1 FOR LOCAL CONTIGUITY REQUIREMENT;
   ENTER 2 FOR GLOBAL CONTIGUITY REQUIREMENT.
   [I1]--> 1
23 HOW MANY GYNANDERS ARE THERE?[I5] 227
24 LANDMARK  1 TO BE USED OUT OF  2 IS:[I2]? 1
25 LANDMARK  2 TO BE USED OUT OF  2 IS:[I2]? 24

26 WHAT IS THE ORDER ALONG THE BLASTODERM OF
   LANDMARK     1 ?[I2] 1
27 WHAT IS THE ORDER ALONG THE BLASTODERM OF
   LANDMARK    24 ?[I2] 2
28 HOW MANY CYCLES ARE DESIRED IN THE EM ALGORITHM?[I4] 10
29 DO YOU WISH TO INITIALIZE THE EM ALGORITHM?[A1]
   IF NOT, THE PROGRAM INITIALIZES BY SETTING ALL POSSIBLE
   BLASTODERM CONFIGURATION PROBABILITIES EQUAL--> N

                    **LEAVING "INPUT" TO BEGIN CALCULATION**

30 THE CHI-SQUARE STATISTIC IS              17.705
   THE LOG-LIKELIHOOD IS           -538.176

31 DO YOU WISH TO RUN THE PROGRAM AGAIN?[A1]
   ENTER Y FOR YES;
   ENTER N FOR NO: N
   WHAT IS THE NAME OF THE OUTPUT FILE FOR THE
   DISTANCE MATRIX?
   *DSTNCE.MTX

32 THE NEXT TIME THAT YOU USE THIS PROGRAM USE
   THE SEED VALUES        24855,     -16599

   STOP --
```

to minimize the error criterion, trial values of the error criterion are reported (pr. 45). At the end of the search, coordinates for each site in the fate map and the map itself are provided (pr. 46, 48).

The package is available on request from D. R. Kankel (Department of Biology, Yale University, Box 6666, 260 Whitney Ave., New Haven, CT 06511, (203) 436-1292).

Work reported here was supported by research grants NS11788 and NS12346 from the National Institutes of Health.

Arnold, J. and D.R. Kankel (1981). Fate mapping multi-focus phenotypes. Genetics 99, 211-229

Dempster, A.P., N.M. Laird, and D.B. Rubin (1977). Maximum likelihood from incomplete data via the EM algorithm. Journal of the Royal Statistical Society, Series B 39, 1-22

Flanagan, J.R. (1976). A computer program automating construction of fate maps of Drosophila. Developmental Biology 53, 142-146

_____________ (1977). A method for fate mapping the foci of lethal and behavioral mutants in Drosophila melanogaster. Genetics 85, 587-601

Garcia-Bellido, A. and J.R. Merriam (1969). Cell lineage of the imaginal discs in Drosophila gynandromorphs. Journal of Experimental Zoology 170, 61-76.

Haberman, S.J. (1974). The Analysis of Frequency Data. The University of Chicago Press, Chicago.

_____________ (1977). Product models for frequency tables involving indirect observation. Annals of Statistics 5, 1124-1147

Hall, J.C., W.M. Gelbart, and D.R. Kankel (1976). Mosaic systems. pp. 265-314. In: The Genetics and Biology of Drosophila, Volume 1a. Edited by M. Ashburner and E. Novitski. Academic Press, NY.

Hotta, Y. and S. Benzer (1973). Mapping of behavior in Drosophila mosaics. pp. 129-167. In: Genetic Mechanisms of Development, 31st Symposium of the Society for Developmental Biology. Edited by F.H. Ruddle, Academic Press, New York.

Koana, T. and Y. Hotta (1978). Isolation and characterization of flightless mutants in Drosophila melanogaster. Journal of Embryological Experimental Morphology 45, 123-143

Merriam, J.R. and K. Lange (1974). Maximum likelihood estimates for fate map locations of behavior in Drosophila. Developmental Biology 38, 196-201

Poulson, D.F. (1950). Histogenesis, organogenesis, and differentiation in the embryo of Drosophila melanogaster mergen. pp. 168-174. In: Biology of Drosophila edited by M. Demerec. Wiley, New York.

Sturtevant, A.H. (1929). The clavet mutant type of Drosophila simulans: a study of chromosome elimination and of cell-lineage, Zeit. wiss. Zool. 135, 323-356

Zalokar, M., I. Erk, and P. Santamaria (1980). Distribution of ring X chromosomes in the blastoderm of gynandromorphic D. melanogaster, Cell 19, 133-141

```
33 R MAPPNG
   PROVIDE NAME OF INPUT FILE
   *DSTNCE.MTX

34 PROVIDE NAME OF FILE TO RECEIVE NEW COORDINATES
   *DSTNCE.MX2

35 PROVIDE NAME OF OUTPUT FILE
   *DSTNCE.001

36 ENTER MAXIMUM NUMBER OF ITERATIONS TO BE PERFORMED: 50

37 YOU MAY ENTER THE UPPER BOUND FOR ALLOWED
   DISTANCE[F7.3] OR YOU MAY ALLOW THE PROGRAM TO SELECT THE
   LARGEST OBSERVED DISTANCE AS A DEFAULT.  SELECT THE DEFAULT
   BY SIMPLY ENTERING A "CARRIAGE-RETURN" -->

38 PROVIDE UPPER LIMIT ON CYCLE VALUE[I3] -->

39 DO YOU WISH TO RECEIVE ONLY THE MINIMAL
   AMOUNT OF PRINTER OUTPUT?  THIS OPTION IS RECOMMENDED
   IN THAT IT SAVES PAPER AND TIME.  ADDITIONAL RESULTS
   ARE ALWAYS AVAILABLE IN THE OUTPUT FILE.  ENTER "Y"
   TO SUPRESS SOME PRINTED OUTPUT --> Y

40 THE PROGRAM CAN FIX THE X,Y COORDINATES OF ONE
   OF THE VARIABLES.  TO DO THIS, JUST ENTER THE VARIABLE
   NUMBER[I3].  A "CARRIAGE-RETURN" ONLY WILL REJECT THIS
   OPTION --> _

41 YOU MAY ALSO FIX  THE ANGULAR RELATIONSHIP BETWEEN
   ANY TWO VARIABLES.  ENTER THE NUMBERS
   OF BOTH VARIABLES IF THIS OPTION IS TO BE SELECTED[2I5]-->

42 WILL INITIAL COORDINATES BE ENTERED FROM KEYBOARD? N

43 DO YOU WISH THE PROGRAM TO GENERATE INITIAL
   OORDINATES?  IF YOU ANSWER "N", THE PROGRAM WILL ASSUME
   THAT THESE ARE TO BE FOUND IN THE DATA INPUT FILE --> Y

44 WILL THE FORM OF THE INPUT MATRIX BE UPPER(U),
   LOWER(L) OR FULL(F)? F

45 MAXIMUM PERMITTED DISTANCE IS  0.706

      1
      2
      3
      4
      5
      6
      7
      8
      9
     10
     11
   INCREASING ERROR ON TWO CONSECUTIVE CYCLES

     13
     14
     15
     16
     17
     18

INCREASING ERROR ON TWO CONSECUTIVE CYCLES

 50

46 FINAL ERROR=        0.00047      FINAL CC=  -1.20

   1  NEW COORD X,Y= 0.00000 1.62439        OLD COORD X,Y= 0.00000 0.70600

   2  NEW COORD X,Y= 0.00000 0.82055        OLD COORD X,Y= 0.00000 0.60900

   3  NEW COORD X,Y= 0.00000 0.74854        OLD COORD X,Y= 0.00000 0.57300

   4  NEW COORD X,Y= 0.00000 0.05000        OLD COORD X,Y= 0.00000 0.00000

   ERROR ON  1 IS     0.00008
   ERROR ON  2 IS     0.00015
   ERROR ON  3 IS     0.00008
   ERROR ON  4 IS     0.00016

47 DO YOU WISH FINAL CONFIGURATION PLOTTED ON THE TERMINAL? Y
```

48

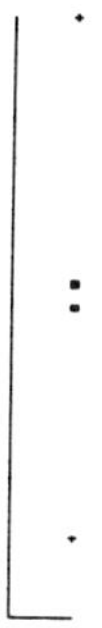

ORIGIN=-0.195,-0.195   XMAX=0.000 YMAX=1.624

AN INTERACTIVE PROGRAM FOR ADAPTIVELY ANALYZING DATA

Michael Brannigan, The University of Georgia

When attempting to model multivariate data sets contaminated by error, it is generally not known what the underlying function is to be approximated, nor the distribution from which the errors derive. One useful method, in this low information content situation, is to choose an approximating function which can be fitted to the data adaptively. This problem subsumes the problems of model size or order. A satisfactory solution to this problem is to use methods from information theory and especially the Akaike Information Criterion (AIC). A discussion of univariate and multivariate numerical techniques using these ideas is presented and an interactive computer procedure is described.

1. Introduction

The need to analyze data efficiently, whether in a univariate or multivariate setting, arises from the ever increasing output of such data from all the scientific, medical and engineering disciplines. It is typical, in such instances, that information concerning the distribution of errors in the data, and the functional relation between the variables, is unknown. We have, therefore, a problem in which the information content of the data set is low, and we need some method to resolve this lack of information to give the owner of the data an idea on how his data behaves.

One method of solving such problems is to consider each individual data set in isolation, which is in many ways the ideal situation. However, this places a heavy, time consuming burden on the data analyst, who has to have a large store of computer software to deal with the variety of data sets he is likely to come across. We need a method which the data owner can use directly on his data set, and which can give satisfactory answers to most problems without the need of a trained data analyst. We present here such a method, namely the use of adaptive approximation techniques accessed interactively by the data owner.

This approach presents its own problems, and it's these problems which motivate our methodology.

The first problem is the data owner. He is typically neither a trained statistician nor a numerical analyst. Here the power of interactive computing is manifest. The possible choices on the menus given to the person analyzing the data can be suitably explained while at the conclusion of each menu we can give:

If in doubt try ...

On the other hand we must not exclude the knowledgeable user, thus each menu should include choices of sufficient variety and complexity.

The second problem is: can we find suitable approximation techniques which will be universal enough to apply to any possible data set? To solve this problem we propose using adaptive approximation of the data. For the univariate case the answer to our question is an unequivocal affirmative, while for multivariate data sets much research is still needed.

Other attempts at adaptively fitting functions to data are given in [14, 23, 30, 31, 32] with reports of success for various data sets. These methods, however, require assumptions concerning the data which we feel to be unnecessary and often inapplicable to general data sets. Thus in [23] uncorrelated errors are looked for to test for trends in the data, in [30, 31] the user is asked to supply an upper bound for the errors in the data and in [14, 32] normality of the distribution of errors is assumed.

We propose a general method applicable to both univariate and multivariate data sets using the model selection criteria of Akaike [2]. This requires the minimal of assumptions on the data set being analyzed.

We can now state the mathematical problem which represents our technique.

2. Mathematical Problem

We presume the existence of a data set (t_i, y_i), $i=1,\ldots,N$; $t_i \varepsilon \mathbb{R}^n$, $y_i \varepsilon \mathbb{R}$, and assume that a relationship between t_i and y_i exists of the form

$$y_i = F(t_i) + e_i \ , \quad i=1,\ldots,N \ ,$$

where F is an unknown underlying function and e_i is the unknown error in the measurement of y_i.

Consider now an approximating set S_k of real-valued functions ϕ defined by

$$S_k = \{\phi(t,\theta_k) : t \varepsilon \mathbb{R}^n, \ \theta_k \varepsilon \mathbb{R}^k\}$$

where θ_k is a vector of unknown parameters.

For a suitable norm we can now pose the regression problem:

find $\theta_k \varepsilon \mathbb{R}^k$ such that

$$||y_i - \phi(t_i,\theta_k)||$$

is minimized over S_k subject to

$$u \leq T\phi \leq v$$

where $u, v \varepsilon \mathbb{R}^n$ and T maps ϕ into $\mathbb{R}^n$.

This is a constrained approximation problem in the given normed space.

If now k becomes a variable then we arrive at the concept of adaptivity.

Definition. The set of approximating functions S_k is adaptive if S_k is defined for all k such that $1 \leq k \leq L$ for some L.

The adaptive regression problem which we wish to solve is:

Find not only a best θ_k *for fixed* k *but that* k *which best solves the data problem presented.*

The software for solving this problem will be hidden to the casual user of the program so it is imperative that the subprograms used are of the highest quality with respect to programming style and numerical stability. This criterion is certainly not satisfied in many existing statistical computer packages.

3. Interactive Program

The visible portions of the technique are the menus presented to the user. In fact we only ask for two choices to be made and our program chooses others based on these, and it is not difficult to envisage an extension to the program outlined here to make the analysis wholly automatic for a general user. For every choice given suitable software has to be provided and we indicate reliable methods according to the state of the art.

The first question which we pose is: (a) *Which norm do you wish to use?* One guideline which is well founded is; if the distribution of errors e_i, i=1,...,N has the form:

$$\exp(-|e|^p/p\sigma)/\sigma$$

then the use of the ℓ_p norm provides maximum likelihood estimates of our parameters θ_k when ϕ depends linearly on θ_k. For a discussion of this and choice of norm see [25]. For a relationship between which ℓ_p norm to use and kurtosis see [22].

Good software exists for values of p = 1, 2, ∞, which are specific approximation problems, see [1, 3, 4, 5, 6, 9, 15, 16, 20]. However, it is not difficult to provide, using optimization methods, software for the general $1 < p < \infty$ value, see [15, 16, 21].

A further question arises, in the context of the direct approximation problem, and that is, does the user want to constrain the result? We feel that the minimum which must be provided are constraints on the resulting y values. This will arise if the experimenter wishes to bound the error for each experimentally determined value y_i, i=1, ...,N. Software for this problem exists, see [7, 12, 16, 18, 24, 29].

On the bottom line of our menu we must put:

If in doubt use $p = 1$

We have chosen here the ℓ_1-norm as we have found this a good general norm for the many data sets we have used, see [8]. However, different situations may dictate other choices, and a reasonable compromise is p = 1.5.

We note here that the choice of p = ∞ should only occur when it is thought that the errors are small and uniformly distributed. Even in this case we have found that p = 1 works equally as well. If the errors are normally distributed, which is not usual in practice, then p = 2 is the theoretical choice.

For a totally automatic data analysis program, where this choice of which norm to use is omitted, then use a subprogram to calculate the $\ell_{1.5}$ norm without constraints.

Our second question posed to the user is: (b) *Which approximating set of functions do you wish to use?* In the general situation, which we consider, where nothing is known of our underlying function F, there does not seem to be any advantage in choosing approximating sets S_k which are non-linear in θ_k. If the data owner has some knowledge on how the variables are related then this must be used, and the method outlined here can easily incorporate such a user defined regression function.

The set of choices for the user will consist of two menus, one for univariate data and the other for multivariate data.

(i) Univariate case Here the choice of approximating functions is simply a choice of which type of spline to use, as the theory of splines shows the undoubted superiority of splines over other functions for univariate approximation. We can also minimize the space complexity of our program by the use of one stable algorithm. Such an algorithm can provide the user with any continuity requirements he wishes, even to the case where there are discontinuities in the underlying function.

To use splines we must first define an interval [a,b] in which the abscissae of the data lies. Let π_{pk} be a p-partition of order k for [a,b], that is $\pi_{pk} = \{\lambda_i,\ i=1-k,\dots,p+k\}$ where

$$\lambda_{1-k} \le \dots \le \lambda_0 = a < \lambda_1 \le \dots \le \lambda_p < \lambda_{p+1} = b \le \dots \le \lambda_{p+k}$$

The set $\{\lambda_i\}$ are referred to as knots and if for some j $\lambda_j = \lambda_{j+1} = \dots = \lambda_{j+r-1}$ then λ_j is said to have multiplicity r.

On this partition π_{pk} we can define the normalized B-splines N_{kj}, j=1,...,p+k, where N_{kj} is a piecewise polynomial such that

$$N_{kj} = \begin{cases} 0 \text{ in the intervals } (-\infty,\lambda_{j-k}) \text{ and } (\lambda_j,\infty), \\ \text{polynomial of degree} < k \\ \text{on each interval } [\lambda_{i-1},\lambda_i],\ i=j-k,\dots,j \end{cases}$$

If knot λ_i has multiplicity r then every B-spline N_{kj} for which $j-k+1 \le i \le j$ has continuity C_{t-1}, where t = k-r, at λ_i. By grouping knots together we can therefore achieve discontinuity at a knot λ_i by placing k knots at that point. On the other hand we can give our B-spline the maximum possible continuity of k-2 by keeping all the knots simple.

The normalized B-spline N_{kj} satisfies the recurrence relationship

$$N_{kj}(t) = \frac{t-\lambda_{j-k}}{\lambda_{j-1}-\lambda_{j-k}} N_{k-1,j-1}(t) + \frac{\lambda_j - t}{\lambda_j-\lambda_{j-k+1}} N_{k-1,j}(t)$$

with

$$N_{1j}(t) = \begin{cases} 1 & t \in [\lambda_{j-1},\lambda_j] \\ 0 & \text{otherwise} \end{cases}$$

This relationship together with the properties:

$$N_{kj}(t) > 0 \quad t \in (\lambda_{j-k},\lambda_j)$$

$$N_{kj}(t) = 0 \quad t \notin [\lambda_{j-k},\lambda_j]$$

$$\sum_{j=1}^{p+k} N_{kj}(t) = 1 \quad t \in [a,b]$$

make their calculation computationally stable. For an analysis see [13].

Having defined these B-splines we can now compute the spline approximation $\phi(t)$ of our data, where

$$\phi(t) = \sum_{j=1}^{p+k} \alpha_j N_{kj}(t) ,$$

by solving the overdetermined system of linear equations given by

$$\phi(t_i) = y_i, \quad i=1,\ldots,N$$

using the norm chosen by the user.

The menu which is presented will include values for k = 1,2,3 as these fit all the usual types of data sets. The other choice is the multiplicity r of each knot. From our own experience we would recommend that the bottom line should read;

If in doubt use k=3 and r=2.

This gives the Hermite cubic piecewise approximation and takes care of any sudden changes in the direction of the underlying function.

The approximation problem is well defined once π_{pk} is given, and it is the choice of partition which makes the problem adaptive. Not only does the position of the knots pose a problem, namely a non-linear optimization problem, but the value of p is unknown and the adaptive procedure must find a 'best' p. These features of the technique we discuss later. For a complete account of the adaptive procedure for the univariate case see [0].

(ii) Multivariate case For this case much research is needed as little has been done in this area. Software for interpolation has been thoroughly tested, see [17], but these programs can only be used when the errors are negligible. Even in this case the resulting function has as many parameters as there are data points which is not a satisfactory situation. For an account of the adaptive procedure for the multivariate case see [10].

The first type of approximating set of functions to consider are the tensor products of splines. Thus, for example if we have two dimensional data scattered over an area given by [a,b] x [c,d] and, π_{pk} is a p-partition of order k on [a,b], π'_{qk} is a q-partition of order k on [c,d] then we can approximate our data by the bicubic-spline, over the grid $\pi_{pk} \times \pi'_{qk}$,

$$\phi(x,y) = \sum_{i=1}^{q+k} \sum_{j=1}^{p+k} \alpha_{ij} N_{ki}(y) N_{kj}(x)$$

Tensor products for n-dimensional data can be also so defined.

This approach causes difficulties. Data sets are not usually regularly distributed over the domain, which results in grid squares containing no data points, and hence the matrix of coefficients for our approximation problem becomes singular with all the attendant computational difficulties. Also if, for example, one extra knot is added to the partition π_{pk} above then q+k more unknowns are added to the approximation, and this subtracts from the power of the adaptive process which performs better when the number of unknowns is not increased at too rapid a rate.

It is for these reasons that we do not recommend that tensor products are included on the menu for multivariate data sets, at least for a general user environment.

If we consider where the problems arise in tensor product approximation we see that they stem from the need to use a grid of lines over the domain. One method of overcoming this problem is to use a triangulation and finite element techniques. This can be done for two or three dimensional data but the computational difficulties of extending this further are prohibitive.

We propose the use of metric approximants to overcome the difficulties associated with a grid and to this end we have begun a study of these methods, see [11].

First a set of 'knots' $\{T_i : T_i \in \mathbb{R}^n, i=1,\ldots,N$ are chosen, where $T_i = (T_{i1}, T_{i2}, \ldots, T_{in})$, which are scattered over the domain $D \subset \mathbb{R}^n$ of our data set. For any $t \in D$ we have the Euclidean metric

$$\rho^2(t,T_i) = \sum_{k=1}^{n} (t_k-T_{ik})^2 ,$$

where $t = (t_1, \ldots, t_n)$. Using this metric we can define the products

$$\pi_\alpha(t,j) = \prod_{\substack{k=1\\k\neq j}}^{N} \rho^{2\alpha}(t,T_k) ,$$

and the functions

$$\gamma_j(t) = \pi_\alpha(t,j)/\sum_{k=1}^{N} \pi_\alpha(t,k), \quad j=1,\ldots,N .$$

We can now define a N(n+1) linear space, elements of which we denote by $\phi(t)$, where

$$\phi(t) = \left\{\sum_{i=1}^{N} \beta_{io} + \sum_{j=1}^{n} \beta_{ij}(t_j-T_{ij})\right\} \gamma_i(t)$$

These functions are C_2 continuous for $\alpha \geq 1$ and

$$\phi(T_k) = \beta_{ko} ,$$

$$\frac{\partial\phi(T_k)}{\partial x_i} = \beta_{ki} ,$$

$$\frac{\partial^2\phi(T_k)}{\partial x_i \partial x_j} = 0 .$$

For $0.5 < \alpha < 1$ we have C_1 continuity,

$$\phi(T_k) = \beta_{ko} ,$$

$$\frac{\partial\phi(T_k)}{\partial x_i} = \beta_{ki} ,$$

and second derivatives do not exist.

Also it is possible to place a further knot, anywhere in the domain, and only increase the number of unknown values by n+1. This is the minimum possible for a domain in n-space. We have thus achieved our objective. For the mathematical properties and numerical experiments see [11].

Although this method does work well we did find that fine tuning of the knot positions was needed. We declare that more research is needed in this area.

The menu for this section is limited and should be reduced to a choice of $\alpha=1$ or $\alpha=0.5$.

(iii) Summary of Menus We have thus arrived at the lists of choices the user is to make

Q. Which norm?
(i) p = 1
(ii) p = 2
(iii) p, uniform
(iv) p = users choice
If in doubt use p = 1.5.

Q. Which approximation?

Univariate
(i) order of spline k=?
(ii) continuity r=?
If in doubt put k=3, r=2

Multivariate
(i) Tensor product spline
(ii) Metric approximant α=0.5
(iii) Metric approximant α=1
If in doubt use (iii).

Q. Do you wish to bound the resulting error?

Having made these choices the rest of the program is automatic.

4. Adaptive Selection Procedure.

The choices above relate to the process by which a best θ_k is computed given a value for k, see our problem definition in section 2. What the program has to find is the correct value of k, at least as best as possible. To solve this problem we suggest the use of the Akaike Information Criterion (AIC).

From our approximation problem we obtain for any $\theta_k \in \mathbb{R}^k$ a $\phi \in S_k$ such that

$$y_i = \phi(t_i,\theta_k) + r_i(\theta_k) \quad i=1,\ldots,N$$

The residuals $r_i(\theta_k)$ of this approximation can be computed and we should compare these known residuals with the unknown errors e_i of the data. The minimum amount of information which we can prescribe to these errors is the form of their distribution.

Let $f(x,\xi)$ be the assumed distribution for the errors, where $x \in \mathbb{R}$ is a random variable and ξ the vector of parameters. For each θ_k the residuals $r_i(\theta_k)$ of the approximation are considered as N observations of the random variable x; the vector ξ is then calculated as the maximum likelihood estimate, given $\theta_k \in \mathbb{R}^k$. Our assumption concerning this choice of distribution is that for some $\Theta \in \mathbb{R}^m$ the residuals $r_i(\Theta)$ equal e_i, i=1, ...,N; the estimate $\xi(\Theta)$ we denote by Ξ. It is our intention, therefore, to compare $f(x,\xi(\theta_k))$ with $f(x,\Xi)$, and to do this we use the mean information for discrimination as defined by

$$I(\Xi,\xi(\theta_k)) = \int f(x,\Xi)\, \ell n \frac{f(x,\Xi)}{f(x,\xi(\theta_k))} dx.$$

We then choose that k which minimizes the value of I; this is related to the maximum entropy principle, where I is the entropy.

Using an analysis described in [2, 10] we obtain an estimate of I and arrive at the following result;

choose that k which minimizes

$$-2\sum_{i=1}^{N} \ell nf(r_i(\theta_k^*),\ \xi(\theta_k^*)) + 2k$$

where θ_k^* is the best approximation vector of coefficients from S_k. This is the AIC used previously in time series analysis.

We note here that if $f(x,\xi)$ is the normal distribution and we use a least squares norm to obtain θ_k^* for each k then the AIC criterion is asymptotically equivalent to the method of generalized cross-validation [10, 19, 20].

To be able to use this criterion we have to assume some distribution $f(x,\xi)$ with ξ unknown. So that the user does not have to make such a choice we suggest that use is made of the extended exponential distribution

$$f(x,\xi) \propto \exp(-|x|^p/p\xi^p)/\xi$$

then we must minimize

$$N \ln \hat{\xi}^p + 2k$$

where the maximum likelihood estimate $\hat{\xi}$ is given

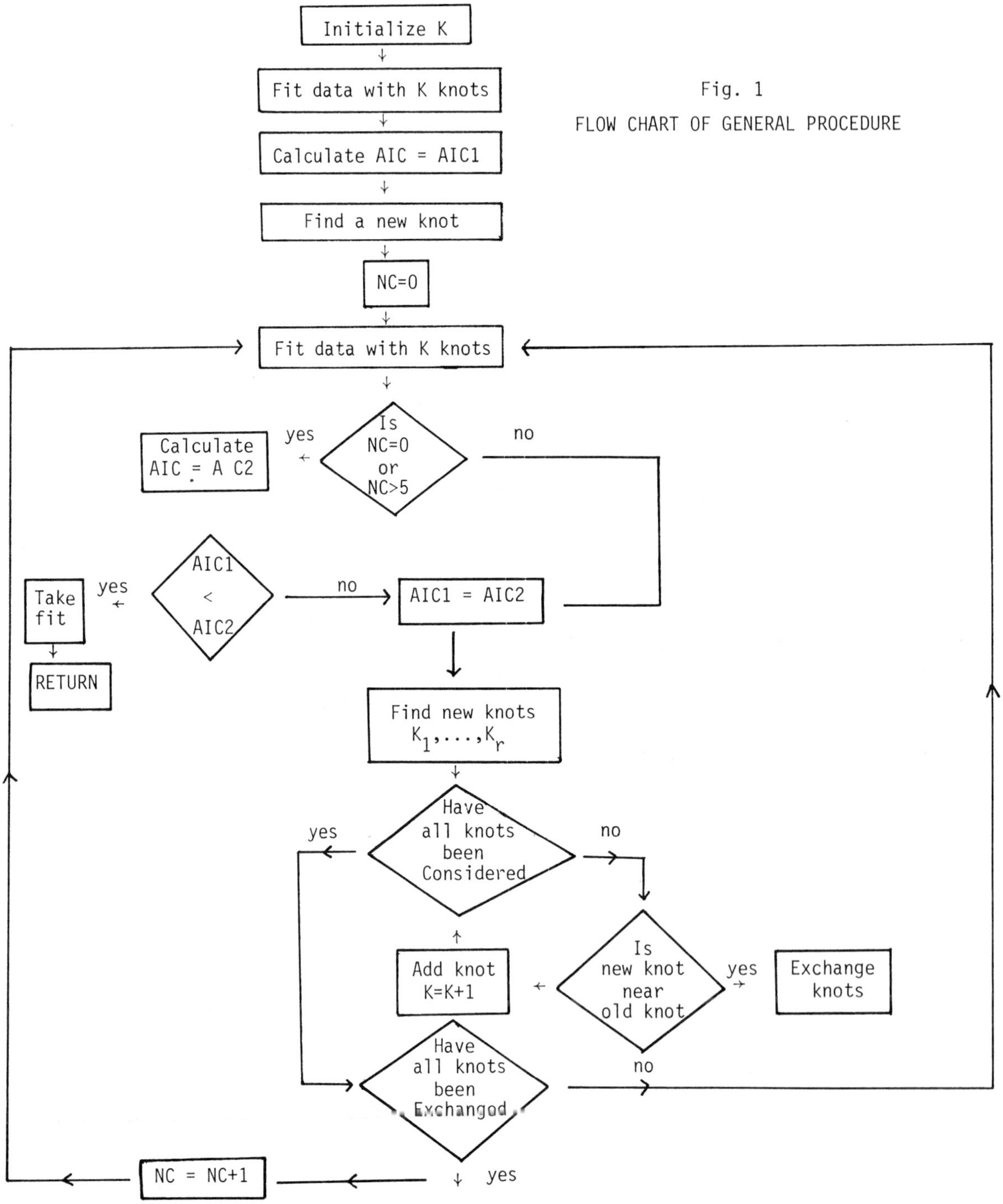

Fig. 1

FLOW CHART OF GENERAL PROCEDURE

by

$$N\hat{\xi}^p = \sum_{i=1}^{N} r_i^{\,p}(\theta_k^*)$$

From the numerical results we have considered to date this seems to be a good guideline.

5. Computational Considerations

Having outlined the procedural techniques used in the program we now present the flow chart for the subroutine. The underlying concept is to increase the number of knots of the approximation until the value of AIC is minimized. Being a discrete problem and because we increase the number of unknowns k by at least 2 for each iteration we can only hope for an estimate of this minimum. However, if the increase in knots is kept low the minimum found will be a good estimate, also because of the type of approximation we use, see section 3, then good approximations to the data are obtained for a small number of knots.

As can be seen from the flow chart Fig. 1 new knots are added to the approximation if AIC1 > AIC2. The question to be asked is where to put the new knots and how many.

For the univariate case a simple procedure is to compare the second moments of the residuals in each interval with the global second moment. That is, if we have k intervals, n_j, $j=1,\ldots,k$, data points for interval j, and the residuals of the present fit are given by r_{ij}, $i=1,\ldots,n_j$; $j=1,\ldots,k$ we compute

$$m_j = \sum_{i=1}^{n_j} r_{ij}^{\,2}/n_j \qquad j=1,\ldots,k$$

and

$$M = \sum_{j=1}^{k} \sum_{i=1}^{n_j} r_{ij}^{\,2}/N$$

We now consider those intervals j for which $m_j > M$. Having found an interval we place the new knot where the present curve fit has a first or second zero derivative. The reason for this becomes evident when we realize that the low degree polynomials used in the approximation have only a small number of turning points and that hence we cannot expect these to follow data with many peaks and valleys.

In some circumstances the new knot X is near an existing knot, say X_i. Nearness in this instance means that the number of data points in the interval (X_i,X) is small (<10). This situation can occur when the initial estimate for X_i is poor and X is a better estimate of the turning point of the underlying function. In this situation X replaces X_i as a knot and no new knot is added to that interval.

For the multivariate metric approximation we again must look for maxima and minima of the underlying function. We have found that the coefficients β_{ij}, $j > 0$, are small. This arises because the function $(x_i-T_{ij})\phi(x)$ tends to infinity as x becomes large hence the coefficients of this basis function should be near zero for the approximation to work best. Having found candidates for new knots we either add them or exchange them as in the univariate case. Here nearness between a new knot T and existing knot T_i is if the hypersphere centre T radius $\rho(T,T_i)$ is small, say it includes <10 data points. We use the number of data points as a measure of closeness so that we can place knots physically close to each other when the density of data points is high and not close when the density of data points is low.

Having found a new set of knots a new approximation is found.

One question which must be answered is whether it is necessary to optimize the position of the knots. If we consider the approximation problem then not only can we find optimal values for the coefficients θ_k but the knot positions can be optimized. The non-linear problem of optimal knot positioning is computationally difficult and the time complexity of the problem grows exponentially with the increase of data points. It has been our experience that the methods described above for finding new knot positions work well for moderate to large sets, say >30 points. However, for small data sets these methods deteriorate but then optimization of knot positions at each iteration becomes computationally acceptable. Whichever procedure is chosen a final optimization should be made when the fit has been accepted using the criteria in the subprogram displayed in Fig. 1.

BIBLIOGRAPHY

1. Abdelmalek, N.N. Chebyshev solutions of overdetermined systems of linear equations. BIT, 15 (1975), 117-129.
2. Akaike, H. Information theory and the extension of the maximum likelihood principle. Proc. 2nd Symp. Inf. Th. (B.N. Petrov and F. Craki Ed.) Akademie Kiado, Budapest (1973), 267-281.
3. Barrodale, I. and Roberts, F.D.K. An improved algorithm for discrete ℓ_1 linear approximation. SIAM J. Numer. Anal. 10 (1973), 839-848.
4. Barrodale, I. and Young, A. Algorithms for best L_1 and L_∞ linear approximations on a discrete set. Numer. Math. 8, (1966), 295-306.
5. Bartels, R.H., Conn, A.R. and Sinclair, J.W. Minimization techniques for piecewise differentiable functions: the ℓ_1 solution to an overdetermined linear system. SIAM J. Numer. Anal. 15 (1978), 224-241.
6. Bartels, R.H. and Golub, G.H. Stable numerical methods for obtaining the Chebyshev solution to an overdetermined system of equations. Comm. ACM 11 (1968), 401-406.

7. Brannigan, M. Theory and computation of best strict constrained Chebyshev approximation of discrete data. IMA J. of Numer. Anal. 1 (1981), 169-184.
8. Brannigan, M. An adaptive piecewise polynomial curve fitting procedure for data analysis. Comm. Stats. A10, 18 (1981), 1823-1848.
9. Brannigan, M. The strict Chebyshev solution of overdetermined systems of linear equations with rank deficient matrix. Numer. Math. to appear.
10. Brannigan, M. A multivariate adaptive data fitting algorithm; in, Numerische Methoden der Approximations theorie. (L. Collatz, Ed.) Vol. 5, ISNM, Birkhauser, (1982), 30-42.
11. Brannigan, M. Multivariate data modelling by metric approximants. University of Georgia Technical Report 137, (1982).
12. Chalmers, B.L. and Taylor, G.D. Uniform approximation with constraints. Jber. dt. Mat. Ver. 81, (1979), 49-86.
13. Cox, M.G. Practical Spline Approximation. NPL Report DITC 1/82, (1982).
14. Craven, P. and Wahba, G. Smoothing noisy data by spline functions; estimating the correct degree of smoothing by the method of cross-validation. Numer. Math. 31 (1979), 377-403.
15. Fischer, J. An algorithm for discrete linear L_p approximation. Numer. Math. 38 (1981), 129-139.
16. Fletcher, R. Practical methods of optimization. Vol. 2, J. Wiley (1981).
17. Franke, R. Scattered data interpolation: Test of some methods. Math. Comp. 38 (1982), 181-200.
18. Gimlin, D.R., Cavin, R.K. and Budge, M.C. A multiple exchange algorithm for calculation of best restricted approximation. SIAM J. Numer. Anal. 11, (1974), 219-231.
19. Golub, G.H., Heath, M. and Wahba, G. Generalized cross-validation as a method for choosing a good ridge parameter. Technometrics. 21, 2 (1979).
20. Golub, G.H. and Reinsch, C. Singular valued decomposition and least squares solutions. Numer. Math. 14 (1970), 407-420.
21. Hettich, R. Semi-infinite programming. Lecture Notes in Control and Information Science. Berlin, Springer-Verlag, (1979).
22. Money, A. lt.; Affleck-Graves, J.F.; Hart, M.L. and Barr, G.D.I. The linear regression model; L_p norm estimation and the choice of p. Comm. Statist. - Simul. Comp., 11 (1), (1982), 89-109.
23. Powell, M.J.D. Curve fitting by splines in one variable. Numer. Approx. to Functions and Data. (J.G. Hayes, Ed.) Athlone Press, (1970), 65-83.
24. Powell, M.J.D. The minimax solution of linear equations subject to bounds on the variables. In Proc. Fourth Manitobe Conference Num. Math. Winnipeg, Utilitatos Mathematica, (1975).
25. Rice, J.R. and White, J.S. Norms for smoothing and estimation. SIAM Rev., 6 (1964), 243-256.
26. Shepard, D. A two dimensional interpolation function for irregularly spaced data. Proc. 1968 ACM National Conference, 517-524.
27. Sposito, V., Smith, W., McCormick, G. Minimizing the sum of absolute deviation. Vadenhoeck and Ruprecht, Gottingen, (1978).
28. Stone, M. An asymptotic equivalence of choice of model by cross-validation and Akaikes criterion. J. R. Statist. Soc. B36, (1977), 44-47.
29. Taylor, G.D. and Winter, M.J. Calculation of best restricted approximations. SIAM J. Numer. Anal. 7, (1970), 248-255.
30. Taylor, G.D. and Hull, J.A. Restricted range adaptive curve fitting. Int. J. Num. Meth. Engng 14 (1979), 379-408.
31. Taylor, G.D. and Avila, P.G. Adaptive ℓ_1 and ℓ_2 curve fitting. Int. J. Num. Meth. Engng 14 (1979).
32. Wahba, G. and Wold, S. A completely automatic French curve: fitting spline functions by cross validation. Comm. Stats. 4, 1, (1975), 1-17.

SOLVING INTEGRAL EQUATIONS WITH NOISY DATA: AN APPLICATION OF SMOOTHING SPLINES IN PATHOLOGY

Douglas Nychka
Department of Statistics
University of Wisconsin

Abstract

Integral equations often provide crucial links between interesting characteristics of a system and the actual data that is collected. In pathology, a version of Abel's equation relates the size distribution of spherical tumors in a block of tissue with the distribution of cross sections that are produced by sectioning the sample. Solving this equation is important for it would facilitate the study of tumor growth and perhaps point toward some of the mechanisms of cancer.

By representing the solution as a smoothing spline a wide class of integral equations including Abel's equation can be solved. The necessity for smoothing the solution arises naturally, especially when the data contain some measurement noise. However, the amount of smoothing must be carefully chosen to insure objective results. A promising approach for determining the appropriate degree of smoothing directly from the data is the method of generalized cross validation. This method will be discussed along with aspects of the spline's computation. The estimate is illustrated for Abel's equation with both Monte Carlo examples and actual experimental data.

Keywords: Abel's equation, cross validation, integral equations, smoothing splines, stereology.

1. INTRODUCTION

Integral equations often provide crucial links between interesting characteristics of a system and the actual data that is collected. In this discussion we consider the general model:

$$Z_i = L_i(f) + e_i \tag{1}$$

where

$$L_i(f) = \int_{\mathbb{R}} k(x_i,r)f(r)dr.$$

$\underset{\sim}{Z}$ is a vector of observations and $\underset{\sim}{e}$ is the corresponding measurement noise. $k(\tilde{\cdot},\cdot)$ is a known integral kernel and f an unknown function. Under reasonable assumptions concerning the smoothness of f and the distribution of the measurement noise, we address the problem of recovering the function f from the data $\underset{\sim}{Z}$. Since in many situations the form of f is not known, or can not be effectively identified from the observations, a non-parametric estimate of f is considered. The proposed estimate is a smoothing spline where the appropriate amount of smoothness in the solution is determined from the data by cross validation. This procedure is illustrated with a version of Abel's integral equation which relates two probability distribution functions, F_2 and F_3, in the following manner:

$$F_2(x) = 1 - \frac{1}{\mu}\int_x^R \sqrt{r^2-x^2}\, dF_3(r), \tag{2}$$

where

$$\mu = \int_0^R r dF_3(r) \text{ and } F_3(r) = 1 \quad \text{for} \quad r \geq R.$$

Given a random sample from the distribution F_2, one is interested in an estimate for the density of F_3. In our particular application of this equation, F_3 is the distribution of tumor radii in a sample of liver tissue and F_2 is the distribution of tumor cross sections observed from slices of the tissue. Although this is a classical problem in the field of stereology, it is not often approached from the context of solving an integral equation.

The next section describes the experimental data which motivated this research and formulates the estimation problem in terms of the general model (1). The following section uses this statistical model as a basis for estimating f_3, the density function of the tumor radii, by regression. Although this estimate is easy to compute, it has the disadvantage that the smoothness in the solution is a function of the number of regression variables. This difficulty motivates the development of the smoothing spline estimate in section 4. Throughout the paper, dissection data from a sample of mouse liver tissue is used as an example. This data has the advantage that the tissue sample has also been exhaustively dissected so that the true distribution of tumor sizes is known. Section 5 compares the spline estimate of f_3 to the actual distribution and discusses possible contributions to the error in the estimate.

2. A MODEL FOR TUMOR DISSECTION DATA

This particular application of Abel's equation was suggested by the data from experiments in pathology studying the growth of micro tumors in the livers of mice. Mice are injected with a carcinogen which over time induces the formation of malignant tumors in the liver. Groups of mice are killed at different times and samples of liver tissue are stained and embedded in parafin. The matrix of parafin enables the sample to be sliced very thin and these slices are mounted on microscope slides. Tumors in the sample will now appear in cross section on these slides.

The validity of different stochastic models for tumor growth can be determined by the distribution of tumor sizes at different times. These growth patterns are important because they might suggest some of the mechanisms which initiate and promote liver cancer. However, by the limitations of the dissection procedure, tumors can only be identified by their cross sections. Since tumors of different sizes can produce the same size cross section, there is not a direct correspondence between the cross sectional data and the distribution of tumor sizes. Although it is possible to take many, closely spaced slices and completely reconstruct each tumor, this procedure is both tedious and costly. What is required is a statistical method that estimates the tumor size distribution from a small number of slices. To accomplish this, the data needs to be placed in the framework of some probability model.

The biology of the liver suggests that the tumors will be uniformly distributed throughout the tissue, while examination of successive cross sections indicates that the tumors are roughly spherical. These assumptions suggest a model from geometric probability. Consider a medium which contains spheres whose centers are distributed uniformly, and whose equitorial radii are distributed according to $F_3(r)$. Now suppose this medium is sliced in a manner independent of the spheres' sizes and locations. Let $F_2(x)$ denote the distribution of the radius of a cross section on the slice. The relationship between F_2 and F_3 is given by equation (2) and was first derived by Wicksell, (1925). Suppose the radius of a cross section can only be observed above a certain size, ε. The integral relationship will still be valid if one interprets F_2 and F_3 as distributions conditional on the radius being larger than ε and if one substitutes for μ the parameter:

$$\mu_\varepsilon = \int_\varepsilon^R \sqrt{r^2-\varepsilon^2}\, dF_3(r).$$

This modification was noticed by Chover and King, (1982), and has practical significance since there is usually a lower limit of detection for cross sections.

Let $\hat{F}_2$ be the sample distribution function of the radii of cross sections and let $\{P_i\}_{i=o,m}$ be a partition of the interval $[\varepsilon,R]$.

$$\hat{F}_2(P_i) - \hat{F}_2(P_{i-1}) = F_2(P_i) - F_2(P_{i-1}) + e_i$$

where the errors, $\underset{\sim}{e}$ will be asymptotically normal with mean zero and only weakly correlated. This still holds when a parallel series of slices cut a tumor more than once.

Let

$$Z_i = \hat{F}_2(P_i) - \hat{F}_2(P_{i-1})$$

Using equation (2) and substituting μ_ε for μ

$$Z_i = L_i\left(\frac{f_3}{\mu_\varepsilon}\right) + e_i\ , \qquad (3)$$

where

$$L_i(h) = \int_{P_{i-1}}^R \sqrt{r^2-P_{i-1}^2}\, f_3(r)dr - \int_{P_i}^R \sqrt{r^2-P_i^2}\, f_3(r)dr.$$

By considering differences in the distribution function to reduce the correlation of the error, a more complicated integral kernel has been introduced. However, (3) is still in the form of the basic integral model presented in the introduction. Estimating the tumor size density from a sample of cross sections is equivalent to solving Abel's equation with noisy data.

3. ESTIMATING A DENSITY BY REGRESSION

To introduce the smoothing spline estimate we first consider a simpler method that estimates f_3 by regression. Let $\{\phi_j\}_{j=1,N}$ be a basis of density functions and represent the tumor size density as

$$f_3 = \sum_{j=1}^N a_j\phi_j, \quad \sum_{j=1}^N a_j = 1\ .$$

If

$$X_{ij} = L_i(\phi_j)$$

then

$$\underset{\sim}{Z} = X\underset{\sim}{\alpha} + \underset{\sim}{e} \quad \text{where} \quad \underset{\sim}{\alpha} = \frac{1}{\mu_\varepsilon}\underset{\sim}{a}\ .$$

The parameters of this linear model can be estimated by least squares and then normalized to yield values for $\underset{\sim}{a}$. Iteratively reweighted least squares could be used if one wanted to account for the different variances in the noise. When the basis is made up of step functions, this method is similar to the unfolding technique proposed by Nicholson and Merckx, (1969). Although this estimate is easy to compute, the procedure ignores the influence of the integral relationship on the linear model. The drawback is that the properties of the estimate are sensitive to the choice of the basis, $\{\phi_i\}_{i=1,N}$. When N is small, unless f_3 is well approximated by the basis, the estimate will miss distinctive features of the size distribution. At the other extreme, a large basis of functions can provide too much flexibility and the resulting estimate may have a rough appearance.

Figure 1 is the cross sectional distribution fit to some dissection data using a large basis. The data consist of 154 tumor cross sections from the liver of a mouse killed 28 weeks after the injec-

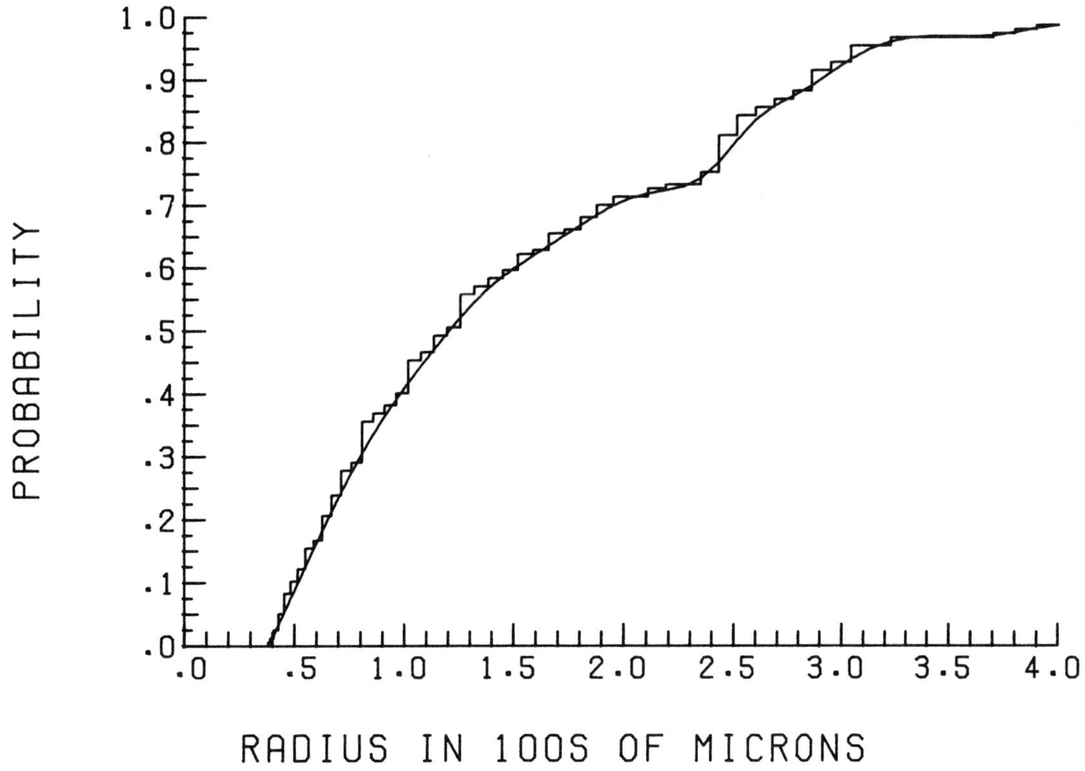

Figure 1. The sample distribution function of the radii from tumor cross sections (step function), and the regression fit (smooth curve) using a large basis of functions. The data are sampled from mouse liver tissue 28 weeks after the injection of DEN. Cross sections below 40 microns (ε) can not be detected.

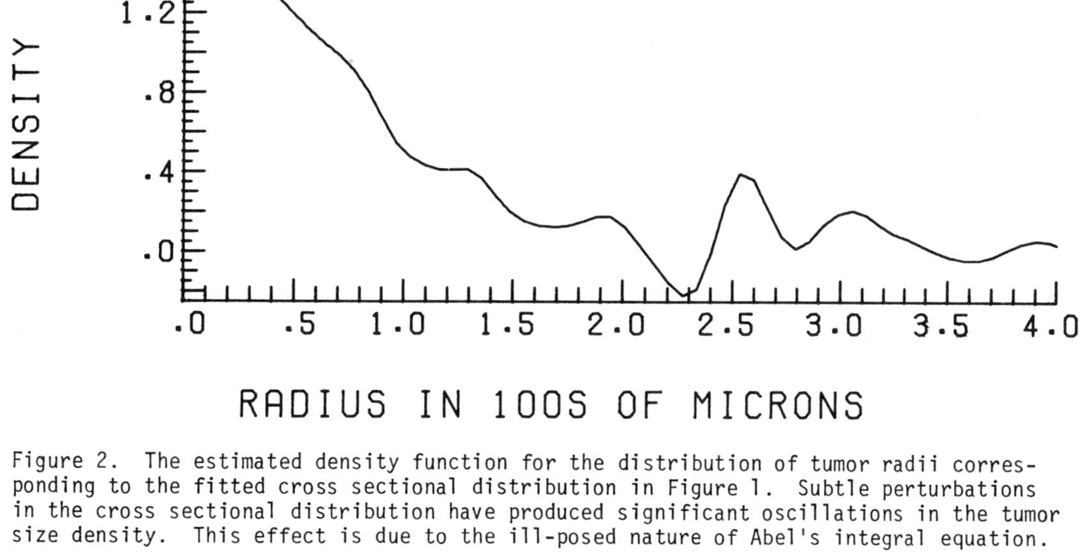

Figure 2. The estimated density function for the distribution of tumor radii corresponding to the fitted cross sectional distribution in Figure 1. Subtle perturbations in the cross sectional distribution have produced significant oscillations in the tumor size density. This effect is due to the ill-posed nature of Abel's integral equation.

tion of diethylnitrosamine. Although the fitted curve is a reasonable match to the data, the resulting tumor size density (Figure 2) is not very smooth and would be difficult to interpret. The fitted cross sectional distribution has incorporated some of the noise due to sampling a finite population. When this cross sectional distribution is translated into the corresponding tumor size distribution, the noise is greatly amplified.

This is a basic feature of most integral equations. When a small perturbation of a function in the range of the integral operator produces a large deviation in the solution the equation is termed ill-posed. In particular, the ill-posed nature of Abel's equation results in the regression matrix, $(X'X)$, being close to singular.

The above discussion demonstrates the dependence of the estimate on the size of the basis. One way of avoiding this problem is to specify an estimate which not only fits the data well, but also is constrained to maintain a certain degree of smoothness. In this manner, a large basis can be used without obtaining results such as in Figure 2. The introduction of smoothing is not only a well accepted technique in numerical analysis (regularization) but also has intuitive appeal. Since biologic phenomenon behave in a continuous manner one expects the growth patterns of tumors to yield smooth distributions. It is reasonable to incorporate this information into any statistical procedure.

4. THE SPLINE ESTIMATE AND GCV

The smoothing spline estimate is best expressed as the solution to a minimization problem.

Let

$$\mathcal{L}(h) = \sum_{i=1}^{m} (L_i(h)-Z_i)^2 + \lambda \int_{\varepsilon}^{R} (h''(r))^2 dr$$

and define the space of functions

$$H = \{h : h,h', \text{ are absolutely continuous}\} \text{ and } h'' \in L^2[\varepsilon,R] \quad .$$

The estimate is

$$\hat{f}_3 = \frac{\hat{h}}{\int_{\varepsilon}^{R} \hat{h}(r)dt}$$

where $\hat{h} \in H$ and satisfies

$$\mathcal{L}(\hat{h}) = \min_{h \in H} \mathcal{L}(h) \ .$$

Note that $\int_{\varepsilon}^{R} \hat{h}(r)dr$ is an estimate for μ_F.

The spline estimate minimizes the sum of two contrasting loss functions. The sum of the squared deviations measures the fidelity of the radial density to the data, while the other loss function characterizes the overall smoothness of the density. Under this smoothness criterion, the spline will tend to join points by lines, since any part of the curve that is close to being linear will have a small second derivative.

The space of functions, H, over which the minimization takes place was chosen because it meshes well with $\mathcal{L}(\cdot)$ and has a Bayesian interpretation with respect to a prior distribution placed on f_3 (Wahba, (1978)).

The parameter λ controls the relative weight given to the two components of $\mathcal{L}(\cdot)$ and can be interpreted the ratio of the noise and the signal variances. When λ is zero, the spline will interpolate the data. This would be appropriate when the measurement noise is negligible. As λ goes to infinity, the spline will become a linear function where the parameters are estimated by least squares. Without an objective method for determining a good value for the smoothing parameter, λ, the smoothing spline estimate encounters the same kind of problems as the regression method. Figure 3 demonstrates the sensitivity of the radial density estimate as the smoothing parameter varies. For large λ, the resulting spline is very smooth, but may have ignored some features of the data. When λ is small, the estimate fits the cross sectional distribution well, but yields an oscillating estimate for the tumor size density. In these particular data, one wonders whether the mode at 280 microns is an actual component of the distribution or rather just an artifact from under smoothing.

One way of choosing a good value for λ is by cross validation (Wahba, (1977)). This method determines λ by measuring how well an excluded data point can be predicted from the remaining data. For any value of λ let

$$\hat{f}_3^{i,\lambda}$$

be the estimate of the tumor size density from the cross sectional data with the ith data point, Z_i, excluded. The generalized cross validation (GCV) function is defined by

$$V(\lambda) = \sum_{i=1}^{m} (L_i(\hat{f}_3^{i,\lambda}) - Z_i)^2 W_i$$

where the weights $\{W_i\}_{i=1,m}$ account for the relative influence of different data points on the solution.

The value of λ which minimizes this function is used to estimate the density. Choosing λ in this manner has some desirable asymptotic properties and has worked well for moderate sample sizes in Monte Carlo experiments.

Although this estimate has been defined in an abstract manner, the actual computation of the spline is a linear problem for fixed λ. There is a matrix, $A(\lambda)$, which depends only on the partition $\{P_i\}_{i=0,m}$ and the parameter λ such that

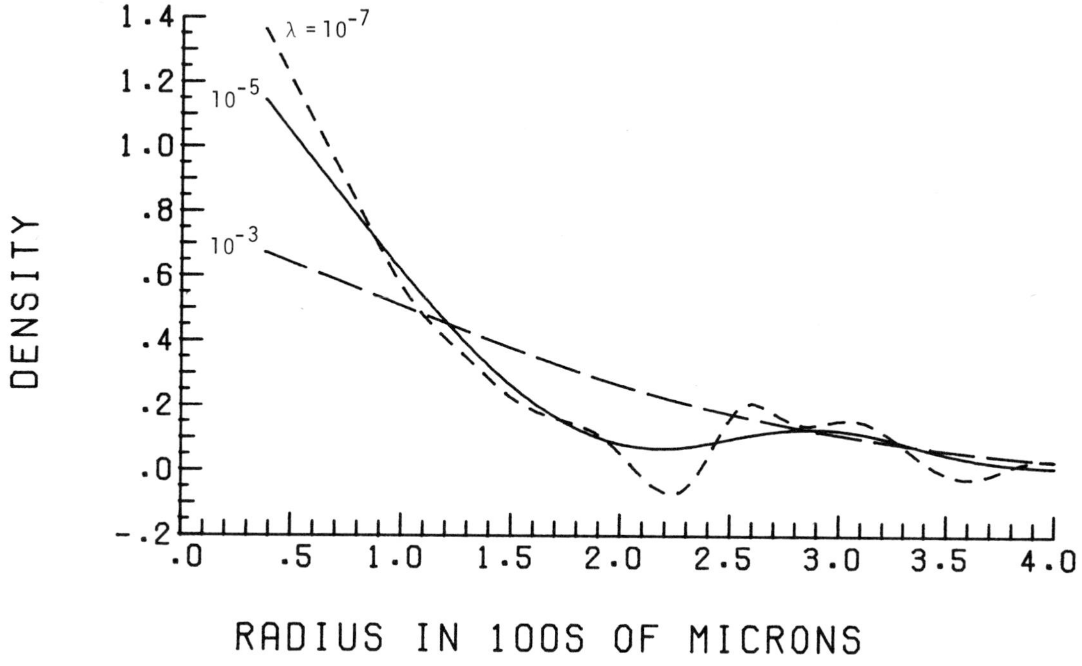

Figure 3. The influence of the smoothing parameter, λ, on the spline estimate. As λ is increased, more emphasis is placed on the smoothness of the spline. When λ = ∞, the spline will be a straight line with the parameters estimated by least squares.

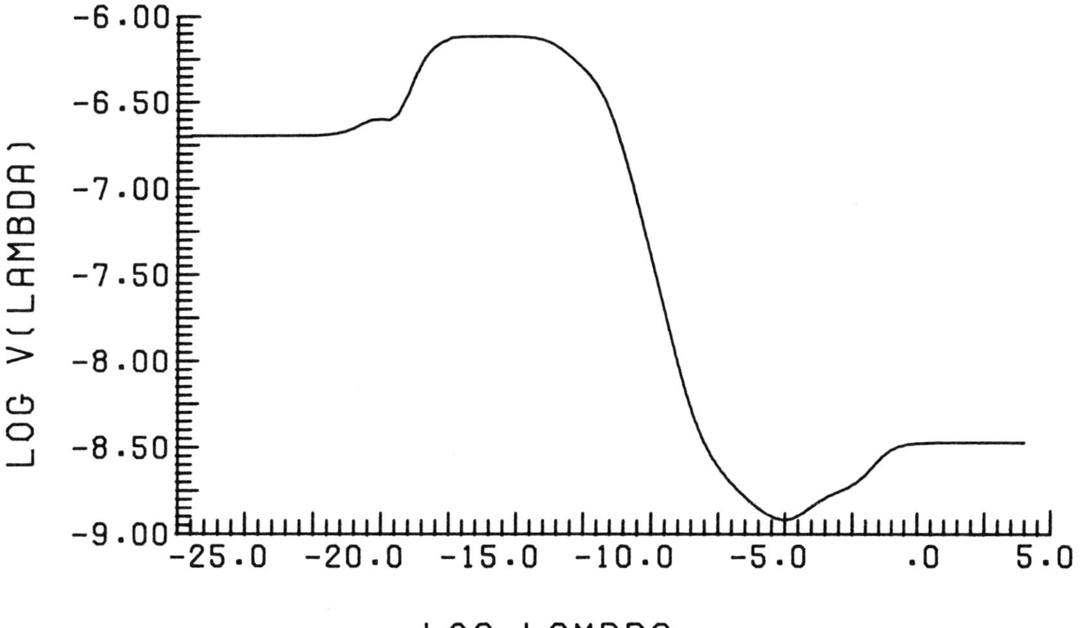

Figure 4. The generalized cross validation (GCV) function for the data. V(λ) measures the ability of the spline to predict an excluded data point from the remaining data. The value of λ which minimizes this function is considered on appropriate amount of smoothing.

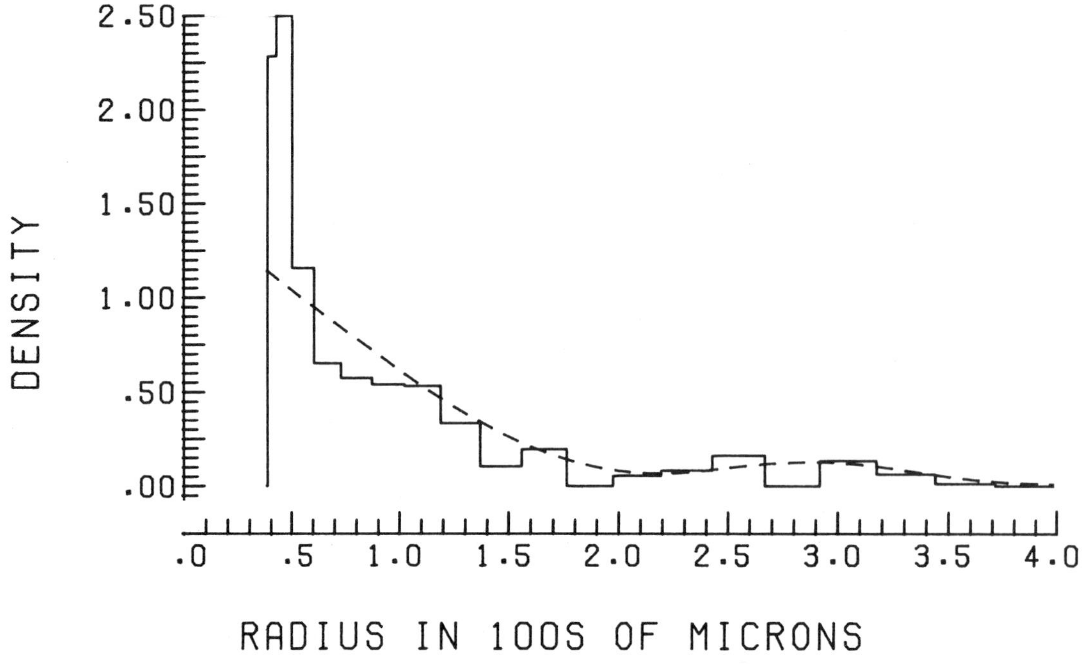

Figure 5. A histogram of the reconstructed tumor radii (solid) and GCV smoothing spline estimated from the cross sectional data (dotted).

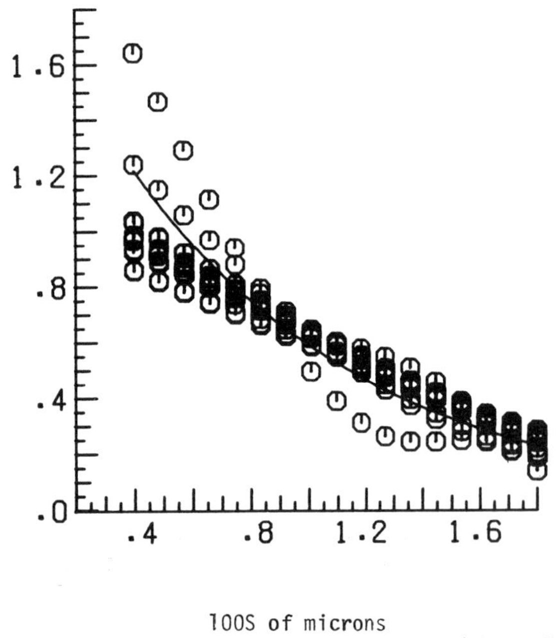

Figure 6. The spline estimates (symbols) from 12 repetitions of a Monte Carlo simulation using an exponential distribution (solid line) for the tumor sizes. The sample size is approximately the same as in the data. The results indicate a slight bias in the estimate near ε .

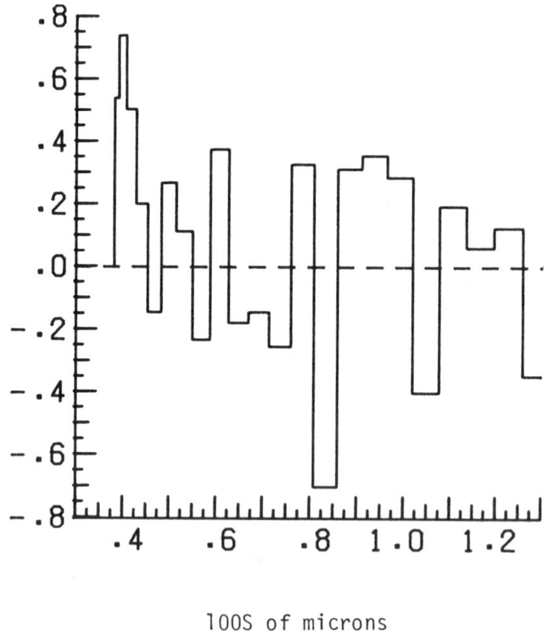

Figure 7. The difference between the histogram of the observed cross sections and the cross sectional distribution predicted from the reconstructed data via Abel's equation. The histograms are normalized to have unit area. The peak below 50 microns can account for the under estimate in Figure 5.

$$\begin{pmatrix} L_1(\hat{f}_3) \\ \vdots \\ L_m(\hat{f}_3) \end{pmatrix} = A(\lambda)\underset{\sim}{Z}$$

This expression simplifies the cross validation function to

$$V(\lambda) = \frac{m\|(I-A(\lambda))\underset{\sim}{Z}\|^2}{(tr(I-A(\lambda)))^2}$$

and avoids the work of reestimating the spline for each excluded point at each value of λ. In fact, the amount of computation needed to estimate the spline using GCV to choose λ is dominated by one singular value decomposition of a matrix. This matrix is positive definite and depends only on the partition $\{P_i\}_{i=1,m}$ and the integral kernel (see Wendelberger, (1981)).

The GCV function for the data (Figure 4) is minimized when the smoothing parameter is about 10^{-5}. This suggests that the middle spline in Figure 3 is a good estimate for the size density. Note that this estimate retains a mode around 280 microns.

5. THE RECONSTRUCTED DATA

For the data set used in this discussion, all the tumors in the sample have also been reconstructed so the exact distribution of tumor sizes is known. Thus, there is a means for judging the validity of the estimate in this example. Overall, the agreement between a histogram of the reconstructed data and the smoothing spline estimated by GCV (Figure 5) is good. These results are particularly striking since there are only 53 reconstructed tumors in the tissue sample. (The greater number of cross sections is due to multiple cuts of the same tumors.)

The concentration of tumors around 280 microns predicted by the spline is an actual feature of the reconstructed data. However, close to the lower limit, ε, the spline underestimates the reconstructed distribution.

This departure can come from several sources. Because the spline is a biased estimate, part of the difference may be due to a statistical bias. However, Monte Carlo results for a distribution of similar shape (Figure 6) suggest that this bias is not large.

Any attempt to recover the reconstructed data from the cross sections will be influenced if the two data sets are not in good correspondence via the integral equation. One way of checking this correspondence is to compare the expected cross sectional distribution predicted from the reconstructions with the observed cross sectional distribution. The expected distribution is computed by substituting the sample distribution function of the reconstructed data into the integral equation (2). For this example there is a slight departure between the two distributions near ε (Figure 7). Since the estimation procedure is sensitive to slight variations in the cross sectional distribution, this small disagreement could also account for the underestimate. The difference between the observed and expected cross sectional distributions can have several explanations. One is the variation in sampling due to the spacing of the slices relative to the tumors' centers. Another explanation is the departure of tumors from the exact sphericity assumed under the derivation of Abel's equation.

6. FUTURE WORK

Although the body of this paper has focused on the solution of a single integral equation, the method can be applied to a wide class of integral kernels. Note that the definition of the estimate in section 4 is not specific to Abel's equation. It would be interesting to investigate the properties of this method under other applications and different kernels.

An important area that needs research is the development of confidence regions for functionals of this estimate. For fixed λ this is not difficult, however, when λ is chosen by GCV the problem is challenging.

ACKNOWLEDGMENT

The author wishes to acknowledge the advice and encouragement of Dr. Grace Wahba. He also would like to thank Dr. Stanley Goldfarb for bringing interesting statistical problems to his attention and making the pathology data available.

REFERENCES

1. Chover, J., King, J. (1981). Personal communication.

2. Nicholson, W. L., Merckx, K. R. (1969). "Unfolding Particle Size Distributions". Technometrics, 11, 707-724.

3. Wahba, G. (1977). "Practical approximate solutions to linear operator equations when the data are noisy," SIAM J. Numer. Anal., 14, 4.

4. Wahba, G. (1978). "Improper priors, spline smoothing and the problem of guarding against model errors in regression", J. Roy. Stat. Soc. Ser. B., 40, 3.

5. Wendelberger, J. (1981). "The computation of Laplacian smoothing splines with examples", University of Wisconsin Statistics Department Technical Report #648.

6. Wicksell, S. D. (1925). "The corpuscle problem, Part I." Biometrika 17, 87-97.

This research supported by ARO contract DAAG29-80-k-0042 and NCI grants CA15664 and CA25522 .

Difficulties in Numerical Computation and Databases

Chair: John W. Wilkinson, Rensselaer Polytechnic Institute

CANSIM, The Canadian Socio–Economic Management Information System
Martin Podehl, Statistics Canada

Some Ideas in Using the Bootstrap in Assessing Model Variability Regression
Gail Gong, Stanford University

Moment Series for Moment Estimators of the Parameters of a Weibull Density
K.O. Bowman, Union Carbide Corp.
L.R. Shenton, University of Georgia, Athens

CANSIM: THE CANADIAN SOCIO-ECONOMIC MANAGEMENT INFORMATION SYSTEM

Martin Podehl, Statistics Canada

INTRODUCTION

Statistical computing requires two basic ingredients: data and analytical software tools. Statistical data are either available in the public domain or are the result of a researcher's own statistical collection program. They are either micro data, for example, the result of a survey, or they are macro data, of aggregated nature, for example, economic statistics. Analytical software tools are available in a wide variety of packages which have been developed over the years and are being refined constantly to take advantage of newly developed algorithms as well as new hardware/software environments.

In the beginning of statistical computing, the main concern was with the development of efficient and sound algorithms. Statistical analysis packages were developed usually by universities and Research Institutes. As these packages matured, data and file handling facilities were added to ease the burden for the researcher. In the commercial environment, on the other hand, data base management packages were developed to ease the burden in organizing, storing, documenting and accessing data in a flexible manner. As these systems matured, flexible retrieval and analytical software of a statistical nature were added in order to explore the full information potential contained in those data bases.

Today these distinctions are of no significance because both the data base management system developer and the statistical package developer have realized the importance of a smooth interface between the two environments.

CANSIM, the Canadian Socio-economic Information management system of Statistics Canada fulfills both needs: an organized data base of statistical information, and analytical tools for statistical and economical modelling and interpretation.

CONCEPT AND PURPOSE

The concept of CANSIM was born in the late sixties as a mechanism to store and make available key statistics to economists and statisticians in Canada. CANSIM brings together under one umbrella, data from Statistics Canada as well as other organizations such as federal departments, provincial governments and the Bank of Canada. Today, in a publicly accessible data base, socio-economic data of time series as well as of cross-classified nature are stored, documented and disseminated to the statistical community in Canada. From a modest start, CANSIM has grown in volume and in importance and is now an integral part of socio-economic analysis in Canada.

The original concept placed primarily emphasis on a simple data organization so that data from different sources could be related to each other. Simple access routine allowed the retrieval of selected time series which then were taken by the user into his own environment for further computation. Over the years much software was developed or interfaced with CANSIM for increasing complex analysis.

EVOLUTION AND OPERATION

Initially, CANSIM was synonymous with time series. In 1968 the foundation was laid with 2,500 series; today the time series module carries over 300,000 time series. In order to handle cross-classified data efficiently, a cross-classified module was added to CANSIM which since 1976 has been used to store data of multi-dimensional nature, referred to as tables. A table can be either retrieved in whole or in part. CANSIM Cross-Classified now carries data from a variety of predominantly social statistical areas, such as health, justice, education, and demography.

Recently a third module was added, the CANSIM Summary Data, which allows access and selective retrieval of data which are also available in the form of User Summary Tapes. At present, our Census data aggregated to small areas are available in this module. That we now have three distinct information systems is not the result of design but rather historical evolution. At some future point unification has to be attempted so that one data model can be used to describe all data regardless of whether they are predominantly of time series or predominantly of cross-classified nature.

The CANSIM systems are maintained and operated by Statistics Canada. They are maintained under contract at a commercial computing service organization and are updated daily. The public has access to these data bases under separate, individual contracts with the supplier. However, under the trade name CANSIM Mini Base, CANSIM data are also available through other computing services companies called Secondary Distributors. Secondary Distributors obtain daily updates to a standard sub-set of the main base. In addition they can obtain supplementary time series as requested by their clientele.

This delivery mechanism of Host Service Bureau and Secondary Distributors offers our users a choice in access and analytical software. Some of the Secondary Distributors are in the information base business and make CANSIM data part of a larger set of economic and statistical information, while others are general purpose computing services companies who had been asked by specific customers to make CANSIM data available at their computing centres.

In Statistics Canada, the CANSIM Division is responsible for all development and operational aspects concerning this information dissemination approach. The CANSIM Division adds new data and maintains existing data in all data bases at the Host Service Bureau, and it produces and distributes printed data directories which describe the data and provide the access identifications. CANSIM Division undertakes a marketing and training program and provides consultation to all users of CANSIM data who are searching for particular data or have difficulties in interpreting them. Last but not least, CANSIM Division maintains and develops new software to explore further the CANSIM data bases for analytical purposes.

ANALYTICAL SOFTWARE

Originally, Statistics Canada had to develop software for retrieval, manipulation, statistical analysis, and representation of results. However, over the years, many packages have been interfaced to CANSIM either by Statistics Canada as part of the Main Base, or by Secondary Distributors who took the CANSIM Mini Base and integrated it into their own software facilities. This was only possible because the data model for the time series data is very simple and follows common conventions within the economic and statistical community. In the beginning of the CANSIM development, the linking of data to software tools needed a lot of attention for reasons of limitations in speed and size of hardware, as well as lack of adequate packages. Today, computing resources are much cheaper and the concern has shifted to developing an environment in which packages can be used easily. Smooth and transparent interfaces among data storage, access systems and analytical tools have to be provided.

Software tools for the exploitation of statistical data bases can be categorized broadly as follows:

a) Basic retrieval and selection

This function is usually provided by the access software to a particular data base environment.

b) Normalization and Transformation

Once retrieved, selected data often need to be normalized and transformed to make them compatible. An example would be two time series which both contain price indexes, but are based on different base years. Before they can be compared, they need to be adjusted to a common base year.

c) Statistical/Econometric Analysis

Here we have a variety of packages. For example, CANSIM data have been interfaced to TROLL for econometric analysis and SAS for statistical analysis. In addition, APL has become the defacto standard as the fall-back software package for manipulation which other packages cannot provide.

d) Reports

A convenient and powerful tool to present data, particularly larger amounts of data, is essential. We have used two approaches.

On one hand, we have interfaced the package TPL as a convenient way to provide cleanly labelled tables; on the other hand, we have developed what we call a chinese menu which provides 20 standard options under which time series data can be presented, together with calculations such as percentage change over periods of time.

e) Graphs

There are many plotting and charting packages available. As well, several APL macros have been developed for that purpose.

In analytical software, the saying holds true: "Different strokes for different folks". CANSIM data are not only used by experts in econometric analysis and statistical analysis, they are used increasingly by less trained users. Thus there must be a range of software tools which strike a balance between power and flexibility on one side and complexity of use on the other. We found it convenient, for purposes of discussions, to plot these analytical software tools on a chart with axes corresponding to the above two terms. Thus we can discuss in which area further work needs to be done.

FUTURE DEVELOPMENTS

CANSIM has become a vital part in the tool kits of statisticians and economists in the public and private sector. This is the result of 14 years of development which started out modestly with a simple basic idea. Enhancements and further developments were undertaken as the result of users' requests and market pressure. We see no reason to change the basic thrust of our approach with CANSIM. However, to lay the foundation for future growth, adjustments to data contents and analytical software may need to be made. The following are our thoughts in that respect.

All our key statistics are available now through the various CANSIM systems. However, with the increase in the costs of assembling, printing, and distributing publications and with limited budgets available, it may be more cost effective to store very detailed statistics only in machine-readable form and to make them accessible either in on-line data bases or in the form of summary tapes. Thus, principal statistics would be available as publications as well as in machine-readable form for analytical purposes. However, subject and geographic detailed data may be offered only through electronic means. As this electronic store-house of information grows, we have to take another look at the way we document and reference this information and data. We have already some keyword search systems, but they are not all encompassing and we are currently undertaking a pilot project in order to see how they can be improved.

Related to this growth of available statistical information is the need to summarize the detailed statistics in the form of fact sheets related to particular topics. These fact sheets could then be available in electronic form as well, or could be produced and printed on paper.

As far as software is concerned, our CANSIM retrieval and analysis software is now 14 years old and is based on batch processing principles. We have to take another look at this whole issue as decreased cost in hardware and increased power in software allow us to establish a complete interactive system. This inter-activity is not only required for the data access but also for the analysis where an analyst asks "what if" questions and receives immediately the answers to those questions.

Most systems of the type of CANSIM which combine large statistical data bases with analytical software run on large main frame computers. I like to present the alternative as the scratchpad concept in which the data base is still maintained at a central location in order to allow control of documentation and access. However, with the advent of powerful mini computers as well as personal work stations in the form of micro computers, we see a scenario where the statistical data required for a particular analytical session is retrieved from such a central store-house of information and transferred into the personal computing environment. Then the analyst can use his tools with which he is familiar to put the data through their analytical paces, so to speak.

Lastly, there is continuing development in the area of videotex services, which in Canada are known under the label Telidon. Statistics Canada is actively participating in the various on-going trials and is paying close attention to the development of this electronic dissemination and presentation medium. While the markets for such services have not yet been firmly established, we believe that Telidon provides an exciting additional medium for disseminating relevant statistical information.

CONCLUSION

Statistics Canada as a central statistical agency is in a key position to develop the infra-structure in which national statistical information and analytical tools are combined. From a presentation of simple fact sheets to powerful econometric models, the needs of the wide spectrum of users have to be addressed. We certainly will continue paying attention to this part of our communication obligation.

SOME IDEAS ON USING THE BOOTSTRAP IN ASSESSING MODEL VARIABILITY

Gail Gong, Stanford University

Abstract.

Variable selection techniques, such as stepwise regression are often used to build a concise model for explaining the data. For example, a variable selection procedure based on forward logistic regression was applied to some chronic hepatitis data from Stanford Hospital, and out of a total of 19 covariates, it chose the model 2,11,14,17 . What is the variability of the model chosen? The bootstrap gives some dramatic results. In the chronic hepatitis experiment, likely models are numerous and diverse.

We make an attempt to define a measure of model variability, and use simulations to see how well the bootstrap estimates this measure.

Keywords.

Bootstrap, logistic regression, stepwise regression, model building, variable selection, model variability.

Variable selection techniques, such as stepwise regression are often used to build a concise model for explaining the data. The covariates which enter into the model are often considered the set of important covariates. An important question is: What is the variability of the model chosen by a variable selection technique such as stepwise regression? Here, we look at how the bootstrap assesses this variability.

This problem had its roots in a chronic hepatitis study conducted at Stanford Hospital by Dr. Peter Gregory. In the keynote address last year, Brad Efron (Efron and Gong 1981) spoke of this study. Of 155 chronic hepatitis patients observed, 33 died from the disease. The last 11 patients are shown in Display 1. In addition to observing whether each patient lived or died, Dr. Gregory recorded 19 covariates summarizing patient history, physical examinations, x-rays, liver function tests, and biopsies. Dr. Gregory wished to obtain a rule for predicting the outcome of a future patient given his or her covariates. The rule Dr. Gregory used is based on forward logistic regression.

The logistic regression model assumes that $x_1 = (t_1,y_1),\ldots,x_n = (t_n,y_n)$ are independent and identically distributed where y_i is a binary variable equal to 1 if the ith patient dies and t_i is a vector of covariates. The logistic model assumes that conditional on t_i, y_i is Bernoulli with probability of death $\theta(t_i)$, where

$$\theta(t) = \frac{\exp(\beta_0 + t\beta)}{1 + \exp(\beta_0 + t\beta)} \quad (1)$$

or equivalently,

$$\text{logit } \theta(t) = \log\left(\frac{\theta(t)}{1 - \theta(t)}\right) = \beta_0 + t\beta \quad .$$

The parameters β_0, β are unknown. However, if we obtained estimates $\hat{\beta}_0$, $\hat{\beta}$, we could substitute

Display 1: Data for the last 11 chronic hepatitis patients. Negative numbers indicate missing observations and were replaced by column averages.

id	y	Age 1	Sex 2	Steroid 3	Antivirals 4	Fatigue 5	Malaise 6	Anorexia 7	Liver Big 8	Liver Firm 9	Spleen Palp 10	Spiders 11	Ascites 12	Varices 13	Bilirubin 14	Alk Phos 15	SGOT 16	Albumin 17	Protime 18	Histology 19
145	1	45	1	2	2	1	1	1	2	2	2	1	1	2	1.90	-1	114	2.4	-1	2
146	0	31	1	1	2	1	2	2	2	2	2	2	2	2	1.20	75	193	4.2	54	2
147	1	41	1	2	2	1	2	2	2	1	1	1	2	1	4.20	65	120	3.4	-1	2
148	1	70	1	1	2	1	1	-1	-1	-1	-1	-1	-1	-1	1.70	109	528	2.8	35	2
149	0	20	1	1	2	2	2	2	2	-1	2	2	2	2	0.90	89	152	4.0	-1	2
150	0	36	1	2	2	2	2	2	2	2	2	2	2	2	0.60	120	30	4.0	-1	2
151	1	46	1	2	2	1	1	1	2	2	2	1	1	1	7.60	-1	242	3.3	50	2
152	0	44	1	2	2	1	2	2	2	1	2	2	2	2	0.90	126	142	4.3	-1	2
153	0	61	1	1	2	1	1	2	1	1	2	1	2	2	0.80	95	20	4.1	-1	2
154	0	53	2	1	2	1	2	2	2	2	1	1	2	1	1.50	84	19	4.1	48	2
155	1	43	1	2	2	1	2	2	2	2	1	1	1	2	1.20	100	19	3.1	42	2

these estimates into equation (1) and get an estimated probability of death $\hat{\theta}(t)$. A reasonable rule predicts death for a patient with covariate vector t if his or her estimated probability of death $\hat{\theta}(t)$ is large.

As in many studies, the number of observations, here 155, is small compared to the number of parameters requiring estimation, here 20. And as is commonly done, Dr. Gregory invoked a variable selection technique to choose a smaller model which hopefully forms a strong predictor. The rule which Dr. Gregory used consists of three parts:

(G.1) Initial screening. For $j = 1,\ldots,19$, assume the simple logistic model

$$\text{(2)} \qquad \text{logit}\ \theta(t) = \beta_0 + t_j\beta_j \quad ,$$

and test $H_0 : \beta_j = 0$. Retain covariate j if the test is significant at $\alpha = 0.05$. The initial screening applied to the chronic hepatitis data retained covariates

17, 12, 14, 11, 13, 19, 6, 5, 18, 10, 1, 4, 2.

(G.2) Forward logistic regression on covariates retained in (G.1). Begin with the logistic model which contains only the constant term and add covariates to the model one at a time. At the k+1-st step, assume covariates $j_1,\ldots,j_k$ have already been added; for $j \neq j_1,\ldots,j_k$, assume the model

$$\text{(3)} \quad \text{logit}\ \theta(t) = \beta_0 + \sum_{\ell=1}^{k} t_{j_\ell}\beta_{j_\ell} + t_j\beta_j \quad ,$$

and test $H_0 : \beta_j = 0$. If at least one of these tests is significant at $\alpha = 0.05$, let j_{k+1} correspond to the most significant test. Stop when no further test achieves significance $\alpha = 0.05$. When applied to the thirteen covariates above, forward logistic regression chose the model with covariates

17, 11, 14, 2

(G.3) Estimate (β_0,β) using maximum likelihood. Let $(\hat{\beta}_0,\hat{\beta})$ be the maximum likelihood estimate based on the logistic model consisting of the covariates chosen by forward logistic regression. It turned out that

$$(\hat{\beta}_0, \hat{\beta}_{17}, \hat{\beta}_{11}, \hat{\beta}_{14}, \hat{\beta}_2)$$

$$= (12.17, -1.83, -1.58, 0.56, -5.17) \ .$$

Gregory's rule chose the model {2,11,14,17}. What is the variability of the model? If Dr. Gregory repeated his experiment, that is obtained 155 new patients and performed an initial screening followed by forward logistic regression, would he get the same model {2,11,14,17}? One way, although not highly practical, of answering this question is to ask Dr. Gregory to obtain $n = 155$ new patients which we label $x_1^*,\ldots,x_n^*$ and apply his rule for getting a model. A second way, although again not practical, is to assume we know the underlying distribution F, use a computer to generate an independent sample $x_1^*,\ldots,x_n^*$ from F, and apply Gregory's rule. The third way, which is practical, is to estimate F with the empirical distribution function $\hat{F}$. This is Efron's (1979) bootstrap. Explicitly, the bootstrap procedure is the following:

(E.1) Generate $x_1^*,\ldots,x_n^*$, a random sample from $\hat{F}$. That is, $x_1^*,\ldots,x_n^*$ is a sample with replacement from the original observations $x_1,\ldots,x_n$.

(E.2) Apply Gregory's rule to $x_1^*,\ldots,x_n^*$, and call the resulting model M^*.

(E.3) Repeat (E.1) and (E.2) a large number B times to get bootstrap models $M_1^*,\ldots,M_B^*$.

Display 2 shows the results of the bootstrap procedure for $B = 50$, and therefore, Display 2 is a list of $M_1^*,\ldots,M_{50}^*$. Keep in mind that if all the bootstrap models are quite similar, we would think that the model variability is small, and if the bootstrap models jumped about erratically, we would think the model variability high. The first bootstrap model was $M_1^* = \{1,2,14,17\}$, perhaps not too different from the original sample model, while the second bootstrap model $M_2^* = \{2,5,10,11,17,19\}$ looks more different. The model $M_{17}^* = \{1,5,12,18,19\}$, having no covariates in common with the original model, looks even more different. In the 50 bootstrap models, there is exactly one model M_{12}^* which coincides precisely with the original model. If we can believe the bootstrap, it seems that Gregory's rule could have chosen any one of many possible models, and so the original sample model {2,11,14,17} is not special.

Studying Display 2 further, we do notice some patterns in the form of repeated occurrences:

$$M_{20}^* = M_{44}^* = \{1,2,11,14,17,18\} \quad ,$$

$$M_{41}^* = M_{48}^* = \{1,2,11,14,17\} \quad ,$$

$$M_{13}^* = M_{35}^* = M_{40}^* = M_{43}^* = \{1,2,11,12,14\} \quad .$$

What does Display 2 tell us about model variability? We would like a single number which summarizes this variability. One one hand, Gregory's rule could have chosen any one of many possibilities, and so the variability is larger than zero. On the other hand, the number of repeated occurences indicates that the models are not totally

Display 2: Models chosen by Gregory's rule applied to 50 bootstrap samples of the chronic hepatitis data.

1	14	17	1	2			
2	17	11	19	2	5	10	
3	11	17	5	3	2		
4	11	17	1	2	14	7	3
5	12	15	1	14	2		
6	14	12	19	17	2		
7	14	17	1	11	12	2	
8	17	13	6	2			
9	12	18	11	8	2	3	14
10	17	13	2	3	1		
11	12	17	11	1	2		
12	17	14	11	2			
13	14	12	11	1	2		
14	12	11	1	2			
15	14	17	5	10	2		
16	14	17	19	6			
17	12	5	18	19	1		
18	12	19	1	14	4		
19	12	13	1	11			
20	17	11	14	18	2	1	
21	17	11	2	1	6	4	10
22	14	17	6	18	19	7	
23	12	14	11	3			
24	14	17	2	1	18		
25	11	17	18	5	2		
26	14	18	1	11	2		
27	12	11	17	2			
28	12	18	6	19	17		
29	17	18	15	11	3	12	
30	17	6	2	10			
31	12	11	18	19	2		
32	14	12	10	2	17	5	
33	13	1	6	2	11	5	
34	12	14	3	1	18	2	
35	14	11	12	1	2		
36	17	11	18	2	1	5	
37	14	13	3	1	18		
38	14	18	6	1			
39	12	11	3				
40	12	11	14	1	2		
41	11	17	2	1	14		
42	17	11	1	6			
43	12	11	14	1	2		
44	11	17	18	2	1	14	
45	14	17	6	10	2	1	
46	11	12	1	2	18	6	7
47	12	14	6	18	2	1	
48	14	1	11	2	17		
49	12	14	3	1			
50	14	11	17	3	12		

random, and so the variability is less than infinity. Also, notice that the repeated occurrences and the original sample model all look very similar. The question of model variability leads to another difficult question, a question concerning distances between models.

We leave the chronic hepatitis problem and turn to some simulations of a much simpler situation.

In these simulations, we will not totally escape the question of distances between models, but we will choose a simple enough situation so that we will be able to enumerate all possible models.

In our simulations, we took the underlying process F to generate $x_1 = (t_1, y_1), \ldots, x_n = (t_{20}, y_{20})$ independently and identically distributed such that t_i is a 4-variate normal random vector with 0 mean and covariance matrix

$$\Sigma = \begin{pmatrix} 1 & 0 & 0 & 0 \\ 0 & 1 & \rho & 0 \\ 0 & \rho & 1 & 0 \\ 0 & 0 & 0 & 1 \end{pmatrix} .$$

where $\rho = .86$, and y_i conditional on t_i is a Bernoulli random variable with probability of death

$$\theta(t) = \frac{\exp(\beta_0 + t\beta)}{1 + \exp(\beta_0 + t\beta)} ,$$

and $\beta_0 = 0$, $\beta' = (1,2,0,0)$.

In the first experiment, 20 observations were generated according to the underlying process above. Applying Gregory's rule to this original sample of 20 observations gave the model $M_1 = \{1,2\}$.

Display 3 shows that Gregory's rule applied to 400 bootstrap samples gave the null model { } 12 times, the model {1} 17 times,..., the model {1,2,3,4} 3 times; {2} was the most popular model, with {1,2} a distant second.

Keep in mind that we would like a way to summarize the variability of the models chosen. If the observed bootstrap models clumped around {2} and {1,2}, we would consider the model variability to be low, and if the observed bootstrap models spread themselves thinly over many possibilities, we would consider the model variability to be high. Display 4 reorders the histogram in Display 3 so that the bootstrap models are in decreasing order of frequency. A steep spike at the left hand side would indicate low model variability while a spread towards the right would indicate high variability. These comments agree with our usual ideas of spread, and in analogy to the interquartile range, we might use the 75-percentile P75 as a measure of spread. In the histogram of Display 4, P75 = 6; 75 percent of the bootstrap models fell in one of 6 possibilities. Because P75 is based on the bootstrap models, we call this statistic the bootstrap P75.

In using P75 as a measure of variability, we circumvent the need to measure distances between models. Indeed, we completely ignore the names of the models and use only their relative ranks. The cost of not considering distances is some loss in information.

We performed a total of 200 experiments each similar

Display 3: Results of Experiment 1. Gregory's rule chose the original sample model 1,2 . The following histogram summarizes 400 bootstrap models.

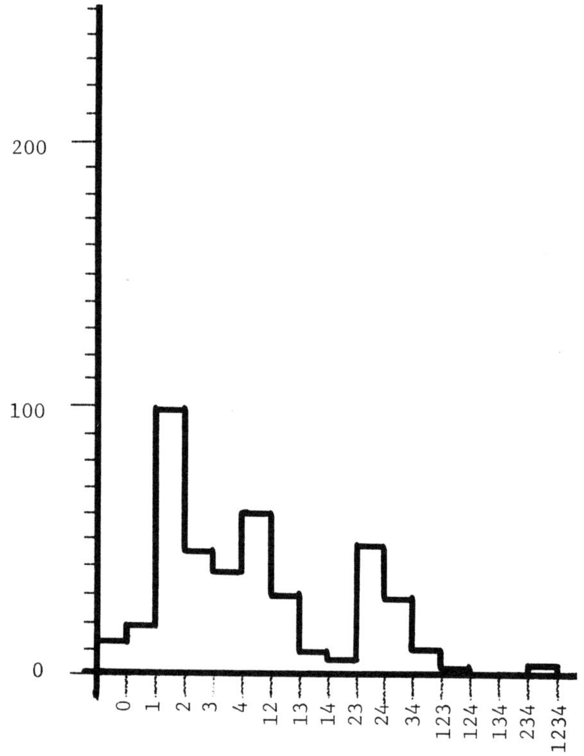

Display 4: Bootstrap models for experiment 1 arranged in order of most frequent occurrence of models.

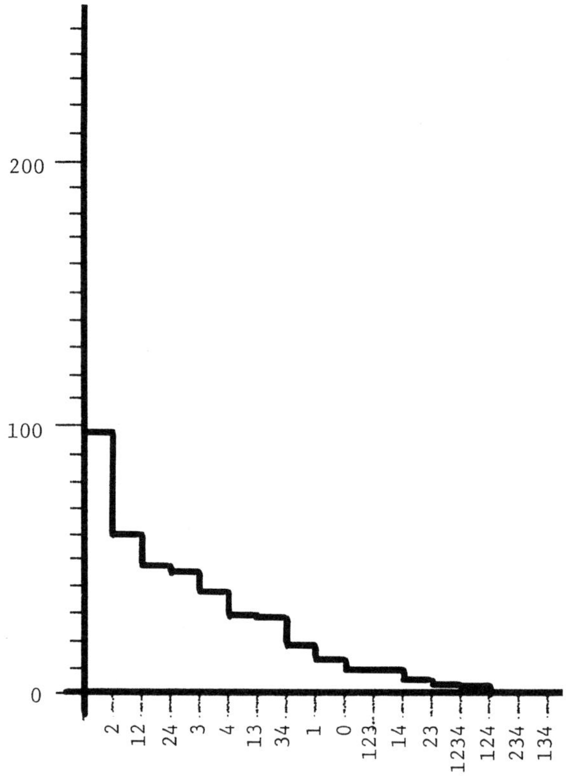

to the first experiment above. In each experiment, we generated a new original sample of 20 observations, and applying Gregory's rule, selected a model. Display 5 shows that the most popular original sample model was {2} with {1,2} being a very distant second. The 75-th percentile of the 200 original sample models is

$$P75 = 2 \ ;$$

75 percent of the original sample models fell into one of 2 possibilities.

If we were experimenters, basing our knowledge on only the first experiment, we would have used the histogram in Display 4 to estimate the histogram in Display 5, and we would have used the bootstrap P75 = 6 to estimate the true P75 = 2. Therefore, we would have badly overestimated the model variability. As we will see in the next paragraph, the first experiment happened to be atypical.

In each of the 200 experiments, just as in the first one, we generated 400 bootstrap samples and calculated the bootstrap P75. Display 6 is a histogram of the bootstrap P75 in the 200 experiments. With a mean of 2.85 and a median of 3, we see that on the average, the bootstrap P75 overestimates slightly the true P75, although with moderate probability, the overestimate can be substantial.

Model variability of stepwise procedures is an important problem, as we have seen in the bootstrap results of the chronic hepatitis study. The work reported here is just a beginning in understanding how the bootstrap can assess model variability.

Display 5: Original sample models of 200 experiments.

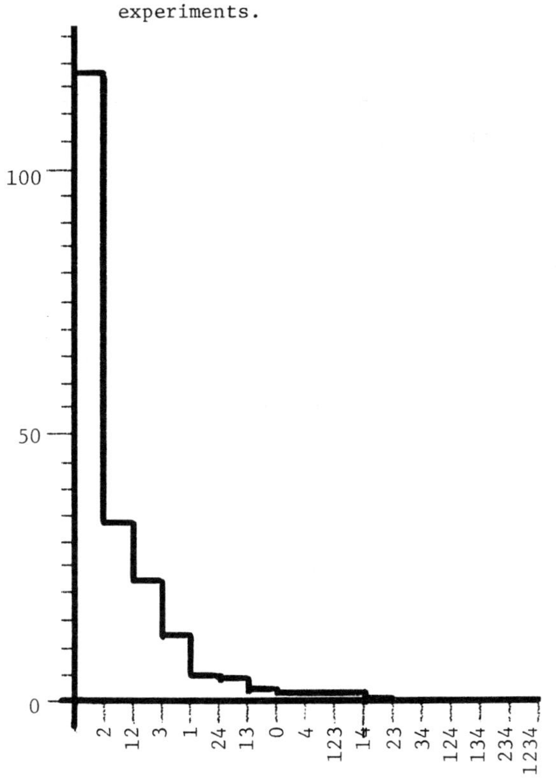

Display 6: Histogram of P75 in 200 experiments.

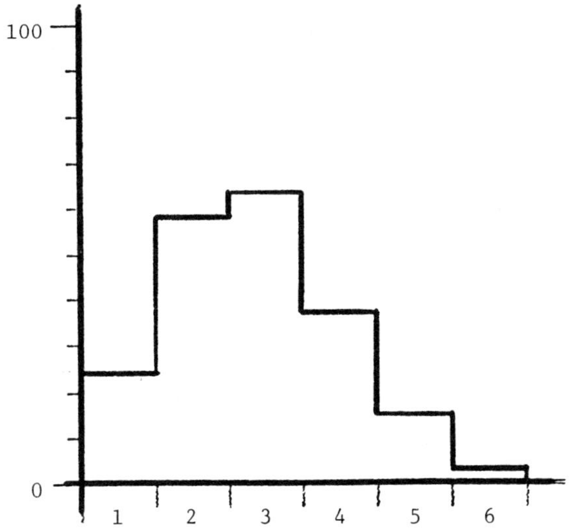

References

Efron, Bradley (1979). Bootstrap methods: Another look at the jackknife, Annals of Statistics, 7, 1-26.

Efron, Bradley and Gong, Gail (1981). Statistical thinking and the computer, Computer Science and Statistics: Proceedings of the 13th Symposium. Springer-Verlag, New York.

MOMENT SERIES FOR MOMENT ESTIMATORS OF THE PARAMETERS OF A WEIBULL DENSITY

K. O. Bowman, Union Carbide Corporation, Nuclear Division
L. R. Shenton, University of Georgia, Athens

ABSTRACT

Taylor series for the first four moments of the coefficients of variation in sampling from a 2-parameter Weibull density are given; they are taken as far as the coefficient of n^{-24}. From these a four moment approximating distribution is set up using summatory techniques on the series. The shape parameter is treated in a similar way, but here the moment equations are no longer explicit estimators, and terms only as far as those in n^{-12} are given. The validity of assessed moments and percentiles of the approximating distributions is studied. Consideration is also given to properties of the moment estimator for 1/c.

Keywords: distribution of statistics, divergent series, Padé approximants, percentile approximations

1. INTRODUCTION

The 3-parameter distribution function is

$$F(t) = 1-\exp\{-(t-s)^c/b^c\} \quad (t\geq s, c, b>0) \qquad (1)$$

where s is the origin, b, and c the scale and shape parameters respectively.

In one form or another (the parameter 1/b is sometimes used) the density has widespread application, the precise reason for its use not being clear always (it has a slight advantage in the simplicity of its distribution function, but this is a minor point in the face of computers of one sort or another). However, it seems well suited to situations involving breaking strengths (Barlow et al., 1979; Cain and Knight, 1981, for example), survival times (Peto and Lee, 1973, for example), etc. It has been used as a model for wind speed (Stewart and Essenwanger, 1978), a main attraction here being the interest in wind power, which is proportional to the cube of wind speed; this translates into changing the value of c in the Weibull model.

Our interest is in the nature of series for the mean, variance, etc., of moment estimators for the parameters in the 3-parameter case. However, the complications here are such as to confine attention more or less to basic asymptotics (a partial study of the situation has so far produced the first 12 terms in the moments of the skewness). Although it is quite likely that properties of estimators in the 3-parameter case will differ considerably from those in the 2-parameter case, the study of the latter should bring out some of the difficulties. The only previous study of the series in this case (Newby, 1980) goes no further than basic asymptotics, and these were not free from error.

1.1 What do we expect from a study of estimators?

Of course, a study of estimation problems should at least have a better than fuzzy aim. Basically estimates of parameters survive only if they lead to passing a satisfactory goodness of fit test. It seems reasonable to assume that refinements predicated on methods of estimation pale in comparison to model selection. Again it is always tempting to base decisions on narrow choices of criteria. Since sample size plays only a minor role in basic asymptotic assessments of variances (and biases), we are deceiving ourselves when decisions are based on asymptotic comparisons. In addition, it is all too easy to introduce a caveat invoking "a large enough sample," a transparent circularity digression.

When we pay some attention to what comes after the first order asymptotic in means and variances, for example, we find a change of attitude to the asymptote, for we may be confronted with a few decreasing terms followed by one or more surges and variegated sign patterns. It is surely time we became aware of the existence of higher order terms and studied ways of using the information they contain. The statistics community seems to be half a century behind the times in this respect and completely unaware of advances and studies due to a school of theoretical physicists (see for example, the preface to Baker and Gammel, 1970).

1.2 Problems with the 3-parameter Weibull and aims of this study.

Moments of the maximum likelihood estimators in this case probably do not exist and other procedures are needed. Fitting by moments is quite straightforward, using the skewness to fix the shape parameter c, then the variance to fix b, and lastly, the mean to fix the start s. But properties of the distribution of these estimators present formidable mathematical difficulties, although a computer assisted approach is feasible. The 2-parameter case has already been studied; Bowman and Shenton (1981) have given details for the first four moments of the coefficient of variation, using summatory algorithms on the series (carried out to terms of order n^{-24}, n being the sample size). Here we discuss characteristics of these series and series for the first four moments of the moment estimator (c^*). Having the four moments for ν^* and c^* we can compare the percentage points of the one against the other using a four moment approximating distribution. Questions of validity are considered. Lastly, some general comments are added concerning the information in (what appear to be) divergent series.

2. LEVIN'S ALGORITHM AND ν^* MOMENTS WHEN $c = 1.5$

2.1 The series (Table 1) alternate in sign and diverge faster than the single factorial series $(1-1!/n+2!/n^2-\ldots)$ but not as fast as the double factorial series $(1-2!/n+4!n^2-\ldots)$. We think the

TABLE 1. Moments of ν^*; c = 1.5.

S	$\mu_1'(\nu^*)$		$\mu_2(\nu^*)$		$\mu_3(\nu^*)$		$\mu_4(\nu^*)$	
0	6.7896869309735	-01						
	-5.6132013492859	-01	2.6772673984050	-01				
	1.6557176844808	-01	-6.2527413386551	-01	3.2420881596408	-01	2.1503282167687	-01
	-1.8474620536721	00	2.8054197020753	00	-2.8812804441747	00	1.0502505615668	-01
	2.1922586200894	01	-3.1740301673027	01	3.0748070794268	01	-1.5448458389139	01
5	-4.3580645232247	02	6.1698213591867	02	-5.8538726736417	02	3.6415327254464	02
	1.2140053990087	04	-1.6985660574568	04	1.6234033676654	04	-1.1056445045515	04
	-4.4319272510179	05	6.1568194941015	05	-5.9254772698640	05	4.2823776889988	05
	2.0203579868046	07	-2.7938852616884	07	2.7053438277634	07	-2.0334982988104	07
	-1.1120346826810	09	1.5329655502103	09	-1.4920295848592	09	1.1530923018020	09
10	7.2096574734542	10	-9.9160099223580	10	9.6926666881294	10	-7.6471743602422	10
	-5.4024459971249	12	7.4175948216140	12	-7.2765971642972	12	5.8332256542299	12
	4.6095483370065	14	-6.3204220814912	14	6.2191074550240	14	-5.0490312473491	14
	-4.4246256616307	16	6.0603265024852	16	-5.9786222434405	16	4.9040292832800	16
	4.7306820232839	18	-6.4738200315179	18	6.4007815420352	18	-5.2953093012828	18
15	-5.5869875796767	20	7.6400548503158	20	-7.5684964011259	20	6.30650928[illegible]133	20
	7.2369947493057	22	-9.8902833121783	22	9.8142882027352	22	-8.2281468998640	22
	-1.0219131662144	25	1.3958391428942	25	-1.3871913557010	25	1.1691746931915	25
	1.5647248801081	27	-2.1362971186825	27	2.1258940610359	27	-1.8000727655091	27
	-2.5858544423711	29	3.5290314664515	29	-3.5160392107693	29	2.9892767600516	29
20	4.5932258200979	31	-6.2663989110185	31	6.2500388332982	31	-5.3328414511363	31
	-8.7373158431193	33	1.1916385088463	34	-1.1896832619930	34	1.0183630563144	34
	1.7739714027278	36	-2.4187672237888	36	2.4169335423533	36	-2.0748600181908	36
	-3.8328687301095	38	5.2247417831321	38	-5.2249959528916	38	4.4971880275419	38
24	8.7887933193700	40	-1.1977722473854	41	1.1987171388092	41	-1.0341841311369	41

($\nu^* = \sqrt{m_2}/m_1'$, where m_2 is the second central moment of the sample, and m_1' the mean.)

Levin algorithm (Levin, 1973) using

$$\alpha_r = \frac{\sum_{j=0}^{r} (-1)^r \binom{r}{j} \left(\frac{j+1}{r+1}\right)^{r-1} \frac{A_{j+1}}{a_j}}{\sum_{j=0}^{r} (-1)^r \binom{r}{j} \left(\frac{j+1}{r+1}\right)^{r-1} \frac{1}{a_j}} \qquad (2.1)$$

where for the series $a_0 + a_1/n + \ldots$,

$$A_{j+1} = a_0 + a_1/n + \ldots + a_j/n^j, \quad (j = 0,1,\ldots)$$

applied to certain divergent series is divergent itself, but there exists a best member of the sequence (or stopping point). Now a peculiar aspect of series for statistical moments is that, for small n, we can often derive exact results using dimension reducing transformations or quadrature; the latter poses problems when n exceeds five or so. In the present case exact results have been found for n=2,3 and 4 using quadrature. Details for the first four moments for these values of n are given in Table 2.

The "boxed" entries are those closest to the true value. In the case of the variance there is not much to choose between r=8 and r=17. The consistency of the stopping point as n increases is noteworthy. In Table 3 we show the sequences for n=5 and n=10.

2.2 Another algorithm (a modified Borel-Padé described in Shenton and Bowman, 1977a) basically considers

$$S(n) \sim e_0 + e_1/n + \ldots \qquad (2.2)$$

$$\sim \int_0^\infty e^{-t} t^{a-1} \{k_0 + k_1(h/n)t + k_2(h/n)^2 t^2 + \ldots\} dt \qquad (a>0; h>0)$$

leading to the summation formula (to be referred to as 2cB)

$$F_r(n;a,h) = N \sum_{s=0}^{r-1} K_s(a,h)\, \Phi_s(N;a) \qquad (N = n/h) \qquad (2.3)$$

where
$$K_s(a,h) = \sum_{r=0}^{s} \binom{s}{r} \frac{e_r}{h^r \Gamma(a+2r)},$$

$$\Phi_s(N;a) = \int_0^\infty \frac{e^{-t} t^{a+2s-1} dt}{(N+t^2)^{s+1}}.$$

$\Phi_s(\cdot)$ can either be calculated by quadrature or using the recurrence

$$4s(s+1)\Phi_{s+1}(N;a) = \sum_{r=0}^{2} G_r \Phi_{s-r}(N;a), \quad (s=2,3,\ldots) \qquad (2.4)$$

with
$$G_0 = 2s(6s+2a-3),$$
$$G_1 = -\{12s^2+8s(a-3)+a^2-7a+12+N\},$$
$$G_2 = (2s+a-3)\,(2s+a-4);$$

and
$$\Phi_0(N;a) = \int_0^\infty e^{-t} t^{a-1} (N+t^2)^{-1} dt,$$

$$\Phi_1(N;a) = \frac{1}{2} a\, \Phi_0(N;a) - \frac{1}{2} \Phi_0(N;a+1),$$

$$\Phi_2(N;a) = \{(4a+6)\Phi_1(N;a) - (a^2+a+N)\Phi_0(N;a) + \Gamma(a)\}/8.$$

Actually these indicate that $\Phi_s(\cdot\cdot)$ is a linear function of the basic functions $\Phi_0(\cdot\cdot)$, and $\Phi_1(\cdot\cdot)$ and indeed

$$\Phi_s(N;a) = N\, \Pi_{s_2}^{(0)}(N) + \Pi_{s_0}^{(1)}(N)\, \Phi_0(N;a) + \Pi_{s_2}^{(2)}(N)\, \Phi_1(N;a) \qquad (s \geq 3) \qquad (2.5)$$

where $s_i = [(s-i-1)/2]$, $i = 1,2,3$

and $\Pi_{s_i}^{(\ )}(\cdot)$ are real polynomials.

TABLE 2. Levin's t-algorithm and the moments series for ν^*, n=2,3,4. (Entries are α_{r-1}; c=1.5).

	r	$\mu_1'(\nu^*)$	$\mu_2(\nu^*)$	$\mu_3(\nu^*)$	$\mu_4(\nu^*)$
n=2	6	.40486185	.06017495	-.01056879	.04307018
	7	.39979784	.06217180	-.00907002	.03302390
	8	.39479750	.06467342	-.00534255	.02057064
	9	.39044492	.06727881	-.00085487	.01098028
	10	.38694110	.06965979	.00356697	.00954210
	11	.38417228	.07149851	.00729993	.01515748
	12	.38196432	.07259348	.01022352	.02266028
	13	.38020300	.07280097	.01228739	.02792580
	14	.37885619	.07204075	.01412681	.02847297
	15	.37795604	.07018375	.01586526	.02370270
	16	.37759054	.06714841	.01863328	.01337855
	17	.37788403	.06275753	.02126346	-.00030514
	18	.37899629	.05713638	.01761667	-.01086268
	19	.38106947	.05199600	-.02680927	.00972894
	20	.38395273	.05679861	-.15955086	.09882317
	True	.382657	.06360	.00649	.008786

	r	$\mu_1'(\nu^*)$	$\mu_2(\nu^*)$	$\mu_3(\nu^*)$	$\mu_4(\nu^*)$
n=3	6	.49557302	.05132049	.00150823	.01928206
	7	.49355822	.05191633	.00191748	.01525018
	8	.49189084	.05253079	.00265513	.01097594
	9	.49068668	.05309256	.00340504	.00837420
	10	.48986117	.05353657	.00403855	.00793691
	11	.48928991	.05382896	.00449792	.00862812
	12	.48888579	.05397361	.00481116	.00943739
	13	.48859966	.05398413	.00500293	.00990738
	14	.48840697	.05388140	.00516034	.00989262
	15	.48829599	.05367738	.00529306	.00946541
	16	.48826233	.05338954	.00548973	.00870570
	17	.48830396	.05302404	.00564607	.00784777
	18	.48842022	.05261345	.00540456	.00730647
	19	.48860605	.05229469	.00304165	.00850647
	True	.488905	.052842	.0047611	.008096

	r	$\mu_1'(\nu^*)$	$\mu_2(\nu^*)$	$\mu_3(\nu^*)$	$\mu_4(\nu^*)$
n=4	6	.54117667	.04353539	.00327633	.01095807
	7	.54021557	.04376028	.00341579	.00900337
	8	.53952911	.04396895	.00363020	.00727274
	9	.53909662	.04414201	.00382233	.00643290
	10	.53883094	.04426374	.00396656	.00631124
	11	.53866334	.04433463	.00405987	.00645609
	12	.53855483	.04436501	.00411736	.00660624
	13	.53848469	.04436465	.00414895	.00668134
	14	.53844185	.04434288	.00417348	.00667184
	15	.53841989	.04430541	.00419236	.00660458
	16	.53841484	.04425801	.00421892	.00650020
	17	.53842363	.04420338	.00423718	.00639565
	18	.53844390	.04414778	.00420655	.00633948
	19	.53847285	.04410983	.00395035	.00647756
	20	.53850428	.04415703	.00336182	.00689265
	True	.5385362	.0441641	.0041379	.0064037

(True given in an appendix on small sample results.)

TABLE 3. Levin's t-algorithm and the moments series for ν^*, n=5,10; c=1.5.

	r	$\mu_1'(\nu^*)$	$\mu_2(\nu^*)$	$\mu_3(\nu^*)$	$\mu_4(\nu^*)$
n=5	7	.56809277	.03766328	.00331170	.00605289
	8	.56776951	.03774945	.00339003	.00527773
	9	.56758617	.03781515	.00345310	.00496769
	10	.56748250	.03785700	.00349608	.00492982
	11	.56742171	.03787906	.00352147	.00497093
	12	.56738511	.03788745	.00353590	.00500903
	13	.56736316	.03788679	.00354316	.00502583
	14	.56735080	.03788075	.00354857	.00502246
	15	.56734505	.03787145	.00355242	.00500770
	16	.56734405	.03786066	.00355762	.00498707
	17	.56734644	.03784916	.00356077	.00496833

	r	$\mu_1'(\nu^*)$	$\mu_2(\nu^*)$	$\mu_3(\nu^*)$	$\mu_4(\nu^*)$
n=10	7	.62353379	.02206202	.00161832	.00179863
	8	.62351206	.02206626	.00162092	.00176415
	9	.62350304	.02206853	.00162229	.00175653
	10	.62349912	.02206957	.00162297	.00175610
	11	.62349733	.02206996	.00162328	.00175668
	12	.62349649	.02207006	.00162341	.00175704
	13	.62349610	.02207003	.00162346	.00175714
	14	.62349594	.02206996	.00162349	.00175709
	15	.62349589	.02206988	.00162351	.00175701
	16	.62349589	.02206981	.00162353	.00175693
	17	.62349591	.02206976	.00162353	.00175688

Results are given in Table 4, and whereas there are slight discrepancies for n=5 and the Levin values (Table 3), the agreement is quite satisfactory. One should notice the reduction in the sizes of the first differences for each moment as n increases. This characteristic also applies to the Levin sequences provided the differences relate to a neighborhood of the best stopping point. It could be that the Borel sequences converge, whereras as noted earlier those for Levin do not.

Our preferred values for the four moments are:

n	$\mu_1'(\nu^*)$	$\mu_2(\nu^*)$	$\mu_3(\nu^*)$	$\mu_4(\nu^*)$
5	0.568	0.0378	0.0035	0.0049
10	0.6236	0.02207	0.00162	0.00175

2.3 We now assume that for higher values of n the stopping rule for the Levin sequences holds. It is possible, in view of the conjectured divergency, that each n has its own best stopping point for each moment. However, the sequence values become tightly packed for larger n; for example for c=1.5, n=50, we have for var(ν^*),

α_{10} = 5.1231738-03	α_{16} = 5.1231117-03
α_{11} = 5.1231473-03	α_{17} = 5.1231104-03
α_{12} = 5.1231320-03	α_{18} = 5.1231096-03
α_{13} = 5.1231228-03	α_{19} = 5.1231090-03
α_{14} = 5.1231173-03	α_{20} = 5.1231087-03
α_{15} = 5.1231138-03	α_{21} = 5.1231085-03

TABLE 4. Borel-Padé sequences for the moments series for ν^* when c=1.5, n=5,10.

	r	$\mu_1'(\nu^*)$	$\mu_2(\nu^*)$	$\mu_3(\nu^*)$	$\mu_4(\nu^*)$
n=5	21	.573267	.037860	.003306	.004785
	22	.572835	.037874	.003312	.004771
	23	.572446	.037886	.003318	.004760
	24	.572094	.037894	.003325	.004752
	25	.571774	.037900	.003332	.004746
	S_3	.568643	.037912	.003016	.004731
	S_5	.567936	.037896	.003470	.005021

	r	$\mu_1'(\nu^*)$	$\mu_2(\nu^*)$	$\mu_3(\nu^*)$	$\mu_4(\nu^*)$
n=10	21	.624125	.022069	.001618	.001754
	22	.624057	.022070	.001618	.001754
	23	.623999	.022070	.001619	.001753
	24	.623947	.022070	.001619	.001753
	25	.623903	.022070	.001619	.001753
	S_3	.623586	.022070	.001635	.001752
	S_5	.623529	.022070	.001622	.001760

(Entries are $F_r(n;1,1)$; see (2.3). S_3, S_5 refer to Shanks' (1955) extrapolates on F_{23}, F_{24}, F_{25} and F_{21}, F_{22}, F_{23}, F_{24}, F_{25}. Indeed

$S_3 \equiv (F_{23} \cdot F_{25} - F_{24}^2)/\Delta^2 F_{24}$, and

$$S_5 = \begin{vmatrix} F_{21} & F_{22} & F_{23} \\ \Delta F_{21} & \Delta F_{22} & \Delta F_{23} \\ \Delta^2 F_{21} & \Delta^2 F_{22} & \Delta^2 F_{23} \end{vmatrix} \div \begin{vmatrix} 1 & 1 & 1 \\ \Delta F_{21} & \Delta F_{22} & \Delta F_{23} \\ \Delta^2 F_{21} & \Delta^2 F_{22} & \Delta^2 F_{23} \end{vmatrix}.$$

These extrapolates are to be used with caution; sometimes they reverse a trend throwing suspicion on the process.)

and α_{16} is the best value flagged from earlier cases. It seems reasonable to take 5.12311-03 as the preferred value. Of course, increasing n still further and choosing a best value would have to take into account the basic accuracy of the moment series coefficients.

2.4 A further set of comparisons for c=2.0 (Table 5) shows that conclusions similar to those drawn for c=1.5 hold.

2.5 A summary of the characteristics of the moment series for ν^* is given in Table 6. It will be noticed that divergency is pronounced for small c, corresponding to marked skewness (and long-tailed) in the Weibull density. The divergency becomes less severe as c increases, but now there is a disruption in the alternating sign pattern, anomolies creeping in for both the initial terms and those for the highest coefficients (n^{-24}, n^{-23}, etc.). It will be recalled that the density itself tends towards symmetry with c slightly larger than three and thereafter achieves negative skewness. We have not carried out extensive studies of the series for c > 4.0.

2.6 Moment assessments for c=0.8(0.1)2.6(0.2)3.2, 3.5,3.8,4.0 and n=13(1)50(5)100 have been tabulated; for $\mu_1'(\nu^*)$, $\mu_2(\nu^*)$, $\mu_3(\nu^*)$, $\mu_4(\nu^*)$ we used

TABLE 5 Moment assessments for ν^*, c=2.0 Levin and Borel (modified).

n		$\mu_1'(\nu^*)$	$\mu_2(\nu^*)$	$\mu_3(\nu^*)$	$\mu_4(\nu^*)$
2	L	.306971(11)	.047562(9)	.006066(7)	.006613(5)
	T	.306853	.047434	.006883	.006036
	DS	.312	.0573	.0120	.00183
3	L	.388759(11)	.037496(9)	.003423(7)	.004547(5)
	T	.388807	.037349	.003626	.004275
	DS	.3848	.0395	.00453	.00635
4	L	.425847(11)	.029815	.002288(7)	.002972(5)
	T	.425863	.029785	.002340	.00288
	DS	.4262	.0293	.00263	.00338
5	L	.446871(11)	.024596(9)	.001640(7)	.002040(5)
	2cB*	.446913	.024645	.001608	.002047
	DS	.44702	.02441	.00177	.002170
10	L	.486309(11)	.013020(9)	.000519(7)	.000559(5)
	2cB*	.486309	.013021	.000518	.000559
	DS	.486299	.013030	.000510	.000563
20	L	.5049	.006696	.000146	.000143
	S_1	.5048	.006708	.000152	.000144
	S_2	.5044	.006675	.000140	.000141

(L is the Levin t-algorithm, the parenthetic entry referring to the best approximant α_r. T refers to values computed by quadrature. 2cB refers to the Borel-Padé algorithm effectively using all the available coefficients (see expression (2.3)); for μ_1' we have used a=2, h=1 with terms up to n^{-4} truncated, and for μ_2, μ_3, and μ_4 we have used a=1, h=1 with the n^{-1} term omitted for μ_2 and no truncations for μ_3 and μ_4. DS refers to the direct sum of the series stopping at the first numerically smallest term. S_1 and S_2 refer to simulations of 10^5 cycles each, the s.d. of the mean being 0.0003 approx.)

13, 18, 12, and 11 coefficients of the corresponding series. A selection is given in Table 7. From these it will be seen that for a sample of n known to come from a Weibull density with parameter c (which fixes ν) the estimate ν^* of ν is expected to underestimate the true ν. Using a least squares procedure on the tabulated values, we have derived the unbiased c, given ν^* and n, namely

$$\bar{c} \sim \{1+b_{01}/n+b_{02}/n^2+\nu^*(b_{10}+b_{11}/n)+\nu^{*2}b_{20}\}/\{a_{00}+a_{01}/n+a_{02}/n^2+\nu^*(a_{10}+a_{11}/n)+\nu^* a_{20}\} \quad (0<\nu^*<1) \qquad (2.6)$$

where

a_{00} =	-0.02586359654	b_{00} =	1.0
a_{01} =	0.1368685508	b_{01} =	-0.03224982824
a_{02} =	0.1941632032	b_{02} =	-0.05540306547
a_{10} =	0.9555907114	b_{10} =	-0.4528195583
a_{11} =	-0.2097962308	b_{11} =	-0.9542316494
a_{20} =	-0.2918002479	b_{20} =	0.08948942647,

TABLE 6. Magnitudes and sign patterns occurring in the first four moment series for the coefficient of variation ν^*, as affected by the shape parameter c.

Moment	$\mu_1'(\nu^*)$		$\mu_2(\nu^*)$		$\mu_3(\nu^*)$		$\mu_4(\nu^*)$	
c	$\lvert v_{24}^{(1)}/v_0^{(1)}\rvert$		$\lvert v_{24}^{(2)}/v_1^{(2)}\rvert$		$\lvert v_{24}^{(3)}/v_2^{(3)}\rvert$		$\lvert v_{24}^{(4)}/v_2^{(4)}\rvert$	
0.9	2.9	67	4.6	67	6.3	66	2.3	67A
1.0	8.6	60	1.7	61	3.6	60	1.1	61A
1.1	4.2	55	1.0	56	3.0	55	7.4	55A
1.2	1.5	51	4.2	51	1.7	51	3.5	51A
1.3	2.5	47	7.4	47	4.0	47	6.9	47A
1.4	1.2	44	3.8	44	2.6	44	3.9	44A
1.5	1.3	41	4.5	41	3.7	41	4.9	41A
1.6	2.6	38	9.4	38	9.2	38	1.1	39A
1.7	7.9	35T	3.0	36	3.4	36	3.5	36A
1.8	3.1	33T	1.2	34	1.6	34	1.4	34A
1.9	1.3	31T	5.0	31	7.4	31	6.1	31A
2.0	3.7	28T	1.5	29	2.4	29	1.9	29A
2.1	2.4	26	9.6	26L	1.7	27L	1.2	27L
2.2	5.7	25B	2.5	26B	5.4	26B	3.5	26B
2.3	1.6	25B	6.7	25B	1.4	26B	8.8	25B
2.4	3.2	26B	1.3	27B	2.3	27B	1.6	27B
2.5	1.2	26B	4.7	26B	1.0	27B	5.9	26B
2.6	5.6	25B	2.3	26B	5.3	26B	2.9	26B
2.8	1.2	25B	4.9	25B	1.2	26B	6.1	25B
3.0	6.0	25B	2.4	26B	6.0	26B	3.0	26B
3.2	1.8	26B	7.3	26B	1.9	27B	8.9	26B
3.5	3.4	26B	1.3	27B	3.4	27B	1.6	27B
3.8	7.3	26B	2.7	27B	6.7	27B	3.2	27B
4.0	2.6	27B	9.6	27B	2.4	28B	1.1	28B

(Introduction of letters of T, L, and B indicate disruption of alternating sign pattern. Disruption occurs at the top (T) of the series, bottom (L), and both top and bottom (B). A refers to a sign pattern with alternation except for the first two terms. In the moment columns each second column refers to the power of ten used as a multiplier. $v_{24}^{(i)}/v_s^{(i)}$, i = 1,2,3,4 refer to coefficients in the series.)

the errors being numerically less than 0.5%. The grid of values used was n=10(1)20,22,25(5)50(10)100 and $0.8 \leq c \leq 4$ involving 575 points.

In a similar way if we need a quick, fairly accurate solution to the equation

$$\frac{\Gamma(1+2/c)}{\Gamma^2(1+1/c)} = 1 + \nu^2, \qquad (2.7)$$

then

$$1/c = \frac{c_1\nu + c_2\nu^2 + c_3\nu^3 + c_4\nu^4}{1 + d_1\nu + d_2\nu^2 + d_3\nu^3} \qquad (2.8)$$

where

$c_1 = 0.779960622$ $\quad d_1 = 0.188028602$

$c_2 = 0.587095391$ $\quad d_2 = 0.609555293$

$c_3 = 0.471569800$ $\quad d_3 = 0.00282363508$

$c_4 = -0.0302146209$

The error in the approximation to c is 0.0004% or less for $0.6 \leq c \leq 6.6$ $(0.178 \leq \nu \leq 1.758)$.

TABLE 7. Moments of ν^* using the Levin sequences.

n	c	1.0	1.5	2.0	2.5	3.0	3.5	4.0
	v	1.000	0.679	0.523	0.428	0.363	0.316	0.281
15	μ_1'	0.914	0.642	0.499	0.409	0.348	0.303	0.268
	σ	0.200	0.125	0.094	0.077	0.067	0.059	0.053
	$\sqrt{\beta_1}$	0.780	0.457	0.300	0.236	0.217	0.219	0.231
	β_2	4.278	3.533	3.227	3.110	3.058	3.036	3.026
20	μ_1'	0.934	0.651	0.505	0.414	0.352	0.306	0.272
	σ	0.182	0.110	0.082	0.067	0.058	0.051	0.046
	$\sqrt{\beta_1}$	0.779	0.421	0.266	0.205	0.186	0.186	0.195
	β_2	4.335	3.460	3.181	3.086	3.046	3.026	3.019
25	μ_1'	0.946	0.657	0.508	0.417	0.354	0.308	0.273
	σ	0.168	0.099	0.073	0.060	0.052	0.046	0.041
	$\sqrt{\beta_1}$	0.766	0.392	0.241	0.184	0.165	0.164	0.172
	β_2	4.332	3.402	3.150	3.070	3.037	3.021	3.015
30	μ_1'	0.954	0.660	0.511	0.419	0.356	0.310	0.275
	σ	0.157	0.091	0.067	0.055	0.047	0.042	0.038
	$\sqrt{\beta_1}$	0.750	0.367	0.222	0.168	0.150	0.149	0.156
	β_2	4.304	3.356	3.128	3.059	3.031	3.018	3.012
35	μ_1'	0.960	0.663	0.513	0.420	0.357	0.311	0.275
	σ	0.148	0.085	0.062	0.051	0.044	0.039	0.035
	$\sqrt{\beta_1}$	0.732	0.347	0.207	0.156	0.139	0.137	0.143
	β_2	4.266	3.319	3.112	3.051	3.027	3.016	3.010
40	μ_1'	0.965	0.665	0.514	0.421	0.358	0.312	0.276
	σ	0.140	0.080	0.058	0.047	0.041	0.036	0.033
	$\sqrt{\beta_1}$	0.714	0.329	0.195	0.146	0.129	0.128	0.134
	β_2	4.224	3.289	3.099	3.045	3.024	3.014	3.009
45	μ_1'	0.969	0.667	0.515	0.422	0.358	0.312	0.277
	σ	0.134	0.075	0.055	0.045	0.038	0.034	0.031
	$\sqrt{\beta_1}$	0.697	0.314	0.185	0.137	0.122	0.120	0.125
	β_2	4.182	3.265	3.089	3.040	3.021	3.012	3.008
50	μ_1'	0.972	0.668	0.516	0.422	0.359	0.313	0.277
	σ	0.128	0.072	0.052	0.042	0.036	0.032	0.029
	$\sqrt{\beta_1}$	0.681	0.301	0.176	0.131	0.115	0.114	0.119
	β_2	4.140	3.244	3.080	3.037	3.019	3.011	3.007
70	μ_1'	0.980	0.671	0.518	0.424	0.360	0.314	0.278
	σ	0.111	0.061	0.044	0.036	0.031	0.027	0.025
	$\sqrt{\beta_1}$	0.624	0.261	0.150	0.110	0.097	0.096	0.100
	β_2	3.992	3.185	3.058	3.026	3.014	3.008	3.005
100	μ_1'	0.986	0.673	0.519	0.425	0.361	0.314	0.279
	σ	0.095	0.051	0.037	0.030	0.026	0.023	0.021
	$\sqrt{\beta_1}$	0.560	0.223	0.126	0.092	0.081	0.080	0.083
	β_2	3.826	3.136	3.042	3.019	3.010	3.006	3.004

(For c=1, there is the special property that ν^* is distributed independently of the mean (see Bowman and Shenton, 1981) so that this special property is used along with Levin's algorithm. For c > 1, we have used Levin's α_{16} for $\mu_1'(\nu^*)$, α_{10} for $\mu_2(\nu^*)$, α_{13} for $\mu_3(\nu^*)$, and α_{10} for $\mu_4(\nu^*)$. If a 4-moment Pearson distribution is now fitted, assuming the value of c is known, our guess is that the middle percentage points (1, 5, 10, 90, 95, and 99) are in error by not more than 5% and very likely less for samples exceeding 30 or so.)

If we replace ν by ν^* then the moment estimator of c is the real solution of

$$\Gamma(1+2/c^*)/\Gamma^2(1+1/c^*) = 1 + \nu^{*2} \qquad (2.9)$$

showing that the distribution of c^* is a function of c only, ν^* being scale free (this is also evident from the tabulated moments of ν^* which do not involve b).

3. THE DISTRIBUTION OF c^*

3.1 Moment series. It will be evident from the equation for c^* that the Taylor series for its moments will be more complicated. However, we use a two-stage process, expressing c^* in terms of ν^*, and ν^* in terms of the moments m_1' and m_2'. Thus we set

$$c^* = c + c_1(\nu^* - \nu) + c_2(\nu^* - \nu)^2/2! + \ldots$$

with

$$c_s = \left.\frac{d^s c^*}{d\nu^{*s}}\right|_{\substack{c^* = c \\ \nu^* = \nu}} . \qquad (3.1)$$

If we wish to carry the series (3.1) and similar ones for higher moments so that in expectation all terms are included contributing to say n^{-12}, then we need all derivatives up to c_{24}. These can be found using Faá di Bruno's formula for a derivative of a function of a function (see for example Shenton and Bowman, 1977b, pp. 14, 130, 169; for several generalizations see Good, 1961).

3.2 Derivatives of c* with respect to ν*. From (1.1)

$$\Gamma(1+2/c^*)/\Gamma^2(1+1/c^*) = 1 + \nu^{*2} \qquad (3.2)$$

so that taking logarithmic derivatives

$$\frac{1}{c^{*2}} \{\psi(1+\frac{1}{c^*}) - \psi(1+\frac{2}{c^*})\} \frac{\partial c^*}{\partial \nu^*} = \frac{1}{2} \{\frac{1}{\nu^*+i} + \frac{1}{\nu^*-i}\} \qquad (3.3)$$

where $\psi(x) = d\ln\Gamma(x)/dx$, $i = \sqrt{(-1)}$. Clearly we can drop the asterisks and replace them when necessary. We write c_r for $\partial^r c/\partial\nu^r$, the modified (3.3) in the form

$$c_1 J(c) = \nu_0. \qquad (3.4)$$

Using the formula of Leibniz for the s-th derivative of a product,

$$\frac{\partial^s J(c)}{\partial c^s} = J^{(s)}(c) = \sum_{r=0}^{s} \binom{s}{r} \frac{(-1)^r}{c^{r+2}} (r+1)!\, H^{(s-r)}(c) \qquad (3.5)$$

where

$$H^{(0)}(c)=H(c)=\psi(1+\tfrac{1}{c})-\psi(1+\tfrac{2}{c}),\ H^{(m)}(c)=d^m H(c)/dc^m.$$

From (3.4)

$$Jc_2 + J^{(1)}c_1^2 = \nu_1 = \partial\nu_0/\partial\nu,$$

$$Jc_3 + 3J^{(1)}c_1c_2 + J^{(2)}c_1^3 = \nu_2, \qquad (3.6)$$

$$Jc_4 + 4J^{(1)}c_1c_3 + 3J^{(1)}c_2^2 + 6J^{(2)}c_1^2c_2 + J^{(3)}c_1^4 = \nu_3$$

and so on, where

$$\nu_s = \frac{\partial^s \nu_0}{\partial \nu^s} = \frac{(-1)^s}{2} s!\, (\frac{1}{(\nu+i)^{s+1}} + \frac{1}{(\nu-i)^{s+1}}).$$

Now the structure of these formulas is the same (Luckacs, 1955) as occurs in the expression of noncentral moments (μ_r') in terms of cumulants. For example,

$$\kappa_2 + \kappa_1^2 = \mu_2',$$

$$\kappa_3 + 3\kappa_2\kappa_1 + \kappa_1^3 = \mu_3', \qquad (3.7)$$

$$\kappa_4 + 4\kappa_3\kappa_1 + 3\kappa_2^2 + 6\kappa_2\kappa_1^2 + \kappa_1^4 = \mu_4'.$$

But these formulas are equivalent to

$$\mu_r' = \sum_{s=0}^{r-1} \binom{r-1}{s} \kappa_{r-s}\mu_s' \quad (r = 2,3,\ldots) \qquad (3.8)$$

giving μ_r' in terms of μ_{r-1}', μ_{r-2}', ..., μ_0' (note $\kappa_1=\mu_1'$, $\mu_0'=1$). Hence the left side members of (3.7) and the generalization can be set up recursively from previous members and awkward combinatorial problems avoided, a distinct advantage in digital implementation.

3.3 Moment series for c*. A tabulation is given in Table 8 for the first four moments for a selection of values from c=0.8(0.1)2.6(0.2)3.2,3.5,3.8, 4.0. The sign pattern for c=1 (apart from one anomoly in each of $\mu_1'(c^*)$ and $\mu_4(c^*)$) is alternating. As c increases this regular pattern is disrupted and the plus signs start to predominate, especially for the higher moments. As for magnitude, very approximately, the coefficient of n^{-12} decreases from (24)!, for c=1, towards (12)! for c=3 for $\mu_1'(c^*)$, with slight increases for the higher moments. See Table 9 for further details.

These properties suggest that E(c*) will exceed c, and Var(c*) will exceed the asymptotic variance ($Var_1(c^*)$) for c in the region of 1.5 or more. Numerical evidence for 0.8 < c < 4.0 and 10 < n < 100 suggests E(c*-c) > 0, and Var(c*)/Var_1(c*) > 1. For example, when c=1.9, n=10, E(c*-c)=0.2, and the variance ratio is 1.4; similarly, when n=10, c=1.5, E(c*-c)=0.8, and the variance ratio is 1.7.

3.4 Summation of the c* series. The diversified structure of the series' coefficients arising from the 100 cases tabulated (25 values of c, for four moments) makes it imperative to diminish the labor involved in a detailed study; so we confine attention generally to samples in the region of 25 or more. This makes less stringent demands on the summatory algorithms chosen.

Again, since magnitudes decrease and sign patterns become irregular as c increases, summatory algorithms successful for small c may fail for large c ($1.6 \leq c < 4$).

For c in the vicinity of unity, we use Levin's t-algorithm or its truncated versions; some illustrations are given in Table 10 and an appendix. We look first of all for monotonicity, and secondly, smallness of first differences.

A word on notation--we use S_3 and S_5 to denote the Shanks' approximant based on **the last three, and last five values computed. (See the footnote to Table 4.) For c*, terms up to the coefficient of n^{-12} are always used.**

In addition L(tr=s,S_r) means a Levin algorithm with s initial terms truncated, with a Shanks' smoothing formula applied to the last r (3 or 5) terms. Similarly, 2cB (a=α, tr=s,S_r) and 1cB (a=α, tr=s,S_r) refer to the Borel-Padé type algorithm described in paragraph 2.2.

We should warn that truncation of a series does not relate linearly to summation algorithms in general. For example, different diagonals of a Padé table are generally distinct, and removing the first term of a series or adding a term at the beginning can drastically change the continued fraction representation.

3.5 Detailed illustrations.

3.5.1. There is undoubtedly a summation problem for small n, so we confine attention for the most part to $n \geq 20$; the difficulties stem from the variety of patterns which emerge for the series,

TABLE 8. Moment series for c*, where $\Gamma(1+2/c^*)/\Gamma^2(1+1/c^*) = 1 + \nu^{*2}$ ($\nu^* = \sqrt{m_2}/m_1'$, the coefficient of variation).

C	S	$\mu_1'(c^*)$	$\mu_2(c^*)$	$\mu_3(c^*)$	$\mu_4(c^*)$
1.0	0	1.00000000000 +00			
		2.64493406685 +00	1.00000000000 +00		
		-1.71123763218 +01	-1.16217622550 +01	-1.30395598911 -01	3.00000000000 +00
		8.53180565368 +02	1.04699772400 +03	4.04537576826 +02	-1.94936949445 +01
		-7.08236389752 +04	-1.18682984508 +05	-7.42938033595 +04	-1.26370978873 +04
	5	9.16919113987 +06	1.93912796742 +07	1.69161175037 +07	6.47275757861 +06
		-1.67242143328 +09	-4.23691027771 +09	-4.70621073393 +09	-2.68301982152 +09
		4.04878601561 +11	1.18709573920 +12	1.59183254710 +12	1.18649611510 +12
		-1.24957512007 +14	-4.13831172021 +14	-6.46747649882 +14	-5.89933637320 +14
		4.77569676051 +16	1.75476767742 +17	3.11777660021 +17	3.34303106097 +17
		-2.21096768650 +19	-8.89115426850 +19	-1.76327643511 +20	-2.16292996989 +20
		1.21859738849 +22	5.30619049143 +22	1.15816021472 +23	1.59366933885 +23
	12	-7.88382598313 +24	-3.68537991717 +25	-8.75534174063 +25	-1.33158479075 +26
1.5	0	1.50000000000 +00			
		2.39460463705 +00	1.53845275798 +00		
		1.06599601622 +00	4.35186733758 +00	5.21738040174 +00	7.10051066563 +00
		2.69713017770 +01	6.48215451578 +01	7.03747501861 +01	8.37131826997 +01
		-3.53721215742 +02	-8.06447688276 +02	-3.95658737729 +02	1.08724472751 +03
	5	9.59416683127 +03	3.05879721603 +04	3.93587343555 +04	2.11853890204 +04
		-3.29037238977 +05	-1.24215369477 +06	-1.97061328158 +06	-1.25192390674 +06
		1.43244108906 +07	6.26518882532 +07	1.22282944586 +08	1.18557479543 +08
		-7.58422614574 +08	-3.74361577598 +09	-8.57722170066 +09	-1.06473968110 +10
		4.75599220101 +10	2.60218037332 +11	6.81247904037 +11	1.02287789404 +12
		-3.46116462749 +12	-2.07055762499 +13	-6.07053476093 +13	-1.06134168661 +14
		2.87708828012 +14	1.86190755390 +15	6.02121347100 +15	1.19499508294 +16
	12	-2.69712794353 +16	-1.87220275839 +17	-6.59986794137 +17	-1.45975868166 +18
2.0	0	2.00000000000 +00			
		2.70621619094 +00	2.49178668783 +00		
		4.09622030667 +00	1.21358171725 +01	1.30938563578 +01	1.86270026930 +01
		1.07750575800 +01	5.87385616295 +01	1.41836390122 +02	3.20518319944 +02
		1.73139719173 +01	2.18087615386 +02	1.04488271269 +03	3.70018540429 +03
	5	1.22861199259 +02	1.22874693140 +03	7.26966573635 +03	3.40537720008 +04
		-6.09643673836 +02	3.01032157428 +02	3.43172490855 +04	2.75931393146 +05
		9.96309999457 +03	6.47799658547 +04	3.33913330334 +05	2.15257142591 +06
		-1.73642702591 +05	-1.03383596766 +06	-1.92966573241 +06	1.01060605221 +07
		3.31904521127 +06	2.21690539839 +07	7.15502179883 +07	1.83808487647 +08
		-7.44175186773 +07	-5.47919534477 +08	-1.91843636327 +09	-3.29254172381 +09
		1.86962029389 +09	1.48340632029 +10	5.72663115649 +10	1.26472136972 +11
	12	-5.20720028160 +10	-4.43006816905 +11	-1.87260123534 +12	-4.66556464359 +12
2.5	0	2.50000000000 +00			
		3.21080683541 +00	3.85125310096 +00		
		5.91359408349 +00	2.11260614720 +01	2.68109244124 +01	4.44964513430 +01
		1.31497936214 +01	9.69408672744 +01	3.02659719099 +02	8.54706236178 +02
		3.19036593715 +01	4.11558422187 +02	2.33021878154 +03	1.01185924436 +04
	5	5.94139796099 +01	1.54260294167 +03	1.48074310784 +04	9.46841021346 +04
		7.69255201951 +00	4.58954031641 +03	8.00056858598 +04	7.53142273523 +05
		-6.67092260119 +02	5.77412371479 +03	3.49142049167 +05	5.16917882133 +06
		-1.90368917783 +03	-3.00588611116 +04	1.05894424669 +06	3.00161450742 +07
		4.02756907485 +04	1.55104573000 +05	2.56936352297 +06	1.45177698170 +08
		5.34231938856 +05	7.52885601116 +06	4.71401051553 +07	7.42259369228 +08
		2.95457913454 +06	9.34343339404 +07	1.03071583918 +09	8.35049082213 +09
	12	-2.61458998108 +07	3.05571651390 +08	1.12854524846 +10	1.30799503718 +11
3.0	0	3.00000000000 +00			
		3.82132187478 +00	5.63714982025 +00		
		7.55069084600 +00	3.24471750061 +01	4.88600986935 +01	9.53323742878 +01
		1.66677744055 +01	1.49609515936 +02	5.64826632612 +02	1.91877256339 +03
		3.53337568366 +01	6.05430408881 +02	4.31019115087 +03	2.30455776023 +04
	5	4.61293354235 +01	2.03314581679 +03	2.61190739435 +04	2.12245487874 +05
		0.30516091291 +01	4.67397937133 +03	1.28212520555 +05	1.81065206363 +06
		-9.58412196960 +01	6.35594863897 +03	5.05747305909 +05	1.02827188568 +07
		1.07237121181 +04	1.11691543390 +05	2.17146313306 +06	5.77578233599 +07
		1.08525524240 +05	2.06596344138 +06	2.22554610008 +07	3.60852002325 +08
		-5.32138022464 +03	1.39651311731 +07	2.64925361942 +08	3.41652787533 +09
		-1.35479035481 +07	-1.18970429170 +08	1.08065423512 +09	3.30646818568 +10
	12	-1.66127616752 +08	-3.89968568664 +09	-3.08174526253 +10	6.47214241681 +10

(Notice the sign pattern irregularities as c increases and the decrease in magnitude in the higher coefficients.)

TABLE 9. Magnitude of coefficients for c* moment series.

Moment	$\mu_1'(c^*)$		$\mu_2(c^*)$		$\mu_3(c^*)$		$\mu_4(c^*)$	
c	$\lvert C_{12}^{(1)}/C_0^{(1)}\rvert$		$\lvert C_{12}^{(2)}/C_1^{(2)}\rvert$		$\lvert C_{12}^{(3)}/C_2^{(3)}\rvert$		$\lvert C_{12}^{(4)}/C_2^{(4)}\rvert$	
0.8	1.1	31	3.4	31	1.2	31	2.5	31
0.9	4.3	27	1.7	28	1.8	28	1.6	28
1.0	7.9	24	3.7	25	6.7	26	4.4	25
1.1	4.4	22	2.3	23	6.1	23	3.2	23
1.2	5.3	20	3.1	21	5.0	21	4.7	21
1.3	1.2	19	7.3	19	9.3	19	1.2	20
1.4	3.9	17	2.6	18	2.9	18	4.3	18
1.5	1.8	16	1.2	17	1.3	17	2.1	17
1.6	1.0	15	7.2	15	7.1	15	1.2	16
1.7	7.2	13	5.0	14	4.6	14	8.2	14
1.8	5.3	12	3.7	13	3.3	13	5.9	13
1.9	4.0	11	2.8	12	2.3	12	4.2	12
2.0	2.6	10	1.8	11	1.4	11	2.5	11
2.1	1.0	09	6.7	09	5.1	09	8.4	09
2.2	4.1	07	3.9	08	4.4	08	1.3	09
2.3	5.3	06	1.9	08	3.9	08	1.8	09
2.4	3.6	06	1.4	08	4.2	08	2.4	09
2.5	1.0	07	7.9	07	4.2	08	2.9	09
2.6	2.2	07	4.3	07	3.3	08	3.2	09
2.8	4.7	07	3.8	08	5.5	07	2.7	09
3.0	5.5	07	6.9	08	6.3	08	6.8	08
3.2	2.9	07	7.6	08	1.1	09	2.4	09
3.5	9.5	07	6.5	07	1.0	09	6.0	09
3.8	2.6	08	1.9	09	7.6	08	3.7	09
4.0	3.0	08	3.1	09	2.6	09	2.3	09

(In the moment columns each second column refers to the power of ten used as a multiplier.)

so that no one approach works for small samples over the parameter space of the shape parameter.

Table 10 gives a general view of the usefulness of the Levin algorithm. Table 11 (c=2.5) treats the four moments of c* and several summation algorithms. The series are noteworthy for the preponderance of positive coefficients and divergence at about the rate of the single factorial series. Higher moments are less easy to sum than lower. Another characteristic to notice is the bumpiness of the coefficients, in contrast to the series for ν^*. As to potential error in the c*-series higher coefficients, we can only say that we have used double-double precision arithmetic on an IBM computer, amounting to the retention of about 30 decimal digits.

3.5.2 Simulation comparisons. A check on the summation algorithm for several values of the shape parameter c with samples of n=20 is shown in Table 12. Agreement with the simulation assessments improves as the skewness of the population decreases (c increases from I towards 3--the Weibull density has zero skewness when c=3.6 approx.).

3.6 Percentage points comparisons. Using the moment series for ν^* and c* along with the mapping in (2.7) we compare standard percentile levels derived from the 4-moment Pearson density approximants (Tables 13a, 13b) for samples of 15, 20, and 25 at five values of c. There are also simulation comparisons for samples of 20. The reader may agree that the results are satisfactory.

Another check on the summatory algorithms arises from a study of Pearson and Tukey (1965) on the relation between distances between percentage points (for Pearson curves) and the mean and standard deviation. For a region of the (β_1,β_2) plane ($\beta_1 < 4$, $\beta_2 < 11$, approximately), we may approximate the mean by $\hat{\mu} = [50\%] + 0.185\Delta$ where $\Delta = [95\%] + [5\%] - 2[50\%]$; here [50%], for example, refers to the median. For the standard deviation Pearson and Tukey give the equations,

$$\hat{\sigma}'_{0.05} = \frac{[95\%] - [5\%]}{\max\{3.29-0.1(\Delta/\hat{\sigma}'_{0.05})^2,\ 3.08\}},$$

$$\hat{\sigma}'_{0.025} = \frac{[97.5\%] - [2.5\%]}{\max\{3.98-0.138(\Delta/\hat{\sigma}'_{0.025})^2,\ 3.66\}}$$

and the final assessment $\sigma \sim \max\{\hat{\sigma}'_{0.05}, \hat{\sigma}'_{0.025}\}$. **We consider these values for the mean and standard deviation of c* using the percentiles of c* derived from the percentiles of ν^* under the mapping (2.7).** The point to notice is our concern for c* moments derived by a complicated numerical process and how these compare with assessments derived from more stable and longer series for ν^* (up to the n^{-24} coefficients). The agreement for samples of 15 or more is quite remarkable (Table 14).

4. THE MOMENT ESTIMATOR FOR 1/c

The equation for the estimator d* of d(=1/c) is

$$\Gamma(1+2d^*)/\Gamma^2(1+d^*) = 1 + \nu^{*2}. \tag{4.1}$$

A quick approximate solution (see 2.8 for a comparison) is

$$d^* \sim 0.908919\nu^* + 0.91081\nu^{*2} \qquad (0 < \nu < 2) \tag{4.2}$$

hinting that the distribution of d* will be close (in some sense) to that of ν^*. A modification of the approach of ¶3 now leads to series developments for the moments of d* up to terms in n^{-12}. From tabulations for the same parameter space as was used for c*, we find the series for d* in general have the same sign and magnitude patterns as ν^* (however, we are limited to fewer coefficients). This development provides yet another check on the validity of moment assessments. As an example, the assessments of moments when n=10, c=1.5 are:

	$\mu_1'(d^*)$	$\sigma(d^*)$	$\sqrt{\beta_1}(d^*)$	$\beta_2(d^*)$
(i) Levin:	0.607184	0.156519	0.4633	3.4253
(ii) Padé:	0.607190	0.156542	0.4634	3.4122

The 4-moment percentiles of d* using (i) are

	1%	5%	10%	90%	95%	99%
d*	0.2924	0.3714	0.4165	0.8125	0.8825	1.0256
Derived ν^*	0.3231	0.4004	0.4437	0.8170	0.8843	1.0257
Direct ν^*	0.3230	0.4006	0.4439	0.8171	0.8846	1.0260

TABLE 10. Levin and Padé approximants for c* moments.

c	r	n=25 μ_1'	μ_2	μ_3	μ_4	n=30 μ_1'	μ_2	μ_3	μ_4
1.0	9	1.0949728	0.0372344	0.0033566	0.0347445	1.0798484	0.0307982	0.0023006	-0.0007795
	10	1.0950276	0.0373526	0.0037434	0.0033054	1.0798738	0.0308527	0.0024777	0.0025505
	11	1.0950562	0.0374226	0.0039414	0.0043164	1.0798864	0.0308835	0.0025660	0.0029895
	12	1.0950702	0.0374535	0.0039704	0.0046815	1.0798921	0.0308958	0.0025749	0.0031664
	13	1.0950773	0.0374746	0.0040353	0.0049112	1.0798948	0.0309041	0.0026012	0.0032735
	S3	1.0950844	0.0375207	0.0039180	0.0053006	1.0798972	0.0309208	0.0025614	0.0034381
	S5	1.0950843	0.0374937	0.0040316	0.0052856	1.0798971	0.0309104	0.0025983	0.0034648
	P10	1.0955000	0.0370200	0.0042100	0.0102000	1.0801000	0.0306700	0.0026870	0.0047570
	P11	1.0947000	0.0346600	0.0035200	0.0041500	1.0797000	0.0289000	0.0023350	0.0028970
1.5	9	1.5987553	0.0718490	0.0131371	0.0205066	1.5817627	0.0580862	0.0085160	0.0127585
	10	1.5987578	0.0718752	0.0132863	0.0205384	1.5817636	0.0580953	0.0085696	0.0127741
	11	1.5987592	0.0718882	0.0133660	0.0206300	1.5817640	0.0580993	0.0085947	0.0128070
	12	1.5987598	0.0718943	0.0134040	0.0207284	1.5817642	0.0581010	0.0086054	0.0128385
	13	1.5987601	0.0718971	0.0134218	0.0208095	1.5817643	0.0581017	0.0086099	0.0128618
	S3	1.5987603	0.0718996	0.0134374	0.0211908	1.5817643	0.0581023	0.0086132	0.0129282
	S5	1.5987603	0.0718996	0.0134373	0.0209189	1.5817643	0.0581023	0.0086132	0.0128849
	P10	1.5987700	0.0719040	0.0134770	0.0214170	1.5817670	0.0581040	0.0086240	0.0130110
	P11	1.5987600	0.0719010	0.0134530	0.0210040	1.5817640	0.0581030	0.0086170	0.0129050
2.0	9	2.1155475	0.1235319	0.0336408	0.0648167	2.0951835	0.0990390	0.0214528	0.0390282
	10	2.1155476	0.1235278	0.0336363	0.0647768	2.0951835	0.0990363	0.0214519	0.0390159
	11	2.1155476	0.1235657	0.0336364	0.0649225	2.0951835	0.0990437	0.0214519	0.0390441
	12	2.1155476	0.1235426	0.0336372	0.0648706	2.0951835	0.0990419	0.0214521	0.0390380
	13	2.1155476	0.1235408	0.0336380	0.0648623	2.0951835	0.0990416	0.0214523	0.0390368
	S3	2.1155476	0.1235406	0.0336559	0.0648608	2.0951835	0.0990416	0.0214531	0.0390365
	S5	2.1155476	0.1235467	0.0336403	0.0648720	2.0951835	0.0990418	0.0214526	0.0390376
	P10	2.1155476	0.1235397	0.0336397	0.0648605	2.0951835	0.0990416	0.0214526	0.0390366
	P11	2.1155475	0.1235402	0.0336390	0.0648594	2.0951835	0.0990416	0.0214525	0.0390364
2.5	9	2.6388235	0.1952872	0.0701416	0.1656667	2.6141264	0.1560170	0.0446131	0.0988083
	10	2.6388232	0.1952872	0.0701420	0.1656683	2.6141263	0.1560170	0.0446132	0.0988085
	11	2.6388233	0.1952872	0.0701416	0.1656727	2.6141263	0.1560170	0.0446131	0.0988091
	12	2.6388233	0.1952872	0.0701413	0.1656633	2.6141263	0.1560170	0.0446131	0.0988065
	13	2.6388233	0.1952869	0.0701469	0.1656434	2.6141264	0.1560171	0.0446134	0.0988021
	S3	2.6388233	0.1952872	0.0701415	0.1656809	2.6141264	0.1560170	0.0446131	0.0988128
	S5	2.6388233	0.1952872	0.0701417	0.1656677	2.6141264	0.1560170	0.0446131	0.0988084
	P10	2.6388233	0.1952873	0.0701419	0.1656175	2.6141264	0.1560170	0.0446132	0.0987839
	P11	2.6388233	0.1952872	0.0701428	0.1656876	2.6141264	0.1560170	0.0446133	0.0988104
3.0	9	3.1660955	0.2887541	0.1286604	0.3648222	3.1364297	0.2303361	0.0818077	0.2169620
	10	3.1660955	0.2887541	0.1285770	0.3648729	3.1364297	0.2303361	0.0818150	0.2169699
	11	3.1660956	0.2887567	0.1286557	0.3650496	3.1364298	0.2303367	0.0818077	0.2169788
	12	3.1660956	0.2887562	0.1286650	0.3648476	3.1364298	0.2303366	0.0818085	0.2169681
	13	3.1660956	0.2887562	0.1286649	0.3648695	3.1364298	0.2303366	0.0818085	0.2169699
	S3	3.1660956	0.2887562	0.1286649	0.3648673	3.1364298	0.2303366	0.0818085	0.2169697
	S5	3.1660956	0.2887562	0.1286648	0.3649202	3.1364298	0.2303366	0.0818085	0.2169717
	P10	3.1660956	0.2887558	0.1286596	0.3649093	3.1364298	0.2303367	0.0818079	0.2169744
	P11	3.1660957	0.2887560	0.1286639	0.3649262	3.1364298	0.2303366	0.0818084	0.2169767

(Notes on Table 10. Sequences for the four moments are those for Levin's t-algorithm (2.1) and refer to α_{r+1} for each moment. S_3 and S_5 refer to the Shank's extrapolates (see footnote to Table 4) based on the last 3 and 5 sequence values respectively. If either of these extrapolates reverses the sequence trend, it should be ignored; generally we look for monotonicity in the sequences. Caution is needed in interpreting the Shanks' extrapolates.

For the Padé fractions we have used the Stieltjes continued fraction forms; for example, for the mean we use

$$\mu_1'(c^*) \sim \frac{nc}{n+} \frac{p_1^{(1)}}{1+} \frac{q_1^{(1)}}{n+} \cdots + \frac{p_5^{(1)}}{1+} \frac{q_5^{(1)}}{n}$$

and P_{10}, P_{11} refer to the approximants stopping at the partial numerators p_5, q_5 respectively. For the variance we use a similar expression, the first partial numerator now being $q_0^{(2)}$. Similarly, $\mu_3(c^*)$ and $\mu_4(c^*)$ have $q_0^{(3)}/n$, and $q_0^{(4)}/n^2$ as first partial numerators.

Generally, there is good agreement in the two types of approximants for $c \geq 2$--five or six decimal place agreement seems to be common. There is a deterioration for smaller c and especially for the 3-rd and 4-th central moments. Thus for c=1, n=25, our preference would be $\mu_3(c^*)$ 0.0040, and $\mu_4(c^*)$ 0.006 with some doubt; the situation for n=30 is only slightly improved. Even so, the effect on the percentiles is surprisingly small (see Tables 13a, 13b).

The reason for the deterioration in the summation algorithms for c < 2 doubtless lies in the largeness of the higher coefficients in the series, together with a "bumpiness" in the early terms especially for μ_3 and μ_4.)

TABLE 11. Assessment of moments of c*, c=2.5, n=20.

$\mu_1'(c^*)$

r	2cB(a=1,tr=1) Fr	Δ	2cB(a=1,tr=0) Fr	Δ	2cB(a=2,tr=0) Fr	Δ
9	2.676077	235	2.668530	1766	2.658901	3744
10	2.676312	172	2.670296	1314	2.662645	2785
11	2.676484	129	2.671610	999	1.665430	2117
12	2.676613	100	2.672609	775	2.667547	1641
13	2.676713		2.673384		2.669188	
S_5	2.67712		2.67864		2.67606	

Direct Sum

r	term
0	2.5
1	0.1605403
2	0.0147840
3	0.0016437
4	0.0001994
5	0.0000186
6	0.0000001
7	-0.0000005
DS(6)	2.677187

The preferred value is 2.67712 because of the small differences in 2cB(a=1,tr=1); this agrees with the direct sum to the n^{-6} term. A simulation of 10^5 cycles gave 2.6777. Levin without truncation gave 2.6772.

$\mu_2(c^*)$

r	2cB(a=2,tr=0) Fr	Δ	2cB(a=1,tr=1) Fr	Δ
9	0.2493811	17514	0.2587758	3567
10	0.2511325	14470	0.2591325	2663
11	0.2525795	11530	0.2593988	2042
12	0.2537325	9340	0.2596630	1600
13	0.2546665		0.2597630	
S_5	0.259590		0.260476	
σ	0.5095		0.5104	

Preferred 2cB is 0.5104. A simulation gave $\sigma_S \sim 0.5105$. The direct sum gave DS(9) = 0.260625 with the n^{-10} coefficient 0.0000007, with $\sigma \sim 0.5104$. The Levin assessment gave 0.5105, our final choice.

$\mu_3(c^*)$

r	2cB(a=1,tr=0) Fr	Δ	2cB(a=1,tr=1) Fr	Δ
9	0.1140509	17471	0.1214065	7610
10	0.1157980	13752	0.1221675	5711
11	0.1171732	11058	0.1227386	4420
12	0.1182790	9049	0.1231806	3496
13	0.1191839		0.1235302	
S_5	0.124287		0.125189	
$\sqrt{\beta_1}$	0.9347		0.9415	

Comparisons are:

2cB $\sqrt{\beta_1} \sim 0.9415$

Simulation $\sqrt{\beta_1} \sim 0.9512$

Levin $\sqrt{\beta_1} \sim 0.9440$

{DS(10) 0.125625 (for $\mu_3(c^*)$)

$\sqrt{\beta_1} \sim 0.9442$

Preferred value $\sqrt{\beta_1} = 0.9442$.

$\mu_4(c^*)$

r	2cB(a=1,tr=0) Fr	Δ	2cB(a=1,tr=1) Fr	Δ
9	0.2630947	76628	0.2966641	45608
10	0.2707575	62896	0.3012249	35777
11	0.2770471	52531	0.3048026	28778
12	0.2823002	44498	0.3070804	23608
13	0.2867500		0.3100412	
S_5	0.318118		0.323717	
β_2	4.684		4.766	

Levin $\beta_2 \sim 4.831$

{DS(12) 0.3283169 (n^{-12} term 0.00003)

$\beta_2 \sim 4.839$

Final choice $\beta_2 \sim 4.84$. A small sample case (c=1.5, n=10) is given in the appendix.

TABLE 12. Moments of c* by series (Levin) and simulation (10^5 runs).

c	n		$\mu_1'(c^*)$	$\sigma(c^*)$	$\sqrt{\beta_1}(c^*)$	$\beta_2(c^*)$
1.0	20	L	1.1177	0.2188	0.6645	3.5796
		S	1.1174	0.2183	0.6751	4.1027
1.5	20	L	1.6248	0.3072	0.8166	4.3727
		S	1.6247	0.3068	0.8240	4.6079
2.0	20	L	2.1470	0.4050	0.9035	4.7211
		S	2.1472	0.4048	0.9106	4.8945
	25	L	2.1155	0.3515	0.7747	4.2498
		S	2.1156	0.3511	0.7705	4.2502
2.5	20	L	2.6772	0.5105	0.9440	4.8307
		S	2.6777	0.5105	0.9512	5.0155
3.0	20	L	3.2123	0.6214	0.9601	4.8627
		S	3.2130	0.6215	0.9669	5.0429

(L ≡ Levin's t-algorithm using all series coefficients to n^{-12}. S ≡ simulation of 10^5 cycles.)

along with a comparison for ν*. In addition we have from the d* percentiles, the c* values 0.975, 1.133, 1.231, 2.401, 2.693, and 3.420 which can be compared with the less reliable (because of the bumpiness of the higher moments) results in Table A1 (appendix).

Further comparisons of moments and percentiles (not reported here) give grounds for confidence in the summation algorithm for the parameter space $1 \leq c \leq 4$ and $n > 15$ approximately. Actually there is reason to believe that if percentage points of c* are needed, it is better to proceed via d*.

5. CONCLUDING REMARKS

(i) The series for the moments of ν* taken as far as the n^{-24} term appear to be divergent. As c, the shape parameter varies from 1 to about 4, the regular alternating sign pattern is increasingly disrupted (especially for the higher moments),

TABLE 13a. Percentage points of ν^* from ν^* moments (direct) and c^* moments (indirect).

	n=15		n=20			n=25	
%	Direct	I	Direct	I	M C	Direct	I
c=1.0							
1	0.5454	0.5475	0.5956	0.5964	0.595	0.6309	0.6315
5	0.6312	0.6249	0.6757	0.6726	0.677	0.7067	0.7048
10	0.6813	0.6743	0.7220	0.7186	0.723	0.7500	0.7481
90	1.1747	1.1736	1.1705	1.1711	1.170	1.1645	1.1649
95	1.2744	1.2479	1.2613	1.2525	1.261	1.2481	1.2441
99	1.4921	1.3651	1.4606	1.4107	1.465	1.4319	1.4099
c=1.5							
1	0.3864	0.3869	0.4243	0.4245	0.425	0.4502	0.4504
5	0.4532	0.4515	0.4840	0.4834	0.484	0.5049	0.5046
10	0.4902	0.4886	0.5171	0.5165	0.518	0.5352	0.5349
90	0.8046	0.8042	0.7942	0.7940	0.794	0.7858	0.7856
95	0.8605	0.8565	0.8427	0.8416	0.842	0.8291	0.8286
99	0.9769	0.9591	0.9429	0.9393	0.943	0.9179	0.9170
c=2.0							
1	0.2985	0.2986	0.3290	0.3290	0.330	0.3496	0.3496
5	0.3523	0.3520	0.3766	0.3765	0.376	0.3929	0.3928
10	0.3821	0.3819	0.4029	0.4028	0.403	0.4168	0.4167
90	0.6212	0.6209	0.6113	0.6110	0.611	0.6039	0.6037
95	0.6606	0.6604	0.6450	0.6448	0.645	0.6338	0.6337
99	0.7394	0.7411	0.7121	0.7127	0.714	0.6930	0.6932
c=2.5							
1	0.2424	0.2425	0.2679	0.2679	0.269	0.2852	0.2852
5	0.2875	0.2873	0.3079	0.3077	0.308	0.3215	0.3214
10	0.3125	0.3123	0.3299	0.3298	0.330	0.3414	0.3413
90	0.5102	0.5100	0.5014	0.5012	0.501	0.4949	0.4948
95	0.5416	0.5412	0.5282	0.5281	0.528	0.5187	0.5186
99	0.6032	0.6026	0.5806	0.5806	0.582	0.5649	0.5650
c=3.0							
1	0.2037	0.2038	0.2256	0.2257	0.226	0.2405	0.2405
5	0.2425	0.2423	0.2601	0.2600	0.260	0.2718	0.2718
10	0.2641	0.2640	0.2792	0.2791	0.279	0.2891	0.2890
90	0.4350	0.4349	0.4271	0.4270	0.427	0.4214	0.4213
95	0.4617	0.4615	0.4499	0.4498	0.450	0.4416	0.4416
99	0.5136	0.5133	0.4941	0.4940	0.495	0.4807	0.4806

(Assessments for ν^* direct were found from moments series; see the footnote to Table 7. Those for Indirect (I) were found from (2.7). M.C. refers to a simulation of 10^5 cycles.)

whereas the magnitude pattern is diluted (the n^{-24} coefficient decreases from about 10^{60} to 10^{25}). The Levin t-algorithm, with stopping point signalled from exact small sample results, works well.

(ii) Series for the shape parameter c^* (taken as far as n^{-12}) are more difficult to sum because of irregular sign and magnitude patterns.

(iii) Series for d^* (estimating $d=1/c$) are similar to those for the coefficient of variation.

(iv) Validation is by numerical investigation--error bounds for moments and percentiles are out of the question. We use several summation

TABLE 13b. Percentage points of c^* from c^* moments (direct) and ν^* moments (indirect).

	n=15		n=20			n=25	
%	Direct	I	Direct	I	M C	Direct	I
c=1.0							
1	0.7439	0.6880	0.7225	0.7008	0.699	0.7229	0.7131
5	0.8075	0.7919	0.8047	0.7996	0.800	0.8098	0.8074
10	0.8554	0.8546	0.8571	0.8576	0.858	0.8615	0.8618
90	1.5112	1.4945	1.4108	1.4037	1.401	1.3512	1.3475
95	1.6420	1.6242	1.5156	1.5078	1.505	1.4406	1.4365
99	1.9000	1.9078	1.7285	1.7311	1.696	1.6233	1.6250
c=1.5							
1	1.0429	1.0237	1.0652	1.0611	1.061	1.0917	1.0906
5	1.1713	1.1657	1.1930	1.1911	1.192	1.2125	1.2118
10	1.2513	1.2507	1.2684	1.2680	1.268	1.2826	1.2823
90	2.1558	2.1480	2.0267	2.0242	2.022	1.9497	1.9484
95	2.3543	2.3449	2.1819	2.1788	2.181	2.0802	2.0786
99	2.7980	2.8015	2.5221	2.5238	2.519	2.3610	2.3621
c=2.0							
1	1.3648	1.3682	1.4234	1.4247	1.420	1.4666	1.4672
5	1.5459	1.5455	1.5867	1.5861	1.587	1.6172	1.6168
10	1.6538	1.6529	1.6830	1.6823	1.684	1.7055	1.7050
90	2.8389	2.8372	2.6747	2.6739	2.673	2.5754	2.5748
95	3.1086	3.1056	2.8844	2.8829	2.885	2.7507	2.7498
99	3.7336	3.7341	3.3524	3.3524	3.344	3.1327	3.1326
c=2.5							
1	1.7089	1.7072	1.7804	1.7805	1.766	1.8349	1.8351
5	1.9242	1.9227	1.9776	1.9769	1.976	2.0177	2.0172
10	2.0555	2.0547	2.0956	2.0950	2.096	2.1259	2.1255
90	3.5518	3.5487	3.3430	3.3417	3.343	3.2175	3.2168
95	3.8968	3.8925	3.6103	3.6085	3.606	3.4405	3.4394
99	4.6964	4.6992	4.2086	4.2092	4.197	3.9281	3.9282
c=3.0							
1	2.0409	2.0395	2.1299	2.1293	2.125	2.1960	2.1958
5	2.2976	2.2964	2.3644	2.3637	2.363	2.4138	2.4134
10	2.4552	2.4547	2.5058	2.5054	2.507	2.5437	2.5434
90	4.2785	4.2753	4.0235	4.0220	4.025	3.8703	3.8695
95	4.7006	4.6967	4.3505	4.3486	4.346	4.1428	4.1417
99	5.6789	5.6835	5.0821	5.0837	5.072	4.7391	4.7398

(For the direct assessments see ¶13.4. For the indirect (I), (2.8) was used. M.C. refers to a simulation of 10^5 cycles.)

algorithms (Levin, Levin with truncation, Padé, simulation) and in them study consistency. There can be difficulties here--for example, adjacent close approximants may still be in error. We have described some highly successful cases and some problematical cases--for example $\mu_4(c^*)$ when c=1.5 or so and n small.

There are outstanding problems, such as:
(a) the response of an algorithm to slight errors in series coefficients for low orders of n^{-1} and large errors in coefficents for high orders of n^{-1}; (b) the choice of algorithm for summation purposes. Levin's t-algorithm works well for alternating series and magnitudes lying between the single and double factorial series. The Padé approach behaves similarly and very likely has

TABLE 14. Mean and standard deviation of c* computed directly from c* series compared to Pearson-Tukey approximants based on percentiles of c* derived from those of ν*.

c		n=15 S	n=15 PT	n=20 S	n=20 PT	n=25 S	n=25 PT
1.0	μ_1'	1.1556	1.1558	1.1177	1.1178	1.0951	1.0951
	σ	0.2589	0.2593	0.2188	0.2186	0.1936	0.1932
1.5	μ_1'	1.6697	1.6696	1.6248	1.6247	1.5988	1.5987
	σ	0.3711	0.3696	0.3072	0.3057	0.2681	0.2664
2.0	μ_1'	2.2023	2.2018	2.1470	2.1468	2.1155	2.1154
	σ	0.4937	0.4928	0.4050	0.4035	0.3515	0.3496
2.5	μ_1'	2.7449	2.7443	2.6772	2.6769	2.6388	2.6387
	σ	0.6245	0.6232	0.5105	0.5086	0.4419	0.4396
3.0	μ_1'	3.2940	3.2933	3.2123	3.2119	3.1661	3.1659
	σ	0.7613	0.7597	0.6214	0.6191	0.5374	0.5345

(S: Levin's t-algorithm, using all available coefficients in the series for $\mu_1'(c^*)$ and $\mu_2(c^*)$. PT: Pearson-Tukey values derived from their $\max\{\hat{\sigma}^1_{0.05}, \hat{\sigma}^1_{0.025}\}$ based on percentiles of c* derived from ν* moment series.)

wide application (see the Baker-Gammel-Wills conjecture (Baker, 1975)); (c) the construction of algorithms which relate specifically to moments of statistics expressable as multiple integrals.

Finally, it should be eminently clear that low order asymptotics to measures such as means, covariances, etc., should be viewed with great caution. Even if the first few coefficients are seductively small, there may be rude awakenings round the corner; for example, an n^{-1} term in a variance may exist but all higher order terms may not.

To those not well acquainted with summation problems reference may be made to: (i) Baker and Gammel (1970), Baker (1975), Graves and Morris (1973), and Brezinski (1980) for modern studies on Padé methods; (ii) Wall (1948), Perron (1950), Stieltjes (1918), Borel (1928) for classical studies; (iii) Van Dyke (1974, 1975) for general remarks on divergent series; (iv) Shohat and Tamarken (1963) for the moment problem.

APPENDIX

A small sample case. To illustrate problems which arise for small samples, we take c=1.5 and n=10. In particular the fourth central moment has the successive coefficients (approximated for convenience)

$$\mu_4(c^*) \sim 0.07 + 0.08 + 0.11 + 0.21 - 1.25 + 11.86 - 106.5 + 1022.9 - 10613.4 + \ldots;$$

it should be noted that the first coefficient is merely three times the square of the variance asymptote and provides no unexpected information. Also note the disrupted sign pattern.

We try the Levin algorithm.

r	$\mu_1'(c^*)$	$\mu_2(c^*)$	$\mu_3(c^*)$	$\mu_4(c^*)$ Truncate & Start at n^{-4} term
		α_r		
2	1.7502	0.1279	0.1080	0.2335
3	1.7418	0.2656	0.1097	0.1679
4	1.6397	0.2403	0.1163	0.1722
5	1.7749	0.2398	0.1244	0.1957
6	1.7675	0.2426	0.1345	0.2229
7	1.7663	0.2457	0.1464	0.1979
8	1.7663	0.2485	0.1585	

We base $\mu_4(c^*)$ on α_6 (adjusted) yielding the value 0.3776. Our preferred assessments are: $\mu_1' = 1.7663$, $\mu_2 = 0.2485$, $\sqrt{\beta_1} = 1.2789(?)$, $\beta_2 = 6.1132(?)$ with rather low confidence in β_2. If we take α_7 instead of α_6, our alternative for the kurtosis is $\beta_2^{(a)} = 5.7102$. We now have the Pearson 4-moment fits for c* (Table A1). Thus the change in β_2 does affect the c* percentiles but this change is damped out in the ν* derived values.

TABLE A1. Percentiles of ν* derived from c* compared to direct values n=10, c=1.5.

%		1	5	10	90	95	99
c*	(a)	0.995	1.134	1.226	2.413	2.628	3.355
	(b)	1.038	1.149	1.230	2.426	2.713	3.360
Derived ν*	(a)	1.005	0.884	0.820	0.442	0.400	0.329
	(b)	0.964	0.873	0.818	0.440	0.400	0.328
ν* direct		1.026	0.885	0.817	0.444	0.401	0.323

((a) uses the moments with kurtosis β_2, and (b) with kurtosis $\beta_2^{(a)}$)

REFERENCES

Baker, G. A., Jr. (1975). Essentials of Padé approximants, Academic Press, New York.

Baker, G. A., Jr. and Gammel, J. L. (1970). The Padé approximant in theoretical physics, Academic Press, New York.

Barlow, R. E., Toland, R. H., and Freeman, T. (1979). Stress-rupture life of Kevlar/epoxy spherical pressure vessels. Lawrence Livermore Laboratory Report UCID-17755, Part 3.

Borel, É. (1920) Leçons sur les series divergentes, Gauthier-Villars, Paris (translated by Charles L. Critchfield and Anna Vakar (1975), Los Alamos Scientific Laboratory).

Bowman, K. O. and Shenton, L. R. (1981). "Moment series for the coefficient of variation in Weibull sampling," Proc. Statis. Comput. Sect. Amer. Statis. Assoc., 148-153.

Bowman, K. O. and Shenton, L. R. (1981). Estimation problems associated with the Weibull distribution. Report ORNL/CSD-79, Union Carbide Corporation.

Brezinski, C. (1980). Padé-Type approximation and general orthogonal polynomials, Birkhäusen Verlag, Basel-Boston-Stuttgart.

Cain, W. D. and Knight, C. E., Jr. (1981). Application of Weibull criterion to failure prediction in composites. Report Y-2235, Oak Ridge Y-12 Plant, Union Carbide Corporation, Nuclear Division.

Good, I. J. (1961). "The multivariate saddlepoint method and chi-squared for the multinomial distribution," Annals of Math. Statis., 32, 535-548.

Graves-Morris, P. R., ed. (1973). Padé approximants and their applications, Academic Press, New York.

Levin, D. (1973). "Development of non-linear transformations for improving convergence of sequences," Internat. J. Computer Math., B3, 371-388.

Lukacs, E. (1955). "Applications of Faá di Bruno's formula in mathematical statistics," Amer. Math. Monthly, 62, 340-348.

Newby, M. J. (1980). "The properties of moment estimators for the Weibull distribution based on the sample coefficient of variation," Technometrics, 22, 2, 187-194.

Pearson, E. S. (1963). "Some problems arising in approximating to probability distributions using moments," Biometrika, 50, 1, 95-111.

Pearson, E. S. and Tukey, J. W. (1965). "Approximate means and standard deviations based on distances between percentage points of frequency curves," Biometrika, 52, 533-546.

Peto, R. and Lee, P. (1973). "Weibull distributions for continuous-carcinogenesis experiments," Biometrics, 29, 457-470.

Shanks, Daniel (1955). "Non-linear transformations of divergent and slowly convergent sequences," J. Math. and Physics, 34, 1-42.

Shenton, L. R. and Bowman, K. O. (1977a). "A new algorithm for summing divergent series: Part 3, applications," J. Computa. and Appl. Math., 3, 35-51.

Shenton, L. R. and Bowman, K. O. (1977b). Maximum likelihood estimation in small samples, Griffin's Statistical Monograph and Courses No. 38, Macmillan Publishing Co., Inc., New York.

Shohat, J. A. and Tamarkin, J. D. (1963). The problem of moments, Amer. Math. Soc., Providence, Rhode Island.

Stewart, D. A. and Essenwanger, A. M. (1970). "Frequency distribution of wind speed near the surface," J. Appl. Meteorology, 17, 1633-1642.

Stieltjes, T. J. (1918). Oeuvres complétes, Vol. 2, P. Noordhoff, Groningen.

Van Dyke, M. (1974). "Analysis and improvement of perturbation series," Quar. J. Mech. Appl. Math. 27, 423-450.

Van Dyke, M. (1975). "Computer extension of perturbation series in fluid mechanics. SIAM J. Appl. Math., 28, 3, 720-734.

Wall, H. S. (1948). Analytic theory of continued fractions, Van Nostrand-Reinhold, Princeton, New Jersey.

ACKNOWLEDGMENT

The first author's research was sponsored by the Applied Mathematical Sciences Research Program, Office of Energy Research, U.S. Department of Energy under contract W-7405-eng-26 with the Union Carbide Corporation.

Categorical Data and Generalized Linear Models

Chair: Michael M. Meyer, Carnegie–Mellon University

GOODNESS OF FIT TESTS FOR SURVEY DATA

Edward J. Bedrick
University of New Mexico

The effect of cluster sample designs of sample χ^2 statistics will be discussed for the class of log-linear models with direct estimates. Closed form expressions for the moments of χ^2 and G^2 are given. A one-moment adjustment of χ^2 and G^2 is proposed which only involves knowledge of cell and marginal design effects.

ESTIMATING GENERALIZED LINEAR MODELS WITH MANY PARAMETERS

Michael M. Meyer
Carnegie-Mellon University

Newton's method is often inappropriate for estimation in generalized linear models. We will discuss alternative optimization techniques which combine the advantages of several methods.

GLIM - A DEVELOPING SYSTEM

Brian Francis, John Hinde
Centre for Applied Statistics
University of Lancaster
Lancaster, England

Mel Slater
Department of Computer Science and Statistics
Queen Mary College
London, England

SUMMARY

This paper introduces the GLIM system and its development into a more comprehensive interactive statistical package. Particular attention is focussed on the facilities for fitting generalised linear models and on the interactive graphics capabilities. Mixing the commands from these modules gives the user powerful facilities for the fitting, displaying and diagnostic checking of a wide class of statistical models, as illustrated in the example.

KEYWORDS: GLIM, GENERALISED LINEAR MODELS, INTERACTIVE GRAPHICS, REGRESSION DIAGNOSTICS.

1. INTRODUCTION

The GLIM system was originally designed for the interactive analysis of generalised linear models. The command language was both simple and flexible and enabled users to do analyses well outside the range of those originally intended. At the same time, the system was not always too convenient for certain standard analyses and there was also a growing pressure for the provision of high quality graphics. These considerations led to the idea of extending GLIM into a modular interactive statistical system. Initially this system will consist of a basic kernel for program control, a module for analysing generalised linear models, an analysis of variance module, an array calculator and an interactive graphics system. This represents a significant extension of the facilities currently available in GLIM and should be released by mid-1983. Obviously the structure is such that other modules can be added at a later date.

This paper gives a brief history of the development of GLIM into the new system, which is tentatively called PRISM (Program for Interactive Statistical Modelling). Section 3 gives a brief description of generalised linear models and their analysis using GLIM. The facilities available in the GRAPH module are outlined in Section 4. Finally, an example is presented to illustrate the flexibility of the GLIM language and the value of interactive graphics for both presenting easily assimulated output and as an integral part of a statistical analysis.

2. DEVELOPMENT OF GLIM

The GLIM system dates back to 1971 when J.A. Nelder proposed the undertaking of "a specific project concerned with specifying and implementing a package related to fitting a wide class of statistical models". The theoretical impetus for this proposal came from the fundamental paper of Nelder and Wedderburn (1972) on generalised linear models. This paper demonstrates that the technique of iteratively reweighted least squares can be used to obtain maximum likelihood estimates for a broad class of regression models, where the observed data is distributed according to some exponential family. The method itself was not new, being exactly the approach given by Finney (1952) for maximum likelihood estimation in probit analysis. This class of generalised linear model includes the standard regression and analysis of variance models for normally distributed data, logit and probit models for binary data, log-linear models for contingency table analysis and random effects models.

The first version of GLIM was released in 1974 and had very limited facilities, but provided the basis for future developments; the ability to interactively analyse generalised linear models using a simple command language. Since then there have been two further releases and the current version, (GLIM-3), Baker and Nelder (1978), provides the user with much more flexibility, but is still a relatively small package specifically for the analysis of generalised linear models. Much of the development of the basic system has consisted of extending the program control elements of the command language, e.g. providing branching, looping and macro facilities. These have enabled users to extend the class of statistical models that can be analysed far beyond the limits originally envisaged by the developers. In addition, the user is also able to access all of the data structures used in the model fitting and so can construct a wide variety of diagnostic information on the particular model under consideration; a very important aspect for good interactive model fitting, see Section 5. It is perhaps worth noting at this point that unlike many statistical packages the amount of output from GLIM is very small, although the user is free to construct any additional output he may want. This has obvious advantages for interactive working and also means that the user is not saddled with the particular set of statistics which the package developers want to give him. Consequently, he can easily modify his methods of analysis to take account of very recent developments.

The current developments of GLIM are designed to extend it to a larger interactive statistical analysis system. They arose originally from two distinct demands; one for an interactive analysis of variance package based on the ANOVA directive in GENSTAT (see Alvey et al, 1977) and the other from the provision of enhanced graphics capabilities in GLIM (GLIM-3 has only very basic line-printer graphics). The decision to incorporate these, and perhaps other capabilities, into the GLIM system was a major break from previous developments, and led to the design of a modular interactive statistical system. The first release of this system is planned for mid-1983 and it will initially consist of five modules:-

(i) the Kernel

this will provide the housekeeping, data manipulation and program control facilities and the link between the other modules. Essentially it will be an enhanced implementation of the features of GLIM-3 which do not directly relate to fitting generalised linear models.

(ii) GLIM

this is release 4 of the generalised linear modelling procedures and again is substantially enhanced.

(iii) AOV

analysis of variance based upon the GENSTAT algorithm of Wilkinson (1970), see also Payne and Wilkinson (1977). This provides complete analysis of variance computations for data from generally balanced designs.

(iv) ACAL

an array calculation with facilities similar to those available in APL. The tabulation of summary statistics and other operations on multi-dimensional arrays will greatly extend the capabilities of the other modules.

(v) GRAPH

an interactive graphics module which is an implementation of the Graphical Kernel system (GKS), the draft ISO standard on computer graphics, see Hopgood (1982). This is not merely interactive in the sense that commands are issued at a terminal but rather that it allows pictures to be created interactively using a graphical input device (such as a light pen).

A complete description of these developments can be found in the GLIM82 proceedings, (Gilchrist, 1982).

3. GLIM

This section briefly covers generlised linear models and the fitting of these models in GLIM. The actual description is in terms of the syntax of GLIM-4, although this is very similar to that of GLIM-3 and the basic ideas remain the same.

3.1 Generalised Linear Models

The concept of a generalised linear model is an extension of the usual normal theory linear model to exponential family distributions with some suitable transformation of the mean having a linear model. The elements are summarized by

(i) a response variable Y having a single parameter exponential family distribution with mean μ

(ii) a set of explanatory variables $X_1,\ldots,X_k$ giving a linear predictor

$$\eta = \beta_o + \beta_1 X_1 + \ldots + \beta_k X_k$$

These explanatory variables can be either continuous variates or categorical, (referred to as factors in GLIM, which are fitted using dummy variables with 0, 1 coding.)

(iii) a link function $g(\mu) = \eta$, relating the mean of the distribution to the linear predictor.

[(i) can be extended to include distributions with an added scale parameter, such as the normal distribution with unknown variance]

Simple examples of such models are

a) normal theory linear regression - here we have a normal distribution, continuous explanatory variables and an identity link function giving

$$\mu = \beta_o + \beta_1 X_1 + \ldots + \beta_k X_k$$

b) analysis of covariance models - these can be fitted as in a) only now some of the explanatory variables are categorical.

c) logit and probit models for binary data - the observations, r successes out of n, are binomially distributed with parameter p (mean np) and the link function is

logit: $\text{logit}(p) = \log\left(\frac{p}{1-p}\right) = \beta_o+\beta_1 X_1+\ldots+\beta_k X_k$

probit: $\Phi^{-1}(p) = \beta_o + \beta_1 X_1 + \ldots + \beta_k X_k$

where Φ^{-1} is the inverse cumulative normal distribution function.

d) log-linear models for contingency tables - these

are based on the Poisson representation of the multinomial distribution and a log link between the Poisson mean and a linear function of the classifying factors.

3.2 Model Specification in GLIM

To specify a generalised linear model in GLIM requires four directives giving the elements described in Section 3.1.

(i) The response variable name is defined using the $YVARIATE directive.

(ii) The probability distribution is defined using the $PROBABILITY directive

```
$PROBABILITY NORMAL
             BINOMIAL  (denominator)
             POISSON
             GAMMA
```

where denominator is an identifier containing the binomial denominator vector.

The default setting is NORMAL.

(iii) The link function giving the relationship between the linear predictor, η, and the mean of the probability distribution, μ, is specified by the $LINK directive:

$LINK	I	identity	$\eta=\mu$
	L	log	$\eta=\log\mu$
	R	reciprocal	$\eta=\mu^{-1}$
	S	square root	$\eta=\mu^{\frac{1}{2}}$
	E *[real]*	exponent	$\eta=\mu$** *[real]*
	G	logit	$\eta=\log\frac{\mu}{n-\mu}$
	P	probit	$\eta=\Phi\ \frac{\mu}{n}$
	C	complementary log-log	$\eta=\log(-\log(1-\mu/n))$

The default setting is the link giving the function of μ which is the natural parameter for the specified distribution, namely

Normal - I, Binomial - G, Poisson - L, Gamma - R

The use of these links gives models with sufficient statistics.

(iv) The regression model to be fitted is defined by using the $FIT directive followed by a structure formula. The syntax of these structure formulae is based on that devised by Wilkinson and Rogers (1973) and allows the combination of factors and variates to provide complex explanatory relationships. The basic elements of these formulae are factors, variates and three operators; . denoting interaction, *crossing and / nesting. The symbol 1 is used for the constant term in the model. In addition it is possible to fit user supplied design matrices and orthogonal polynomials.

Examples: If A, B are factors and X is a variate then

```
$FIT 1 + A + B          gives a main effects model
$FIT 1 + X              a simple linear regression
$FIT 1 + A * B         )
                       )  main effects with
equivalently
$FIT 1 + A + B + A.B   )      interaction
                       )
$FIT 1 + A + X          main effects for A with
                        parallel within-groups
                        regression on X.
```

The output from a $FIT directive consists simply of the deviance, and the degrees of freedom. In normal models the deviance is just the residual sum of squares and in non-normal models it is

-2log(likelihood of fitted model/likelihood of saturated model)

where the saturated model is the model which reproduces the data. The deviance can be used to compare different models and also to assess the goodness-of-fit of any particular model. The $DISPLAY directive allows the user to obtain additional output, such as the parameter estimates and standard errors, standardised residuals and fitted values, and the covariance matrix of the parameter estimates.

3.3 Additional user facilities

GLIM, unlike many statistical packages, also contains most of the features of a high level programming language, including branching, looping and the ability to define subroutines. Scalar, vector and array manipulations are available through the $CALCULATE and $ACAL directives. In addition, many of the structures used and produced by a fit are available to the user, and this facilitates the production of extra diagnostic information after a fit.

In GLIM-4, these structures are stored as system variates or scalars, and have names starting with the symbol "%" (so distinguishing them from user-defined identifiers). Most of them become available to the user immediately after each fit, but some structures need to be extracted from the program into the user's worksheet. Some commonly used system structures are:-

%FV - the fitted values vector
%LP - the linear predictor vector
%YV - the y-variate vector
%VL - the variances of the linear predictor vector
%DF - the number of degrees of freedom
%NU - the number of observations
%DV - the deviance of the current model
%X2 - the value of the generalised Pearson χ^2 statistic for the current model

but many other structures, including parameter estimates, and the SSP matrix, can be obtained.

Another useful facility is the ability to mix

freely directives from all modules. GRAPH directives can be combined with GLIM-4 directives, enabling user defined plots of diagnostic information to be produced simply and quickly. Commonly used collections of directives can be stored in subroutine-like structures called macros, and the user may build up a collection of macros which he or she finds particularly useful.

All the above facilities are illustrated in Section 5. GLIM, however, also contains many other facilities, such as user defined probability distributions and link functions, which are not described here, but allow the fitting of any generalised linear model.

4. GRAPH

The graphics module is a radical departure for the GLIM system. It is an interactive graphics program based on the new I.S.O. standard on computer graphics, the Graphical Kernel System, or GKS (Hopgood, 1982). GKS is itself similar to the widely used CORE system.

The facilities available to the user of GRAPH are useful not only to aid data analyses, but also to produce high quality output for presentation. This makes the GRAPH module a useful software tool for the general user as well as the statistician.

GRAPH contains output primitives for plotting points, lines, areas and text, and these are all available to the user with a wide variety of styles. In addition, the following facilities are also available:

i) Extensive screen management capabilities exist, including multiple windows and viewports, and zooming.

ii) A picture may be constructed in segments, and these segments may be manipulated independently in order to create the final desired image.

iii) Interactive graphics features, such as locator input, and the construction and use of menus can be implemented. Hence, a picture may be created or a menu option chosen using an input device such as a mouse on a tablet or a light pen.

iv) Graphical facilities allow the possibility of saving a permanent file representation of a picture, which can then be replayed back into the system in a subsequent session. For example, a picture drawn interactively may be saved in this way. In a similar fashion, the user can simultaneously activate several different graphics devices; this allows the user to copy pictures from one device to another and provides a convenient method of producing hard copy on a plotter.

v) Many graphical displays of special interest to statisticians, such as histograms, scatter plots, contours and 3-D surface views, are provided as standard features.

Embedding a graphics system such as GKS within the GLIM system gives the programmer an extremely powerful tool, especially when used in conjunction with the other modules.

5. EXAMPLE

Henderson and Velleman (1981) presented an analysis of data on fuel consumption of 32 cars tested by Motor Trend magazine, originally described by Hocking (1976). Their aim was to use interactive regression modelling to develop a model for fuel consumption, MPG, as a function of up to 10 explanatory variables : shape of engine S (straight or V), number of cylinders C, transmission type T (manual or automatic), number of gears G, engine displacement DISP, horsepower HP, number of carburettors CB, final drive ratio DRAT, weight WT and quarter-mile time QMT. The fuel consumption data is used here to illustrate features of the GLIM system; because of this, the data is only partially analysed and we do not end up with a final model. Emphasis is instead placed on outlier detection and regression diagnostics within GLIM, and the ease of including recent developments in this area into an analysis.

We start by plotting the response variate against each of the explanatory variables in turn. Exhibits 1(a) and 1(b) show scatter plots of MPG plotted against H and DISP. These scatter plots are produced with the GRAPH command

```
$DRAW SCATTER x y
```

[Different scatter plots are drawn in different regions of the display area by selecting viewports in a similarly simple manner. In addition, the user can request for the points to be joined and the plotting symbol for the points can be selected using the $STYLE directive.] Both show distinct non-linearity with increasing variability as the explanatory variables increase. These scatter plots suggest that MPG, HP and DISP should be transformed to a log scale. Exhibits 1(c) and 1(d) show the results of such transformations.

```
$CALC LMPG = %LOG(MPG)
   :  LHP = %LOG(HP)
   :  LDISP = %LOG(DISP)
```

(The : indicates repetition of the previous directive)

Both plots look linear, with no obvious heterogeneity. Similar plots for the other explanatory variables do not show anything unusual except for WT, where again the log scale is appropriate giving the new variable LWT.

We now proceed to fit a normal multiple regression of LMPG on all of the explanatory variables using HP, DISP and WT on the log scale. The normal model is declared using

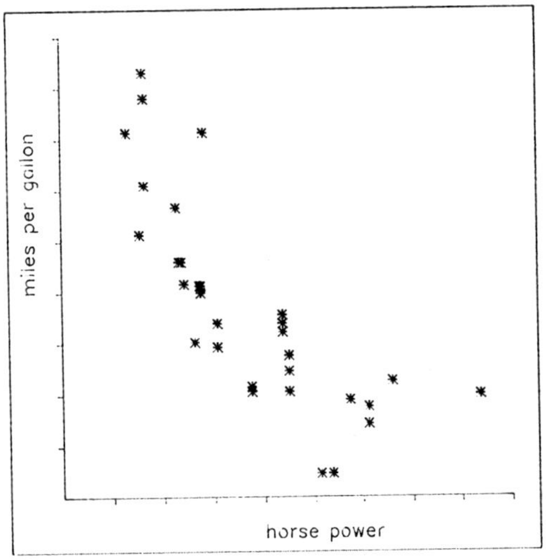

1(a)

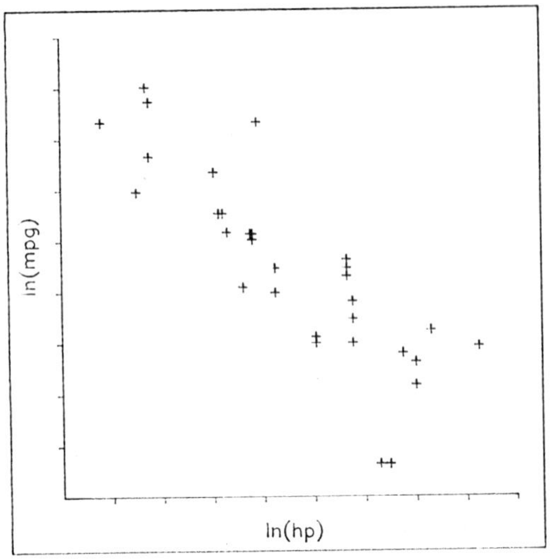

1(c)

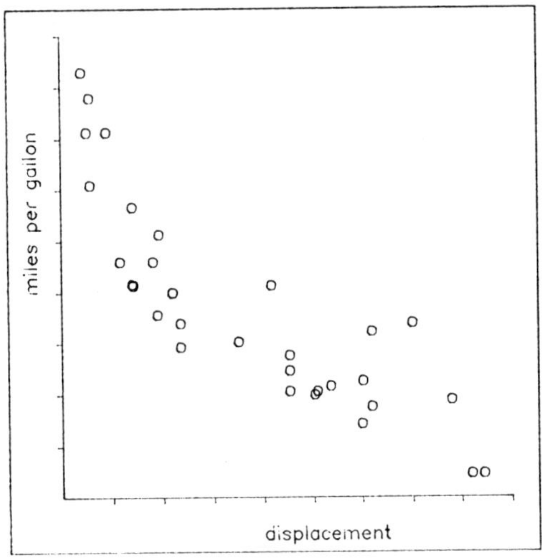

1(b)

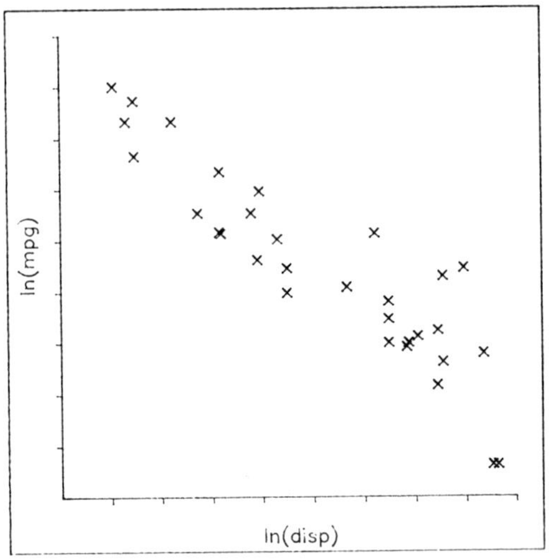

1(d)

EXHIBIT 1

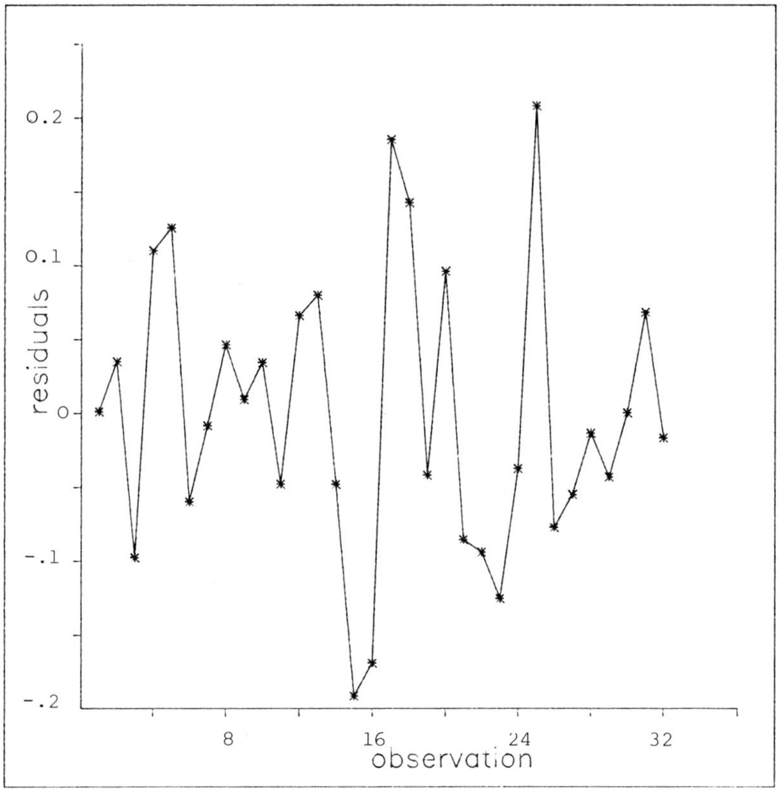

Exhibit 2(a)

Index plot

of row

residuals, e

Exhibit 2(b)

Index plot

of
leverages, v

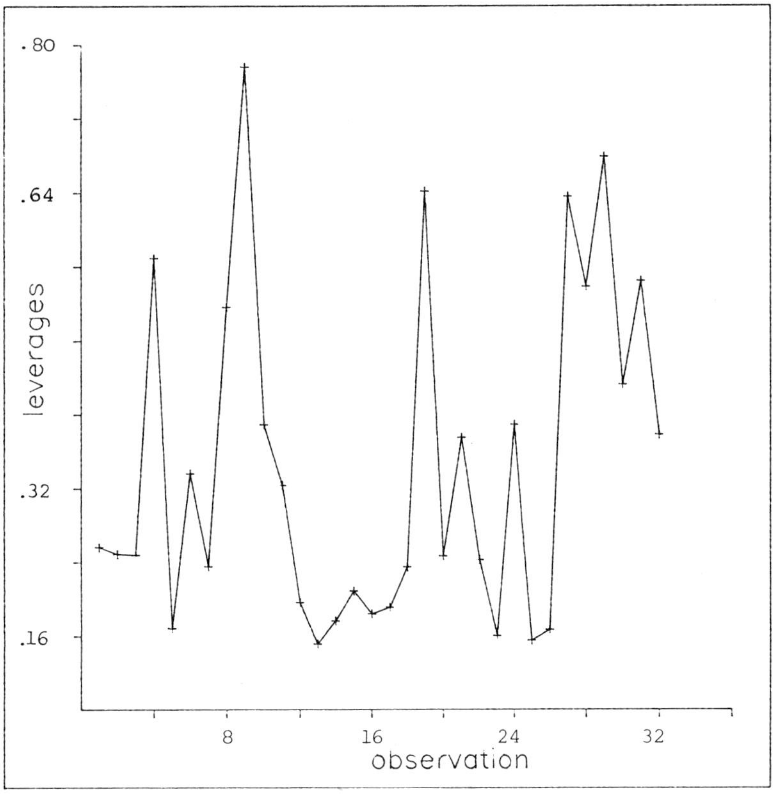

```
$YVAR LMPG $PROBABILITY N $LINK I
```

although the probability and link directives can be omitted since they take the default values.

```
$FIT 1+S+C+T+G+LDISP+LHP+CB+DRAT+LWT+QMT
$DISPLAY ESTIMATES$
```

fits the full model and displays the parameter estimates along with their standard errors; these show that LHP and LWT are important variables, while several variables are apparently irrelevant.

Several authors have proposed a variety of diagnostic procedures for detecting outliers, influential observations or failure of the distributional assumption. Further details of possible approaches for the normal theory model can be found in Hoaglin and Welsch (1978), Atkinson (1982) and Henderson and Velleman (1981). A brief summary can be found in Pregibon (1981), who also extends the ideas to the class of generalised linear models. In the standard normal model (n observations, p regression parameters)

$$\underline{y} = X\underline{\beta} + \underline{\varepsilon} \quad , \quad \underline{\varepsilon} \sim N(0,\sigma^2 I)$$

with fitted values $\hat{\underline{y}} = X\hat{\underline{\beta}}$, the basic elements for constructing diagnostics are the residuals $\underline{e} = \underline{y}-\hat{\underline{y}}$ and the leverage values $\underline{v}$, which are the diagonal elements of the projection matrix $X(X'X)^{-1}X'$. Rewriting the leverage values in the form

$$v_i = \mathrm{Var}(x_i\hat{\underline{\beta}})/\hat{\sigma}^2$$

it is clear that they are easily obtained in GLIM from %VL, the variance of the linear predictor. Exhibits 2(a) and 2(b) show plots of $\underline{e}$ and $\underline{v}$ against the index number of the observation, IND.

```
$CALC E = %YV - %FV
  :   V = %DV/%DF
$C    %V IS THE VARIANCE ESTIMATE
$CALC V = %VL/%V
$DRAW SCATTER IND E JOINED = YES
$DRAW SCATTER IND V JOINED = YES
```

The residual plot shows no particular pattern and only one of the leverage values (observation 9) has a value exceeding 2p/n, (2 x 11/32 = 0.69, for the full model), the rough guide suggested by Hoaglin and Welsch for detecting particularly influential points

From these basic quantities it is possible to derive other diagnostics:

Adjusted residuals : $f_i = e_i/\widehat{\mathrm{Var}(e_i)}^{\frac{1}{2}}$

Jack-knife residuals : $j_i = f_i/\left(\dfrac{n-p-f_i^2}{n-p-1}\right)^{\frac{1}{2}}$

Modified Cook statistics : $h_i = \left(\dfrac{n-p}{p} \cdot \dfrac{v_i}{1-v_i}\right)^{\frac{1}{2}} \cdot j_i$

Various plots of these quantities can be used to detect outlying or influential observations; for example, plots against explanatory variables, index plots (as above), and normal or half-normal probability plots. Exhibit 3 shows index plots and half-normal plots for j_i and h_i. The half-normal plots are obtained using a short macro HPLOT, which is written for a general variable ZY.

```
$MACRO HPLOT
$C HALF-NORMAL PLOT
$CALC HZ = %ND((%GL(%NU,1)/(%NU+1)+1)/2)!
! Quantities for half-normal distribution
  : ZY = %IF(%LT(ZY,0),-ZY,ZY)! forms absolute
!                                       values
$SORT ZY
$DRAW SCATTER HZ ZY
$ENDMAC

$CALC SDE = %SQRT(%V-%VL) : F = E/SDE
  :     J = F/%SQRT((%DF-F**2)/(%DF-1))
  :     H = %SQRT(%DF*V/((%NU-%DF)*(1-V)))*J
$DRAW SCATTER IND  J  JOINED = YES
$DRAW SCATTER IND  H  JOINED = YES
$CALC ZY = J $USE HPLOT
$CALS ZY = H $USE HPLOT
```

Examination of the residual plots reveals little, except for the two largest absolute values (observations 15 and 25) being slightly smaller than expected. The half-normal plot of the Cook's statistic is much more dramatic with one clearly isolated point (observation 4), which has both a moderately large residual and leverage value and so is possibly influential on the fit.

Pregibon suggests summarizing the basic information on outlying and influential observations using a simple scatter plot of the relative individual components of the chi-squared statistic (χ^2_i/χ^2) against the leverage values (v_i). For the normal model

$$\frac{\chi^2_i}{\chi^2} = \frac{e_i^2}{\sum_{j=1}^{n} e_j^2} \qquad i = 1,\ldots,n$$

and these are the same as the relative components of deviance. These plots will indicate points which are badly fitted (large χ^2_i/χ^2), extreme in the design space (large v_i) or both; the identification of such points is made easier by superimposing contours of constant $v_i^* = \chi^2_i/\chi^2 + v_i$ on these plots. Exhibit 4 shows such a scatter plot with a single contour for v_i^* set at $2 \times \mathrm{ave}(v_i^*)$. Only observation 9 (large v_i) looks in any way extreme.

Having identified potentially suspect points the next stage is to assess their effect on the analysis. The simplest methods involve looking at the effect of deleting single observations and two simple criterion suggestion by Hoaglin and Welsch are

(i) change in coefficients, $\hat{\underline{\beta}}-\hat{\underline{\beta}}_{(i)}$, where $\hat{\underline{\beta}}_{(i)}$ is the vector of parameter estimates obtained having deleted the ith observation;

(ii) change in fit at point i, $\underline{x}_i(\hat{\underline{\beta}}-\hat{\underline{\beta}}_{(i)})$.

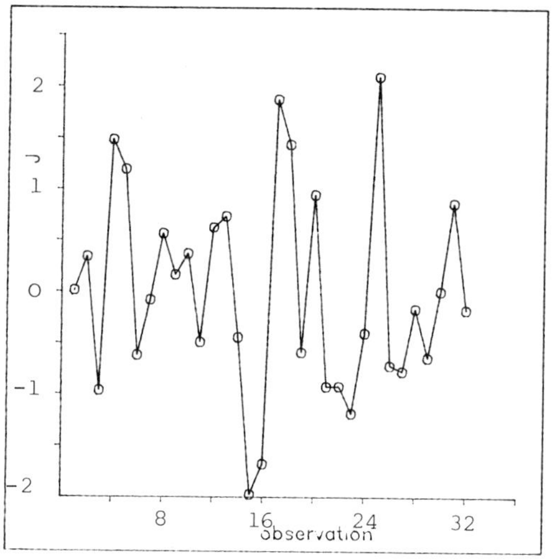

Exhibit 3(a)

Index plot of
jack-knife residuals, j

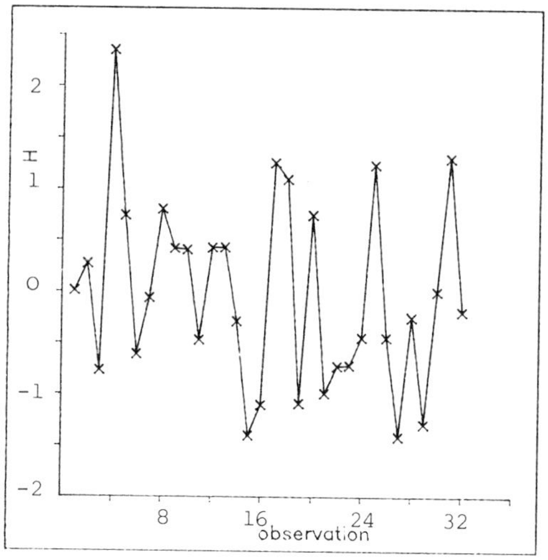

Exhibit 3(b)

Index plot of
modified Cook statistics, h

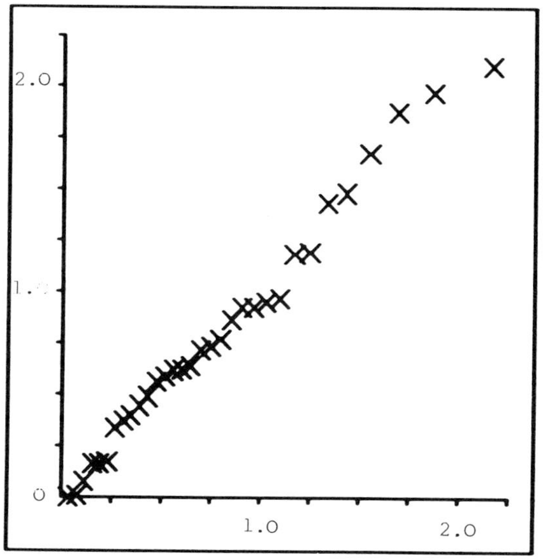

Exhibit 3(c)

Half normal plot for j

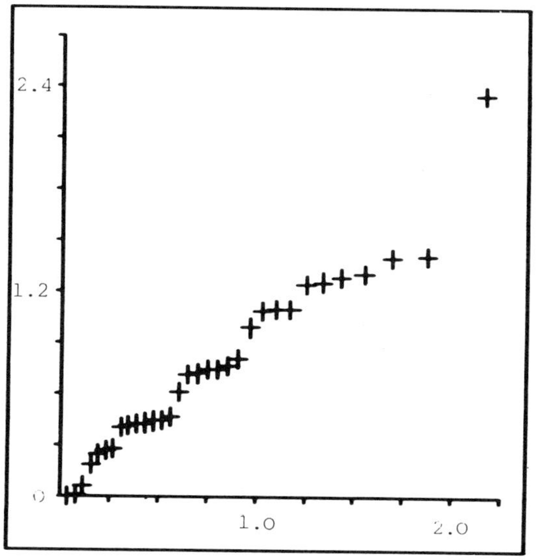

Exhibit 3(d)

Half normal plot for h

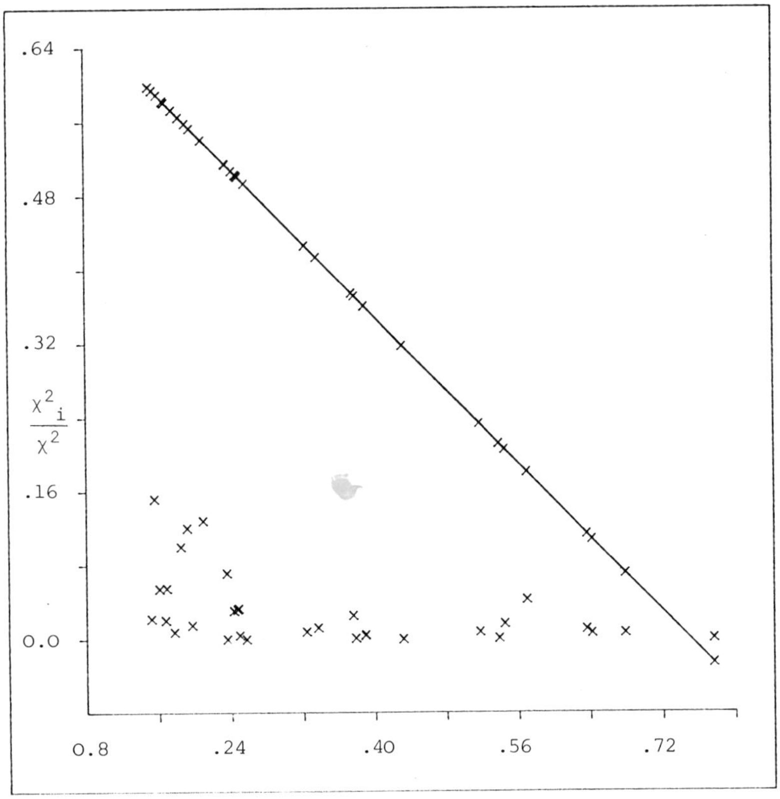

Exhibit 4

Scatterplot of χ^2_i/χ^2 vs. v_i.

Solid line corresponds to $2*\text{ave}(v_i*)$.

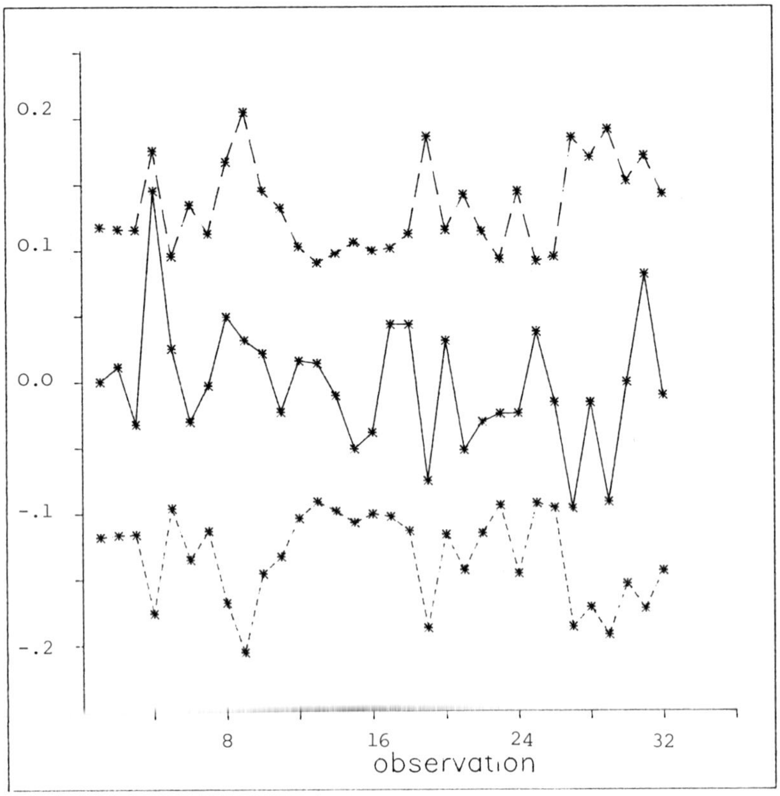

Exhibit 5

Change in fit at point i.

These are both easily calculated in GLIM using a general macro with a single argument specifying the point to be dropped from the fit. However, the change in fit statistics are more easily calculated using.

$$\underline{x}(\hat{\underline{\beta}}-\hat{\underline{\beta}}_{(i)}) = v_i e_i/(1-v_i) ,$$

which only involves information available from the full fit. The quantities are most conveniently summarized using index plots, and can be compared with suitable measures of scale either by standardisation or by including appropriate bands on the plots. Exhibit 4 is an index plot for the change in fit at point i, due to deleting the ith observation, with bands at $\pm 2 * \sqrt{\mathrm{Var}(\hat{y}_i)}$.

More complex procedures for determining coefficient sensitivity and neighbouring effects (the effect of deleting the ith point on the remaining n-1 points) are discussed by Pregibon, and Cook (1979) goes on to consider the effect of the deletion of two or more observations.

In the above we have made no reference to what is clearly the most important element of interactive statistical modelling, namely model selection. There are a number of possible strategies and one approach is to use a backward elimination procedure to obtain a parsimonious model (see Aitkin (1974)). Once again various diagnostic procedures can be useful, such as the partial regression plot, Mosteller and Tukey (1977); this is easily programmed as a GLIM macro with a single argument, the particular explanatory variable under consideration.

REFERENCES

Aitkin, M.A. (1974). Simultaneous inference and the choice of variable subsets in multiple regression. *Technometrics* 16, 221-227.

Alvey, N. et al. (1977). *The Genstat Manual.* Rothamsted Experimental Station.

Atkinson, A.C. (1982). Regression diagnostics, transformations and constructed variables (with discussion). *J.R.Statist.Soc.B.* 44, 1-36.

Baker, R.J. and Nelder, J.A. (1978). *The GLIM Manual : Release 3.* Numerical Algorithms Group: Oxford, U.K.

†
Finney, D.J. (1952). *Probit Analysis.* 2nd ed. Cambridge : University Press.

Gilchrist, R. (1982). GLIM82 : *Proceedings of the International conference on generalised linear models.* Springer Verlag : New York.

Henderson, H.V. and Velleman, P.F. (1981). Building multiple regression models interactively. *Biometrics* 37, 391-412.

Hoaglin, D.C. and Welsch, R.E. (1978). The hat matrix in regression and ANOVA. *American Statistician* 32, 17-22.

Hocking, R.R. (1976). The analysis and selection of variables in linear regression. *Biometrics* 32, 1-44.

Hopgood, F.R.A. (1982). GKS - The First Graphics Standard, (Science and Engineering Research Council). Graphical Kernel System, Draft International Standard, ISO/TC97/SC5/WG2/N117.

Mosteller, F. and Tukey, J. (1977). *Data analysis and regression.* Reading, Massachusetts : Addison-Wesley.

Nelder, J.A. and Wedderburn, R.W.M. (1972). Generalized linear models. *J.R.Statist.Soc.A.* 135, 370-384.

Payne, R.W. and Wilkinson, G.N. (1977). A general algorithm for the analysis of variance. *Appl. Statist.* 26. 251-260.

Pregibon, D. (1981). Logistic regression diagnostics. *Ann. Statist.* 9, 705-724.

Wilkinson, G.N. (1970). A general recursive algorithm for analysis of variance. *Biometrika* 57, 19-46.

Wilkinson G.N. and Rogers, C.A. (1973). Symbolic description of factorial models for analysis of variance. *Appl. Statist.* 22, 392-399.

+
Cook, R.D. (1979). Influential observations in linear regression. *J.Amer. Statist. Ass.* 74, 169-174.

Computer Science, Statistics and Graphics: The Interface

Chair: Carolyn B. Morgan, General Electric Company
Organizer: Gerald J. Hahn, General Electric Company

Packages for Statistical Computer Graphics
Patricia M. Caporal and Gerald J. Hahn, General Electric Company

Interactive Color Graphics for Multivariate Data
Wesley J. Nicholson and Richard J. Littlefield, Pacific Northwest Laboratory

Integrating Color into Statistical Software
Richard A. Becker, Bell Laboratories

PACKAGES FOR STATISTICAL COMPUTER GRAPHICS

Patricia M. Caporal and Gerald J. Hahn
General Electric Company, Schenectady, NY 12345

ABSTRACT

The availability of output devices, such as CRT display terminals and special plotters, provides the statistician and data analyst new opportunities for presenting and analyzing data using high quality graphics.

In this paper, we summarize and discuss the capabilities of some of the currently available statistical graphics software. We consider a wide variety of offerings providing both presentation graphics and data analysis/exploration capabilities, directed at users with varying levels of statistical sophistication, and involving acquisition costs ranging from $150 to $40,000 or more. However, all of the software that we discuss includes some statistical analysis features.

The discussion will be under the following headings:

- Offerings for Desktop Computers
- Interfaces with or Extensions of Existing Statistical Packages
- Integrated Software for Minicomputers and Mainframes
- Specialized Software

The paper should help the user of statistical graphics decide upon the offering that best meets current and future needs.

KEYWORDS

Automation, computers, CRT, data analysis, desktop computers, display devices, graphics, plotters

I. INTRODUCTION AND OVERVIEW

Output devices, such as CRT display terminals and special plotters, which are now available for high-quality graphics, provide the analyst new opportunities for presenting and exploring data. In addition to summarizing data and performing statistical evaluations, the computer can now be used directly to present the results through attractive and meaningful graphical displays. These are being further enhanced by the increasing accessibility of color graphics. As a result, individuals with limited statistical training can obtain simple, but incisive, graphical presentations of the data, while a trained analyst can gain an improved understanding of complex data sets by using graphical tools for exploratory data analysis. Moreover, obtaining such displays on a computer, rather than manually, can significantly reduce the elapsed time to get the desired graphics and allows the analyst to operate in an iterative manner.

The marriage of statistical data analysis and high-quality graphics has become possible through the development of statistical graphics software by software houses, graphics hardware suppliers, universities and others. This paper, which surveys some currently available statistical graphics software, is a logical sequel to two previous papers (Caporal and Hahn [1981a and 1981b]) in which we described software for high-quality graphical displays. In these earlier papers, we dealt principally with offerings for presentation graphics, many of which have only limited capabilities for statistical data analysis. In this paper, we concentrate on software that permits one to integrate the data analysis and data display functions, i.e., offerings that have non-trivial statistical, as well as data display, capabilities. We will, however, deal only with software that provides high-quality graphical output. Thus, we will not, for example, consider programs that only produce plots on standard line printers although these are often sufficient in the exploratory stages of a data analysis. We will, however, consider software for a wide variety of computers, ranging from desktops to mainframes.

Fienberg (1979) reviews modern graphical methods in statistics, covering both presentation and analytical graphics and gives numerous references. Some examples, using the offerings discussed in this paper, are provided by Figures 1 through 13 (These are interspersed with the discussion of the packages with which they deal). We will, however, not emphasize the graphics per se, but only the software for obtaining them.

Chambers (1980) discusses the history and trends of statistical computing and Francis (1981) gives a comparative review of statistical computing.

Our review is broken down as follows:

- Statistical graphics software for desktop computers (Section II)
- Interfaces with, or extensions of, existing statistical packages (Section III)
- Integrated statistical graphics software for minicomputers and mainframes (Section IV)
- Some specialized software for statistical graphics (Section V)

Tables 1, 2, and 3 provide a comprehensive overview of the offerings described in Sections II, III, and IV. Table 1 indicates the primary user of each package and provides some brief descriptive comments. Table 2 shows the acquisition costs (ranging from $150 to $40,000 or more), the software source and the associated host computers and graphic output devices. The graphical and statistical features of the various offerings are summarized in Table 3. Since these tables are self-explanatory, the information contained in them generally will not be repeated in the body of the paper.

Our major purpose is to report on the various offerings — not to evaluate them. We have tried to be objective in our comments and descriptions. However, some degree of judgment invariably enters into such a presentation. Also, in most cases, lack of time and resources has prevented us from obtaining hands-on experience with most of the software. Therefore, the information presented in this paper relies heavily on material obtained from the software suppliers and conversations and correspondence with them.

Finally, we must emphasize that we provide only a sampling—although certainly not a random one—of software for statistical graphics. Obviously, we could include only offerings that we knew about and, undoubtedly, some relevant packages have escaped our attention. Due to the rapid growth of this field, there will likely be further additions by the time this paper is in print. We offer our apologies to the suppliers of those offerings we have omitted and invite them, and other readers, to contact us.

Table 1

SUMMARY OF SOFTWARE FOR STATISTICAL GRAPHICS

SOFTWARE	PRIMARY USERS	COMMENTS
Software for Desktop Computers:		
HP System 35 Statistical Software	General	Basic statistical capabilities for HP System 35
HP 9825A/S Statistics Library	General	Basic statistical capabilities for HP 9825A/S
HP 9845 Statistics Library	General	Extensive statistical capabilities for HP 9845
Tektronix Plot 50 Applications Library	General	Extensive statistical capabilities for Tektronix 4050 series
Trend-Spotter '82	Business	Software for Trend-Spotter '82 Graphics Management Information System
Extensions to Statistical Packages:		
SAS and SAS/Graph Interface	General and statisticians	Graphics interface for SAS statistical package
SAS and Tell-A-Graf Interface	General and statisticians	Interface between SAS and Tell-A-Graf graphics package
Datagraf	General and statisticians	Conversational program interfacing SAS, SAS/GRAPH, and DISSPLA.
SPSS and SPSS Graphics Option	General and statisticians	Graphics interface for SPSS statistical package with Tell-A-Graf interface option
StatII/PlotII Interface	General and statisticians	Graphics interface for StatII program on GE Mark III time-sharing service
Sharp APL Statistics Library and Superplot Interface	Mainly statisticians	Graphics interface for Sharp APL Statistics Library
Integrated Software:		
Dataplot	Mainly engineers, scientists, and statisticians	Developed at National Bureau of Standards; mathematical, as well as extensive statistical capabilities
Statgraphics	General and statisticians	Developed at Princeton University; extensive statistical capabilities
S Package	Mainly statisticians	Expression language developed at Bell Labs; add-on capabilities emphasized; not supported

Table 2

SOURCE AND COST FOR SOFTWARE AND HARDWARE OF STATISTICAL GRAPHICS

SOFTWARE	SOURCE	ACQUISITION COST*	HOST COMPUTER	GRAPHICS OUTPUT DEVICES
Software for Desktop Computers				
HP System 35 Statistical Software	Hewlett-Packard 3404 E. Harmony Road Fort Collins, Colorado 80525	$1500 (one-time fee)	Hewlett-Packard 35A Desktop Computer	Hewlett-Packard 9872A, 7245A Plotters
HP 9825A/S Statistics Library	Hewlett-Packard 3404 E. Harmony Road Fort Collins, Colorado 80525	$250 (one-time fee)	Hewlett-Packard 9825A/S Desktop Computer	Hewlett-Packard 9872A, 7225A, 7245A Plotters
HP 9845 Statistics Library	Hewlett-Packard 3404 E. Harmony Road Fort Collins, Colorado 80525	$1500 (one-time fee)	Hewlett-Packard 9845 Desktop Computer	Hewlett-Packard 9872 Plotter
Tektronix Plot-50 Applications Library	Tektronix, Inc. P.O. Box 1700 Beaverton, Oregon 97075 Phone: (800) 547-1512	Statistics Library $2800. Other software $1000-$4000	Tektronix 4050 Series Desktop Computer	Tektronix 4610 or 4631 Hard Copy Unit, 4662 or 4663 Plotter, 4641 Matrix Printer
Trendspotter '82	Computer Pictures Corporation 20 Broad Street Boston, Massachusetts 02109 Phone: (617) 720-1700	The basic system includes the CRT and the software and costs $35,900. The price can range to $116,000 depending on the options chosen.	Supplied with system	Supplied with system
Extensions to Statistical Packages				
SAS and SAS/Graph Interface	SAS Institute, Inc. Box 8000 Cary, NC 27511 Phone: (919) 467-8000	SAS $5000 1st year; $2500 annual renewal SAS/GRAPH $3000 1st year; $1500 renewal fee.	IBM 360/370 mainframe or compatible machine under OS,OS/VS, and VM/CMS.	Output device independent
SAS and Tell-A-Graf Interface	ISSCO 4186 Sorrento Valley Blvd. San Diego, California 92121 Phone: (714) 452-0170	Same as SAS	Same as SAS	Output device independent
Datagraf	M/A-COM Sigma Data, Inc. 5515 Security Lane Rockville, Maryland 20852 Phone: (301) 984-3636	Standard time-sharing rates, or end-user license	IBM 360/370 mainframe or compatible machines under 0S/VS and VM/CMS.	Output device independent
SPSS and SPSS Graphics Option Interface	Marketing Dept. SPSS, Inc. 444 North Michigan Ave. Chicago, Illinois 60611 Phone: (312) 329-2400	SPSS $7000 1st year; $3500 annual renewal. SPSS Graphics $6000 1st year; $4000 renewal fee.	IBM 360,370,4300,0S,CMS; DEC Systems 10,20, VAX; Prime 400-750; Univac 1100.	Output device independent
StatII/PlotII Interface	GEISCO 401 North Washington St. Rockville, MD 20850 Phone: (800) 638-8730	GEISCO time-sharing service rates	GEISCO Mark III service	Output device independent
Sharp APL and Superplot Statistics Library Interface	I.P. Sharp Associates Limited 2 First Canadian Place Suite 1900 Toronto, Ontario MX5 1E3 Canada Phone: (416) 364-5361	Superplot $1600 per month or $40,000 one time fee. Statistics $800/month or $20,000 one time fee.	IBM 370 or any compatible machine (i.e., IBM 3031, 3081, AMDAHL 470, ITEL, HITACHI NAS)	Zeta 1453, Tektronix 4662, HP 7221 series, CalComp 81 plotters; Tektronic 4013, 4015 terminals; HP 2647A, 7220 series, 9872 series, and others.
Integrated Software				
Dataplot	National Technical Information Service United States Dept. of Commerce Springfield, Virginia 22161 Phone: (703) 487-4807	$900 (one-time fee)	IBM,CDC,DEC,Honeywell Univac,Cray,Burroughs, VAX, Interdata, Data General, HP	Calcomp,Versatec,Tektronix, Zeta plotters; Tektronix 40XX terminals; Tektronix 4112,4114 terminals.
Statgraphics	Statistical Graphics Corp. P.O. Box 1558 Princeton, NJ 08540 Phone: (609) 924-9374	$12,000 1st year; $8000 annual renewal fee	IBM 360/370,303X,3081, or 4300 series machine or compatible system with APL under VM/CMS or TSO.	Output device independent
S Package	Bell Laboratories Computer Information Service 600 Mountain Avenue Murray Hill, NJ 07974 Phone: (201) 582-7330	$150 (one-time fee)	Requires modern UNIX** operating system	HP 7221,Tektronix 4662 plotters Tektronix 4006, 4010, 4012, 4014; HP 2623, 2648, Ramtek 6211; Advanced Electronics Design 512.

*Approximate cost as of Nov. 1981. Some offerings are available under other arrangement (e.g., rental or time-sharing services).

**UNIX is a trademark of Bell Laboratories

Table 3

FEATURES OF SOFTWARE FOR STATISTICAL GRAPHICS

Software \ Feature	Color	3-Dimensonal Plots	Crossplots	Pie Charts	Histograms	Probability Plots	Process Control Charts	Linear Regression	Polynomial Regression	General Non-Linear Regression
Software for Desktop Computers										
HP System 35 Statistical Library	✓	✓	✓		✓	✓		✓	✓	✓
HP 9825 A/S Statistics Library	✓		✓		✓		✓	✓	✓	
HP 9845 Statistics Library	✓	✓	✓		✓	✓		✓	✓	✓
Tektronix Plot-50 Applications Library	✓		✓	✓	✓	✓		✓	✓	✓
Trendspotter '82	✓	✓	✓	✓	✓			✓	✓	
Extensions to Statistical Packages										
SAS and SAS/Graph Interface	✓	✓	✓	✓	✓	✓		✓	✓	✓
SAS and Tell-A-Graf Interface	✓		✓	✓	✓	✓		✓	✓	✓
Datagraf	✓	✓	✓	✓	✓	✓		✓	✓	✓
SPSS and SPSS Graphics Option Interface	✓		✓	✓	✓	✓		✓	✓	
Stat II/Plot II Interface	✓		✓	✓	✓	✓		✓	✓	
Sharp APL Statistics Library and Superplot Interface	✓		✓	✓	✓			✓	✓	✓
Integrated Software										
Dataplot	✓	✓	✓	✓	✓	✓	✓	✓	✓	✓
Statgraphics	✓	✓	✓	✓	✓	✓	✓	✓	✓	✓
S Package	✓	✓	✓	✓	✓	✓		✓		

Software \ Feature	Spline Fitting	Confidence Limits on Fitted Line	Residual Plots	Analysis of Variance	Non-Parametric Statistics	Time Series Analysis	Cluster Analysis	Factor Analysis and/or Principal Com-ponents	Discriminant Analysis	Other Extensive Statistical Analyses
Software for Desktop Computers										
HP System 35 Statistical Library			✓							
HP 9825 A/S Statistics Library		✓		✓	✓					✓
HP 9845 Statistics Library			✓	✓	✓			✓		✓
Tektronix Plot-50 Applications Library		✓	✓	✓		✓				✓
Trendspotter '82	✓	✓				✓				
Extensions to Statistical Packages										
SAS and SAS/Graph Interface	✓	✓	✓	✓	✓	✓	✓	✓	✓	✓
SAS and Tell-A-Graf Interface	✓	✓	✓	✓	✓	✓	✓	✓	✓	✓
Datagraf	✓	✓	✓	✓	✓	✓	✓	✓	✓	✓
SPSS and SPSS Graphics Option Interface	✓	✓	✓	✓	✓	✓		✓	✓	✓
Stat II/Plot II Interface		✓	✓	✓	✓	✓				✓
Sharp APL Statistics Library and Superplot Interface	✓		✓	✓	✓	✓		✓	✓	✓
Integrated Software										
Dataplot	✓	✓	✓	✓		✓				✓
Statgraphics	✓	✓	✓	✓	✓	✓	✓			✓
S Package			✓		✓	✓	✓	✓	✓	✓

II. STATISTICAL GRAPHICS SOFTWARE FOR DESKTOP COMPUTERS

A. Introduction

Boardman (1982) in an article on the future of statistical computing on desktop computers describes various desktop computers and includes a representative list of manufacturers. The use of these computers for data analysis is rapidly increasing. Many suppliers now offer and sell statistical graphics packages. These offerings have the following characteristics:

1. Their use is generally limited only to the desktop computer model for which it was developed (or to systems that emulate it).
2. The packages are generally highly user-friendly and appear to be directed mainly at data analysts with a limited statistical background, rather than at the (smaller) specialized audience of statisticians. As a result, they tend, in general, to be more user-friendly, more flexible, and less statistically sophisticated than most of the offerings for mainly minicomputers and mainframes described in the next two sections. However, the graphical features of the offerings for desktop computers are comparable to those discussed in the other sections.
3. Just as the size and cost of desktop computers varies appreciably, so do the features available in the statistical graphics offerings. Among the offerings we examined, we found the most extensive statistical capabilities in the Statistics Library for the HP 9845 and the Plot 50 Statistics Software for the Tektronix 4050 series desktop computers.

In this section we describe the following offerings for desktop computers:

- HP System 35 Statistical Software
- HP 9825A/S Statistics Library
- HP 9845 Statistics Library
- Tektronix Plot 50 Applications Library
- Trend Spotter '82 Graphics Management Information System

These five packages involve only three manufacturers and only two of the 11 listed by Boardman (1982) in his "Representative List of Desktop Computer Manufacturers," although we suspect that they are among the more sophisticated of the currently available offerings.

B. HP System 35 Statistical Software

The HP System 35 Statistical Software consists of sublibraries for:

- Basic Statistics
- Statistical Graphics
- Regression Analysis
- Nonlinear Regression Analysis.

The statistical software contains the capability of creating graphical output.

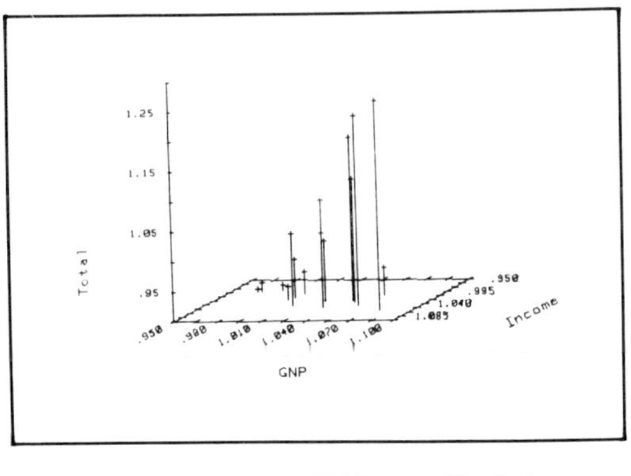

Figure 1. XYZ Plot Using HP System 35A Software

C. HP 9825A/S Statistics Library

The HP 9825A/S Statistics Library contains sublibraries for:

- General Statistics
- Analysis of Variance and Regression Analysis
- Nonparametrics

An additional package is available for stepwise regression analysis. Capabilities for plotting statistical results are contained within the sublibraries.

D. HP 9845 Statistics Library

The HP 9845 Statistics Library contains sublibraries for:

- Basic Statistics and Data Manipulation
- General Statistics
- Statistical Graphics
- Regression Analysis
- Nonlinear Regression Analysis
- Analysis of Variance
- Monte Carlo Simulation Utilities
- Principal Components and Factor Analysis

Prompts guide the user through the programs. Most have the capability of producing graphical displays of the statistical results. A similar library is available for the HP 9826/9836 desktop computer.

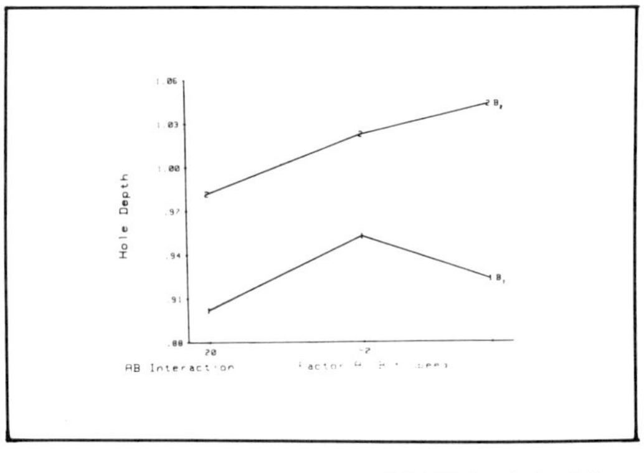

Figure 2. Interaction Plot Using HP 9845 Statistics Library

E. Tektronix PLOT 50 Applications Library

The Tektronix PLOT 50 Applications Library consists of a statistical library as well as other software. The statistical library consists of sublibraries for

- Tests and Distributions
- Analysis of Variance
- Multiple Linear Regression
- Nonlinear Estimation

Menus and prompts guide the user. The statistical sublibraries contain capabilities for plotting statistical results. A separate time series analysis and forecasting package is also available.

F. Trend-Spotter '82 Graphics Management Information System

Unlike the other packages for desktop computers described in this section, the Trend-Spotter '82 basic system includes both a color CRT and the statistical software. Additional options, including hardware for hard copy output, can be ordered with the system. As suggested by its name, Trend-Spotter is aimed principally at business people and administrators and is claimed to be "a graphics system designed by managers, for use by managers." For example, it permits estimation of trends and forecasts and includes adjustments for cost-of-living, anticipated inflation, and seasonal effects.

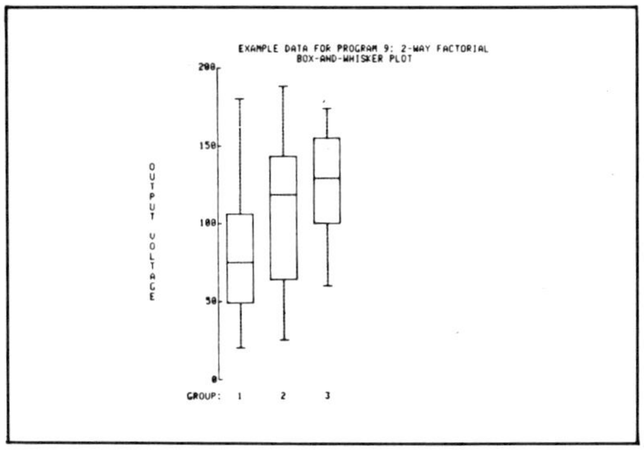

Figure 3. Boxplot Using Plot 50 Statistics Library

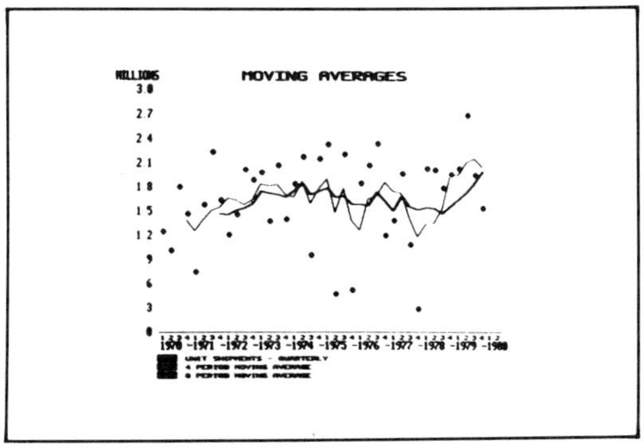

Figure 4. Moving Averages Plot Using Trendspotter '82

III. INTERFACES WITH, OR EXTENSIONS OF, EXISTING STATISTICAL PACKAGES

A. Overview

Sophisticated computer packages for statistical analysis have gained prominence during the last decade and are used extensively by statisticians and other data analysts. Some prominent examples are BMDP (Biomedical Computer Programs P-Series), Minitab, SAS (Statistical Analysis System), SPSS (Statistical Package for the Social Sciences), and P-Stat. These offerings, and many others, are compared by Francis (1981). Most were developed prior to the general availability of high-quality computer graphics. As a result, extensions for, or interfaces with, high-quality graphics have recently been developed. We will consider:

- Three offerings involving the SAS package:

  – the SAS/Graph extension to SAS
  – an interface between SAS and the Tell-A-Graf graphics program
  – Datagraf, an interface to SAS, SAS/Graph, and the Disspla graphics package, available on the Boeing Computer Services time-sharing service

- The interface between SPSS and the SPSS Graphics Option, including an interface option with the Tell-A-Graf graphics program.
- The interface between the StatII statistical analysis package and the PlotII program, both available on the General Electric Information Service Company (GEISCO) MarkIII time-sharing service.
- The interface between Sharp Associates APL Functions for Statistical Analysis and their Superplot data display package.
- Plans for the development of graphical capabilities for BMDP, Minitab, and P-Stat.

B. The SAS/Graph Extensions to SAS

The SAS/Graph extension to SAS allows users to obtain high-quality graphical displays of the output generated during a SAS run. SAS/Graph procedures are similar to SAS procedures and can be included in SAS runs. SAS/Graph also interfaces with the SAS/ETS (Economic Time Series) Library.

C. Interface between SAS and Tell-A-Graf

An interface between SAS and the Tell-A-Graf graphics package is achieved through a SAS procedure called PROC TAG. This transforms SAS files into Tell-A-Graf data sets. PROC TAG is available from ISSCO (see Table 2).

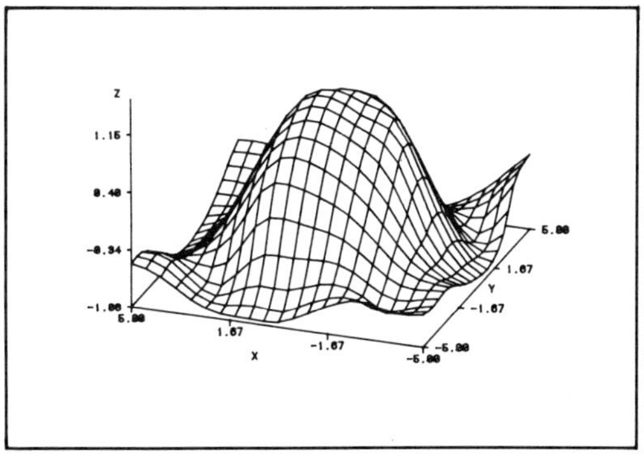

Figure 5. Spline Interpolation Using SAS/GRAPH

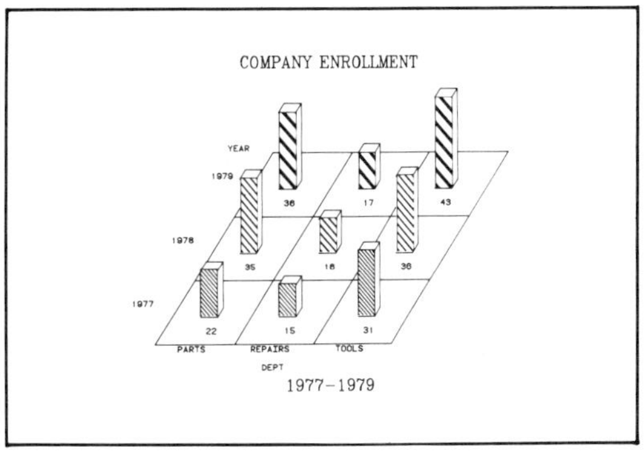

Figure 6. Three-Dimensional Bar Chart Using SAS/GRAPH

D. Datagraf

Datagraf, developed by M/A-COM Sigma Data, Inc., and available on the Boeing Computer Services national time-sharing service, provides interfaces to SAS, SAS/Graph, and the Disspla graphics sub-routine package. The interface is achieved through a conversational language that prompts the user for information and does not require the user to learn either the SAS or the Disspla language. Thus, unlike the other packages described in this section, Datagraf appears as a new offering to the user. It also has various additional features beyond those of SAS and Disspla (e.g., a database consisting of demographic, socioeconomic and other data by county from the Bureau of the Census).

E. The SPSS Graphics Option and Tell-A-Graf Interface

The SPSS Graphics Option permits the use of graphics commands within SPSS that are similar in form to the standard SPSS commands. In addition, SPSS Graphics permits SPSS users to interface with Tell-A-Graf by allowing the user to write files that can be accessed by Tell-A-Graf.

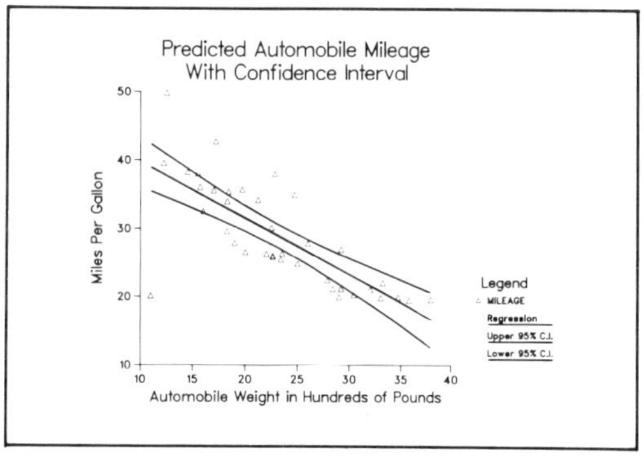

Figure 7. Regression Plot Using SPSS Graphics

F. The StatII/PlotII Interface

StatII is an extensive statistical package on the MarkIII time-sharing service of the General Electric Information Services Company (GEISCO). It interfaces with PlotII, a graphics package for the same system.

G. Interface of Sharp APL Statistical Function Library and Superplot

The Sharp APL Functions for Statistical Analysis is a library of sophisticated routines organized under the following headings:

- General Statistical Functions
- Model Parameter Estimation
- Probability Functions and Distributions
- Analysis of Variance
- Multivariate Analysis
- Time Series Analysis

The statistical library appears to be directed at relatively knowledgeable analysts. It interfaces with Superplot, a Sharp APL graphics package, to provide graphical displays.

H. Plans for BMDP, Minitab and P-STAT

BMDP, Minitab and P-Stat do not currently have interfaces with graphics packages, but there are plans for developing such interfaces. In particular, we received the following responses to our inquiries from the suppliers of these packages:

BMDP: "BMDP does not currently interface with high-resolution graphics devices.

   One of our current projects is implementation of BMDP on a desktop microcomputer which features a graphics terminal. We expect to be able to drive the graphics terminal with modified versions of our current programs."

Minitab: "Minitab does not currently have high resolution graphics capabilities. We do plan to add such capabilities, but the first edition of this will not be available in a regular release before January 1983......Several of our users have added graphic capabilities to Minitab.....(we) expect initially to develop graphics for one or two environments, probably Tektronix 4010 and Siggraph Standard, and to begin with some basic capabilities.... The attempt will be to: (1) Emphasize data analysis graphics (as opposed to presentation graphics.) (2) Support medium as will as high resolution graphics.

P-Stat: "P-Stat does not yet offer high quality graphics.......We have looked at graphics interfaces, and this seems to be the direction in which we will eventually follow......"

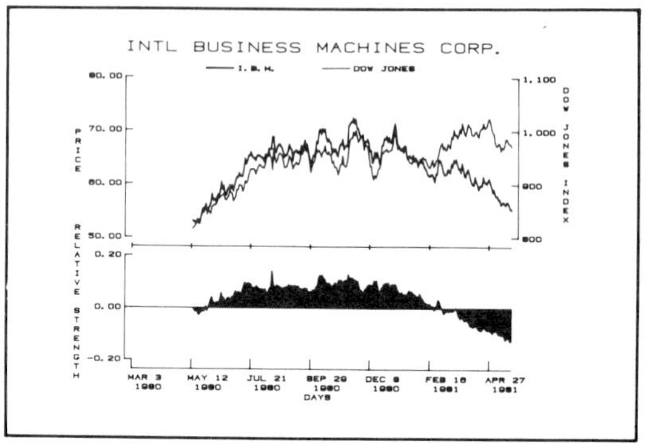

Figure 8. Line Chart Using Superplot

IV. INTEGRATED STATISTICAL GRAPHICS SOFTWARE FOR MINICOMPUTERS AND MAINFRAMES

A. Overview

Ideally, users of statistical graphics would like graphical and statistical capabilities integrated into a single package. This is the way most statistical graphics offerings for desktop computers, such as those described in Section II, are written. In contrast, the software described in Section III marry previously written statistical routines with more recently developed graphics software. (Datagraph appears to be an in-between case.)

A new generation of software that integrates statistical analysis with high-quality computer graphics into a single package is now being developed. We will consider

- Dataplot — developed at the National Bureau of Standards
- Statgraphics — developed at Princeton University
- S — developed at Bell Labs

These three offerings differ appreciably with regard to primary user (see Table 1), cost (see Table 2) and user-friendliness. (Statgraphics seems to be the most friendly to the general user; S appears to be aimed at the most limited audience).

A fourth offering, called Grafstat, developed at the IBM Watson Research Center, has recently come to our attention. This has been described by its developers [Heidelberger, Welch, and Wu (1982)] as "an APL workspace, designed for interactive scientific and engineering plotting and interactive data analysis. The workspace runs with a full-screen editing interface on the IBM 3277GA dual screen terminal." However, Grafstat is currently not generally available.

B. Dataplot

Dataplot uses Tektronix Plot-10 graphics software to create statistical graphics. According to its developers, "Dataplot was developed originally in 1977 in response to data analysis problems encountered at the National Bureau of Standards (NBS). It has subsequently been the most heavily-used interactive graphics and non-linear fitting language at NBS. It is a ... tool not only for 'raw' graphics, but also for manuscript preparation, modeling, data analysis, data summarization, and mathematical analysis. Dataplot may be run either in batch mode or interactively, although it was primarily designed for (and is most effectively used in) an interactive environment." Its capabilities are grouped under the following headings:

- General Graphics Diagrammatic
- Diagrammatic Graphics
- Fitting
- Graphical Data Analysis
- Non-Graphical Data Analysis
- Mathematical

Filliben (1980 and 1981) provides more information on Dataplot.

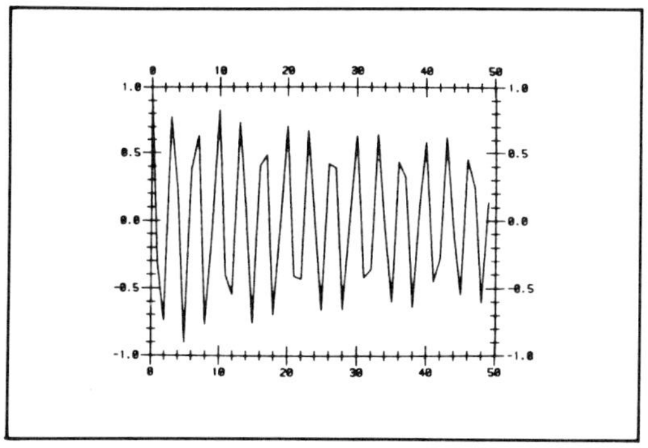

Figure 9. Autocorrelation Plot Using Dataplot

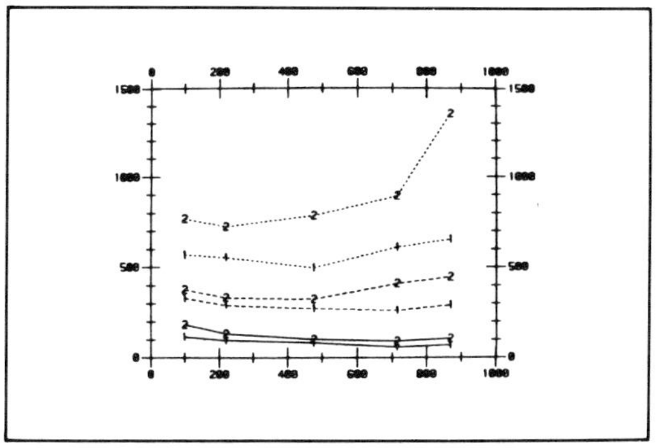

Figure 10. Graphical ANOVA Plot Using Dataplot

C. Statgraphics

Statgraphics, developed at Princeton University, is a new package with broad statistical and graphical capabilities. It contains an optional menu control scheme for general users. Experienced users can access the APL program functions directly and create new ones. Functions are organized into 24 chapters devoted to analysis of variance, basic plotting functions, cluster analysis, descriptive methods, estimation and testing, distribution functions, simulation and random numbers, forecasting, data input/output, exploratory data analysis, basic draw functions, categorized data analysis, multivariate statistics, nonparametric statistics, numerical analysis, sampling, quality control, regression analysis, smoothing, time series analysis, stochastic modeling, experimental design, special math functions and mathematical programming. Pohlemus (1982a and 1982b) provides more information on Statgraphics.

D. The S Package

S is an interactive language and system developed by the Bell Laboratories statistics research departments to reflect modern concepts in data analysis, data display techniques and computing. S is an expression language; the expressions used include algebraic and functional expressions, which are interpreted and evaluated by S. The emphasis is not on all-inclusiveness of currently available capabilities, but on making it easy for a knowledgeable user to add desired capabilities. External support for S is not provided by Bell Labs. In fact, the description of S states that "It is essential that any group hoping to make the best use of S have a local facility for counselling and program development... This means someone...willing and able to learn a reasonable amount about S and the UNIX software environment." Becker and Chambers (1976 and 1978) provide further information on the S package.

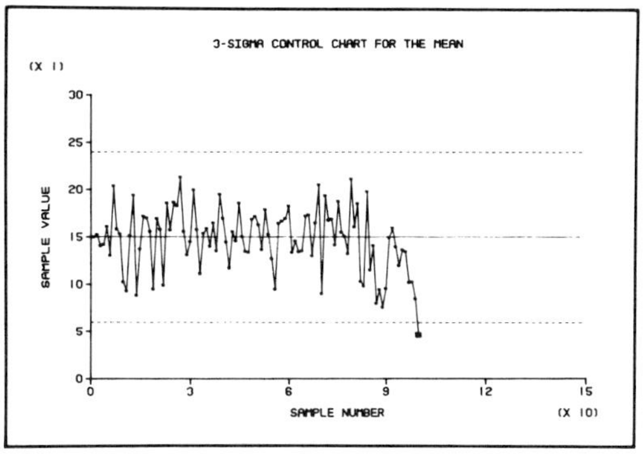

Figure 11. Control Chart Using Statgraphics

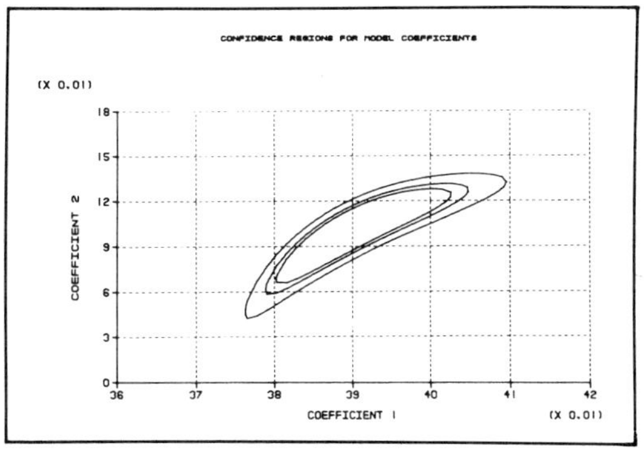

Figure 12. Plot of Coefficients Confidence Regions Using Statgraphics

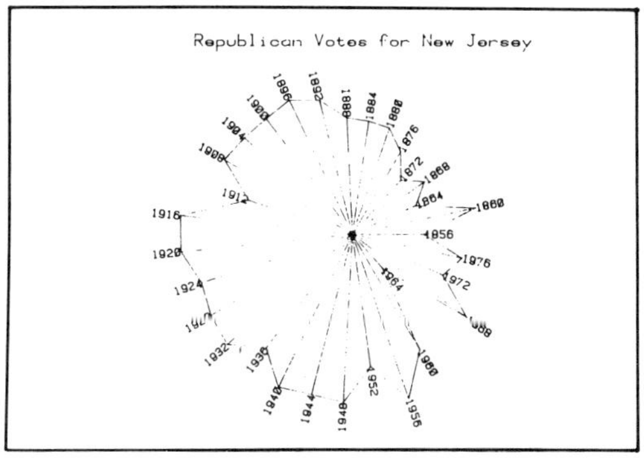

Figure 13. Star Symbol Plot Using S

V. SPECIALIZED SOFTWARE

There is a great deal of specialized software for statistical graphics. To illustrate the type of specialized software that is available, we indicate a few offerings with which we happen to be familiar.

- Regression I/II is a two-part regression analysis graphics package (approximate cost: $48) for the Atari, Apple, TRS-80, Pet/CBM, North Star and CP/M desktop computers. It is available from DYNACOMP, Inc., 1427 Monroe Avenue, Rochester, NY 14618.

- Curve Fit is a curve-fitting graphics program (approximate cost: $100) and Curve II is a general purpose one- and two-dimensional graphics data display package (approximate cost $275) for the Apple II, TRS-80, PET, North Star, Atari 800 and NEC PC-8001 desktop computers. These programs are available from West Coast Consultants, 1775 Lincoln Blvd, Tracy, CA 95376.
- DRFACE is a program developed at the Los Alamos Scientific Laboratory to summarize multivariate data by computer-drawn faces, see Bruckner and Mills (1979). It has recently been used to obtain color face plots (see Hahn, Morgan and Lorensen [1981]).
- ALDS (Analysis of Large Data Sets) is a new interactive color graphics offering for multivariate data, using an extended Minitab statistics package and including RAMTEK multi-dimensional color plotting commands (see Nicholson [1982]).

VI. CONCLUDING REMARKS

The last two offerings described in the preceding section illustrate how one can use color graphics to impart additional information. Each of the offerings described in the previous sections also provide color outputs, even though they may not currently be used in that manner, due to equipment limitations. We expect that these limitations will gradually disappear and that the clever use of color in high-quality graphics will be an important future development.

We have tried to provide an overview of some of the software for integrating statistical analyses with high-quality graphics that has come to our attention. We have described

1. Offerings for both presentation graphics and data analysis/exploration graphics.
2. Software for desktop computers, minicomputers and mainframes.
3. Packages directed at managers and business people, engineers and scientists, data analysts and statisticians, and various combinations thereof.
4. Offerings where the required level of statistical and/or computing knowledge of the user varies from little to fairly extensive.
5. Offerings with acquisition costs ranging from $150 to $40,000 or more (various time-sharing and licensing arrangements are also available for many of the offerings).

We hope these comments will provide a useful starting point for those who would like to select the software that best meets current and future needs.

REFERENCES

Becker, R.A. and Chambers, J.M. (1976), "On Structure and Portability in Graphics for Data Analysis," Proceedings of the 9th Symposium on the Interface of Computer Science and Statistics. (S Package)

Becker, R.A. and Chambers, S.M. (1978), "Design and Implementation of the S System for Interactive Data Analysis," Proceedings of the IEEE Compsac, pp. 626-629.

Boardman, T.J. (1982), "The Future of Statistical Computing on Desktop Computers," The American Statistician, Vol. 36, February 1982, pp. 49-58.

Bruckner, L.A. and Mills, C.F. (1979), "The Interactive Use of Computer Drawn Faces to Study Multidimensional Data," Technical Report LA-7752-MS, Los Alamos Scientific Laboratory, Los Alamos, New Mexico.

Caporal, P.M. and Hahn, G.J. (1981a), "Tools for Automated Statistical Graphics," IEEE Computer Graphics and Applications, Fall 1981, pp. 72-82.

Caporal, P.M. and Hahn, G.J. (1981b), "Computer Offerings for Statistical Graphics — An Overview," Proceedings of the 13th Symposium on the Interface of Computer Science and Statistics, pp. 352-355.

Chambers, J. (1980), "Statistical Computing: History and Trends," *The American Statistician 34*, pp. 238-243.

Fienberg, S.E. (1979), "Graphical Methods in Statistics," The American Statistician, Vol. 33, pp. 165-178.

Filliben, J.J. (1980), "A review of DATAPLOT -- An Interactive High-Level Language for Graphics, Non-Linear Fitting, Data Analysis, and Mathematics," Proceedings of the Statistical Computing Section of the American Statistical Association.

Filliben, J.J. (1981), "DATAPLOT -- An Interactive High-Level Language for Graphics, Non-Linear Fitting, Data Analysis, and Mathematics," *Computer Graphics 15* (3), pp. 199-213.

Francis, I. (1981), *Statistical Software, A Comparative Review*, Elsevier North Holland, Inc., 52 Vanderbilt Avenue, New York, NY 10017.

Hahn, G.J., Morgan, C.B., and Lorenson, W.E. (1981), "Color Face Plots for Product Quality Assessment," Proceedings of the Statistical Computing Section of the American Statistical Association, pp. 252-255.

Heidelberger, P., Welch, P. D., and Wu, L. S. Y. (1982), "The Application of Dual Screen Graphics and APL to Interactive Data Analysis," Proceedings of the 14th Symposium on the Interface of Computer Science and Statistics.

Nicholson, W.L. (1982), "Interactive Color Graphics for Multivariate Data," Proceedings of the National Computer Graphics Association Conference.

Polhemus, N.W. (1982a), "STATGRAPHICS: An Interactive Statistical Graphics System in APL," Proceedings of the National Computer Graphics Association Conference.

Polhemus, N.W. (1982b), "Interactive Statistical Graphics in APL: Designing a Versatile User-Efficient Environment for Data Analysis," Proceedings of the 14th Symposium on the Interface of Computer Science and Statistics. (Statgraphics)

INTERACTIVE COLOR GRAPHICS FOR MULTIVARIATE DATA

Wesley L. Nicholson and Richard J. Littlefield, Pacific Northwest Laboratory

ABSTRACT

Meaningful display of data structure in more than two dimensions is a challenge to statistical graphics. The Analysis of Large Data Sets Project (ALDS) utilizes a VAX 11/780 and a RAMTEK 9400 high resolution color graphics display device to evaluate potential tools such as motion, color, glyphs and stereo 3-D for display of pseudo higher-dimensional data. This paper describes some of the ALDS research on the use of color and glyphs. Color is helpful but not essential. It is particularly useful for accent, for redundant expression of geometric cues and for identifying categories. Carefully selected color sets can display an ordered scale of a quantitative back variable. Glyphs can display quantitative back variables in a higher-dimensional scatterplot or summary statistics on back variables in each cell of a plot cellulated on two front variables. Examples illustrate the simultaneous use of color and glyphs in these two situations.

The ALDS Project has developed a general purpose glyph description language (GDL) which is embedded in an expanded MINITAB statistics package. GDL provides easy definition of arbitrary glyphs and flexible binding of glyph characteristics to back variables. Thus, GDL is a powerful tool for the evaluation of glyphs in an interactive graphics environment.

Key Words

interactive statistical graphics, color graphics, glyph language, higher-dimensional scatterplots, cellulation plots

1. INTRODUCTION

The Analysis of Large Data Sets Project (ALDS) (Hall, 1982) is a research effort to describe the process of analyzing large data sets, to capitalize on the analysis opportunities of large data sets, and to develop special purpose tools for large data set analysis. The results of this research are implemented in the ALDS statistical laboratory described by Nicholson, Carr and Hall (1980).

Some large data sets consist of many cases, each involving a number of variables with unknown interrelationships. The initial phase of analysis (called exploratory data analysis or EDA) on large data sets seeks to understand structure patterns among the cases by visualization. The higher the dimensionality of the space in which cases are viewed, the more likely the analyst is to discern these patterns. Thus, there is a continuing effort on the part of data analysts to develop methods of looking at data in higher-dimensional space. These methods are focusing in diverse directions. Motion is being used by Huber and Donoho (1982) and by Friedman, McDonald and Stuhtzle (1982) to create a three-dimensional cue. Anderson (1957) introduced glyphs which allow back variables to be indicated with the plotting symbol. Shading and color have been used for back variables (with varying degrees of success). Stereo has been used to add a third dimension. ALDS research on use of motion and anaglyph stereo 3-D is described by Nicholson and Littlefield (1982). In this paper, we describe the use of color and glyphs to create higher-dimensional views. Our basic research aim is to use the best of all available techniques to create a broad multi-faceted tool for viewing higher-dimensional data.

There are few postulates to guide this research. Fienberg (1979), in a review of graphical methods in statistics, commented "We have come far ..., we know how to prepare some forms of statistical graphics well, yet in other areas we have much to learn." Multidimensional scatterplotting is one of the areas where there is much to learn. Tukey and Tukey (1982) describe a number of ideas for multidimensional, static displays. Huber in a review of multidimensional motion displays (Kolata, 1982) states that "computer graphics will lead to a whole new style of data analysis". As techniques evolve the final proof of their utility will rest on whether they actually provide new and/or improved data analysis capability. The ALDS project through its research computing facility with a VAX 11/780 computer and RAMTEK 9400 high resolution color display provides a flexible environment to evaluate techniques. The glyph language and the color plotting capability described here are some of the tools that are available. Our goal is to allow the data analyst the flexibility to go from a mind vision of a data analysis plot to reality on the screen with no outside assistance. We envision the programming of a short glyph program, the construction of a color scale and a rocking loop and then the final plot or series of plots all accomplished in a matter of minutes.

This paper has four major sections. The first two sections discuss some general aspects of color and glyphs. The third section illustrates these concepts with several displays of multidimensional data. Finally, the fourth section describes our Glyph Definition Language (GDL), a unique software tool for developing display techniques.

2. COLOR

The effectiveness of color in statistical graphics is unknown. There are few examples of color statistical graphics in the published literature. Those that appear receive a mixed evaluation from data analysts. With the arrival of color graphics devices and hardcopy units, statistical graphics displays in color are easy to produce and record, although publication of color in statistical journals may be delayed because of high cost. Thus, the challenge of doing something useful with color to enhance the information content of statistical graphics is upon us. Our approach to the use of color in statistical graphics is pragmatic. The few color examples done so far provide a starting point for our experimentation in the practical application of color in statistical graphics.

Current ALDS research in the use of color is a follow-on to that reported by Carr (1981), who identifies four uses of color. We paraphrase these as aesthetics, categories, ordered scales, and anaglyphic stereo 3-D as follows:

Aesthetics - We live in a colored world. Hence, effective use of color as accent or in redundancy with a geometric cue can make a statistical graphics display easier to look at and possibly more informative. However, here as in all uses of color to convey information, individual differences in color perception may distort the information transfer or may completely eliminate it. Most aesthetic uses of color are not critical, just more pleasing. An example is the well known pie chart for partitioning a whole into variable size subsets. Using a different color for each wedge is attractive if the colors are properly selected. However, shades of gray or distinct cross hatchings convey the information as well.

Categories - Color is an excellent means to distinguish subsets of points in a scatterplot. Morse (1979), in an article on effective data display, references a number of papers that substantiate this claim. Color is particularly useful because it is perceived independently of other graphical variables such as symbol shape. In Exhibit 3, the three varieties of iris are identified by the dot size of the plotting symbol. While there is no ambiguity in the identification, there is some confounding of dot size with ray length which depicts sepal width. A more effective solution is to use a distinct color for each variety. Unfortunately we cannot show this in a black-and-white paper. For scatterplots with many more points, say in the thousands, there does not seem to be any effective alternative to color for separating categories.

Another use of color is to identify overlapping points in different categories. On many display devices, colors for different categories can be chosen to form distinct combinations. In our system, for example, overlapping red and green points are displayed as yellow. If the number of categories is small (two or three), all of the distinct overlap combinations can be uniquely identified.

Ordered Scales - Our attempts to select a set of colors which are viewed as well ordered, and hence provide a quantitative scale, have been limited to selecting paths through the color cube illustrated in Exhibit 1.

The eight vertices of the cube are the full saturation mixtures of all possible subsets of the primary colors red, green, and blue. These primaries correspond to the three guns in a color CRT display. Thus, to the resolution of the intensity scale in the display device, all colors in the interior and on the boundary of the color cube are possible. The major diagonal connecting the black and the white vertices is the same lightness axis as in the ISCC-NBS standard color solid. The remaining two dimensions of hue and saturation in the standard color solid are non-linearly transformed into the color cube. Saturation increases with distance from the black/white lightness axis and hue is the remaining dimension. Saturation does not remain constant on the surface of the cube and hence the color progression on the surface represents more than change in hue.

One path through the color cube that we have found useful is the red-gray-green curve illustrated in Exhibit 1. From either the red or the green full saturation vertex, the path decreases in saturation and increases in lightness continuously up to the symmetrically located gray center point. This curve can be viewed as the joining of two light/dark achromatic scales, with color being used to identify

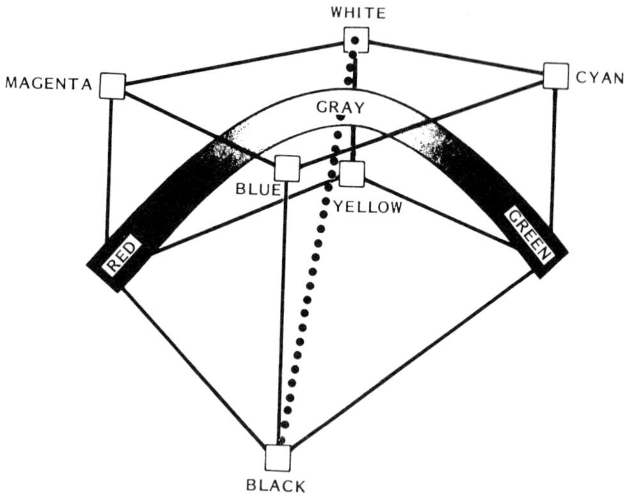

EXHIBIT 1: An Ordered Path Through The Color Cube

the scales. It is particularly useful if there is a natural center to the quantitative variable being displayed. An example would be in plotting residuals, where gray corresponds to zero and full saturation red and green correspond to the most extreme positive and negative residuals.

The shape of the curve through the color cube can be modified to improve its usefulness. It is basically parabolic. However, trial and error suggests that there are more discernible levels near the vertex when the exponent is 1.5 instead of 2. This aspect depends heavily on the exact display device and ambient illumination, and would differ for different displays and media.

It appears that ordering hue scales is much more complicated. Gnanadesikan (1977) describes several experiments to obtain ordered hues using multidimensional scaling. While there was some success, the fact that a complex algorithm was needed for the ordering suggests a certain futility to the process. There are successes in the sense that some hue scales are almost universally recognized. Probably the best example is the cartographer's terrain scale, with Florida in green and Colorado in hues of red and brown. As a learned response this hue scale is successful. In our use of color to display a quantitative back variable, we want an almost immediate understanding of the scale and only a minimal amount of effort in extracting the information content conveyed by its use. We have tried other curves, such as the red/green diagonal and a red-yellow-green parabolic curve. These choices do not give the uniformity of interpretation obtained from the curve in Exhibit 1.

Overlapping data points must be handled differently than for categorical data displayed with color. With ordered color scales combinations of colors are not meaningful. With raster scan display devices, an effective solution is to display only the last color plotted at each position. This method is also versatile because the plotting sequence can be ordered according to an arbitrary back variable.

Anaglyphic Stereo 3-D - The ALDS project has investigated the use of red and green images viewed with red-green filter glasses for creating a stereoptic third dimension. The computer science aspects of this work are described by Littlefield (1982). Carr (1981) and Nicholson and Littlefield (1982) discuss examples of this stereoptic approach to viewing three-dimensional scatterplots.

There are two facets of this work which give promise for the display of more than three dimensions. First, the glyph language can be used to produce plotting symbols which involve one or more additional dimensions. Thus, our basic view can be a three-dimensional scatterplot with higher dimensions cued by glyphs. Second, it may be possible to extend the anaglyphic technique to incorporate some color cueing, as is currently done in broadcast stereo television. The idea is to use only colors that have nonzero components for red and for green or blue. The depth cue is provided by horizontal disparity between the red and green-plus-blue components, while the viewer's eyes recombine the components to produce a perception of the original colors.

We expect considerable variation in viewers' success with color-cued anaglyph stereo. Indeed, it may be asked why we bother to try, since there are other full color methods of stereo presentation. The answer is that the anaglyphic approach is well suited for on-screen stereo displays because it maintains the full spatial resolution of the device and can be seen simultaneously by several viewers. Even with its limitations, anaglyphic stereo appears to be the most practical method for CRT displays for the near future.

3. GLYPHS

Our definition of "glyph" is rather broad. We consider a glyph to be any plotting symbol which displays data by changing the appearance of the symbol. This concept encompasses a wide variety of graphical forms, including Anderson's original glyphs and metroglyphs, plus the weathervanes, k-sided polygons, and Chernoff faces developed by other authors. Fienberg (1979) gives an overview and references many of the specific forms. In this paper, we will discuss general aspects of the glyph technique. As with many other graphical techniques, glyphs have two main uses: exploration (EDA) and presentation. The motivations and corresponding glyph designs are different.

For presentation use, the display is intended to convey a specific impression. Some glyph designs, particularly Chernoff faces, seem well suited for this task. One can carefully assign data dimensions to glyph features, and there is no need to maintain neutrality or independence between dimensions. In addition, one can select the number of data points and dimensions as necessary to best display the important aspects.

For exploratory use, the purpose of the glyph is to display as many dimensions and points as possible, in a neutral fashion. An ideal EDA glyph would enable the viewer to consider any combination of dimensions simultaneously, from singly to all combined. It is important that the glyph display the data dimensions independently, and that no dimension be allowed to overwhelm another.

Another important consideration is the tradeoff between glyph complexity and number of data points displayed. It is clear that a glyph which works quite well with 50 data points can be useless with 1000. There are two problems. One is that the glyphs will usually overlap as the number of data points rises, and the overlapping glyphs can be quite difficult to interpret. The second is that the human visual system can handle only a few features (at a glance). If the glyph is so complicated that study is required to understand it, then it is too complicated for use with large numbers of points.

ALDS investigations have taken two major approaches to these problems. The first is to use a simple glyph that can be interpreted at a glance. For example, the "ray" glyph in Exhibit 2 displays four dimensions: color, angle, dot size, and ray length. When many data points are viewed in the aggregate, an overall texture is seen. By concentrating on the color, orientation, lightness, or coarseness of the pattern, one can easily consider the four dimensions either independently or together.

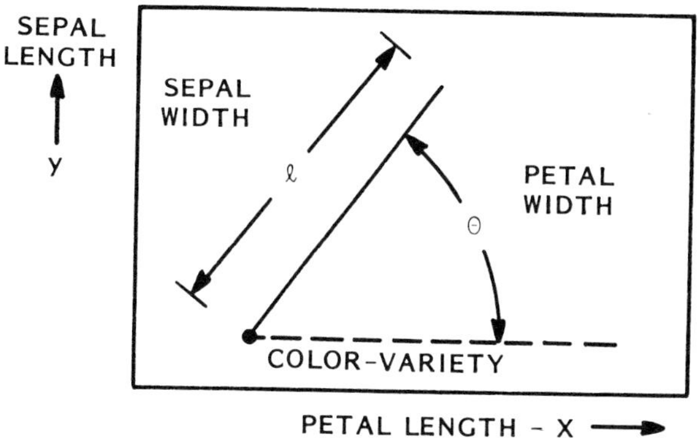

EXHIBIT 2: The "Ray"Glyph

The second approach is to reduce the number of displayed points by aggregation. The data are grouped and some summary statistics are calculated for each group. The summary statistics are then displayed by a glyph. This technique is not new, and in fact the concept encompasses many of the classical displays. For example, a histogram can be viewed as an aggregation across one variable, with one summary statistic (count) displayed by a particularly simple glyph (box with variable height). Similarly, the box-and-whisker plot can be viewed as an aggregation across one variable, with five summary statistics (minimum, maximum, median, and two hinges) displayed with a somewhat more complicated glyph.

It is clear that the aggregation technique, summary statistics, and display style are all independent issues. The difference between our work and more familiar displays such as the box-and-whisker plot is the display style. We believe that a simple, well chosen glyph can be interpreted more easily and consistently in some applications. This is particularly true when glyphs are scattered around the plot in a 2-D array as in Exhibit 8.

4. EXAMPLES OF COLOR AND GLYPH APPLICATIONS

The use of the ALDS color and glyph system is best explained by examples. The first example shows how four-dimensional data set can be displayed using glyphs and categorical color. The second example shows how a large three-dimensional data set can be

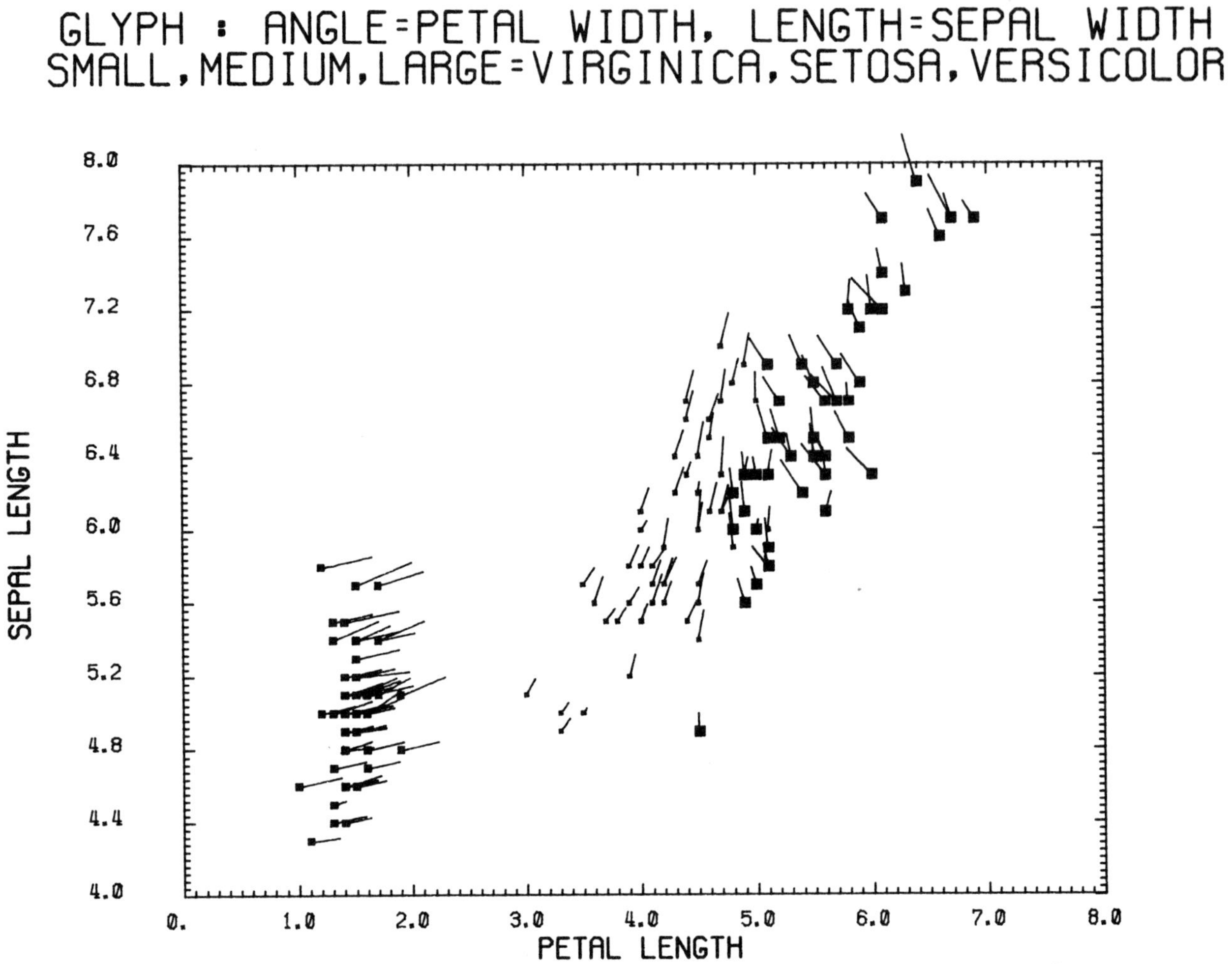

EXHIBIT 3: Anderson Iris Data, Four Measurements on Each of 50 Flowers From 3 Varieties

displayed using aggregation, glyphs, and ordered color scales.

Our first example uses the Edgar Anderson (1935) iris data, consisting of four measurements on each of 50 flowers from each of three varieties. Exhibit 3 is a simple glyph plot displaying the data set. The scatterplot shows the relationship between sepal length and petal length for these flowers, with the dot size of the plotting symbol identifying iris variety. The remaining two measurements, sepal width and petal width, are indicated by the glyph. As described earlier, this display shows some confusion of dot size and ray length. A better display uses distinct colors to code for variety.

The glyph used to display the iris data is illustrated in Exhibit 2. The length of the ray is proportional to sepal width. The angle that the ray subtends from horizontal is proportional to petal width. The maximum length and maximum angle for the ray are determined by trial and error so that the display best conveys four dimensions. Here a maximum length of 0.7 inches on the display screen gave enough resolution that the relative sepal widths for the three varieties could be discerned and yet the rays did not excessively overlap. A maximum angle of 135 degrees was selected so that there would be no confusion between 0 and 180 degrees.

Tukey and Tukey (1982) illustrate a plotting scheme consisting of the six, two-variable views for displaying four-dimensional data. It is very easy to see the positive correlations among petal length, petal width, and sepal length and the negative correlations of these three with sepal width. These pairwise correlations are also evident in Exhibit 3. The ray angle increases from left to right and from bottom to top, while ray length decreases from left to right and from bottom to top.

While Exhibit 3 may not convey new information, it is a concise way of plotting the four measurements and of identifying the three iris varieties. Even two-dimensional plots make it clear that setosa iris are a separate cloud. However, Exhibit 3 clearly shows that virginica and versicolor iris are not separate even in four dimensions. Also, there is some question whether a casual view of a number of two-dimensional plots would pick out some of the higher-dimensional characteristics. For example, the four virginica runts and the single versicolor runt are perhaps more obvious in the four-dimensional glyph plot.

Our second example is more complicated. This data set started out as a set of 21,862 short time series. The problem was to determine the number of distinct patterns that were present. From the physics of the problem, we knew several things about the data. The first few points are irrelevant. The late part of each series is due to a different physical phenomenon from earlier portions. Several different phenomena are at work simultaneously in the early part of the series. Finally, consecutive points are highly correlated.

To reduce the dimensionality of the data while preserving the physics, we constructed three time averages for each series over an early, a middle, and a late time interval. Thus, each of the 21,862 series is reduced to a three-dimensional variable representing averages across three time intervals. For brevity, and to emphasize that for display purposes these are simply three nominally independent variables, we shall call these "early", "middle", and "late".

The resulting three-dimensional data set is illustrated as three pair-wise scatterplots in Exhibits 4, 5, and 6. Clearly, there are a number of clusters. Exhibit 4 identifies a large diffuse cluster near the origin, a distinct rod-shaped cluster in the center, a pipe stem shape extending to the upper right-hand corner of the plot, and a thin needle crossing or possibly lying outside the base of the pipe stem. To varying degrees, the same structure is discernible in Exhibits 5 and 6. Can we add to our understanding with enhanced scatterplots that provide information on a back variable?

Our approach is to start with the middle versus late scatterplot of Exhibit 4, and to add some information about the early variable shown in Exhibits 5 and 6. First, we use a cellulation technique illustrated by Bachi (1978) and Tukey and Tukey (1982) to divide the two front variables, middle and late, into a rectangular grid of 16 by 16 cells. In each cell, we plot a glyph that conveys information about the number of (middle, late) pairs falling in the cell and the distribution of early for those pairs.

An octile ray glyph for conveying this information is depicted in Exhibit 7. The glyph consists of a variable size solid dot with three rays emanating from the dot center. The area of the dot is proportional to the logarithm plus one of the count in the cell. The addition of one guarantees that there will be a dot for cells with one observation. Within each cell, the first octile, fourth octile (median), and seventh octile were calculated for the distribution of early. The angles of the three rays from horizontal are proportional to the octile values, scaled so that the minimum and maximum possible values are displayed as 0 and 180 degrees, respectively.

Exhibit 8 is the cellulation plot constructed from the scatterplot of Exhibit 4. We observe that the largest dot sizes are in the lower left corner, indicating that the preponderance of data is in the large diffuse cloud. A relatively large dot is in the extreme upper right corner, indicating a large number of data points there. The left end of the centrally located rod-shaped cluster has a higher density of data than the rest of the cluster. This information is not visible in the two-dimensional scatterplots because there are so many overlapping points that it is impossible to see the density differences.

SCATTERPLOT OF TWO TIME AVERAGES

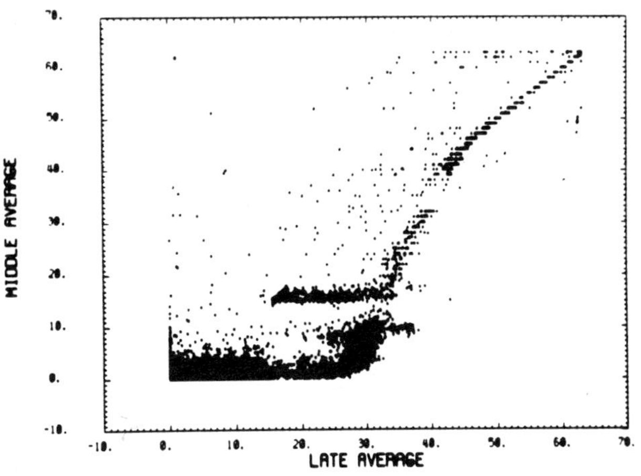

EXHIBIT 4: First Pairwise Scatterplot

SCATTERPLOT OF TWO TIME AVERAGES

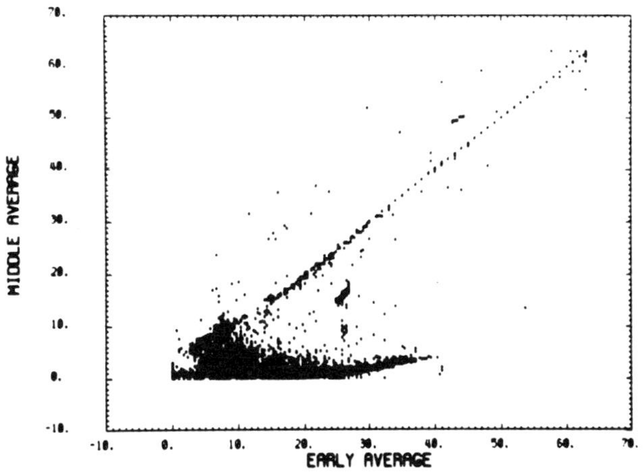

EXHIBIT 5: Second Pairwise Scatterplot

SCATTERPLOT OF TWO TIME AVERAGES

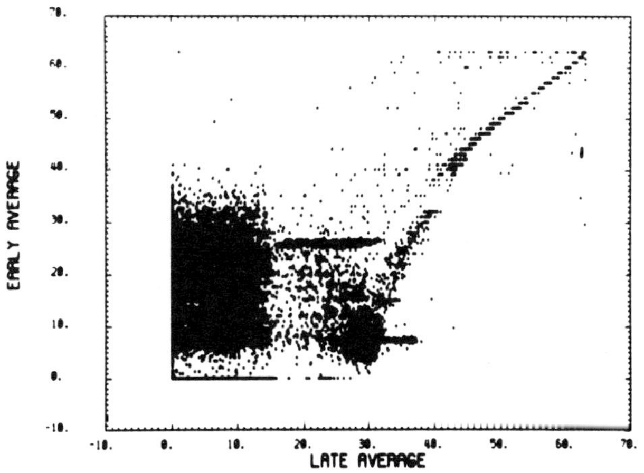

EXHIBIT 6: Third Pairwise Scatterplot

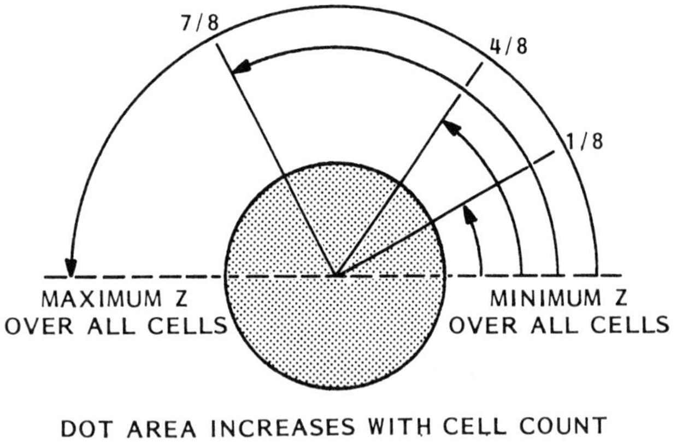

EXHIBIT 7: Octile Ray Glyph

What additional information is conveyed by the octiles of the "early" distribution? Consider the diffuse cluster at the lower left, and note that within this cluster the ray angles become smaller and closer together toward the right. This indicates that the cluster extends out furthest for small late values and diminishes as late gets larger (i.e., towards the right). In the rod-shaped cluster in the lower center, the rays are all close together except where the cluster crosses the pipe stem (the diagonal linear structure). This indicates that the cluster has little depth. In addition, glyphs in the rod-shaped cluster have slightly more vertical rays than those in the surrounding area, indicating that the rod is slightly in front. Finally, the tightness of the rays in the pipe stem and their increasing angle indicate that the pipe stem lies diagonal to the middle-late plane and has little depth.

A few outlier points are discernible even in this low resolution plot. The cluster of points in the upper left corner, which are clearly middle-late outliers, are not early outliers since they line up with the upper end of the pipe stem. Immediately to the left and below the left end of the rod-shaped cluster is a small set of variable early values, indicated by a wide spread in the rays.

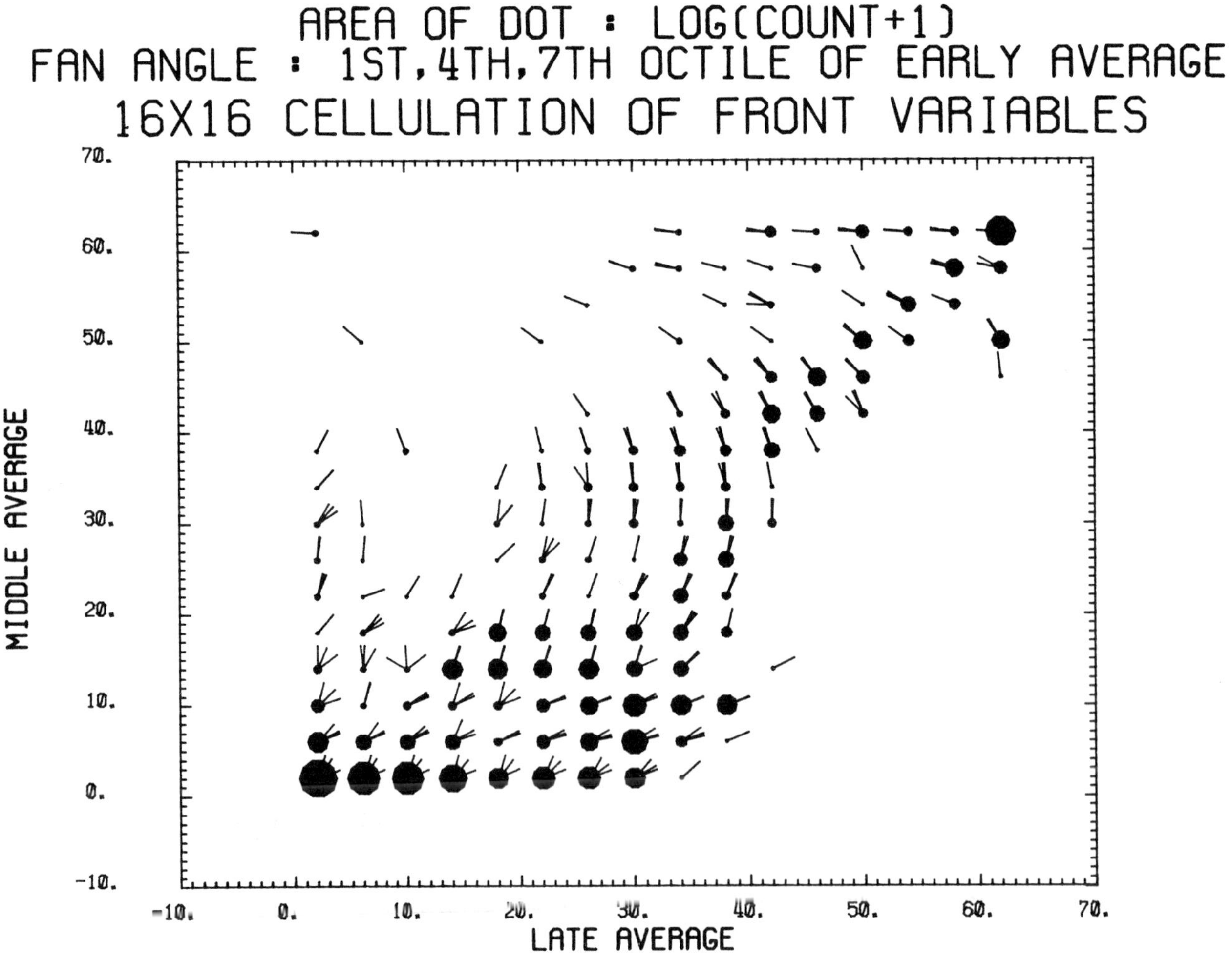

EXHIBIT 8: Glyph Plot of Summary Statistics From Cellulation

Color is not essential to display this glyph plot, since all the features described above can be seen in this black and white version. However, we have tried other versions of the plot in color and in shades of gray and can state quite firmly that they are easier to interpret. For example, using gray dots makes the rays stand out better and visually separates count and distributional information. Using red dots and yellow rays does the same thing and also makes the display more attractive. It is possible that the black and white version could be improved by changing the glyph design, such as using an open circle instead of a filled dot. Nonetheless, it seems clear that using color or gray scale is the preferred solution if available, because less effort is required to get a useful plot.

One problem with the cellulation display of Exhibit 8 is the loss of resolution in the front variables. This can be partially offset by reducing the size of the cells and glyphs. However, smaller glyphs are harder to read. For example, the glyph used in Exhibit 8 is not effective for 32 x 32 cells.

With smaller cells, the glyphs must be simpler and hence convey less information. Something must be left out. In this data set, for 32 x 32 cells the octiles are only marginally useful and are the candidates for omission. This leaves cell count and median.

One effective display method is to use the ordered color scale of Exhibit 1 for the median, and dot size for the count. Because early is highly correlated with middle, the color display shows the bottom of the plot mainly in shades of green, the top in shades of red, and the center in gray. Outliers appear as spots of color contrasting against the overall gradation.

We have used this display technique at resolutions of up to 64 x 64 cells, at which point three-dimensional outliers are easily picked out. Unfortunately, the printing process cannot reproduce such a plot.

5. SOFTWARE TOOLS

5.1 General Capabilities

The ALDS software system provides a unique capability for experimenting with glyphs. It is easy first, to define new glyphs, in terms of appearance and how appearance changes with different data, and, second, to exercise the glyphs on a variety of data.

The first aspect is provided by using a specialized Glyph Definition Language (GDL) for describing glyphs. GDL is flexible but is easy to learn and use. In addition, the supporting software is built such that there is little effort involved in changing a glyph definition. This encourages experimenting with different glyph forms.

The second aspect is provided by integrating glyph plotting into the MINITAB statistical analysis package (Ryan et al (1981)). This provides a rich environment of data selection, transformation, and analysis tools that complement the basic plotting capabilities. This environment encourages experimenting with different data sets.

5.2 Concepts of Glyph Plotting Software

We find it useful to think of glyph plots as an extension of standard two-dimensional scatter plots. In a scatterplot, two "front variables" are displayed as the position of a plotting symbol. "Back variables" are displayed by changing the symbol type, size, or color. Glyph plots have more flexibility in the display of back variables. Typical techniques include changing the symbol angle, aspect ratio or relative proportions of parts of the glyph.

At present, there is little computer software for generating glyph plots. Programs for scatterplots are widespread, but it appears that few are general enough to plot most glyphs. Viewing glyph plots as an extension of scatterplots provides a solution to this problem. Because both plots use front variables in the same way, any scatterplotting program can be made to draw glyphs. Two modifications are required:

1) The data management interfaces and command language must handle several back variables.

2) The inner loop of the plotting software must draw a user-definable glyph at each data point, instead of some fixed symbolism.

These modifications permit a wide range of implementations. For example, in the ALDS system high resolution scatterplotting was available in a local version of MINITAB. We used this package because its data management and command language were already in place. Our glyph definition language was then designed to be similar to the MINITAB command language. This minimized user training and implementation effort.

5.3 Sample Application

Exhibit 3, described in the preceding section, was produced by loading the data into the ALDS version of MINITAB and then executing the following commands:

```
GLYPHDEF  RAY.DEF
RGPLOT 'SL' 'PL' 5 'RAY' 'COLOR' 'RLEN' 'ANGLE'
   'DOTSIZ'
```

The GLYPHDEF command assembles the glyph definitions from file RAY.DEF, making them available for subsequent plotting. This is done only once unless the glyphs are changed. RGPLOT then sets up the plot by drawing axes, labels, etc., and draws the glyphs by executing the appropriate glyph program at each data point.

The GLYPHDEF and RGPLOT commands are not part of GDL. Rather, they are commands to the application program that tell it to execute the GDL support software. The same commands could produce a wide variety of plots depending on the glyph definitions loaded by GLYPHDEF. It is these definitions that are coded in GDL.

The following list shows the GDL program that defines our sample glyph. This is the content of file RAY.DEF in our example.

```
  ;  Glyph #4: Slanting ray
  ;      color = param1, length = param2,
  ;      theta = param3, dotsize = param4

  -LABEL,L4              entry point for glyph
  NEWPEN,P1              set "pen number" = param 1
  MARK,P4                draw dot, size = param 4
  COS,P3,M1              set M1 = cosine (param 3)
  SIN,P3,M2              set M2 = sine (param 3)
```

```
MULT,P2,M1,M11          set M11 = M1 * param 2
MULT,P2,M2,M12          set M12 = M2 * param 2
PLOT,M11,M12            draw line to endpoint of ray
RETURN
```

5.4 Software Design Approach

In our experience, previous glyph programs have been coded in a general purpose language such as FORTRAN and embedded directly in an application program. This approach is simple in concept, but cumbersome in practice. At best, considerable expense and delays are caused by having to rebuild the entire application to change a glyph definition. At worst, the prospective glyph author may have to learn a lot about the application's internal data structures. In any case, experimenting with new glyphs is discouraged to some degree.

The ALDS system takes a different approach. Only the GDL support software is embedded in the application program. GDL programs to define particular glyph formats are written separately. They are interpreted by the support software when the application program is executed.

This approach has the following potential advantages:

1) Changing a glyph requires only editing the GDL program. There is little effort in trying a new glyph.

2) Glyphs are coded in a language that is easy to learn and use. An analyst can make his own glyphs without becoming a computer programmer.

3) The language hides the application program's internal data structures from the glyph author, providing him with a simple view of the data.

To actually provide these advantages, it is important that the GDL language be flexible. Enough power must be available to the GDL user to code any glyph. Modifying the GDL support software, which is embedded in the application program, is too expensive to do on a regular basis.

In our large data set environment, an additional requirement is that execution of GDL programs must be efficient enough to regularly plot hundreds or thousands of data points.

5.5 Major Features of GDL Language

In terms of meeting the design goals, the most important features of GDL are the following:

1) GDL is procedural, not descriptive. Statements are executed in a prescribed order established by the programmer. In connection with GDL's low-level drawing commands, this lets the GDL programmer make totally arbitrary glyphs. He is never tied into a set of standard templates.

2) GDL is a complete programming language. GDL programs can do arithmetic and evaluate mathematical functions. They have local memory (independent of the application program). GDL also provides a full set of conditional and subroutine branch instructions (not shown in the example). This flexibility precludes having to modify the GDL support software.

3) GDL is concise. Even though GDL commands are low level, typical glyph programs are short. Our most complicated glyph program to date required only 50 lines.

The exact syntax of GDL is largely irrelevant. Our current GDL is a simple language with low-level commands, one per line. This required only a modest implementation effort, but has proved to be effective. Coding a new glyph is quick and easy compared with designing and evaluating it.

Other languages could also be used for glyph definition. For example, the LOGO language with "turtle graphics" (Abelson, 1982) might be effective. Assuming that a suitable interpreter were available, it could be interfaced with scatterplotting software as outlined in the following section. However, we expect that this would be more effort than our GDL implementation, because of the size and complexity of most such interpreters.

5.6 GDL Interface with Scatterplotting Software

The interface between GDL and an existing scatterplotting program is straightforward. In any scatterplotting program there is a loop that plots one data point at a time. This loop is simply modified to call the GDL interpreter, once per point, passing as arguments the values of the front and back variables at that point. The GDL interpreter thus needs no knowledge of the plotting program's data structures and can confine itself to plotting the glyph. This independence facilitates installing the interpreter in a variety of application programs.

Scaling and labeling of back variables are important issues. In our system, scaling must be done manually using the data manipulation tools in the analysis package, and knowing what range of values is expected by the GDL program. This task could be automated.

Automatic labeling is more difficult. Our system has no features for automatic labeling or legend generation. Typically the user works without labels during exploration, and supplies textual descriptions or separate diagrams of the glyph parameters during presentations. It seems impossible to automatically generate a legend when glyphs can display back variables in literally any imaginable fashion. Probably this problem will be solved by agreeing on a set of standard glyphs and corresponding legends. However, our current knowledge of glyph designs is so limited that we are unwilling to sacrifice flexibility just to get automatic labeling.

6. CONCLUSIONS

Any evaluation of the usefulness of specific techniques, such as color and/or glyphs, for displaying data in more than two dimensions must involve whether the techniques are for data analysis or for presentation of summary results. Clearly, because of the individual differences of color perception, there are problems in using color for presentation graphics. We make no pretense of evaluating the degree of usefulness of our techniques in this sense. Our evaluation is limited to the potential usefulness of color and glyphs during the analysis stage of an investigation into higher-dimensional structure.

With the above caveat, our current conclusions are as follows:

1) Distinct color hues are useful to identify categories and/or accent important characteristics in a statistical graphics display. Of course there are alternatives, so while color is useful and appears to speed up the identification process, we cannot say that color is essential.

2) For the display of quantitative information "ordered" color scales appear useful but must be carefully selected. Clearly, a single hue scale with varying lightness or saturation is just an accented version of the familiar gray scale. Linking two single hue scales together symmetrically by attaching the gray ends gives a useful extension, particularly for situations where the quantitative variable has symmetry about a central value. We have little positive to offer about the selection of ordered scales using a number of distinct hues.

3) The GDL glyph language provides a powerful tool for development and display of arbitrary glyph symbols. The simplicity of the language and the capability of arbitrary binding to data variables provides a flexible interactive tool for experimentation on the usefulness of glyphs.

4) The general usefulness of both color and glyphs for displaying higher-dimensional data is clearly analyst specific. For some analysts the back variable cues are strong and higher dimensions are visualized. For others the results are far from satisfactory.

5) The full impact of color on statistical graphics cannot be realized until color reproduction is both a more accurate and a more economical process. In the ALDS system, some of the display techniques involving color are limited to the RAMTEK screen because film cannot accurately reproduce the image. On the other hand, the era of table top, minicomputer work stations with high resolution color graphics capability is just around the corner. Research on the use of color as a tool for higher-dimensional display is important.

7. ACKNOWLEDGMENT

The ALDS project and, in particular, the work reported in this paper was supported by the U.S. Department of Energy, Applied Mathematical Sciences, under contract DE-AC06-76RLO 1830.

8. REFERENCES

Abelson, H. (1982). A Beginners Guide to LOGO. Byte Magazine, August 1982, Vol. 7, No. 8, pp. 88-112.

Anderson, E. (1935). The irises of the Gaspe Peninsula. Bull. Amer. Iris Soc. 59:2-5.

Anderson, E. (1957). A semigraphical method for the analysis of complex problems. Proc. Nat. Academy of Sciences, 13:923-27 (reprinted in Technometrics (1960), 2:387-91).

Bachi, R. (1978). Graphical statistical methodology in the automation era. Graphic Presentation of Stat. Inf.: Presented at the 136th Ann. Meet. Am. Stat. Assoc., Soc. Stat. Sect. Sess. Graphical Meth. Stat. Data, Boston, 1976. Tech. Rep. 43:23-68.

Carr, D.B. (1981). Raster color displays - examples, ideas and principles, Proceedings of the 1980 DOE Statistical Symposium, October 29-31, 1980, Berkeley, Calif., CONF-801045:116-126.

Donoho, D.L., Huber, P.J., Ramos, E. and Thomas, H.M. (1982). Kinematic display of multivariate data. Proceedings of the Third Annual Conference and Exposition of the National Computer Graphics Association, Inc. - Vol. 1, June 13-17, 1982, Anaheim, CA; 393-8.

Fienberg, Steven E. (1979). Graphical methods in statistics. American Statistician, 33, 4:165-178.

Friedman, Jerome H., McDonald, John Alan, and Stuetzle, Werner (1982). An introduction to real-time graphical techniques for analyzing multivariate data. Proceedings of the Third Annual Conference and Exposition of the National Computer Graphics Association, Inc. - Vol. 1, June 13-17, 1982, Anaheim, CA; 421-7.

Gnanadesikan, R. (1977). Methods for Statistical Data Analysis of Multivariate Observations. New York: Wiley.

Hall, D.L. (Editor)(1982). ALDS 1980 Panel Review, Pacific Northwest Laboratory, Richland, WA, January 1982. PNL-SA-10008.

Kolata, Gina (1982). Computer Graphics Comes to Statistics, Science 217, September 3, 198?: 919-20.

Littlefield, R.J. (1982). Stereo and motion in the display of 3-D scatterplots, Proceedings of the 8th Annual Computer Graphics Conference, May 4-6, 1982, Detroit, MI, Engineering Society of Detroit, Detroit.

Morse, Alan (1979). Some Principles for the Effective Display of Data," Comput. Graphics 13(2): 94-101.

Nicholson, W.L., Carr, D.B. and Hall, D.L. (1980). The analysis of large data sets, 1980 Statistical Computing Section Proceedings of the American Statistical Association: 59-65.

Nicholson, Wesley L. and Littlefield, Richard J. (1982). The use of color and motion to display higher-dimensional data. Proceedings of the Third Annual Conference and Exposition of the National Computer Graphics Association, Inc. Vol. 1, June 13-17, 1982, Anaheim, CA: 476-85.

Ryan, T.A. Jr., Joiner, B.L., and Regan, B.F. (1981). MINITAB Reference Manual, March 1981. Dunbury Press, Boston, MA.

Tukey, P.A. and Tukey, J.W., (1982). Graphic display of data sets in three and more dimensions, Interpreting Multivariate Data, John Wiley & Sons, London.

Integrating Color into Statistical Software

Richard A. Becker, Bell Laboratories

ABSTRACT

Recent hardware advances have made color graphical output devices generally available to statisticians. This, combined with the general attractiveness and eye-catching ability of color, has brought about a desire to produce colorful statistical displays.

Pen plotters form one class of color devices. They are able to change the colors of the lines and characters that they draw by changing pens, and some can automatically control a number of pens. Raster scan color scopes have, in addition to line color, the ability to produce areas of color. This capability is exploited in typical presentation graphics, e.g. bar graphs and pie charts, and in more sophisticated displays such as color contour plots.

To facilitate the production of color displays, statistical software must allow the user to:

- specify colors
- fill areas based on hardware capabilities (either filling of polygonal areas or seed fills)
- control color look-up tables using an appropriate user-oriented color model.

Keywords: *color graphics, raster scan, polygonal areas.*

Why Color?

At present, there is a wide ranging interest in color graphics for statistical displays. Why is this? There are several apparent reasons. First, the new raster-scan graphics device technology has made color displays possible. Second, the same technology has made color terminals available at an affordable cost. Many medium-resolution color terminals are now on the market for $5000 to $20000. Third, and perhaps equally important, is that people *like* color displays. Our world is a colorful one, and there is a natural desire to make our computer graphics world colorful, too. After all, who wants a black and white television when a color one is economically available?

A related concept is that a colorful display draws attention to itself, and thus may be seen by important users (e.g. the company president) where a less colorful display might be passed over. If the display presents an important message, color might be justified solely on these grounds.

The desire to produce statistical displays using color does present some problems, however. One such problem is that of judging the effect that human color perception has on the perception of a color plot. Cleveland and McGill (1981) conducted experiments on the distortion that color can have in graphical displays. Their experiment involved judging relative areas on two color maps; for example, subjects were asked whether there was more red area, more green area, or the same of each. With intense colors such as red and green, the red areas were consistently judged larger even when the regions were the same size. With pastel colors, such distortions did not occur.

A problem related to perception is that there is little empirical justification for color displays. The question that needs to be answered is "how much do we gain from using colors as opposed to textures and gray scales?"

Another major problem with color graphical displays is that of obtaining hard copy output. It will be some time before we become a "paperless society" with video display screens everywhere. In the meantime, it will be necessary to show the color displays to others via papers, publications, and memoranda. At present, facilities for duplicating color originals are not common and are still relatively costly.

Line Color or Area Color

When most people talk of using color in statistical displays, they have in mind more than the line-drawn color available on pen plotters. Indeed, colored lines from pen plotters have been available for quite some time. The big change that raster-scan displays have made is that they can produce areas of color, and this is what most people have in mind when discussing color in statistical graphics.

Some of the most prevalent statistical graphical forms are often drawn using area color: bar graphs, pie charts, maps. Somewhat more sophisticated uses of area color are topographical maps (contour plots) and computerized tomography displays. In any case, such displays are relatively familiar, and it is tempting to demand similar things from statistical software.

The Place of Color in a Statistical Graphics System

Given a decision to implement area color capabilities, it is necessary to integrate the capability into the overall statistical graphics system. Refer to exhibit 1

Exhibit 1

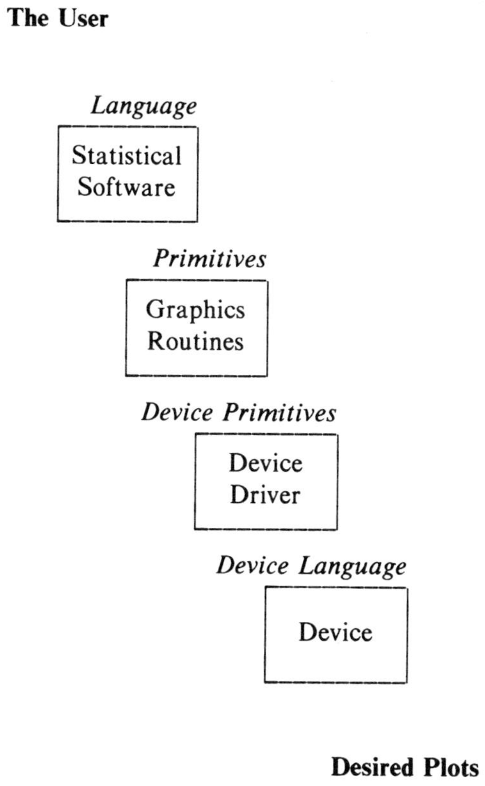

where the path from the user to the desired plots is broken down into a series of steps involving different hardware/software domains. At the top level, the user communicates to statistical software using a language such as S, (Becker and Chambers, 1980). This communication is typically expressed in statistical terms: for example, "produce a scatter plot with a superimposed regression line". At the next level, the statistical software communicates with general-purpose graphical software, at the level of the SIGGRAPH CORE graphics proposal (SIGGRAPH, 1980). At this level, device independent graphical operations are translated into low level primitives that are carried out by the device dependent portion of the graphics system—the device driver. The device driver knows what commands must be transmitted to a particular graphical device to produce pictures.

The integration of area color, then, must be natural at the user level and must eventually map into the capabilities of the device at the other. Most of the user interaction with the statistical software will depend on the specifics of the language syntax, system concepts, and similar things. From the user's perspective, colors can often be presented as extra parameters to the statistical graphics routines. For the most part, a convenient method of doing this is to assign a small integer color numbers to each area and to later specify the mapping between the integer and the desired color. This provides the opportunity to defer decisions about the actual colors used in the picture until the entire picture is available. The next section describes how this may be implemented.

At the other end of the graphics chain we have the capabilities (or lack thereof) of the graphical device. Device area filling capabilities are presented in exhibit 2.

Exhibit 2

Device Area-Filling Capabilities

Device	Hardware Fill Capability	
Plotters	None	Fine spacing of lines to simulate (see plotter ads)
Raster	Rectangle	May allow textures
Raster	Seed or Polygon Fill	Textures and Color Map Available
Bitmap	Rectangle	Do your own polygon fill

As the table notes, line-drawing devices such as plotters have no capabilities for filling areas except by drawing potentially enormous numbers of contiguous lines. The time consumed during such operations rules out such devices for most serious applications with filled areas.

A number of devices provide rectangle filling, which satisfies user needs for bar graphs and other simple displays. Some also have circle sector filling to provide pie chart capabilities. The most capable devices, however, can fill polygons, and thus can produce many other forms of area color graphics.

There are basically two mechanisms used by devices which fill arbitrary polygonal areas. The *polygon fill* capability requires that the outline of a polygon be transmitted to the device and the device then locally fills the area. The other form of area filling is depends on a *seed fill* algorithm, in which previously drawn lines are used as boundaries for the area to be filled. The device driver directs the device to fill the area containing a selected *seed pixel*. The device locally scans its picture memory to find boundaries of the area surrounding the seed pixel.

Although these two methods of polygon filling for the most part are equivalent, there are significant differences in the way that they must be handled by the graphics software. Seed fill algorithms may at times have difficulty adequately coloring odd-shaped areas. (Consider an hour-glass shaped area: as the middle becomes more and more narrow, pixels on opposite sides eventually touch, effectively dividing it into two regions. It is difficult for any high-level routine to know when this will happen, since when the pixels touch depends on details of the line-drawing algorithms in the device.) Polygon fill algorithms, on the other hand, require more complicated data structures. Exhibit 3 shows the differences between the way a figure composed of four rectangular areas may be drawn using seed fill or polygon fill techniques. Notice how the data structures for polygon filling must recognize the connected sets of lines segments that make up each region, while for seed fills only the boundaries need be drawn, in any order. While neither approach is difficult for this example, consider the differences needed for drawing a map showing the States in the USA, for example.

Exhibit 3

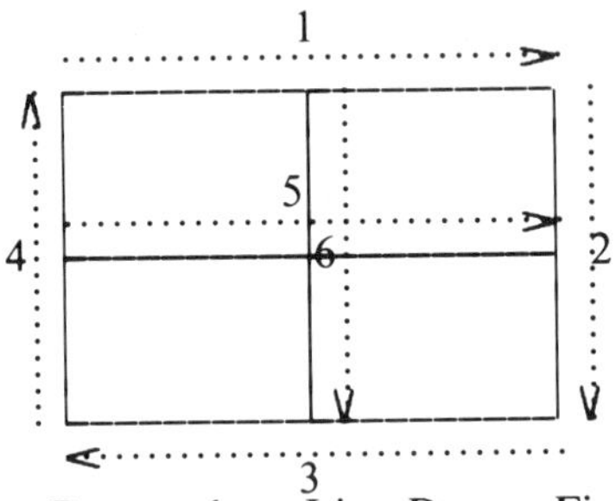

Four Rectangles—Line Drawn Figure

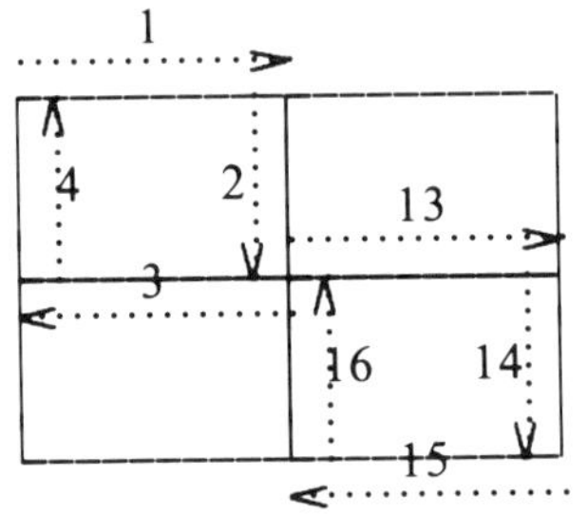

Four Rectangles—Polygon Drawn Figure

User Control of Color

In the previous section, we glossed over actual color choices by allowing colors to be represented by small integer color numbers. A nice solution to this problem is provided by a hardware feature of many of the display devices—the *color map*. The color map describes a mapping between small integers and colors represented, for example, by hue, lightness and saturation. The meaning of a color number is device dependent: on certain devices, the color map is nothing more than a fixed relation between color numbers and actual colors, e.g., red is 1, green is 2. On other devices the color map relates a color number to a color chosen from a fixed palette of, say, 64 colors. On the most flexible devices the palette is much larger.

On devices with non-fixed color maps, the user can have external control over the mapping, allowing the colors in the picture to be changed *after* the picture has been drawn. The user can then see color choices in the context of the full picture. (Many devices with color maps can also provide forms of dynamic displays through color-table animation.)

It helps to provide a natural method of controlling color choices. The raster extensions to the CORE system (SIGGRAPH 1980) allow color specification by means of hue, lightness, and saturation. This HLS system appears adequate for specifying colors. However, Berk, et al. (1982) present empirical evidence that other techniques for color specification may be superior.

Conclusions

The technology is available for producing color displays of statistical data. Techniques for area filling and color specification are readily available, often supported by hardware in the graphical devices. Nonetheless, there are substantial challenges for those who wish to use color in statistical displays. In particular, we need a more thorough understanding of what effect color has on a particular display and how important it is to communicating meaning.

References

Becker, R. A., and Chambers, J. M., *S: A Language and System for Data Analysis,* Bell Laboratories, January 1981.

Berk, T., Brownston, L., and Kaufman, A., "A New Color-Naming System for Graphics Languages", *IEEE Computer Graphics and Applications,* May 1982, pp. 37-44.

Cleveland, W. S. and McGill, R., "Color Induced Distortion in Graphical Displays", *The Harvard Library of Computer Graphics,* Mapping Collection, Vol. 17, 1981.

SIGGRAPH, "Status Report of the Graphics Standards Planning Committee," *Computer Graphics,* **13** No. 3, August 1980.

Implementation Strategies for Statistical Methods

Chair: Marcello Pagano, Harvard University and Sidney Farber Cancer Institute

Calculating Distributions for Nonparametric Statistics
Marcello Pagano and David Tritchler, Harvard University and Sidney Farber Cancer Institute

On the Use of Linear Harmonic Forms to Simultaneously Generalize Certain Statistical Computations
Michael E. Tarter, University of California, Berkeley

Quantiles, Parametric-Select Density Estimation, and Bi-Information Parameter Estimators
Emanuel Parzen, Texas A & M University

CALCULATING DISTRIBUTIONS FOR NONPARAMETRIC STATISTICS*

Marcello Pagano and David Tritchler
Harvard University and Sidney Farber Cancer Institute

Algorithms are presented for finding the exact distributions of a number of common nonparametric statistics. The algorithms require polynomial time for execution as opposed to the exponential time required by complete enumeration. The recursive algorithm is cast in terms of the characteristic function, which lends itself to several extensions of the algorithm.

Key Words: Permutation distributions; Fast Fourier Transform; Non-parametrics.

Introduction

For ease of exposition, consider the case of two samples $x_1, x_2, \ldots, x_m$ and $y_1, y_2, \ldots y_n$ which when combined may be written $z_1, z_2, \ldots, z_N$ $(N = m+n)$.

Define the statistics $S = \sum_{j=1}^{N} z_j I_j$ where I_j is a binary indicator. The permutation distribution of the random variable (r.v.) S is obtained by keeping the z_j fixed and letting $I = (I_1, \ldots, I_N)$ index each of the ${}_NC_m$ equally likely subsamples, of fixed size m, from the first N natural numbers.

The obvious approach to calculate the distribution of S is the one which requires the total enumeration of all ${}_NC_m$ subsamples. In the worst case, (m=n) this increases as $4^n/n^{\frac{1}{2}}$. The computational problems with permutation distributions led researchers to find other methods. Pitman (1937/38) found the asymptotic distributions for the test statistics, but for small samples the problem remained unsolved. Wilcoxon (1945) replaced the observation by the rank of z_j amongst $z_1, \ldots, z_N$. This breakthrough led to other nonparametric tests that had a number of advantages. One of these is that it is practical to tabulate their distributions in a number of important situations.

But even with nonparametric tests based on ranks, there are still some situations that defy tabulation, such as, for example, stratified samples, censored observations, and ties. In the next section we present an algorithm to calculate the distribution of S (when S is a sum of the original observations or when S is a function of the ranks) in polynomial time. As a result it is feasible to obtain distributions that would previously have been infeasible. Furthermore, these distributions are useful not only for testing purposes but also for point estimation, confidence intervals, etc. (see for example, Kempthorne and Doerfler (1969), Hollander and Wolfe (1973), and Tritchler (1980)).

*This research was supported in part by grants from the National Institutes of Health, DHS, CA-28066 and CA-09337.

Computing Permutation Distributions

Let

$$\Phi_S(\Theta) = E[\exp(i\Theta S)]$$

be the characteristic function of S and introduce the notation

$$\Phi_S(\Theta) = \Phi(m,N,\Theta)$$

for given m, N, Θ and let

$$\psi(m,N,\Theta) = \Phi(m,N,\Theta) \times {}_NC_m \ . \quad (1)$$

Pagano and Tritchler (1980A) show how $\Phi(m,N,\Theta)$ can be obtained in polynomial time, as opposed to the exponential time needed for enumeration of all possible samples. That is, the time required by their algorithm is bounded above by a polynomial in N. The calculation of the characteristic function is based on the difference equation

$$\psi(j,k,\Theta) = \exp(i\Theta z_k)\psi(j-1,k-1,\Theta) + \psi(j,k-1,\Theta) \text{ for } 1 \le j \le k \le N. \quad (2)$$

After the characteristic function is calculated at the Q frequencies

$$\Theta_j = \frac{2\pi j}{Q} \quad j = 0, 1, \ldots, Q-1 \quad Q \ge \max S \quad (3)$$

it can be inverted by the Fast Fourier Transform algorithm (FFT) (Cooley and Tukey (1965)) to obtain the exact permutation distribution of S. The total time required is approximately m N Q operations for the Q characteristic function evaluations plus 2 Q log Q operations for the FFT, where an 'operation' is a complex multiplication and addition. Thus, the order of work is dominated by the calculation of the characteristic function. The algorithm requires that the r.v. S be non-negative integer valued. To insure this, the data is subjected to an initial transformation if necessary. The implications of data transformation to integer form are discussed in Section 2.2 of Pagano and Tritchler. Essentially, if the data are given to a precision of k decimal places, multiplying each data value by 10^k yields an equivalent problem and inferences are unchanged. The number of frequencies Q and hence execution time and storage will be increased. Q may be reduced by using a multiplier less than 10^k and truncating. In that case, the inferences become approximate.

An important feature of their algorithm is that

$$\psi(j,N,\Theta) \quad j=0,1,2,\ldots,m \qquad (4)$$

are automatically calculated in the process of obtaining $\psi(m,N,\Theta)$. These quantities are required by the algorithms to be presented.

Note that due to the linearity property of the Fourier Transform, the Fourier inverse of $\psi(m,N,\cdot)$ is the vector F whose j^{th} element is

$$f_j = {}_N C_m \cdot P(S = j)$$

$$= \text{no. of size m samples with Sum S.} \quad (5)$$

Thus, the ψ-function may be used to enumerate subsample means. This property will be of use in the computation of confidence intervals.

The methods presented in this paper are based on an algorithm which computes the permutation distribution for any set of scores. The various specific techniques result from generating scores particular to that technique, a trivial process. For example, the score function

$$a(z_{(i)}) = i$$

yields the Wilcoxon test where

$$S = \sum_{j=1}^{N} a(z_{(j)}) I_j.$$

The Multi-sample Problem

An important generalization of the proposed algorithm is to the case of more than two samples. In order to avoid overly cumbersome notation, we restrict ourselves to the case of three samples. The ideas easily extend to more than three samples.

Define $S^{(1)}$, $S^{(2)}$ and $S^{(3)}$ to be the sums in each of the samples respectively; in an obvious notation,

$$S^{(1)} = \sum_{j=1}^{m_1} z_j$$

$$S^{(2)} = \sum_{j=m_1+1}^{m_1+m_2} z_j$$

$$S^{(3)} = \sum_{j=m_1+m_2+1}^{N} z_j.$$

The characteristic function is now bivariate (since $S^{(1)} + S^{(2)} + S^{(3)}$ is fixed) and can be obtained from the ψ function, as before, where

for $j,k=1,2,\ldots$ such that $j+k \leq \ell=1,2,\ldots$

$$\psi(j,k,\ell_1,\Theta_1,\Theta_2) = \exp(i\Theta_1 z_\ell)\psi(j-1,k,\ell-1,\Theta_1,\Theta_2) + \exp(i\Theta_2 z_\ell)\psi(j,k-1,\ell-1,\Theta_1,\Theta_2) + \psi(j,k,\ell-1,\Theta_1,\Theta_2). \quad (6)$$

Fourier inversion is performed using the multivariate FFT (Singleton (1969)) to obtain the joint distribution of $S^{(1)}$ and $S^{(2)}$.

Another k-sample test is the Jonckheere statistic for testing equality against ordered alternatives (see Hollanders and Wolfe (1973)). The proposed algorithm can be modified to calculate the distribution of this statistic (Pagano and Tritchler (1980A)).

Stratification

Another generalization is to convolutions of random variables, such as in stratification. For example, suppose two treatments are to be compared, and sex and age may affect the response being measured. Then, one would stratify according to these factors so as not to confound any differences due to them with possible treatment differences. If one does stratify, then the correct permutation distribution is not the one previously defined. One must take the stratification into account.

Suppose, as before, that $x_1,\ldots,x_m$ and $y_1,\ldots,y_n$ represent the two samples. But now there are k strata and m_j of the x's and n_j of the y's come from the jth stratum. THen, because of the stratification, the ${}_N C_m$ samples of size m from $z_1,\ldots z_N$ are not equally likely. The samples that are equally likely are the $\sum_{j=1}^{k} {}_{N_j} C_{m_j}$ (where $N_j = m_j + n_j$) samples of size, where each sample has m_j elements from stratum j, for $j=1,\ldots,k$.

In order to find the distribution of S for stratified samples, express

$$S = \sum_{j=1}^{k} \sum_{\ell} z_\ell I_{j,\ell} = \sum_{j=1}^{k} S^{(j)} \qquad (7)$$

where the second summation in (7) is over the jth stratum and m_j of the $I_{j,\ell}$ are equal to one. Now (2), suitably modified, can be used to find the characteristic function of each $S^{(j)}$. Whence the characteristic function of S is the product of these k characteristic functions.

Multivariate Applications

The algorithm also generalizes to multivariate observations. Suppose that we have 2 samples $\underset{\sim}{x}_1, \underset{\sim}{x}_2, \ldots, \underset{\sim}{x}_m$ and $\underset{\sim}{y}_1, \underset{\sim}{y}_2, \ldots, \underset{\sim}{y}_n$ where each observation is say, a vector of length 3. The two-sample statistic is now also a vector $S = (s_1, s_2, s_3)$. Then in the trivariate case (2) generalizes to

$$\psi(j,k,\underset{\sim}{\theta}) = \exp(i(\theta_1 x_{k1} + \theta_2 x_{k2} + \theta_3 x_{k3}))\psi(j-1, k-1, \underset{\sim}{\theta}) + \psi(j, k-1, \underset{\sim}{\theta})$$
$$\text{for } \underset{\sim}{\theta} = (\theta_1, \theta_2, \theta_3,)^T \text{ and}$$
$$\underset{\sim}{x}_k = (x_{k1}, x_{k2}, x_{k3})^T. \qquad (8)$$

Censored Data

An interesting result that we present here because of the complications caused by the censoring, is that the above methods extend to an important nonlinear statistic. Suppose that $x_1, \ldots, x_{m1}$ and $c_1, \ldots, c_{n1}$ are the observations from population 1, and $y_1, \ldots, y_{m2}$ and $d_1, \ldots, d_{n2}$ are observations from population 2. Suppose further that the c and d are censored observations. Then the F-statistic to test the equality of the two populations (see for example, Lagakos (1979) p. 146) is

$$F = \frac{(\sum_{j=1}^{m_1} x_j + \sum_{j=1}^{n_1} c_j)/m_1}{(\sum_{j=1}^{m_2} y_j + \sum_{j=1}^{n_2} d_j)/m_2}$$

Define

$$T = \sum_{j=1}^{m_1} x_j + \sum_{j=1}^{n_1} c_j + \sum_{j=1}^{m_2} y_j + \sum_{j=1}^{n_2} d_j,$$

$w=n_1+n_2$, $r=m_1+m_2$, $N_1=m_1+n_1$, $N_2=m_2+n_2$ and $N=N_1+N_2$.

We wish to find

$$p = \Pr\{F > k\}$$

for a given constant k. Which permutation distribution induces this probability must be determined. If one considers only the partitions where sample one always consists of m_1 uncensored observations, then there are ${}_rC_{m_1} \cdot {}_wC_{n_1}$ points in the sample space. Furthermore, the algorithm previously given for stratified samples applies. If on the other hand m_1 is allowed to vary, then we must consider all ${}_NC_{N_1}$ different partitions.

To this end, a little algebra leads to

$$p = \Pr\{ \sum_{j=1}^{m_1} x_j + \sum_{j=1}^{n_1} c_j > T\, m_1 k/(m_2 + k m_1)\}.$$

In order to account for the fact that m_1 is itself random,

$$p = \sum_{i=v_1}^{v_2} \Pr(m_1=i)\Pr\{ \sum_{j=1}^{m_1} x_j + \sum_{j=1}^{n_1} c_j > \frac{T m_1 k}{(m_2+km_1)} \Big| m_1 = i\} \quad (9)$$

where $v_1 = \max(0, N_1-n_1-n_2)$ and $v_2 = \min(r, N_1)$. This suggests an algorithm for finding p.

Write the combined sample of observed death times as $z_1, z_2, \ldots, z_r$ and likewise let $e_1, e_2, \ldots, e_w$ be the censored observations. Let S_z represent the sum of a size m_1 sample of z's and let S_e be the sum of a size n_1 sample of e's. Here m_1 is random while $N_1 = m_1+n_1$ is fixed. If each of the ${}_NC_{N_1}$ points in the sample space are equally likely then $\Pr(m_1=j) = {}_rC_{m_1} \cdot {}_wC_{n_1} / {}_NC_{N_1}$. Of course, other specifications for this probability can be entertained. The conditional probabilities on the right in (9) are given by the distributions of $T = S_z+S_e$ conditional on $m_1=j$. Given m_1, S_z and S_e are mutually independent, so the conditional distribution of T is the convolution of the conditional distributions of S_z and S_e. Thus, conditional on $m_1=j$, the characteristic function of T is given by

$$\phi_T^{(j)}(\theta) = \psi_z(j,r,\theta)\psi_e(N_1-j,w,\theta)/({}_{N_1}C_N \cdot \Pr(m_1=j))$$

where $\psi_z(j,r,\theta)$ is computed from the z's and $\psi_e(N_1-j,w,\theta)$ is computed from the e's. This characteristic function may be calculated and inverted for $j = V_1, V_1+1, \ldots, V_2$ to obtain the probabilities needed in (9). By the recursive nature of (2), it can be seen that when $\psi_e(V_2,r,\theta)$ is calculated, $\psi_e(j,r,\theta)$ for $j=0,1,\ldots,V_2-1$ are automatically obtained in the process, and similarly for $\psi_z(N_1-V_2,w,\theta)$, so no extra computation is required to obtain ψ_e and ψ_z.

The One Sample Problem

It is often of interest to test the hypothesis that a population distribution is symmetric about zero. Suppose that the data consist of the dependent observations $x_1, x_2, \ldots, x_N$ and let $z_1 = |x_i|$ $i = 1,2,\ldots,N$. Assign positive integer scores $a_1, a_2, \ldots, a_N$ to the z_i, based on either the ranks or the magnitudes of the z_1. The test statistic is of the form

$$S = 2 \sum_{i=1}^{N} a_i\, I(x_i)$$

or equivalently

$$S' = \sum_{i=1}^{N} a_i I'(x_i) = S - T$$

where

$$I(x_i) = \begin{cases} 1 \text{ if } x_1 > 0 \\ 0 \text{ if } x_1 \leq 0 \end{cases}$$

$$I'(x_i) = \begin{cases} 1 \text{ if } x_i > 0 \\ -1 \text{ if } x_i \leq 0 \end{cases}$$

and $T = \sum_{i=1}^{N} a_i$.

See, for example, Maritz (1979).

Under the null hypothesis and conditionally on $z_1, z_2, \ldots, z_N$

$$P(I(x_i) = 1) = P(I'(x_i) = 1) = \tfrac{1}{2}$$

and

$$\Phi_{S'}(\Theta) = \prod_{j=1}^{N} [\exp(i\Theta a_i) + \exp(-i\Theta a_i)]/2$$

$$= \prod_{j=1}^{N} \cos(\Theta a_i)$$

is computed at the Fourier frequencies

$$\Theta_j = \frac{2\pi}{Q} j \text{ for } j = 0,1,\ldots,Q-1, \text{ and } Q \geq 2T.$$

Since S takes only positive values, we invert

$$\Phi_S(\Theta) = \exp(i\Theta T) \quad \Phi_{S'}(\Theta).$$

Interval and Point Estimation Based on Typical Values

Nonparametric interval and point estimation for location and shift parameters may be carried out by procedures which are not rank-based but are related to permutation tests. The method for interval estimation will be described, but the technique also yields point estimates. The method also extends to estimation for a shift parameter in blocked experiments. See Tritchler (1980) for a discussion.

For the one-sample case, let $z_1, z_2, \ldots, z_N$ be a random sample and consider the null hypothesis that the distribution of $z_i - \mu$ is symmetric about zero, where μ is a location parameter, that is H_0: $F_i(z_i-\mu-\varepsilon) = 1-F_i(z_i-\mu+\varepsilon)$ for all ε. Such a hypothesis arises, for example, when z_1 is a difference score resulting from a paired comparison.

Confidence statements concerning μ may be based on the typical value theorem (Hartigan (1969)). Let $E = \{\xi_{(1)}, \xi_{(2)}, \ldots, \xi_{(2^N-1)}\}$ be the ordered set of all subsample means from $z_1, z_2, \ldots, z_N$, omitting the empty sample. Then the intervals $(-\infty, \xi_{(1)}), (\xi_{(1)}, \xi_{(2)}), \ldots, (\xi_{(2^N-1)}, \infty)$ each include the location parameter μ with equal probability, so a $1-2r/2^N$ C.I. for μ is $(\xi_{(r)}, \xi_{(2^N-r)})$. Enumerating the set of typical values E is done by the proposed algorithm (2), due to (4) and (5). Once the typical values are enumerated, intervals of any confidence level may be trivially derived.

The procedure was applied to Darwin's data on the differences in heights of matched pairs of cross-fertilized and self-fertilized plants. The differences in 15 pairs are, in eight's of an inch, 49, -67, 8, 16, 6, 23, 28, 41, 14, 29, 56, 24, 75, 60, -48. Selected confidence intervals for μ are (3.75, 38.14), (-.167, 41), (-9.5, 47) for confidence levels of 90%, 95%, and 99% respectively. The algorithm required 3.2 CPU seconds to execute on a CDC 6600 computer. When the first 10 observations were repeated, the execution time rose to 11.2 CPU seconds for the resulting sample of 25 observations.

Typical values for the shift parameter in the two-sample problem can also be found. Consider two samples $x_1, x_2, \ldots, x_m$ and $y_1, y_2, \ldots, y_n$ which, when combined, may be written $z_1, z_2, \ldots, z_N (N=m+n)$, where

$$z_i = \begin{cases} x_i & i=1,2,\ldots,m \\ y_{i-m} & i=m+1,\ldots,N. \end{cases}$$

Suppose that the probability law of the data is given by

$$\Pr(X_i \leq x) = F(x-\Delta) \quad i=1,2,\ldots,m$$
$$\Pr(Y_j \leq y) = F(y) \quad j=1,2,\ldots,n.$$

The parameter of interest is the location shift parameter Δ.

Let $X^\circ = \{x_1, x_2, \ldots, x_m\}$

$Y^\circ = \{y_1, y_2, \ldots, y_n\}$

$C(A)$ = # elements in the finite set A

$$D = \{d_{(j)};\ d_{(j)} = (\textstyle\sum_\alpha y_i - \sum_\beta x_i)/C(\alpha), \alpha \subseteq X^\circ, \beta \subseteq Y^\circ$$

such that $0 < C(\alpha) = C(\beta)$

$$d_{(1)} \leq d_{(2)} \leq d_{(3)} \leq \cdots \leq d_{({}_NC_m - 1)}\}.$$

Then each of the intervals

$$(-\infty, d_{(1)}), (d_{(1)}, d_{(2)}), (d_{(2)}, d_{(3)}), \ldots, (d_{(M-1)}, \infty)$$

where $M = {}_N C_m$ covers the shift parameter Δ with probability $1/M$.

The enumeration of the set D provides intervals of any confidence level. These intervals are related to the inversion of the two-sample permutation test. The elements of D may be thought of as convolutions of means of x's and y's. The proposed algorithm and the convolution theorem of Fourier analysis are used to enumerate D.

To illustrate the efficiency of the algorithm, data from Snedecor and Cochran (1967, p. 118) on the effect of sleep on the basal metabolism of 26 college women were analyzed. The measurements in calories per square meter per hour are:

7 or more hours of sleep: 35.3 35.9 37.2
33.0 31.9 33.7 36.0 35.0 33.3
33.6 37.9 35.6 29.0 33.7 35.7

6 or less hours of sleep: 32.5 34.0 34.4
31.8 35.0 34.6 33.5 33.6 31.5
33.8 34.6.

Selected confidence intervals for the shift parameter are (-2.114, .386), (-2.34, .650), (-2.814, 1.180) for confidence levels of 90%, 95%, and 99% respectively. The algorithm required 2.6 CPU seconds to execute on a CDC 6600 computer. When each observation was repeated, the execution time rose to 14.5 CPU seconds for the total sample of 52 observations.

Noether (1978) points out that the two-sample location shift interval can be used to provide a two-sample scale shift interval using a log transformation.

Rank-based Intervals

Confidence intervals based on the Wilcoxon rank-sum and signed rank statistics have been well known for over 20 years. Noether (1978) includes a general approach for converting tests based on linear rank statistics for the one- and two-sample problems into C.I.'s for the appropriate parameters. The calculation of the linear rank test differs from the more general permutation test on the observations in that, as the parameter value varies, the distribution of the test statistic remains fixed while the value of the test statistic varies discontinuously, since the rank scores are fixed. The algorithm (2) can be used to automate Noether's procedure by allowing the (fixed) distribution of the linear rank statistic to be machine calculated rather than relying on tables, so the Noether procedure can be programmed to compute confidence intervals with only the data as input. Such a program could accommodate any linear rank scores, sample sizes, and confidence levels. Since tabulated distributions are not required, this method also allows the original observations to be treated as a fixed set of rank scores for the purpose of computing C.I.'s. The rank procedure demands less computing time and much less storage than the permutation algorithms for interval estimation.

For a given two-sample linear rank test statistic T Noether's procedure obtains the function $T(\Delta)$, the value of the test statistic considered as a function of the shift parameter Δ. The critical value of $T(\Delta)$ for a given significance level is constant over Δ. Consider a stratified experiment of k blocks as in Section 5. Then if T_i is the test statistic for block i, the summary test statistic $T = T_1+T_2+\ldots+T_k$ can be described as a function of Δ by $T(\Delta) = T_1(\Delta)+T_2(\Delta)+\ldots+T_k(\Delta)$. Thus $T(\Delta)$ is a sum of k functions, each of which is easily obtained by Noether's procedure. The critical value of the summary test statistic is constant over Δ and may be obtained by the technique for stratified analyses given by Pagano and Tritchler (1980, Section 3.1). Thus, blocked experiments are easily accommodated.

Logistic Regression

The logistic regression model is a powerful tool for the analysis of discrete data. Due to properties of the exponential family of distributions, conditioning on sufficient statistics for nuisance parameters yields exact hypothesis tests for regression parameter values in the logistic framework (Cox (1970)). The conditional distributions for the exact test statistics for regression parameters may be calculated by the multivariate algorithm (8).

A special case of exact logistic regression is the method for the analysis of k 2 x 2 contingency tables given by Zelen (1971). In that case, the permutation distribution reduces to the hypergeometric. The use of the characteristic function representation for the distributions facilitates the calculation of districution of sums of random variables resulting from the combination of tables (Pagano and Tritchler (1980B)).

References

Cooley, J.W. and Tukey, J.W. (1965). An algorithm for machine calculation of complex Fourier series. Mathematical Computation, 19, 297-301.

Cox, D.R. (1970). The Analysis of Binary Data. Methuen, London.

Cox, D.R. (1972). Regression models and life-tables. Journal of the Royal Statistical Society, B34, 187-202.

Hartigan, J.A. (1969). Using subsample values as typical values. Journal of the American Statistical Association, 64, 1303-1317.

Hollander, M. and Wolfe, D.A. (1973). Nonparametric Statistical Methods. Wiley, New York.

Kempthorne, O. and Doerfler, T.E. (1969). The behavior of some significance tests under experimental randomization. Biometrika, 56, 231-248.

Lagakos, S.W. (1979). General right censoring and its impact on the analysis of survival data. Biometrics, 35, 139-156.

Maritz, J.S. (1979). A note on exact robust confidence intervals for location. Biometrika, 66, 163-166.

Noether, G.E. (1978). Distribution-free confidence intervals. Statistica Neerlandica, 32, 109-122.

Pagano, M. and Tritchler, D.L. (1980A). On obtaining permutation distributions in polynomial time. Technical Report 118Z, Department of Biostatistics, Sidney Farber Cancer Institute, Boston, MA.

Pagano, M. and Tritchler, D.L. (1980B). An algorithm for the analysis of several 2x2 contingency tables. Technical Report 89Z, Department of Biostatistics, Sidney Farber Cancer Institute, Boston, MA.

Pitman, E.J.G. (1937/38). Significance tests which may be applied to samples from any population. Journal of the Royal Statiscal Society, B4, 119-130, 225-237. Biometrika, 29, 322-335.

Singleton, R.C. (1969). Multivariate complex Fourier transform, computed in place using mixed-radix Fast Fourier Transform algorithm. Stanford Research Institute.

Snedecor, G.W. and Cochran, W.C. (1967). Statistical Methods, 6th edition. The Iowa State University Press, Ames.

Tritchler, D.L. (1980). On inverting permutation tests. Unpublished report.

Wilcoxon, F. (1945). Individual comparisons by ranking methods. Biometrics, 1, 80-83.

Zelen, M. (1971). The analysis of several 2x2 contingency tables. Biometrika, 58, 129-137.

ON THE USE OF LINEAR HARMONIC FORMS TO SIMULTANEOUSLY GENERALIZE CERTAIN STATISTICAL COMPUTATIONS

Michael E. Tarter, University of California, Berkeley

ABSTRACT

It is shown that a large class of statistical procedures can be implemented by computational methods based on linear combinations of sample trigonometric moments, i.e., linear harmonic forms. An estimator is presented which, as the number of terms of the harmonic form increases, approaches the Wilcoxon test statistic but which does not require the input of ranked data. It is shown that this estimator can be expressed as the sum of two statistics, the first of which is proportional to the difference between the means of the two samples used to compute either the conventional Wilcoxon or the new estimator. Both the new estimator and many other linear harmonic forms are shown to be easily generalizable to deal with densities conditioned by a concommitant variable.

It is shown that with the exception of the Gaussian case, the log likelihood function of any Pearson family location parameter can be expressed as a simple function of two linear harmonic forms. It is shown that linear harmonic forms can be used to compute a wide variety of scale parameter estimators.

A general theorem is presented which in a manner analogous to the Gauss-Markoff Theorem, yields equations (analogous to the normal equations) for the optimal estimation of linear harmonic forms.

Key words: Linear harmonic; Fourier series; Wilcoxon test; log likelihood function; scale parameter; Pearson family; Gauss-Markoff Theorem; nonparametric regression; smoothing.

1. INTRODUCTION

It usually goes without saying that there are many methods which can be used to implement individual estimators, e.g., the various computational formulas for the sample variance. However, it appears to be equally true that many diverse and distinct estimators can often utilize a single implementation procedure, i.e, algorithm. For example, by making use of Fourier series implementation a single computational strategy can be used to obtain a wide variety of options and displays, most of which are associated with a particular linear combination of sample trigonometric moments.

This paper will primarily illustrate and elaborate the following paradigm: Let $\{X_j\}$, $j=1,\ldots,n$, be an i.i.d. random sample with c.d.f. F. Define the k-th sample trigonometric moment as

$$\hat{B}_k = n^{-1} \sum_{j=1}^{n} \exp(-2\pi i k X_j) \ . \tag{1.1}$$

The finite sequence $\{\hat{B}_k\}$, $k=-m,-m+1,\ldots,m$, and its bivariate generalization, where $m << n$ can be used for almost all univariate and bivariate data analysis computations.

Ideally, the sequence $\{\hat{B}_k\}$ contains most of the statistical information within $\{X_j\}$. Notice that in classical statistics, for a given underlying model, the analog to $\hat{B}_k$ would consist of the minimal sufficient statistics. It will be demonstrated in later sections of this paper that for many exploratory data analysis applications the sequence $\{\hat{B}_k\}$ is much more convenient to work with than the original sample $\{X_j\}$.

A surprisingly large number of statistics can be expressed in terms of either series or finite linear combinations of coefficients $\hat{B}_k$. For example if all points of the sample $\{X_j\}$ from F are pretransformed to the open interval (1/4, 3/4), a common estimate of F's variance σ^2, i.e.,

$$n^{-1} \sum_{j=1}^{n} (X_j-\bar{X})^2 \tag{1.2}$$

equals

$$1/12 + \sum_{k\neq 0} (-1)^k \hat{B}_k \exp(2\pi i k\bar{X})/(2\pi^2 k^2) \ . \tag{1.3}$$

Note that expression (1.3) can be interpreted as a Fourier series expansion of a function evaluated at the sample mean $\bar{X}$ where coefficients are functionally related to the data through the $\hat{B}_k$. (The simplest way of obtaining expression (1.2) from expression (1.3) is to use Series 516 of Jolley (1962) taking note of the interval over which Series 516 is known to converge.)

The use of harmonic or Fourier series methods in data analysis is similar in many ways to the Parzen (1962) and Rosenblatt (1956) kernel methods of nonparametric estimation. In fact the author and Raman (1972) showed that weighted Fourier series density estimators [Watson (1969); Kronmal and Tarter (1967, 1968, 1970)] could, under fairly general conditions, be considered to be identical to kernel estimators and that for all most practical applications the two approaches could be treated as different means of expressing the same function. It should also be mentioned that K. Davis (1974), H. D. Brunk (1974, 1976) and W. H. Fellner (1974) have generalized the Fourier series approach by methods which include application of Fourier transforms and in essence removed the troublesome restriction of series procedures to estimation over a finite interval.

Because it is convenient in terms of exposition and computation to regard $\{\hat{B}_k\}$ as a sequence of m statistics, in this paper we will retain the series representation and henceforth make the simplifying assumption that the support of F is on the unit interval. In several sections we utilize results described by the author and Silvers covering applications to the bivariate case. In particular, we will make use of the following assumptions and relationships: Suppose $\{(X_j,Y_j)\}$, j=1,...n, represents a sample of bivarite data from an L_2 (see Edwards, 1967) density with support on the unit square. Let $B_{s,k}$ represent the s,k-th Fourier coefficient of the random variate (X,Y)'s density and $f(x_0)$ represent the non-zero marginal density of $X=x_0$. The conditional density of Y=y given x_0 can then be expressed as

$$g(y|x_0) = \sum_k B_k^{(x_0)} \exp(2\pi iky) \tag{1.4}$$

where

$$B_k^{(x_0)} = \sum_s B_{s,k} \exp(2\pi iksx_0)/f(x_0) . \tag{1.5}$$

The reason for including relations (1.4) and (1.5) in this introductory section is that together with variance expression (1.3) they can be used to illustrate four of the general principles underlying what is here referred to as the use of harmonic forms for data analysis and statistical implementation: 1) Perhaps most importantly, note that expression (1.5) is a linear function of $B_{s,k}$ for any fixed value of x_0. 2) The bivariate sample trigonometric moments,

$$\hat{B}_{s,k} = n^{-1} \sum_{j=1}^{n} \exp[-2\pi i(kY_j+sX_j)] \tag{1.6}$$

can be used to form estimates of each $B_k^{(x_0)}$ by substitution of $b_s \hat{B}_{s,k}$ for $B_{s,k}$ in expression (1.5) where weight b_s can be estimated by procedures described in Section 5 of this paper. 3) For any individual value of x_0 all n data points contribute to an estimate of $g(y|x_0)$ based on expression (1.6) no matter what their distance, in the x-direction, from x_0. 4) An estimate of $B_k^{(x_0)}$ can be substituted for $\hat{B}_k$ of variance expression (1.3) and yield an estimate of the variance of a Y variate for a given value of x, i.e., $\sigma^2_{Y|x}$. A generalization of Wilcoxon's test to multivariate data based on $B_k^{(x_0)}$ will be introduced in section 3. In Sections 2, 3 and 4 many diverse statistical operations will be considered in terms of estimated linear combinations of Fourier coefficients, B_k. Following this we will present a basic theorem for utilizing sequences of sample trigonometric moments of form (1.1) or (1.6) to estimate a linear combination of Fourier coefficients B_k.

2. LINEAR HARMONIC FORMS

The usefulness of harmonic implementation procedure stems from the wide variety of statistical operations that can be placed within a single computational framework. Specifically, distributional transformation and scale change, subcomponent isolation and editing, the estimation of conditionals and their moments, "age" adjustment and ridit transformation and a data grouping correction operation can all be performed using modifications of one basic algorithm. For example, consider the sequence of "modified trigonometric moments" $\{\tilde{B}_k\}$; $k=0,\underline{+}1,\underline{+}2,\ldots$, where for some double sequence of weights $\{w_{s,k}\}$

$$\tilde{B}_k = \sum_s w_{k,s} B_s \tag{2.1}$$

and

$$B_s = E[\exp(-2\pi isX)] \tag{2.2}$$

where X is a random variable with density f(x). If T is a one-to-one differentiable function such that X = T(Y), then as is well known, Y is a random variate from g(y), where $t \equiv T'$ and

$$g(y) = f[T(y)]t(y) . \tag{2.3}$$

If

$$g(y) = \sum_k \tilde{B}_k \exp(2\pi iky) \tag{2.4}$$

then we obtain the special case of (2.1) where

$$w_{k,s} = \int \exp[-2\pi i(kT^{-1}(x)-sx)]dx . \tag{2.5}$$

In the remainder of this section, estimators based on relations of form (2.1) will be referred to as "linear harmonic forms."

The computational option which we call PERTURB is an example of the use of a linear harmonic form. Consider that a scale change with fixed point 1/2 can be conceptualized as a special case of transformation T^{-1} where for a certain value of scale change constant, $\tilde{\sigma}$

$$T^{-1}(X) \equiv \tilde{\sigma}(x-1/2)+1/2. \tag{2.6}$$

By substituting expression (2.6) into (2.5) we can approximate a new density estimator $\tilde{f}$ obtained by slightly expanding or contracting the scale of the original sample, without the necessity of recomputing the original sample trigonometric moments $\hat{B}_k$. The computational procedure PERTURB provides one of several alternative checking procedures. Specifically, it is designed to help decide whether bumps or other observed distributional features have been induced by the original scaling process much in the way one would check on the effect the leftmost class interval beginning and rightmost class interval end points have on the construction of a conventional histogram. Due to the use of linear harmonic form (2.1), PERTURB is quite computationally efficient.

The particular sequence of $w_{k,s}$ which will be described now forms an important part of many of our subtroutines. This sequence can be treated as a combination of two processes. Gregor (1969), Kronmal (1964), Medgyessy (1954, 1961), Tarter and Raman (1972) used the univariate coefficient $\exp[2\pi^2k^2\lambda^2]$ and Tarter and Silvers (1975) used the bivariate coefficient $\exp[-2\pi^2\underline{k}'\Lambda\underline{k}]$ where $\underline{k} = (k_1,k_2)^t$ and Λ is a two-by-two matrix of elements λ_{11}, λ_{12}, λ_{21}, λ_{22} to change the second moment in the univariate case and the variance-covariance matrix in the case of a bivariate estimated density $\hat{f}$. Recent trials using the new options have indicated that this is a more general process than had once been suspected. Specifically, the use of weights $\exp[2\pi^2k^2\lambda^2]$ does not require the assumption that the original density is expressible as a superposition of normal frequencies as had previously been assumed (see Tarter, 1979b).

Now suppose one wishes to find a Fourier coefficient $\tilde{B}_k$ of a bivariate density f truncated within a finite box with edges parallel to and within the unit square where the s-th edge extends from ω_1 to Ω_1 in the x-direction and ω_2 to Ω_2 in the y-direction. Here,

$$\begin{aligned}\tilde{B}_{\underline{k}} &= \int_{\omega_1}^{\Omega_1}\int_{\omega_2}^{\Omega_2} f(x,y)\exp[2\pi i(k_1x+k_2y)]dxdy\\ &= \sum_{\underline{j}\neq\underline{k}} B_{\underline{j}} \prod_{u=1}^{2} \{(\exp[2\pi i(j_u-k_u)\Omega_u]\\ &\quad - \exp[2\pi i(j_u-k_u)\omega_u])/2\pi i(j_u-k_u)\}\\ &\quad + B_{\underline{k}} \prod_{s=1}^{2} (\Omega_s-\omega_s) \; . \qquad (2.7)\end{aligned}$$

Expression (2.7) is a linear harmonic form, i.e., a special case of expression (2.1). Even more importantly, the estimator formed by multiplying each B_k by $\exp[2\pi^2k^2\lambda^2]$ (or its bivariate equivalent) and then multiplying each $\tilde{B}_k$ by the reciprocal $\exp[-2\pi^2k^2\lambda^2]$ is also a linear harmonic form. Hence we can first use $\exp[2\pi^2k^2\lambda^2]$ to separate distributional subcomponents, then use a graphical display unit light pen to indicate values of ω and Ω to isolate a separated component and finally reverse the component separation process after the desired distributional subcomponent has been isolated. To implement this process computationally one needs only evaluate linear form (2.1). Tarter, et al. (1976) gave several examples of the use of this option for the analysis of cholesterol-tryglyceride data.

3. COMPUTATION AND GENERALIZATION OF THE WILCOXON TEST STATISTIC

From Section 3 of Kronmal and Tarter (1968) one finds that as integer $m\to\infty$, for any order statistic $x_{(j)}$, $j=1,\ldots,n$, associated with the i.i.d. sample $\{Xj\}$, $j=1,\ldots,n$; $\hat{F}_m(x_{(j)})$ will approach $(j-1/2)/n$ where

$$\hat{F}_m(z) = 1/2 + z-\bar{x} + \sum_{k\in M} \exp(2\pi ikz)\hat{B}_k/(2\pi ik) \qquad (3.1)$$

the set M contains all negative and positive integers between and including minus and plus m and of course $\bar{x} = n^{-1}\sum_{j=1}^{n} X_j$.

Now suppose one combines two i.i.d. samples $\{X_j^{(1)}\}$, $j=1,\ldots,n_1$ and $\{X_j^{(2)}\}$, $j=1,\ldots,n_2$. As defined by expression (1.1) the k-th sample trigonometric moment $B_k^{(1,2)}$, of this composite sample will equal

$$\hat{B}_k^{(1,2)} = [n_1\hat{B}_k^{(1)}+n_2\hat{B}_k^{(2)}]/(n_1+n_2) \qquad (3.2)$$

where $\hat{B}_k^{(1)}$ represents the k-th trigonometric moment associated with the first and $\hat{B}_k^{(2)}$ represents the k-th trigonometric moment associated with the second sample.

The conventional rank sum statistic T will then equal the limit as $m\to\infty$ of

$$\begin{aligned}T_m &= \sum_{j=1}^{n_1} [(n_1+n_2)\hat{F}_m(X_j^{(1)}) + 1/2]\\ &= n_1/2 + (n_1+n_2) \sum_{j=1}^{n_1} [1/2 + \bar{X}^{(1)}-\bar{X}^{(1,2)}\\ &\quad + \sum_{k\in M} \exp(2\pi ikX_j^{(1)})\hat{B}_k^{(1,2)}/(2\pi ik)]\end{aligned}$$

where $\bar{X}^{(1,2)}$ represents the mean of the composite sample, which of course, in terms of $\bar{X}^{(1)}$ and $\bar{X}^{(2)}$, (the means of the individual samples) equals $(n_1\bar{X}^{(1)}+n_2\bar{X}^{(2)})/(n_1+n_2)$. Furthermore,

$$\begin{aligned}T_m &= n_1/2 + n_1(n_1+n_2)/2 + n_1n_2(\bar{X}^{(1)}-\bar{X}^{(2)})\\ &\quad + n_1(n_1+n_2) \sum_{k\in M} \hat{B}_{-k}^{(1)}\hat{B}_k^{(1,2)}/(2\pi ik) \qquad (3.4)\end{aligned}$$

and thus after defining $\bar{T}$ as $n_1(n_1+n_2+1)/2$

$$\begin{aligned}T_m-\bar{T} &= n_1n_2(\bar{X}^{(1)}-\bar{X}^{(2)}) + n_1^2 \sum_{k\in M} \hat{B}_k^{(1)}\hat{B}_{-k}^{(1)}/(2\pi ik)\\ &\quad + n_1n_2 \sum_{k\in M} \hat{B}_k^{(2)}\hat{B}_{-k}^{(1)}/(2\pi ik) \; . \qquad (3.5)\end{aligned}$$

Coincidentally, as described in Hoel (1962, p. 334) under the null hypothesis of density identity, for large sample sizes "T can be approximated satisfactorily by the proper normal distribution". The proper normal distribution has mean and variance given by the formulas.

$$E(T) = n_1(n_1+n_2+1)/2 \qquad (3.6a)$$

$$\sigma_T^2 = n_1 n_2 (n_1+n_2+1)/12 \; . \qquad (3.6b)$$

Thus, if n_1, n_2 and m are large, the distribution of $(T-\overline{T})/\sigma_T$ will be approximated satisfactorily by the standard normal distribution.

Now note the following eight properties of $T-\overline{T}$ as defined by expression (3.5):

1) To compute $T-\overline{T}$ no data ranking is necessary.

2) In practice, reasonable term inclusion rules for the choice of set M will suggest that M contain $-k$ whenever k is a member of M. Hence the second term $n_1^2 \sum_{k\varepsilon M} \hat{B}_k^{(1)}\hat{B}_{-k}^{(1)}/(2\pi ik)$. of expression (3.5) can be set equal to zero.

3) Whenever n_1 is sufficiently large to allow $\overline{X}^{(1)}$ and $\hat{B}_k^{(1)}$; $k = \pm 1, \pm 2, \ldots, \pm m$ to be treated as constants, $T-\overline{T}+n_1n_2\overline{X}^{(2)}$ is a linear harmonic form where w_s of expression (2.1) equals $n_1n_2\hat{B}_{-s}^{(1)}/(2\pi is)$.

4) As n_2 increases the linear form $\Sigma\hat{B}_k^{(2)}\hat{B}_{-k}^{(1)}/(2\pi ik)$ will approach $\Sigma B_k^{(2)}B_{-k}^{(1)}/(2\pi ik)$ where $B_k^{(2)}$ and $B_{-k}^{(1)}$ represent respectively the k-th Fourier coefficients of the two densities f_1 and f_2 whose identity is to be gauged by the non-parametric test, i.e., $X_j^{(s)} \varepsilon f_s$, $j=1,\ldots,n_s$ for $s=1,2$. As described by Kronmal and Tarter (1968) for most densities encountered in applied statistics B_k will approach zero extremely rapidly as k increases. Hence the terms $B_k^{(2)}B_{-k}^{(1)}/(2\pi ik)$, the products of two components which themselves decrease rapidly and which, in addition, are divided by $(2\pi ik)$, will decrease extremely rapidly.

5) Expression (3.5) separates into two components the first of which is $n_1n_2(\overline{X}^{(1)}-\overline{X}^{(2)})$. Thus, the second component to some degree tends to measure distributional difference not attributable to difference between the means of f_1 and f_2.

6) By using expressions (1.5) and (1.6), a test of the identity between the two conditional densities $f_1(y|x)$ and $f_2(y|x)$ can be constructed where $\overline{X}^{(1)}$ and $\overline{X}^{(2)}$ of expression (3.5) can be evaluated by nonparametric regression procedures and expression (1.5) can be used to replace each $\hat{B}_k^{(2)}$ and $\hat{B}_k^{(1)}$ with its conditional counterpart.

In many applications one would like to graph a measure of the difference or distance between $f_1(y|x)$ and $f_2(y|x)$ against values of a concomitant variate x. For very large samples one can of course divide one's data into subsets on the basis of x, then compute separate t statistics for each subset and finally plot these t statistics against x. However, as described in section 1, the methods described in this paper allow all n_1 and n_2 data points to contribute to the overall estimator for any fixed value of x.

7) Following the notation used in Tarter and Marshall (1978), let $\hat{B}_k^{(j)} = \hat{c}_k^{(j)} + i\,\hat{s}_k^{(j)}$ for $j=1,2$, where $\hat{c}_k^{(j)}$ and $\hat{s}_k^{(j)}$ are real valued. Then if the inclusion of the index s within M implies that $-s$ is also contained in M,

$$\frac{T-\overline{T}}{n_1n_2} = (\overline{X}^{(1)}-\overline{X}^{(2)})+(1/\pi)\sum_{k\varepsilon M'}[\hat{c}_k^{(1)}\hat{s}_k^{(2)}-\hat{c}_k^{(2)}\hat{s}_k^{(1)}]/k$$

where M' is the set of all positive members of M.

8) All variances and covariances of $\hat{c}_k^{(u)}$ and $\hat{s}_\ell^{(u)}$ for u=1,2; and all integer values of k and ℓ can be computed using simple formulas presented by Tarter and Marshall (1978, p. 286). Hence, whenever n_1 is sufficiently large, the variance of linear harmonic form

$$T' = \sum_{k\varepsilon M'} [\hat{c}_k^{(1)}\hat{s}_k^{(2)}-\hat{c}_k^{(2)}\hat{s}_k^{(1)}]/k$$

can easily be computed in terms of the population coefficients $c_k^{(2)}$ and $s_k^{(2)}$, $k\varepsilon M'$ defined as the limit of $\hat{c}_k^{(2)}$ and $\hat{s}_k^{(2)}$ respectively as $n\to\infty$. Since $c_k^{(2)}$ and $s_k^{(2)}$, $k\varepsilon M'$ are very easy to evaluate for most common statistical distributions (see Kronmal and Tarter, 1968), this provides a convenient way to evaluate the variance of T' for commonly used densities.

4. THE HARMONIC ANALYSIS OF LIKELIHOOD FUNCTIONS

We will now demonstrate that many maximum likelihood estimators can be computed by means of linear harmonic forms. The formula for a constant times the sample standard deviation given by expression (1.3) will be shown to be a special case of a very large class of such maximum likelihood estimators.

Consider an i.i.d. sample $\{X_j\}$, $j=1,\ldots,n$; $X_j \sim f(x|\{\theta\})$ where $\{\theta\}$ is a set of parameters such that for any θ value, f has support on the unit interval and

$$\int_0^1 [\ln f(x|\{\theta\})]^2 \, dx < \infty \ . \tag{4.1}$$

Using basic relationships described in Edwards (1967) one can show that

$$L = \sum_{n=1}^{n} \ln f(X_j|\{\theta\})$$

$$= \lim_{m\to\infty} \sum_{j=1}^{n} \int_0^1 \delta_m(x-X_j) \ln f(x|\{\theta\})dx \tag{4.2}$$

for almost every x when

$$\delta_m(x) = \sum_{k=-m}^{m} \exp[2\pi ikx] \ . \tag{4.3}$$

Since n is infinite and

$$\exp[2\pi ik(x-X_j)] = \exp[2\pi ikx]\exp[-2\pi ikX_j)$$

one finds that

$$L = \lim_{m\to\infty} n \sum_{k=-m}^{m} \hat{B}_k w_k \tag{4.4}$$

where

$$w_k = \int_0^1 \exp[2\pi ikx]\ln[f(x|\{\theta\})]dx \tag{4.5}$$

Thus the likelihood function, before or after differentiation with respect to θ, estimates the limit as $m\to\infty$ of a linear harmonic form

$$\sum_{k=-m}^{m} B_k w_k \ . \tag{4.6}$$

The use of expression (4.4) has been investigated in terms of both theoretical and practical implications (see Tarter, 1975, 1979). We have found for example that the restriction of f's support to the unit interval does not prevent maximum likelihood estimators obtained by means of expression (4.4) from being identical to non-truncated estimators (provided that data is initially pretransformed to the unit interval). At the end of this section we will demonstrate this finding for the case of the sample variance of normal variates. However, several new general theoretical results will be presented first.

Suppose

$$f(x|\{0_k=B_k\}) = 1 + \sum_{\substack{k\neq 0 \\ -m}} B_k \exp[2\pi ikx] \tag{4.7}$$

If we set

$$\partial L/\partial 0_k = \int_0^1 [[(\Sigma \hat{B}_j \exp(2\pi ijx))]/[(\Sigma B_j \exp(2\pi ijx))]] \cdot \exp(2\pi ikx)dx \tag{4.8}$$

equal to zero for all values of k, then the uniqueness theorem of Fourier expansion [Edwards (1967)] implies that any maximum likelihood estimator of B_k is a constant times $\hat{B}_k$. However under the assumption that $\int_0^1 f(x)dx = 1$, then $E\hat{B}_k = B_k$ and thus $\hat{B}_k$ is an unbiased maximum likelihood estimator of B_k.

Now suppose each B_k is itself expressible as a function of S parameters $\{\lambda_s\}$, s=1,...,S. The chain rule implies

$$\frac{\partial L}{\partial \gamma_s} = \sum_k \frac{\partial L}{\partial B_k} \frac{\partial B_k}{\partial \gamma_s} \tag{4.9}$$

and therefore

$$\frac{\partial L}{\partial \gamma_s} = \int_0^1 \frac{\Sigma \hat{B}_v \exp[2\pi ivx]}{\Sigma B_v \exp[2\pi ivx]} \Sigma \frac{\delta B_v}{\delta \gamma_s} \exp[2\pi ivx]dx \tag{4.10}$$

Several types of densities allow one to greatly simplify the use of these new likelihood procedures. For example, suppose one wishes to estimate the location parameter of a variety of truncated Pearson family densities (see Elderton, 1953), defined by

$$\frac{f'(x-\theta)}{f(x-\theta)} = \frac{x\, I_{[0,1]}(x)}{(\beta x-\alpha_1)(\beta x-\alpha_2)} \tag{4.11}$$

where

$$I_{[0,1]}(x) = 1 \text{ for } 0 \leq x \leq 1$$

$$= 0 \text{ elsewhere} \ .$$

Here

$$\frac{\partial L}{\partial \theta} = \lim_{m\to\infty} \sum_{k=-m}^{m} \hat{B}_k \exp[2\pi ik\theta]\tilde{w}_k \tag{4.12}$$

where

$$\tilde{w}_k = \int_0^1 \frac{x \exp[2\pi ikx]}{(\beta x-\alpha_1)(\beta x-\alpha_2)} dx \ .$$

If $\beta\neq 0$, (4.12) implies that a likelihood equation solution must approach a solution of the equality

$$\alpha_1 \sum_{k=-m}^{m} \tilde{w}_{1k} \hat{B}_k \exp[2\pi ik\theta] \tag{4.13}$$

equals

$$\alpha_2 \sum_{k=-m}^{m} \tilde{w}_{2k} \hat{B}_k \exp[2\pi ik\theta]$$

as $m\to\infty$ where

$$\tilde{w}_{vk} = \int_0^1 \frac{\exp[2\pi ikx]}{\beta x-\alpha_v}\, dx$$

$$= [\cos 2\pi k\alpha_v/\beta + i \sin 2\pi k\alpha_v/\beta]*\{[Ci(2\pi k(\beta-\alpha_v)/\beta)$$

$$+ i\ Si(2\pi k(\beta-\alpha_v)/\beta)]$$

$$- [Ci(-2\pi k\alpha_v/\beta) + i\ Si(-2\pi k\alpha_v/\beta)]\}/\beta \qquad (4.15)$$

v=1,2 and Ci and Si are the cosine and sine integrals, respectively (Abromowitz and Stegum, 1964).

If $\beta=0$, which would imply in the non-truncated case that f has a normal distribution, then

$$\tilde{w}_k = C(-1)^k/(2\pi ik) \qquad (4.16)$$

where the constant C plays no role in the likelihood estimation process when expression (4.12) is set equal to zero. Applications of expressions (4.16) and (4.12) for nonparametric regression purposes will be demonstrated separately. We will now consider the use of harmonic likelihood techniques to obtain an estimator of a scale parameter.

Let

$$f(x|\theta_1,\theta_2) = (2\theta_2)^{-1}\exp[-|x-\theta_1-1/2|/\theta_2]I_{[0,1]}(x). \qquad (4.17)$$

Here

$$\ln L = n[-\ln\theta_2-\ln 2-\theta_2^{-1}/4] - n \sum_{k\neq 0} \frac{\hat{B}_k[(-1)^k-1]\theta_2^{-1}}{2\pi^2 k^2}$$

$$\cdot \exp[2\pi ik(\theta_k+1/2)] , \qquad (4.18)$$

and thus the likelihood estimator $\hat{\theta}_2$

$$= 1/4 + \sum_{k\neq 0} \hat{B}_k[(-1)^k-1]\exp(2\pi ik(\theta_1+1/2))/(2\pi^2k^2)$$

which if all data points X_j satisfy the inequality $1/4 < X_j < 3/4$,

$$= 1/4 -2(\pi^2 n)^{-1}\sum\sum \frac{\cos 2\pi(2k-1)(\tilde{x}-X_j)}{k^2} \cdot$$

$$= 1/4 -2(\pi^2 n)^{-1} \sum_{j=1}^{n} \frac{\pi}{8} [\pi-4\pi|\tilde{x}-X_j|]$$

$$= n^{-1} \sum_{j=1}^{n} |\tilde{x}-X_j| \quad , \qquad (4.20)$$

where $\tilde{x}$, as can be shown by methods similar to those used here, is the sample median. Thus, as long as all sample values are transformed to within the appropriate interval, the computation of both the sample variance (see expression (1.3), whose derivation is almost identical to the above) and absolute deviation can be based on a linear harmonic form.

5. A GENERAL THEOREM FOR HARMONIC DATA ANALYSIS

Up to this point emphasis has been placed on the uses of specific linear harmonic forms. This section will concern the general question of how one can choose the best linear function of $\hat{B}_k$ to estimate any linear combination of population Fourier coefficients B_k. Early work on a related topic included the following results: (1) Under the usual mean integrated square error, MISE, criterion, an integral of the optimal density estimator, based on $\hat{B}_k$, is an optimal estimator of the population cumulative [Kronmal and Tarter (1978)]. (2) If one sets out to estimate a function

$$g(x) = \sum w_k B_k \exp[2\pi ikx] \qquad (5.1)$$

by means of an estimator

$$\hat{g}(x) = \sum_{k\in M} w_k \hat{B}_k \exp[2\pi ikx] \qquad (5.2)$$

then the same set M will optimize the MISE fit of g to $\hat{g}$ for all sequences of w_k containing nonzero elements [Tarter and Raman (1972)]. This enables one to change the variance or covariance of a display by multiplying each $\hat{B}_k$ by a weight $\exp[2\pi^2k^2\lambda^2]$ without readjusting the basic underlying estimator.

In this section we will consider a very general result involving linear harmonic forms expressible as

$$\tilde{g} = \int_{R^p} g(\underline{x})\hat{f}(\underline{x})d\underline{x} \qquad (5.3)$$

where for uniformly convergent

$$\hat{f}(\underline{x}) = \sum_{\underline{k}} b_{\underline{k}}\hat{B}_{\underline{k}} \exp(2\pi i\underline{k}^t\underline{x}) \qquad (5.4)$$

$$\hat{B}_{\underline{k}} = n^{-1} \sum_{j=1}^{n} \exp(-2\pi i\underline{k}^t\underline{X}_j) \qquad (5.5)$$

$\{X_j\}$, j=1,...,n, is an i.i.d. sample of p-variate vectors from a density f whose support is on the unit hypercube R^p where it has a uniformly convergent Fourier expansion, $\underline{k}$ represents a row vector of integers and $\underline{k}^t$, its transpose. Here g will be defined as an arbitrary L_2 function such that $g(\underline{x})f(\underline{x})$ is continuous within R^p. In almost all applications, the weight w_s of expression (2.1) will equal the s-th Fourier coefficient of g.

For ease of notation define the vector of coefficients

$$\hat{\underline{b}} = (b_{k_1}, b_{k_2}, \ldots)^t ,$$

where $(k_1, k_2, \ldots)$ is an arbitrary ordering of the indices of summation k of (5.4). Then one can show that the value of b which minimizes mean square error

$$E[\tilde{g}-E(\tilde{g})]^2 \tag{5.6}$$

can be expressed as

$$C\,\hat{\underline{b}} = n\,c \tag{5.7}$$

where the s-th element of c equals

$$B_{\underline{s}} \sum_{\underline{k}} \overline{B}_{\underline{k}} \int_{R^p} g(\underline{x}) \exp[-2\pi i \underline{k}^t \underline{x}] d\underline{x} \tag{5.8}$$

and the (k,s)-th element of C equals

$$(B_{\underline{s-k}} + (n-1) B_{\underline{s}} \overline{B}_{\underline{k}}) \int_{R^p} g(\underline{x}) \exp[-2\pi i \underline{k}^t \underline{x}] d\underline{x}. \tag{5.9}$$

Proof: The assumed uniform convergence of the Fourier series of f and $\hat{f}$ together with the assumption that $g(\underline{x})f(\underline{x})$ is continuous and hence bounded within R^p assure that

$$E[\tilde{g}-E(\tilde{g})]^2 = E\left|\sum_{\underline{k}} (b_{\underline{k}}\hat{B}_{\underline{k}} - B_{\underline{k}}) \int_{R^p} g(\underline{x}) \exp[2\pi i \underline{k}^t \underline{x}] d\underline{x}\right|^2 . \tag{5.10}$$

Now

$$H \equiv E\left|\sum_{\underline{k}} (b_{\underline{k}}\hat{B}_{\underline{k}} - B_{\underline{k}}) \int_{R^p} g(\underline{x}) \exp[2\pi i \underline{k}^t \underline{x}] d\underline{x}\right|^2 \tag{5.11}$$

when considered as a function of a given $b_{\underline{k}}$, say $b_{\underline{k}_0}$, and $\{X_j\}$, j=1,...,n, satisfies the assumption of Leibnitz's rule (see Taylor, 1955, p. 523). Hence,

$$\frac{\partial E[\tilde{g}-E(\tilde{g})]^2}{\partial b_{\underline{k}_0}} = 2E\Big([\hat{B}_{\underline{k}_0} \int_{R^p} g(\underline{x}) \exp[2\pi i \underline{k}_0^t \underline{x}] d\underline{x}$$

$$\cdot \overline{\sum_{\underline{k}} (b_{\underline{k}}\hat{B}_{\underline{k}} - B_{\underline{k}}) \int_{R^p} g(\underline{x}) \exp[2\pi i \underline{k}^t \underline{x}] d\underline{x}}\Big) \tag{5.12}$$

which from the assumptions of uniform convergence equals

$$2 \int_{R^p} \exp[2\pi i \underline{k}_0^t \underline{x}] d\underline{x} \sum_{\underline{k}} (b_{\underline{k}} E[\hat{B}_{\underline{k}_0} \overline{\hat{B}_{\underline{k}}}] - B_{\underline{k}_0} \overline{B}_{\underline{k}})$$

$$\int_{R^p} g(\underline{x}) \exp[-2\pi i \underline{k}^t \underline{x}] d\underline{x}. \tag{5.13}$$

Since the author and Kronmal (1970) showed that

$$E\,\hat{B}_{\underline{k}_0} \overline{\hat{B}_{\underline{k}}} = n^{-1}[B_{\underline{k}_0-\underline{k}} - B_{\underline{k}_0} \overline{B}_{\underline{k}}] + B_{\underline{k}_0} \overline{B}_{\underline{k}}$$

$$= n^{-1} B_{\underline{k}_0-\underline{k}} + (n-1) B_{\underline{k}_0} \overline{B}_{\underline{k}}/n \tag{5.14}$$

one obtains expression (5.7) by setting (5.13) equal to zero for all $\underline{k}$ and substituting (5.14) into the resulting equations.

This theorem shows that it is not only computationally but also statistical convenient (as far as optimal data usage is concerned) to express certain data analytic procedures in terms of linear harmonic forms.

6. THE SMOOTHING, COMPONENT SEPARATION HIERARCY

Mathematicians, statisticians, physicists and engineers have accumulated a large body of practical experience with the idiosyncrasies of harmonic methods. One by-product of the work done by Dirichlet, Fejer and their contemporaries concerning the convergence of Fourier series has been the development of highly sophisticated filtering and smoothing techniques. One way of conceptualizing the Fourier series approaches to density estimation is to regard these procedures as "ways to do translation-invariant smoothing" (see J. Tukey's published discussion of Kronmal, Tarter, 1974, p. 398). In this section we will illustrate techniques for control of the smoothing process by use of certain linear harmonic forms.

Our earliest attempt to systematically control the smoothing process was based on the use of Fejer partial summation. As described in Lanzos (1961, p. 209-11), consider an unweighted truncated Fourier series with coefficients c_k, s_k; k=0,...,m. $f_m(z) = 1/2\, c_0 + c_1 \cos x + \ldots + c_m \cos mx + s_1 \sin x + \ldots + s_m \sin mx$, where $f_m(x) \to f(x)$ as $m \to \infty$. Truncated series f_m can be expressed as

$$f_m(x) = \int_{-\pi}^{\pi} f(x)\delta_m(x-t)dt \tag{6.1}$$

where $\delta_m(x)$ "is the so-called Dirichlet kernel"

$$\delta_m(z) = \frac{\sin(m + 1/2)z}{2\pi \sin(z/2)} . \tag{6.2}$$

If instead of (6.2) we utilize Fejer kernel

$$\tilde{\delta}_m(z) = \frac{\sin^2(mz/2)}{2\pi m \sin^2(z/2)} \tag{6.3}$$

we find that "this kernel possesses the strong focusing properties expressed by

$$\lim_{m\to\infty} \int_{\varepsilon}^{\pi} |\tilde{\delta}_m(z)|dz = 0 \quad \text{and} \quad \lim_{m\to\infty} \int_{-\varepsilon}^{\varepsilon} |\tilde{\delta}_m(z)|dz = 1$$

where "ε is a prescribed arbitrary small positive number, independent of [m]."

As discussed by Kronmal and Tarter (1968) and illustrated in Tarter and Kronmal (1976), Section 5, a Fejer weighting system does tend to smooth a harmonic estimator. The implementation of the Fejer kernal method is extremely easy since one need only multiply the k-th term, where k is the subscript of c or s by $b_k = [1-k/(m+1)]$.

Probably due to the fact that m of $[1-k/(m+1)]$ takes on integer values, we have found that the Fejer process does not usually possess the potential for fine tuning necessary in many applications. We have, however, designed the univariate option FEJERIZE which estimates a value of the constant m by a hueristic measure of display smoothness.

We were greatly helped in our search for a more refined method to display smoothing by the realization that smoothing is the conceptual opposite of density component separation. Specifically, if we choose variance "reducing" constants λ_{11} and λ_{22} or for the univariate case, λ^2 of $\exp[2\pi^2k^2\lambda^2]$, to be negative rather than positive values, we will in effect tend to increase rather than decrease the overlap between separate components. Once we removed the checks in our programs which had restricted λ to take on positive values, we were able to conduct trials with the new method.

Ironically we had already designed a univariate option called REDUCE which used the $b_k = \exp[2\pi^2k^2\lambda^2]$ weights to automatically reduce the variance of an estimator in order to compensate for the variance inflating effects of various Parzen-Rosenblatt kernel choices. Let $\hat{f}$ represent an estimator of f based on a kernel $\delta(z) = \Sigma b_k \exp[2\pi ikz]$ where f and δ satisfy certain general conditions described in detail by the author and Raman (1972). Specifically

$$\hat{f}(x) = n^{-1} \sum_{j=1}^{n} \delta(x-Xj) . \qquad (6.5)$$

Then

$$\mu'_k - E \int_0^1 x^k \hat{f}(x)dx$$

$$= \sum_{j\neq 0} (1-b_j)B_j \left[\frac{1}{2\pi ij}\right.$$

$$\left. + \sum_{s=1}^{k-1} (-1)^s k!(2\pi ij)^{-(s+1)}/(k-s)!\right] \qquad (6.6)$$

where μ'_k represents the k-th moment of f about the origin and

$$\hat{f}(x) = n-1 \sum_{j=1}^{n} \delta(x-X_j) = \sum_s b_s \hat{B}_s \exp[2\pi isx]. \qquad (6.7)$$

Thus the linear harmonic form

$$\sum_{j\neq 0} (1-b_j)\hat{B}_j\left[\frac{1}{2\pi ij} + \sum_{s=1}^{k-1} (-1)^s k!(2\pi ij)^{-(s+1)}/(k-s)!\right] \qquad (6.8)$$

is an unbiased estimator of the difference between the moment of a density and the corresponding moment of its estimator $\hat{f}$.

The option REDUCE simply uses expression (6.8) where k=2, to estimate the amount of desired variance reduction, and the weight $b_j = \exp[2\pi^2j^2\lambda^2]$ to implement this reduction. The question of the limitations of REDUCE will be described elsewhere.

7. ACKNOWLEDGEMENTS

This research was supported by National Cancer Institute Grant No. 1 R01 CA28142-01A1 and National Institute of General Medical Sciences Grant No. 1 R01 GM25386-03. The author would like to thank Mr. Bill Freeman and Ms. Seemin Qayum for their technical assistance and Bonnie Hutchings for her typing services.

REFERENCES

Abramowitz, M. and Stegun, I.A., eds. (1964), Handbook of Mathematical Functions with Formulas, Graphs and Mathematical Tables, Applied Mathematics Series 55, National Bureau of Standards, U.S. Government Printing Office, Washington, D.C.

Brunk, H.D. (1976), "Univariate Density Estimation by Orthogonal Series," Technical Report No. 51, Dept. of Statistics, Oregon State University, Corvallis, Oregon.

Brunk, H. D. and Pierce, D.A. (1974), "Estimation of Discrete Multivariate Densities for Computer-aided Differential Diagnosis of Disease," Biometrika, 61, 493-499.

Davis, K.B. (1974), "Fourier Integral Estimates for Probability Density Functions," Ph.D. Dissertation, Dept. of Biostatistics, University of Washington.

Edwards, R.E. (1967), Fourier Series, A Modern Introduction, Vol. I, New York: Holt, Rinehart and Winston, Inc.

Fellner, W. H. (1974), "Heuristic Estimation of Probability Densities," Biometrika, 61, 485-492.

Gregor, J. (1969), "An Algorithm for the Decomposition of a Distribution Into Gaussian Componets, " Biometrics, 25, 79-93.

Hoel, P.G. (1962), Introduction to Mathematical Statistics, 3rd ed., New York: Wiley.

Jolley, L.B.W. (1961), Summation of Series, 2nd ed., New York: Dover Publications, Inc.

Kronmal, R.A. (1964), "The Estimation of Probability Densities," unpublished doctoral dissertation, Department of Public Health, University of California, Los Angeles.

Kronmal, R.A. and Tarter, M.E. (1968), "The Estimation of Probability Density and Cumulatives by Fourier Series Methods," Journal of the American Statistical Association, 63, 925-952.

Kronmal, R.A. and Tarter, M.E. (1974), "The Use of Density Estimates Based on Orthogonal Expansions," in Dixon, W. and Nicholson, W. L., eds., Exploring Data Analysis: The Computer Revolution in Statistics, Los Angeles: University of California Press.

Medgyessy, P. (1954), "Some Recent Results Concerning the Decomposition of Compound Probability Distributions," MTA Alk Mat. Int. Kozl III, 155-69.

Medgyessy, P. (1961), Decomposition of Superpositions of Distribution Functions, Budapest: Publishing House of the Hungarian Academy of Science.

Parzen, E. (1962), "On Estimation of a Probability Density Function and Mode," Annals of Mathematical Statistics 33, 1065-1076.

Rosenblatt, M. (1956), "Remarks on Some Nonparametric Estimates of a Density Function," Annals of Mathematical Statistics, 27, 832-837.

Tarter, M.E. (1975), "A Method for Maximum Likelihood Parameter Estimation Based Upon a Reduced Data File," Proceedings of the Conference on Computer Graphics, Pattern Recognition and Data Structure, Institute of Electrical and Electronics Engineers, IEEE Catalogue No. 75CH0981-1C, 249-252.

Tarter, M.E. (1979a), "Trigonmetric Likelihood Estimation and Application to the Analysis of Incomplete Survival Information" Journal of the American Statistical Association, 74 132-139.

Tarter, M.E. (1979b), "Biocomputational Methodology an Adjunct to Theory and Applications," Biometrics, 35, 9-24.

Tarter, M.E. (1970), "On Multivariate Density Estimates Based On Orthogonal Expansions," Annals of Mathematical Statistics, 41, 718-722.

Tarter, M.E. (1976), "An Introduction to the Implementation and Theory of Nonparametric Density estimation," The American Statistican, 3, 105-112.

Tarter, M.E. and Marshall, J.S. (1978), "A New Nonparametric Procedure Designed for Simulation Studies," Comm. Statist. B7(3), 283-293.

Tarter, M.E., Marshall, J.S., Lum, S.B., Rigsbee, E.O., and Wong, J.T. (1976), "Interactive Editing of Biomedical Data," Computer Programs in Biomedicine, 6, 117-123.

Watson, Geoffrey (1969), "Density Estimation by Orthogonal Series," Annals of Mathematical Statistics, 40, 1496-1498.

QUANTILES, PARAMETRIC-SELECT DENSITY ESTIMATION, AND BI-INFORMATION PARAMETER ESTIMATORS*

Emanuel Parzen, Texas A&M University

ABSTRACT This paper describes the FUN.STAT approach to statistical data science; it combines (1) density-quantile function signatures of distributions, (2) entropy and information measures, and (3) functional statistical inference. In functional inference problems the parameters to be estimated are density functions. Exponential models and autoregressive models are approximating densities which can be justified as maximum entropy for respectively the entropy of a probability density and the entropy of a quantile density. It is proposed that bi-information estimation of a density function can be developed by analogy to the problem of identification of regression models.

KEY WORDS Statistical data science, functional inference, information divergence of index α, bi-information, comparison distribution functions, density estimation.

1. FUN.STAT Approach to Statistical Data Science

This paper reports on our research program in statistical data science which is attempting to convey to conventional statistical problems (both parametric and non-parametric) the viewpoints characteristic of signal processing and time series analysis. To describe and detect phenomena of interest one seeks "signatures" which distinguish them. Various functions and indices in the quantile domain are introduced to provide signatures of statistical distributions.

A quantile based approach to statistical science can be developed to reach conclusions by comparing graphs rather than numbers, and is thus teachable to introductory students without advanced mathematics. On the other hand, advanced math is needed by statisticians to develop the theory, and to enjoy its features of elegance and rigor. One should question the long range vitality of the discipline of statistics when many statisticians claim they do not need to know much theory to do "real" statistics.

We propose the name FUN.STAT for the approach to statistical data science that our research program is attempting to develop. The FUN.STAT domain of statistical data model identification and parameter estimation combines (1) density-quantile function signatures of distributions, (2) entropy and information measures, and (3) functional statistical inference.

Quantile and density-quantile functions provide a world that is dual to distribution functions and isomorphic with spectral density functions.

Information and entropy permit us to form two or more estimators for the parameters of a model by using different information divergence criteria. The fit of a model can be tested by comparing different estimators, preferably by comparing a measure of entropy estimated using different parameter estimators.

Functional inference is our name for the concept of "abstract inference" formulated by Grenander. The word "functional" is used with three interpretations: (a) functional = useful; (b) functional = functional analysis as one applies techniques of numerical analysis, solutions of linear equations, and approximation theory; (c) functional = estimation of functions, and fitting curves and surfaces to a discrete grid of points.

FUN.STAT connotes the name of a library of computer programs for statistical data analysis whose output provides both graphs of functions and numerical diagnostics of the fit and complexity of the functions. FUN.STAT is an approach to statistical graphics which argues that a graph should be a picture of a function which is a signature of a probability model. We currently have available computer packages ONESAM, TWOSAM, and BISAM.

2. Functions that describe probability distributions

The probability law of a continuous random variable X has traditionally been described by the distribution function $F(x) = \Pr[X \le x]$, and the probability density function $f(x) = F'(x)$.

Quantile domain signatures of probability distributions are:

(1) Quantile Function $Q(u) = F^{-1}(u)$

$= \inf \{x\colon F(x) \ge u\}$

$= \inf \{x\colon F(x) = u\}$ if F is continuous

$= x$ such that $F(x) = u$ if F increasing at x

(2) Quantile-Density Function $q(u) = Q'(u)$

(3) Density-Quantile Function $fQ(u) = f(Q(u))$

Theorem: For F continuous $FQ(u) = u$, $fQ(u)\, q(u) = 1$.

The quantile function permits normalizations for easy display and comparison of the sample quantile function of data. We call

$$IQ(u) = \frac{Q(u)-Q(0.5)}{2\{Q(.75)-Q(.25)\}}$$

the "informative quantile" function. We call

$$Q_1(u) = fQ(.5)Q(u)$$

the "unitized quantile" function.

3. Raw functions that describe samples

Data $X_1,\ldots,X_n$ is called a random sample of X when $X_1,\ldots,X_n$ are independent random variables identically distributed as X. An important role in the analysis of a sample is played by the order statistics $X_{(1)} < X_{(2)} < \ldots < X_{(n)}$

(1) Sample Distribution

$\tilde{F}(x) = \frac{j}{n}$, $X_{(j)} \le x < X_{(j+1)}$

*Research supported by the U.S. Army Research Office Grant DAAG 29-80-C-0070.

(2) Sample Probability Density, or Histogram, estimates $f(x)$ by a numerical derivative

$$\tilde{f}(x) = \frac{\tilde{F}(x+h) - \tilde{F}(x-h)}{2h}$$

(3) Sample Quantile $\tilde{Q}(u) = \tilde{F}^{-1}(u)$

$$= X_{(j)}, \frac{j-1}{n} < u \leq \frac{j}{n}$$

A universal display of any data set is provided by the quantile box plot, introduced in Parzen (1979), computed for the informative quantile function. A sample quantile-density is a numerical derivative (for some h>0)

$$\tilde{q}(u) = \{\tilde{Q}(u+h) - \tilde{Q}(u-h)\}/2h.$$

A sample density-quantile is defined by $\tilde{f}\tilde{Q}(u) = 1/\tilde{q}(u)$. An important formula is

$$\tilde{f}(X_{(j)}) = \tilde{f}\tilde{Q}(\frac{j}{n+1}) = 2\{(n+1)(X_{(j+1)}-X_{(j-1)})\}^{-1}$$

4. Smooth functions that describe samples and estimate probability distributions

The functions F, f, Q, q, fQ that represent the true probability distribution of a random variable X are estimated by smooth functions $\hat{F}$, $\hat{f}$, $\hat{Q}$, $\hat{q}$, $\hat{f}\hat{Q}$ which are derived from the raw descriptive functions $\tilde{F}$, $\tilde{f}$, $\tilde{Q}$, $\tilde{q}$, $\tilde{f}\tilde{Q}$. One distinguishes between parametric and non-parametric methods of estimating smooth functions.

A parametric estimation method: (1) assumes a family F_θ, f_θ, Q_θ, q_θ, $f_\theta Q_\theta$ of functions, called parametric models, which are indexed by a parameter $\theta = (\theta_1,\ldots,\theta_k)$; (2) forms estimators $\hat{\theta} = (\hat{\theta}_1,\ldots,\hat{\theta}_k)$ of θ; (3) forms smooth functions by

$$\hat{F}(x) = F_{\hat{\theta}}(x),\ \hat{f}(x) = f_{\hat{\theta}}(x),$$

$$\hat{Q}(u) = Q_{\hat{\theta}}(u),\ \hat{q}(u) = q_{\hat{\theta}}(u),$$

$$\hat{f}\hat{Q}(u) = f_{\hat{\theta}}Q_{\hat{\theta}}(u).$$

A non-parametric estimation method forms estimators which are not based on parametric models. Important examples of non-parametric estimators of a probability density $f(x)$ and a quantile-density $q(u)$ are respectively

$$\hat{f}(x) = \frac{1}{\delta}\int_{-\infty}^{\infty} K(\frac{x-y}{\delta})\, d\tilde{F}(y)$$

$$\hat{q}(u) = \frac{1}{\delta}\int_{0}^{1} K(\frac{u-t}{\delta})\, d\tilde{Q}(t)$$

for suitable kernels $K(\cdot)$ and bandwidth δ.

5. Parameter estimation and information divergence

When a parametric model f_θ is assumed, parameter estimators $\hat{\theta}$ are often determined by minimizing a "distance" between $\tilde{f}(x)$ and $f_\theta(x)$. A "distance" between two probability densities $f(x)$ and $g(x)$ is denoted $I(f;g)$ and is called an information divergence between $f(x)$ and $g(x)$. It is usually not symmetric in f and g. It does not satisfy the triangle inequality for a metric. But it does satisfy $I(f;g) > 0$ and $I(f;g) = 0$ if and only if $f = g$.

The most famous, and most important, definition of information divergence is

$$I_1(f;g) = \int_{-\infty}^{\infty} -\log\{\frac{g(x)}{f(x)}\}\, f(x)\, dx$$

called the information divergence of order 1, or Kullback-Liebler information divergence. Information divergence of order α is defined for $\alpha>0$ (but $\alpha \neq 1$) by

$$I_\alpha(f;g) = \frac{-1}{1-\alpha}\log\int_{-\infty}^{\infty}\{\frac{g(x)}{g(x)}\}^{1-\alpha} f(x)\, dx.$$

The most important values of α are $0.5 \leq \alpha \leq 2$.

Bi-information divergence is defined by

$$II(f;g) = \int_{-\infty}^{\infty}\left|\log\{\frac{g(x)}{f(x)}\}\right|^2 f(x)\, dx;$$

it may be regarded as related to $I_2(g;f)$.

Information divergence of order 1 has an important decomposition

$$I_1(f;g) = H(f;g) - H(f)$$

defining

$$H(f;g) = \int_{-\infty}^{\infty}\{-\log g(x)\}\, f(x)\, dx,$$

$$H(f) = H(f;f) = \int_{-\infty}^{\infty}\{-\log f(x)\}\, f(x)\, dx.$$

We call $H(f;g)$ the cross-entropy of f and g, and call $H(f)$ the entropy of f.

Maximum likelihood parameter estimation can be shown to be equivalent to minimum cross-entropy estimation. The likelihood function of a parametric model f_θ is defined by

$$L(f_\theta) = \log f_\theta(X_1,\ldots,X_n)$$

$$= \sum_{t=1}^{n} \log f_\theta(X_t)$$

One may verify that

$$L(f_\theta) = n\int_{-\infty}^{\infty} \log f_\theta(x)\, d\tilde{F}(x)$$

$$= -n\, H(\tilde{f};\, f_\theta).$$

The maximum likelihood parameter estimator $\hat{\theta}$, defined by

$$L(f_{\hat{\theta}}) = \max_\theta L(f_\theta),$$

clearly satisfies

$$H(\tilde{f};f_{\hat{\theta}}) = \min_\theta H(\tilde{f};f_\theta).$$

It also satisfies

$$I_1(\tilde{f};f_{\hat{\theta}}) = \min_\theta I_1(\tilde{f};f_\theta).$$

In general parameter estimators $\hat{\theta}$ are found by minimizing $I_\alpha(\tilde{f};f_\theta)$ or $I_\alpha(f_\theta;\tilde{f})$. Chi-squared estimators minimize $I_2(f_\theta;\tilde{f})$ while modified chi-squared estimators minimize $I_2(\tilde{f};f_\theta)$.

To compute $I_1(f;f_\theta)$ one needs to compute $H(f)$. A useful formula for accomplishing this is

$$H(f) = \int_{-\infty}^{\infty}\{-\log f(x)\}\, dF(x)$$

$$= \int_0^1 \{-\log fQ(u)\}\, du$$

$$= \int_0^1 \log q(u)\, du.$$

The value of $I_1(f;f_{\hat{\theta}})$ can be used to test the goodness of fit of the parametric model f_θ.

6. Information and bi-information parameter estimation, and comparison distribution functions

Given a sample with sample probability density function $\tilde{f}$ and parametric model f_θ, one can form diverse parameter estimators, denoted $\hat{\theta}$ and $\check{\theta}$, corresponding to two choices of information divergence which we take to be: (1) $I_1(\tilde{f};f_\theta)$, and (2) $I_2(f_\theta;\tilde{f})$ or $II(\tilde{f};f_\theta)$. We call $\hat{\theta}$ and $\check{\theta}$ diverse parameter estimators. For greater precision we call $\hat{\theta}$ the (order 1) information estimator, and $\check{\theta}$ the bi-information estimator.

When the parametric model f_θ is exact, the diverse parameter estimators have equivalent statistical properties; they are both asymptotically efficient estimators, and are not significantly different from each other.

When the values of $\hat{\theta}$ and $\check{\theta}$ computed from a sample are significantly different one should suspect that the parametric model f_θ does not fit the data. The Shapiro-Wilk statistics for testing normality and exponentiality can be regarded as comparing diverse estimators which minimize information of order 1 and 2 respectively.

One can interpret $\hat{\theta}$ and $\check{\theta}$ as parameter values of "best approximating" models.

One wishes to evaluate $F_{\hat{\theta}}(x)$ and $F_{\check{\theta}}(x)$ as smooth estimators of $F(x)$. For any parameter value θ, define

$$\tilde{D}_\theta(u) = F_\theta(\tilde{Q}(u))$$

which is the sample quantile function of the transformed random variables

$$U_1 = F_\theta(X_1),\ldots,U_n = F_\theta(X_n).$$

The true parameter value θ has the property that $U_1,\ldots,U_n$ are distributed with a uniform [0,1] distribution. Then parameter estimators $\hat{\theta}$ and $\check{\theta}$ are compared by the character of the closeness to the identity function $D(u) = u$ of $\tilde{D}_{\hat{\theta}}(u)$ and $\tilde{D}_{\check{\theta}}(u)$.

We call $\tilde{D}_\theta(u)$ a comparison distribution function. Its derivative

$$\tilde{d}_\theta(u) = \{\tilde{D}_\theta(u)\}'$$

plays a basic role and is called a comparison density; formulas for the comparison density are

$$\tilde{d}_\theta(u) = f_\theta(\tilde{Q}(u))\,\tilde{q}(u) = \frac{f_\theta(\tilde{Q}(u))}{\tilde{f}\,\tilde{Q}(u)}$$

An alternative comparison density introduced in Parzen (1979), is

$$\tilde{d}(u) = f_0Q_0(u)\,\tilde{q}(u) \div \tilde{\sigma}_0,$$

$$\tilde{\sigma}_0 = \int_0^1 f_0Q_0(u)\,\tilde{q}(u)\,du,$$

$$D(u) = \int_0^u d(t)\,dt$$

where $f_0Q_0(u)$ is a specified density-quantile function.

Parameter estimators can be justified as minimizing information divergence

$$I_1(\tilde{d}_\theta) = \int_0^1 -\log \tilde{d}_\theta(u)\,du = I_1(\tilde{f};f_\theta)$$

$$II(\tilde{d}_\theta) = \int_0^1 |\log \tilde{d}_\theta(u)|^2 du = II(\tilde{f};f_\theta)$$

$$I_\alpha(\tilde{d}_\theta) = \frac{-1}{1-\alpha}\log \int_0^1 \{\tilde{d}_\theta(u)\}^{1-\alpha} du$$

$$\int_0^1 |\tilde{d}_\theta(u) - 1|^2\,du = \int_0^1 |\tilde{d}_\theta(u)|^2\,du - 1 \quad .$$

These measure the closeness to 1 of $\tilde{d}_\theta(u)$, or the closeness to $D(u) = u$ of $\tilde{D}_\theta(u)$. However the final decision about parameter estimators should be based on visual inspection of the graph of $\tilde{D}_\theta(u)$.

Another consequence of considering information of order α is that we can unify the estimation criterion used to form maximum likelihood estimators with the estimation criterion used to form Gaussian time series parameter estimators:

$$I_{sp}(\tilde{f};f_\theta) = \log \int_0^1 \frac{\tilde{f}(w)}{f_\theta(w)}\,dw\ ,$$

where $\tilde{f}$ and f_θ are spectral densities. It is comparable to

$$I_2(\tilde{d}_\theta) = \log \int_0^1 \frac{\tilde{f}\tilde{Q}(u)}{f_\theta \tilde{Q}(u)}\,du$$

7. Statistical inference reduced to density estimation

The quantile approach to statistical data analysis being developed by Parzen [since Parzen (1979)] is based on the proposition that conventional problems of statistical inference concerning (1) a random sample $X_1,\ldots,X_n$, (2) a bivariate sample $(X_1,Y_1),\ldots,(X_n,Y_n)$, or (3) two samples $X_1,\ldots,X_m$ and $Y_1,\ldots,Y_n$ should be transformed to problems of functional inference, estimating and testing hypotheses about density functions $d(u)$, $d(u_1,u_2)$, $\ldots,d(u_1,\ldots,u_k)$, on the unit interval $0\le u\le 1$, unit square $0\le u_1,u_2\le 1$, unit hypercube $0\le u_1,\ldots,u_k\le 1$. To illustrate how this is done consider the following problems.

Modeling bivariate data and tests for independence. Let X and Y be continuous random variables with joint density function $f_{X,Y}(x,y)$. The hypothesis, Ho: X and Y are independent can be expressed

$$\text{Ho: } f_{X,Y}(x,y) = f_X(x)\,f_Y(y)$$

or in terms of information divergence

$$I(f_{X,Y};f_Xf_Y) = \int_{-\infty}^{\infty}\int_{-\infty}^{\infty}\{-\log \frac{f_X(x)f_Y(y)}{f_{X,Y}(x,y)}\}\,f_{X,Y}(x,y)\,dx\,dy$$

by

$$\text{Ho: } I(f_{X,Y};f_Xf_Y) = 0 \quad .$$

Define

$$D(u_1,u_2) = F_{X,Y}(Q_X(u_1),Q_Y(u_2))$$

$$d(u_1,u_2) = \frac{\partial^2}{\partial u_1 \partial u_2} D(u_1,u_2) = \frac{f_{X,Y}(Q_X(u_1),Q_Y(u_2))}{f_XQ_X(u_1)\,f_YQ_Y(u_2)}$$

We call $d(u_1,u_2)$ the quantile dependence density. The hypothesis Ho can be expressed

$$\text{Ho: } D(u_1,u_2) = u_1u_2, \quad d(u_1,u_2) = 1.$$

One can verify that

$$I_1(f_{X,Y};f_Xf_Y)=\int_0^1\int_0^1 \{\log d(u_1,u_2)\}\, d(u_1,u_2)du_1du_2$$

$$= -H_1(d(u_1,u_2))$$

Thus estimating the information divergence between $f_{X,Y}$ and f_Xf_Y is equivalent to estimating the negative of the entropy of $d(u_1,u_2)$. Estimators $\hat{d}_m(u_1,u_2)$ dependent on a finite number of parameters can be formed from the raw estimator

$$\tilde{D}(u_1,u_2) = \tilde{F}_{X,Y}(\tilde{Q}_X(u_1),\ \tilde{Q}_Y(u_2)).$$

Modeling likelihood ratios and testing equality of distributions. Let X and Y be continuous random variables. The hypothesis

$$\text{Ho: } F_X(x) = F_Y(x), \text{ or } f_X(x) = f_Y(x)$$

can be expressed in terms of information divergence

$$I(f_Y;f_X) = \int_{-\infty}^{\infty} -\log \frac{f_X(x)}{f_Y(x)}\, dF_Y(y)$$

$$= \int_0^1 -\log d(u) \quad du$$

$$= -\text{Hqd}\ (d(u))$$

defining the comparison distribution function and comparison density function

$$D(u)=F_XQ_Y(u), \quad d(u) = \frac{d}{du}D(u)=\frac{f_X(Q_Y(u))}{f_Y(Q_Y(u))}$$

Estimating the information divergence between f_Y and f_X is equivalent to estimating the negative of the entropy in the quantile-density sense of the comparison density $d(u)$.

8. Parametric-select density estimation and Maximum Entropy Densities

A density $d(u) = D'(u)$ can be approximated in many ways by sequences $d_m(u), m=1,2,\ldots$ of functions which converge to $d(u)$. For $m=1,2,\ldots$, let $\hat{d}_m(u)$ be an estimator of $d_m(u)$; the sequence $\hat{d}_m(u)$ then estimates $d(u)$.

If $d_m(u)$ corresponds to a standard finite parameteric model $d(u)$ for which one could consider testing the hypothesis that $d_m(u)$ provides an exact model, we call $d_m(u)$ a parametric-select representation, and $\hat{d}_m(u)$ a parametric-select estimator, to indicate that we are free to select the number of parameters in $d_m(u)$ to provide an adequate approximation or representation of $d(u)$.

We call $d_m(u)$ a non-parametric representation, and $\hat{d}_m(u)$ a non-parametric estimator, if $d_m(u)$ does not correspond to a standard finite parameter model which could be interpreted as an exact model.

An important criterion for developing the functional form of exact models for densities is the maximum entropy principles.

A density $f(x)$, $-\infty<x<\infty$, which maximizes entropy $H(f) = \int_{-\infty}^{\infty}\{-\log f(x)\}f(x)\,dx$ subject to constraints

$$\int_{-\infty}^{\infty} T_j(x)f(x)\,dx = \tau_j, \quad j=1,\ldots,k,$$

where $T_j(x)$ are specified functions (called sufficient statistics) and τ_j are specified moments can be shown to have the representation, called an exponential model,

$$\log f(x) = \sum_{j=1}^{k} \theta_jT_j(x) - \Psi(\theta_1,\ldots,\theta_k)$$

where

$$\Psi(\theta_1,\ldots,\theta_k)=\log \int_{-\infty}^{\infty}\exp \sum_{j=1}^{k} \theta_jT_j(x) \quad dx$$

guarantees that $f(x)$ integrates to 1.

A quantile density $q(u)$, $0<u<1$, which maximizes entropy $\text{Hqd}(q) = \int_0^1 \log q(u)\,du$ subject to the constraints

$$\frac{\int_0^1 \exp(2\pi iuv)\ f_0Q_0(u)q(u)du}{\int_0^1 f_0Q_0(u)\ q(u)\ du} = \rho(v), v=0,\pm1,\ldots,\pm m$$

where $f_0Q_0(u)$ is a specified density quantile function must have the representation, called an autoregressive model [Parzen (1982)],

$$q(u)=q_0(u)\sigma_m^2|1+\alpha_m(1)e^{2\pi iu}+\ldots+\alpha_m(m)e^{2\pi ium}|^{-2}$$

9. Exact-parametric and parameter-select estimation of probability density functions using exponential models

Two important exponential models for a density $f(x)$, $-\infty<x<\infty$ are the normal density and the gamma density.

The normal density, denoted Normal (μ,σ)

$$f_{\mu,\sigma}(x) = \frac{1}{\sigma}\,\phi\left(\frac{x-\mu}{\sigma}\right),$$

$$\phi(x) = \frac{1}{\sqrt{2\pi}} \exp -\frac{1}{2}x^2$$

is exponential with sufficient statistics $T_1(x)=x$ and $T_2(x) = x^2$.

The Gamma density, denoted Gamma (r,λ) where $\lambda=1/\sigma$,

$$f_{r,\sigma}(x) = \frac{1}{\sigma} f_r\left(\frac{x}{\sigma}\right),$$

$$f_r(x) = \frac{1}{\Gamma(r)} x^{r-1} e^{-x}, \quad x>0,$$

$$= 0, \quad x<0,$$

is exponential with sufficient statistics $T_1(x)=x$ and $T_2(x) = \log x$.

A location scale parameter Gamma density

$$f_{r,\mu,\sigma}(x) = \frac{1}{\sigma} f_r\left(\frac{x-\mu}{\sigma}\right)$$

is not an exponential model. We can treat it as one by estimating μ (say, by the minimum $X_{(1)}$ of the random sample $X_1,\ldots,X_n$), and treating $X_j-\hat{\mu}$ as a sample from $f_{r,\sigma}(x)$.

The hypothesis that the data is fit by a normal distribution versus the hypothesis that the data is fit by a Gamma distribution can be tested by forming an over-parametrized exponential model with sufficient statistics

$$T_1(x)=x,\quad T_2(x)=x^2,\quad T_3(x)=x^3,\quad T_4(x)=\log x.$$

The (order 1) information divergence, or maximum likelihood, estimators $\hat{\theta}_1, \hat{\theta}_2, \hat{\theta}_3, \hat{\theta}_4$, which minimize information divergence of order 1, $\int_0^1 -\log \tilde{d}_\theta(u)\,du$, may be found for an exponential model by solving

$$\hat{\tau}_j = E_{\hat{\theta}}[T_j]$$

where $\tau_j = E_\theta[T_j]$ is estimated by

$$\hat{\tau}_j = \bar{T}_j = \frac{1}{n}\sum_{j=1}^{n} T_j(X_{(j)}) \quad .$$

The bi-information divergence estimators θ_1, θ_2, θ_3, θ_4, which minimize information divergence $\int_0^1 |\log \tilde{d}_\theta(u)|^2 du$, may be found using least squares regression analysis techniques by minimizing with respect to $\theta_1,\ldots,\theta_k$ the sum of squares

$$\sum_{j=2}^{n-1} \Big|\log f(X_{(j)}) - \overline{\{\log f(X_j)\}}$$
$$-\theta_1(T_1(X_{(j)})-\bar{T}_1)-\ldots-\theta_k(T_k(X_{(j)})-\bar{T}_k)\Big|^2$$

Stepwise regression is used to suggest parsimonious parametrizations.

Graphical procedures to determine which parameter values fit best are as follows: estimate $\tilde{D}_\theta(\frac{j}{n+1})$, $j=2,\ldots,n-1$, by adding

$$\tilde{d}_\theta(\tfrac{j}{n+1}) = f_\theta(X_{(J)}) \div \tilde{f}(X_{(j)})$$

and normalizing the sum to go from 0 to 1. One inspects its graph to see how it deviates from $D(u) = u$.

10. Case study

Density estimators, using bi-information parameters, are presented for the data set of Buffalo snowfall 1910-1972. Bi-information select regression estimation of the parameters of a 4-paramential exponential model with sufficient statistics x, x^2, x^3, and $\log x$ leads to the conclusion that Buffalo snowfall obeys a gamma distribution. It is equally well fit by a normal distribution whose parameters are estimated by minimizing bi-information rather than order 1 information. The hypothesis that Buffalo snowfall is normal seems to be acceptable, but one can question whether the maximum likelihood estimators (sample mean and variance) provide the best-fitting normal distribution for Buffalo snowfall. As in Parzen (1979), we reject a trimodal shape probability density estimate for Buffalo snowfall, which has been found by several non-parametric density estimation techniques.

The maximum likelihood estimators of a normal distribution for the Buffalo snowfall data are the sample mean $\hat{\mu} = 80.5$ and sample variance $\hat{\sigma}^2 = 487$. The bi-information divergence parameter estimators are $\check{\mu} = 41.9$ and $\check{\sigma}^2 = 644$. The parsimonious four parameter exponential density fitted by bi-information divergence is a gamma distribution whose parameters correspond to a mean of 83 and a variance of 692. Their graphs show that the fitted gamma and normal densities are similar. The $\tilde{D}(u)$ plots also are similar for both distributions and show that they provide satisfactory fits of the data.

REFERENCES

Parzen, E. (1979) Nonparametric statistical data modeling. Journal of the American Statistical Association, 74, 105-131.

________. (1982) Maximum entropy interpretation of autoregressive spectral densities. Statistics and Probability Letters, 1, 2-6.

$\tilde{D}(u)$ FOR BI-INF-DIV NORMAL (81.9, 644)

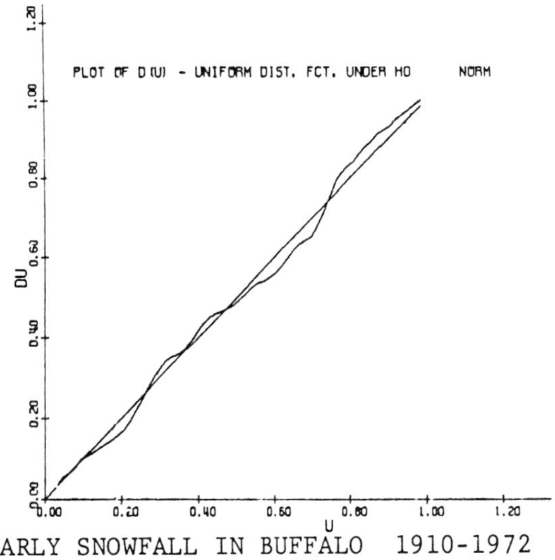

YEARLY SNOWFALL IN BUFFALO 1910-1972
Mean 80.5, Variance 487

Contributed Papers

Design A Form: A Full Screen Data Entry, Verification, Updating, and Display System
Michael A. Fox, UCLA Hospital Computing Facility, Los Angeles

The Documentation of Statistical Software in GAMS: The Guide to Available Mathematical Software
Sally E. Howe, National Bureau of Standards

Statistical Computing: A Necessary Tool in Energy Research
David L. Nelson, Boeing Computer Services Company

"What To Do 'Til the Nonlinear Model Comes": Integrating a Plethora of Computational and Graphic Tools for Analysis of Multivariate Data
James M. Malone II, Innovative Information Technology

Exact Sampling Distributions of Two Measures of Skewness – A Computer Approach
Derrick S. Tracy, University of Windsor
William C. Conley, University of Wisconsin, Green Bay

A Collection of Happy Endings for Incomplete Beta Functions
Lester Klein, The American University

A Portable Interactive FORTRAN Verifier
Lon–Mu Liu, University of Illinois at Chicago
Laszlo Engleman, University of California, Los Angeles

A Graph–Decomposition Method Based on the Density–Contour Clustering Model
M. A. Wong, S. E. Madnick, and J. M. Lattin, Massachusetts Institute of Technology

A Comparison of Robust Methods and Detection of Outliers Techniques When Estimating a Location Parameter
Jeffrey S. Simonoff, New York University

Identifying Influential Observations in Time Series Data
James M. Lattin, Massachusetts Institute of Technology

On Methodologies of Computer Simulations to Evaluate Ridge Estimators
W.S. Luk, Simon Fraser University

Optimal Production Run For a Process Subject to Drift, Shift, and Changes in Variance
M.A. Rahim and R.S. Lashkari, University of Windsor

Recursive Algorithms in Statistics
Norman Neff, Trenton State College

A Bayesian Treatment of Nonresponse when Sampling from a Dichotomous Population
James H. Albert, Bowling Green State University

DESIGN A FORM:
A FULL SCREEN DATA ENTRY, VERIFICATION, UPDATING, AND DISPLAY SYSTEM

Michael A. Fox, UCLA Hospital Computing Facility Los Angeles 90024

Abstract

Display screens or forms are described by a specification language. A particular definition can be automatically generated by graphically designing a form on a screen. This specification is data for a compiler which generates PL/1 code. This instance of reusable code will display the form and perform single and multiple field verification. Facsimiles of the "filled-in forms" are printed and the records, implied by the data, can be written to a standard system's file, or can be used as transactions to data base management systems. A variety of options exist for updating. Generated code frees the user from constraints imposed by the specification language. Field translation, the sharing of single physical records between many screens, and multiple views of the same data files are other options. Existing files can be formatted to the screen for display, post hoc field validation, and restructuring.

The system is complete in itself, with overtones of a data base management system. It interfaces directly to other systems and can provide building blocks for other full screen applications.

Key words and phrases: full screen, data entry, edit, display, reusable code, design specification, code generator, form design, IBM W3270, reliable code, data management, file management.

Introduction

The design of reliable programs is expensive and time consuming. In recent years we have seen an emphasis in methodologies aimed at providing robust, comprehensible, and maintainable systems. This thrust manifests itself in such areas as design specifications, reusable code, and program generators. This paper presents a practical working example of these software practices.

The motivation for this work lies in reducing and rendering less cumbersome the bulk of the statistical worker's task, casually described as data management. To perform analysis one collects data, which must be validity checked and arranged in suitable order. Occasions arise when fairly complex edit rules have to be applied to data and there is always the desire to view, in a formatted easy to read manner, individual cases for possible update.

These tasks are essentially the same for all data sets. Passing from one study to the next should not therefore require repetition of mundane tasks. Finesse at the specification level is needed. Design A Form addresses this need.

System Requirements

The initial requirements for the system are a full screen data entry method which to the user looks like a form. This "form" should allow single-field and across-field validation to be performed, to any degree of complexity. Facsimiles of the filled in forms should be available. Files created by the system should be simple data files. Other systems could immediately use these files and conversely such files would be readable by this system. A mechanism should be available to pass the data entered or derived in other ways, such as transactions. Retrieval, updating, restructuring, and post hoc data validation should be supported.

Except for a field's attributes (numeric etc) a form or tableau is pictorial. This visual aspect can therefore be described by typing on to a display screen. Non visual components require a language for their description. In this system a high level language is used to define all aspects of a form. Instances of this language, the graphical aspects, can be automatically produced using the terminal. The clauses so generated are available for addition or modification.

In any system, as the number of options increase so does the richness of the definition language. To create a system which will not suffer from artificial constraints imposed by the definition language it would appear that the latter would have to evolve into a programming language. Extreme simplicity and a high degree of flexibility are not, however, mutually exclusive. The reconciliation of these requirements has been realized in a program generator. The target language chosen was PL/1 and the display device the IBM 3270 series of both monochrome and color terminals.

It must be emphasised that although the system generates PL/1 source code, in the vast majority of cases, the specification language captures all that is required and going from form design to data entry and updating requires no programming knowledge. It is a task easily accomplished by nontechnical people. Complex situations involving multiple forms with context-dependent decisions, will require some intervention. Experience has shown that this open-ended feature is welcomed by those who use packaged programs but have needs that transcend them.

System Design Considerations

In writing programs the most serious errors are those involving control structures (dynamic conditions for following a particular path are incorrectly computed) and data structures (bounds of arrays are erroneous). Syntax errors are, for the most part, found by the compiler. Generating source code, via a specification language, offers a number of advantages. The most important is that the production of error free programs is an achievable goal. Simple applications can be "brought up" in a few minutes.

Customizing starts off with complete correct code and is therefore at minimal risk with respect to the introduction of errors. This is because all the "hard" error prone program facets such as management of data structures and screen handling code are produced automatically. Adapting the code to perform such operations as complicated table look ups and embedded computations can of course introduce errors. These, however, will be confined to small domains and are easily detectable.

This system is an example of "reusable code", each new application can be thought of as a progeny varying from its parent in its speciific function, yet sharing a common, reusable, core.

The concept of abstract data types and encapsuled modules is used in code that is "hidden", from the user thereby retaining its viability. Part of the generated code is, however, open to the user. Hidden code ensures that it can only be approached and used in a controlled way. Open code provides for easy and swift customization. The capsule "screen" which consists of the abstact data type used to hold and manage data going to and from the display device is available as hidden code. This means that the user can control what is displayed, and recieves back the analyzed replies to the screen. Each screen is represented by an open code PL/1 procedure which contains three distinct parts. A PL/1 structure which brings together all the replies, the actual stream of characters sent to the controller, and a "case" block (called select in PL/1). In this case block each field which has a reply is represented and is available to the user. A developer who wishes to use the system beyond that which is generated, via the specification language, has only to know the specifics of his data and not how screen management is accomplished.

Since logic between screens is independent of the hidden code versatile applications can be designed with ease. For example, in a financial planning example three screen were used for each case. The first to collect data and the others to display computed results. A procedure was written to do the required computations. The only system housekeeping required was declaring the PL/1 structures defining the three screens to this procedure and steering, via calls, the display of each individual screen. Indeed skeletal steering procedures are part of the system and are generated when multiple screen applications are defined. A user then had available a system that dyamically displayed the consequences of, for example, a fluctuating dollar value on the cash flow situation of a company that deals with puchasing and leasing goods.

Form or Screen Design

A program "BLANK" presents a screen to the user, on to which the form or tableau is typed. This will consist of legends or narrative material, field names, and reply fields denoted by asterisks. Lateral movement of objects on the screen is accomplished via the terminal's positioning keys. When the desired result is achieved a function key is pressed resulting in the translation of the screen into an instance of the specification language. If Income ****** were typed on line 10 column 5 on the screen it would be translated into

```
Income (10,5,6)      This is of the form

Legend or field name (row,column,length)
```

This would define a character string field. To specify conditions on the field a series of attributes may be specified.

```
Thus Income (10,5,6,NB)
```

instructs the system to generate code to write the word "Income" on the screen at line 10 column 5 and to accept up to six numeric characters (N) insisting that this field be entered i.e. non blank (B). For the field "Sex" to take on only the values "M" or "F" with a user defined message the specification is

```
    Sex (6,3,1)
:¬='M' &¬='F' Sex can only be M or F :
```

Erroneous entries will be signaled by writing a message, sounding a bell, positioning the cursor and, highlighting the offending field. The operator can either correct the field, or by pressing a function key force the reply to be accepted.

Other field attributes include date, right justification, full replies, default values compute fields, and value carry over (from one form to the next). The most general specification of a field is

```
Legend (row,column,length,attributes)
: failure condition message ;
  failure condition message ; ... :
```

Retrieval and Updating

Retrieval is by example. An empty form is presented on to which search criteria is typed. This in conjunction with a condition (equality, greater than, less than, or range) is used to find cases. In addition, all cases can be sequentially displayed, or a search for cases that fail an edit rule selected. This is the situation required for *post hoc* editing. In the update mode, cases can be altered with dynamic recalculation of compute fields. Pressing a function key will redisplay the changed case. Editing criteria and reformatting data can be respecified.

It is unfortunate that designers of data-gathering forms still continue the archaic practice of encoding items at source rather than leaving this to the computer (males=1 etc required by some packages for grouping variables). *Design A Form* takes the position that source data should be readable and therefore provides a translation mechanism to go from a source of one size to a target of another. The default value in the printed facsimile of the form is the source while the target value is written to the file. On retrieval both the stored value and the inverse translation can be displayed.

Interface Considerations

In the normal situation the files created by the system are standard system's files, with the data appearing as characters without any embedded control information. Such files can immediately be read by any other program as raw data. Since "ghost" fields (usually filled with blanks) can be specified variable values can be separated from each other to facilitate "free form" entry in other packages.

This detachment of the files from the system provides for complete data independence. This makes feasible the use of the system as a "front end" to a data base system for situations where the data is too voluminous for simple files. In this situation transactions would be sent between the two systems.

System Limitations

Functional separation and modularity are the design philosopy of this product. Features that rightly belong in other systems are excluded. In light of the overtones that this system has to a data base management systems (DBMS), the important differences must be stressed.

Here data is looked at in a case by case manner, a DBMS is more global in approach. In a good DBMS searches do not usually require passing the whole file. In inverted systems much logic can be performed on the reference files or directories before looking at the actual data. Retrieval using logical expressions is limited, in this system, to "AND". Here the "OR" is accomplised with multiple searches. Although hierarchical cases are supported by this system, there is no connectivety maintained between the various record types (relations). Cross case computation (means, minima, etc.) is a simple customization task, however, anything more complex is the province of a statistical package. A DBMS excels in handling volatile data. This system is geared towards changes to data items rather than deletion of whole cases. File, rather than data base functions, are then performed thus new cases are added sequentially at the end of the file, while insertions and deletions are treated as transactions and are generally processed at the end of a session.

For a very large file the overhead in computer cost, storage, and more complex operator training required by a DBMS is warrented. There are, however, occations when data management should be restricted to files. In such situations a DBMS would be too complex. Many studies fall into this category. Instances exist where data remains static and essentially lost because no suitable means is available to read and comprehend the data. A large series of files containing encoded information concerning land utilization lay unused because of the difficulty in using it. A translator to these files was incorporated into this system which was used to display the data in English in an pleasant format that encouraged use. A DBMS would have been too costly and too difficult for the casual user.

This system because of its ease of use, its file handling features, its simple interface to other packages, its flexibility, and its parsimony can play in important part in data management.

THE DOCUMENTATION OF STATISTICAL SOFTWARE IN GAMS: THE GUIDE TO AVAILABLE MATHEMATICAL SOFTWARE

Sally E. Howe, National Bureau of Standards

ABSTRACT

In the first phase of a project to organize and publicize the mathematical and statistical software available to scientists at the National Bureau of Standards, Ron Boisvert, David Kahaner, Janice Knapp-Cordes, Martin Knapp-Cordes, and I have produced an approximately 400-page Guide to Available Mathematical Software (GAMS). All of the software which this guide documents is available on the Univac 1100/82 computer at NBS in Gaithersburg, Maryland, and most is available on the CDC Cyber 750 at the Department of Commerce laboratories in Boulder, Colorado, where some NBS staff are located. GAMS was produced by systematically querying a database management system designed for this project using DMS-1100, Univac's CODASYL database management system.

GAMS is based on an extensive scheme for classifying both statistical software and software for mathematical computations of interest to statisticians -- such as special functions, linear algebra, integrals, differential equations, and optimization. The current edition classifies and contains documentation for approximately 2300 subroutines in the IMSL, NAG, and PORT proprietary libraries and three dozen high-quality public-domain packages including LINPACK, FFTPACK, and QUADPACK. A future edition will include programs and interactive systems as well as more subroutines, and will take the form of a more easily maintained and searched on-line database.

KEYWORDS

classification scheme, data base, mathematical software, scientific computing, statistical computing, statistical software

INTRODUCTION

The development of GAMS was motivated by the need to provide up-to-date information about mathematical and statistical software available to NBS scientistics using a wide variety of computers to analyse scientific data. There are approximately 3400 NBS employees, approximately half of whom are physical scientists and engineers, many of them involved in collecting and analysing data. NBS computing facilities include two central computers (a Univac 1100/82 and a CDC Cyber 750), more than one hundred minicomputers, and several hundred microcomputers. The data analysis needs cover the full spectrum of scientific computing and are best met by providing state-of-the-art scientific software. The NBS Center for Applied Mathematics in general and its Scientific Computing Division in particular are responsible for providing much of this software, and GAMS is one important vehicle for disseminating information about software.

Certain constraints influenced the form of the first edition of GAMS, which was distributed in October, 1981. First, since there was no single computer which all NBS scientists used, the first edition was in hard-copy, so all NBS staff have access to the information. Second, since there were so many NBS computers, public-domain software was well-organized and clearly identified. Third, because it was important to make the information available as soon as possible, and because this was a first step in a long-term project, no attempt was made to document all mathematical and statistical software available at NBS. Rather, the first edition documented only libraries and packages of subroutines which, as of June, 1981, had been installed and were being maintained by the Scientific Computing Division for use by NBS staff. (There are many other software products, both public-domain and commercial, which may provide additional, equal, or better facilities. The omission of any such software does not imply its unsuitability for use.) Other useful subroutines and stand-alone programs and interactive systems will be added in later editions.

The first edition of GAMS provides information about approximately 2300 subroutines, all but a few of which are written in FORTRAN. Each of these subroutines belongs to one of five "libraries." Three proprietary libraries provide software for solving problems in many areas of mathematics and statistics: 1) the 443-subroutine IMSL (1980) library, 2) the 932-subroutine NAG (1981) library, and 3) the 269-subroutine PORT (1976) library. The fourth library is the NBS Core Math Library (CMLIB), which contains several hundred high-quality public-domain FORTRAN subroutines acquired from universities and government laboratories or written by NBS staff. CMLIB consists of several dozen packages, each of which comes from a single developer and usually solves a narrow set of problems. For example, three packages of particular interest to statisticians are 1) LINPACK (Dongarra, et al., 1979), subroutines to analyse and solve various systems of linear algebraic equations, 2) QUADPACK (DeDoncker, et al., in press), subroutines to evaluate definite integrals of functions of one variable, and 3) FFTPACK (Swarztrauber, 1982), subroutines to compute the fast Fourier transform in various forms. Subroutines in CMLIB can easily be moved to other computers. The fifth library, MATHWARE, like CMLIB contains packages of public-domain software obtained from several sources, but MATHWARE packages are more difficult to move.

THE GAMS DOCUMENT

GAMS is divided into six sections, which are now

described.

Section 1. GAMS Classifications

The tree-structured GAMS classification scheme is organized by mathematical problem rather than by method whenever practical, and is strongly influenced by the authors' knowledge of generally available software and the needs of the NBS scientific community. Because the same mathematical problem can be described in different ways, there are "pointers" between entries in the scheme. These pointers make replicating subsections of the scheme unnecessary.

The classification scheme in the first edition of GAMS is a direct descendant of the Bolstad (1975) scheme. Since the distribution of GAMS in 1981, however, the first edition's scheme has been substantially revised. While retaining Bolstad's tree structure and problem orientation, the current (1982) GAMS scheme has abandoned compatibility with the Bolstad scheme and its predecessors, thereby freeing the scheme for a major reorganization. The current GAMS scheme, along with a description of its historical development and underlying philosophy, will appear in a forthcoming SIGNUM Newsletter (Boisvert _et al_., in preparation).

The classes at the highest level of the current scheme are:

A. ARITHMETIC, ERROR ANALYSIS
B. NUMBER THEORY
C. ELEMENTARY AND SPECIAL FUNCTIONS
D. LINEAR ALGEBRA
E. DIFFERENTIATION AND INTEGRATION
F. DIFFERENTIAL AND INTEGRAL EQUATIONS
G. INTEGRAL TRANSFORMS
H. INTERPOLATION AND APPROXIMATION
I. SOLUTION OF NONLINEAR EQUATIONS
J. OPTIMIZATION
K. OPERATIONS RESEARCH
L. STATISTICS AND PROBABILITY
M. COMPUTATIONAL GEOMETRY
N. GRAPHICS
O. SYMBOLIC COMPUTATION
P. DATA HANDLING
Q. SERVICE ROUTINES
R. SOFTWARE DEVELOPMENT TOOLS

Classes at the next level of the scheme have letter and number designations (e.g., A1). Alternate letters and numbers are appended for more specific classes. The following is a subset of Chapter L (Statistics and Probability), in which the organization and naming attempt to reflect the way statisticians label data and analyses.

L. STATISTICS AND PROBABILITY
L1. Data summarization
L1a. Univariate data
L1a1. Quantitative
L1a2. Qualitative (proportional)
L1b. Multivariate data
L2. Data manipulation
L2a. Transform
L2b. Sort
L2c. Group
L2d. Sample
L2e. Subset
L3. Graphics
L3a. Histograms
L3b. Distribution functions
L3c. Scatter diagrams
L3c1. Symbol plots
L3c2. Multiple plots
L3c3. Vertical plots
L3c4. Probability plots
<further classified by distribution>
L3d. EDA graphics
L4. Elementary statistical inference and hypothesis testing
L4a. Univariate data
L4a1. Parameter estimation
L4a2. Goodness-of-fit tests
L4a3. Randomness tests
L4a4. Nonparametric
L4b. Multivariate data
L4b1. Parameter estimation
L4b2. Nonparametric
L5. Function evaluation
L5a. Univariate functions
L5a1. Distribution and density functions
<further classified by distribution>
L5a2. Inverse distribution and density functions
<further classified by distribution>
L5b. Multivariate functions
L5b1. Distribution and density functions
<further classified by distribution>
L6. Pseudo-random number generation
L6a. Univariate
<further classified by distribution>
L6b. Multivariate
<further classified by distribution>
L6c. Service routines
L7. Experimental design, including analysis of variance
L7a. One-way analysis of variance and covariance
L7b. Balanced multi-way design
L7b1. Complete
L7b1a. Two-way
L7b1b. Factorial
L7b1c. Nested
L7b2. Incomplete
L7c. General linear model (unbalanced design)
L7d. Multivariate analysis of variance
L8. Regression
L8a. Linear least squares (L_2)
L8a1. Simple
L8a2. Polynomial
L8a3. Piecewise polynomial (spline)
L8a4. Multiple
L8a5. Several multiple regressions
L8a6. Multivariate
L8a7. Diagnostics
L8a8. Inference
L8b. Linear least absolute value (L_1)
L8c. Linear minimax (L_∞)

L8d. Biased (ridge)
L8e. Robust
L8f. Nonparametric
L8g. Nonlinear
L9. Categorical data analysis
L9a. 2-by-2 tables
L9b. Two-way tables
L9c. Log-linear model
L9d. EDA (e.g., median polish)
L10. Time series analysis
L10a. Smoothing and filtering
L10b. Transforms
L10c. Autocorrelation analysis
L10d. ARIMA modeling and forecasting
L10e. Spectral analysis
L10f. Cross-correlation analysis
L11. Correlation analysis
L12. Discriminant analysis
L13. Factor analysis
L13a. Principal components analysis
L14. Cluster analysis
L15. Life testing and survival analysis

Section 2. Modules by Class

This section has the same organization as the GAMS classification scheme (Section 1). For all classes at the highest level of the scheme and for some at lower levels, Modules by Class contains a discussion of the particular mathematical or statistical problem and a list of references. The discussion often addresses computational issues and problems of which a user should be aware. For example, under "L6. Pseudo-random number generation" appears a discussion of the uses of pseudo-random numbers, the central place taken by the generation of uniform pseudo-random numbers, and two issues which should be considered in selecting subroutines, namely quality of results and portability of the software. One reference given is to Kennedy and Gentle (1980). A list of modules (subroutines) appears under more specific classifications. A module is listed at the classification(s) which most specifically but completely describe the problem that the module software solves. For example, there are four subroutines classified under "L9. Categorical data analysis" at the node "L9b. Two-way tables." These subroutines are CTPR and CTRBYC from IMSL, and G01AFF and G01AFE from NAG (these latter two are double and single precision versions of the same subroutine).

Section 3. Module Dictionary

For each of the modules, listed in alphabetical order, the following information is provided:

a. Name

b. Short description

c. Name of library containing the module

d. Name of package containing the module (this is the same as the library if the library is not partitioned into packages)

e. Language in which the module is coded

f. Precision (e.g., integer, single, double)

g. Portability

Proprietary: module is purchased or leased for a specific computer; although the source code may run on other computers, permission to move the module must be obtained from the module originators

Portable: module source code is freely available and will probably run on most computers with only minor adjustments

Not portable: module source code is freely available, but will probably not run on other computers without substantial changes

h. NBS Univac 1100/82 command to obtain detailed documentation for the module

i. Calling sequence for the module

j. Name of the file element on the NBS Univac 1100/82 containing a source program to test the module (when available)

k. Coroutines (a list of other modules which are almost always used with this module)

An example of a Module Dictionary entry is:

RGM computes estimates of simple linear regression parameters for a geometric mean regression | CMLIB | SLRPACK | FORTRAN | Single precision | Portable | Documentation: @PRT,S CMLIB*DL.800-RGM/SLRPACK | CALL RGM (N, X, Y, OUTPUT, WORK, IER) | Tests: CMLIB*TL.800-RGM/SLRPACK.

Sections 4 and 5. Package and Library Dictionaries

For each of the packages in CMLIB and MATHWARE, listed in alphabetical order, the following information is provided:

a. Name

b. Short description

c. Name of library containing the package

d. Version name or date installed

e. Name of organization which produced this software, including at least one contact

f. Portability (proprietary, portable, or not portable -- defintions are given in the description of the Module Dictionary)

g. Support level

3: actively supported at NBS; at least one of the software authors is on staff

2: actively supported at NBS

1: support provided by package originators; minimal support available at NBS

0: not supported at NBS

h. Machines / compilers at NBS on which the package is readily available

i. NBS Univac 1100/82 command to obtain detailed documentation for the package

j. Reference to other generally available documentation

The entry for the single precision version of LINPACK is:

LINPACKS analyse and solve various systems of linear algebraic equations | CMLIB | Version 1978 | Originated by Argonne National Laboratory, Argonne, IL (J.J. Dongarra) | Portable | Support level 3 | Available on Univac 1100/82 / FTN, Cyber 750 / FTN | Documentation: @PRT,S CMLIB*DD.201/LINPACKS | Reference: J.J. Dongarra et al., LINPACK Users' Guide, SIAM, Philadelphia.

The Dictionary entry for each of the five libraries is similar to that for a package.

Section 6. Index

A keyword and phrase index points either to other Index entries or into the classification scheme. For example, for Nonlinear regression the Index says "see APPROXIMATION, see REGRESSION." A representative subset of the REGRESSION section of the Index is:

REGRESSION
  Biased (ridge) L8d
  Linear least squares (L_2) L8a
  Nonlinear L8g
  Spline L8a3

Indices such as this one supplement a tree-structured classification scheme. With an index, different terminology can be used to point to the same class, eliminating the need to replicate portions of the scheme using the terminology of various scientific disciplines.

PREPARATION OF THE GAMS DOCUMENT

Sections 2, 3, 4, and 5 (Modules by Class and the three Dictionaries) are the output of computer programs that systematically query a database system designed for this project with the help of DMS 1100, Univac's CODASYL data management system. The final GAMS document was then typeset using the NBS typographic system with camera-ready copy printed on a Versatec electrostatic printer-plotter.

DISCUSSION

GAMS was distributed to several hundred NBS staff members in October, 1981, and was well received. Enhancements to GAMS since its distribution include the addition of several packages to CMLIB and of on-line documentation retrieval, by which a user can obtain documentation for several subroutines by executing a simple one-line command.

In addition to having a new classification scheme, the second edition of GAMS will use the Relational Information Management System (RIM) (1982) data management system. RIM promises to be an easy-to-use tool for maintaining up-to-date information about scientific software.

ACKNOWLEDGEMENTS

Responsibility for the creation of the GAMS data base, the query software, and production of the camera-ready document, belong to R.F. Boisvert, D.K. Kahaner, and M. Knapp-Cordes. J. Knapp-Cordes was responsible for the documentation of IMSL, NAG, and PORT subroutines in the data base. IMSL and NAG provided much of the data for modules in their libraries. A long list of people were consulted in designing the classification scheme; those contributing to the statistics and probability chapter include J.R. Donaldson, K. Eberhardt, K. Kafadar, J. Koontz, and B.W. Rust. I thank L. DeLeonibus for preparing this document.

REFERENCES

Boisvert, R.F., S.E. Howe, and D.K. Kahaner. "The GAMS Classification Scheme for Mathematical and Statistical Software," to appear in SIGNUM Newsletter.

Bolstad, J. (1975). "A Proposed Classification Scheme for Computer Program Libraries," SIGNUM Newsletter, v. 10, no. 2-3, pp. 32-39.

DeDoncker, E., D.K. Kahaner, R. Piessens, and C. Überhuber. QUADPACK - a Subroutine Package for Automatic Integration, to appear in Springer Series in Computational Mathematics.

Dongarra, J.J., J.R. Bunch, C.B. Moler, and G.W. Stewart (1979). LINPACK Users' Guide, SIAM, Philadelphia.

IMSL Library Reference Manual (1980). IMSL, Inc., Houston.

Kennedy, W.J. and J.E. Gentle (1980). Statistical Computing, Marcel Dekker, New York, 591 pp.

NAG FORTRAN Library Manual (1981). Numerical Algorithms Group, Oxford, England.

PORT Mathematical Subroutine Library (1976). Bell Laboratories, Murray Hill, NJ.

Swarztrauber, P.N. (1982). "Vectorizing the FFT's," in: G. Rodriguez (ed.) Parallel Computations, Academic Press, New York.

User Guide: RIM 5.0 (Univac) (1982). Boeing Commercial Airplane Company, P.O.Box 3707, Seattle, Washington 98124. (The document was stamped "Preliminary Information.")

STATISTICAL COMPUTING: A NECESSARY TOOL IN ENERGY RESEARCH

David L. Nelson, Boeing Computer Services Company

Any solution of our energy problems is going to require the concerted efforts of scientists and researchers from a large variety of disciplines. This paper points out the contributions from statistical computing that are vital to current energy research. For electric power utilities, as an example, work is going on to model system loads probabilistically and to simplify these models using statistical properties of demand and environment. Utilities are also interested in extracting useful information from data on customer demographics, fuel availability, outages and system reliability. In fossil fuel exploration, statistical computing is used to analyze seismic and drill hole data, to model an underground source's shape, and to satisfy environmental impact concerns by analyzing large data bases for soils, hydrology, wildlife, and vegetation. In nuclear power production, key applications are probabilistic risk assessment, which allows a systematic analysis of power plant safety, epidemiologic studies, and material accounting data and methods. In solar applications, statisticians are involved in the safety aspects of new solar thermal generation systems and in data analysis for photovoltaic experiments. These and other examples in the paper describe work that is being done by computing statisticians in enhancing the prospects of meeting our growing energy demands.

Keywords:

Statistical Computing in Energy Research
Statistical Analysis of Energy Data
Statistical Problems in Energy
Probabilistic Risk Assessment
Energy System Safety

1. INTRODUCTION

These days, no one needs to be told that energy, the demand for it, and the long-term outlook for supply are very much a part of our everyday concern. As individuals, as nations, as members together in a crisis of worldwide proportion, all of us are interested in ways in which major problems with energy supply can be softened, postponed or eliminated. These problems crop up under a number of headings: supply - where the energy comes from; distribution - how it gets to the ultimate user; safety - how to protect people and the environment from adverse impacts due to energy production or consumption; research - finding new or better ways of producing energy; and management - how to manage and conserve our energy resources.

In each of these areas, scientists and engineers from a wide variety of backgrounds are needed in order to form a complete front in attacking the technical problems that arise in energy. Since one thing that characterizes almost all such problems is the gathering and analysis of large amounts of data, it is not surprising that among the technological disciplines working on energy-related programs, statistics, and specifically statistical computing, is an ubiquitous one. A few examples of important activites in which computing statisticians are taking a lead are analysis of large and complex data sets; data structuring, storage and retrieval; exploratory data analysis; report generation; forecasting energy needs and supplies; assessing new energy technologies; searching for fuel; and optimimum processing of fuels.

This paper highlights the role of analytical and computing statisticians in helping to solve some of our energy problems. The problems are categorized according to the form of energy to be produced, but the reader will recognize the elements of many of the headings described above in each of these areas. Hopefully, the reader will also recognize ways in which solutions achieved by statisticians working in one field can be applied successfully to problems faced in others.

2. ELECTRIC POWER

Some of the principal sponsors of research in electric power in which statisticians are involved are the U.S. Department of Energy (DOE) and the Electric Power Research Institute (EPRI). In addition, many private and public utilities are making use of greater numbers of statistical tools in their rate setting, load forecasting, reporting and environmental impact estimation.

DOE funds several large studies requiring high-level statistical skills. One of these, sponsored by the Applied Mathematical Sciences Research Program, is on Analysis of Large Data Sets. This project, being performed at Pacific Northwest Laboratories, is a joint project by statisticians and computer scientists. The effort is aimed at general-purpose ways in which a massive amount of data can be stored, maintained, accessed and analyzed. Questions to be answered concern both hardware requirements (interactive computing, fast input/output, high-resolution color raster graphics, and high performance virtual-memory computers) and software needs (statistical algorithms, data management, graphics software, user interfaces, and overall system integration software). The application areas for the results of this study are very wide, including analysis of data from energy-related materials studies, health and environmental concerns, energy usage, natural energy resources and their depletion and real-time monitoring and experimentation. The results can also be expected to have broad usability outside the energy area.

Another significant area of statistical research sponsored by DOE is in the electric power systems load modeling area. The Division of Electric Energy Systems has funded Boeing Computer Services and GE, among others, to look at ways in which physically-based models of electric power system loads can be constructed with appropriate probabilistic and statistical assumptions. See Nelson et al (1981).

The models that have resulted from these studies go a long way toward enabling load researchers to describe what it means to aggregate loads (say, thousands of resistance heaters in an electrical network) to see what the properties of the combined load might be.

Another result is that time-of-day metered electric usage can be disaggregated (with the help of appliance survey information and weather data) to see what part of the total load is due to each of several major appliance categories. Probability, statistical computing and statistical theory all have played a major part in the success of this research.

Load modeling studies like the one mentioned above are only one aspect of the larger need of utilities to understand their customer set, the demand on their services, impact of rate structures and conservation measures, and the economic risks involved in expansion of generation capacity. In each of these areas, data (or the potential to obtain it) speak to the need for computing statisticians to be involved at an early stage in a wide variety of utility studies. Far-thinking utilities are discovering more and more the need for statistical tools in their planning, life testing and management functions. As an example, Puget Sound Power and Light Company not only has collected data which was useful in validating the models constructed in the DOE load modeling study, but is making use of SAS in constructing a Customer Sampling and Reporting System. This system will give planners and rate analysts access to the utility's own billing data base that they have not had, and will facilitate a high level of responsiveness to federal guidelines on rate structures.

EPRI is a non-governmental body whose utility members produce about 70% of the electricity generated in the United States.

The institute plans and manages research and development that will advance capabilities in electric power generation, delivery and use. Many of the projects sponsored by EPRI, whose overall budget is approximately $260 million, involve data collected in literally scores of areas of utility concern: power outages, material corrosion, nuclear safety, system reliability, economics, environment, and many more.

Examples of research projects sponsored by EPRI with a significant amount of work by computing statisticians are load modeling studies complementing those sponsored by DOE, load shape estimation, economic forecasting, and data analysis on underground cable corrosion and steam generator deterioration.

3. FOSSIL FUELS

Research involving fossil fuels is relatively advanced in its use of statistical computing. Statisticians working with oil, coal, and natural gas companies have, in fact, been at the forefront of a new subset of statistical computing called "geostatistics". Some of the critical fossil fuel problems that have, in part, a statistical solution include estimation of oil reservoir potential, which has obvious impact on a company's exploration strategy and on economic decisions; using seismic data to pinpoint likely sites for exploration; understanding the variables that influence the costs of drill holes (see Eddy and Kadane, 1982); and contour plotting of underground reservoirs for oil and coal, of surface tailings and of environmental data, all of which are being solved by a surface fitting method called Kriging that relies on statistics (David, 1977).

An imaginitive use of statistical computing by a major Northwest coal mining company has great potential for use in other energy-related applications. This company is having its entire data management and reporting system for geology, environment and hydrology data bases written in SAS. This work, performed by Boeing Computer Services, involves some of the most ambitious coding of combined SAS and IBM full-screen capabilities to date, and is resulting in a reporting system that will give scientists and managers a high level of access to data that is critical for environmentally sound and economically viable mining strategies.

4. NUCLEAR POWER

The contributions of statisticians in solving problems in nuclear power would make a lengthy list. Three major areas that statisticians are working on are nuclear material accounting and safeguards, probabilistic risk assessment, and analysis of radiation effects data. Research in these areas is sponsored variously by DOE, EPRI and the Nuclear Regulatory Commission.

In the nuclear material accounting and safeguards area, statisticians are working on several projects sponsored by NRC through its Office of Nuclear Regulatory Research and Oak Ridge National Laboratory. "Safeguards" itself is a term used to describe methods that insure the integrity of ownership of nuclear material used in power reactors. Part of the measures in place involve accounting procedures that enable a high probability of detection if nuclear material is lost or diverted by some unauthorized party. Described properly, detection becomes a statistical problem, and some sophisticated ways of dealing with measurements have evolved out of the application of statistical methods.

One example is in the comparison of the weight of containers of nuclear material as determined by a shipper and by a receiver. Because of measurement error and random effects, the two weights seldom coincide. How big do the discrepancies have to be in order to give cause for alarm? How many small losses does one tolerate before becoming convinced that a diverter is deliberately trickling material out of many shipments in order to escape detection? These and other questions have been approached by statisticians through hypothesis tests, cumulative techniques, and software for accounting and for Monte Carlo simulation of diversion scenarios. See Rose et al (1982).

Since about 1975, the NRC has encouraged the use of another statistical technique, probabilistic risk assessment (PRA) in the quantitative analysis of nuclear reactor safety. The first major application of this technique took place in the Reactor Safety Study (WASH-1400), which demonstrated that the systematic analysis of nuclear power plant safety could reasonably be accomplished. PRA uses a collection of fault trees and event trees, which decompose the events that can lead to an accident to their lowest quantifiable level, and then show how the failures of minor components can build up to the failure of large subsystems and even the plant itself. NRC has recently accelerated its use of PRA to help reexamine the rationale behind NRC's collection of regulatory processes. As a result statisticians are currently involved with industry and regulatory representatives in giving technical guidance on PRA methods and procedures. A draft PRA Procedures Guide (NUREG/CR-2300) was recently released for peer review, and has been the subject of workshops and conferences in which statisticians have been active.

A third area of contribution by statisticians in nuclear power is in determining health effects due to radiation exposure. Here, the techniques of small population statistics must be brought to bear in a very sensitive arena. An example of work done in this important area is Gilbert (1980).

5. SOLAR POWER

Solar power is one of the interesting new areas of increased energy activity that falls under the category of renewable resources (since the sun is essentially an infinite source of energy). Computing statisticians are contributors to several major solar studies, of which two are mentioned here.

DOE has sponsored several solar thermal electrical generation experiments, a major one of which is being conducted in the desert south of Albuquerque, New Mexico. Here, a 200-foot tower is surrounded by mirrors which follow the sun's path and focus rays on a solar collector atop the tower. The hot gases from the collector in turn run a power generator. The entire system, since it is experimental, is subject to uncertainties in its safety. As a result, EPRI, representing its utility subscribers, has funded a safety study similar to the nuclear PRA techniques mentioned above. This study is pointing out ways in which the total thermal generating plant can be made a safe and viable means of providing needed power to sun belt utilities.

A second experiment, and one that involves the collection and analysis of large amounts of data, is the Solar Photovoltaic Data Reduction Center (DRC), sponsored by DOE at Sandia National Laboratory, New Mexico. DOE has awarded design contracts to several companies and institutions for various photovoltaic system application experiments. The prime goal of DRC is to collect and archive data from the experimental sites across the U.S. and make the data available to DRC users. Reports generated by the DRC project go to experimenters and statisticians at Solar Energy Research Institute, National Oceanic and Atmospheric Administration and other locations for analysis. The result is an important advance in the state of the art of solar collector photovoltaics.

6. CONCLUDING REMARKS

Since solar power was the only renewable energy resource highlighted, is is worth mentioning just a few other areas in which statisticians are making contributions: wind energy (safety);

wave energy (frequency/amplitude studies); and biomass (estimation of quantities, often through remote sensing).

In total, it is easy to see that the computing statistician is working hand in hand with other researchers and scientists in practically every field of energy development, production, and distribution. The problems represented by the energy demands of our society and the shortfall of supply on the near horizon are by no means solved. As a result, the need for statisticians and their computational tools can be expected to continue growing for many years to come.

7. REFERENCES

Burnett, B. (1979). The Analysis of Large Data Sets project - computer science research areas. Proc. 1979 DOE Statistical Symposium, D. A. Gardiner and T. Truett, eds. Oak Ridge National Laboratory. pp. 205-208.

Carr, D. B. (1979). The Many Facets of Large. Proc. 1979 DOE Statistical Symposium, D. A. Gardiner and T. Truett, eds. Oak Ridge National Laboratory. pp. 201-204.

David, M. (1977). Geostatistical oil reserve estimation, Elsevier, New York.

Eddy, W. F., and J. B. Kadane (1982). The cost of drilling for oil and gas. J. Amer. Statist. Assoc. 77, pp. 262-269.

Gilbert, E. S. (1980). An evaluation of methods for assessing the effects of occupational exposure to radiation. Paper presented at Joint Statistical Meetings, Houston, Texas.

Nelson, D. L., D. S. Newman, Y. K. Chan, B. Dembart, F. W. Scholz and E. Yip (1981). A physically based methodology for constructing load models for power systems. Boeing Computer Services document 40236-5, prepared under Department of Energy contract DE-AC01-78ET29020.

Nuclear Regulatory Commission (1981). PRA procedures guide, Review draft. Document NUREG/CR-2300. Prepared under the auspices of the American Nuclear Society and the Institute of Electrical and Electronics Engineers.

Rose, D. M., F. W. Scholz, and A. Matsumoto (1982). Statistical analysis of cumulative shipper-receiver data. Boeing Computer Services document 40384-0, prepared under Nuclear Regulatory Commission contract NRC-01-81-012-01.

"WHAT TO DO 'TIL THE NONLINEAR MODEL COMES": INTEGRATING A PLETHORA OF COMPUTATIONAL AND GRAPHIC TOOLS FOR ANALYSIS OF MULTIVARIATE DATA

James M. Malone II, Innovative Information Technology, Schenectady, N.Y.

This presentation will describe coordinated use of a variety of new and little known computer-based methods to (1) screen many variables for nonlinear predictive power, (2) separate or combine predictors to reduce dimension of predictor spaces for nonlinear response modeling, (3) effectively display response curves or hypersurfaces for one or several predictors, (4) fit intermediate or final models subject to global "qualitative" constraints.

KEY WORDS: multivariate homogeneity, iterative partitioning, nonparametric regression, stereograms, nonlinear estimation, iconic displays, curve fitting, cluster analysis, explanatory power.

Because of the scope of this tutorial and limitations of space only an outline of the topics will be given.

PROBLEM STAGE	NEW SOLUTIONS
1. Can y vector be predicted by x vector?	1. Let f(x,y)=joint distribution of x, y, $f_X(x)$=marginal distribution of x, $f_Y(y)$=marginal distribution of y, $g(x,y)=f_X(x)f_Y(y)$=distribution of randomly paired x, y. Test homogeneity of distributions f(x,y),g(x,y).
2. Which components of x vector predict y vector?	2. Partition x-space into regions heterogeneous with respect to y. Measure powers of x components to explain the partitioning.
3. What factors (linear combinations of salient x components) best predict a particular y component?	3.1. A method based on finding hyperplanes tangent to response surface and parallel to regression hyperplanes. 3.2. A method using measures of nonlinear association between y and combinations of x's.
4. How is y nonlinearly related to predictive factors?	4.1. Graphical display using contour stereograms and extensions. 4.2. "Rubber sheet" curve and surface fitting.
5. Having conjectured a model, how obtain acceptable parameter estimates?	5. Estimation with sign or monotonicity constraints via semi-infinite programming.

1. Method. Test homogeneity of multivariate distributions given samples from n populations of real vectors.

A. By selection of observation points without replacement form n(n-1)/2 samples of between population interpoint distances and n samples of within population interpoint distances.

Remarks: Requires an algorithm to achieve desirable sizes for distance samples. Possibly desirable to perform rotations and dilatations before computing Euclidean distance.

B. Test homogeneity of resulting n(n+1)/2 univariate samples.

Possibilities: Use Barton and David (1957) multiple runs statistic. Pool "between" distances and "within" distances and use any univariate two-sample homogeneity test.

Applications:

A. To test independence of x and y vectors given (x,y) observations, divide sample into two parts. In one part randomly permute the x vectors paired with y vectors, giving sample with same marginals and x,y independent. Test multivariate homogeneity of the two resulting (x,y) samples.

B. To test "distribution symmetry" of x and y vectors (f(x,y)=f(y,x)) divide sample into two parts and exchange x and y in one part. Test homogeneity of resulting samples. (Note: For scalars, symmetry of x and y is equivalent to distribution of x-y conditioned on x+y being symmetric about zero.)

C. To test fit of a hypothesized distribution generate monte carlo samples from it and test homogeneity with observed sample. (Alternatively use Levy-Rosenblatt transformation $x_i'=Pr(X_i \leq x_i | x_1,\ldots,x_{i-1})$ to obtain "observed" independent uniform variates then use principle suggested by A to verify independence.

2. Method. Partition predictor space into regions with heterogeneous responses (prediction oriented partitioning or POP).

A. Initially all observations form one group.

B. At each stage consider group "most dissimilar to self" (heterogeneous). For each predictor with more than one level dichotomize observations in this group by agglomerative clustering:

(1) Initially each level of the predictor defines a cluster.
(2) Combine the two most similar clusters into a cluster. (If levels of predictor are ordered, possibly combine the two most similar clusters with adjacent levels.) Repeat until there are exactly two clusters.

Retain the dichotomy with the most dissimilar pair of clusters, i.e., split the group into two groups based on levels of the selected variable (if resulting groups are of sufficient size and sufficiently dissimilar).
C. Continue to split groups until no group can be split or is sufficiently dissimilar to self or there are "enough" groups.
Remarks: Any measure of similarity of two groups of responses can be used. (Responses may be multivariate.) Selection of variables on which to split groups and estimation of similarities may be carried out by working with random subsets of the data.
D. Similarity measures produced in the process of evaluating dichotomies (potential splits) may be aggregated for each predictor to give indices of potential explanatory power or PEP of each predictor as interacting with all others.
E. To show structure of final groups display responses in typical observations of each group using metroglyphs or shadow boxes. A <u>shadow box</u> is a matrix of symbols encoding levels of variables, and is the line-printer substitute for metroglyphs or other icons (e.g. Chernoff faces).

3. <u>Method</u>. Find linear combinations of x's which predict y.

3.1. Let $u_i = \Sigma a_{ij} x_j$, $y \simeq f(u_1, \ldots, u_m)$, $(\Sigma_j a_{ij}^2 = 1)$.

$$\frac{\partial y}{\partial x_j} = \Sigma_{i=1}^{m} \frac{\partial f}{\partial u_i} a_{ij}$$

The $\partial y/\partial x_j$'s have an m-dimensional basis in function space. Representing them in terms of such a basis gives the a's. There is a correspondence between such representation in the space and representation at a finite set of points in x-space, say S. Therefore:
A. Perform several multiple linear regressions of y on the x's.
B. If there is a hyperplane tangent to the response surface y(x) and parallel to the "true" regression hyperplane then $\partial y/\partial x_j$ equals the regression coefficient of x_j at points of tangency. Take such a point of tangency for each regression to be a point of S (parallel hyperplane heuristic or PH^2. In actual computations the empirical regressions may be weighted according to goodness of fit.)
C. Brillinger (1977) has shown that for m=1 if the x's are a random sample from a multivariate normal distribution, then there <u>is</u> a parallel hyperplane with probability one.

<u>Further applications of parallel hyperplane heuristic</u>.

Among several further models which may be treated by PH^2 is $y \approx \Sigma f_i(x_i)$.
A. Divide x space into subregions. Do linear regressions. Assume parallel hyperplane approximately tangent at centroid of subregion. Then $f_i'(\bar{x}_i)$ approximately equals regression coefficient of x_i.
B. Plot $f_i'(\bar{x}_i)$ against $\bar{x}_i$. Identify form of f_i' thus form of f_i. (This model may of course be treated in other ways.)

3.2. Choose a predictor u based on a measure of nonlinear association with y. Let $w_{ij} = 1/(y_i - y_j + \varepsilon)^2$.
Possible measures (Cliff and Ord, 1973):
$\Sigma w_{ij}(u_i - \bar{u}_i)(u_j - \bar{u}_j)$ Moran's generalized I
$\Sigma w_{ij}(u_i - u_j)^2$ Geary's generalized c (also used by Carroll for "parametric mapping" and interpretation of nonmetric scaling solutions).
Correlation between y and a smoothing of y as a function of u via a Tukey nonlinear filter (Friedman's "projection pursuit regression").
Correlation between y and u (special case of 3.1 with m=1 and S a single point).

It can be readily shown that extremizing I and c lead to symmetric eigenvalue problems with the a's as eigenvectors. The correlation-based approaches may be used to produce u_i's one at a time, either orthogonal to preceding u_i or fitted to residuals from a model f based on the preceding u_i. Related methods may be used to achieve nonlinear association between y and any specified function of the x's with undetermined parameters--often by iterative schemes resulting from taking u to be a linearized Taylor series approximation.

4. <u>Method</u>. New graphical display techniques.

4.1. Display response (and possibly other predictors) as function of three predictors by a contour (or glyph) stereogram.

A (metro)glyph is a configuration of rays emanating from a point, orientation of a ray identifying a variable and length encoding its value at the point. A "contour" is here a symbol placed at a point encoding the value of a single variable at the point.

The stereogram is a representation of objects in three dimensional space by a binocular pair of plane images viewed through a stereoscope.* A point (x,y,z) in the unit cube is projected into the pair of points $(X_1,Y),(X_2,Y)$ where +x is "right", +y is "forward", +z is "up" and
$X_1=0.74+r(x-.32)$ $Y=0.84+r(y-0.50)$
$X_2=3.26+r(x-.68)$ $r=2.74/(2.64-z)$

*For example "stereo opticon viewer" sold by Taylor-Merchant Corporation, 25 W. 45th St., New York.

4.2. Consider a traditional plane contour plot of z as a function of x and y (z=z(x,y)) drawn on an elastic membrane. Perform a continuous invertible distortion of the x-y plane. Project the contour plot and the original x-y grid vertically on the u-v plane. Suppose the resulting contour plots x(u,v), y(u,v) and z(u,v) are readily modeled. Then by eliminating u and v the form of z(x,y) is identified.

Similarly and more usefully consider the plot of y vs. x (y=y(x)) and distort x. (Piecewise linear distortions are easily handled mechanically by "fanfolding" the plotting paper or in interactive graphics.) Project x (x=x(x)) and y on u, identify x(u) and y(u) then eliminate u. This is "rubber sheet curve fitting". A special case is Hastings' (1955) transformation.

5. Method. Fit parameters subject to sign or monotonicity constraints on the model.

Let the model be $f(x,\theta)$ where x and θ are vectors with θ to be estimated. Let the constraints be: $g_i(x,\theta)\geq 0$ for all x in X_i. Typically $g_i \equiv f$ or $\partial f/\partial\theta_j$ for some component θ_j.

A. Let the active constraint set be empty.
B. Find the θ of best fit subject to $g_{i_k}(x_k,\theta) \geq 0$ for all pairs (i_k,x_k) in the active constraint set (replacing previous θ). Use any applicable mathematical programming algorithm.
C. Let $z_i=g_i(x_{(i)},\theta)$ minimize $g_i(x,\theta)$ for x in X_i. If $z_i<0$ add $(i,x_{(i)})$ to the active constraint set. If $z_i\geq 0$ for all i stop.
D. If $g_{i_k}(x_k,\theta)\geq \varepsilon>0$ remove (i_k,x_k) from the active constraint set.
E. Return to step B.

This usually successful method is called semi-infinite programming (finite number of parameters, infinite number of constraints).

References

Barton, D.E. and David, F.N. (1957) "Multiple Runs," Biometrika 44, 168-178.

Brillinger, D.R. (1977) "The Identification of a Particular Time Series System," Biometrika 64, 509-515.

Cliff, A.D. and Ord, J.K. (1974) Spatial Autocorrelation, Pion Ltd., London.

Hastings, C. Jr., Hayward, J.T. and Wong, J.P., Jr. (1955) Approximations for Digital Computers, Princeton University Press, Princeton, p. 106.

EXACT SAMPLING DISTRIBUTIONS OF TWO MEASURES OF SKEWNESS - A COMPUTER APPROACH

Derrick S. Tracy and William C. Conley
University of Windsor and University of Wisconsin at Green Bay

ABSTRACT

Sampling distributions of the ratio statistic $k_3/k_2^{3/2}$ are calculated for the discrete uniform distribution using computer techniques. The same algorithm is used to calculate the sampling distribution of the measure of skewness

$$sk = \frac{(Q_3-M)-(M-Q_1)}{(Q_3-M)+(M-Q_1)} .$$

It is pointed out that computer techniques can be used to find the exact sampling distribution of virtually any statistic from any underlying distribution for small samples.

Graphs of selected sampling distributions are presented.

Keywords: Exact sampling distributions, measures of skewness, algorithm, Calcomp plotter

1. INTRODUCTION

The ratio statistic $k_3/k_2^{3/2}$, Kendall and Stuart [1], is a measure of skewness (lack of symmetry) of a distribution. Finding the sampling distribution of this ratio statistic can by very complicated using traditional methods. Using computer techniques we obtained the sampling distribution of $k_3/k_2^{3/2}$ for sampling without replacement from the discrete uniform distribution for the following values of $\binom{N}{n}$: $\binom{15}{3}$, $\binom{15}{4}$, $\binom{15}{5}$, $\binom{15}{6}$, $\binom{15}{7}$, $\binom{15}{8}$, $\binom{15}{9}$, $\binom{15}{10}$, $\binom{125}{3}$, $\binom{60}{4}$, $\binom{40}{5}$, $\binom{30}{6}$ and $\binom{25}{8}$.

We define the discrete uniform distribution to be $f(x) = \frac{1}{N}$, $x = 1,2,\dots,N$.

Several sampling distributions of $k_3/k_2^{3/2}$ were calculated for the discrete unform distribution for sampling with replacement. The results were similar to the corresponding "without replacement" sampling distributions.

The statistic $sk = \frac{(Q_3-M)-(M-Q_1)}{(Q_3-M)+(M-Q_1)}$ is a measure of skewness, where Q_1 is the first quartile, M is the median, and Q_3 is the third quartile, Yule and Kendall [2]. Its value ranges between ± 1. We obtained the sampling distributions of sk for the discrete uniform distribution for sampling without replacement when the population size is N=15 and 20 and the sample size is $n = 3,4,5,\dots,10$ using the computer algorithm.

However, the computer technique is general enough to allow us to calculate the sampling distribution of any univariate (and some bivariate and multivariate) statistic for any sampling scheme applied to any finite underlying distribution. Finite approximations to continuous underlying distributions can also be used.

2. THE COMPUTER ALGORITHM

The computer program used to calculate a sampling distribution can essentially be divided into two parts. The first part consists of the statistic in question, the underlying distribution, and the type of sampling to be done (with or without replacement, etc.). The second part consists of the histogram which records the location of each sample statistic value and its corresponding probability.

Usually nested DO-loops are used to consider all possible samples and about a 10 statement series with IF statements in a loop are required for the histogram. The authors used FORTRAN IV on an I.B.M. 360-65 computer with a Calcomp plotter attached to the computer to draw the graphs. However, any computer language that has IF statements, DO-loops, and subscripted variables would suffice for sampling distribution work.

The upper and lower bounds for the histograms can be selected by the researcher and fixed ahead of time. Then this region is just divided up into 8, $16,32,64,128,\dots,2^r$ intervals depending on the accuracy required for the study being undertaken.

It is not necessary to limit oneself to sampling from the discrete uniform distribution. The previously discussed program can be modified to sample from any finite distribution, the only limitations being the speed and capacity of the computer being used in the study. For sampling without replacement the probability of each sample can be unequal. If so, each probability is calculated and stored for later use in constructing the sampling distribution histogram. If storage is not feasible the probabilities can be calculated in the actual histogram loop.

Figures 1 and 2 show some examples of sampling distributions of $k_3/k_2^{3/2}$. Figures 3 and 4 show the graphs of some sampling distributions of sk . Sampling distributions of a variety of statistics from different sampling situations and the programming details are available from the authors.

FIGURE 1

$k_3/k_2^{3/2}$

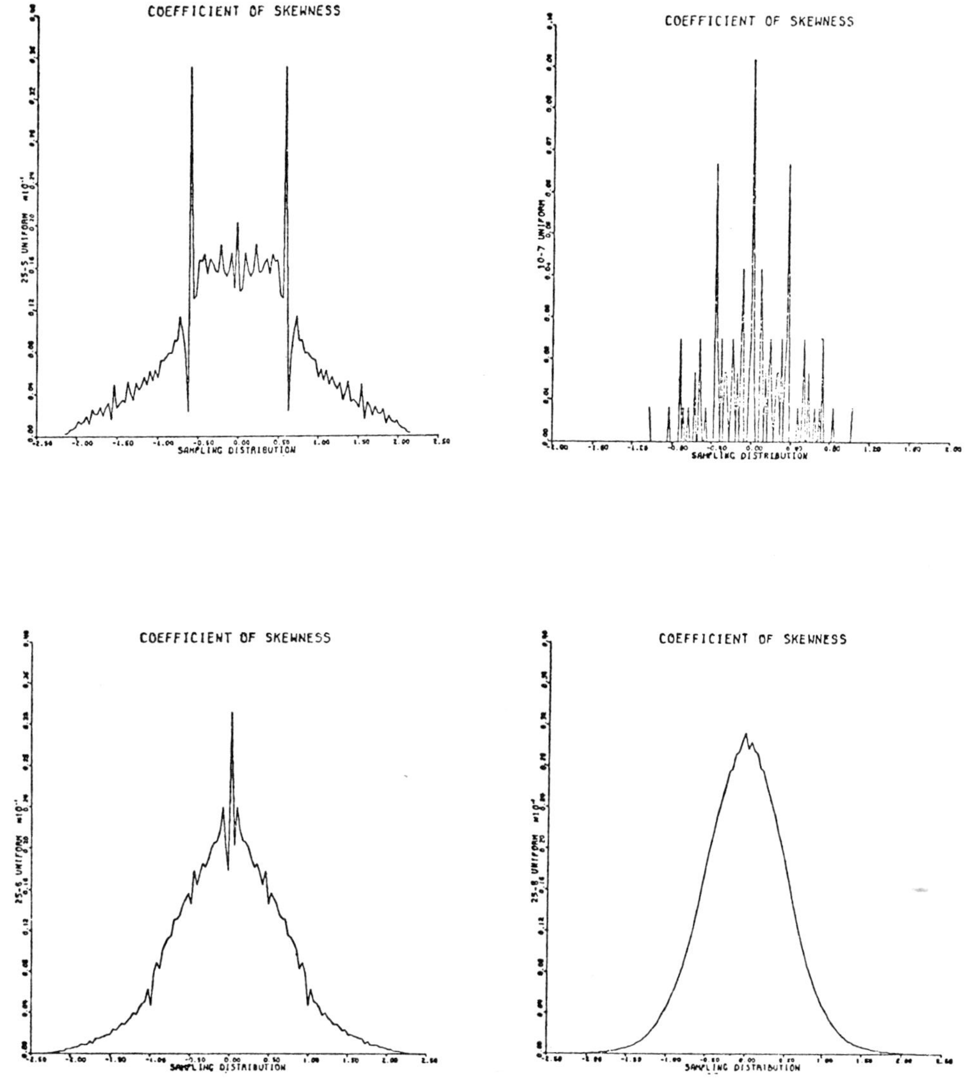

FIGURE 2

$k_3/k_2^{3/2}$

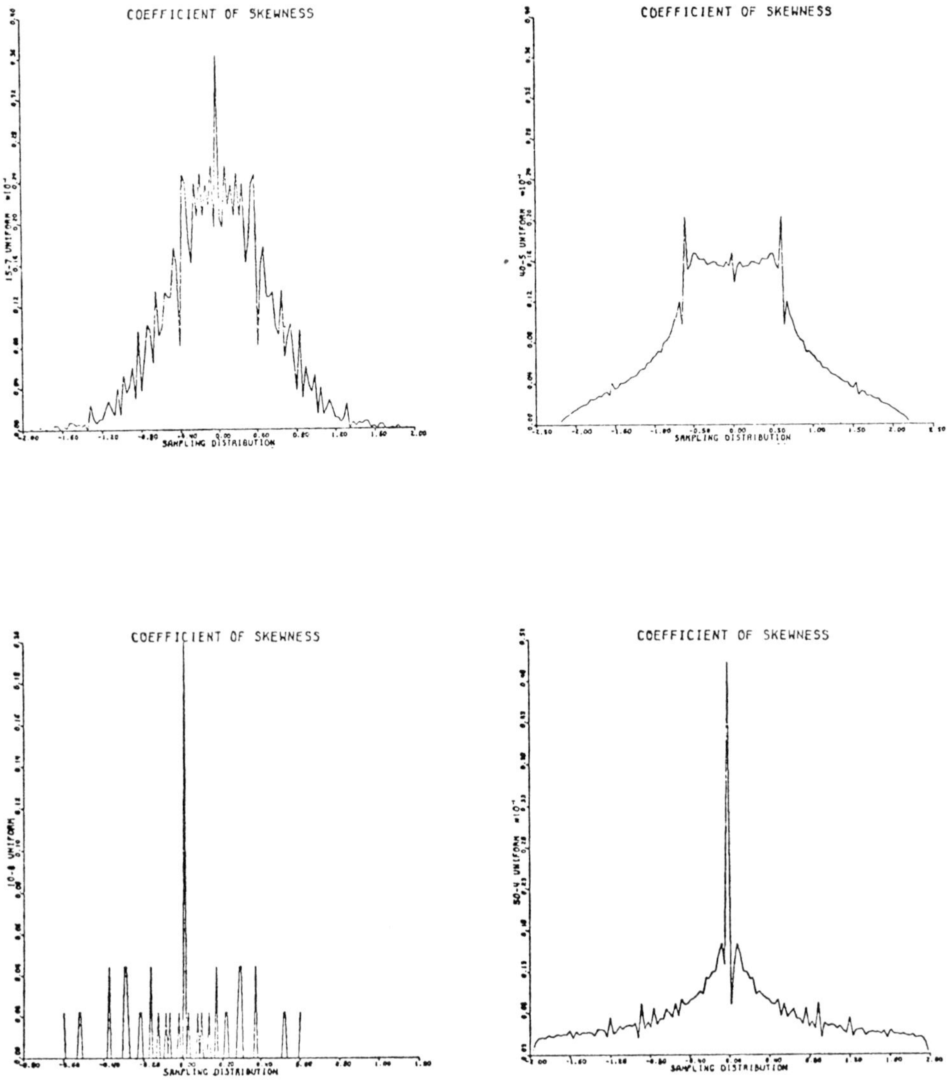

FIGURE 3

sk

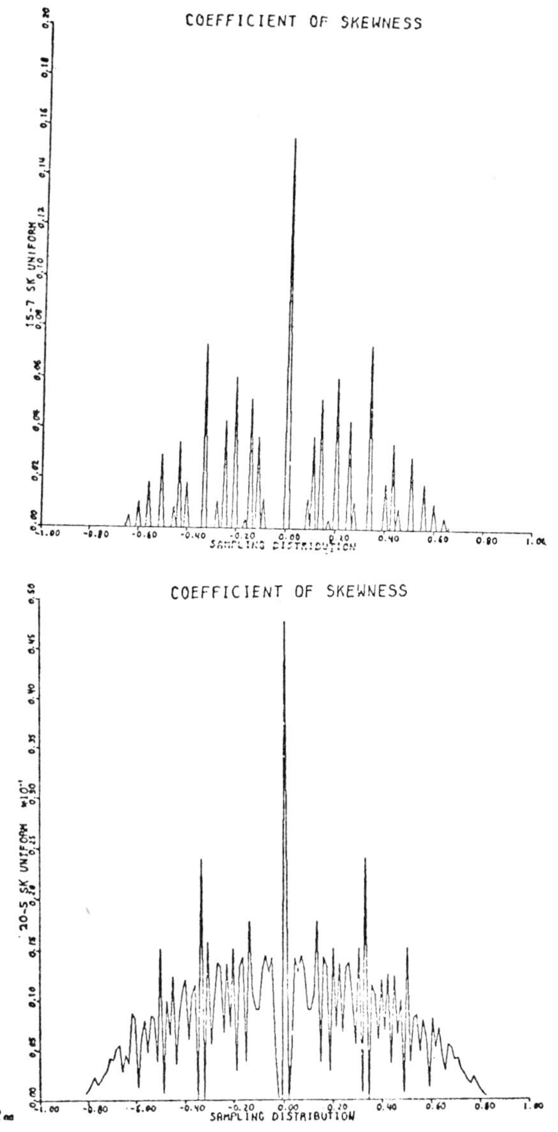

FIGURE 4

sk

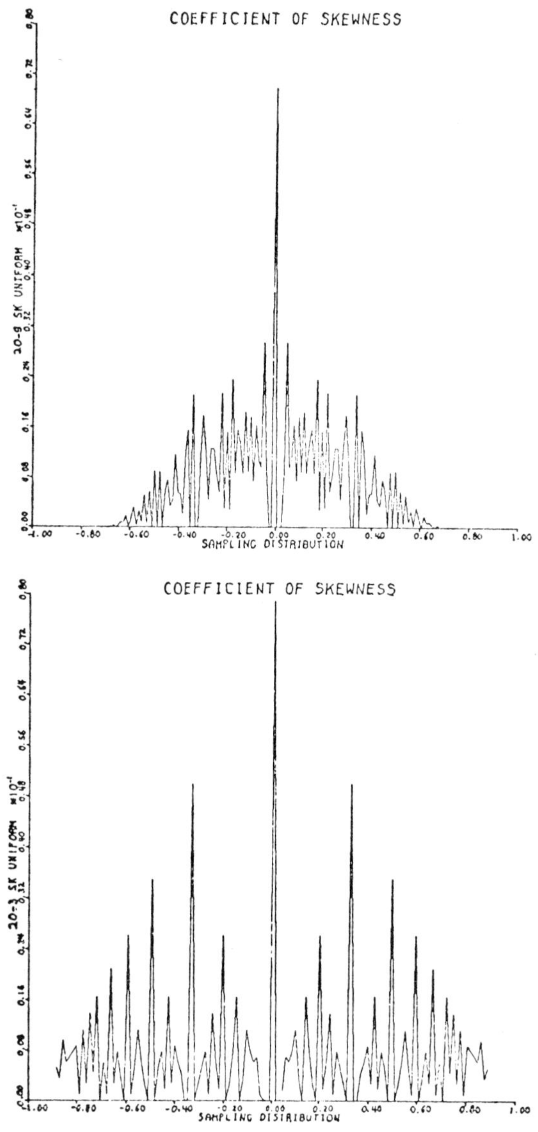

3. CONCLUSION

Our technique is similar to the Monte Carlo approach to sampling distributions in that with both techniques we examine thousands or millions of samples. However with our technique we examine all possible samples and hence find the exact sampling distribution of the statistic in question. Until very recently this approach to a theoretically difficult sampling distribution problem was technologically impossible. But with the recent and future advances in speed (Ware [3]) and capacity (Houston [4]) of computers our technique for finding exact sampling distributions can be useful in a variety of applications when classical techniques become complicated.

REFERENCES

[1] Kendall, M.G. and Stuart, A. (1958). The Advanced Theory of Statistics, 1, London: Charles Griffin and Company.

[2] Yule, G.U. and Kendall, M.G. (1945). An Introduction to the Theory of Statistics, 13th Edition; London, Charles Griffin and Company, Ltd.

[3] Ware, W.H. (1972). The Ultimate Computer, I.E.E.E. Spectrum, March, 84-91.

[4] Houston, G.B. (1973). Trillion Bit Memories. Datamation, October, 52 58.

A COLLECTION OF HAPPY ENDINGS FOR INCOMPLETE BETA FUNCTIONS

Lester Klein, The American University

ABSTRACT

Methods of generating random numbers with Exponential, Gamma, Beta, Cauchy, and Normal distributions in digital computers is given. These distributions are all obtained from appropriate transformation of the U(0,1) r.v.

A simple method for estimating $P(x \leq a)$, where x is either Beta, Gamma, or Exponential, and a is any value in the domain of x is also shown.

INTRODUCTION

Most installations and most high level languages provide a library function to yield pseudo-random numbers uniformly distributed on the unit interval. For example, at IBM installations, RANDU may be invoked in any FORTRAN program.

$U(0,1)$ to $N(m,s^2)$

From the well-known fact that if x is uniformly distributed on (0,1) we have $E(x)=\frac{1}{2}$, $Var(x)=1/12$, we may quickly and easily obtain a random number with mean 0.0 and variance 1.0 by adding 12 observations from U(0,1), subtracting 6.0, which is normally distributed by virtue of the Central Limit Theorem. The linear transformation $z'=sz+m$ quickly yields a random number with any desired mean and variance.

Uniform to Exponential

The cumulative distribution function of an Exponential distribution with parameter b is

$$F(x) = b\int_0^x e^{-bt}dt$$

F(x) represents a probability and hence is a number in the unit interval. The integral equation above may be solved for x yielding

$$x = \frac{-\ln(1.0 - F(x))}{b}$$

By using a random number from U(0,1) for F(x) above we obtain a new random number which is exponentially distributed with parameter b. It's easy to confirm that for any positive value of b and any F(x) in (0,1) the value of x will be in $(0, \infty)$.

EXPONENTIAL TO GAMMA

The characteristic function of the Exponential distribution with parameter b is

$$C_x(t) = \frac{b}{b - it}$$

If $y = x_1+x_2+ \ldots +x_n$ where each x is Exponential with parameter b then the characteristic function of y is

$$C_y(t) = \left[\frac{b}{b - it}\right]^n$$

This form is easily recognized as the c.f. of a Gamma r.v. with parameters n and b. Thus, to abtain random numbers that have a Gamma distribution with parameters n and b, for example, we need only generate n exponential numbers with parameter b and add them together.

GAMMA TO BETA

We state as a Theorem a result which frequently appears as an exercise in textbooks on Mathematical Statistics.

Theorem 1. If x and y are independently distributed Gamma random variables with parameters (m,b) and (n,b), respectively, then the distribution of

$$u = \frac{x}{x + y}$$

is Beta with parameters m,n.

Proof:

By virtue of independence, the joint density of x and y is

$$f(x,y) = Cx^{m-1}y^{n-1}\exp(-b(x+y))$$

$$x > 0, y > 0$$

where

$$C = \frac{b^{m+n}}{(m-1)!(n-1)!}$$

Let $u=x/(x+y)$ and $v=y$.
Solving for x and y, we obtain

$$x = \frac{uv}{(1-u)} \qquad y = v$$

The jacobian of this transformation is easily computed and found to be

$$|J| = v/(1-u)^2$$

The joint density of u and v may now be written as

$$h(u,v) = C\left(\frac{uv}{1-u}\right)^{m-1} v^{n-1} \exp\left[\frac{-bv}{1-u}\right]$$

$$0 < u < 1, v > 0$$

The marginal density of u may be found by integrating with respect to v,i.e.,

$$g(u) = Cu^{m-1}(1-u)^{-m-1}\int_0^\infty v^{m+n-1} \exp\left[\frac{-bv}{1-u}\right] dv$$

The integrand is easily recognized as a Gamma function with parameters (m+n) and (b/(1-u)). Hence, the integral above is equal to

$$(m+n-1)!\, b^{-m-n}(1-u)^{m+n}$$

The desired result,

$$h(u) = \frac{(m+n-1)!}{(m-1)!(n-1)!} u^{m-1}(1-u)^{n-1}$$

$$0 < u < 1$$

follows after some cancellation.qed.

Thus Beta distributed random numbers may be generated by first generating a Gamma distributed random number with parameters m,b (the value of b is irrelevant as long as it is greater than 0),then another Gamma distributed number with parameters n,b, and finally computing $x/(x+y)$.

NORMAL TO CAUCHY

Here is a cleverly worded problem that the author has seen on a comprehensive examination:

If x and y are independently distributed normal random variables with means 0 and variances 1 show that the mean of

$$u = x/y$$

does not exist.

Of course, the way to answer such a question is to find the probability distribution function of u and to show that it is the Cauchy distribution.

i.e.,

$$f(x,y) = \frac{1}{2\pi}\exp(-\tfrac{1}{2}(x^2+y^2))$$

$$-\infty < x,y < \infty$$

from $u=x/y$, $v=y$ we obtain, $x=uv, y=v$, with the Jacobian, $J = v$

The joint density of u and v is then

$$g(u,v) = \frac{1}{2\pi} v \exp(-\tfrac{1}{2}v^2(1+u^2))$$

$$-\infty < u,v < \infty$$

Letting $w=v^2$ we get $v=w^{\frac{1}{2}}, dv/dw=\frac{1}{2}w^{-\frac{1}{2}}$, and

$$h(u,w) = \frac{1}{4\pi}\exp(-\tfrac{1}{2}w(1+u^2))$$

$$-\infty < w < \infty$$

In order to get the density of u we must integrate with respect to w.
We observe that w is an even function hence

$$g(u) = \frac{1}{2\pi}\int_0^\infty \exp(-\tfrac{1}{2}w(1+u^2))dw$$

from which the result follows.

$$g(u) = \frac{1}{\pi(1+u^2)} \qquad \text{qed}$$

This result also holds if x and y have equal variances other than 1.0.

EXAMPLES

The algorithms herein described were executed on IBM equipment and the FORTRAN language. 10,000 random numbers with each of the five distributions were generated and histograms produced with the results. The first 2 moments about the mean are also given.

It is easy to see that they all pass the "eyeball" test, that is, the normal, exponential, Gamma, and Beta distributions all have the correct shape. The values of the first 2 moments about the mean all agree very well with theory.

The histogram of the Cauchy distributed random numbers demonstrates that the pdf of that distribution approaches 0 very slowly as x approaches plus and minus infinity.

```
10,000 RANDOM NUMBERS DISTRIBUTED AS N(0,1),

< -2,25         ***
                 105

-2,25,-1,75     *******
                 301

-1,75,-1,25     **************
                 654

-1,25,-0,75     *************************
                1209

-0,75,-0,25     ***********************************
                1735

-0,25, 0,25     ***************************************
                1949

 0,25, 0,75     ************************************
                1784

 0,75, 1,25     ************************
                1167

 1,25, 1,75     ***************
                 712

 1,75, 2,25     ******
                 278

>  2,25         ***
                 106

MEAN = 0,0019888  VARIANCE = 0,9949487
```

```
EXPONENTIAL DISTRIBUTION WITH PARAMETER 2,0

<  0,25         ***************************************
                3884

 0,25, 0,50     *************************
                2444

 0,50, 0,75     ****************
                1502

 0,75, 1,00     *********
                 848

 1,00, 1,25     ******
                 510

 1,25, 1,50     ****
                 300

 1,50, 1,75     **
                 187

 1,75, 2,00     **
                 123

 2,00, 2,25     *
                  84

 2,25, 2,50     *
                  49

 2,50, 2,75     *
                  30

>  2,75         *
                  39

MEAN = 0,4998574  VARIANCE = 0,2499766
```

```
GAMMA DISTRIBUTION WITH PARAMETERS 5 AND 2,0

<  0,50         *
                  43

 0,50, 1,00     *****
                 508

 1,00, 1,50     *************
                1320

 1,50, 2,00     *******************
                1902

 2,00, 2,50     ******************
                1869

 2,50, 3,00     ***************
                1525

 3,00, 3,50     **********
                1054

 3,50, 4,00     *******
                 784

 4,00, 4,50     ****
                 450

 4,50, 5,00     **
                 258

>  5,50         *
                 154

MEAN = 2,4919949  VARIANCE = 1,2524490
```

```
BETA DISTRIBUTED RANDOM NUMBERS WITH PARAMETERS 5 AND 6

<  0,10         *
                  14

 0,10, 0,20     ***
                 301

 0,20, 0,30     ***********
                1172

 0,30, 0,40     *********************
                2193

 0,40, 0,50     *************************
                2507

 0,50, 0,60     ********************
                2075

 0,60, 0,70     ************
                1241

 0,70, 0,80     ****
                 434

 0,80, 0,90     *
                  59

>  0,90         *
                   4

MEAN = 0,4564340  VARIANCE = 0,0210918
```

CAUCHY DISTRIBUTION WITH PARAMETER 0,0

< -2,25	*************	1300
-2,25,-1,75	****	327
-1,75,-1,25	*****	488
-1,25,-0,75	*********	816
-0,75,-0,25	*************	1265
-0,25, 0,25	***************	1560
0,25, 0,75	*************	1334
0,75, 1,25	********	786
1,25, 1,75	*****	497
1,75, 2,25	***	287
> 2,25	*************	1340

APPLICATIONS

The obvious application of these algorithms is in Monte Carlo simulation models where it is necessary to sample populations that have any of distributions herein described. For example, in a queueing problem it may be necessary to generate some "waiting times" which are Gamma distributed. Gyrocompass "drift" is often simulated with a Gamma distributed random number and a 50/50 assignment of sign.

Another application is in the evaluation of incomplete Beta and Gamma functions without recourse to tables. Suppose, for example, that some problem being solved with a computer requires probabilities of the form $P(x \leq a)$ or $P(x \geq b)$ where x is either Gamma or Beta distributed and (a,b) are any numbers in the allowable ranges of x. All one need do to get good approximations of such probabilities is generate a large number of random numbers having the required distribution and count the frequency above or below a and b, respectively. The fraction of the total will then be the required probability.

For example, $P(x \leq 2.0)$ where x is a Gamma random variable with parameters 5 and 2.0 is approximately .1871. This is read directly from the histogram of the Gamma distributed random numbers on the previous page, i.e.

$$\frac{(43+508+1320)}{10000}$$

It is worthwhile to note that these algorithms not only produce random numbers that have the required shape and moments about the mean but are also very "well-behaved" in the tails.

BIBLIOGRAPHY

Rohatgi, V.K., An Introduction to Probability Theory and Mathematical Statistics, John Wiley & Sons.

A PORTABLE INTERACTIVE FORTRAN VERIFIER

Lon-Mu Liu
Department of Quantitative Methods
University of Illinois at Chicago
Box 4348, Chicago, Illinois 60680

Laszlo Engleman
Department of Biomathematics
University of California, Los Angeles
Los Angeles, California 90024

ABSTRACT

The PIF (Portable Interactive Fortran) verifier is a software tool that performs static analysis for Fortran programs. It is designed to analyze Fortran programs and report the possible errors and non-portable features within and between program units. Its capability is roughly a combination of the PFORT (Ryder 1974) and the DAVE (Osterweil and Fosdick 1976) systems. The PIF verifier stores the attributes of the variables in common blocks and dummy arguments in a subprogram in an information file as soon as the program unit is analyzed. Such information in turn is used to check subsequent usages of the common blocks and subprograms. Because a subprogram can be individually checked, the PIF system can verify Fortran software of any size. The cost for each program unit remains the same even if the total size of the software is large. In addition to program validation, the PIF verifier generates a ready-to-use documentation for each analyzed program unit and produces an inter-program-unit flow graph at any specified program unit.

Keywords: Fortran, static analysis, portability, automatic documentation, call-graph.

1. INTRODUCTION

The PIF (Portable Interactive Fortran) verifier is a software tool that performs static analysis for Fortran programs. It is designed to analyze Fortran programs and report the possible errors and non-portable features within and between program units. Its capability is roughly a combination of the PFORT (Ryder, 1974) and the DAVE (Osterweil and Fosdick, 1976) systems. The PFORT verifier checks a program for adherence to portable Fortran (Ryder, 1974) and inter-program-unit communication. The DAVE system performs data flow analysis in addition to checking inter-program-unit communication. It is capable of detecting a wide variety of data flow anomalies, such as undefined or unused variables. The PIF system is designed to be used interactively and is convenient even for a large scale software development project.

The PIF system stores the attributes (e.g. type, input and/or output, scalar or array) of the variables in common blocks and dummy arguments in a subprogram in an information file as soon as the program unit is analyzed. Such information in turn is used to check subsequent usages of the common blocks and subprograms. Because a subprogram can be individually checked, the PIF system can verify Fortran software of any size. The cost for each program unit remains the same even if the total size of the software package is large. The information file is portable and can therefore, once it is generated, be used on different computing systems.

In an interactive environment, the output of a verification system must be appropriately tailored and must allow the user to control the amount of output. In such environment, even the listing of the source statements can be quite prohibitive. The PIF verifier avoids this problem by associating error messages for a statement with the line number of the statement. In addition, the user can specify the amount of output by using PIF control statements which are similar to Fortran statements. The control statements can also be used to turn off and on diagnostic messages, create call-graph, compress the information file, etc.

The PIF system is designed to verify programs written in either Fortran-66 or Fortran-77. (The current version only handles Fortran-66 programs.) One major difference between these two standards is the usage of the character variables, which is the main source of non-portability in Fortran-66. Its effect on Fortran-77 remains to be seen. Character variable usage in Fortran-77 is more restrictive than that in Fortran-66. By using the PIF pseudo-Fortran statements, Fortran-77 standard for character variable usage can be enforced on the programs which run under Fortran-66 compilers. Thus, it provides a smooth transition from Fortran-66 to Fortran-77.

In addition to program validation, the PIF verifier generates a ready-to-use documentation for each analyzed program unit. The inter-program-unit flow graph (referred to here as call-graph) can also be produced at any specified program unit.

2. PIF USAGE

The PIF verifier assumes that the Fortran code to be analyzed is stored in a file. This file may contain a single subprogram, a group of subprograms, or a main program and subprograms. The verifier analyzes the program units sequentially and stores the checking information in the information file one by one. When a particular subprogram (program unit) is analyzed all information relevant to that unit which have been stored as a result of previous analyses are utilized for checking correct inter-program-unit-communications. Hence to facilitate a more complete inter-progrom-unit-communications checking the calling subprograms ought to be analyzed (or re-analyzed) after all called subprograms have been processed. The record length for the source code file must be 80 and the columns between 73 and 80 of each record must contain a record (statement) number. The record numbers must be in strictly increasing order within each program unit. There is no limit on the size of each program unit or the total number of program units in a file. However, it is desirable to break a large program into several groups of subprograms, and verify them group by group.

To meet various needs, the user may use the PIF control statements to specify the options of analysis and output. A PIF control statement has the following syntax:

```
C&    CONTROL /keyword/ options
```

The character "C&" must appear in the first two columns and the word CONTROL must appear after the sixth column. The continued lines (if needed) are also preceded by the "C&" characters and have a non-blank character in the sixth column. The control statements can be inter-mixed with the Fortran statements. Their usage will be discussed later. Note that it is not necessary to remove the control statements after the program is verified because they are treated as comment cards by Fortran compilers.

In addition to Fortran and PIF control statements, the source file can also contain pseudo-Fortran statements. A pseudo-Fortran statement is a valid Fortran statement (under Fortran-66 or Fortran-77) preceded by "C&" in the first two columns. Thus a pseudo-Fortran statement is also treated as a comment statement by Fortran compilers but is considered by the verifier to be a valid statement. The use of pseudo-Fortran statements enables enforcement of Fortran-77 standard on a program to be compiled under Fortran-66 compilers.

The syntax of the PIF control statements is explained in the next section. Examples of the PIF usage are listed in Section 4.

3. CONTROL STATEMENTS

The PIF verifier has ten control statements. Each statement usually has several options. Four of them are described below:

(1) The PROFILE statement

Syntax

```
C&    CONTROL /PROFILE/ LISTING(YES or NO),
C&    *                 SUMMARY(YES or NO),
C&    *                 NEWFILE(YES OR NO),
C&    *                 LEVEL(i)
```

The PROFILE statement is used to control the general features of the PIF verifier. It can be repeatedly used anywhere in a program unit. The specified options will be in effect immediately. The meanings of the options are described below:

LISTING -- controls listing of the Fortran source code. The default is NO.

SUMMARY -- controls reporting of usage of variables and statement labels. The default is NO.

NEWFILE -- tells PIF if the information file is a new file (YES) or previously existing information file (NO) to which current information is to be added. The default is NO.

LEVEL -- specifies the call-graph level for this group of program units. The argument i must be a positive integer. This option is used in conjunction with the CALLGRAPH control statement.

(2) The MESSAGE statement

Syntax

```
C&    CONTROL /MESSAGE/ OFF(i, ..., i),
C&    *                 ON (i, ..., i)
```

The MESSAGE statement is used to control the amount of diagnostic messages. It is used to turn off and on the printing of certain diagnostics which may be less or more relevant in the programmer's environment. All diagnostic messages of the PIF verifier have unique numbers associated with them. The user may use the MESSAGE statement to turn off or on the printing of a specific diagnostic message. A pre-assigned (default) action will be taken if a diagnostic message number is not specified in the MESSAGE control statement. As an example, the following statement turns off the diagnostic messages 2302, 2510, and turns on the messages 904, 2508, and 702. Since the default action for 904, 2508, and 702 is ON, the ON specification can be omitted.

```
C&    CONTROL /MESSAGE/ OFF(2302,2510),
C&    *                 ON (904,2508,702)
```

(3) The LIBRARY statement

Syntax

```
C&     CONTROL /LIBRARY/ name(i), ..., name(i)
```

The LIBRARY statement allows the user to use the subprogram checking information from existing libraries where names are the names of the libraries and the i's are the corresponding logical units. When a subprogram is not found in the primary information file, the verifier will check the names in the libraries according to the order specified in the LIBRARY statement. The following statement will cause the verifier to check the subprogram usage against the information in the libraries LINPACK (first) and EISPACK (second).

```
C&     CONTROL /LIBRARY/ LINPACK(20), EISPACK(21)
```

(4) The CALLGRAPH statement

Syntax

```
C&     CONTROL /CALLGRAPH/ LEVEL(i),
C&     *            ENTRIES(name, ..., name)
```

The CALLGRAPH statement generates a call-graph for the user according to the specified entries and level. The subroutines with higher levels (specified by the PROFILE statement) than that specified in the CALLGRAPH statement will not be listed in the call-graph.

4. EXAMPLES

Below are two examples illustrating the capabilities of the PIF verifier. In the first example, the verifier reports undefined and unused variables. Most of the compilers do not report unused variables. Some compilers report undefined variables when the statement is executed (e.g., WATFIV). PIF provides such information all at once. In the second example, the verifier checks the consistency for the arguments between the calling and the called subprograms. Most of compilers also provide such information during program execution. Some compilers do not report the errors at all.

Example (1) Undefined and unused variables

Program Listing

```
00040  C&     CONTROL /PROFILE/ NEWFILE(YES)
00050  C
00060  C      CHECK THE USAGE OF A VARIABLE
00070  C
00080         SUBROUTINE SUBA(X,A)
00090         B=X
00100         A=1.0
00110         IF(X.GE.1.0) X=X+1.0
00120         A=X+1.0
00130         RETURN
00140         END
00230  C
00240         FUNCTION FUNA(A)
00250         A=B*10.0+1.0
00260         FUNA=FUNA*A
00270         IF(A.GT.10.0) FUNA=FUNA*A*A
00280         RETURN
00290         END
```

PIF Output

```
PROGRAM NAME: SUBA

*5012*   THE VARIABLE  A  IN STATEMENT 00000120
         HAS BEEN DEFINED AT LEAST TWICE BEFORE
         IT IS REFERENCED

*5020*   THE VARIABLE  B  IN STATEMENT 00000090
         IS DEFINED, BUT IS NEVER REFERENCED

END OF THE INFORMATION FOR PROGRAM SUBA
==========================================

PROGRAM NAME: FUNA

*5014*   THE VARIABLE  B  REFERENCED IN
         STATEMENT 00000250 IS NOT DEFINED

*5014*   THE VARIABLE  FUNA  REFERENCED IN
         STATEMENT 00000260 IS NOT DEFINED

END OF THE INFORMATION FOR PROGRAM FUNA
==========================================
```

Example (2) Consistency checking for the arguments between the calling and the called subprograms

Program Listing

```
00040  C&     CONTROL /PROFILE/ NEWFILE(YES)
00050  C
00060  C      CHECK THE ATTRIBUTES OF THE
00065  C      ACTUAL ARGUMENTS
00070  C
00080         SUBROUTINE SUBB(A,B,C,D,E,F,G,EXT)
00090         DIMENSION D(1),F(1)
00100         EXTERNAL EXT
00110         E=EXT(A)
00120         C=A+B
```

```
| 00130      15 FORMAT(1X,10F7.1)                     |
| 00140         IPRT=6                                |
| 00150         WRITE(IPRT,15) A,B,C,D,E,F,G          |
| 00160         RETURN                                |
| 00170         END                                   |
| 00180         SUBROUTINE SUBA(A,B,C,F,G,I)          |
| 00190         DIMENSION G(2),D(1)                   |
| 00200         EXTERNAL C                            |
| 00210         I=10                                  |
| 00220         B=15                                  |
| 00230         AB=3.0                                |
| 00240         CALL SUBB(A,I,C,1.0,1.0,F,G,EXT)      |
| 00250         CALL SUBB(A,B,AB+1.0,D,E,G,F,C)       |
| 00260         CALL SUBB(A,B)                        |
| 00270         RETURN                                |
| 00280         END                                   |
|                                                     |
```

PIF Output

```
*2730*  THE CHECKING INFORMATION FOR THE
        SUBPROGRAM  EXT  IN STATEMENT 00000110
        IS UNAVAILABLE

PROGRAM NAME: SUBB

END OF THE INFORMATION FOR PROGRAM SUBB
=======================================

*0114*  THE 8-TH ARGUMENT OF THE SUBPROGRAM
        SUBB  IN STATEMENT 00000240 SHOULD
        BE AN EXTERNAL FUNCTION

*0124*  THE 7-TH ARGUMENT OF THE SUBPROGRAM
        SUBB  IN STATEMENT 00000240 SHOULD
        BE A SCALAR, NOT AN ARRAY

*0122*  THE 6-TH ARGUMENT OF THE SUBPROGRAM
        SUBB  IN STATEMENT 00000240 SHOULD
        BE AN ARRAY, NOT A SCALAR

*0120*  THE 5-TH ARGUMENT OF THE SUBPROGRAM
        SUBB  IN STATEMENT 00000240 IS AN
        OUTPUT VARIABLE, CANNOT BE A CONSTANT
        OR AN EXPRESSION

*0118*  THE 4-TH ARGUMENT OF THE SUBPROGRAM
        SUBB  IN STATEMENT 00000240 SHOULD
        BE AN ARRAY, CANNOT BE A CONSTANT
        OR AN EXPRESSION

*0116*  THE 3-TH ARGUMENT OF THE SUBPROGRAM
        SUBB  IN STATEMENT 00000240  SHOULD
        NOT BE AN EXTERNAL FUNCTION

*0112*  THE 2-TH ARGUMENT OF THE SUBPROGRAM
        SUBB  IN STATEMENT 00000240 SHOULD
        BE REAL TYPE

*0120*  THE 3-TH ARGUMENT OF THE SUBPROGRAM
        SUBB  IN STATEMENT 00000250 IS AN OUTPUT
        VARIABLE, CANNOT BE A CONSTANT OR AN
        EXPRESSION

*2734*  THE NUMBER OF ARGUMENT(S) FOR THE
        SUBPROGRAM  SUBB  IN STATEMENT 00000260
        SHOULD BE 8, NOT 2

PROGRAM NAME: SUBA

*5014*  THE VARIABLE  D  REFERENCED IN STATEMENT
        00000250 IS NOT DEFINED

*5020*  THE VARIABLE  EXT  IN STATEMENT
        00000240 IS DEFINED.  BUT IS NEVER
        REFERENCED.

*5020*  THE VARIABLE  E  IN STATEMENT 00000250
        IS DEFINED.  BUT IS NEVER REFERENCED

END OF THE INFORMATION FOR PROGRAM SUBA
=======================================
```

5. DISCUSSION

Software development is labor intensive, especially program debugging and documentation. We find the tool of static analysis can alleviate such burden substantially. In addition, a verifier can also improve the reliability and quality of software, and enforce consistent programming style. The software tool development has been rapid in recent years. Among those, an integrated software tool, called TOOLPACK, is developed by Osterweil (1981).

We have employed the PIF verifier to develop large statistical software, the SCA system (Liu and Hudak 1982), which has approximately 90,000 statements, divided into approximately 400 subprograms. The PIF system has proven extremely useful. It shortens the debugging effort and also improves portability and reliability of the program.

ACKNOWLEDGEMENT The development of the PIF verifier was supported in part by grants from College of Business Administration, University of Illinois at Chicago, and Scientific Computing Associates. The authors wish to thank Judy Curry for her editorial assistance.

REFERENCES

[1] Liu, L.-M. and Hudak, G.B. (1982). "An Integrated Time Series Analysis Computer Program: the SCA System." To appear in the Proceedings of the International Time Series Meeting in Cincinnati.

[2] Osterweil, L.J. and Fosdick, L.D. (1976). "DAVE -- A Validation Error Dectection and Documentation System for FORTRAN Program." Software -- Practice and Experience 6: 473-496.

[3] Osterweil, L.J. (1981). "TOOLPACK Architectural Design," Department of Computer Science, University of Colorado at Boulder.

[4] Ryder, B.G. (1974). "The PFORT Verifier." Software -- Practice and Experience 4: 359-378.

A Graph-Decomposition Method Based on the Density-Contour Clustering Model

M. A. Wong, S. E. Madnick, and J. M. Lattin, Massachusetts Institute of Technology

Abstract

In this paper, a computationally efficient graph-decomposition procedure is proposed, which is based on the density-contour clustering model and the minimum spanning tree algorithm. The effectiveness of this procedure will be illustrated by a constructed example and its practical utility will also be pointed out.

Key Words. Graph-decomposition, density-contour clusters, minimum spanning tree algorithm, computational complexity.

1. INTRODUCTION

In this study, our objective is to develop a graph decomposition technique with the following properties: (1) it would partition a graph into densely-intraconnected subgraphs with minimal cross-links among these subgraphs; (2) it would require no prior knowledge of the number of such subgraphs present in the graph; and (3) it would be computationally efficient so that large graph networks would be effectively partitioned. The desirability of such a procedure has been indicated in the architectural design literature (see for example, Alexander 1964) and the social network literature (Lattin and Wong, 1982). In Section 2, a survey of the graph-decomposition literature is presented, and it leads to the conclusion that none of the existing techniques have all of the aforementioned properties. The density-contour clustering model on a graph is then defined in Section 3, and a graph-decomposition technique based on this model is described in Section 4. In Section 5, a discussion of the applications of the developed procedure is given.

2. REVIEW OF THE GRAPH-DECOMPOSITION LITERATURE

The graph-decomposition techniques found in the literature can be divided into two types: (a) the criterion-optimizing techniques--in which a partition of the given graph is obtained by optimizing a goodness-of-partition criterion, and (b) the node-tearing or bond-energy techniques--in which clusters of nodes are identified by searching for densely-intraconnected subgraphs which are inter-connected by relatively few cross-links.

2.1 Criterion-optimizing techniques

These techniques can be formulated as attempts to partition a graph so as to optimize some predetermined criterion. For example, many of them attempt to minimize the sum of the weights of the cross-links between subgraphs. (See Kernighan and Lin (1970), Lukes (1974, 1975), and Christofides and Brooker (1976) for methods that operate under some size constraints on the subgraphs, and see Ford and Fulkerson (1962) for an unconstrained approach.) These methods also operate under the assumption that the number of subgraphs (or clusters of nodes) the graph is to be partitioned into has been decided *a priori* by the investigator.

The differences between the methods lie primarily in the optimality of the final solution and the efficiency of the computational algorithm. Gorinshteyn (1969), Lukes (1975), and Christofides and Brooker (1976) all set out to find the globally optimal solution; however, Gorinshteyn uses a branch-and-bound strategy and Lukes take the dynamic programming approach, while Christofides and Brooker adopt the tree search method. On the other hand, Kernighan and Lin (1970) and Huff (1979) use an efficient interchange heuristic to search for a locally optimal solution.

A major drawback of these criterion-optimizing techniques is that they are not useful in determining the number of loosely-interconnected densely-intraconnected subgraphs present in a given graph. For a given graph, the "natural" concept of clustering suggests that one should be looking for subgraphs in which the nodes are densely-connected, separated from other such subgraphs by relatively few cross-links. (For related concepts in Euclidean space, see Zahn (1971), Hartigan (1975), and Wong and Lane (1981).) Graph decomposition methods which use this approach of seeking densely-intraconnected subgraphs in a graph will be described next.

2.2 Node-tearing and bond-energy techniques

The first method we will consider is the bond-energy algorithm due to McCormick et. al. (1972). By permuting the rows and columns of the graph adjacency matrix in such a way that numerically larger array elements are blocked together, their algorithm serves to identify the "natural " (or densely-intraconnected) subgraphs in the graph, as well as the interconnectedness of these subgraphs. Therefore, this bond-energy algorithm is useful in suggesting the number of natural subgraphs present in a graph, although it tends to give excessive weights to large elements in the graph-adjacency matrix. Its main drawback is that the best partition is not explicitly given and personal judgment has to be exercised to identify the subgraphs. Moreover, its computational time increases with N^3, where N is the number of nodes in the graph. The central idea underlying the node-tearing techniques (see Sangiovanni-Vincentelli, et. al, 1977) is to locate the smallest separating sets -- that is, the set of nodes with the lowest cardinality such that their removal from the graph splits the graph into two or more unconnected subgraphs. In effect, this type of technique searches for nodes which do not belong to any densely-intraconnected subgraph, and hence their removal will reveal the natural subgraphs. An efficient heuristic algorithm for node tearing is given in Sangiovanni-Vincentelli et. al. (1977), whose computational time is of order $O(Nb)$, where b is the numberof edges or links in the graph. However, the fact that the solution produced by this algorithm is only locally optimal remains a major concern.

The above survey indicates that there is still a gap in the graph decomposition literature. The criterion-optimizing techniques assume that the number of subgraphs has been decided a priori by the investigator, and hence do not address the problem of identifying the "appropriate" number of subgraphs. The node-tearing algorithm is an efficient heuristic for tearing large-scale networks, but it is only applicable to unweighted graphs. Moreover, it is not clear how the subgraph-membership of the nodes that are identified and removed by the node-tearing process can be determined. In this paper, an efficient graph decomposition procedure based on the minimum spanning tree algorithm is developed, using a concept similar to the Euclidean density-contour clustering model given in Hartigan (1975) and Wong and Lane (1981). (For an extensive review of the connection between graph theory and clustering, see Hubert (1974).) In the next section, density-contour clusters on a graph will be defined.

3. DENSITY-CONTOUR CLUSTERS ON A GRAPH

For a given graph, clusters of nodes may be thought of as densely-intraconnected subgraphs separated from other such subgraphs by relatively few cross-links. To formalize this concept, we need to first define the density contour on the link between any two nodes i and j; the level of the contour is used to signify the extent of linkage on connectedness between the two nodes. Using a neighborhood concept that corresponds to the nearest neighbor density estimation technique in statistics, the density contour on the link between any two linked nodes i and j on an unweighted graph is defined as follows:

$$d_{ij} = \frac{\cap N_{ij}}{\cup N_{ij}},$$

where $\cap N_{ij}$ = # of nodes connected to both i and j (i and j included) and $\cup N_{ij}$ = # of nodes connected to either i or j or both. (The density contour between two unlinked nodes is defined to be zero.) For weighted graphs, the corresponding definition is:

$$d_{ij} = \frac{2W_{ij} + \frac{1}{2}\sum_{k \in C}(W_{ik} + W_{jk})}{\cup N_{ij}},$$

where W_{ij} = weight on the link between nodes i and j, and C is the set of nodes connected to both i and j (i and j excluded). The computation of the density contour on each of the links of an unweighted graph is illustrated in Figure 1 below.

Now, we are ready to define the density-contour clusters on a graph. For all $d^* > 0$, a density-contour cluster at level d^* on a graph G is defined to be a subgraph S such that S is maximal among linked sets of nodes whose pairs of nodes can be connected by links with density contour $\geq d^*$. It is easy to show that the family T of density-contour clusters on a graph G forms a tree in that $A \in T$, $B \in T$ implies either $A \supset B$, $B \supset A$, or $A \cap B = \Phi$, the empty set. (See Figure 2 for an example of a tree of density-contour clusters on a graph.) Since the level d* of a density- contour cluster signifies its degree of internal-binding, the densely-intraconnected subsets of a graph can be identified from the tree of density-contour clusters defined on it.

It should also be noted that when the density level is lowered, a density-contour cluster usually expands into a larger cluster by including an extra node. However, sometimes a density-contour cluster would expand to form a much larger density-contour cluster by coalescing with another disjoint density-contour cluster. These "branching clusters", which cannot be expanded smoothly, are defined as follows: a density-contour cluster S is a branching cluster if every cluster properly including it contains a cluster disjoint from S. And a modal cluster is a branching cluster which does not properly contain another such cluster. Since the disjoint modal clusters are the most densely-intraconnected subgraphs, they are useful in indicating the number of "natural" subgraphs that are present in a given graph as well as identifying these subgraphs. The computational procedure for finding the tree of density-contour clusters on a graph is described in the next section.

4. THE COMPUTATIONAL ALGORITHM

For a given graph G = (N, A), where N is the set of nodes in G and A is the set of (weighted) links connecting the nodes in G, the computational procedures for finding the tree of density-contour clusters can be described as follows:

PRELIMINARY STEP: For each link ℓ_{ij} in A, compute the density contour d_{ij} defined on it using formulation stated in the above section.

STEP 1: Let i and j be the pair of nodes with the largest d_{ij}, amalgamate them to form a cluster C, and define the density contour between C and any other node k by:

$$d_{kC} = \max \{d_{ik}, d_{jk}\}.$$

STEP 2: Repeat STEP 1 treating C as a node and ignoring the individual nodes i and j in all future steps. The amalgamation continues until all nodes are grouped into one large cluster. (All clusters obtained in the course of the algorithm are density-contour clusters on the graph.)

It should be noted that this algorithm is equivalent to the classical minimum spanning tree (MST) algorithm. (For published algorithm that would produce the MST, see for example, Ross (1969) and Hartigan (1975).) However, in order that the MST algorithm can be usefully applied to the partitioning of a graph, it is important to have density-contours defined on the links of the graph. And the introduction of the density-contour clustering model on a graph is a key contribution of this paper.

The computational complexity of the graph-decomposition procedure described above is dominated by the complexity of the PRELIMINARY STEP. Moreover, since there are $|A|$ links, and each density contour calculation requires $|A|/|N|$ comparisons on the average, a careful implementation of this step would require $O(|A|^2/|N|)$ comparisons. Hence, the amount of computations is directly proportional to $|N|^3$, as $|A|$ is of order $|N|^2$. However, due to the sparsity of most graph-adjacency matrices, the proposed grah decomposition is practicable for moderately-sized graphs. To illustrate, the CPU times requred to do the graph-decomposition for graphs of various sizes on an IBM 370/168 computer are given in the following table:

$\|N\|$	$\|A\|$	CPU time (sec)
22	39	0.05
27	96	0.14
69	203	0.85
77	289	0.99
250	889	2.23

Furthermore, in order to illustrate the effectiveness of the proposed graph-decomposition technique, it is applied to the unweighted graph shown in Figure 2. (The computed density contours on the links are in parentheses.) The tree of density-contour clusters computed for this 13-nodes graph is given in Figure 3, while the partition-tree corresponding to the modal clusters is shown in Figure 4. (For a detailed description of the algorithm for constructuing the partition-tree, see Lattin (1981).) It can be seen that the three densely-intraconnected subgraphs present in this constructed example are correctly identified.

5. DISCUSSION

In this paper, a computationally efficient graph-partitioning procedure is developed. A key contribution of this effort is the introduction of the concept of density-contour clustering model on a graph. However, it should also be pointed out that the practical utility of this procedure has also been demonstrated in several applications areas. For example, in Lattin (1981), this procedure is shown to be useful in decomposing complex software design problems into manageable subproblems. And in Lattin and Wong (1982), it is shown to be effective in exploring the structure of social networks.

6. REFERENCES

Alexander, C. (1964). Notes on the synthesis of forms. Harvard University Press, Cambridge.

Christofides, N. and Brooker, P. (1976). "The optimal partitoning of graphs", SIAM Journal of Applied Mathematics, 30, 55-69.

Ford, L. R. and Fulkerson, D. R. (1962). Flows in Networks, Princeton University Press.

Gorinshteyn, L. L. (1969). "Partitioning of graphs", Engineering Cybernetics, 76-82.

Hartigan, J. A. (1975). Clustering Alogorithms. New York: John Wiley.

Huff, S. L. (1979). "Decomposition of weighted graphs using the interchange partiioning algorithm", Technical Report #8, CISR, M.I.T.

Hubert, L. J. (1974). "Some applications of graph theory to clustering", Psychometrika, Vol. 39, No. 3, 283-309.

Kernighan, B. W. and Lin, S. (1970). "An efficient heuristic for partitioning graphs", Bell System Technical Journal, 49, 291-307.

Lattin, J. M. (1981). "Implementation and evaluation of a graph-partitioning techniqe based on a high-density clustering model", Technical Report #15, CISR, M.I.T.

Lattin, J. M., and Wong M. A. (1982). "A high-density clustering approach to exploring the structure of social networks", Connections, Vol. V, No. 1, 21-28.

Lukes, J. A. (1974). "Efficient algorithm for the partitioning of trees", IBM Journal of Research and Development, 18, 217-224.

Lukes, J. A. (1975). "Combinatorial solutions to the partitioning of general graphs", IBM Journal of Research and Development, 19, 170-190.

McCormick, W. T., Schwietzer, P. J., and White, T. W. (1972). "Problem decomposition and data reorganization by a clustering technique", Operations Research, 20, 993-1007.

Ross, G. J. S. (1969). "Minimum spanning tree", Algorithm AS12, Applied Statistics, 18, 103-114.
Sangiovanni-Vincentelli, A., Chen, L., and Chua, L. O. (1977). "An efficient heuristic cluster algorithm for tearing large-scale networks", IEEE Transactions on Circuits and Systems, CAS-24, 12, 709-717.

Wong, M. A. and Lane, T. (1981). "A kth nearest neighbor clustering procedure", Proceedings of the 13th Symposium on the Interface between Computer Science and Statistics, W. F. Eddy (ed.), 308-311. Spring Verlag.

Zahn, C. T. (1971). "Graph-theoretic methods for detecting and describing gestalt clusters", IEEE Transactions on Computers, Vol. C20, 68-86.

Fig. 1

Density Contours on an unweighted graph, and the corresponding tree of high-density clusters.

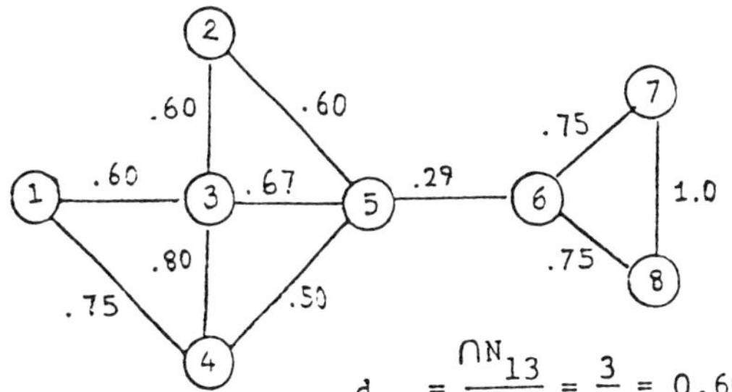

$$d_{13} = \frac{\cap N_{13}}{\cup N_{13}} = \frac{3}{5} = 0.60$$

$$d_{68} = \frac{\cap N_{68}}{\cup N_{68}} = \frac{3}{4} = 0.75$$

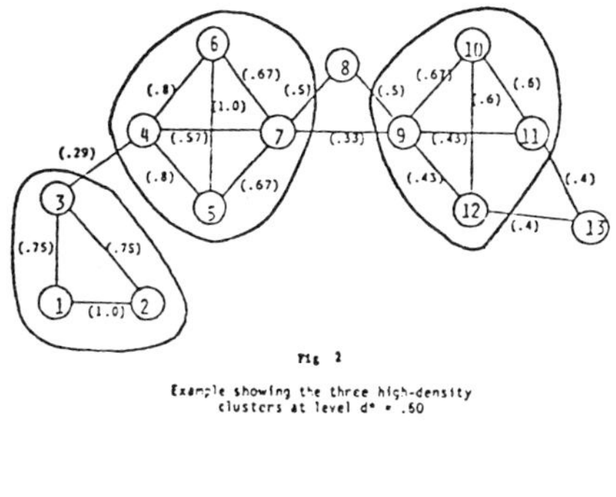

Fig 2

Example showing the three high-density clusters at level d* = .60

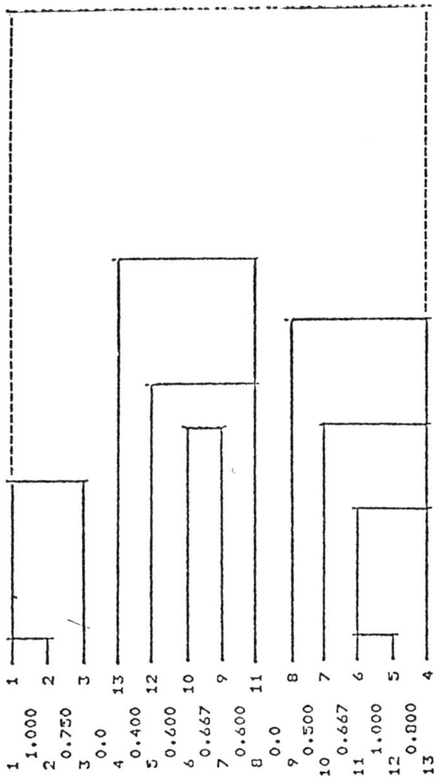

Figure 4

Partition tree for the 13 node example

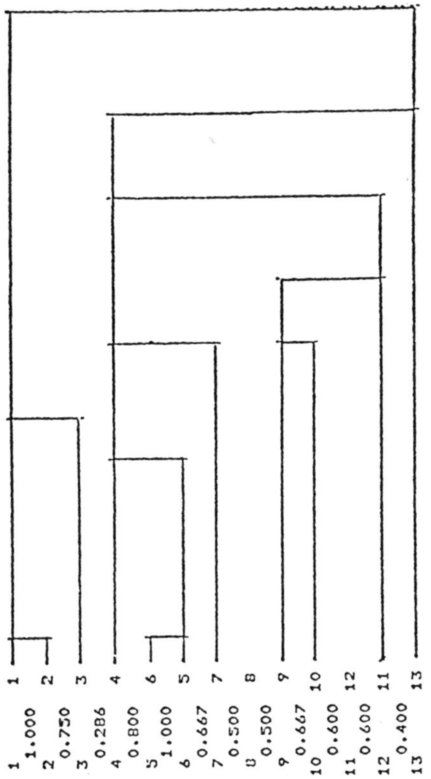

Figure 3

High-density clustering tree for 13 node example

A COMPARISON OF ROBUST METHODS AND DETECTION OF OUTLIERS TECHNIQUES WHEN ESTIMATING A LOCATION PARAMETER

Jeffrey S. Simonoff, New York University

ABSTRACT

Although the poor performance of the mean as a location estimate when outliers are present in the data is well-known, there has been no clear concensus as to whether robust estimation or outlier detection is the appropriate corrective procedure. In this paper, 27 robust estimation and outlier detection techniques (including the mean and an adaptive detection technique introduced here) are compared with regards to accuracy of estimation. Computer simulations are generated modelling both symmetric and asymmetric contamination; the techniques are also evaluated on the real data of Stigler (1977). It is shown that the proper class of estimates depends on the degree of contamination, and whether the contamination is symmetric or asymmetric. It is also shown that while adaptive estimation is effective on the large real data sets, the most effective technique overall on the real data sets is a detection of outliers procedure.

KEYWORDS

Robust estimation; Detection of outliers; Simulation; Contamination models; Mean squared error; Real data.

INTRODUCTION

A large part of the statistical literature, particularly of the past 15 years, has dealt with the handling of unusual observations (or outliers) in the data. The proposals that have been presented can be grouped into two major areas: robust statistical methods (whereby outlying observations are automatically given less weight in estimation) and detection of outliers techniques (whereby outlying observations are deleted from the sample using objective criteria). Despite the obviously close conceptual nature of these two strategies, there has been little interaction of comparison of techniques.

It is the purpose of this paper to provide such a comparison in the particular problem of location estimation. It is well known that a common estimation strategy is to remove points that seem unusual (either by subjective or objective criteria) and then use a standard estimation technique such as the mean. It can be argued (see Hawkins 1980, pp. 3-4) that this provides a better strategy than robust techniques, since it only throws out (or discounts) demonstrably bad data. However, Huber (1981, pp. 4-5) argues the opposite conclusion, saying robust procedures "are superior because they can make a smooth transition between full acceptance and full rejection of an observation." Clearly, there is a basic conflict here that needs to be resolved.

The effectiveness of the many robust estimation has been treated in the literature. In particular the Princeton simulation study (Andrews et.al. 1972) examined the accuracy of 65 location-estimation techniques subject to varying degrees of symmetric contamination. Stigler (1977) studied the effectiveness of several robust estimation techniques on a collection of real data sets. Ansell (1973) examined several robust estimation techniques on data subject to asymmetric contamination. The results of these studies will be considered in more detail in later sections.

It is not the case however, that detection of outlier techniques have been evaluated in this fashion. The typical evaluation method for these techniques is to determine the power of the outlier test (as the proportion of generated outliers detected); see, for example, Jain (1981). This is not the appropriate evaluation criterion for an applied statistician, since ultimately it is accurate estimation that is desired. That is, an "outlier" should only be rejected if it adversely affects the estimation process.

Relles and Rogers (1977) conducted an experiment designed to compare robust procedures with outlier detection; rather than use the objective outlier detection procedures in the literature, however, they used the subjective opinions of several statisticians to trim off outliers. They found that the outlier detection procedure worked fairly well, although not as well as the robust procedures.

Another reason power considerations are not important here is that the level of significance of the test (which is obviously related to the power) is only a nuisance parameter here. The choice of significance level depends only on the resultant accuracy of the mean of the reduced sample for estimating the true mean.

In Section 2 the robust methods and outlier detection techniques tested here are outlined. The behavior of the estimation techniques in samples subject to symmetric contamination is considered in Section 3; asymmetric contamination is treated in Section 4. Finally, the performance of the estimation techniques on Stigler's data sets is studied in Section 5.

The evaluations in Sections 3 and 4 are performed through the use of computer simulations. First 20 standard normal deviates were generated using the IMSL (1980) routine GGNML. Then, a binomial (20,p) random variable Y is generated (using GGBN), where p is the probability of a data value coming from the contaminant distribution. Finally, Y of the original variates are transformed by $X \to uX+w$. This model is denoted by 100p%(uN+w).

ROBUST ESTIMATION AND DETECTION OF OUTLIERS

Let $X_1,\ldots,X_n$ be a sample of size n; $Y_{(i)}$ is the ith order statistic.

A. Robust estimators (details concerning these estimators can be found in Andrews et.al. 1972; they are only briefly outlined here)

R1: The mean, X (denoted M in this study)

R2,R3: The 10% and 25% trimmed means ("10%" and "25%", respectively).

R4,R5: Huber proposal 2. The estimator is indexed

on the parameter K; we try K=1.5(H15) and K=1.2 (H12).

R6: the Jaeckel adaptive trimmed mean (JAE).

R7: the Hodges-Lehmann estimate (H/L)

R8: the adaptive estimator proposed by Vernon Johns (JOH).

R9: Andrews "sine" M-estimator (AMT)

R10,R11: Hampel's descending M-estimators. The choices of a, b and c determining where the curve ascends and descends used here are: $a = 2.1$, $b = 4.0$, $c = 8.2$ (21A) and $a = 1.7$, $b = 3.4$, $c = 8.5$ (17A)

R12: the median (50%)

B. Detection of outliers techniques (details concerning these techniques can be found in Hawkins 1980).

Let $S_0 = \{X_1,\ldots,X_2\}$, and subsets S_i, $i = 1,\ldots,k-1$ be formed be deleting an observation farthest from the mean of the subset S_{i-1} (or from the mean of the trimmed sample in the case of the RST procedures defined later); k corresponds to the number of suspected outliers in the sample.

Several statistics have been suggested to detect multiple outliers in a sample; the ones considered here are the following:

(1) Tietjen and Moore's (1972) E_k statistic:

$EK_i=(s^2(S_i)/s^2(S_o))[(n-i-1)/(n-1)]$ $i = 1,\ldots,k$

where $s^2(S_i)$ is the variance of the observations in subset S_i

(2) the extreme studentized deviate (ESD) statistic:

$ESD_i = |X^{(S_{i-1})} - \overline{X}(S_{i-1})|/s(S_{i-1})$ $i = 1,\ldots,k$

where $X^{(S_{i-1})}$ is the observation farthest from $\overline{X}(S_{i-1})$ in S_{i-1}

(3) the RST statistic:

$RST_i = |X^{(S_{i-1})} - a|/b$ $i = 1,\ldots,k$

where $X^{(S_{i-1})}$ is the observation farthest from the trimmed mean a in the subset S_{i-1}; b^2 is the trimmed variance.

(4) the kurtosis (KUR) statistic:

$KUR_i=(n-i+1)\sum_{j=1}^{n-i+1}[X_j(S_{i-1})-\overline{X}(S_{i-1})]^4/(s^2(S_{i-1})(n-i))^2$

$i=1,\ldots,k$

These statistics are used to estimate a location parameter through the following "backwards-stepping" procedure:

(a) sample values of the statistics are compared with critical values for $i = k$

(b) if a sample value is found to be greater than (for EK, less than) the critical value, i outliers are declared to be present

(c) otherwise, i is decreased to i-1, and step(b) is repeated

(d) if no sample value is found to be significant, the number of outliers is set $i = 0$.

(e) the final estimator of the center of location of the population is $\overline{X}(S_i)$ (that is, the mean of the non-outliers)

Clearly, the implementation of these tests depends on knowledge of the critical values. As was pointed out be Rosner (1975), these critical values depend on the largest number of outliers tested (in order to guar ntee the right level of significance α). That is, the test is a simultaneous test depending on k.

Although this provides a test with the correct level of significance, it is quite restrictive, since it requires tables of critical values for each value of k. For this reason, we also examine a sequential application of the procedure, where the critical value at each step (b) above is taken as the critical value for $k = 1$. The significance level of this procedure will not be α (Hawkins 1980, p. 72, conjectures a true level of 1.25α for the ESD statistic when using this technique), but tables for all values of k are not necessary.

A problem common to all of these techniques is the arbitrariness of the choice of the significance level α. Since α determines the strictness of the test (the probability of falsely rejecting a point as an outlier), it seems reasonable to want α to be flexible, depending on the data itself (that is, data that seems to exhibit many outliers will be screened less strictly, and rejection will be easier; data that has few outliers will be screened more strictly). This is an idea of the same sort as adaptive robust estimation.

We develop an adaptive detection technique through the following mechanism. We assume a model of ϵ-contamination; that is, $F(X)=(1-\epsilon)\Phi(X)+\epsilon G(X)$, where G is the contaminant distribution. If ϵ is small, we want the detection test to be very strict (that is, rejection should be difficult); that is, α should be small. If ϵ is close to 1, then G is the true parent distribution, and again α should be small. However, if ϵ is close to .5, we want rejection to be easier, so α should be large. A functional relationship between α and ϵ that satisfies these conditions is $\alpha = a\epsilon(1-\epsilon)$, $a > 0$. The choice of a is obviously fairly arbitrary; the choice used here is $a = 5/9$. In this way,a typical significance level ($\alpha = .05$) is equated with a typical level of contamination ($\epsilon = .1$; see Huber 1981 p. 3).

The final ingredient needed to calculate α is an estimate of ϵ. The estimate should depend on the data (it should be adaptive); Jaeckel's adaptive trimmed mean provides the estimate. If JAE says to trim $\hat{t}$ off of each side, then the estimate of ϵ is $\hat{\epsilon} = 2\hat{t}$. This means that the final functional form is $\hat{\alpha} = 10\hat{t}(1-2\hat{t})/9$.

In order to use this, a test statistic must be used where the critical value can be evaluated for any $\hat{\alpha}$; Hawkins (1980, p.136) provides such a formula for the ESD statistic. The ESD statistic is calculated sequentially and compared to the critical value obtained from $\hat{\alpha}$.

The 15 different detection of outliers procedures are the following:

D1,D2: Tietjen and Moore's E_k, for $\alpha = .10$(EK10) and $\alpha = .05$(EK05). This is a simultaneous procedure; critical values are tabulated for, and the initial number of outliers tested is, $k = 10$.

D3,D4: The simultaneous RST procedure; $\alpha = .10$(RSTSM10) and $\alpha = .05$(RSTSM05). The initial number of outliers tested is $k = 5$.

D5,D6: The simultaneous ESD procedure (ESDSM10 and ESDSM05); $k = 5$

D7,D8: The simultaneous KUR procedure (KURSM10 and KURSM05); $k = 5$

D9,D10: The sequential ESD procedure (ESD10,ESD05); $k = (n-1)/2$

D11,D12: the sequential RST procedure (RST10,RST05) $k = (n-3)/2$

D13,D14: the sequential KUR procedure (KUR10,KUR05) $k = (n-1)/2$

D15: The sequential adaptive procedure (ADEST)

SYMMETRIC CONTAMINATION

All of the robust estimators considered here were evaluated under symmetric contamination by Andrews et.al. (1972); the main thrust of this section will be to compare these results with the behavior of the outlier detection procedures. The results of the simulations ($n = 20$) under symmetric contamination are contained in Table 1. The Princeton study noted that while the mean M has the best behavior when there is no contamination, it quickly becomes deficient when contamination occurs.

Under small contamination (10%3N,5%10N), the best estimators were the Huber proposal 2 H12, the Hampels 21A,17A and AMT and a 10% trimmed mean. Larger contamination (25%3N) causes the 25% trimmed mean to be more effective; the Hampel 17A is also highly effective. In the case of large contamination (25%10N), the 25% trimmed mean and 17A are again highly effective; they also found the adaptive estimator JOH effective.

Examination of Table 1 illustrates several facts concerning the outlier detection techniques. When there is no contamination, all of the techniques work similarly, except EK and RST; both of these procedures result in too many outliers being rejected. There are probabily two different mechanisms at work here; EK has a higher initial level of $k(=10)$, while RST is unstable due to the instability of the trimmed variance.

Under small contamination (10%3N,5%10N) and moderate contamination (25%3N), the detection technique do not, in general, work as well as the robust methods; in fact, in all three cases, the best detection technique is beaten by both 21A and AMT. When there is gross contamination (25%10N), the story is a little better, but 17A still beats all of the detection techniques.

It should also be noted that the relationship of α and ϵ hypothesized earlier comes through here. This is reflected by the fact that for five of the seven procedures, the $\alpha = .10$ level worked better for gross contamination than $\alpha = .05$. This is also reflected by the strong performance of the adaptive test ADEST; under gross contamination, its effectiveness is quite close to that of 17A, and clearly beats the adaptive robust estimators JAE and JOH.

ASYMMETRIC CONTAMINATION

The behavior of the estimators under asymmetric contamination is considerably different from the behavior under symmetric contamination. The study of Ansell (1973) brought this out, since (of the limited class of robust estimators considered there) the median (which performed poorly under symmetric contamination) performed the best in the case of asymmetry.

The position taken here is that the asymmetric portion of the parent distribution is contaminant; the parameter being estimated is the mean parameter being estimated is the mean of the uncontaminated distribution. Accuracy is measured through the mean squared error (MSE).

Table 2 provides the pertinent information about the estimators. When the parent distribution is subject to small amounts of moderate contamination (10%(N+3)), the heavy trimmed means (25% and 50%, the median) and the Hampel 17A are more effective than any detection procedure. However, when there is a smaller amount of gross contamination (5%(N+10)), this is no longer the case; although the Hampels AMT, 21A and 17A are again effective, the detection techniques ESDSM05, KURSM05, ESD10, ESD05 and KUR05 are equally effective.

When there is a large amount of moderate contamination (25%(N+3)), the median is the most effective estimator. The sequential RST procedures are (surprisingly) almost as effective. Under the model of a large amount of gross contamination (25%(N+10)), the median is again the most effective estimator, with the sequential procedures ESD10, ESD05 and KUR05 being similarly effective. The adaptive detection technique also provides a fairly strong performance (considerably better than the adaptive trim JAE it is derived from).

REAL DATA

The possible inappropriateness of relating simulation models to the real world was examined through the use of real data sets by Stigler (1977). He tested several estimators (including M, 10%, 25%, a one-step version of H15, AMT and 50%) on these data, taking advantage of the fact that the "true values" being estimated at the time are now known. It is instructive to do the same for the other estimation techniques proposed here.

Two indices proposed by Stigler are used for the evaluation of the estimation procedures. For each data set j the quantity $s_j = \frac{1}{27}\sum_{i=1}^{27}(\hat{\theta}_{ij}-\theta_j)$ is computed, where θ_j denotes the "true value" for the jth data set, and $\hat{\theta}_{ij}$ is the value of the ith estimator for the jth data set (estimators R1-R12 correspond to numbers 1-12; estimators D1-D15 correspond to numbers 13-27). The performance of estimator i for data set j is measured by the relative error $e_{ij}=|\hat{\theta}_{ij}-\theta_j|/s_j$. Finally, the index of relative error RE(i) for estimator i is computed as the average across data sets $RE(i)=n^{-1}\sum_{j=1}^{n} e_{ij}$.

The other index is the relative rank RR(i); it is calculated by substituting r_{ij} for e_{ij}, where r_{ij} is the rank of the estimator based on the criterion $|\hat{\theta}_{ij} - \theta_j|$. The values of e_{ij} are calculated, and then used to get RE(i) and RR(i). Qualitative groupings are given in Table 3.

As can be seen, the results when analyzing the real data are considerably different from either the symmetric of asymmetric simulated data sets. As Stigler pointed out, the mean itself works well on the small data sets, as does a 10% trimmed mean; we also see the Huber H15 is effective. However, the detection procedures ESD10 and ESD05 are as effective as any robust estimator.

For the large data sets, the effectiveness of the detection techniques is even more apparent, since the only robust technique in the top eight is the adaptive JOH. Although this is consistent with the recommendations of Andrews et.al. (1972) (that adaptive estimation becomes effective for $N \geq 50$), it is important to note that the adaptive estimator JOH is the worst technique on the small samples. In contrast to this instability, ESD10 and ESD05 are consistently effective, for both large and small data sets. For this reason, the sequential ESD techniques seem to be the most preferable.

CONCLUSION

It was the purpose of this paper to compare the effectiveness of robust estimation and outlier detection procedures. Using computer simulations, it was shown that the proper technique depends on the degree of contamination present, and whether the contamination is symmetric or asymmetric.

When there is symmetric contamination, the robust estimators are overall most effective (particularly the Hampels). If there is a fair amount of gross outliers, the adaptive detection procedure seems promising.

The proper choice of estimation tool is particularly sensitive to the degree of asymmetric contamination. When there is a small amount of contamination, Hampels again are very effective; however, the median is more effective when there is more contamination. The sequential ESD and KUR techniques are effective when there are gross asymmetric outliers, as is the adaptive detection proposal.

The picture is less clear when using the real data sets, but overall the sequential ESD procedure seems the most consistently effective. Although light trimming (10%) works well on small data sets it is not as effective as other techniques on large ones; the opposite is true for the adaptive JOH.

If a composite recommendation can be gleaned from these results, it would be that Hampels are basically effective, except if there are large asymmetries; then the median is better. Further, sequential application of the ESD procedure is usually appropriate, particularly if the contamination is asymmetric.

REFERENCES

1. Andrews, D.F., Bickel, P.J., Hampel, F.R., Huber, P.J., Rogers, W.H., Tukey, J.W., (1972) Robust estimates of location: survey and advances, Princeton, N.J.: Princeton University Press
2. Ansell, A.M. (1973), "Robustness of location estimators to asymmetry", Appl. Statist. 22, 249-254
3. Hawkins, D.M. (1980), Identification of outliers New York:Chapman and Hall
4. Huber, P.J. (1981), Robust Statistics, New York John Wiley and sons
5. International Mathematical and Statistical Libraries (1980), Subroutines GGNML, GGBN, Houtston, Texas
6. Jain, R.B. (1981), Detecting outliers: power and some other considerations", Comm. in Statist. A10, 2299-2314
7. Relles, D.A. and Rogers, W.H. (1977),"Statisticians are fairly robust estimators of location" J. Amer. Statist. Assoc. 72, 107-111
8. Rosner, B. (1975), "On the detection of many outliers", Technom. 17, 221-227.
9. Stigler, S.M. (1977), "Do robust estimators work with real data?", Ann. Statist. 5, 1055-1098 (with discussion)
10. Tietjen, G.L. and Moore, R.M. (1972), "Some Grubbs-type statistics for the dection of several outliers", Technom. 14, 583-597

TABLE 1: Mean squared errors x n for estimators subject to symmetric contamination (average number of outliers detected in parentheses); n = 20

	0%	10%3N	25%3N	5%10N	25%10N
M	1.004	1.827	2.868	6.048	25.232
10%	1.062	1.320	1.926	1.308	7.857
25%	1.189	1.376	1.732	1.336	2.554
H15	1.042	1.326	1.954	1.267	5.905
H12	1.077	1.305	1.809	1.253	3.833
JAE	1.115	1.336	1.800	1.267	3.011
H/L	1.065	1.343	1.839	1.269	3.699
JOH	1.145	1.393	1.831	1.284	2.908
AMT	1.070	1.304	1.873	1.125	2.618
21A	1.077	1.299	1.834	1.135	2.462
17A	1.121	1.308	1.748	1.170	2.184
50%	1.494	1.695	2.002	1.640	2.510
EK10	1.687(2.5)	2.505(5.1)	3.175(6.6)	3.055(6.4)	3.922(9.8)
EK05	1.221(.9)	1.970(3.3)	2.755(4.7)	2.661(5.3)	3.869(9.7)
RSTSM10	1.066(.3)	1.570(.7)	2.378(1.3)	1.333(1.2)	3.841(3.6)
RSTSM05	1.029(.2)	1.600(.5)	2.425(.9)	1.328(.9)	4.233(3.3)
ESDSM10	1.129(.3)	1.425(.8)	2.117(1.3)	1.215(1.1)	3.377(3.6)
ESDSM05	1.069(.1)	1.462(.6)	2.193(1.0)	1.173(.9)	3.553(3.4)
KURSM10	1.130(.3)	1.439(.8)	2.147(1.3)	1.194(1.0)	3.049(3.6)
KURSM05	1.085(.2)	1.469(.6)	2.203(1.0)	1.152(.9)	3.304(3.5)
ESD10	1.092(.2)	1.431(.7)	2.133(1.1)	1.167(.9)	2.586(3.5)
ESD05	1.035(.1)	1.439(.5)	2.253(.7)	1.136(.8)	3.492(3.1)
RST10	2.383(6.0)	2.515(6.4)	2.795(6.6)	2.491(6.3)	2.784(7.4)
RST05	2.246(5.5)	2.426(5.9)	2.762(6.2)	2.355(5.8)	2.710(7.2)
KUR10	1.223(.5)	1.595(1.1)	2.186(1.4)	1.308(1.2)	2.273(4.0)
KUR05	1.108(.2)	1.483(.7)	2.260(.9)	1.208(.9)	2.582(3.6)
ADEST	1.451(1.2)	1.705(1.8)	2.192(2.4)	1.512(1.9)	2.246(4.7)

TABLE 2: Mean squared errors x n for estimators subject to asymmetric contamination (average number of outliers detected in parentheses); n = 20

	10%(N+3)	25%(N+3)	5%(N+10)	25%(N+10)
M	3.662	13.793	11.081	144.102
10%	2.656	11.482	2.918	104.515
25%	2.198	9.040	1.500	48.367
H15	2.792	12.212	2.006	116.285
H12	2.499	11.124	1.552	89.940
JAE	2.488	11.456	1.490	96.408
H/L	2.633	11.529	1.642	129.556
JOH	2.832	13.948	2.030	226.052
AMT	2.609	11.518	1.131	42.199
21A	2.523	11.208	1.148	30.120
17A	2.317	10.255	1.182	23.473
50%	2.378	7.862	1.716	17.200
EK10	3.296(5.1)	10.429(4.5)	3.229(7.4)	21.722(10.0)
EK05	3.261(3.0)	12.050(2.5)	3.074(6.8)	21.939(10.0)
RSTSM10	3.215(.7)	12.796(.6)	1.370(1.4)	94.491(2.5)
RSTSM05	3.378(.4)	13.312(.3)	1.283(1.2)	94.758(2.4)
ESDSM10	2.924(.9)	12.000(.9)	1.229(1.3)	64.601(3.4)
ESDSM05	3.112(.6)	12.709(.6)	1.171(1.2)	65.160(3.3)
KURSM10	3.005(.9)	12.111(.9)	1.222(1.3)	43.667(3.9)
KURSM05	3.183(.6)	12.676(.6)	1.171(1.2)	56.775(3.5)
ESD10	3.032(.7)	12.680(.6)	1.161(1.2)	19.426(5.1)
ESD05	3.289(.4)	13.286(.3)	1.115(1.1)	19.416(5.0)
RST10	3.000(6.4)	8.339(5.9)	2.411(6.3)	21.333(7.0)
RST05	3.014(6.0)	8.861(5.5)	2.261(5.9)	21.285(6.9)
KUR10	3.018(1.1)	12.251(1.1)	1.300(1.5)	20.304(5.3)
KUR05	3.259(.6)	12.922(.6)	1.170(1.2)	19.480(5.1)
ADEST	2.751(2.0)	11.303(1.9)	1.571(2.2)	19.754(5.6)

TABLE 3: Qualitative groupings of estimation techniques based on relative error and relative rank

	Small Samples		Large Samples	
	Relative Error	Relative Rank	Relative Error	Relative Rank
Best	ESD10, H15, ESD05, 10%, M	H15, M, 10%, ESD05, KUR10, ESD10	JOH, ESD05	JOH, ESD05, ESDSM10
Good	AMT, 21A, H/L, H12, KURSM05, ESDSM05, RSTSM05, RSTSM10, KURSM10, 17A	ESDSM10, KURSM05, KURSM10, ESDSM05, RSTSM10, RSTSM05, 21A, KUR05, H12, AMT, ADEST, H/L, EK05	ESDSM10, RSTSM10, RSTSM05, ESDSM05, ESD10, ADEST	RSTSM10, RSTSM05, ESDSM10, ESD10, ADEST, 10%
Average	JAE, ESDSM10, 25%, 50%, ADEST, EK05, KUR10, EK10, KUR05	25%, 17A, EK10, 50%	M, 10%, H15, H12, H/L, 21A, AMT, KUR05, KURSM10, KURSM05, 17A, KUR10, JAE, 25%	KUR05, KURSM10, H/L, AMT, 21A, M, 17A, KURSM05, H12, KUR10, H15, JAE, 25%
Poor	RST05, RST10, JOH	JAE, RST10, RST05, JOH	50%, EK10, EK05, RST10, RST05	50%, RST10, RST05, EK10, EK05

IDENTIFYING INFLUENTIAL OBSERVATIONS IN TIME SERIES DATA

James M. Lattin, Sloan School of Management, M.I.T.

ABSTRACT

We propose and develop a diagnostic technique for assessing the sensitivity of the sample autocorrelation function to individual time series observations. The technique, intended as an aid in the diagnosis step of ARIMA modeling, enables the analyst to identify extremely influential points and to adjust outlying observations according to a more internally consistent realization of the autocorrelation function without first specifying the underlying model. We apply the technique to a series of residential telephone demand in Australia.

key words: sensitivity diagnostic, time series, outlier detection, ARIMA modeling, sample autocorrelation function

I. Introduction

Time series observations that are made during periods characterized by atypical activity (e.g. promotion, strike, holiday) or that are recorded incorrectly can substantially distort the sample autocorrelation function ($\underline{r}$) of the series and disguise the nature of the underlying ARIMA model. While some extremely elegant robust methods exist for ARIMA modeling, they require some initial specification of an underlying model, which must be diagnosed from prior, uncontaminated data or from some more resistant measure of the autocorrelation process (see e.g. Martin, Samarov, and Vandaele (1980)). When the analyst has weak priors about the true underlying model, a diagnostic approach has considerable appeal.

In this paper, we present a simple diagnostic technique for assessing the sensitivity of the sample autocorrelation function to single time series observations. Our approach is similar to one used in econometrics (see Belsley, Kuh, and Welsch (1980)), where the effect on the estimated regression coefficients is assessed for each observation in the data. Our technique enables the analyst to identify troublesome, influential points and to ascertain the approximate influence of each on the sample autocorrelation function. We also present a straightforward heuristic for adjusting these outlying observations according to a more internally consistent autocorrelation function. Our approach provides a convenient, computationally manageable means for identifying influential or non-characteristic time series observations during the diagnosis stage of ARIMA modeling, as well as an alternative for adjusting these observations without first specifying the underlying model.

The paper follows in several sections. Section II describes the sensitivity diagnostic, and suggests a helpful diagnostic plot from which to identify the most influential observations in the series. Section III discusses ways of achieving a more internally consistent realization of the sample autocorrelation function, denoted $\underline{r}^*$, and section IV outlines a heuristic technique for adjusting one or a few outlying points to be highly consistent with $\underline{r}^*$. Section V concludes the paper with the application of the technique to a series of residential telephone demand in Australia.

II. Sensitivity Diagnostic

The potentially distorting effect of extremely influential observations has been a concern in cross-sectional models and in time series ARIMA models. For cross-sectional econometric models, Belsley, Kuh, and Welsch (1980) introduce a set of computationally efficient diagnostics for determining the impact of the deletion of a single observation on the overall regression. For example, they introduce a scaled measure of change called $DFBETAS_{ij}$, which is the change in the estimate of the jth out of p coefficients due to the deletion of the ith out of N observations. By examining the N x p matrix of DFBETAS for relatively large absolute values, it is possible to identify those observations with substantial influence in the determination of one or more of the coefficients in the model. In addition, the diagnostic is quite computationally efficient, requiring that the regression be run only once, rather than once for each of the N distinct sets of N-1 observations.

For the sample autocorrelation function of a time series variable, however, the elimination of a single row does not necessarily correspond to the deletion of an observation. Because $\underline{r}$ involves lagging the time series variable $\underline{y}$ against itself, an observation y_i may appear twice in the cross-product calculation for r_k: as $(y_i-\bar{y})(y_{i+k}-\bar{y})$ and as $(y_{i-k}-\bar{y})(y_i-\bar{y})$, where $k<i<N-k$, as well as in the mean. We now introduce the following notation for our time series diagnostic:

$\underline{y}$ = time series of N observations

$\underline{r}_k(i)$ = the autocorrelation of $\underline{y}$ at lag k with the ith observation removed

$\bar{y}(i)$ = the mean of the time series variable $\underline{y}$ with the ith observation removed

$$V = \sum_{t=1}^{N} (y_t-\bar{y})^2$$

$$V(i) = \sum_{t=1}^{N} (y_t-\bar{y}(i))^2 - (y_i-\bar{y}(i))^2$$

$$L_k = \sum_{t=k+1}^{N-k} y_t$$

$$C_k = \sum_{t=1}^{N-k} (y_t-\bar{y})(y_{t+k}-\bar{y})$$

and

$$C_k(i) = \sum_{t=1}^{N-k} (y_t - \bar{y}(i))(y_{t+k} - \bar{y}(i)) - c,$$

where c will depend upon the relative values of i, N, and k as shown below. While most time series applications adopt $r_k = C_k/V$, in this paper we will set $r_k = (NC_k)/((N-k)V)$. We then define

$$r_k(i) = \begin{cases} ((N-1)/(N-k-1))(1/V(i))\{C_k(i) - (y_i - \bar{y}(i))(y_{i+k} - \bar{y}(i))\}, & i \leq k \\ ((N-1)/(N-k-2))(1/V(i))\{C_k(i) - (y_i - \bar{y}(i))(y_{i-k} + y_{i+k} - 2\bar{y}(i))\}, & k < i \leq N-k \\ ((N-1)/(N-k-1))(1/V(i))\{C_k(i) - (y_i - \bar{y}(i))(y_{i-k} - \bar{y}(i))\}, & N-k < i \end{cases}$$

By using the equations below, it is possible to calculate all values of $r_k(i)$ in a number of operations proportional to N x L (where L is the number of lags considered in $\underline{r}$), which is the same order of work required to calculate $\underline{r}$:

$$V(i) = V - (N/(N-1))(\bar{y}^2 - 2\bar{y}y_i + y_i^2)$$

$$C_k(i) = \begin{cases} C_k - (1/(N-1)^2)\{2k(N-1)\bar{y}^2 - 2kN\bar{y}y_i + ky_i^2\} + (1/(N-1))(y_i - \bar{y})\{L_k - Ny_{i+k}\}, & i \leq k \\ C_k - (1/(N-1)^2)\{(N^2+2kN-k)\bar{y}^2 - (N^2+2kN+N)\bar{y}y_i\} + (1/(N-1))(y_i - \bar{y})\{L_k - N(y_{i-k} + y_{i+k})\}, & k < i \leq N-k \end{cases}$$

(Note that the remaining case where $N-k<i$ is exactly the same as for $i \leq k$, except that y_{i-k} replaces y_{i+k}).

We can now form the N x L matrix of $r_k - r_k(i)$ and identify the relatively large absolute values indicating influential observations. However, unlike the case with cross-sectional data, the influence of observation y_i on the autocorrelation coefficients is not limited to the ith row of the diagnostic matrix and will appear not only along row i, but also along diagonals above and below row i in the matrix. In order to simplify the process of identifying the most influential points, we can calculate some measure R_t that will suitably indicate the impact of each observation across all coefficients of $\underline{r}$. If we denote $r_k - r_k(i)$ by $DFR_{i,k}$, then one such measure might be

$$R_i = (1/4L)\sum_{k=1}^{L} (2DFR_{i,k}^2 + DFR_{i-k,k}^2 + DFR_{i+k,k}^2)$$

(Note that suitable corrections must be made when $i<L$ and $N-L<i$.)

For a different approach to assess the sensitivity of $\underline{r}$ to a single observation, see Polasek (1982).

III. Determining $\underline{r^*}$

In the event that the autocorrelation diagnostic indicates only a few extremely influential points, it may be appropriate to form $\underline{r^*}$, a less sensitive realization of the sample autocorrelation function, by calculating $\underline{r}$ without the indicated observations. We might use this approach when faced with what Martin (1980, p. 6) characterizes as "isolated additive outliers." If, however, there is evidence of sensitivity but no clear indication of a small subset of influential points, it might be better to employ some resistant technique for determining $\underline{r^*}$, as suggested by Huber (1981) and in several forms by Devlin, Gnanadesikan, and Kettenring (1975). In fact, Polasek (1982) has taken Huber's (1981, p. 202f) formulation and applied it to time series data. Ideally, we might like to estimate r_k^* by the slope of a resistant line regressed through a scatter plot of y_t^* vs. y_{t+k}^*, where $\underline{y^*}$ is the robustly standardized series. The trade-off, of course, is an additional computational burden.

Regardless of the approach employed, the desensitized function $\underline{r^*}$ should reflect an autocorrelation process that is largely consistent with the greater part of the data. To the extent that $\underline{r^*}$ differs from $\underline{r}$, it may well aid the analyst in diagnosing the underlying ARIMA model, which may have been disguised by the impact of a few influential or non-characteristic points.

IV. Adjusting Observations

Once the appropriate time series model has been diagnosed, there exist estimation techniques that will adjust outlying observations so as to be consistent with the underlying model. Brubacher and Wilson (1976) have developed an interpolation technique for filling in missing data or adjusting observations specified a priori. Martin, Samarov, and Vandaele (1980) have presented an elegant robust estimation method for ARIMA models that iteratively adjusts inconsistent points (robust filter) while refining parameter estimates.

Without recourse to these techniques, however, there appears to be very little else to fall back on. According to Durbin, (as cited by Martin, Samarov, and Vandaele (1980, p. 1)), "...all the Box-Jenkins packages known to me make no provision for outliers and contamination of various kinds." The autocorrelation diagnostic presented above is a computationally straightforward technique that might be included with any existing ARIMA package as an aid in model diagnosis. However, in the absence of some resistant estimation technique, it must be possible to adjust the extremely influential or atypical observations to avoid distortion of the ordinary ARIMA parameter estimates.

We now propose a simple heuristic technique for adjusting one or a few influential observations identified in the diagnostic process. The approach is conceptually superior to linear interpolation in that it adjusts the points so as to be highly consistent with $\underline{r^*}$. Also, it does not require a priori specification and estimation of a model and parameters as does Brubacher and Wilson's (1976) interpolation technique.

To adjust the observation y_i, we simply set $y_i=y$, where y minimizes

$$\sum_{k=1}^{L} \{(C_k(y)/V(y)) - r_k*\}^2,$$

where $C_k(y)$ and $V(y)$ are the quantities C_k and V written as functions of the ith observation. Both $C_k(y)$ and $V(y)$ are quadratic functions of y, so it is not difficult to determine the functional form of the first derivative and to search for the best value of y.

When two or three observations need to be adjusted, the simplest approach is a heuristic one, adjusting one point at a time and then iterating until a reasonably stable configuration is reached. (If these points are extreme outliers, it helps to begin by replacing each point with the trimmed mean of the series).

V. Application

In this section, we apply the techniques outlined above to a time series of residential telephone demand in Australia (see Roberts (1980, p. 70)). The data, presented in Figure 1, are 56 quarterly observations spanning the period 1962:3 to 1976:2. Roberts (1980) indicates that the series becomes stationary after consecutive and seasonal (i.e. quarterly) differencing.

We applied the autocorrelation diagnostic to the stationary series and calculated R_t according to the equation above. The plot of R_t vs. t, shown in Figure 2, reveals that the 37th and 41st observations in the twice differenced series (corresponding to the values $(y_{42}-y_{41} - y_{38}+y_{37})$ and $(y_{46}-y_{45} - y_{42}+y_{41})$, respectively) are the most influential in the series. (The plot also reflects the rather turbulent period of the early 1970's in the data.) It turns out that most of the impact introduced by these points can be traced to the failure of the original observation y_{42} to exhibit a characteristic fourth quarter drop, and to the relatively high value of y_{45}. In this situation, however, any action we might take with regard to a particular observation in the stationary series may not correspond directly to an action on some point in the original series.

Figure 3 compares the autocorrelation function of the stationary series to $\underline{r*}$ computed by eliminating the 37th and the 41st observations, and reveals that they are divergent at several different lags. The shape of $\underline{r*}$ might well suggest a somewhat different underlying ARIMA process. While Roberts (1980) was concerned in his modeling efforts with accommodating the relatively large spikes at lags 8 and 12, these seem to be principally a result of the observations indicated by the autocorrelation diagnostic, as there are no spikes at r_8* and $r_{12}*$.

In the following table, we present the results of estimating two ARIMA models on the stationary series and on the stationary series with the 37th and 41st observations adjusted according to the heuristic proposed in section IV above. The results of such an adjustment, unfortunately, cannot be traced exactly to the original observations $\underline{y}$, which might lead us to attempt some approach other than differencing to achieve stationarity (as suggested by Martin, Samarov, and Vandaele (1980, pp. 22-23) in the presence of outliers), or to alter the adjustment process to reflect changes to the original series.

The two ARIMA models are suggested by the spikes in the sample autocorrelation function at r_1*, r_4*, and r_5*. In fact, Roberts (1980, p. 116) reports satisfactory results in fitting the moving average model to total telephone demand (business plus residential), but uses a more elaborate model on the residential series alone in an attempt to explain the spikes in $\underline{r}$ at lags 8 and 12.

As shown in the table, in all four cases the model results are satisfactory, in that they all produce an acceptable pattern of residuals. There are, however, striking differences in the parameter values for the moving average model. These differences are directly attributable to two influential observations in the stationary series, which may ultimately stem from the noncharacteristic value of y_{42}. To the extent that this point or some small number of atypical observations are inflating the ARIMA parameter estimates, it may have some very undesirable implications for forecasting the series.

	Stationary Series	Stationary Series (Adjusted)
AR 1	.199	.141
(std.err)	(.142)	(.138)
AR 4	-.387	-.409
(std.err)	(.143)	(.142)
Std.dev. Residuals	5095	3908
Chi Sq (D.F.=15)	14.03	5.57
MA 1	.545	.249
(std.err)	(.068)	(.106)
MA 4	.984	.704
(std.err)	(.072)	(.106)
Std.dev. Residuals	4155	3740
Chi Sq (D.F.=15)	12.51	7.61

(Note: in each case a constant was estimated which was not significant. The chi square statistic tests whether or not the residuals from the model are significantly different from white noise, using an autocorrelation function with 15 lags.)

We can present here only a fraction of the detailed investigation that should accompany such a time series analysis, especially when forecasting the series is the ultimate goal. Nonetheless, the diagnostic process as a whole seems to provide valuable additional insight in the early stages of the modeling process, and can help to reduce the distortion of ARIMA parameter estimates caused by a few influential observations in the series.

REFERENCES

Belsley, D.A., E. Kuh, and R.E. Welsch (1980). Regression Diagnostics. New York, John Wiley and Sons.

Box, G.E.P., and G.M. Jenkins (1967). Time Series Analysis: Forecasting and Control. San Francisco, Holden-Day.

Brubacher, S.R., and G.T. Wilson (1976). "Interpolating time series with application to the estimation of holiday effects on electricity demand," JRSS C, 25(2):107-116.

Devlin, S.J., R. Gnanadesikan, and J.R. Kettenring (1975). "Robust estimation and outlier detection with correlation coefficients," Biometrika, 62(3):531-545.

Durbin, J. (1979). "Discussion of the paper by Drs. Kliener, Martin, and Thomson," JRSS B, 41(3):338-339.

Fox, A.J. (1972). "Outliers in time series," JRSS B, 34:350-363.

Huber, P. (1981). Robust Statistics. New York, John Wiley and Sons.

Martin, R.D. (1980). "Robust methods for time series," invited talks delivered at the International Time Series Meetings, Nottingham, England, March 26-30, 1979, and the second Applied Time Series Symposium, Tulsa, OK, March 3-5, 1980.

Martin, R.D., A. Samarov, and W. Vandaele (1980). "Robust methods for ARIMA models," Center for Computational Research in Economics and Management Science Technical Report, Sloan School of Management, M.I.T.

Polasek, W. (1982). "Robust estimation and resistance analysis for the autocorrelation function," Preprint 47, Institute of Statistics and Computer Science, University of Vienna.

Roberts, J.H. (1980). "A comparative study of short term forecasting techniques used to plan a telephone network," unpublished M.Comm. thesis, University of Melbourne, Australia.

Tukey, J. (1977). Exploratory Data Analysis. Reading, MA, Addison Wesley.

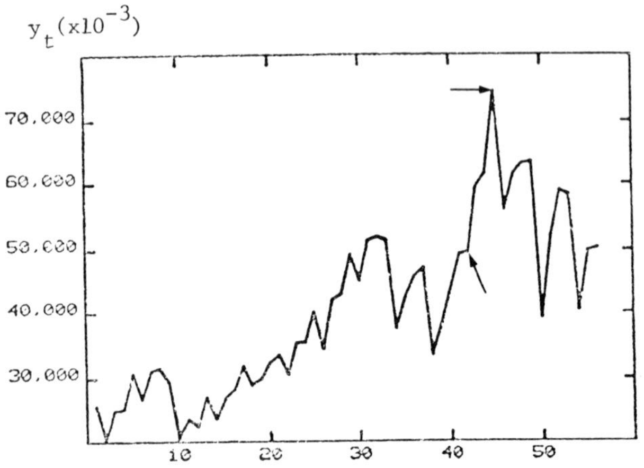

FIGURE 1

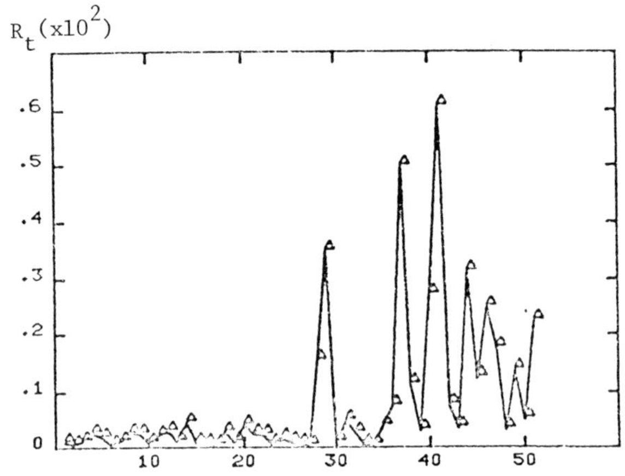

FIGURE 2

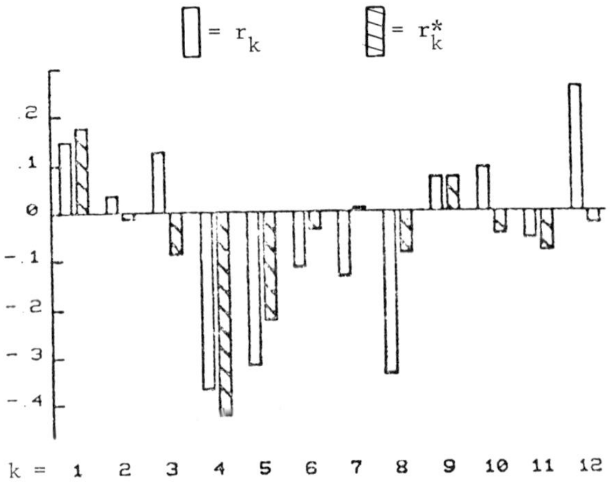

FIGURE 3

On Methodologies of Computer Simulations to Evaluate Ridge Estimators

W. S. Luk
Department of Computing Science
Simon Fraser University
Burnaby, B.C., Canada

Abstract: Numerous algorithms have been proposed to find a good value for the ridge parameter k such that the resulting ridge estimators yield a small mean-square-error. Computer simulation is by far the only effective tool to evaluate ridge estimators, and hence a k-selecting algorithm. Unfortunately, due to the differences in setting up a simulation, results obtained from various simulations are incompatible. This paper analyses the setups of these simulations and points out that the choice of data scale is the single important factor that is responsible for these seemingly incompatible results. In addition, the performance of k-selecting algorithms are compared in two different data scales.

Index Terms: Ridge Regression, Multicollinearity, Simulation, Data Scaling.

Introduction:

Since it was proved in [9] that there exists a value of the ridge parameter k such that the mean-square-error (MSE) of the corresponding ridge estimators is smaller than that of ordinary-least-square (OLS) estimators, many k-selecting algorithms have been proposed. The performance of many of these algorithms is domenstrated by simulation experiments. [3] contains a comprehensive bibliography of the simulation experiments reported in the literature. It is difficult to draw firm conclusions from these experiments due to the lack of uniformity in the setups of these simulations. Some k-selecting algorithms are rated good in some simulations and not so good in others.

The prime motive of this paper is to explain why the simulation results are incompatible. This goal is achieved by analysing the differences in the setups of various simulations. We include in our comparison study the following papers: [4], [6], [7], [8], [11], [13], [14] and [19]. Each simulation is labelled by the paper describing it. [10] and [18] are not inculded since they have identical setups as some of the above. We shall compare them in four aspects: data scale, evaluation criterion, simuluation parameter set and data generation.

Data Scale:

Data scale is the scale of measurement of the predictor variables that is used in the regression process. Two data scales are considered in this paper.

Consider the usual linear regression model:

(1) $Y=\beta o+X\beta+\varepsilon$

where X is an n x p matrix of predictor variables of rank p, β is an unknown vector of regression coefficients and ε is a vector of independent, normally distributed random variables with mean zero and variance σ^2. For comparison purpose, we choose βo to be zero. We call this model the original model, which is adopted by [6], [14] and [19].

If the design matrix X is standardized so that $X'X$ is an identity matrix, we have the standardized model, which is usually expressed as follows:

(2) $Y=Z\alpha+\varepsilon$

where $Z=XQ$ and $\alpha=Q'\beta$. Q is a p x p orthogonal matrix such that $Q'X'XQ=D=\text{diag}\{\lambda 1,\ldots,\lambda p\}$, $\lambda 1,\ldots,\lambda p$ being the eigenvalues of the correlation matrix $X'X$ (before standardization).

The two models differ in the procedure of calculating MSE. We shall first consider the standardized model. Given a value for the ridge parameter k, to be determined by some k-selecting algorithm, the ridge estimator of α is as follows:

(3) $\hat{\alpha}i(k)=[D+kI]^{-1}Z'Y,\ i=1,\ldots,p$

If k=0, (3) yields the least square estimator $\hat{\alpha}i(0)$ or simply $\hat{\alpha}i$. (This notation will be used for all least square estimates). For $k\neq 0$, (3) becomes

(4) $\hat{\alpha}i(k)=[\lambda i/(\lambda i+k)]\hat{\alpha}i,\ i=1,\ldots,p$

To calculate ridge estimator $\hat{\beta}i(k)$ in the original model, the X and Y are first standardized and $\hat{\alpha}i(k)$ is obtained by (4) and then the ridge estimator in the original model is given by

(5) $\tilde{\beta}(k)=Q\hat{\alpha}(k)$

$\tilde{\beta}(k)$ is then converted to $\hat{\beta}(k)$ in the original model as follows:

(6) $\hat{\beta}j(k)=\tilde{\beta}j(k)Yo/(Xj)o,\quad \hat{\beta}o(k)=\bar{Y}-\sum_{i=1}^{p}\hat{\beta}j(k)\bar{X}j$

where $\bar{X}j$ and $(Xj)o$ are the mean and standard deviation respectively of the jth column of X, and $\bar{Y}$ and Yo are similarly defined. Note that [6] ignores the adjustment of βo and considers $\beta o(k)$ to be identically zero. This however does not alter the results in any significant way, as will be shown later.

The difference between the standardized and the original models is one of scaling. In standardizing the predictor variables, the mean is subtracted from each variable ('centering') and then the centered variable is divided by its standard deviation ('scaling'). The ridge estimator has been proved in [1] to be location invariant by introducing the ridge estimator $\beta_0(k)$ for the constant term β_0, as in (6). The ridge regression however is not scale invariant. In fact, [16] concludes that 'the choice of scales is perhaps the single most important phase of ridge analysis'. The findings of this paper agree with this statement.

Evaluation Criterion:
As the theory of ridge regression was developed on the basis of minimizing the MSE of the regression coefficient estimators, most of the simulations adopt it as the measure of performance of a k-selecting algorithm. However, there are several versions of MSE in use. The following definition of MSE is most commonly used:

$$(7) \quad MSE(k)= \sum_{i=o}^{p}(\hat{\beta}i(k)-\beta i)^2, \text{ or } \sum_{i=1}^{p}(\hat{\alpha}i(k)-\alpha i)^2$$

depending on which model to be used.

In [13], a weighted MSE, which is related to the MSE of prediction is defined as follows:

$$(8) \quad MSE(k)= \sum_{i=1}^{p}\lambda i(\hat{\alpha}i(k)-\alpha i)^2$$

In [7], (7) is modified so that $MSE(k)/\sigma^2$ is used as the evaluation criterion. Since comparison is made when the signal-to-noise is fixed, this scaled MSE will yield identical results as (7).

Simulation Parameter set:
In order to calculate MSE, we need values of a set of variables. We call this set of variables the simulation parameter set. Obviously, if the entire model according to (1) or (2) is known, then all versions of MSE can be calculated. In this case, the simulation parameter set consists of X, β(or α) and ε. Alternatively, one can take a sufficient statistics approach whereby values are directly assigned to only those variables that appear in the MSE formula, e.g. (7) or (8). For example, in (8), only λ's, $\hat{\alpha}i(k)$, and α's are involved. αi and k are used in (4) to calculate $\hat{\alpha}i(k)$. Most k-selecting algorithms make use of the value of σ to derive an appropiate value of k. The value of $\hat{\sigma}$ can be generated based on a value of σ. Likewise, the value of $\hat{\sigma}$ can be generated based on a value of α. Thus, $\{\lambda,\hat{\alpha},\alpha,\hat{\sigma},\sigma\}$ is a simulation parameter set.

[4] and [13] propose their own k- selecting algorithms based on the Bayesian theory and show them to be good heuristics in their simulations which employ $\{ \lambda, \hat{\alpha}, \alpha, \hat{\sigma}, \sigma\}$ as the simulation parameter set. In commenting [4], both [5] and [17] point out that the sufficient statistics approach, coupled with the fact that both and are generated from some normal distribution, tends to favour algorithms with Bayesian assumptions.

Data Generation:
Data for a variable in a chosen simulation parameter set can either be assigned directly so that they are similar to some known data sets, or be generated through a random number generator based on some known distributions. In [11], well-known multicollinear data sets are used for simulation experiments. They are also used in other experiments such as [13]. When the design matrix X is randomly generated, the random data generation is designed such that the predictor variables bear a certain degree of multicollinearity.

Most of the simulations being considered here use only a few design matrices. Surprisingly, this is true even for simulations where matrices are randomly generated. Obviously, it is not very meaningful to compare the simulation results when different design matrices are used. Besides, it is difficult to explain the results conclusively. In [19] for example, one design matrix is generated for each degree of multicollinearity. One of matrices generated which is supposed to possess a higher degree of multicollinearity than the other matrix, actually has a smaller λ-ratio (i.e. ratio of the largest eigenvalue over the smallest eigenvalue). This situation would not have happened had a number of design matrices been generated for each degree of multicollinearity.

Another Simulation:
As we have seen, the setup of each simulation experiment under consideration here differs from others in several ways. Some differences may be superificial while others may be important enough to alter the results significantly. We set up a simulation of our own as a test-bed, which is much more comprehensive than the others. The primary purpose of this simulation is to determine which factors in a simulation set make important differences. We accomphish this objective by running simulations in parallel, with identical setups and data, except for a particular factor in question.

We generate X randomly using a 2-parameter method as described in [19]. Fifty design matrices are randomly generated for each of the five degrees of multicollinearity. To be compatible with [11] and for computational considerations, the dimension of X's are 13 x 4 (i.e. 4 predictor variables). For each X, five values of β are used: Va, 3Va/4+Vb/4, Va/2+Vb/2, Va/4+3Vb/4 and Vb, where Va and Vb are the eigenvectors corresponding to the largest and the smallest eigenvalues of X. (According to [15], MSE(k) is minimised or maximized when β is Va or Vb.) For each value of β, there are five values of σ: 0.01, 0.1, 0.5, 1.0 and 5.0; i.e. five signal-to-noise ratios $\beta'\beta/\sigma^2$, as is normalized. Based on each value of σ, 100 sets of n $N(0,\sigma^2)$ variates as values of ε are generated. Therefore, there are 100x50x5 = 25,000 models for each degree of multicollinearity and each degree of signal-to-noise ratio, covering the whole spectrum of β. For each model and each k-selecting algorithm (see below), a k value is obtained and then calculation is proceeded as described earlier.

k-selecting Algorithms:
There are five k-selecting algorithms we choose for evaluation. The first three, i.e. RIDGM [4], L&W [13] and HKB [11] have done quite well in those simulations using the standardized model. We shall call them collectively Group 1 algorithms. [19] using the original model finds the performance of L&W and HKB unsatisfactory. Instead it rates M&G [14] to be the best of the five evaluated in that paper. K&S [12] is included because it is in the class of M&G, as its performance in our simulation is similar to that of M&G. These two algorithms are called collectively Group 2 algorithms. For each model, we search for an optimal value of k through an algorithm called BEST, such that MSE(k) is minimized for this value of k.

Conclusion:
The details of the simulation and tabulation of results are included in [20]. We summarize our findings as follows:

1. The constant term in the original model does not matter. We find that the term $\beta o(k)$ in (6) contributes very little to the value of MSE.

2. There are significant differences in the simulation results, when the evaluation criteria (7) and (8) are used in turn. However, the rankings of the k-selecting algorithms are the same. It seems though that it is more difficult for any k-selecting algorithm to improve over OLS if (8) is used as the evaluation criterion, especially in the good fit region.

3. Using sufficient statistics approach in data generation does not affect the ranking of the k-selecting algorithms. We use $\{X, \beta, \varepsilon\}$ as the simulation parameter set and our results do not differ significantly from that of [4], [8] and [13].

4. Perhaps quite surprisingly, our comprehensive simulation does not produce significantly different results in comparison with other experiments using only a few design matrices.

5. We find that the choise of model is the only factor that may alter the performance ranking of the k-selecting algorithms.
5.1. Original Model: In the good fit regions, Group 2 algorithms do better than Group 1, generally speaking. In poor fit region, the reverse is true.
5.2. Standardized Model: HKB and RIDGM in Group 1 outperform Group 2 algorithms across the board. Although L&W in Group 1 still does poorly in good fit regions, its performance greatly improves with standardized model in use. It outperforms all others in poor fit regions. We also observe from the performance of BEST that ridge regression is more effective when the standardized model is used.

6. Although it is not the prime purpose of this paper to evaluate various k-selecting algorithms, we cannot help but observe the following:

6.1. Within Group 1, K&S does overall better than M&G.
6.2. Within Group 2, HKB and RIDGM perform equally well in good fit region, though HKB tends to do better in case of high degree of multicollinearity. L&W does the worst in the good fit regions. Nevertheless, its performance in the poor fit region is almost perfect.

References:

[1] Brown, P.J. "Centering and Scaling in Ridge Regression", Technometrics 19 (1977), pp.35-36
[2] Coniffe, D. and Stone, J. "A Critical Review of Ridge Regression", The Statistician, 24 (1973), pp.67-68.
[3] Draper, N.R. and Van Nostrand, R.C. "Ridge Regression and James-Stein Estimation: Review and Comments", Technometrics, 21 (1979), pp.451-466
[4] Dempster, A.P., Schatzoff, M. and Wermuth, N. "A Simulation Study of Alternatves to Ordinary Least Squares", JASA, 72 (1977), pp.77-106
[5] Efron, B. and Morris, C. "Comment", JASA, 72 (1977), pp.91-93
[6] Gibbons, D.I. "A Simulation Study of Some Ridge Estimators", General Motors Research Lab. Research Publication No. GMR-2659, March, 1978
[7] Gunst, R.F. and Mason, R.L. "Biased Estimation in Regression: An Evaluation Using Mean Square Error", JASA, 72 (1977), pp.616-628
[8] Hoerl, A.E. "Comment", JASA, 72 (1977), pp.94-95
[9] Hoerl, A.E. and Kennard, R.W. "Ridge Regression: Biased Estimation for Non-orthogonal Problems", Technometrics, 12 (1970), pp.55-67
[10] Hoerl, A.E. and Kennard, R.W. "Ridge Regression: Iterative Estimation of the Biasing Parameter", Comm. in Stat., A5 (1976), pp.77-88
[11] Hoerl, A.E., Kennard, R.W. and Baldwin, K.F. "Ridge Regression: Some Simulations", Comm. in Stat. 4 (1975), pp.105-123
[12] Kasarda, J.D. and Shih, W.-F. P. "Optimal Bias in Ridge Regression Apporaches to Multicollinearity", Sociological Methods & Research, 4 (1977), pp.461-470
[13] Lawless, J.F. and Wang, G. "A Simulation Study of Ridge and Other Regression Estimators", Comm. in Stat. A5 (1976), pp.307-323
[14] McDonald, G.C. and Galarneau, D.J. "A Monte Carlo Evaluation of Some Ridge Type Estimators", JASA, 70 (1975), pp.407-416
[15] Newhouse, J.P. and Oman, S.D. "An Evaluation of Ridge Estimators", Rand Corp. R-716-PR (1971)
[16] Obenchain, R.L. "Ridge Analysis Following a Preliminary Test of the Shrunken Hypothesis", Technometrics, 17 (1975), pp.431-445
[17] Thisted, R.A. "Comment", JASA, 72 (1977), pp.102-103

[18] Vinod, H.D. "Simulation and Extension of a Minimum Mean Squared Error Estimator in Comparison with Stein's", Technometrics, 18 (1976), pp.491-496

[19] Wichern, D.W. and Churchill, G.A. "A comparison of Ridge Estimators", Technometrics, 20 (1978), pp.301-311

[20] Luk, W.S. "On Methodologies of Computer Simulations to Evaluate Ridge Estimators", Technical Report 81-1, Dept. of Computing Science, Simon Fraser University, Burnaby, B.C. (1981)

OPTIMAL PRODUCTION RUN FOR A PROCESS SUBJECT TO DRIFT, SHIFT, AND CHANGES IN VARIANCE

M.A. Rahim & R.S. Lashkari
University of Windsor

ABSTRACT

This paper describes how to determine the optimal production run for an industrial process which is subject to a negative drift in its mean over time, a shift due to an assignable cause, and changes in the variance of its output.

Optimal decision rules are developed to determine the length of the production period, at the beginning of which the process is in control, and at the end of which it is shut-down for resetting. A cost function is developed which consists of the cost of resetting the process, the cost of rejected items, and the lost product cost due to shut-down. To determine the optimal production run, the cost function is minimized using a search algorithm, as well as a graphical method which relies on a digital plotter.

(PRODUCTION PLANNING; QUALITY CONTROL; OPTIMIZATION)

INTRODUCTION

In any production process, some variations in product quality are unavoidable. These variations, which in general are attributed to chance causes or to assignable causes, may result in an unacceptable level of process mean, process variance or both. Variations due to chance causes are random in nature. Their occurrence is not predictable and they do not occur in repetitive cycles. The resulting variations are rarely produced by only one cause; rather, they are mostly due to a number of interactive causes [3]. Some typical chance causes of variations are [5]: slight variations in raw materials, slight vibration of machine, lack of operator perfection in reading instruments and setting controls. Variations due to assignable causes are non-random in nature. Their occurrence is predictable and repetitive, and they may result in a large amount of variation in product quality. Some typical assignable causes of variations are [5]: defective raw materials, faulty set up, untrained operator, cummulative effects of heat, vibration, shock, etc.

Generally, quality control procedures are required to maintain the production process in such a way that the output of the process meets the required production specifications. Traditionally, the specification limits are set based on the knowledge of variability due to chance effects. During the production cycle, the variability due to assignable cause may drive the process into an out-of-control state. In controlling a process, the objective is, to detect the shift in process mean and eliminate the assignable cause. This is done by inspecting a sample of the product output after regular intervals of time. Numerous articles have been published relating to the optimal control of process mean. For a review of the literature, see Montgomery [6].

In some industrial processes, change in the process mean is time dependent and continuous for a given length of time. That is, the mean of an operating process drifts steadily with time from an in-control state to an out-of-control state. There can be as many causes as one can imagine for a process to exhibit a systematic trend in the process mean during the course of operation. The drift can be positive or negative. For example, the positive drift is said to occur when tool wears out and the negative drift may occur when the diameter of a spray nozzle is being clogged/rebuilt continuously when a liquid is sprayed upon a surface. To keep the process in control the magnitude of the drift is to be maintained within a specified range. This is obtained by resetting the tool or cleaning the spray nozzle. There exists a relationship between the magnitude of the drift and the length of the production run. Processes that drift slowly from an in-control state have received little analytical attention. Gibra [2,3] investigated the optimal determination of production run to monitor a process involving tool wear in which the mean of the quality characteristic exhibits a trend in positive direction. His optimal control procedures establish decision rules for adjustment due to drift as well as for the occurrence of an assignable cause. The control rules minimize the adjustment cost and the costs due to the production of defective items. However, the study did not consider the cost of the process shutdown and no attempt was made to study the effect of negative drift in the process mean. Considering the cost of the process shut down, Rahim & Lashkari [7] proposed models for determining the optimal production runs for a process having negative drift. In developing the models they assumed that the drift may be accompanied by a shift in the process mean. However, an assumption common to the works mentioned above [2,3,6,7] is that, the process mean changes while variance remains constant throughout the production period. The assumption of constant variance, while providing some convenience in formulation of models, is not a general one. For example, an improper tool set up may cause certain irregular variations in the operations of the production process. Consequently the variance of the product will not remain constant throughout the process. Variance may also change within a production period as machine's precision deteriorates due to lack of proper maintenance.

On occasions, the quality characteristic in question may be one of the properties of the material, such as density, tensile strength, resistance, coefficient of expansion and so on. Shewhart [8] reported that in the case of the physical property of a material there is some relationship between the mean value of the product quality and its standard deviation. Thus, if mean changes during the production period, the variance changes consequently. Changes in variance may also be experienced in production processes where drift and shift are in effect.

This paper describes how to determine the optimal production run, at the beginning of which the process produces the output under a correct setup, and at the end of which the process is shutdown for resetting. The process mean is subject to a gradual change and/or a step-change during the production period. Subsequently, changes in the process variance are experienced. Changes in the variance may also be due to lack of proper maintenance of the process. As the production process operates over time, its mean experiences a negative drift below the specified range, which has to be controlled by resetting. A longer production run is desirable, because each resetting involves time and cost. A balance must be maintained between the cost of resetting and the loss due to defective items.

The model presented here considers single specification limit for the process mean. A cost function per unit of finished item is developed which consists of the following elements: (1) the resetting cost; (2) the cost of rejected items, and (3) the lost product cost due to resetting. The cost function is then minimized using a search method as well as a graphical method to obtain the optimal production run.

ASSUMPTIONS OF PROCESS MODEL

The process is assumed to start in a state of "in-control". The measurable characteristic of the process variable, x, is assumed to be normally distributed with mean μ_0 and variance σ_0^2. The process mean drifts constantly and linearly in the negative direction as time goes on. In addition, it is assumed that, during the production run, the process may be disturbed by the occurrence of an assignable cause which shifts the current mean by an amount $\delta\sigma_0$, where δ is constant (positive or negative). Furthermore, it is assumed that with the change in process mean, the process variance, σ_0^2 changes to σ_t^2 where $\sigma_t^2 > \sigma_0^2$. Based on the general outlines of the works of Gibra [2,3] the following notation will be used:

- δ = the shift parameter
- μ_t = process mean at time t when only drift is in effect $= \mu_0 - \theta t$
- σ_t^2 = process variance at time t
- θ = the drift in the process mean per unit time
- $\bar{w}_1$ = the average proportion of non-defective items produced per unit time when only the effect of the drift is assumed
- $\bar{w}_2$ = the average proportion of non-defective items per unit time due to the combined effect of the drift and the shift
- r = production rate in pieces per unit time
- $\delta\sigma_0$ = the magnitude of the shift in the process mean due to the occurrence of the assignable cause
- k = coefficient of the specification limit for the mean
- L_1^2 = coefficient of the lower specification limit for variance
- L_2^2 = coefficient of the upper specification limit for variance
- γ = average proportion of time within the production period, which the process is subject to drift
- K_r = the resetting cost
- τ_r = the resetting time
- u = the penalty incurred per defective item
- t_a = the length of production run
- V_0 = the cost per unit of finished item
- F(x) = the cumulative distribution function of the standardized normal variate X
- f(x) = the probability density function (pdf) of the standardized normal variate X
- z = standard normal variate
- $F_{\chi^2;n-1}(x)$ = the cumulative distribution function of the chi-square variate x with n-1 degrees of freedom
- n = sample size
- $\hat{\sigma}_s^2$ = sample variance at sampling point
- P = probability of defective item at time t
- P_1 = probability that output variable falls outside of its mean specification limit at time t
- P_2 = probability that output variable falls outside of its variance specification limit at time t

DETERMINATION OF OPTIMAL PRODUCTION RUN

As the production process operates over time, the process mean is subject to change due to shift and/or drift; concurrently the process variance changes. These changes in the process mean and variance may cause the quality of the output to deterioriate, depending on both the magnitude and the direction of the drift and the shift. Some degree of deterioration may be tolerated at a cost. It may be less costly, however, to intervene, by overhauling, adjusting or resetting the production process after a specified production run. The following model describes how to determine the optimum production run length.

Suppose that the specification limit for mean is expressed as $\mu_0 - k\sigma_0$, that is, the acceptable process mean varies between μ_0 and $\mu_0 - k\sigma_0$. It is assumed that the negative drift is in effect. The mean shifts further by an amount $\delta\sigma_0$ in the negative direction in case there is an assignable cause. The shift remains effective throughout the production period until the process is shutdown for resetting. At time t=0, the mean is μ_0 and at the end of the production run, that is, at time $t=t_a$ the mean is $\mu_0 - t_a\theta - \delta\sigma_0$.

Suppose that the coefficient of lower specification limit for variance is $L_1^2=0$, and that the coefficient of upper specification limit of variance is L_2^2. That is the upper specification limit for variance is $L_2^2\sigma_0^2$. Therefore, the probability of a defective item at time t when both drift and shift are in effect is

$$P = P_1 + P_2 - P_1P_2$$

where

$$P_1 = P_r[x_t \leq \mu_0 - k\sigma_0 | \mu = \mu_t, \sigma = \sigma_t]$$

$$= P_r[z \leq \frac{\mu_0 - k\sigma_0 - \mu_t}{\sigma_t}] = F(\frac{\theta}{\sigma_t} t - k\frac{\sigma_0}{\sigma_t} - \delta\frac{\sigma_0}{\sigma_t}),$$

$$P_2 = P_r[\hat{\sigma}_s^2 > L_2^2\sigma_0^2 | \mu = \mu_t, \sigma^2 = \sigma_t^2]$$

$$= P_r[\chi^2 > L_2^2(n-1)\frac{\sigma_0^2}{\sigma_t^2}]$$

$$= 1 - F_{\chi^2;n-1}(a)$$

where, $a = (n-1)L_2^2\frac{\sigma_0^2}{\sigma_t^2}$. Thus, the probability of a non-defective item at t is:

$$= 1 - P$$

$$= F(k\frac{\sigma_0}{\sigma_t} - \frac{\theta}{\sigma_t}t - \delta\frac{\sigma_0}{\sigma_t}) \cdot F_{\chi^2;n-1}(a) \qquad (1)$$

Now, we have:

$$\bar{w}_2 = \frac{r}{t_a}\int_0^{t_a} F(k\frac{\sigma_0}{\sigma_t} - \frac{\theta}{\sigma_t}t - \delta\frac{\sigma_0}{\sigma_t})F_{\chi^2;n-1}(a)\,dt$$

$$= \frac{\sigma_t}{\theta}\frac{r}{t_a}F_{\chi^2;n-1}(a)\,[(k\frac{\sigma_0}{\sigma_t} - \delta\frac{\sigma_0}{\sigma_t})F(k\frac{\sigma_0}{\sigma_t} - \delta\frac{\sigma_0}{\sigma_t})$$

$$- (k\frac{\sigma_0}{\sigma_t} - \frac{\theta}{\sigma_t}t_a - \delta\frac{\sigma_0}{\sigma_t})F(k\frac{\sigma_0}{\sigma_t} - \frac{\theta}{\sigma_t}t_a - \delta\frac{\sigma_0}{\sigma_t})$$

$$+ f(k\frac{\sigma_0}{\sigma_t} - \delta\frac{\sigma_0}{\sigma_t}) - f(k\frac{\sigma_0}{\sigma_t} - \frac{\theta}{\sigma_t}t_a - \delta\frac{\sigma_0}{\sigma_t})] \qquad (2)$$

In order to obtain $\bar{w}_1$, we substitute $\delta=0$ in Equation (2). Assuming that the sampling cost and the number of defective items produced during the period τ_r, are negligible, and that the parameter γ is known, the expected total cost during the production run is:

$$E(T.C.) = k_r + \gamma u t_a(r-\bar{w}_1) + (1-\gamma)ut_a(r-\bar{w}_2) + \tau_r V_0 r.$$

Therefore, the expected total cost per unit is:

$$E(T.C.) = \frac{k_r + \gamma u t_a(r-\bar{w}_1) + (1-\gamma)ut_a(r-\bar{w}_2) + \tau_r V_0 r}{\gamma\bar{w}_1 t_a + (1-\gamma)\bar{w}_2 t_a}$$

$$= \frac{k_r + ut_a r + r\tau_r V_0}{\gamma\bar{w}_1 t_a + (1-\gamma)\bar{w}_2 t_a} - u \qquad (3)$$

Differentiating Equation (3) with respect to t_a and equating to zero, we have:

$$(k_r + ut_a r + \tau_r V_0 r)[\gamma\bar{w}_1 + \gamma t_a\frac{\partial\bar{w}_1}{\partial t_a} + (1-\gamma)\bar{w}_2$$

$$+ (1-\gamma)t_a\frac{\partial\bar{w}_2}{\partial t_a}] = \gamma t_a\bar{w}_1 + (1-\gamma)t_a\bar{w}_2 \qquad (4)$$

From Equation (2), we obtain:

$$\frac{\partial\bar{w}_1}{\partial t_a} = \frac{\gamma F(k\frac{\sigma_0}{\sigma_t} - \frac{\theta}{\sigma_t}t_a)F_{\chi^2;n-1}(a) - \bar{w}_1}{t_a}$$

$$\frac{\partial\bar{w}_2}{\partial t_a} = \frac{\gamma F(k\frac{\sigma_0}{\sigma_t} - \frac{\theta}{\sigma_t}t_a - \delta\frac{\sigma_0}{\sigma_t})F_{\chi^2;n-1}(a) - \bar{w}_2}{t_a}$$

Substituting these values in Equation (4) and simplifying the expression, we have

$$\frac{k_r}{u_r} + t_a + \frac{\tau_r V_0}{u} = \frac{M}{N} \qquad (5)$$

where

$$M = \gamma\frac{\sigma_t}{\theta}[k\frac{\sigma_0}{\sigma_t}F(k\frac{\sigma_0}{\sigma_t}) - (k\frac{\sigma_0}{\sigma_t} - \frac{\theta}{\sigma_t}t_a)F(k\frac{\sigma_0}{\sigma_t} - \frac{\theta}{\sigma_t}t_a)$$

$$+ f(k\frac{\sigma_0}{\sigma_t}) - f(k\frac{\sigma_0}{\sigma_t} - \frac{\theta}{\sigma_t}t_a)]$$

$$+ (1-\gamma)\frac{\sigma_t}{\theta}[(k\frac{\sigma_0}{\sigma_t} - \delta\frac{\sigma_0}{\sigma_t})F(k\frac{\sigma_0}{\sigma_t} - \delta\frac{\sigma_0}{\sigma_t})$$

$$- (k\frac{\sigma_0}{\sigma_t} - \frac{\theta}{\sigma_t}t_a - \delta\frac{\sigma_0}{\sigma_t})F(k\frac{\sigma_0}{\sigma_t} - \frac{\theta}{\sigma_t}t_a - \delta\frac{\sigma_0}{\sigma_t})$$

$$+ f(k\frac{\sigma_0}{\sigma_t} - \delta\frac{\sigma_0}{\sigma_t}) - f(k\frac{\sigma_0}{\sigma_t} - \frac{\theta}{\sigma_t}t_a - \delta\frac{\sigma_0}{\sigma_t})]$$

$$N = \gamma F(k\frac{\sigma_0}{\sigma_t} - \frac{\theta}{\sigma_t}t_a) + (1-\gamma)F(k\frac{\sigma_0}{\sigma_t} - \frac{\theta}{\sigma_t}t_a - \delta\frac{\sigma_0}{\sigma_t})$$

To obtain the optimal production run length t_a, Equation (5) can now easily be solved numerically or graphically. The following examples demonstrate the procedure.

Example 1: Consider the production process which is free from the occurrence of an assignable cause and that it is to be terminated for adjustment or for resetting due to the effect of the drift. Thus we set $\delta = 0$ and $\gamma = 1.0$ in Equation (5). The specification limit for mean is set at $\mu_0 - 3\sigma_0$, and the upper specification limit for variance is $1.4\sigma_0^2$. The other parameters are given as follows: k_r = \$100.00; τ_r = 0.25 hours; $\sigma_0 = 1.50$; $\mu_0 = 10$; $\sigma_t/\theta = 2$ per unit time; V_0 = \$112.0; r = 25 pieces per hour; u = \$4.0; $\theta = 1.0$. Using these parameters, Equation (5) is solved for the optimal value of t_a, using a computer program based on the search method developed by Leavenworth [1]. The optimal production run indicates that the process should be reset every 5.52 hours.

The graphical solution is shown in Figure 1, where the straight line represents the left-hand side of Equation (5), and the curve represents the right-hand side. Drawing a perpendicular to the abscissa, from the intersection of the two lines, the solution for t_a is found to be approximately 5.51 hours.

When computer facilities are available, the procedure for representation of Equation (5) in graphical form could be easily programmed on the computer, and displayed on a terminal.

It is interesting to note that, if the variance is assumed to remain constant during the production process, i.e., if $\sigma_t^2 = \sigma_0^2$, the optimal value of t_a is 5.21 hours.

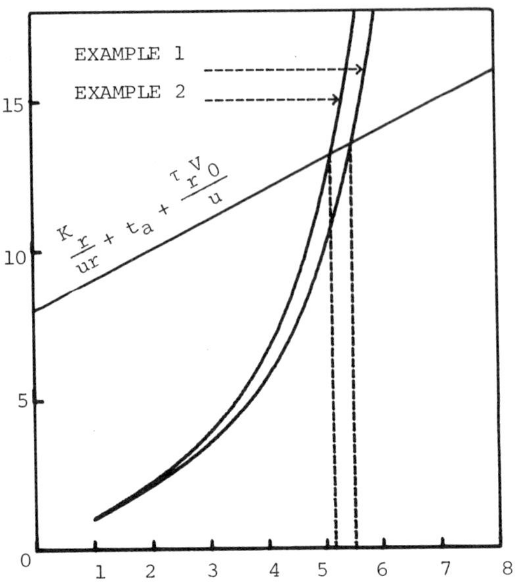

Figure 1: DETERMINATION OF PRODUCTION RUN

Example 2: Consider that the process is to be terminated due to the drift as well as the occurrence of the assignable cause. The specification limit is set at $\mu_0 - 3\sigma_0$, the shift parameter $\delta = 1.0$, and $\gamma = 0.55$ and other parameters are the same as in Example 1. The optimal solution results in a production run length of 5.16 hours whereas the graphical solution obtained from Figure 1 is 5.15 hours. However, if the process variance is regarded as uniformly distributed, that is, $\sigma_t^2 = \sigma_0^2$, the plan results in a production length of 4.83 hours.

CONCLUSIONS

The optimal decision rules are derived for determining the length of the production run for various industrial situations, where the process mean changes due to drift and/or shift, and the process variance is also subject to change. In the light of the findings it may be stated that the optimal production run depends upon the magnitude and the direction of the drift and the shift. The results also indicate that the assumption of constant variance has a sizeable effect on the production run length. The model presented here does not take into account the sampling costs in determining the production run lengths; such costs (as well as other parameters) could, however, be easily incorporated into the model. The graphical solution procedure provides near optimal values in most cases and could be easily utilized at workshop level where computer facilities may not be readily available.

ACKNOWLEDGEMENTS

The financial support provided by the Natural Sciences and Engineering Research Council of Canada for conducting this study is gratefully acknowledged. The authors would like to acknowledge the assistance provided by Mr. K. Tsuchiya with computing aspects of this study.

REFERENCES

1. Leavenworth, B., "Algorithm 25: Real Zeros of an Arbitrary Function", Comm. of A.C.M., No. 3, Vol. 12, pp. 602, 1960.
2. Gibra, I.N., "Optimal Control of Process Subject to Linear Trends", The J. of Ind. Engg., No. 1, Vol. 14, pp. 35-41, 1967.
3. Gibra, I.N., "Optimal Production Run of Processes Subject to Systematic Trends", Int. J. Prod. Res., No. 4, Vol. 12, pp. 511-512, 1974.
4. Halper, N.S., The Assurance Sciences: An Introduction to Quality Control and Reliability, Prentice-Hall, Englewood Cliffs, New Jersey, 1978.
5. Juran, J.M., Quality Control Handbook, (Second Edition), McGraw Hill Book Company, Inc., Section 13, pp. 42, 1962.
6. Montgomery, D.C., "The Economic Design of Control Charts: A Review and Literature Survey", Journal of Quality Technology, No. 2, Vol. 12, pp. 75-87, April 1980.
7. Rahim, M.A. and Lashkari, R.S., "Modelling of a Production Process Having a Negative Drift", Proceedings of International AMSE Conference: Modelling and Simulation, Paris-Sud, France, July 1-3, 1982.
8. Shewhart, W.A., Economic Control of Quality Manufactured Product, D. Van Nostrand Company, Inc., pp. 261, 1931.

RECURSIVE ALGORITHMS IN STATISTICS

Norman D. Neff, Trenton State College

Abstract: We present two applications of recursive algorithms to statistics. We develop a recursive algorithm for a nonparametric permutation test, and include PL/I code in recursive and nonrecursive form. In a second application, the values of a function $f(\underline{x})$ involving determinants must be generated as $\underline{x}=(x_1,\ldots,x_n$ ranges over a finite subset of R^n. We express $f(\underline{x})$ as $f_n(\underline{x})$ where there is a recurrence of the form

$$f_r(\underline{x}) = g(r,f_{r-1}(\underline{x}),x_r) \quad r=1,2,\ldots,n$$

with $f_r(\underline{x})$ depending only on $(x_1,x_2,\ldots,x_r)$. The tuples $(x_1,\ldots,x_r)$ are generated by depth-first traversal of a tree, the computation of $f_r(\underline{x})$ is intermeshed with the traversal, and an order-of-magnitude gain in efficiency is obtained.

Keywords: Backtracking, depth-first search, permutation tests, recursion

Application 1: A permutation test. Fisher [3] proposed a nonparametric version of the paired-sample t test for cases where the assumption of normality could not be accepted. Assume that $X_1,\ldots,X_n$ is a random sample from a symmetric but otherwise unspecified distribution. To test the null hypothesis that the population media is zero versus the alternative of a positive population median, the procedure is as follows. Let C be the cardinality of the set of all n-tuples $(d_1,\ldots,d_n)$ such that

$d_i=0$ or 1, $\quad i=1,\ldots,n$, and

$$\Sigma_{i=1}^n d_i|X_i| \geq \Sigma_{i=1}^n \max(X_i,0)$$

Reject the null hypothesis at significance level α If $C \leq \Sigma\alpha\, 2^n$. This test is UMP unbiased against the class of normal alternatives $N(\mu,\sigma^2)$, $\mu>0$. Lehmann [4] develops the theory of permutation tests and the related "randomization" tests in which we are willing to accept distributional assumptions about treatment effects but not about experimental unit effects. Edgington [2] gives numerous FORTRAN programs for randomization tests, but not much explanation of how such programs work or how they are developed. In this section we use the example of the Fisher test to show how recursive techniques sometimes lead to simple, efficient algorithms for such problems

The brute force approach to this problem generates all n-tuples $(d_1,\ldots,d_n)$ where $d_i=0$ or 1. For each n-tuple we check whether we have a "solution", i.e. whether

$$\Sigma_{i=1}^n d_i y_i \geq t$$

where $y_i=|X_i|$ and $t=\Sigma_{i=1}^n \max(X_i,0)$. The set of all n-tuples may be identified with the set of leaves in a full binary tree of depth n. Figure 1 illustrates the case $n=2$, $y_1=2$, $y_2=1$, $t=2$. Solutions are circled in the Figure. A depth-first traversal of a tree is recursively effected by CALL TRAV($\emptyset$,1) where TRAV is

```
PROCEDURE TRAV(d,k)
   FOR EACH child d' of d,
      CALL TRAV(d',k+1)
RETURN
```

If the children are always generated in the order left, right, then for Figure 1 the succession of first arguments $\underline{d}$ to calls of TRAV is $\emptyset$, 0, 00, 01, 1, 10, 11. The traversal goes as deep as possible before backing up to explore other parts of the tree. Note that the sequence of nodes is exactly the sequence of states for the index variables of doubly nested loops on d_1, d_2.

To refine the brute force approach, note that if $\underline{d}_k = (d_1,\ldots,d_k)$, k<n satisfies

$$\Sigma_{i=1}^k d_i y_i + \Sigma_{i=k+1}^n y_i < t$$

then no descendant of $\underline{d}_k$ can be a solution. We need only generate those children $\underline{d}_k$ satisfying the bounding predicate $P_k(\underline{d}_k)$ defined by $s_k \geq g_k$, where $s_k=\Sigma_{i=1}^k d_i y_i$, $g_k=t-\Sigma_{i=k+1}^n y_i$, $k<n$, and $g_n=0$ In most applications the bounding predicate is merely a necessary condition for the existence of descendants that are solutions. In this example the bounding predicate is minimal in that it is also a sufficient condition; the search for solutions never enters a blind alley.

An example of a second refinement occurs at node (1) in Figure 1. If $s_k \geq t$, then all leaves of the subtree rooted at $\underline{d}_k$ are solutions, and the count may be increased by 2^{n-k} without traversing the subtree. If $\underline{d}_k$ satisfies this condition, then the subtree rooted at $\underline{d}_k$ may be collapsed to a single solution node of depth k and value $f(\underline{d}_k)=2^{n-k}$. The problem is reduced to the summation of $f(\underline{d}_k)$ over the leaves of a subtree of the original tree.

The PL/I program of Figure 2 recursively computes the permutation test. For maximum effectiveness of pruning, the y_k are stored in nonincreasing order. Omitted is the initialization of global arrays containing the g_k and powers of 2. We assume $0<t\leq\Sigma_{i=1}^n y_i$. Each time RTEST is called, d_{k-1} satisfies the bounding predicate but

is not a solution of depth k-1. If $d_k=1$, we need not test the depth k bounding predicate, and if $d_k=0$, we need not test for a solution of depth k. By testing the child $d_k=1$ first, the algorithm tries to quickly find solutions at shallow depths bearing large values of 2^{n-k}. If a particular significance level α is specified, then each change of COUNT can be followed by a test terminating the algorithm with the message "not significant" if COUNT $\geq \alpha 2^n$.

Nonrecursive coding. In most implementations of general purpose scientific languages, recursive subroutine calls are illegal or expensive. Depth-first search may alternatively be programmed iteratively, either as a nest of loops or as a "backtrack" program [1,7]. Figure 3 is a backtrack version of Figure 2. On an IBM 370/158 with PL/I Optimizer compiler, the backtrack version needs about 70% of the execution time required by the recursive version. Backtracking is based on an iterative description of depth-first traversal. During the traversal, maintain a record of the set of unvisited children of the current node and of all ancestors of the current node. Given the current node v, the successor v′ in the traversal is defined as follows. If v has unvisited children, pick one as v′. If v has no unvisited children, backtrack to its parent, grandparent,...until either an ancestor of v with an unvisited child (v′) is found, or no further backtracking is possible (traversal complete).

Application 2: A probability computation. In application 1, the computation of s_k is effected by the recursion $s_k = s_{k-1}+y_k d_k$. In terms of nested loops, this corresponds to replacing a nest containing the complete computation of s_n with a nest where all but the recursion step has been factored out of each loop. Neff and Naus [5] found a similar recursion in the following problem which arose in connection with the calculation of the probability of the existence of a subinterval containing at least n points with N points are uniformly distributed on the unit interval.

Given natural numbers n and L, generate the values of $\det(H_{(L+1)x(L+1)})\det(G_{LxL})$ for all integer sequences $(s_1,\ldots,s_{2L+1})$ satisfying constraints of the form

$$b_1(j,s_{j-1}) \leq s_j \leq b_2(j,s_{j-2}),\ j=1,\ldots,2L+1,$$

where b_1 and b_2 are given functions, $s_{-1}=s_0=0$, and H and G are positive definite matrices,

$$h_{ij} = 1/(s_{2i-1} - s_{2j-2} - (i-j)n)!$$

$$g_{ij} = 1/(s_{2i} - s_{2j-1} - (i-j)n)!$$

Here the nodes of the tree are k-tuples $\underline{s}_k = (s_1, \ldots, s_k)$. To efficiently generate det(H)det(G) at each leaf of the tree, the determinants are recursively computed using the Crout form of Gaussian elimination without pivoting [6]. In the Crout method, the column-reduced form B of a matrix A satisfies

$$b_{i1} = a_{i1}$$

$$b_{ij} = a_{ij} - \Sigma_{k-1}^{j-1} b_{ik} b_{kj} \qquad i \geq j \geq 2$$

$$=(a_{ij} - \Sigma_{k=1}^{i-1} b_{ik} b_{kj})/b_{ii} \qquad i<j$$

Elements b_{ij} of B are recursively defined in terms of elements of B above and to the left of the b_{ij}. When node $\underline{s}_{2k+1}$ is entered, the Crout recursion allows the successive computation of entries $b_{k+1,1},\ldots,b_{k+1,k+1}$ in the column-reduced form of h, requiring a total of $k(k+1)/2$ multiplications. the innermost loop, corresponding to depth 2L+1, has a cost on the order of $L^2/2$, compared with a cost on the order of $L^3/3$ for the conventional computation of a single determinant of order L+1.

This sort of gain in efficiency is generally available when $f(\underline{x})=f_n(\underline{x})$ and there is a recurrence of the form

$$f_r(x_1,\ldots,x_n)=g(r,f_{r-1}(\underline{x}),x_r),\ r=1,\ldots,n$$

with $f_r(\underline{x})$ depending only on $(x_1,\ldots,x_r)$. If the generation of the $\underline{x}_n$ is coded as a nest of loops, the content of each loop is the computation of $g(r,f_{r-1}(\underline{x}),x_r)$ followed by preparation for the next loop in the nest.

References:

1. Bitner, J.R. and Reingold, E.M., Backtrack programming techniques, Communications of the ACM, v.18 1975, 651-656.

2. Edgington, E.S., Randomization Tests, Marcel Dekker, New York, 1980.

3. Fisher, R.A., The Design of Experiments, Hafner, New York, 1935, 44-49.

4. Lehmann, E. L., Testing Statistical Hypotheses, Wiley, New York, 1959, 183-199.

5. Neff, N.D. and Naus, J.I., The distribution of the size of the maximum cluster of points on a line. Volume 6 of Selected Tables in Mathematical Statistics, American Mathematical Society, Providence, R.I., 1980, 14-21.

6. Stoutmeyer, D. R., PL/I Programming for Engineering and Science, Prentice-Hall, Englewood Cliffs, N.J., 1971

7. Wells, M.B., Elements of Combinatorial Computing, Pergamon, Oxford and New York, 1971, 27-31, 93-106.

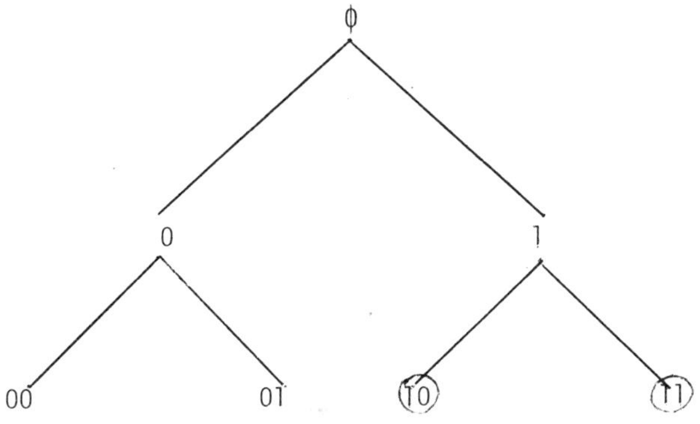

Figure 1

```
PERMTEST:  PROC OPTIONS(MAIN);
 DCL  (COUNT,(G,S,TWO,Y)(0:25)) FIXED BIN#31);
 GET LIST(N,T);
  /* OMITTED:                            */
  /* INPUT Y(*) IN NONINCREASING ORDER */
  /* INITIALIZE ARRAYS G(*), TWO(*)     */
 S(0)=0; COUNT=0;
 CALL RTEST(1);
RTEST: PROC(K) RECURSIVE;
 /* D(1), ... , D(K-1) DEFINED */
 /* TRY CHILDREN */
 /* D(K)=+1 */
 S(K)=S(K-1)+Y(K);
 /* CHECK FOR SOLUTION */
 IF S(K)>=T THEN COUNT=COUNT+TWO(N-K);
 ELSE CALL RTEST(K+1);
 /* D(K)=0; */
 S(K)=S(K-1);
 IF S(K)>=G(K) THEN CALL RTEST(K+1);
END RTEST;
PUT SKIP DATA(COUNT);
END PERMTEST;
```

Figure 2

```
PERMTEST:  PROC OPTIONS(MAIN);
 DCL  (COUNT,(L,G,S,TWO,Y)(0:25)) FIXED BIN(31);
 GET LIST (N,T);
  /* OMITTED:                            */
  /* INPUT Y(*) IN NONINCREASING ORDER */
  /* INITIALIZE ARRAYS G(*), TWO(*)     */
 K=1; L(1)=1; S(0)=0; COUNT=0;
BTEST:  DO WHILE (K>0);
 /* D(1), ... , D(K-1) DEFINED */
 /* L(K) IS LARGEST UNUSED D(K) VALUE */
 IF L(K)=-1 THEN GOTO BACKTRACK;
 VISIT:;
 /* D(K)=+1 */
 IF L(K)=1 THEN DO;
    L(K)=0;
    S(K)=S(K-1)+Y(K);
   /* CHECK FOR SOLUTION */
   IF S(K)>=T THEN COUNT=COUNT+TWO(N-K);
    ELSE DO;K=K+1; L(K)=1; GOTO VISIT;
          END;
    END;
 /* D(K)=0; */
    L(K)=-1;
    S(K)=S(K-1);
    IF S(K)>=G(K) THEN DO;
       K=K+1; L(K)=1; GOTO VISIT;
       END;
BACKTRACK: K=K-1;
END BTEST;
PUT SKIP DATA(COUNT);
END PERMTEST;
```

Figure 3

A BAYESIAN TREATMENT OF NONRESPONSE WHEN SAMPLING FROM A DICHOTOMOUS POPULATION

James H. Albert, Bowling Green State University

ABSTRACT. Suppose a sample survey is taken to learn about the proportion of a population in favor of a particular statement. A significant proportion of the sample does not respond to the survey and a priori the experimenter feels that the groups of respondents and nonrespondents possess different attitudes towards the statement. A prior distribution is developed which can reflect vague prior beliefs about the differences in the attitudes of respondents and nonrespondents. This distribution is used to develop an interval estimate of the population proportion.

Key words and phrases: Cross-product ratio, Dirichlet mixture, credible interval.

1. INTRODUCTION. Suppose a mail survey is sent to learn about the attitudes of a population toward a particular subject. Let n denote the total number of surveys sent out and let n_r (n_s) denote the number of people who respond (don't respond). The n_r respondents are classified dichotomously into the two groups "favorable" and "unfavorable"; let n_{fr} (n_{ur}) denote the number observed in the favorable (unfavorable) group. The observed counts and corresponding probability model are shown below.

	Resp.	Nonresp.				
Fav.	n_{fr}			p_{fr}	p_{fs}	p_f
Unfav.	n_{ur}			p_{ur}	p_{us}	p_u
	n_r	n_s	n	p_r	p_s	

(Note that two cells in the count table are empty, since these counts are unobservable.) If the population is assumed infinite, the probability of observing the triple $\underset{\sim}{x} = (n_{fr}, n_{ur}, n_s)$ is proportional to $p_{fr}^{n_{fr}} p_{ur}^{n_{ur}} (p_{fs}+p_{us})^{n_s}$. One general problem of interest is to estimate p_f, the probability that a given member of the population is favorable.

From a classical point of view, there is no data available to estimate p_{fs} (the probability an individual does not respond and is favorable), and therefore the probability $p_f = p_{fr} + p_{fs}$ is not estimable. The usual practice is to use the statistic n_{fr}/n_r, the proportion of respondents in favor, as an estimate of p_f. This estimator is unbiased for p_{fr}/p_r, the conditional probability that a respondent is favorable. However, if the bias $p_{fr}/p_r - p_f$ is large, n_{fr}/n_r will be an unsuitable estimate of the probability of interest p_f. (Birnbaum and Sirken (1950) and Hansen and Hurwitz (1946) have studied the errors incurred from using the estimate n_{fr}/n_r.)

This classical problem of estimability can be avoided by means of the Bayesian method. A user states his prior beliefs about the vector $\underset{\sim}{p} = (p_{fr}, p_{fs}, p_{ur}, p_{us})$ in terms of a prior distribution placed on $\underset{\sim}{p}$ and a posterior distribution for $\underset{\sim}{p}$ is computed which combines the prior beliefs of the user with the observed sample counts. The posterior distribution is then used to provide point and interval estimates for p_f. This Bayesian method of estimating p_f, of course, depends strongly on the form of the prior distribution chosen. The most convenient family of prior distributions on $\underset{\sim}{p}$ is the Dirichlet, with density given by

$$(1.1)\quad \pi_D(\underset{\sim}{p}|K,\underset{\sim}{\eta}) \propto p_{fr}^{K\eta_{fr}-1}\, p_{fs}^{K\eta_{fs}-1}\, p_{ur}^{K\eta_{ur}-1}\, p_{us}^{K\eta_{us}-1},$$

where $K > 0$, $\eta_{ij} > 0$ for all i,j, $\eta_{fr} + \eta_{fs} + \eta_{ur} + \eta_{us} = 1$ and $\underset{\sim}{\eta} = (\eta_{fr}, \eta_{fs}, \eta_{ur}, \eta_{us})$. To use this family of prior distributions, a user specifies $\underset{\sim}{\eta}$, which represents a guess at the vector of probabilities $\underset{\sim}{p}$, and K, which reflects the precision of the guess $\underset{\sim}{\eta}$. Kaufman and King (1973) use the Dirichlet family of priors to develop a posterior mean estimate of p_f and, in addition, develop solutions to various two-stage sampling problems.

The Bayesian method of estimating p_f using the Dirichlet family of priors is attractive because of its computational simplicity. However, before this Bayesian procedure is recommended in practice, we should investigate whether typical prior beliefs about $\underset{\sim}{p}$ can be modeled by the Dirichlet family. One common prior belief that the user may possess is that the group of respondents are not representative of the entire population. To state in terms of conditional probabilities, it may be believed that $p_{f\cdot r} = p_{fr}/p_r$, the probability a respondent is favorable, is significantly different than $p_{f\cdot s} = p_{fs}/p_s$, the probability a nonrespondent is favorable. Alternately, the user may believe that $p_{r\cdot f} = p_{fr}/p_f$, the probability a favorable subject responds is much smaller or larger than $p_{r\cdot u} = p_{ur}/p_u$, the probability an unfavorable subject responds. In either case, the user is making a statement a priori about the association structure in the 2×2 table formed by the classes response/nonresponse and favorable/unfavorable.

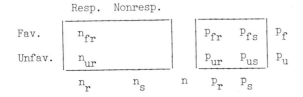

One implication of the Dirichlet prior is that the conditional probabilities $p_{f\cdot r}$ and $p_{f\cdot s}$ (or $p_{r\cdot f}$ and $p_{r\cdot u}$) are independent. Thus this convenient class of priors will be unsuitable for reflecting prior beliefs about the similarity or dissimilarity of these conditional probabilities. In other words, the Dirichlet family is not a rich enough family to incorporate certain prior beliefs about the bias due to the non-availability of all the subsets.

In the estimation of cell probabilities from a 2×2 table, Albert and Gupta (1982) introduced a class of priors, a mixture of Dirichlet distributions, which is designed to reflect prior beliefs about the association structure of the table. This class of priors accepts the input of two parameters α_0 and K. The parameter α_0 is a guess at the cross product ratio $\alpha = (p_{fr}p_{us})/(p_{fs}p_{ur})$, reflecting one's prior belief about the cross-classification structure. To understand how one guesses at α in this situation, note that the measure can be rewritten as

$$(1.2)\qquad \alpha = \frac{p_{f\cdot r}/(1-p_{f\cdot r})}{p_{f\cdot s}/(1-p_{f\cdot s})}$$

or

$$(1.3)\qquad \alpha = \frac{p_{r\cdot f}/(1-p_{r\cdot f})}{p_{s\cdot f}/(1-p_{s\cdot f})}\ .$$

In either expression, α is written as a ratio of odds of conditional probabilities. To illustrate the use of (1.2), one interpretation of the guess $\alpha_0 = 2$ is that the odds of a respondent favoring is believed twice as large as the odds of a nonrespondent favoring. The parameter K reflects the precision of the guess at α, or equivalently the sureness of one's prior belief about the association in the table.

Using the prior of Albert and Gupta (1982), section 2 gives the posterior distribution for p_f and uses this distribution to find posterior moments for p_f. Since this prior is a mixture of Dirichlets, these results are built on results in the Dirichlet prior case given in Kaufman and King (1973). These posterior moments are then used in the development of an approximate $(1-\gamma)100$ percent credible interval for p_f. In section 3, we conclude our discussion by illustrating the computation of the posterior moments in examples. Our main concern is to investigate the effect of the choice of α_0 and K on the estimate and the precision of the estimate of p_f.

2. PRIOR TO POSTERIOR ANALYSIS.

Albert and Gupta (1982) introduced the following two-stage prior distribution to reflect prior beliefs about association in a 2×2 table:

Stage I: The vector $\underset{\sim}{p}$ possesses the Dirichlet density (1.1), where the components in $\underset{\sim}{\eta}$ have row margins η_f, $1-\eta_f$, column margins η_r, $1-\eta_r$, and cross product ratio α_0. That is, the prior means satisfy the configuration

(2.1)

$\eta_{fr}(\eta_f,\eta_r)$	$\eta_f-\eta_{fr}(\eta_f,\eta_r)$	η_f
$\eta_r-\eta_{fr}(\eta_f,\eta_r)$	$1-\eta_r-\eta_f+\eta_{fr}(\eta_f,\eta_r)$	$1-\eta_f$
η_r	$1-\eta_r$	

where $\alpha_0 = [\eta_{fr}(\cdot,\cdot)(1-\eta_r-\eta_f+\eta_{fr}(\cdot,\cdot))]/[(\eta_f-\eta_{fr}(\cdot,\cdot)\ (\eta_r-\eta_{fr}(\cdot,\cdot))]$. From (2.1), it can be shown that

$$\eta_{fr}(\eta_f,\eta_r) = d-\text{sgn}(\alpha_0-1)[d^2-\alpha_0(\alpha_0-1)^{-1}\eta_f\eta_r]^{\frac{1}{2}} \qquad \alpha_0 \neq 1$$

$$= \eta_f\eta_r \qquad \alpha_0 = 1,$$

where $d = [(\alpha_0-1)^{-1}+\eta_f+\eta_r]/2$.

Stage II: The parameters η_f and η_r represent guesses at the probability of favoring p_f and the probability of responding p_r, respectively. We assume that the user is unable to make guesses at either probability, and therefore, (η_f,η_r) is given a noninformative uniform distribution on the unit square.

The resulting prior density for $\underset{\sim}{p}$ is given by

$$(2.2)\qquad \pi_1(\underset{\sim}{p}) = \int_0^1\int_0^1 \pi_D(\underset{\sim}{p}|K,\underset{\sim}{\eta}^*)d\eta_f d\eta_r,$$

where $\underset{\sim}{\eta}^* = (\eta^*_{fr},\eta^*_{fs},\eta^*_{ur},\eta^*_{us})$ is the vector of of prior means with configuration (2.1). To use the prior (2.2), the user need only specify two parameters α_0 and K. As mentioned in section 1, the parameter α_0 is a guess at the cross-product ratio of the table. The prior parameter K represents the precision of this guess. Typically, vague prior information will exist about the association structure in the table and a small positive value will be chosen for K.

If $\underset{\sim}{p}$ is given the Dirichlet $(\underset{\sim}{\eta},K)$ prior, then Kaufman and King (1973) show that the posterior density of p_f can be represented by

$$(2.3)\qquad \pi_2(p_f|\underset{\sim}{x},\underset{\sim}{\eta}) = C\sum_{j=0}^{n_s} f_{Bb}(j|K\eta_{fs},K\eta_s,n_s)$$

$$\cdot f_\beta(p_f|K\eta_f+n_{fr}+j,K\eta_u+n_{ur}+n_s-j),$$

where $f_\beta(\cdot|a,b)$ is the beta density with parameters a,b, $f_{Bb}(\cdot|a,b,c)$ is the beta-binomial mass function as defined in Raiffa and Schlaifer (1961), p. 218, C is a proportionality constant, and η_s, η_f and η_u are the prior means of p_s, p_f and p_u respectively. Using this representation, one can show that the posterior mean and variance of p_f are given by

$$(2.4)\quad E(p_f|\underset{\sim}{x},\underset{\sim}{\eta}) = \frac{n_{fr}+K\eta_f+n_s\eta_{fs}/\eta_s}{n+K}$$

and

$$(2.5)\quad Var(p_f|\underset{\sim}{x},\underset{\sim}{\eta}) = \frac{1}{n+K+1}E(p_f|\underset{\sim}{x},\underset{\sim}{\eta})(1-E(p_f|\underset{\sim}{x},\underset{\sim}{\eta}))$$

$$+\frac{n_s}{(n+K)(n+K+1)}\frac{\eta_{fs}\eta_{us}}{\eta_s^2}\frac{(n_s+K\eta_s)}{(1+K\eta_s)}.$$

Note that (2.3) is the posterior distribution of p_f conditional on a value of the prior mean $\underset{\sim}{\eta}$. If $\underset{\sim}{p}$ is given the two-stage prior (2.2), then the posterior distribution of p_f is given by

$$(2.6)\quad \pi_4(p_f|\underset{\sim}{x}) = \int_0^1\int_0^1 \pi_2(p_f|\underset{\sim}{x},\underset{\sim}{\eta}^*)$$

$$\cdot\pi_3(\eta_f,\eta_r|\underset{\sim}{x})d\eta_f d\eta_r,$$

where

$$(2.7)\quad \pi_3(\eta_f,\eta_r|\underset{\sim}{x}) \propto$$

$$\frac{\Gamma(K\eta_{fr}^*+n_{fr})\Gamma(K\eta_{ur}^*+n_{ur})\Gamma(K(1-\eta_r)+n_s)}{\Gamma(K\eta_{fr}^*)\quad\Gamma(K\eta_{ur}^*)\quad\Gamma(K(1-\eta_r))}.$$

Using conditioning arguments, we can use the representation (2.6) together with (2.4) and (2.5) to find posterior moments of p_f. To illustrate, the posterior mean of p_f is given by

$$(2.8)\quad E(p_f|\underset{\sim}{x}) = E[E(p_f|\underset{\sim}{x},\eta_f,\eta_r)]$$

$$= E\left[\frac{n_{fr}+K\eta_f+n_s\eta_{fs}^*/(1-\eta_r)}{n+K}\Bigg|\underset{\sim}{x}\right]$$

$$= \frac{n_{fr}+KE(\eta_f|\underset{\sim}{x})+n_sE(\eta_{fs}^*/(1-\eta_r)|\underset{\sim}{x})}{n+K}.$$

Using similar techniques, the posterior variance of p_f can be computed and is given by

$$(2.9)\quad Var(p_f|\underset{\sim}{x}) = (n+K+1)^{-1}E(p_f|\underset{\sim}{x})(1-E(p_f|\underset{\sim}{x}))$$

$$+(n+K)^{-1}(n+K+1)^{-1}$$

$$\cdot[n_sE(\eta_{f\cdot s}^*(1-\eta_{f\cdot s}^*)\frac{n_s+K(1-\eta_r)}{1+K(1-\eta_r)})$$

$$+Var(K\eta_f+n_s\eta_{f\cdot s}^*)],$$

where $\eta_{f\cdot s}^* = \eta_{fs}^*/(1-\eta_r)$.

The posterior mean (2.8) can be used as a point estimate of the probability p_f. A credible interval for p_f can be easily developed by assuming that the central portion of the distribution is approximately normally distributed. With this assumption, a $(1-\gamma)100$ per cent credible interval is given by

$$(2.10)\quad (E(p_f|\underset{\sim}{x})-z_{\gamma/2}[Var(p_f|\underset{\sim}{x})]^{\frac{1}{2}},$$

$$E(p_f|\underset{\sim}{x})+z_{\gamma/2}[Var(p_f|\underset{\sim}{x})]^{\frac{1}{2}}),$$

where $z_{\gamma/2}$ is the upper $\gamma/2$ percentage point of a standard normal distribution.

3. EXAMPLE. In this section, we will conduct a preliminary investigation of the behavior of the posterior distribution of p_f (2.6). In particular, we will investigate the effect of one's choice of α_0 and K on the posterior mean and variance of p_f.

To begin, a few comments are necessary about the computation of the posterior quantities (2.8) and (2.9). These expressions all involve expectations using the posterior density of (η_f,η_r) (2.7), which is not expressible in closed form. Thus it is necessary to compute expectations of the form

$$(3.1)\quad E[g(\eta_f,\eta_r)|\underset{\sim}{x}] = \frac{\int_0^1\int_0^1 g(\eta_f,\eta_r)\pi_3(\eta_f,\eta_r)d\eta_f d\eta_r}{\int_0^1\int_0^1 \pi_3(\eta_f,\eta_r)d\eta_f d\eta_r},$$

where g is an arbitrary function of η_f and η_r. One efficient way of computing the integrals in (3.1) uses the notion of importance sampling. First if $\alpha_0 = 1$ and the parameter K approaches infinity, then it can be shown that

$$(3.2)\quad \lim_{K\to\infty}\pi_3(\eta_f,\eta_r|\underset{\sim}{x}) = \pi_L(\eta_f,\eta_r|\underset{\sim}{x})$$

$$= f_\beta(\eta_f|n_{fr}+1,n_{ur}+1)f_\beta(\eta_r|n_r+1,n_s+1),$$

a product of two beta densities. The limiting distribution (3.2) can serve as a rough approximation to $\pi_3(\eta_f,\eta_r)$ for values of α_0 near one and moderate values of K. Next rewrite the expectation (3.1) as

$$(3.3)\quad E[g(\eta_f,\eta_r)|\underset{\sim}{x}] =$$

$$\frac{\int_0^1\int_0^1 g(\eta_f,\eta_r)\left[\frac{\pi_3(\eta_f,\eta_r)}{\pi_L(\eta_f,\eta_r)}\right]\pi_L(\eta_f,\eta_r)d\eta_f d\eta_r}{\int_0^1\int_0^1 \left[\frac{\pi_3(\eta_f,\eta_r)}{\pi_L(\eta_f,\eta_r)}\right]\pi_L(\eta_f,\eta_r)d\eta_f d\eta_r}.$$

Finally, to approximate the integrals in (3.3) using simulation, n_0 values of (η_f, η_r) are randomly generated from the beta densities in (3.2). Call the randomly generated values (e_{fi}, e_{ri}), $i = 1, \ldots, n_0$. Then (3.3) is approximated by

$$(3.4)\quad \frac{\sum_{i=1}^{n_0} g(e_{fi}, e_{ri})\pi_3(e_{fi}, e_{ri})/\pi_L(e_{fi}, e_{ri})}{\sum_{i=1}^{n_0} \pi_3(e_{fi}, e_{ri})/\pi_L(e_{fi}, e_{ri})}$$

In Table I, the posterior mean (2.8) and posterior variance (2.9) have been computed for the table of counts $\underset{\sim}{x} = (70,48,78)$ and for different values of the prior parameters α_0 and K. In each case, the approximation (3.4) was used with $n_0 = 10000$ iterations. A few general observations can be made about these posterior estimates. First, note that the posterior mean of p_f (2.8) can be expressed as a weighted mean of three terms:

$$(3.5)\quad E(p_f|\underset{\sim}{x}) = \frac{n_r}{n+K}\frac{n_{fr}}{n_r} + \frac{K}{n+K}E(\eta_f|\underset{\sim}{x}) + \frac{n_s}{n+K}E(\eta^*_{f\cdot s}|\underset{\sim}{x}).$$

The parameter $\eta^*_{f\cdot s}$ represents the user's prior guess at $p_{f\cdot s}$, the probability a nonrespondent is in favor, and the posterior expectation $E(\eta^*_{f\cdot s}|\underset{\sim}{x})$ appears to roughly satisfy the equality

$$\frac{(n_{fr}/n_f)/(1-n_{fr}/n_f)}{E(\eta^*_{f\cdot s}|\underset{\sim}{x})/(1-E(\eta^*_{f\cdot s}|x))} = \alpha_0.$$

The posterior mean (3.5) appears to use the n_s nonrespondent counts by first partitioning them into the (fs), (us) cells so that the cross-product ratio of the 2×2 table of counts is α_0, and then pooling the counts in the favorable cells to estimate p_f. A second general comment is that the posterior variance of p_f appears to be a decreasing function of K and $|\alpha_0 - 1|$. These posterior variance values can be contrasted in size with the variance of the "usual" estimate n_{fr}/n_r, which is equal to $(n_{fr}/n_r)(1-n_{fr}/n_r)/n_r = .00205$. Typically, the user will possess vague prior beliefs about the differences between respondents and nonrespondents and thus will choose a small value of K. As indicated in Table I, this choice of K will result in a much larger posterior variance than the classical variance .00205. Thus, in this brief example, the posterior distribution appears to reflect both the belief in association (inputted through α_0) and the strength of the belief in the association (inputted through K).

TABLE I

Computed Values of Posterior Means and Posterior Variances. $\underset{\sim}{x} = (70,48,78)$

	α_0 .06	.25	1	4	16
K = 4					
$E(p_f\|\underset{\sim}{x})$	.702	.648	.592	.520	.467
$Var(p_f\|\underset{\sim}{x})$	.0078	.0125	.0167	.0145	.0159
K = 25					
$E(p_f\|\underset{\sim}{x})$	.716	.665	.592	.514	.420
$Var(p_f\|\underset{\sim}{x})$	.0021	.0041	.0053	.0047	.0042
K = 100					
$E(p_f\|\underset{\sim}{x})$	.713	.682	.591	.500	.414
$Var(p_f\|\underset{\sim}{x})$	.0010	.0018	.0028	.0022	.0012

REFERENCES

1. Albert, J. H., and A. K. Gupta (1982). Bayesian estimation methods for 2×2 contingency tables using mixtures of Dirichlet distributions. Department of Mathematics and Statistics, Bowling Green State University, Technical Report.

2. Birnbaum, Z. W., and M. G. Sirken (1950). Bias due to nonavailability in sample surveys. *J. Amer. Statist. Assoc.*, 45, 98-111.

3. Hansen, M. H., and W. N. Hurwitz (1946). The problem of non-response in sample surveys. *J. Amer. Statist. Assoc.*, 41, 517-529.

4. Kaufman, G. M., and B. King (1973). A Bayesian analysis of nonresponse in dichotomous processes. *J. Amer. Statist. Assoc.*, 68, 670-678.

5. Raiffa, H., and R. O. Schlaifer (1961). *Applied Statistical Decision Theory*, Boston: Harvard Business School.

List of Participants

Participants

Varol Akman
2106 Mass. Ave., Apt.2A
Troy, NY 12180

James H. Albert
Dept of Math & Statistics
Bowling Green State Univ
Bowling Green, OH 43403

Cynthia Alexander
303 Troy Building
Rensselaer Polytechnic Inst
Troy, NY 12181

David Allen
Dept of Statistics
Univ of Kentucky
Louisville, KY 40506

Michael B. Anderson
Inter-American Devel. Bank
808 17th St. N.W.
Washington, DC 20577

Ronn Andrusco
Box 468 Postal Station J
Toronto, Ontario
Canada M4J 4Z2

John A. Antoinetti
Life Insurance Marketing
and Research Association
P.O. Box 208
Hartford, CT 06141

Jonathan Arnold
Hill Center, Busch Campus
Dept of Statistics
Rutgers University
New Brunswick, NJ 08903

E. Neely Atkinson
Dept of Biomathematics
M.D. Anderson Hospital
Texas Medical Center
Houston, TX 77030

Reo Audette
Computing Centre
Simon Fraser University
Burnaby, B.C.
Canada V5A 1S6

Jenny A. Baglivo
Sloan-Kettering Institute
1275 York Avenue
New York, NY 10021

John Barnard
N.Y.S Agric. Exper. Station
Geneva, NY 14456

Jeff Barnes
N.Y.S. Dept of Social Svcs
Suite 16-B
40 N. Pearl St.
Albany, NY 12243

Teresa L. Beam
American Statistical Assoc.
8534 Selendine
San Antonio, TX 78239

Richard A. Becker
Bell Laboratories
600 Mountain Ave.
Murray Hill, NJ 07974

Edward J. Bedrick
Dept of Statistics
Univ of New Mexico
Albuquerque, NM 87131

Morton M. Belinsky
Concordia University
1455 Maisonneuve West
Montreal, Quebec
Canada H3G 1M8

Michael E. Bellow
462 S. Aihen St., Apt. 7
Pittsburgh, PA 15232

Jon L. Bentley
Dept of Computer Science
Carnegie-Mellon University
Pittsburgh, PA 15213

Patrick Beynon
University of Ottawa
33 Goodwood Dr.
Ottawa, Ontario
Canada K2C 3H2

Lynne Billard
Dept of Stat & Comp Sci
Univ of Georgia
Athens, GA 30602

Giselle Binstok
Ayerst Laboratories
685 Third Ave.
New York, NY 10017

Eric C. Blair
Dept of Indus & Mgmt Engr
Rensselaer Polytechnic Inst
Troy, NY 12181

Alvin Blum
IBM Watson Research Center
P.O. Box 218
Yorktown Heights, NY 10598

Charles G. Boncelet, Jr.
8-317 Engineering Quad
Princeton University
Princeton, NJ 08544

Dennis Boos
Dept of Statistics
North Carolina State Univ
Raleigh, NC 27650

Robert M. Boudreau
Dept of Math & Stat
Univ of Pittsburgh
Pittsburgh, PA 15260

K.O. Bowman
Union Carbide Corp
Nuclear Division
P.O. Box Y, Bldg. 9704-1
Oak Ridge, TN 37830

James Bozik
Zimmite Corporation
810 Sharon Dr.
Westlake, OH 44145

M. Brannigan
Univ of Georgia
Athens, GA 30602

D.F. Bray
Health and Welfare Canada
675 Denbury Ave.
Ottawa, Ontario
Canada K2A 2P2

Kent M. Brothers
Div of Health Systems
Univ of British Columbia
Vancouver, B.C.
Canada V6T 126

Thomas A. Bubolz
Statistical Laboratory
Iowa State University
Ames, IA 50011

Roald Buhler
P-STAT, Inc.
Box 285
Princeton, NJ 08540

Shirrel Buhler
P-STAT, Inc.
Box 285
Princeton, NJ 08540

Andreas Buja
Dept of Statistics
Stanford University
Stanford, CA 94306

David Butler
136 Sage Annex
Rensselaer Polytechnic Inst
Troy, NY 12181

Luis Z. Cabeza
44 Brinsmade Terr.
Troy, NY 12180

William Ford Calhoun
Mt. Sinai School of Medicine
100th St. & 5th Ave.
Annen 24-92
New York, NY

Linnda Caporael
Dept of Psychology
Rensselaer Polytechnic Inst
Troy, NY 12181

Patricia M. Caporal
General Electric Company
P.O. Box 43
2 River Road
Schenectedy, NY 12345

Daniel B. Carr
Pacific Northwest Labs
P.O. Box 999
Richland, WA 99352

John Chakmakas
N.Y.S. Dept of Social Svcs
40 North Pearl Street
Twin Towers, Fourth Floor
Albany, NY 12243

John Chambers
Bell Laboratories
600 Mountain Rd. 5C-114
Murray Hill, NJ 07974

Douglass Chapman
Statistics Dept.
Covenant House
460 W. 41st St.
New York, NY 10036

Ron Charron
Agriculture Canada
930 Carling Ave.
Ottawa, Ontario
Canada K1A OCI

Chan-Fu Chen
Dept of Math & Stat
SUNY at Albany
Albany, NY 12222

Mike Cheng
Statistics Canada
R. H. Coats Bldg.
Tunney's Pasture
Ottawa, Ontario
Canada K1A OT6

Herman Chernoff
Dept of Statistics
M.I.T.
Cambridge, MA 02139

Christy Chuang
Dept of Biostatistics
Univ of Rochester
Rochester, NY 14642

John O. Church
General Foods, Inc.
250 North Street (T12-3)
White Plains, NY 10625

Daniel J. Clark
106 Third St.
Troy, NY 12180

William D. Commins, Jr.
National Science Foundation
1800 G. St., N.W.
Washington, DC 20550

John E. Conroy
Texas Instruments Inc.
P.O. Box 225012- MS 82
Dallas, TX 75265

Michael A. Contino
Penn State University
University Park, PA 16802

Isabel Cordon
Bryckwyck, Apt. C-11
Rensselaer Polytechnic Inst
Troy, NY 12180

Luis O. Cordon
Bryckwyck, Apt. C-11
Rensselaer Polytechnic Inst
Troy, NY 12180

Christopher Cox
Division of Biostatistics
Univ of Rochester Medical Ctr
633 Claybourne Rd.
Rochester, NY 14618

Giles L. Crane
C.C.S.
73 Philip Dr.
Princeton, NJ 08540

Glen Culbertson
Dept of Psychology
Rensselaer Polytechnic Inst
Troy, NY 12181

Lawrence Danziger
IBM Corporation
3 Spur Way
Poughkeepsie, NY

Gerarda Darlington
University of Guelph
Guelph, Ontario
Canada N1G 2W1

Sara Dearing
Union College
Computer Services
Schenectady, NY 12308

Joseph Deken
School of Business
Univ of Texas at Austin
Austin, TX 78712

Thomas A. Delhanty
Dept of Stat, Mgmt & Info Sci
Rensselaer Polytechnic Inst
Troy, NY 12181

Barry deVille
Carleton University
Colonel By Drive
Ottawa, Ontario
CANADA

Kieron A. Dey
IIT Research Institute
RADC/RBRAC
Griffiss Air Force Base
Rome, NY

Gregg Diffendal
Bureau of the Census
3551 Federal Bldg 3
Washington, DC 20233

Jan Dijkstra
Technological University
P.O. Box 51/33
Eindhofen
The Netherlands

David P. Doane
School of Econ & Mgmt
Oakland University
Rochester, MI 48063

Eileen Driscoll
254 Ives Hall
Cornell University
Ithaca, NY 14853

Joseph Duncan
Retina Foundation
20 Staniford St.
Boston, MA 02114

Charles W. Dunnett
Dept of Mathematical Sciences
McMaster University
Hamilton, Ontario
Canada L8S 4K1

Neal Van Eck
Institute for Social Research
P.O. Box 1248
Ann Arbor, MI 48106

William F. Eddy
Dept of Statistics
Carnegie-Mellon University
Pittsburgh, PA 15213

Lawrence J. Emrich
Roswell Park Memorial Inst
666 Elm Street
Buffalo, NY 14263

Norma J. Faris
D204 Colonie Apt.
Troy, NY 12180

Brian D. Feeney
Boston College
Casson 1
Chestnut Hill, MA 02167

Paul W. Fingerman
Boeing Computer Services Co.
7980 Gallows Ct.
Vienna, VA 22180

Robert A. Fisher
Canadian Forestry Service
Box 4000
Fredericton, N.B.
Canada E3B 5L1

Daniel J. Fox
University of Michigan
106 Rackham
Ann Arbor, MI 48109

Michael A. Fox
Hospital Computing Facility
UCLA
10833 LeConte Ave.
Los Angeles, CA 90024

Brian Francis
Centre for Applied Statistics
University of Lancaster
Bailrigg, Lancaster
United Kingdom LA1 4YL

Bruce Frederick
Div of Criminal Justice Svcs
Stuyvesant Plaza
Albany, NY 12203

Herman P. Friedman
IBM Systems Research Inst.
205 E. 42nd Street
New York, NY 10017

Karole Friemann
United Services Auto Assoc
9800 Fredericksburg Rd.
San Antonio, TX 78288

K.R. Gabriel
Dept of Statistics
Univ of Rochester
Rochester, NY 14627

William A. Gale
Bell Laboratories
600 Mountain Ave.
Murray Hill, NJ 07079

Robert G. Garrett
Geological Survey of Canada
601 Booth St.
Ottawa, Ontario
Canada K1A 0E8

Miriam Gasko
Graduate School of Business
Univ. Of Chicago
1101 E 58th St.
Chicago, IL 60637

Paul H. Geissler
Patuxent Wildlife Research Ctr
Laurel, MD 20811

Thomas J. Gildea
G. D. Searle and Co.
4901 Searle Parkway
Skokie, IL 60077

Herb Ginsburg
Westinghouse-Bettis A.P.L.
P.O. Box 79
West Mifflin, PA 15122

Marvin Glasser
New York Medical College
Valhalla, NY 10595

Bernard Goldsmith
Lally Management Center
Rensselaer Polytechnic Inst
Troy, NY 12181

Eva Goldwater
9 Forest Edge Road
Amherst, MA 01002

Gail Gong
Dept of Statistics
Stanford University
Stanford, CA 94305

Flavio Rocha Gorini
SQS 315, Bl."K"
Apto 604
70 000 Brazilia-D.F.
Brazil

Misa Gratton
Statistics Canada
R. H. Coats Bldg.
Tunney's Pasture
Ottawa,Ontario
Canada K1A OT6

Michael Greenacre
Div of Biostatistics
Box 630
Univ of Rochester Medical Ctr
Rochester, NY 14642

Steven C. Greenstein
SUNY at Albany
CS-25 1400 Washington Ave.
Albany, NY 12222

Malcolm Greig
Computer Center
Univ of British Columbia
Vancouver, B.C.
Canada V6T 1W5

Malcolm Griffin
Queens University
307 Frontenae St.
Kingston, Ontario
Canada KL7 3S9

Alan M. Gross
Bell Laboratories
3 Corporate Place, Rm 2D215
Piscataway, NJ 08854

Gerald J. Hahn
Corp. Research & Development
General Electric Company
1 River Road
Schenectady, NY 12345

Charles Hallahan
U.S. Dept of Agriculture
4800 Little Falls Rd.
Arlington, VA 22207

Christian J. Haller
C.C.S., 51 Warren Hall
Cornell University
Ithaca, NY 14853

Bruce Hammer
136 Sage Lab Annex
Rensselaer Polytechnic Inst
Troy, NY 12181

Effat M. Hamouda
Dept of Mathematics
DePaul University
2323 N. Seminary #517
Chicago, IL 60614

Yangsook Han
N.Y.S. Dept of Health
Empire State Plaza
Albany, NY 12024

C. David Hardison
Lilly Research Laboratories
307 E. McCarty St.
Indianapolis, IN 46285

Frederick Hartwig
Union College
Schenectady, NY 12308

Erin Harvey
University of Waterloo
Waterloo, Ontario
Canada N2L 3G1

Karl W. Heiner
Dept of Stat, Mgmt & Info Sci
Rensselaer Polytechnic Inst
Troy, NY 12181

Michael Hennesey
136 Sage Lab Annex
Rensselaer Polytechnic Inst
Troy, NY 12181

Ronald I. Herman
Federal Reserve Board
20th and Constitution Ave
Washington, DC 20551

Peter M. Herzfeld
N.Y.S. Dept of Health
Empire State Plaza
Tower Bldg, Room 382
Albany, NY 12237

Jay Hilfiger
Statistical Computing Group
61 Warren Hall
Cornell University
Ithaca, NY 14853

John Hinde
Center for Applied Statistics
Univ of Lancaster
Bailrigg, Lancaster
United Kingdom LA1 4YL

R. Jeanette O'Hara Hines
University of Guelph
Guelph, Ontario
Canada N1G 2W1

David J. Hogan
Dept of Comp & Info Science
Ohio State University
2036 Neil Avenue Mall
Columbus, OH 43210

Myles Hollander
Dept of Statistics
Florida State University
Tallahassee, FL 32306

Donald S. Holmes
Inst of Admin and Management
Union College
Schenectady, NY 12308

Harvard Holmes
1 Cyclotron Rd.
Building 50-B, Rm 3238
Lawrence Berkeley Laboratory
Berkeley, CA 94720

John D. Holt
Dept of Math & Statistics
University of Guelph
Guelph, Ontario
Canada N1G 2W1

Jean B. Holzer
Southern New England Tel
227 Church St., 7th Flr.
New Haven, CT 06506

Trina Hosmer
Computing Center
Univ of Massachusetts
85 Buttam Road
Pelham, MA 01002

George Houghton
Box 130, RD #1
Berkshire, NY 13736

Whaylon House
136 Sage Lab Annex
Rensselaer Polytechnic Inst
Troy, NY 12181

Sally E. Howe
National Bureau of Standards
A151 Technology Building
Washington, DC 20234

Chuck Humphrey
Computing Services
University of Alberta
Edmonton, Alberta
Canada T6G 2H1

Princess Humphrey
160 Elgin St.
Ottawa, Ontario
Canada KIG 3J4

Joyce M. Hutchins
American Statistical Assoc.
160 Rilla Vista
San Antonio, TX 78216

Ho-Ling Hwang
29 Proctor Ave.
Watervliet, NY 12189

Albyn C. Jones
Yale University
Box 2179 Yale Station
New Haven, CT 06520

Arthur Kanzaki
Greenwich Research Assoc
26-43 210 Place
Bayside, NY 11360

Bruce A. Kaplan
Educational Testing Service
E.T. 20
Rosedale Road
Princeton, NJ 08540

Alex W. Kask
Ernst and Whinney
153 East 53rd St.
New York, NY 10022

Myron Katzoff
Bureau of the Census
Rm 3524-3
Washington, DC 20233

H. Mark Keintz
Univ of Pennsylvania
Criminolgy/CR
Philadelphia, PA 19104

William J. Kennedy
Statistical Laboratory
Iowa State University
Ames, IA 50011

R. P. Kershner
Sterling Winthrop Res Inst
Columbia Turnpike
Rensselaer, NY 12144

Geung-Ho Kim
NOAA
Sandy Hook Lab
Highlands, NJ 07732

Lester Klein
114 Melbourne Ave.
Silver Spring, MD 20901

Edward Kobialka
FAA Technical Center
ACT-220
Atlantic Cty Airport, NJ

David P. Kopcso
Babson College
Wellesley, MA 02157

John Koval
Dept of Statistics
Univ of Western Ontario
London, Ontario
Canada N6A 5B9

Ken Krallman
SUNY at Buffalo
4250 Ridge Lea Rd.
Amherst, NY 14226

William S. Krasker
Harvard Business School
Boston, MA 02163

Robert Kusiak
400 University Avenue
8th Floor
Toronto, Ontario
Canada

James Lancaster
Sterling Winthrop Res Inst
Columbia Turnpike
Rensselaer, NY 12144

Nicholas Lange
School of Public Health
Harvard University
Boston, MA 02115

R. S. Lashkari
Dept of Industrial Engineering
Univ of Windsor
Windsor, Ontario
Canada N9B 3P4

James M. Lattin
Sloan School of Management
M.I.T.
50 Memorial Drive
Cambridge, MA 02174

Charles E. Lawrence
N.Y.S. Dept of Health
Empire State Plaza
Albany, NY 12237

Greg Layhew
Bell Canada
Rm. 1100
160 Elgin St.
Ottawa, Ontario
Canada KIG 3J4

Chin-Hui Lee
Verbex/Exxon
Two Oak Park
Bedford, MA 01730

S. K. Lee
Bell Laboratories
Rm. FJ 1B-112
Crawfords Corners Rd.
Holmdel, NJ 07733

Samuel Leinhardt
Sch of Urban & Public Affairs
Carnegie-Mellon University
Pittsburgh, PA 15213

Anne Leney
Sidney Farber Cancer Inst
44 Binney St.
Boston, MA 02215

John H. Leong
Dept of Statistics
Univ of Vermont
Burlington, VT 05405

Howard Levene
10 Park Ave.
Larchmont, NY 10938

Peter A. W. Lewis
Naval Postgraduate School
Monterey, CA 93940

William S. Lin
2100 Burdett Ave.
Troy, NY 12180

William Lisowski
A T & T
295 N. Maple Ave.
Basking Ridge, NJ 07920

Arthur S. Littell
School of Public Health
Univ of Texas
Box 20186
Houston, TX 77025

Lon-Mu Liu
Dept of Quantitative Methods
Univ of Illinois
Box 4348
Chicago, IL 60680

Robert A. Lochner
Dept of Math, Stat, & Comp Sci
Marquette University
Milwaukee, WI 53233

Robert G. Lovell
Michigan Dept of Social Svcs
528 Highland Av.
E. Lansing, MI 48823

Edith H. Luchins
Dept of Mathematical Sciences
Rensselaer Polytechnic Inst
Troy, NY 12181

Wo-Shun Luk
Dept of Computer Science
Simon Fraser University
Burnaby, B.C.
Canada V5A 1S6

Robert Lum
Bell Canada
620 Belmont Room 1120
Montreal, Quebec
Canada H3B 2MS

Gregory A. Mack
Battelle Memorial Institute
505 King Avenue
Columbus, OH 43201

Mary Maggio
Eastman Kodak
Kodak Park Division
1669 Lake Ave.
Rochester, NY

James M. Malone, II
Innovative Information Tech.
8 Vine St.
Scotia, NY 12303

Durwood Marshall
639 Park Ave., Apt 1W
Albany, NY

R. Douglas Martin
Dept of Statistics
Univ of Washington
Seattle, WA 98195

Gerald Mayfield
Greenwich Research Associates
Office Park 8
Greenwich, CT 06830

Leslie J. McCain
SUNY at Buffalo
Academic Computing Services
4250 Ridge Lea
Amherst, NY 14226

Allen McIntosh
Bell Laboratories
600 Mountain Ave.
Murray Hill, NJ 07974

John D. McKenzie, Jr.
Babson College
Wellesley, MA 02157

Jeff B. Meeker
Research Statistics
CIBA-Geigy Corporation
Summit, NJ 07901

William Q. Meeker
Dept of Statistics
Iowa State University
Ames, IA 50011

Chao-Ho Meng
Dept of Forest Engineering
Univ of New Brunswick
Bag Service #44555
Fredericton, NB
Canada E3B 6C2

Michael M. Meyer
Dept of Statistics
Carnegie-Mellon University
Pittsburgh, PA 15213

Douglas Mills
University Computing Center
Princeton University
87 Prospect Ave.
Princeton, NJ 08544

George Minich
World Bank
1818 H St., NW
Washington, DC 20433

Susan Mitchell-Herzfeld
N.Y.S. Dept of Social Svcs
40 N. Pearl St. 16B
Albany, NY 12343

John F. Monahan
Dept of Statistics
North Carolina State Univ
P.O. Box 5457
Raleigh, NC 27650

S. Monteiro
Dept of Chemical Engr
Rensselaer Polytechnic Inst
Troy, NY 12181

Carolyn B. Morgan
General Electric Company
1 River Road
Building 37 Rm 578
Schenectady, NY 12345

Robert Muenchen
Univ of Tennessee
200 Stokely Mgmt. Center
Knoxville, TN 37996

Ian Munro
Dept of Computer Science
Univ of Waterloo
Waterloo, Ontario
Canada N2L 3G1

Thomas A. Murphy
I.B.M.
South Rd. D284 B928-1
Poughkeepsie, NY 12602

Daniel Naggar
Dept of Transportation
400 7th St, SW
Washington, DC 20590

John C. Nash
Univ of Ottawa
Ottawa, Ontario
Canada KIN 9B5

Howard Neckowitz
A T & T
4A 210 Rte 202/206
Bedmanster, NJ 07921

Norman Neff
Trenton State College
Trenton, NJ 08625

David L. Nelson
Boeing Computer Services
565 Andover Park W.
Tukwila, WA 98188

Sandra Newsome
Dept of Psychology
Rensselaer Polytechnic Inst
Troy, NY 12181

Wesley L. Nicholson
Battelle,Pacific Northwest Lab
P.O. Box 999
Richland, WA 99352

Phillip Nickerson
Sch of Urban & Public Affairs
Carnegie-Mellon University
Pittsburgh, PA 15213

Douglas Nychta
Univ of Wisconsin, Madison
640 W. Badger Rd. #9
Madison, WI 53713

Charles L. Odoroff
Box 630
Univ of Rochester Medical Ctr
Univ of Rochester
Rochester, NY 14642

Kenneth Offord
Medical Research Statistics
Mayo Clinic
Rochester, MN 55905

Ingram Olkin
Dept of Statistics
Stanford University
Stanford, CA 94305

Jane E. Oppenlander
GE/Knolls Atomic Power Lab
P.O. Box 1072
Schenectady, NY 12301

George Ostrouchov
Dept of Statistics
Iowa State University
315A Snedecor Hall
Ames, IA 50011

Edvard Outrata
Statistics Canada
R. H. Coats Bldg.
Tunney's Pasture
Ottawa,Ontario
Canada K1A OT6

Marcello Pagano
Dept of Statistics
Harvard University
Boston, MA 02163

William F. Page
Veterans Administration
810 Vermont Ave., N.W.
Washington, DC 20420

Vito Pagnotti
Division of Air
Bureau of Impact Assessment
and Meteorolgy
50 Wolf Rd.
Albany, NY

Frederick C. Parmenter
Babson College
Wellesley, MA 02157

Emanuel Parzen
Institute of Statistics
Texas A&M University
College Station, TX 77843

Albert S. Paulson
Dept of Stat, Mgmt, & Info Sc
Rensselaer Polytechnic Inst
Troy, NY 12181

Mary Burr Paxton
Clement Associates
1515 Wilson Blvd.
Arlington, VA 22209

Sally Peavy
National Bureau of Standards
Washington, DC 20234

Gary Perlman
Dept of Psychology
Univ of Calif at San Diego
La Jolla, CA 92093

Thomas J. Perrone
National Weather Service
Techniques Development Lab
Room 804, 8060 13th Street
Silver Spring, MD 20740

Arthur V. Peterson
Hutchinson Cancer Research Ctr
1124 Columbia Street
Seattle, WA 98104

Robert Pfeiffer
SUNY at Albany
Computing Center - CS17
Albany, NY 12222

Walter W. Piegorsch
Cornell University
337 Warren Hall
Ithaca, NY 14853

Roger Pinkham
Stevens Inst of Technology
Hoboken, NJ 07030

Walter R. Pirie
Dept of Statistics
Virginia Poly Inst & State U.
Blacksburg, VA 24061

Martin Podehl
Statistics Canada
CANSIM Division
R. H. Coats Bldg.
Tunney's Pasture
Ottawa, Ontario
Canada K1A OT6

Neil W. Polhemus
Dept of Civil Engineering
Princeton University
Princeton, NJ 08544

David Pollard
Yale University
Yale Station
Box 2179
New Haven, CT 06520

Daryl Pregibon
Bell Laboratories
600 Mountain Ave.
Murray Hill, NJ 07974

Mark A. Presser
General Foods Corp.
250 North St., T12-3
White Plains, NY 10625

Peter Ratener
Univ of Washington
19610 Redmond Rd.
Redmond, WA 98052

Peter A. Reese
Roswell Park Memorial Inst
666 Elm St.
Buffalo, NY 14263

Andrea A. Reilly
N.Y.S. Dept of Health
Empire State Plaza
Albany, NY 12237

Anthony H. Riccardi
DeSeve Economics
17 First St.
Troy, NY 12180

M.G. Richardson
Numerical Algorithms Group
NAG Central Office
Mayfield House
256 Banbury Road
Oxford
United Kingdom OX2 7DE

John A. Ritts
Rohm and Haas Company
727 Norristown Rd.
Spring House, PA 19477

Ed Robison
249 Hooker
Poughkeepsie, NY 12603

Luiz Antonio Coelho de Rose
SQN 108, Bl."K", Apto. 107
70 744 Brazilia -D.F.
Brazil

Stephen de Rosenroll
160 Elgin St.
Ottawa, Ontario
Canada K1A OT6

J. Rostami
Sterling Winthrop Res Inst
Columbia Turnpike
Rensselaer, NY 12144

Daniel L. Rourke
Univ of Michigan
106 Rackham
Ann Arbor, MI 48109

Michael F. Russin
I.B.M.
South Rd.
Poughkeepsie, NY 12602

Barbara F. Ryan
Minitab Project
215 Pond Laboratory
University Park, PA 16802

Thomas A. Ryan, Jr.
Minitab Project
215 Pond Laboratory
University Park, PA 16802

Richard S. Sacher
Alan M Voorhees Computing Ctr
Rensselaer Polytechnic Inst
Troy, NY 12181

William M. Sallas
IMSL, Inc.
Sixth Floor NBC Bldg.
7500 Bellaire Blvd.
Houston, TX 77036

Alexander Samarov
CCREMS
M.I.T.
E40-139
1 Amherst St.
Cambridge, MA 02146

Jim Sampson
I.B.M.
Dept. 312
Bldg. 416
South Rd.
Poughkeepsie, NY 12601

Stephen M. Samuels
Dept of Statistics
Purdue University
W. Lafayette, IN 47907

James Sandy
Hansford Data Systems Inc.
3055 Brighton-
Henrietta Townline Rd.
Rochester, NY 14623

Elliot D. Saroff
Bur of Forecasting & Planning
N.Y.S. Dept of Mental Health
44 Holland Ave.
Albany, NY 12229

James L. Schmidhammer
Dept of Math & Statistics
University of Pittsburgh
Pittsburgh, PA 15260

J.D. Schmitz
MDS
200 Fifth Avenue
Waltham, MA 02254

Larry Schneider
Sandoz, Inc.
46 Route 10
E. Hanover, NJ

Robert C. Schriver
Smith Kline and French Labs
1500 Spring Garden St.
Philadelphia, PA 19101

Phillip C. Schroth
975 Foster Drive
Los Angeles, CA 90048

Karl F. Schutz
Rand Corporation
1700 Main St.
Santa Monica, CA 90406

David W. Scott
Dept of Mathematical Sciences
Rice University
Houston, TX 77001

Therese A. Shady
N.Y.S. Dept of Social Services
40 N. Pearl St. 16B
Albany, NY 12343

Arthur Shapiro
Stevens Inst of Technology
Hoboken, NJ 67030

Anupam K. Sharma
Wyeth Ltd.
4455 Chesswood Dr.
Downsview, Ontario
Canada M3J 2C2

Larry R. Shenton
Dept of Statistics
Univ of Georgia
Athens, GA 30602

Larry A. Shepp
Bell Laboratories
600 Mountain Ave.
Murray Hill, NJ 07974

Glenn Shorrock
Ecole Polytech de Montreal
C.P. 6079, Succ. A
Montreal, Quebec
Canada H3C 3A7

Richard Shorrock
Bell Canada
Suite 1120 -620 Belmont
Montreal,Quebec
Canada H3B 2M3

Jeffrey Simonoff
New York University
100 Trinity Place
New York, NY 10006

M. Slater
Queen Mary College
20 Upper Tooting Park
London
United Kingdom SW1 7SR

Eric Small
Modulation Sciences Inc.
99 Myrtle Avenue
Brooklyn, NY 11201

David Spooner
Dept of Mathematical Sciences
Rensselaer Polytechnic Inst
Troy, NY 12181

Herbert Stander
Sterling Winthrop Res Inst
Columbia Turnpike
Rensselaer, NY 12144

Bruce H. Stanley
N.Y.S. Agric Expt Station
Cornell University
Geneva, NY 14456

J. Michael Steele
Dept of Statistics
Stanford University
Stanford, CA 94305

Walter B. Studdiford
Office of the Registrar
Princeton University
Box 70
Princeton, NJ 08544

Paul Swanson, Jr.
College of Business Admin
University of Cincinnati
Cincinnati, OH 45221

Michael Tarter
Dept of Biostatistics
Univ of California, Berkeley
Berkeley, CA 94720

Robert F. Teitel
Teitel Data Systems
Suite 727 East
7315 Wisconsin Avenue
Bethesda, MD 20814

James J. Thomas
Battelle,Pacific Northwest Lab
Mathematics Bldg.
P.O. Box 999
Richland, WA 99352

Brian Thompson
Agriculture Canada
Building 54, C.E. Farm
Ottawa, Ontario
Canada K1A 0C6

John C. Thornton
Mt. Sinai School of Medicine
100th St. & 5th Ave.
Annen. 24-92
New York, NY

James M. Tien
Dept of Elec, Comp & Sys Engr
Rensselaer Polytechnic Inst
Troy, NY 12181

Janet Titlow
Smith Kline and French Labs
1500 Spring Garden Street
Philadelphia, PA 19101

Derrick S. Tracy
Dept of Mathematics
Univ of Windsor
Windsor, Ontario
Canada N9B 3P4

Mitchell Trager
U.S. Census Bureau
3607 Osborne Court
Waldorf, MD 20601

Thomas Triscari, Jr.
79 Colehamer Ave.
Troy, NY 12180

David Tritchler
Dept of Statistics
Harvard University
Boston, MA 02163

Michael C. Tsianco
Marck & Co.
Rahway, NJ

John W. Tukey
Bell Laboratories
600 Mountain Ave.
Murray Hill, NJ 07974

Paul A. Tukey
Bell Laboratories
600 Mountain Ave.
Murray Hill, NJ 07904

Sarah Tung
Computing Services
Univ of Delaware
015 Smith Hall
Newark, DE 19711

Wayne R. Ugolik
N.Y.S. Dept of Transportation
Bldg 4, Room 209
Albany, NY 12232

Dana L. Ulery
Louviers 3178
E. I. Du Pont de Nemours & Co
Wilmington, DE 19898

Andrew Walaszek
SPSS, Inc.
444 N. Michigan
Chicago, IL 60611

Bruce W. Weide
Dept of Computer & Info Sci
Ohio State University
2036 Neil Avenue Mall
Columbus, OH 43210

Norris Weimer
Computing Services
General Services Building
Univ of Alberta
Edmonton, Alberta
Canada T6G 2H1

Peter D. Welch
IBM Watson Research Center
P.O. Box 218
Yorktown Heights, NY 10598

Roy E. Welsch
M.I.T.
50 Memorial Drive, E53-383
Cambridge, MA 02146

Carl Wetzstein
Eastman Kodak Company
MSD B56 Kodak Park
Rochester, NY 14650

Sherry A. Wilhelm
American Statistical Assoc.
5810 Mission Bend
San Antonio, TX 78233

John W. Wilkinson
Dept of Stat, Mgmt & Info Sci
Rensselaer Polytechnic Inst.
Troy, NY 12181

Allan Wilks
Dept of Statistics
Princeton University
Princeton, NJ 08540

Ronald Woan
Computing Services Office
Univ of Illinois
Champaign, IL 61820

Barbara B. Wolfe
Computing Center
SUNY at Albany
Albany, NY 12222

Chi Song Wong
University of Windsor
3510 Roxborough
Windsor, Ontario
Canada N9B 3P4

M. Anthony Wong
Sloan School of Management
M.I.T.
50 Memorial Drive
Cambridge, MA 01730

Ernest Woodward
Northwestern University
2129 Sheridan Rd.
Evanston, IL 60201

Ronald J. Wooldridge
Bur of Forecasting & Planning
N.Y.S. Dept of Mental Health
44 Holland Ave.
Albany, NY 12229

Lilian Shiao-Yen Wu
IBM Watson Research Center
PO Box 218
Yorktown Heights, NY 10598

William J. Wunderlin
General Foods
Prospect Plains Rd.
Cranbury, NJ 07731

Mark Wysoski
Union College
Computing Services
Schenectady, NY 12308

Altan Yazici
Inst of Admin & Management
Union College
Schenectady, NY 12308

Richard R. Zeller
Babcock & Wilcox - ARC
984 Mill Creek, #96
Alliance, OH 44601

Lecture Notes in Statistics

Vol. 1: R. A. Fisher: An Appreciation. Edited by S. E. Fienberg and D. V. Hinkley. xi, 208 pages, 1980.

Vol. 2: Mathematical Statistics and Probability Theory. Proceedings 1978. Edited by W. Klonecki, A. Kozek, and J. Rosiński. xxiv, 373 pages, 1980.

Vol. 3: B. D. Spencer, Benefit-Cost Analysis of Data Used to Allocate Funds. viii, 296 pages, 1980.

Vol. 4: E. A. van Doorn, Stochastic Monotonicity and Queueing Applications of Birth-Death Processes. vi, 118 pages, 1981.

Vol. 5: T. Rolski, Stationary Random Processes Associated with Point Processes. vi, 139 pages, 1981.

Vol. 6: S. S. Gupta and D.-Y. Huang, Multiple Statistical Decision Theory: Recent Developments. viii, 104 pages, 1981.

Vol. 7: M. Akahira and K. Takeuchi, Asymptotic Efficiency of Statistical Estimators. viii, 242 pages, 1981.

Vol. 8: The First Pannonian Symposium on Mathematical Statistics. Edited by P. Révész, L. Schmetterer, and V. M. Zolotarev. vi, 308 pages, 1981.

Vol. 9: B. Jørgensen, Statistical Properties of the Generalized Inverse Gaussian Distribution. vi, 188 pages, 1981.

Vol. 10: A. A. McIntosh, Fitting Linear Models: An Application of Conjugate Gradient Algorithms. vi, 200 pages, 1982.

Vol. 11: D. F. Nicholls and B. G. Quinn, Random Coefficient Autoregressive Models: An Introduction. v, 154 pages, 1982.

Vol. 12: M. Jacobsen, Statistical Analysis of Counting Processes. vii, 226 pages, 1982.

Vol. 13: J. Pfanzagl (with the assistance of W. Wefelmeyer), Contributions to a General Asymptotic Statistical Theory. vii, 315 pages, 1982.

Vol. 14: GLIM 82: Proceedings of the International Conference on Generalised Linear Models. Edited by R. Gilchrist. v, 188 pages, 1982.

Vol. 15: K. R. W. Brewer and M. Hanif, Sampling with Unequal Probabilities. ix, 164 pages, 1983.

Vol. 16: Specifying Statistical Models: From Parametric to Non-Parametric, Using Bayesian or Non-Bayesian Approaches. Edited by J. P. Florens, M. Mouchart, J. P. Raoult, L. Simar, and A. F. M. Smith. xi, 204 pages, 1983.

Vol. 17: I. V. Basawa and D. J. Scott, Asymptotic Optimal Inference for Non-Ergodic Models. ix, 170 pages, 1983.

Vol. 18: W. Britton, Conjugate Duality and the Exponential Fourier Spectrum. In prep, 1983.

Springer Series in Statistics

L. A. Goodman and W. H. Kruskal, Measures of Association for Cross Classifications. x, 146 pages, 1979.

J. O. Berger, Statistical Decision Theory: Fouindations, Concepts, and Methods. xiv, 425 pages, 1980.

R. G. Miller, Jr., Simultaneous Statistical Inference, 2nd edition. xvi, 299 pages, 1981.

P. Brémaud, Point Processes and Queues: Martingale Dynamics. xviii, 354 pages, 1981.

E. Seneta, Non-Negative Matrices and Markov Chains. xv, 279 pages, 1981.

F. J. Anscombe, Computing in Statistical Science through APL. xvi, 426 pages, 1981.

J. W. Pratt and J. D. Gibbons, Concepts of Nonparametric Theory. xvi, 462 pages, 1981.

V. Vapnik, Estimation of Dependences based on Empirical Data. xvi, 399 pages, 1982.

H. Heyer, Theory of Statistical Experiments. x, 289 pages, 1982.

L. Sachs, Applied Statistics: A Handbook of Techniques. xxviii, 706 pages, 1982.

M. R. Leadbetter, G. Lindgren and H. Rootzen, Extremes and Related Properties of Random Sequences and Processes. xii, 336 pages, 1983.